# BRITISH RAILWAYS
# LOCOMOTIVES & COACHING STOCK
# 2009

The Complete Guide to all
Locomotives & Coaching Stock which
operate on the National Rail network and
Eurotunnel

Robert Pritchard, Peter Fox & Peter Hall

ISBN 978 1 902336 70 1

© 2009. Platform 5 Publishing Ltd., 3 Wyvern House, Sark Road, Sheffield,
S2 4HG, England.

# CONTENTS

# CONTENTS

## SECTION 4 – ELECTRIC MULTIPLE UNITS

## SECTION 5 – UK Light Rail & Metro Systems

## SECTION 6 – CODES

## COVER PHOTOGRAPHS

**Front Cover:** East Midlands Trains-liveried HST 43055 and 43048 pass Milford, between Belper and Duffield with the 10.27 Sheffield–London St. Pancras International on 15/08/08. Most Sheffield–London services are now covered by Class 222 DEMUs.

**Rear Cover:** Northern-liveried 156 443 passes the signal box at Blaydon with the 08.30 Carlisle–Newcastle on 27/09/08. **Robert Pritchard (2)**

# PROVISION OF INFORMATION

This book has been compiled with care to be as accurate as possible, but in some cases information is not officially available and the publisher cannot be held responsible for any errors or omissions. We would like to thank the companies and individuals which have been co-operative in supplying information to us. The authors of this book will be pleased to receive notification of any inaccuracies readers may find in the series, and also any additional information to supplement our records and thus enhance future editions. Please send comments to:

Robert Pritchard, Platform 5 Publishing Ltd., 3 Wyvern House, Sark Road, Sheffield, S2 4HG, England.

**Tel:** 0114 255 2625 **Fax:** 0114 255 2471
**e-mail:** robert@platform5.com

This book is updated to January 2009.

# ACKNOWLEDGEMENTS

The author would like to thank all Train Operating Companies, Freight Companies, Rolling Stock Leasing Companies and spot-hire companies that have helped with the compilation of this book.

Thanks are also due to those who sent reports of changes observed during 2008 for the **Today's Railways UK** magazine "Stock Changes" column and for corrections given to the 2009 "pocket book" series.

# BRITAIN'S RAILWAY SYSTEM

## INFRASTRUCTURE & OPERATION

Britain's national railway infrastructure is owned by a "not for dividend" company, Network Rail. Many stations and maintenance depots are leased to and operated by Train Operating Companies (TOCs), but some larger stations remain under Network Rail control. The only exception is the infrastructure on the Isle of Wight, which is nationally owned and is leased to South West Trains.

Trains are operated by TOCs over Network Rail, regulated by access agreements between the parties involved. In general, TOCs are responsible for the provision and maintenance of the locos, rolling stock and staff necessary for the direct operation of services, whilst NR is responsible for the provision and maintenance of the infrastructure and also for staff to regulate the operation of services.

## DOMESTIC PASSENGER TRAIN OPERATORS

The large majority of passenger trains are operated by the TOCs on fixed term franchises. Franchise expiry dates are shown in the list of franchisees below:

| Franchise | Franchisee | Trading Name |
|---|---|---|
| Chiltern Railways | Deutsche Bahn (until 1 March 2022) | Chiltern Railways |
| Cross-Country[1] | Arriva Trains Ltd. (until 1 November 2013) | Cross-Country |
| East Midlands[2] | Stagecoach Holdings plc (until 11 November 2013) | East Midlands Trains |
| Greater Western[3] | First Group plc (until 1 April 2013) | First Great Western |
| Greater Anglia[4] | National Express Group plc (until 1 April 2011) | National Express East Anglia |
| Integrated Kent[5] | GoVia Ltd. (Go-Ahead/Keolis) (until 3 March 2012) | Southeastern |
| InterCity East Coast[6] | National Express Group plc (until 9 November 2013) | National Express East Coast |
| InterCity West Coast | Virgin Rail Group Ltd. (until 31 March 2012) | Virgin Trains |
| London Rail[7] | MTR/Laing Rail (until 11 November 2014) | London Overground |
| LTS Rail[8] | National Express Group plc (until 25 May 2011) | c2c |
| Merseyrail Electrics[9] | Serco/NedRail (until 20 July 2028) | Merseyrail Electrics |
| Northern Rail[10] | Serco/NedRail (until 12 September 2011) | Northern |
| ScotRail | First Group plc (until 8 November 2014) | First ScotRail |
| South Central[11] | GoVia Ltd. (Go-Ahead/Keolis) (until 20 September 2009) | Southern |

| South Western[12] | Stagecoach Holdings plc (until 4 February 2014) | South West Trains |
| Thameslink/Great Northern[13] | First Group plc (until 1 April 2012) | First Capital Connect |
| Trans-Pennine Express[14] | First Group/Keolis (until 1 February 2012) | First Trans-Pennine Express |
| Wales & Borders | Arriva Trains Ltd. (until 6 December 2018) | Arriva Trains Wales |
| West Midlands[15] | GoVia Ltd. (Go-Ahead/Keolis) (until 19 September 2013) | London Midland |

## Notes:

[1] Awarded for six years to 2013 with an extension for a further two years and five months to April 2016 if performance targets are met.

[2] Awarded for six years to 2013 with an extension for a further one year and five months to April 2015 if performance targets are met.

[3] Awarded for seven years to 2013 with an extension for a further three years to April 2016 if performance targets are met.

[4] Awarded for seven years to 2011 with an extension for a further three years to April 2014 if performance targets are met. Franchise was branded "One" from April 2004 to February 2008.

[5] The Integrated Kent franchise started on 1 April 2006 for an initial period of six years to 2012, with an extension for a further two years to April 2014 if performance targets are met.

[6] Awarded for five years and 11 months to 2013 with an extension for a further one year and five months to April 2015 if performance targets are met. National Express took over the new East Coast franchise following the financial difficulties experienced with GNER's holding company Sea Containers.

[7] The London Rail Concession is different from all other rail franchises, as fares and service levels are set by Transport for London instead of the DfT. Incorporates the North and West London lines, the Gospel Oak–Barking line and Euston–Watford local services.

[8] The LTS Rail franchise is due to be rebranded as part of National Express Group's adoption of a new unified identity for all of its operations, but the new brand had not been selected at the time of going to press.

[9] Now under control of Merseytravel PTE instead of the DfT. Franchise due to be reviewed after seven years (in July 2010) and then every five years to fit in with the Merseyside Local Transport Plan.

[10] Awarded for six years and nine months to 2011 with an extension for a further two years to September 2013 if performance targets are met.

[11] The South Central franchise termination date has been brought forward by three months to ensure that the winner of the new franchise has already taken over before any major timetable changes are made in December 2009.

[12] Awarded for seven years to 2014 with an extension for a further three years to February 2017 if performance targets are met.

[13] Awarded for six years to 2012 with an extension for up to a further three years to April 2015 if performance targets are met.

[14] Awarded for eight years to 2012 with an extension a further five years to February 2017 if performance targets are met.

[15] Awarded for six years to 2013 with an extension for a further two years to September 2015 if performance targets are met.

All new franchises officially start at 02.00 on the first day. Because of this the finishing date of an old franchise and the start date of its successor are the same.

Where termination dates are dependent on performance targets being met, the earliest possible termination date is given. However, with Chiltern and Merseyrail, the termination dates are based on the maximum franchise length.

The following operators run non-franchised services only:

| Operator | Trading Name | Route |
|---|---|---|
| BAA | Heathrow Express | London Paddington–Heathrow Airport |
| First Hull Trains | First Hull Trains | London King's Cross–Hull |
| Grand Central | Grand Central | London King's Cross–Sunderland |
| North Yorkshire Moors Railway | North Yorkshire Moors Railway | Pickering–Grosmont–Whitby/Battersby |
| West Coast Railway Company | West Coast Railway Company | Birmingham–Stratford-upon-Avon Fort William–Mallaig* York–Harrogate–Leeds–York–Scarborough* Machynlleth–Porthmadog/Pwllheli* |
| Wrexham, Shropshire & Marylebone Railway | Wrexham & Shropshire | London Marylebone–Wrexham General |

* Special summer-dated services only.

# INTERNATIONAL PASSENGER OPERATIONS

Eurostar (UK) operates passenger services between the UK and mainland Europe, jointly with the national operators of France (SNCF) and Belgium (SNCB/NMBS). Eurostar (UK) is a subsidiary of London & Continental Railways, which is jointly owned by National Express Group and British Airways.

In addition, a service for the conveyance of accompanied road vehicles through the Channel Tunnel is provided by the tunnel operating company, Eurotunnel.

# FREIGHT TRAIN OPERATIONS

The following operators operate freight train services under "Open Access" arrangements:

DB Schenker (formerly EWS)
Freightliner
First GBRf
Direct Rail Services (DRS)

Fastline (Jarvis)
Advenza (Cotswold Rail)
Colas Rail
West Coast Railway Company

# 1. LOCOMOTIVES

# INTRODUCTION

## SCOPE

This section contains details of all locomotives which can run on Britain's national railway network, plus those of Eurotunnel. Locomotives which are owned by, for example, DB Schenker and Freightliner which have been withdrawn from service and awaiting disposal are listed in the main part of the book. Locos which are awaiting disposal at scrapyards are listed in a new "Locomotives Awaiting Disposal" section.

Only preserved locomotives which are currently used on the National Rail network are included. Others, which may be Network Rail registered but not at present certified for use, are not included, but will be found in the twelfth edition of the Platform 5 book, "Preserved Locomotives and Multiple Units".

## LOCO CLASSES

Loco classes are listed in numerical order of class. Principal details and dimensions are quoted for each class in metric and/or imperial units as considered appropriate bearing in mind common UK usage.

**Builders:** These are shown in class headings. Abbreviations used are found in section 6.6.

All dimensions and weights are quoted for locomotives in an "as new" condition with all necessary supplies (e.g. oil, water and sand) on board. Dimensions are quoted in the order length x width. Lengths quoted are over buffers or couplers as appropriate. All widths quoted are maxima. Where two different wheel diameter dimensions are shown, the first refers to powered wheels and the second refers to non-powered wheels.

## NUMERICAL LISTINGS

Locomotives are listed in numerical order. Where numbers actually carried are different from those officially allocated, these are noted in class headings where appropriate. Where locomotives have been recently renumbered, the most immediate previous number is shown in parentheses. Each locomotive entry is laid out as in the following example:

| RSL No. | Detail | Livery | Owner | Pool | | Allocn. | Name |
|---------|--------|--------|-------|------|--|---------|------|
| 57302 d | | **VT** | P | ATTB | | MA | VIRGIL TRACY |

**Detail Differences**. Only detail differences which currently affect the areas and types of train which locomotives may work are shown. All other detail differences are specifically excluded. Where such differences occur within a class or part class, they are shown in the "Detail" column alongside the individual locomotive number.

Standard abbreviations used for the locomotives section are:

| | |
|---|---|
| a | Train air brake equipment only. |
| b | Drophead buckeye couplers. |
| c | Scharfenberg couplers. |
| d | Fitted with retractable Dellner couplers. |
| k | Fitted with Swinghead Automatic "buckeye" combination couplers. |
| p | Train air, vacuum and electro-pneumatic brakes. |
| r | RETB fitted |
| s | Slow Speed Control equipment. |
| v | Train vacuum brake only. |
| x | Train air and vacuum brakes ("Dual brakes"). |
| + | Additional fuel tank capacity. |
| § | Sandite laying equipment. |

In all cases use of the above abbreviations indicates the equipment indicated is normally operable. Meaning of non-standard abbreviations and symbols is detailed in individual class headings.

**Codes.** Codes are used to denote the livery, owner, pool and depot of each locomotive. Details of these will be found in section 6 of this book.

**Names.** Only names carried with official sanction are listed. Names are shown in UPPER/lower case characters as actually shown on the name carried on the locomotive.

# GENERAL INFORMATION

## CLASSIFICATION AND NUMBERING

All locomotives are classified and allocated numbers by the Rolling Stock Library under the TOPS numbering system, introduced in 1972. This comprises a two-digit class number followed by a three-digit serial number. Where the actual number carried by a locomotive differs from the allocated number, or where an additional number is carried to the allocated number, this is shown by a note in the class heading.

For diesel locomotives, class numbers offer an indication of engine horsepower as shown in the table below.

| Class No. Range | Engine h.p. |
|---|---|
| 01–14 | 0–799 |
| 15–20 | 800–1000 |
| 21–31 | 1001–1499 |
| 32–39 | 1500–1999 |
| 40–54, 57 | 2000–2999 |
| 55–56, 58–69 | 3000+ |

For electric locomotives class numbers are allocated in ascending numerical order under the following scheme:

| | |
|---|---|
| Class 70–80 | direct current and DC/diesel dual system locomotives. |
| Class 81 onwards | alternating current and AC/DC dual system locos. |

Numbers in the 89xxx series are allocated by the Rolling Stock Library to locomotives which have been de-registered but subsequently re-registered for use on the Network Rail network and whose original number has already been re-used. 89xxx numbers are normally only carried inside locomotive cabs and are not carried externally in normal circumstances.

## WHEEL ARRANGEMENT

For main line locomotives the number of driven axles on a bogie or frame is denoted by a letter (A = 1, B = 2, C = 3 etc.) and the number of non-powered axles is denoted by a number. The use of the letter "o" after a letter indicates each axle is individually powered, whilst the "+" symbol indicates bogies are inter-coupled.

For shunting locomotives, the Whyte notation is used. In this notation the number of leading wheels are given, followed by the number of driving wheels and then the trailing wheels.

# HAULAGE CAPABILITY OF DIESEL LOCOMOTIVES

The haulage capability of a diesel locomotive depends upon three basic factors:

1. Adhesive weight. The greater the weight on the driving wheels, the greater the adhesion and more tractive power can be applied before wheelslip occurs.

2. The characteristics of its transmission. To start a train the locomotive has to exert a pull at standstill. A direct drive diesel engine cannot do this, hence the need for transmission. This may be mechanical, hydraulic or electric. The present British Standard for locomotives is electric transmission. Here the diesel engine drives a generator or alternator and the current produced is fed to the traction motors. The force produced by each driven wheel depends on the current in its traction motor. In other words, the larger the current, the harder it pulls. As the locomotive speed increases, the current in the traction motor falls, hence the *Maximum Tractive Effort* is the maximum force at its wheels the locomotive can exert at a standstill. The electrical equipment cannot take such high currents for long without overheating. Hence the *Continuous Tractive Effort* is quoted which represents the current which the equipment can take continuously.

3. The power of its engine. Not all power reaches the rail, as electrical machines are approximately 90% efficient. As the electrical energy passes through two such machines (the generator or alternator and the traction motors), the *Power at Rail* is approximately 81% (90% of 90%) of the engine power, less a further amount used for auxiliary equipment such as radiator fans, traction motor blowers, air compressors, battery charging, cab heating, Electric Train Supply (ETS) etc. The power of the locomotive is proportional to the tractive effort times the speed. Hence when on full power there is a speed corresponding to the continuous tractive effort.

# HAULAGE CAPABILITY OF ELECTRIC LOCOMOTIVES

Unlike a diesel locomotive, an electric locomotive does not develop its power on board and its performance is determined only by two factors, namely its weight and the characteristics of its electrical equipment. Whereas a diesel locomotive tends to be a constant power machine, the power of an electric locomotive varies considerably. Up to a certain speed it can produce virtually a constant power. Hence power rises with speed according to the formula given in section three above, until a maximum speed is reached at which tractive effort falls, such that the power also falls. Hence the power at the speed corresponding to the maximum tractive effort is lower than the maximum speed.

# BRAKE FORCE

The brake force is a measure of the braking power of a locomotive. This is shown on the locomotive data panels so operating staff can ensure sufficient brake power is available on freight trains.

## ELECTRIC TRAIN SUPPLY (ETS)

A number of locomotives are equipped to provide a supply of electricity to the train being hauled to power auxiliaries such as heating, cooling fans, air conditioning and kitchen equipment. ETS is provided from the locomotive by means of a separate alternator (except Class 33 locos, which have a DC generator). The ETS index of a locomotive is a measure of the electrical power available for train supply.

Similarly, most loco-hauled coaches also have an ETS index, which in this case is a measure of the power required to operate equipment mounted in the coach. The sum of the ETS indices of all the hauled vehicles in a train must not exceed the ETS index of the locomotive.

ETS is commonly (but incorrectly) known as ETH (Electric Train Heating), which is a throwback to the days before loco-hauled coaches were equipped with electrically powered auxiliary equipment other than for train heating.

## ROUTE AVAILABILITY (RA)

This is a measure of a railway vehicle's axle load. The higher the axle load of a vehicle, the higher the RA number on a scale from 1 to 10. Each Network Rail route has a RA number and in general no vehicle with a higher RA number may travel on that route without special clearance.

## MULTIPLE & PUSH-PULL WORKING

Multiple working between vehicles (i.e. two or more powered vehicles being driven from one cab) is facilitated by jumper cables connecting the vehicles. However, not all types are compatible with each other, and a number of different systems are in use, each system being incompatible with any other.

**Association of American Railroads (AAR) System:** Classes 59, 66, and 67.
**Blue Star Coupling Code:** Classes 20, 25, 31, 33, 37 40 and 73.
**DRS System:** Classes 20/3, 37 and 47.
**Green Circle Coupling Code:** Class 47 (not all equipped).
**Orange Square Coupling Code:** Class 50.
**Red Diamond Coupling Code:** Classes 56 and 58.
**SR System:** Classes 33/1, 73 and various electric multiple units.
**Within Own Class only:** Classes 43 and 60.

Many locomotives use a time-division multiplex (TDM) system for push-pull and multiple working which utilises the existing RCH jumper cables fitted to coaching stock vehicles. Previously these cables had only been used to control train lighting and public address systems.

Class 47 locos 47701–47717 were equipped with an older non-standard TDM system.

# 1.1. DIESEL LOCOMOTIVES

## CLASS 08          BR/ENGLISH ELECTRIC          0-6-0

**Built:** 1955–1962 by BR at Crewe, Darlington, Derby Locomotive, Doncaster or Horwich Works.
**Engine:** English Electric 6KT of 298 kW (400 h.p.) at 680 r.p.m.
**Main Generator:** English Electric 801.
**Traction Motors:** Two English Electric 506.
**Maximum Tractive Effort:** 156 kN (35000 lbf).
**Continuous Tractive Effort:** 49 kN (11100 lbf) at 8.8 m.p.h.
**Power At Rail:** 194 kW (260 h.p.).          **Train Brakes:** Air & vacuum.
**Brake Force:** 19 t.                         **Dimensions:** 8.92 x 2.59 m.
**Weight:** 49.6–50.4 t.                       **Wheel Diameter:** 1372 mm.
**Design Speed:** 20 m.p.h.                    **Maximum Speed:** 15 m.p.h.
**Fuel Capacity:** 3037 litres.                **RA:** 5.
**Train Supply:** Not equipped.
**Multiple Working:** m Equipped for multiple working. All others not equipped.

**Notes:** † – Equipped with remote control (Hima Sella system) for working at Celsa, Cardiff Tidal.

§ – Equipped with remote control (Cattron system) for evaluation purposes.

Actual locations for all operational shunters are given where known, apart from DB Schenker and Freightliner-operated locos which generally move about on a more regular basis.

Certain Class 08s that don't have Network Rail engineering acceptance are classed as "in industrial service" and can be found in section 1.4 of this book.

08850 is registered for use between Battersby and Whitby only, for rescue purposes.

**Non-standard liveries/numbering:**

08308 All over ScotRail "Caledonian Sleeper" purple.
08442 Dark grey lower bodyside with light grey upper bodyside. Carries no number.
08480 Yellow with a red bodyside band. Carries number "TOTON No 1".
08499 Pullman Rail blue & white.
08616 Carries number 3783.
08701 Carries number "Tyne 100".
08715 "Day-glo" orange.
08721 As **B**, but with a black roof & "Express parcels" branding with red & yellow stripe.
08810 Two-tone light grey.
08824 Carries number "IEMD01".

Originally numbered in series D3000–D4192.

**Class 08/0. Standard Design.**

| 08077 | **FL** | P | DFLS | LH (S) |

| | | | | | |
|---|---|---|---|---|---|
| 08308 a | **0** | RL | MRSO | IS | |
| 08389 a | **E** | DB | WSSN | TO | |
| 08393 a | **E** | DB | WSSI | TO | |
| 08397 a | **E** | DB | WZTS | AN | |
| 08401 a | **DG** | DB | WSXX | IM | |
| 08402 a | **E** | X | ~~WNSO~~ S | ~~ML~~ | |
| 08405 a | **E** | DB | WSSM | TO | |
| 08410 a | **GL** | FG | EFSH | PZ | |
| 08417 a | **BS** | SO | CDJD | ZA | |
| 08418 a | **E** | DB | WZTS | BS | |
| 08428 a | **E** | DB | WNTR | DR | |
| 08442 a | **0** | DB | WSXX | EH | RICHARD J. WENHAM EASTLEIGH DEPOT DECEMBER 1989–JULY 1999 |
| 08451 | **GB** | AM | ATZZ | MA | |
| 08454 | **K** | AM | ATLO | WB | |
| 08466 a† | **E** | DB | WSSI | TO | |
| 08472 a | **WA** | WA | RFSH | EC | |
| 08480 a | **0** | DB | WSXX | TO | |
| 08482 a | **E** | DB | WSSN | TO | DON GATES 1952–2000 |
| 08483 a | **GL** | FG | EFSH | OO | DUSTY Driver David Miller |
| 08485 a | **B** | DB | WZTS | Carlisle Yard | |
| 08489 a | **E** | X | WNSO | MH | |
| 08495 | **E** | DB | WNTS | DR | NOEL KIRTON OBE |
| 08499 a | **0** | PU | | CF | |
| 08500 | **E** | DB | WNTS | DR | |
| 08502 | **NO** | HN | HNRL | HT | |
| 08507 a | **HN** | HN | HNRL | CZ | |
| 08509 a | **F** | X | WNSO | IM | |
| 08510 a | **B** | X | WNSO | EH | |
| 08512 a | **E** | DB | WNTS | DR | |
| 08514 a | **E** | DB | WNTS | DR | |
| 08516 a | **E** | DB | WSXX | BK | |
| 08525 | **MA** | EM | EMSL | NL | |
| 08527 | **FA** | HN | HNRL | RR | |
| 08528 | **DG** | ~~DB~~ | WNTS | ~~BS~~ Batt | |
| 08530 | **FL** | P | DFLS | FD | |
| 08531 a | **DG** | P | DFLS | FD | |
| 08536 | **B** | PO | | DY (S) | |
| 08538 | **DG** | DB | WSSN | TO | |
| 08540 | **E** | DB | WNTS | TO | |
| 08543 | **DG** | DB | WNYX | BS | |
| 08561 | **B** | DB | WNXX | DR | |
| 08567 | **E** | DB | WSSN | TO | |
| 08569 | **E** | DB | WNYX | DR | |
| 08571 a | **WA** | WA | HBSH | BN | |
| 08575 | **FL** | P | DFLS | FD | |
| 08577 | **E** | DB | WNTS | BS | |
| 08578 | **E** | DB | WSSN | TO | |
| 08580 | **E** | DB | WNYX | BS | |
| 08582 a | **DG** | X | WNSO | DR | |
| 08585 | **FL** | P | DFLS | FD | Vicky |

| 08587 | E | X | WNSO | MG | |
| 08593 | E | DB | WNTS | TO | |
| 08596 at | WA | WA | RFSH | BN | |
| 08597 | E | DB | WNTS | TE | |
| 08605 | E | DB | WSSI | TO | |
| 08611 | V | AM | ATLO | LL | DOWNHILL C.S. |
| 08615 | WA | WA | RFSH | EC | |
| 08616 | LM | LM | EJLO | TS | TYSELEY 100 |
| 08617 | K | AM | ATLO | WB | |
| 08623 | E | DB | WSSI | TO | |
| 08624 | FL | P | DFLS | FD | |
| 08630 | E | DB | WNTS | MG | BOB BROWN |
| 08632 | E | DB | WNTS | BS | |
| 08633 | E | DB | WSSM | TO | |
| 08641 | FB | FG | EFSH | LA | |
| 08644 | GL | FG | EFSH | LA | |
| 08645 | FB | FG | EFSH | LA | Mike Baggott |
| 08646 | F | DB | WSSI | MG | |
| 08651 a | DG | DB | WNYX | BS | |
| 08653 | E | DB | WSSN | BS | |
| 08662 | E | DB | WNTS | EH | |
| 08663 a | GL | FG | EFSH | PM | |
| 08664 | E | DB | WNTS | DR | |
| 08665 | E | X | WNSO | HM | |
| 08669 a | WA | WA | RFSH | ZB | Bob Machin |
| 08670 a | E | X | WNSO | ML | |
| 08676 | E | DB | WSSN | TO | |
| 08685 | E | DB | WSSI | TO | |
| 08689 a | E | DB | WNTS | TO | |
| 08690 | MA | EM | EMSL | NL | |
| 08691 | FL | FL | DFLS | FD | Terri |
| 08696 a | G | AM | ATLO | MA | LONGSIGHT TMD |
| 08697 | B | EM | EMSL | DY (S) | |
| 08698 a | E | DB | WNTS | TE | |
| 08701 a | RX | DB | WSSN | TO | |
| 08703 a | E | DB | WSSN | TO | |
| 08706 | E | DB | WSSM | TO | |
| 08709 | E | DB | WNTS | BS | MOLLY'S DAY |
| 08711 k | RX | DB | WSSN | TO | |
| 08714 | E | DB | WSSI | TO | Cambridge |
| 08721 | 0 | AM | ATLO | MA | M.A. Smith |
| 08724 | WA | WA | HBSH | NL | |
| 08735 | E | DB | WSSI | TO | |
| 08737 a | E | DB | WSSN | TO | |
| 08738 m | ECR | DB | WSSN | TO | |
| 08742 | RX | DB | WSSN | TO | |
| 08745 | FE | P | DHLT | SZ (S) | |
| 08750 a | K | RL | MRSO | HE | |
| 08752 † | E | DB | WSSI | TO | |
| 08757 | RG | DB | WNTS | TO | |
| 08765 | E | DB | WNTS | EH | |

| 08770 | a | **DG** | DB | WNTS | Newport Docks | |
| 08776 | a | **DG** | DB | WNTS | Tees Yard | |
| 08782 | at | **CU** | DB | WSSI | TO | CASTLETON WORKS |
| 08783 | | **E** | DB | WNTS | TO | |
| 08784 | | **E** | DB | WSSK | TO | |
| 08785 | a | **FL** | P | DFLS | FD | |
| 08786 | a | **DG** | DB | WNTS | WY | |
| 08788 | | **RT** | RL | MRSO | IS | |
| 08790 | | **B** | AM | ATLO | OY | STARLET |
| 08795 | | **GL** | FG | EFSH | LE | |
| 08798 | | **E** | DB | WNTS | DR | |
| 08799 | a | **E** | DB | WSSN | TO | ANDY BOWER |
| 08802 | | **E** | DB | WSSI | TO | |
| 08804 | | **E** | DB | WNTS | EH | |
| 08805 | | **B** | LM | EJLO | SI | CONCORDE |
| 08810 | a | **O** | LW | MBDL | CP | |
| 08822 | | **GL** | FG | EFSH | LE | |
| 08824 | ak | **K** | DB | WSXX | CE | |
| 08828 | a | **E** | DB | WSXX | BS | |
| 08834 | | **DR** | HN | HNRL | CR | |
| 08836 | | **GL** | FG | EFSH | OC | |
| 08842 | | **E** | DB | WNTS | BS | |
| 08844 | | **E** | DB | WSSN | TO | CHRIS WREN 1955–2002 |
| 08847 | | **CD** | RL | MRSO | NC | |
| 08850 | | **G** | NY | MBDL | NY | |
| 08853 | a | **WA** | WA | RFSH | ZB | |
| 08854 | † | **E** | DB | WNTS | MG | |
| 08856 | | **B** | DB | WNXX | DC | |
| 08865 | | **E** | DB | WSSK | TO | |
| 08866 | | **E** | DB | WNTS | DR | |
| 08868 | | **B** | HN | HNRL | CP | |
| 08872 | | **E** | DB | WZTS | IM | TONY LONG STRATFORD DEPOT 1971–2002 |
| 08874 | | **SL** | RL | MRSO | NC | |
| 08877 | | **DG** | DB | WSXX | SP | |
| 08879 | | **E** | DB | WSSA | TO | |
| 08884 | | **B** | DB | WZTS | BS | |
| 08886 | § | **E** | DB | WNTS | TO | |
| 08887 | a | **VP** | AM | ATZZ | MA | |
| 08888 | | **E** | DB | WNTS | DR | |
| 08890 | | **DG** | X | WNSO | EH | |
| 08891 | | **FL** | P | DFLS | FD | J.R 1951–2005 |
| 08892 | | **DR** | HN | HNRL | RR | |
| 08897 | | **E** | DB | WSSN | TO | |
| 08899 | | **MA** | EM | EMSL | DY | |
| 08904 | | **E** | DB | WSSN | TO | |
| 08905 | | **E** | DB | WNTS | BS | |
| 08907 | | **E** | DB | WSSN | TO | |
| 08908 | | **MM** | EM | EMSL | DY | |
| 08909 | | **E** | DB | WSSN | TO | |
| 08918 | | **DG** | DB | WNTS | OC | |
| 08920 | | **F** | DB | WNXX | BS | |

| 08921 † | E | DB | WNTS | SP |
|---------|---|----|------|-----|
| 08922 | DG | DB | WNTS | DR |
| 08924 | E | DB | WNTS | ML |
| 08925 | B | DB | WNXX | DR |
| 08933 | E | X | WNSO | Hoo Jn. |
| 08934 a | VP | AM | ATLO | WB |
| 08939 m | ECR | DB | WSEN | TO |
| 08941 | E | DB | WNTS | DR |
| 08948 c | EP | EU | GPSS | TI |
| 08950 | MA | EM | EMSL | NL |
| 08951 † | E | DB | WSSI | TO | FRED |
| 08953 a | DG | DB | WNXX | DR |
| 08954 | F | DB | WNXX | AN |
| 08955 | F | X | WNSO | BS |
| 08956 | BS | SO | CDJD | Old Dalby |

**Class 08/9. Reduced height cab.** Converted 1985–1987 by BR at Landore.

| 08993 | E | DB | WSSN | TO |
|-------|---|----|------|-----|
| 08994 a | E | DB | WNTS | DR | SPIRIT OF INNOVATION |
| 08995 a | E | DB | WSSN | TO |

# CLASS 09    BR/ENGLISH ELECTRIC    0-6-0

**Built:** 1959–1962 by BR at Darlington or Horwich Works.
**Engine:** English Electric 6KT of 298 kW (400 h.p.) at 680 r.p.m.
**Main Generator:** English Electric 801.
**Traction Motors:** English Electric 506.
**Maximum Tractive Effort:** 111 kN (25000 lbf).
**Continuous Tractive Effort:** 39 kN (8800 lbf) at 11.6 m.p.h.

| | |
|---|---|
| **Power At Rail:** 201 kW (269 h.p.). | **Train Brakes:** Air & vacuum. |
| **Brake Force:** 19 t. | **Dimensions:** 8.92 x 2.59 m. |
| **Weight:** 49 t. | **Wheel Diameter:** 1372 mm. |
| **Design Speed:** 27 m.p.h. | **Maximum Speed:** 27 m.p.h. |
| **Fuel Capacity:** 3037 litres. | **RA:** 5. |
| **Train Supply:** Not equipped. | **Multiple Working:** Not equipped. |

Class 09/0 were originally numbered D3665–D3671, D3719–D3721, D4099–D4114.

**Class 09/0. Built as Class 09.**

| 09001 | E | DB | WSSN | TO |
|-------|---|----|------|-----|
| 09003 | E | DB | WNTS | MG |
| 09005 k | E | DB | WSSN | TO |
| 09006 | E | DB | WNTS | DR |
| 09007 | ML | DB | WSSN | TO |
| 09008 | E | DB | WNTS | BS |
| 09009 | E | DB | WNXX | SL | Three Bridges C.E.D. |
| 09010 | DG | DB | WNTS | HG |
| 09011 | DG | DB | WNTS | MG |
| 09012 | DG | DB | WNXX | HG |

| 09013 | **DG** | DB | WNTS | TO | |
| 09014 | **DG** | DB | WSSN | TO | |
| 09015 | **E** | DB | WNTS | MG | |
| 09016 | **E** | DB | WNXX | BZ | |
| 09017 | **E** | DB | WNTS | Newport ADJ Yard | |
| 09018 | **E** | DB | WNXX | HG | |
| 09019 | **ML** | DB | WSSN | TO | |
| 09020 | **E** | DB | WNTS | MG | |
| 09022 a | **E** | DB | WNTS | BS | |
| 09023 a | **E** | DB | WSSI | TO | |
| 09024 | **ML** | DB | WNTS | EH | |
| 09026 a | **G** | SN | HWSU | BI | Cedric Wares |

**Class 09/1. Converted from Class 08. 110 V electrical equipment.**
**Converted:** 1992–1993 by RFS Industries, Kilnhurst.

| 09101 (08833) | **DG** | DB | WNTS | DR |
| 09102 (08832) | **DG** | DB | WNTS | MG |
| 09103 (08766) | **DG** | DB | WNTS | AY |
| 09104 (08749) | **DG** | DB | WNXX | TE |
| 09105 (08835) | **DG** | DB | WSSN | TO |
| 09106 (08759) | **E** | DB | WSSN | TO |
| 09107 (08845) | **E** | DB | WNTS | DR |

**Class 09/2. Converted from Class 08. 90 V electrical equipment.**
**Converted:** 1992 by RFS Industries, Kilnhurst.

| 09201 (08421) | ak **DG** | DB | WSSM | TO |
| 09202 (08732) | **DG** | DB | WNYX | DR |
| 09203 (08781) | **DG** | DB | WNYX | CE |
| 09204 (08717) | **DG** | DB | WNXX | TY |
| 09205 (08620) | **DG** | DB | WNTS | TE |

---

# CLASS 20          ENGLISH ELECTRIC          Bo-Bo

**Built:** 1957–1968 by English Electric Company at Vulcan Foundry, Newton-le-Willows or by Robert Stephenson & Hawthorn at Darlington.
**Engine:** English Electric 8SVT Mk. II of 746 kW (1000 h.p.) at 850 r.p.m.
**Main Generator:** English Electric 819/3C.
**Traction Motors:** English Electric 526/5D or 526/8D.
**Maximum Tractive Effort:** 187 kN (42000 lbf).
**Continuous Tractive Effort:** 111 kN (25000 lbf) at 11 m.p.h.

| | |
|---|---|
| **Power At Rail:** 574 kW (770 h.p.). | **Train Brakes:** Air & vacuum. |
| **Brake Force:** 35 t. | **Dimensions:** 14.25 x 2.67 m. |
| **Weight:** 73.4–73.5 t. | **Wheel Diameter:** 1092 mm. |
| **Design Speed:** 75 m.p.h. | **Maximum Speed:** 75 m.p.h. |
| **Fuel Capacity:** 1727 litres. | **RA:** 5. |
| **Train Supply:** Not equipped. | **Multiple Working:** Blue Star. |

**Non-standard liveries/numbering:**

20088 & 20105 RFS grey.
20132 Carries number D8132.
20138 and 20215 As **FO** but with a red solebar stripe.
20906 Carries no number.
Originally numbered in series D8007–D8190, D8315–D8325.

## Class 20/0. Standard Design.

| | | | | | |
|---|---|---|---|---|---|
| 20016 | B | HN | HNRS | LM | |
| 20032 | B | HN | HNRS | LM | |
| 20057 | B | HN | HNRS | LM | |
| 20072 | B | HN | HNRS | LM | |
| 20081 | B | HN | HNRS | LM | |
| 20088 | 0 | HN | HNRS | LM | |
| 20092 | U | HN | HNRS | BH | |
| 20096 | F | HN | HNRL | BH | |
| 20105 | 0 | HN | HNRS | BH | |
| 20107 | F | HN | HNRS | BH | |
| 20119 | B | HN | HNRS | BH | |
| 20121 | B | HN | HNRS | BH | |
| 20132 | G | HN | HNRS | BH | Barrow Hill Depot |
| 20138 | 0 | HN | HNRS | LM | |
| 20197 | B | HN | HNRS | LM | |
| 20215 | 0 | HN | HNRS | LM | |

**Class 20/3. Direct Rail Services refurbished locos.** Details as Class 20/0 except:

**Refurbished:** 1995–1996 by Brush Traction at Loughborough (20301–20305) or 1997–1998 by RFS(E) at Doncaster (20306–20315). Disc indicators or headcode panels removed.

| | |
|---|---|
| **Train Brakes:** Air. | **Maximum Speed:** 75 m.p.h. |
| **Weight:** 76 t. | **Fuel Capacity:** 2900 (+ 4909) litres. |
| **Brake Force:** 35 t. | **RA:** 6. |

**Multiple Working:** DRS system.

| | | | | | |
|---|---|---|---|---|---|
| 20301 | (20047) | + | **DR** | DR XHSS | KM | Max Joule 1958–1999 |
| 20302 | (20084) | | **DR** | DR XHSS | KM | |
| 20303 | (20127) | + | **DR** | DR XHNC S | KM CS | |
| 20304 | (20120) | | **DR** | DR XHNC | KM | |
| 20305 | (20095) | | **DR** | DR XHSS | KM | |
| 20306 | (20131) | + | **DR** | DR XHSS | KM | |
| 20307 | (20128) | + | **DR** | DR XHSS S | CR CS | |
| 20308 | (20187) | + | **DS** | DR XHNC | KM | |
| 20309 | (20075) | + | **DS** | DR XHNC | KM | |
| 20310 | (20190) | + | **DR** | DR XHSS | KM | Gresty Bridge |
| 20311 | (20102) | + | **DR** | DR XHSS | CR | Class 20 'Fifty' |
| 20312 | (20042) | + | **DS** | DR XHSS | KM | |
| 20313 | (20194) | + | **DR** | DR XHSS S | KM CS | |
| 20314 | (20117) | + | **DS** | DR XHNC S | KM CS | |
| 20315 | (20104) | + | **DR** | DR XHSS | CR | |

**Class 20/9. Harry Needle Railroad Company (former Hunslet-Barclay/DRS) locos.** Details as Class 20/0 except:

**Refurbished:** 1989 by Hunslet-Barclay at Kilmarnock.
**Train Brakes:** Air.                    **Fuel Capacity:** 1727 (+ 4727) litres.

| | | | | |
|---|---|---|---|---|
| 20901 (20101) | **F** | HN HNRL | BH |
| 20902 (20060) + | **DR** | HN HNRS | LM |
| 20903 (20083) + | **DR** | HN HNRS | LM |
| 20904 (20041) | **DR** | HN HNRS | BH |
| 20905 (20225) + | **F** | HN HNRL | BH |
| 20906 (20219) | **DR** | HN HNRS | CP |

# CLASS 25 BR/BEYER PEACOCK/SULZER Bo-Bo

**Built:** 1965 by Beyer Peacock at Gorton.
**Engine:** Sulzer 6LDA28-B of 930 kW (1250 h.p.) at 750 r.p.m.
**Main Generator:** AEI RTB15656.          **Traction Motors:** AEI 253AY.
**Maximum Tractive Effort:** 200 kN (45000 lbf).
**Continuous Tractive Effort:** 93 kN (20800 lbf) at 17.1 m.p.h.
**Power At Rail:** 708 kW (949 h.p.).      **Train Brakes:** Air & vacuum.
**Brake Force:** 38 t.                      **Dimensions:** 15.39 x 2.73 m.
**Weight:** 71.5 t.                         **Wheel Diameter:** 1143 mm.
**Design Speed:** 90 m.p.h.                 **Maximum Speed:** 60 m.p.h.
**Fuel Capacity:** 2270 litres.            **RA:** 5.
**Train Supply:** Not equipped.            **Multiple Working:** Blue Star.

Original number is D7628, which the loco currently carries.

**Note:** Only certified for use on Network Rail metals between Whitby and Battersby, as an extension of North Yorkshire Moors Railway services.

| | | | | | |
|---|---|---|---|---|---|
| 25278 | **GG** | NY MBDL | NY | SYBILLA |

# CLASS 31 BRUSH/ENGLISH ELECTRIC A1A-A1A

**Built:** 1958–1962 by Brush Traction at Loughborough.
**Engine:** English Electric 12SVT of 1100 kW (1470 h.p.) at 850 r.p.m.
**Main Generator:** Brush TG160-48.        **Traction Motors:** Brush TM73-68.
**Maximum Tractive Effort:** 160 kN (35900 lbf).
**Continuous Tractive Effort:** 83 kN (18700 lbf) at 23.5 m.p.h.
**Power At Rail:** 872 kW (1170 h.p.).     **Train Brakes:** Air & vacuum.
**Brake Force:** 49 t.                      **Dimensions:** 17.30 x 2.67 m.
**Weight:** 106.7–111 t.                    **Wheel Diameter:** 1092/1003 mm.
**Design Speed:** 90 m.p.h.                 **Maximum Speed:** 90 m.p.h.
**Fuel Capacity:** 2409 litres.            **RA:** 5 or 6.
**Train Supply:** Not equipped.            **Multiple Working:** Blue Star.

Originally numbered D5520–D5699, D5800–D5862 (not in order).

**Non-standard numbering:**

31190 Also carries number D5613.

**Class 31/1. Standard Design.** RA: 5.

| 31105 | Y | NR | QADD | DF | |
|--------|------|------|------|------|------|
| 31106 | FR | HJ | RVLO | DF | SPALDING TOWN |
| 31107 | K | X | QSTR | DF | |
| 31190 | G | PO | RVLO | DF | |
| 31233 a | Y | NR | QADD | DF | |
| 31285 | Y | NR | QADD | DF | |

**Class 31/4. Electric Train Supply equipment.** RA: 6.
**Train Supply:** Electric, index 66.

| 31423 | B | HN | HNRS | LM | |
|--------|------|------|------|------|------|
| 31454 | IC | RL | RVLO | DF | |
| 31459 | K | RE | RVLO | DF | CERBERUS |
| 31465 | RR | NR | QADD | DF (S) | |
| 31468 | FR | RL | RVLO | DF (S) | HYDRA |

**Class 31/6. ETS through wiring and controls.** RA: 5.

| 31601 | (31186) | WX | RL | RVLO | DF | GAUGE 'O' GUILD 1956–2006 |
|--------|---------|------|------|------|------|------|
| 31602 | (31191) | Y | RE | RVLO | DF | DRIVER DAVE GREEN |

# CLASS 33          BRCW/SULZER          Bo-Bo

**Built:** 1960–1962 by the Birmingham Railway Carriage & Wagon Company at Smethwick.
**Engine:** Sulzer 8LDA28 of 1160 kW (1550 h.p.) at 750 r.p.m.
**Main Generator:** Crompton Parkinson CG391B1.
**Traction Motors:** Crompton Parkinson C171C2.
**Maximum Tractive Effort:** 200 kN (45000 lbf).
**Continuous Tractive Effort:** 116 kN (26000 lbf) at 17.5 m.p.h.
**Power At Rail:** 906 kW (1215 h.p.).   **Train Brakes:** Air & vacuum.
**Brake Force:** 35 t.                   **Dimensions:** 15.47 x 2.82 (2.64 m. 33/2).
**Weight:** 76-78 t.                     **Wheel Diameter:** 1092 mm.
**Design Speed:** 85 m.p.h.              **Maximum Speed:** 85 m.p.h.
**Fuel Capacity:** 3410 litres.          **RA:** 6.
**Train Supply:** Electric, index 48 (750 V DC only).
**Multiple Working:** Blue Star.

Originally numbered in series D6500–D6597 but not in order.

**Class 33/0. Standard Design.**

| 33025 | WC | WC | MBDL | CS | Glen Falloch |
|--------|------|------|------|------|------|
| 33029 | WC | WC | MBDL | CS (S) | Glen Loy |
| 33030 | DR | WC | MBDL | CS (S) | |

**Class 33/2. Built to former Loading Gauge of Tonbridge–Battle Line.**
All equipped with slow speed control.

| 33202 | B | CD | CREL | GL (S) | |
|--------|------|------|------|------|------|
| 33207 | WC | WC | MBDL | CS | Jim Martin |

## CLASS 37          ENGLISH ELECTRIC          Co-Co

**Built:** 1960–1965 by English Electric Company at Vulcan Foundry, Newton-le-Willows or by Robert Stephenson & Hawthorn at Darlington.
**Engine:** English Electric 12CSVT of 1300 kW (1750 h.p.) at 850 r.p.m.
**Main Generator:** English Electric 822/10G.
**Traction Motors:** English Electric 538/A.
**Maximum Tractive Effort:** 245 kN (55500 lbf).
**Continuous Tractive Effort:** 156 kN (35000 lbf) at 13.6 m.p.h.
**Power At Rail:** 932 kW (1250 h.p.).        **Train Brakes:** Air & vacuum.
**Brake Force:** 50 t.                        **Dimensions:** 18.75 × 2.74 m.
**Weight:** 102.8–108.4 t.                    **Wheel Diameter:** 1092 mm.
**Design Speed:** 90 m.p.h.                   **Maximum Speed:** 80 m.p.h.
**Fuel Capacity:** 4046 (+ 7678) litres.      **RA:** 5 (§ 6).
**Train Supply:** Not equipped.
**Multiple Working:** Blue Star († DRS system).

Originally numbered D6600–D6608, D6700–D6999 (not in order).

**Non-standard liveries/numbering:**

37402 Light grey lower bodyside & dark grey upper bodyside.
37411 Also carries number D6990.

**Class 37/0. Standard Design.** Details as above.

| | | | | | |
|---|---|---|---|---|---|
| 37029 § | **DR** | HN | ADFL | BH | |
| 37038 † | **DR** | DR | XHSS | KM | |
| 37042 + | **E** | DB | WNXX | DR | |
| 37046 a | **CE** | X | WNSO | TY | |
| 37057 + | **E** | HN | HNRS | BH | |
| 37058 a+ | **CE** | X | WNSO | TY | |
| 37059 a+† | **DR** | DR | XHSS | CR | |
| 37069 a+† | **DS** | DR | XHNC | KM | |
| 37077 a | **ML** | X | WNSO | EH | |
| 37087 a† | **DR** | DR | XHNC | KM | Keighley & Worth Valley Railway 40th Anniversary 1968–2008 |
| 37108 + | **WC** | TT | TTTC | CS (S) | |
| 37165 a+ | **CE** | HN | HNRS | CS | |
| 37194 † | **DR** | DR | XHSS | KM | |
| 37196 a | **CE** | X | WNSO | TY | |
| 37197 | **DS** | DR | XHHP | LB | |
| 37198 + | **ML** | NR | QSTR | Quorn, GCR | |
| 37201 | **CE** | HN | HNRS | BH | |
| 37203 | **ML** | DB | WNXX | BS | |
| 37214 | **WC** | WC | MBDL | CS (S) | Loch Laidon |
| 37218 † | **DS** | DR | XHSS | CR | |
| 37221 a | **F** | X | WNSO | TY | |
| 37229 † | **DS** | DR | XHNC | KM | Jonty Jarvis 8-12-1998 to 18-3-2005 |
| 37238 a+ | **F** | X | WNSO | TY | |
| 37248 + | **WC** | TT | MBDL | CS | Loch Arkaig |
| 37259 † | **DR** | DR | XHNC | KM | |
| 37261 a+† | **DR** | DR | XHSS | KM | |

| 37293 | a+ | **ML** | X  | WNSO | TY |
|-------|----|--------|----|------|-----|
| 37294 | a+ | **CE** | X  | WNSO | CD |

**Class 37/3. Re-geared (CP7) bogies.** Details as Class 37/0 except:

**Maximum Tractive Effort:** 250 kN (56180 lbf).
**Continuous Tractive Effort:** 184 kN (41250 lbf) at 11.4 m.p.h.
**Design Speed:** 80 m.p.h.

| 37372 |   | **ML** | HN | HNRS | BH |
|-------|---|--------|----|------|-----|
| 37377 | + | **U**  | X  | WNSO | EH |

**Class 37/4. Refurbished with electric train supply equipment.** Main generator replaced by alternator. Re-geared (CP7) bogies. Details as Class 37/0 except:
**Main Alternator:** Brush BA1005A.     **Power At Rail:** 935 kW (1254 h.p.).
**Traction Motors:** English Electric 538/5A.
**Maximum Tractive Effort:** 256 kN (57440 lbf).
**Continuous Tractive Effort:** 184 kN (41250 lbf) at 11.4 m.p.h.
**Weight:** 107 t.
**Design Speed:** 80 m.p.h.
**Fuel Capacity:** 7678 litres.
**Train Supply:** Electric, index 30.

| 37401 | r  | **E**  | DB | WKBN | EH |                                        |
|-------|----|--------|----|------|-----|----------------------------------------|
| 37402 |    | **0**  | DB | WNXX | TO | Bont Y Bermo                           |
| 37405 | r  | **E**  | DB | WNTS | TO |                                        |
| 37406 | r  | **E**  | DB | WFMU | EH | The Saltire Society                    |
| 37409 |    | **F**  | DR | XHSS | BH |                                        |
| 37410 | r  | **E**  | DB | WNTS | EH |                                        |
| 37411 |    | **G**  | DB | WNTS | EH | CAERPHILLY CASTLE/CASTELL CAERFFILI    |
| 37412 |    | **F**  | DR | XHSS | BH |                                        |
| 37415 |    | **E**  | DB | WNXX | MG |                                        |
| 37416 |    | **GS** | DB | WNXX | EH |                                        |
| 37417 | ra | **E**  | DB | WNXX | EH | Richard Trevithick                     |
| 37419 |    | **E**  | DB | WNTS | OC |                                        |
| 37421 | r  | **E**  | PO | WNSO | ML |                                        |
| 37422 | r  | **E**  | DB | WNTS | EH | Cardiff Canton                         |
| 37423 | †  | **DS** | DR | XHNC | KM |                                        |
| 37425 |    | **BL** | DB | WNTS | EH | Pride of the Valleys/ Balchder y Cymoedd |
| 37426 |    | **E**  | DB | WNXX | CD |                                        |
| 37427 | r  | **E**  | DB | WNXX | ML |                                        |
| 37428 |    | **GS** | DB | WNXX | MG |                                        |

**Class 37/5. Refurbished without train supply equipment. Main generator replaced by alternator. Re-geared (CP7) bogies.** Details as Class 37/4 except:
**Maximum Tractive Effort:** 248 kN (55590 lbf).
**Weight:** 106.1–110.0 t.

| 37503 | r§    | **E**  | DB | WNXX | DR     |
|-------|-------|--------|----|------|--------|
| 37510 | a†    | **DS** | DR | XHNC | KM     |
| 37515 | a†    | **DR** | DR | XHHP | BH     |
| 37516 | s§    | **LH** | X  | WNSO | DR     |
| 37517 | as§   | **LH** | WC | MBDL | CS (S) |
| 37521 | r§    | **E**  | DB | WNXX | DR     |

**Class 37/6. Originally refurbished for Nightstar services.** Main generator replaced by alternator. UIC jumpers. Details as Class 37/5 except:
**Maximum Speed:** 90 m.p.h.                    **Train Brake:** Air.
**Train Supply:** Not equipped, but electric through wired.
**Multiple Working:** DRS system.

| | | | | | |
|---|---|---|---|---|---|
| 37601 | **DS** | DR | XHNC | KM | |
| 37602 | **DS** | DR | XHSS ⚡ | ~~KM~~ CS | |
| 37603 | **DS** | DR | XHNC | KM | |
| 37604 | **DS** | DR | XHNC | KM | |
| 37605 | **DR** | DR | XHNC | KM | |
| 37606 | **DR** | DR | XHSS | CR | |
| 37607 | **DR** | DR | XHNC | KM | |
| 37608 | **DR** | DR | XHSS | KM | |
| 37609 | **DR** | DR | XHSS | CR | |
| 37610 | **DS** | DR | XHSS | KM | T.S.(Ted) Cassady 14.5.61–6.4.08 |
| 37611 | **DR** | DR | XHNC | KM | |
| 37612 | **DR** | DR | XHNC ⚡ | ~~KM~~ CS | |

**Class 37/5 continued.**

| | | | | | |
|---|---|---|---|---|---|
| 37667 | s† **DR** | DR | XHNC | KM | |
| 37668 | s§ **E** | WC | MBDL | CS (S) | |
| 37669 | r  **E** | DB | WNXX | MG | |
| 37670 | r  **E** | DB | WFMU | KY | St. Blazey T&RS Depot |
| 37671 | a  **F** | DB | WNXX | TY | |
| 37672 | as **F** | HN | HNRS | BH | |
| 37675 | as§**F** | DB | WNXX | MG | Margam TMD |
| 37676 | a§ **WC** | WC | MBDL | CS | Loch Rannoch |
| 37680 | a§ **F** | HN | HNRS | HP | |
| 37682 | rt **DS** | DR | XHNC | KM | |
| 37683 | a  **DS** | DR | XHHP | BH | |
| 37684 | ar§ **E** | DB | WNXX | MG | Peak National Park |
| 37685 | a§ **IC** | WC | MBDL | CS (S) | |
| 37688 | † **DR** | DR | XHNC | KM | Kingmoor TMD |
| 37689 | a§ **F** | DB | WNXX | DR | |
| 37692 | s§ **F** | X | WNSO | MG | Didcot Depot |
| 37693 | as **F** | DB | WNXX | TY | |
| 37696 | as **F** | HN | HNRS | LM | |
| 37698 | a§ **LH** | DB | WNXX | MG | |

**Class 37/7. Refurbished locos. Main generator replaced by alternator. Re-geared (CP7) bogies.** Ballast weights added. Details as Class 37/5 except:
**Main Alternator:** GEC G564AZ (37796–803) Brush BA1005A (others).
**Maximum Tractive Effort:** 276 kN (62000 lbf).
**Weight:** 120 t.                    **RA:** 7.

| | | | | | |
|---|---|---|---|---|---|
| 37702 | s **GIF** | X | WNSO | ES | |
| 37703 | **GIF** | DB | WZKS | ES | |
| 37706 | **WC** | WC | MBDL | CS | |
| 37707 | **E** | DB | WNXX | BS | |
| 37709 | **F** | DB | WNXX | MH | |
| 37710 | **LH** | WC | MBDL | CS (S) | |

| | | | | | |
|---|---|---|---|---|---|
| 37712 | a | **WC** | WC | MBDL | CS |
| 37714 | a | **GIF** | DB | WZKS | ES |
| 37716 | | **GIF** | DB | WZKS | ES |
| 37717 | | **E** | WC | MBDL | CS (S) |
| 37718 | | **GIF** | DB | WZKS | ES |
| 37796 | as | **F** | X | WNSO | TY |
| 37798 | | **ML** | X | WNSO | MG |
| 37799 | as | **GIF** | X | WNSO | ES |
| 37800 | a | **GIF** | DB | WZKS | ES |
| 37801 | s | **GIF** | X | WNSO | ES |
| 37883 | | **GIF** | DB | WZKS | ES |
| 37884 | | **GIF** | DB | WZKS | ES |
| 37886 | | **E** | DB | WNXX | MH | Sir Dyfed/County of Dyfed |
| 37888 | | **GIF** | X | WNSO | ES |
| 37890 | a | **F** | DB | WNXX ~~Sc~~ | ~~MG~~ |
| 37891 | a | **F** | DB | WNXX | TY |
| 37893 | | **E** | DB | WNXX | BS |
| 37895 | s | **E** | DB | WNXX | BS |
| 37896 | s | **F** | DB | WNXX ~~Sc~~ | MG |
| 37898 | s | **F** | HN | HNRS | LM |

**Class 97/3. Class 37s refurbished for Network Rail for use on the Cambrian Lines pilot ERTMS signalling project.** Details as Class 37/0.

| | | | | | |
|---|---|---|---|---|---|
| 97301 | (37100) | **Y** | NR | QETS | BH |
| 97302 | (37170) | **Y** | NR | QETS | BH |
| 97303 | (37178) | **Y** | NR | QETS | BH |
| 97304 | (37217) | **Y** | NR | QETS | BH | John Tiley |

# CLASS 40    ENGLISH ELECTRIC    1Co-Co1

**Built:** 1958–1962 by the English Electric Co. at Vulcan Foundry, Newton-le-Willows.
**Engine:** English Electric 16SVT Mk2 of 1490 kW (2000 h.p.) at 850 r.p.m.
**Main Generator:** English Electric 822/4C.
**Traction Motors:** English Electric 526/5D or EE526/7D.
**Maximum Tractive Effort:** 231 kN (52000 lbf).
**Continuous Tractive Effort:** 137 kN (30900 lbf) at 18.8 m.p.h.

| **Power At Rail:** 1160 kW (1550 h.p.). | **Train Brakes:** Air & vacuum. |
|---|---|
| **Brake Force:** 51 t. | **Dimensions:** 21.18 x 2.78 m. |
| **Weight:** 132 t. | **Wheel Diameter:** 914/1143 mm. |
| **Design Speed:** 90 m.p.h. | **Maximum Speed:** 90 m.p.h. |
| **Fuel Capacity:** 3250 litres. | **RA:** 6. |
| **Train Supply:** Steam. | **Multiple Working:** Blue Star. |

Originally numbered D345.

| | | | | | |
|---|---|---|---|---|---|
| 40145 | **BL** | 40 | ELRD | BQ | East Lancashire Railway |

# CLASS 43      BREL/PAXMAN      Bo-Bo

**Built:** 1976–1982 by BREL at Crewe Works.
**Engine:** Paxman Valenta 12RP200L of 1680 kW (2250 h.p.) at 1500 r.p.m.
(* Paxman 12VP185 of 1565 kW (2100 h.p.) at 1500 r.p.m.).
(m MTU 16V4000 R41R of 1680kW (2250 h.p.) at 1500 r.p.m.). Fitted to the all
FGW, NXEC and XC power cars.
**Main Alternator:** Brush BA1001B.
**Traction Motors:** Brush TMH68–46 or GEC G417AZ, frame mounted.
**Maximum Tractive Effort:** 80 kN (17980 lbf).
**Continuous Tractive Effort:** 46 kN (10340 lbf) at 64.5 m.p.h.
**Power At Rail:** 1320 kW (1770 h.p.).     **Train Brakes:** Air.
**Brake Force:** 35 t.     **Dimensions:** 17.79 x 2.71 m.
**Weight:** 70.25 t.     **Wheel Diameter:** 1020 mm.
**Design Speed:** 125 m.p.h.     **Maximum Speed:** 125 m.p.h.
**Fuel Capacity:** 4500 litres.     **RA:** 5.
**Train Supply:** Three-phase electric.
**Multiple Working:** Within class, jumpers at non-driving end only.

**Notes:** † Buffer fitted.

43013, 43014 & 43062 are fitted with measuring apparatus & front-end cameras.

43053 & 43056 are at Brush, Loughborough for fitting with mtu power units
prior to transfer to FGW, having transferred from NXEC.

| | | | | | |
|---|---|---|---|---|---|
| 43002 | m | **FB** | A | EFPC | LA |
| 43003 | m | **FB** | A | EFPC | LA | ISAMBARD KINGDOM BRUNEL |
| 43004 | m | **FB** | A | EFPC | LA | First for the future/ |
| | | | | | | First ar gyfer y dyfodol |
| 43005 | m | **FB** | A | EFPC | LA |
| 43009 | m | **FB** | A | EFPC | LA | First transforming travel |
| 43010 | m | **FB** | A | EFPC | LA |
| 43012 | m | **FB** | A | EFPC | LA |
| 43013 | † | **Y** | P | QCAR | EC |
| 43014 | † | **Y** | P | QCAR | EC |
| 43015 | m | **FB** | A | EFPC | LA |
| 43016 | m | **FB** | A | EFPC | LA |
| 43017 | m | **FB** | A | EFPC | LA |
| 43018 | m | **FB** | A | EFPC | LA |
| 43020 | m | **FB** | A | EFPC | LA |
| 43021 | m | **FB** | A | EFPC | LA | David Austin – Cartoonist |
| 43022 | m | **FB** | A | EFPC | LA |
| 43023 | m | **FB** | A | EFPC | LA |
| 43024 | m | **FB** | A | EFPC | LA |
| 43025 | m | **FB** | A | EFPC | LA |
| 43026 | m | **FB** | A | EFPC | LA |
| 43027 | m | **FB** | A | EFPC | LA | Glorious Devon |
| 43028 | m | **FB** | A | EFPC | LA |
| 43029 | m | **FB** | A | EFPC | LA |
| 43030 | m | **FB** | A | EFPC | LA | Christian Lewis Trust |
| 43031 | m | **FB** | A | EFPC | LA |

| 43032 m | FB | A | EFPC | LA | |
| 43033 m | FB | A | EFPC | LA | Driver Brian Cooper |
| | | | | | 15 June 1947–5 October 1999 |
| 43034 m | FB | A | EFPC | LA | TravelWatch SouthWest |
| 43035 m | FB | A | EFPC | LA | |
| 43036 m | FB | A | EFPC | LA | |
| 43037 m | FB | A | EFPC | LA | |
| 43040 m | FB | A | EFPC | LA | Bristol St. Philip's Marsh |
| 43041 m | FB | A | EFPC | OO | |
| 43042 m | FB | A | EFPC | OO | |
| 43043 * | MN | P | EMPC | NL | |
| 43044 * | MN | P | EMPC | NL | |
| 43045 * | MN | P | EMPC | NL | |
| 43046 * | ST | P | EMPC | NL | |
| 43047 * | MN | P | EMPC | NL | |
| 43048 * | ST | P | EMPC | NL | T.C.B. Miller MBE |
| 43049 * | MN | P | EMPC | NL | Neville Hill |
| 43050 * | ST | P | EMPC | NL | |
| 43052 * | MN | P | EMPC | NL | |
| 43053 m | FB | P | EFPC | OO | |
| 43054 * | MN | P | EMPC | NL | |
| 43055 * | ST | P | EMPC | NL | |
| 43056 m | FB | P | EFPC | OO | |
| 43058 * | ST | P | EMPC | NL | |
| 43059 * | MN | P | EMPC | NL | |
| 43060 * | MN | P | EMPC | NL | |
| 43061 * | MN | P | EMPC | NL | |
| 43062 Y | | P | QCAR | EC | John Armitt |
| 43063 m | FB | P | EFPC | OO | |
| 43064 | MN | P | EMPC | NL | |
| 43065 † | GC | ST | GCHP | HT | |
| 43066 * | MN | P | EMPC | NL | |
| 43067 † | GC | ST | GCHP | HT | |
| 43068 † | GC | ST | GCHP | HT | |
| 43069 m | FB | P | EFPC | OO | |
| 43070 m | FB | P | EFPC | OO | The Corps of Royal Electrical and |
| | | | | | Mechanical Engineers |
| 43071 m | FB | P | EFPC | OO | |
| 43072 * | MN | P | EMPC | NL | Derby Etches Park |
| 43073 * | MN | P | EMPC | NL | |
| 43074 * | MN | P | EMPC | NL | |
| 43075 * | MN | P | EMPC | NL | |
| 43076 * | MN | P | EMPC | NL | |
| 43078 m | FB | P | EFPC | OO | |
| 43079 m | FB | P | EFPC | OO | |
| 43080 † | GC | ST | GCHP | HT | |
| 43081 * | MN | P | EMPC | NL | |
| 43082 * | MN | P | EMPC | NL | |
| 43083 * | ST | P | EMPC | NL | |
| 43084 † | GC | ST | GCHP | HT | |
| 43086 m | FB | P | EFPC | OO | |

| 43087 | m | FB | P | EFPC | OO | |
| 43088 | m | FB | P | EFPC | OO | |
| 43089 | | ST | P | EMPC | NL | |
| 43091 | m | FB | P | EFPC | OO | |
| 43092 | m | FB | FG | EFPC | OO | |
| 43093 | m | FB | FG | EFPC | OO | |
| 43094 | m | FB | FG | EFPC | OO | |
| 43097 | m | FB | FG | EFPC | OO | Environment Agency |
| 43098 | m | FB | FG | EFPC | OO | |
| 43122 | m | FB | FG | EFPC | OO | |
| 43123 | † | GC | ST | GCHP | HT | |
| 43124 | m | FB | A | EFPC | LE | |
| 43125 | m | FB | A | EFPC | LE | |
| 43126 | m | FB | A | EFPC | LE | |
| 43127 | m | FB | A | EFPC | LE | Sir Peter Parker 1924–2002 |
| | | | | | | Cotswold Line 150 |
| 43128 | m | FB | A | EFPC | LE | |
| 43129 | m | FB | A | EFPC | LE | |
| 43130 | m | FB | A | EFPC | LE | |
| 43131 | m | FB | A | EFPC | LE | |
| 43132 | m | FB | A | EFPC | LE | We Save the Children – Will You? |
| 43133 | m | FB | A | EFPC | LE | |
| 43134 | m | FB | A | EFPC | LE | |
| 43135 | m | FB | A | EFPC | LE | |
| 43136 | m | FB | A | EFPC | LE | |
| 43137 | m | FB | A | EFPC | LE | |
| 43138 | m | FB | A | EFPC | LE | |
| 43139 | m | FB | A | EFPC | LE | Driver Stan Martin |
| | | | | | | 25 June 1960 – 6 November 2004 |
| 43140 | m | FB | A | EFPC | LE | |
| 43141 | m | FB | A | EFPC | LE | |
| 43142 | m | FB | A | EFPC | LE | |
| 43143 | m | FB | A | EFPC | LE | Stroud 700 |
| 43144 | m | FB | A | EFPC | LE | |
| 43145 | m | FB | A | EFPC | LE | |
| 43146 | m | FB | A | EFPC | LE | |
| 43147 | m | FB | A | EFPC | LE | |
| 43148 | m | FB | A | EFPC | LE | |
| 43149 | m | FB | A | EFPC | LE | |
| 43150 | m | FB | A | EFPC | LE | |
| 43151 | m | FB | A | EFPC | LE | |
| 43152 | m | FB | A | EFPC | LE | |
| 43153 | m | FB | FG | EFPC | OO | |
| 43154 | m | FB | FG | EFPC | OO | |
| 43155 | m | FB | FG | EFPC | OO | |
| 43156 | m | FB | P | EFPC | OO | Dartington International Summer School |
| 43158 | m | FB | FG | EFPC | OO | |
| 43159 | m | FB | P | EFPC | OO | |
| 43160 | m | FB | P | EFPC | OO | |
| 43161 | m | FB | P | EFPC | OO | |
| 43162 | m | FB | P | EFPC | OO | |

| 43163 | m | FB | A  | EFPC | OO |                       |
|-------|---|----|----|------|----|-----------------------|
| 43164 | m | FB | A  | EFPC | OO |                       |
| 43165 | m | FB | A  | EFPC | OO | Prince Michael of Kent |
| 43168 | m | FB | A  | EFPC | OO |                       |
| 43169 | m | FB | A  | EFPC | OO | THE NATIONAL TRUST    |
| 43170 | m | FB | A  | EFPC | OO |                       |
| 43171 | m | FB | A  | EFPC | OO |                       |
| 43172 | m | FB | A  | EFPC | OO |                       |
| 43174 | m | FB | A  | EFPC | OO |                       |
| 43175 | m | FB | A  | EFPC | OO |                       |
| 43176 | m | FB | A  | EFPC | OO |                       |
| 43177 | m | FB | A  | EFPC | OO |                       |
| 43179 | m | FB | A  | EFPC | OO | Pride of Laira        |
| 43180 | m | FB | P  | EFPC | OO |                       |
| 43181 | m | FB | A  | EFPC | OO |                       |
| 43182 | m | FB | A  | EFPC | OO |                       |
| 43183 | m | FB | A  | EFPC | OO |                       |
| 43185 | m | FB | A  | EFPC | OO | Great Western         |
| 43186 | m | FB | A  | EFPC | OO |                       |
| 43187 | m | FB | A  | EFPC | OO |                       |
| 43188 | m | FB | A  | EFPC | OO |                       |
| 43189 | m | FB | A  | EFPC | OO |                       |
| 43190 | m | FB | A  | EFPC | OO |                       |
| 43191 | m | FB | A  | EFPC | OO |                       |
| 43192 | m | FB | A  | EFPC | OO |                       |
| 43193 | m | FB | P  | EFPC | OO |                       |
| 43194 | m | FB | FG | EFPC | OO |                       |
| 43195 | m | FB | P  | EFPC | OO |                       |
| 43196 | m | FB | P  | EFPC | OO |                       |
| 43197 | m | FB | P  | EFPC | OO |                       |
| 43198 | m | FB | FG | EFPC | OO | Oxfordshire 2007      |

**Class 43/2. Rebuilt NXEC and XC power cars.** Power cars have been renumbered by adding 200 to their original number.

| 43206 | (43006) | m | GN | A | IECP | EC | Kingdom of Fife       |
|-------|---------|---|----|---|------|----|-----------------------|
| 43207 | (43007) | m | XC | A | EHPC | EC |                       |
| 43208 | (43008) | m | NX | A | IECP | EC |                       |
| 43238 | (43038) | m | NX | A | IECP | EC |                       |
| 43239 | (43039) | m | NX | A | IECP | EC |                       |
| 43251 | (43051) | m | NX | P | IECP | EC |                       |
| 43257 | (43057) | m | NX | P | IECP | EC |                       |
| 43277 | (43077) | m | NX | P | IECP | EC |                       |
| 43285 | (43085) | m | XC | P | EHPC | EC |                       |
| 43290 | (43090) | m | NX | P | IECP | EC | mtu fascination of power |
| 43295 | (43095) | m | NX | A | IECP | EC |                       |
| 43296 | (43096) | m | GN | A | IECP | EC | Stirling Castle       |
| 43299 | (43099) | m | NX | P | IECP | EC |                       |
| 43300 | (43100) | m | NX | P | IECP | EC | Craigentinny          |
| 43301 | (43101) | m | XC | P | EHPC | EC |                       |
| 43302 | (43102) | m | NX | P | IECP | EC |                       |
| 43303 | (43103) | m | XC | P | EHPC | EC |                       |

| 43304 | (43104) | m | XC | A | EHPC | EC | |
| 43305 | (43105) | m | NX | A | IECP | EC | |
| 43306 | (43106) | m | NX | A | IECP | EC | |
| 43307 | (43107) | m | NX | A | IECP | EC | |
| 43308 | (43108) | m | NX | A | IECP | EC | |
| 43309 | (43109) | m | NX | A | IECP | EC | |
| 43310 | (43110) | m | NX | A | IECP | EC | |
| 43311 | (43111) | m | NX | A | IECP | EC | |
| 43312 | (43112) | m | NX | A | IECP | EC | |
| 43313 | (43113) | m | GN | A | IECP | EC | The Highlands |
| 43314 | (43114) | m | GN | A | IECP | EC | East Riding of Yorkshire |
| 43315 | (43115) | m | NX | A | IECP | EC | |
| 43316 | (43116) | m | NX | A | IECP | EC | |
| 43317 | (43117) | m | NX | A | IECP | EC | |
| 43318 | (43118) | m | GN | A | IECP | EC | City of Kingston upon Hull |
| 43319 | (43119) | m | NX | A | IECP | EC | |
| 43320 | (43120) | m | NX | A | IECP | EC | |
| 43321 | (43121) | m | XC | P | EHPC | EC | |
| 43357 | (43157) | m | XC | P | EHPC | EC | |
| 43366 | (43166) | m | XC | A | EHPC | EC | |
| 43367 | (43167) | m | NX | A | IECP | EC | DELTIC 50 1955–2005 |
| 43378 | (43178) | m | XC | A | EHPC | EC | |
| 43384 | (43184) | m | XC | A | EHPC | EC | |

# CLASS 47          BR/BRUSH/SULZER          Co-Co

**Built:** 1963–1967 by Brush Traction, at Loughborough or by BR at Crewe Works.
**Engine:** Sulzer 12LDA28C of 1920 kW (2580 h.p.) at 750 r.p.m.
**Main Generator:** Brush TG160-60 Mk4 or TM172-50 Mk1.
**Traction Motors:** Brush TM64-68 Mk1 or Mk1A.
**Maximum Tractive Effort:** 267 kN (60000 lbf).
**Continuous Tractive Effort:** 133 kN (30000 lbf) at 26 m.p.h.
**Power At Rail:** 1550 kW (2080 h.p.).      **Train Brakes:** Air.
**Brake Force:** 61 t.                        **Dimensions:** 19.38 x 2.79 m.
**Weight:** 111.5–120.6 t.                    **Wheel Diameter:** 1143 mm.
**Design Speed:** 95 m.p.h.
**Maximum Speed:** 95 m.p.h. (* 75 m.p.h.).  **RA:** 6 or 7.
**Fuel Capacity:** 3273 (+ 5550).
**Train Supply:** Not equipped.
**Multiple Working:** † DRS system, m Green Circle (operational locos only).

Originally numbered in series D1100–D1111, D1500–D1999 but not in order.

**Non-standard liveries/numbering:**

47145 Dark blue with Railfreight Distribution logos.
47773 Also carries number D1755.
47812 Also carries number D1916.
47815 Also carries number D1748.
47829 "Police" livery of white with a broad red band outlined in yellow.
47851 Also carries number D1648.
47853 "XP64 blue" with red cabside panels. Also carries number D1733.
47972 BR Central Services red & grey.

**Class 47/0 (Dual-braked locos) or Class 47/2 (Air-braked locos). Standard Design.** Details as above.

| | | | | |
|---|---|---|---|---|
| 47145 + | **0** | HN | HNRS | GL |
| 47150 *+ | **FL** | HN | HNRS | BA |
| 47194 | **F** | WC | MBDL | CS (S) |
| 47236 + | **FE** | WC | MBDL | CS (S) |
| 47237 + | **AZ** | CD | ADFL | GL |
| 47245 x+m | **WC** | WC | MBDL | CS |
| 47289 *+ | **FF** | HN | HNRS | BA |

**Class 47/3 (Dual-braked locos) or Class 47/2 (Air-braked locos).**
Details as Class 47/0 except:                    **Weight:** 113.7 t.

| | | | | |
|---|---|---|---|---|
| 47295 a | **FF** | HN | HNRS | LM |
| 47355 m | **K** | X | MBDL | CS (S) |
| 47363 | **F** | WC | MBDL | CS (S) |
| 47368 x | **F** | WC | MBDL | CS (S) |
| 47370 *+ | **FF** | X | DHLT | IP |
| 47375 + | **AZ** | CD | ADFL | GL |

**Class 47/4. Electric Train Supply equipment.**
Details as Class 47/0 except:

**Weight:** 120.4–125.1 t.                    **Fuel Capacity:** 3273 (+ 5887) litres.
**Train Supply:** Electric. ETH 66.          **RA:** 7.

| | | | | | |
|---|---|---|---|---|---|
| 47489 x | **RG** | WC | MBDL | CS (S) | |
| 47492 x | **RX** | GD | MBDL | CS (S) | |
| 47501 x† | **DS** | DR | XHNC | KM | Craftsman |
| 47525 x | **FE** | WC | MBDL | CS (S) | |
| 47526 x | **BL** | WC | MBDL | CS (S) | |
| 47575 x | **RG** | RV | RTLS | 5< ~~CQ~~ | |
| 47580 x | **BL** | 47 | MBDL | TM | County of Essex |

**Class 47/7. Previously fitted with an older form of TDM.**

Details as Class 47/4 except:
**Weight:** 118.7 t.                    **Fuel Capacity:** 5887 litres.
**Maximum Speed:** 100 m.p.h.

| | | | | | |
|---|---|---|---|---|---|
| 47703 x | **FR** | HN | HNRS | LW | |
| 47709 x† | **DS** | DR | XHNC | KM | |
| 47712 x† | **DS** | DR | XHNC | KM | Pride of Carlisle |
| 47714 xm | **AR** | HN | HNRS | LB | |

**Class 47/7. Former Railnet dedicated locos.** All have twin fuel tanks.

| | | | | | |
|---|---|---|---|---|---|
| 47727 m | **CS** | CS | COLO | TJ | Rebecca |
| 47739 m | **CS** | CS | COLO | TJ | Robin of Templecombe |
| 47747 | **E** | RV | RTLO | CP (S) | |
| 47749 m | **CS** | CS | COLO | TJ | Demelza |
| 47760 | **WC** | WC | MBDL | CS | |
| 47769 | **V** | RV | RTLO | CP | Resolve |
| 47772 x | **RX** | WC | MBDL | CS (S) | |
| 47773 x | **GG** | 70 | MBDL | TM | |
| 47776 x | **RX** | WC | MBDL | CS (S) | |

| 47786 | **WC** | WC | MBDL | CS | Roy Castle OBE |
| 47787 | **WC** | WC | MBDL | CS | |
| 47790 † | **DS** | DR | XHHP | DF | |
| 47791 | **RX** | DR | XHSS | BH | |

**Class 47/4 continued.** RA6. Most fitted with extended-range fuel tanks (+).

**Note:** 47804 renumbered from 47792.

| 47798 | **RP** | NM | MBDL | CS (S) | Prince William |
| 47799 | **RP** | DB | WNXX | OC | |
| 47802 +† | **DS** | DR | XHNC | KM | Pride of Cumbria |
| 47804 | **WC** | WC | MBDL | CS | |
| 47805 +m | **RV** | RV | RTLO | CP | TALISMAN |
| 47810 + | **CD** | CD | CRRH | NC | Captain Sensible |
| 47811 + | **GL** | FL | DFLH | Dagenham | |
| 47812 +m | **GG** | RV | RTLO | CP | |
| 47813 +m | **CD** | CD | CRRH | NC | John Peel |
| 47815 +m | **GG** | RV | RTLO | CP | GREAT WESTERN |
| 47816 + | **GL** | FL | DFLH | BA | |
| 47818 + | **1** | CD | CRRH | NC | Emily |
| 47826 + | **WC** | WC | MBDL | CS | |
| 47828 +m | **CD** | CD | CRRH | NC | Joe Strummer |
| 47829 + | **0** | HN | HNRS | LM | |
| 47830 + | **GL** | FL | DFLH | BA | |
| 47832 +† | **DS** | DR | XHNC | KM | Solway Princess |
| 47839 +m | **RV** | RV | RTLO | CP | PEGASUS |
| 47841 + | **DS** | DR | XHHP | KM | |
| 47843 +m | **RV** | RV | RTLO | CP | VULCAN |
| 47847 +m | **BL** | RV | RTLO | CP | |
| 47848 +m | **RV** | RV | RTLO | CP | TITAN STAR |
| 47851 + | **GG** | WC | MBDL | CS | Traction Magazine |
| 47853 +m | **0** | RV | RTLO | CP | RAIL EXPRESS |
| 47854 + | **WC** | WC | MBDL | CS | |
| 47972 | **0** | WC | MBDL | CS (S) | |

# CLASS 50          ENGLISH ELECTRIC          Co-Co

**Built:** 1967–1968 by English Electric at Vulcan Foundry, Newton-le-Willows.
**Engine:** English Electric 16CVST of 2010 kW (2700 h.p.) at 850 r.p.m.
**Main Generator:** English Electric 840/4B.
**Traction Motors:** English Electric 538/5A.
**Maximum Tractive Effort:** 216 kN (48500 lbf).
**Continuous Tractive Effort:** 147 kN (33000 lbf) at 23.5 m.p.h.
**Power At Rail:** 1540 kW (2070 h.p.).
**Brake Force:** 59 t.
**Weight:** 116.9 t.
**Design Speed:** 105 m.p.h.
**Fuel Capacity:** 4796 litres.
**Train Supply:** Electric, index 61.

**Train Brakes:** Air & vacuum.
**Dimensions:** 20.88 x 2.78 m.
**Wheel Diameter:** 1092 mm.
**Maximum Speed:** 90 m.p.h.
**RA:** 6.
**Multiple Working:** Orange Square.

Originally numbered D431, D444 & D449.

| 50031 | **BL** | PO | CFOL | KR | Hood |
|-------|--------|-----|------|-----|------|
| 50044 | **GG** | 50 | CFOL | KR | EXETER |
| 50049 | **BL** | 50 | CFOL | TM | Defiance |

## CLASS 52                   BR/MAYBACH                   C-C

**Built:** 1961–1964 Swindon Works.
**Engine:** Two Maybach MD655 of 1007 kW (1350 h.p) at 1500 r.p.m.
**Transmission:** Hydraulic. Voith L630rV.
**Maximum Tractive Effort:** 297 kN (66700 lbf).
**Continuous Tractive Effort:** 201 kN (45200 lbf) at 14.5 m.p.h.
**Power At Rail:** 1490 kW (2000 h.p.).      **Train Brakes:** Air & vacuum.
**Brake Force:** 83 t.                        **Dimensions:** 20.7 m x 2.78 m.
**Weight:** 110 t.                            **Wheel Diameter:** 1092 mm.
**Design Speed:** 90 m.p.h.                   **Maximum Speed:** 90 m.p.h.
**Fuel Capacity:** 3900 litres.               **RA:** 6.
**Train Supply:** Steam.                      **Multiple Working:** Not equipped.

Never allocated a number in the 1972 number series.

Registered on TOPS as No. 89416.

| D1015 | **M** | DT | MBDL | KR | WESTERN CHAMPION |
|-------|-------|-----|------|-----|------------------|

## CLASS 55              ENGLISH ELECTRIC              Co-Co

**Built:** 1961 by English Electric at Vulcan Foundry, Newton-le-Willows.
**Engine:** Two Napier-Deltic D18-25 of 1230 kW (1650 h.p.) each at 1500 r.p.m.
**Main Generators:** Two English Electric 829/1A.
**Traction Motors:** English Electric 538/A.
**Maximum Tractive Effort:** 222 kN (50000 lbf).
**Continuous Tractive Effort:** 136 kN (30500 lbf) at 32.5 m.p.h.
**Power At Rail:** 1969 kW (2640 h.p.).      **Train Brakes:** Air & vacuum.
**Brake Force:** 51 t.                        **Dimensions:** 21.18 x 2.68 m.
**Weight:** 100 t.                            **Wheel Diameter:** 1092 mm.
**Design Speed:** 105 m.p.h.                  **Maximum Speed:** 100 m.p.h.
**Fuel Capacity:** 3755 litres.               **RA:** 5.
**Train Supply:** Electric, index 66.         **Multiple Working:** Not equipped.

Originally numbered D9016 & D9000.

55022 registered on TOPS as No. 89500.

| 55016 | **GG** | DR | XHSS | BH | GORDON HIGHLANDER |
|-------|--------|-----|------|-----|-------------------|
| 55022 | **B**  | MW | ELRD | BQ | ROYAL SCOTS GREY |

# CLASS 56     BRUSH/BR/RUSTON     Co-Co

**Built:** 1976–1984 by Electroputere at Craiova, Romania (as sub contractors for Brush) or BREL at Doncaster or Crewe Works.
**Engine:** Ruston Paxman 16RK3CT of 2460 kW (3250 h.p.) at 900 r.p.m.
**Main Alternator:** Brush BA1101A.
**Traction Motors:** Brush TM73-62.
**Maximum Tractive Effort:** 275 kN (61800 lbf).
**Continuous Tractive Effort:** 240 kN (53950 lbf) at 16.8 m.p.h.
**Power At Rail:** 1790 kW (2400 h.p.).    **Train Brakes:** Air.
**Brake Force:** 60 t.                    **Dimensions:** 19.36 x 2.79 m.
**Weight:** 126 t.                     **Wheel Diameter:** 1143 mm.
**Design Speed:** 80 m.p.h.         **Maximum Speed:** 80 m.p.h.
**Fuel Capacity:** 5228 litres.      **RA:** 7.
**Train Supply:** Not equipped.     **Multiple Working:** Red Diamond.

**Note:** All equipped with Slow Speed Control.

**Non-standard liveries:**

56311 Light grey with yellow cabsides.
56312 Purple with yellow cabsides & green lining.

| | | | | |
|---|---|---|---|---|
| 56006 | B | DB | WNXX | BH |
| 56007 | FER | DB | WZGF | CE |
| 56011 | E | HN | HNRS | LM |
| 56018 | FER | DB | WZGF | WA |
| 56021 | LH | HN | HNRS | LM |
| 56025 | F | X | WNSO | IM |
| 56027 | LH | HS | WNSO | IM |
| 56031 | FER | DB | WZGF | CD |
| 56032 | FER | DB | WZGF | OC |
| 56033 | F | DB | WNXX *Sc* | HM |
| 56037 | E | DB | WZTS | OC |
| 56038 | FER | DB | WZGF | CD |
| 56041 | E | DB | WNXX | HM |
| 56043 | F | X | WNSO | IM |
| 56046 | CE | DB | WNXX | TO |
| 56048 | CE | DB | WZTS *Sc* | HM |
| 56049 | FER | DB | WZGF | OC |
| 56051 | FER | DB | WZGF | OC |
| 56052 | F | X | WNSO | IM |
| 56053 | F | DB | WNXX | HM |
| 56054 | F | DB | WNXX | FB |
| 56055 | LH | DB | WNXX | HM |
| 56056 | F | DB | WNXX *Sc* | HM |
| 56058 | FER | DB | WZGF | OC |
| 56059 | FER | DB | WZGF | OC |
| 56060 | FER | DB | WZGF | OC |
| 56062 | E | DB | WNXX | MG |
| 56064 | F | X | WNSO | IM |
| 56065 | FER | DB | WZGF | CD |

| | | | | |
|---|---|---|---|---|
| 56067 | E | DB | WNXX | FB |
| 56068 | E | DB | ~~WNXX~~ Sc | ~~HM~~ |
| 56069 | FER | DB | WZGF | CD |
| 56070 | F | DB | WNXX | OC |
| 56071 | FER | DB | WZGF | OC |
| 56072 | F | DB | WNXX | HM |
| 56073 | F | DB | WNXX | TO |
| 56074 | FER | DB | WZGF | OC |
| 56076 | F | X | WNSO | IM |
| 56077 | LH | DB | WNXX | CD |
| 56078 | FER | DB | WZGF | CD |
| 56079 | F | DB | ~~WNXX~~ Sc | ~~HM~~ |
| 56081 | FER | DB | WZGF | OC |
| 56082 | F | X | WNSO | IM |
| 56083 | LH | DB | WNXX | FB |
| 56084 | LH | X | WNSO | IM |
| 56085 | LH | DB | WNXX | TE |
| 56086 | F | X | WNSO | IM |
| 56087 | FER | DB | WZGF | CD |
| 56088 | E | DB | WNXX | TE |
| 56089 | E | X | WNSO | IM |
| 56090 | FER | DB | WZGF | OC |
| 56091 | FER | DB | WZGF | EH |
| 56093 | F | DB | WNXX | HM |
| 56094 | FER | DB | WZGF | OC |
| 56095 | FER | DB | WZGF | OC |
| 56096 | FER | DB | WZGF | OC |
| 56099 | F | DB | WNXX | HM |
| 56100 | LH | DB | WNXX | MG |
| 56101 | F | PO | WNSO | IM |
| 56102 | LH | DB | WNXX | TE |
| 56103 | FER | DB | WZGF | OC |
| 56104 | FER | DB | WZGF | OC |
| 56105 | FER | DB | WZGF | OC |
| 56106 | FER | DB | WZGF | CD |
| 56107 | LH | DB | WNXX | FB |
| 56108 | F | DB | WNXX | TE |
| 56109 | LH | DB | WNXX | FB |
| 56110 | LH | DB | WNXX | HM |
| 56111 | LH | DB | WNXX | TE |
| 56112 | LH | DB | WNXX | OC |
| 56113 | FER | DB | WZGF | OC |
| 56114 | E | HS | WNSO | IM |
| 56115 | FER | DB | WZGF | EH |
| 56116 | LH | DB | ~~WNXX~~ Sc | ~~HM~~ |
| 56117 | FER | DB | WZGF | EH |
| 56118 | FER | DB | WZGF | OC |
| 56119 | E | DB | WNXX | HM |
| 56120 | E | DB | WNXX | FB |
| 56127 | F | DB | WNXX | TE |
| 56129 | F | DB | WNXX | TE |

| 56133 | F | DB | WZTS | OC |
| 56134 | F | DB | WZTS | HM |

| 56301 | (56045) | **FA** | FA | RCJA | RR | |
| 56302 | (56124) | **FA** | FA | RCJA | RR | Wilson Walshe |
| 56303 | (56125) | **FA** | RE | RCJA | RR | |

| 56311 | (56057) | **0** | HS | HTLX | WF | |
| 56312 | (56003) | **0** | HS | HTLX | WF | ARTEMIS |
| 56313 | (56128) | | HS | | | |

# CLASS 57       BRUSH/GM       Co-Co

**Built:** 1964–1965 by Brush Traction at Loughborough or BR at Crewe Works as Class 47. Rebuilt 1997–2004 by Brush Traction at Loughborough.
**Engine:** General Motors 12 645 E3 of 1860 kW (2500 h.p.) at 904 r.p.m.
**Main Alternator:** Brush BA1101D.
**Traction Motors:** Brush TM64-68 Mark 1 or Mark 1a.
**Maximum Tractive Effort:** 244.5 kN (55000 lbf).
**Continuous Tractive Effort:** 140 kN (31500 lbf) at ?? m.p.h.
**Power at Rail:** 1507 kW (2025 h.p.).    **Train Brakes:** Air.
**Brake Force:** 80 t.    **Dimensions:** 19.38 x 2.79 m.
**Weight:** 120.6 t.    **Wheel Diameter:** 1143 mm.
**Design Speed:** 75 m.p.h.    **Maximum Speed:** 75 m.p.h.
**Fuel Capacity:** 5550 litres.    **RA:** 6
**Train Supply:** Not equipped.    **Multiple Working:** † DRS system.

**Class 57/0. No Train Supply Equipment. Rebuilt 1998–2000.**

| 57001 | (47356) | | **FL** | P | SBXL | LB |
| 57002 | (47322) | † | **DS** | P | XHHP | KM |
| 57003 | (47317) | † | **DS** | P | XHHP | CR |
| 57004 | (47347) | † | **DS** | DR | XHNC | KM |
| 57005 | (47350) | | **AZ** | St CD | ADFL | GL |
| 57006 | (47187) | | **AZ** | CD | ADFL | GL |
| 57007 | (47332) | † | **DS** | P | XHNC | KM |
| 57008 | (47060) | † | **DS** | P | XHNC | KM |
| 57009 | (47079) | † | **DS** | P | XHNC | KM |
| 57010 | (47231) | † | **DS** | P | XHNC | KM |
| 57011 | (47329) | † | **DS** | P | XHNC | KM |
| 57012 | (47204) | † | **DS** | P | XHNC | KM |

**Class 57/3. Electric Train Supply Equipment. Virgin Trains locos. Rebuilt 2002–2004.** Details as Class 57/0 except:

**Engine:** General Motors 12645F3B of 2050 kW (2750 h.p.) at 954 r.p.m.
**Main Alternator:** Brush BA1101F (recovered from a Class 56) or Brush BA1101G.
**Fuel Capacity:** 5887 litres.    **Train Supply:** Electric, index 100.
**Design Speed:** 95 m.p.h.    **Maximum Speed:** 95 m.p.h.
**Brake Force:** 60 t.    **Weight:** 117 t.

**Note:** 57313–316 are on sub-lease to Arriva Trains Wales and are used on the Holyhead–Cardiff loco-hauled service.

**Non-standard livery**: 57313 & 57316 All over blue.

| | | | | | | |
|---|---|---|---|---|---|---|
| 57301 | (47845) | d | **VT** | P | ATTB | MA | SCOTT TRACY |
| 57302 | (47827) | d | **VT** | P | ATTB | MA | VIRGIL TRACY |
| 57303 | (47705) | d | **VT** | P | ATTB | MA | ALAN TRACY |
| 57304 | (47807) | d | **VT** | P | ATTB | MA | GORDON TRACY |
| 57305 | (47822) | d | **VT** | P | ATTB | MA | JOHN TRACY |
| 57306 | (47814) | d | **VT** | P | ATTB | MA | JEFF TRACY |
| 57307 | (47225) | d | **VT** | P | ATTB | MA | LADY PENELOPE |
| 57308 | (47746) | d | **VT** | P | ATTB | MA | TIN TIN |
| 57309 | (47806) | d | **VT** | P | ATTB | MA | BRAINS |
| 57310 | (47831) | d | **VT** | P | ATTB | MA | KYRANO |
| 57311 | (47817) | d | **VT** | P | ATTB | MA | PARKER |
| 57312 | (47330) | d | **VT** | P | ATTB | MA | THE HOOD |
| 57313 | (47371) | d | **0** | P | ATTB | MA | |
| 57314 | (47372) | d | **AB** | P | ATTB | MA | |
| 57315 | (47234) | d | **AB** | P | ATTB | MA | |
| 57316 | (47290) | d | **0** | P | ATTB | MA | |

**Class 57/6. Electric Train Supply Equipment. Prototype ETS loco. Rebuilt 2001.** Details as Class 57/0 except:

**Main Alternator:** Brush BA1101E.  **Fuel Capacity:** 3273 litres.
**Train Supply:** Electric, index 100.  **Weight:** 113 t.
**Design Speed:** 95 m.p.h.  **Maximum Speed:** 95 m.p.h.
**Brake Force:** 60 t.

| | | | | | |
|---|---|---|---|---|---|
| 57601 | (47825) | **WC** | WC MBDL | CS | |

**Class 57/6. Electric Train Supply Equipment. First Great Western locos. Rebuilt 2004.** Details as Class 57/3.

| | | | | | | |
|---|---|---|---|---|---|---|
| 57602 | (47337) | **FB** | P | EFOO | OO | Restormel Castle |
| 57603 | (47349) | **GL** | P | EFOO | OO | Tintagel Castle |
| 57604 | (47209) | **GL** | P | EFOO | OO | Pendennis Castle |
| 57605 | (47206) | **FB** | P | EFOO | OO | Totnes Castle |

# CLASS 58          BREL/RUSTON          Co-Co

**Built:** 1983–1987 by BREL at Doncaster Works.
**Engine:** Ruston Paxman 12RK3ACT of 2460 kW (3300 h.p.) at 1000 r.p.m.
**Main Alternator:** Brush BA1101B.  **Traction Motors:** Brush TM73-62.
**Maximum Tractive Effort:** 275 kN (61800 lbf).
**Continuous Tractive Effort:** 240 kN (53950 lbf) at 17.4 m.p.h.
**Power At Rail:** 1780 kW (2387 h.p.).  **Train Brakes:** Air.
**Brake Force:** 60 t.  **Dimensions:** 19.13 x 2.72 m.
**Weight:** 130 t.  **Wheel Diameter:** 1120 mm.
**Design Speed:** 80 m.p.h.  **Maximum Speed:** 80 m.p.h.
**Fuel Capacity:** 4214 litres.  **RA:** 7.
**Train Supply:** Not equipped.  **Multiple Working:** Red Diamond.

**Notes:** All equipped with Slow Speed Control.

Locos in use in The Netherlands currently carry the following numbers: 58039; 5811, 58044; 5812 and 58038; 5814.

**Non-standard liveries:**

58001 As **F0** but with a red solebar stripe.
58038 Vos Logistics (black with a broad orange stripe).

| | | | | |
|---|---|---|---|---|
| 58001 | **0** | DB | WZFF | BH |
| 58002 | **ML** | DB | WZTS | EH |
| 58003 | **F** | DB | WZTS | TO |
| 58004 | **FER** | DB | WZFF | EH |
| 58005 | **ML** | DB | WZFF | TO |
| 58006 | **F** | DB | WZFF | EH |
| 58007 | **SCO** | DB | WZFF | EH |
| 58008 | **ML** | DB | WZTS | TO |
| 58009 | **SCO** | DB | WZFF | EH |
| 58010 | **FER** | DB | WZFF | EH |
| 58011 | **FER** | DB | WZFF | EH |
| 58012 | **F** | DB | WZTS | TO |
| 58013 | **ML** | DB | WZFF | EH |
| 58014 | **ML** | DB | WZTS | TO |
| 58015 | **CON** | DB | WZFS | ES |
| 58016 | **FER** | DB | ~~WZTS~~ | OC  *Bat* |
| 58017 | **F** | DB | WZTS | EH |
| 58018 | **FER** | DB | WZFF | EH |
| 58019 | **F** | DB | WZTS | TO |
| 58020 | **GIF** | DB | WZFS | ES |
| 58021 | **FER** | DB | WZFF | EH |
| 58022 | **F** | DB | WZTS | CD |
| 58023 | **ML** | DB | WZTS | TO |
| 58024 | **GIF** | DB | WZFS | ES |
| 58025 | **GIF** | DB | WZFS | ES |
| 58026 | **F** | DB | WZFF | EH |
| 58027 | **CON** | DB | WZFS | ES |
| 58028 | **F** | DB | WZTS | TO |
| 58029 | **GIF** | DB | WZFS | ES |
| 58030 | **GIF** | DB | WZFS | ES |
| 58031 | **GIF** | DB | WZFS | ES |
| 58032 | **FER** | DB | WZFF | EH |
| 58033 | **TSO** | DB | WZFF | EH |
| 58034 | **FER** | DB | WZFF | EH |
| 58035 | **FER** | DB | WZFF | EH |
| 58036 | **ML** | DB | WZFF | TO |
| 58037 | **E** | DB | WZFS | EH |
| 58038 | **0** | DB | WZFH | TB |
| 58039 | **ACT** | DB | WZFH | TB |
| 58040 | **SCO** | DB | WZFF | EH |
| 58041 | **GIF** | DB | WZFS | ES |
| 58042 | **ML** | DB | WZFF | EH |
| 58043 | **GIF** | DB | WZFS | ES |
| 58044 | **ACT** | DB | WZFH | TB |
| 58045 | **F** | DB | WZTS | OC  *Bratt* |
| 58046 | **FER** | DB | WZFF | EH |
| 58047 | **CON** | DB | WZFS | ES |

| 58048 | **E** | DB | WZTS | OC |
| 58049 | **TSO** | DB | WZFF | EH |
| 58050 | **CON** | DB | WZFS | ES |

# CLASS 59          GENERAL MOTORS          Co-Co

**Built:** 1985 (59001/59002/59004) or 1989 (59005) by General Motors, La Grange, Illinois, USA or 1990 (59101–59104), 1994 (59201) and 1995 (59202–59206) by General Motors, London, Ontario, Canada.
**Engine:** General Motors 16-645E3C two stroke of 2460 kW (3300 h.p.) at 904 r.p.m.
**Main Alternator:** General Motors AR11 MLD-D14A.
**Traction Motors:** General Motors D77B.
**Maximum Tractive Effort:** 506 kN (113 550 lbf).
**Continuous Tractive Effort:** 291 kN (65 300 lbf) at 14.3 m.p.h.
**Power At Rail:** 1889 kW (2533 h.p.).     **Train Brakes:** Air.
**Brake Force:** 69 t.                      **Dimensions:** 21.35 x 2.65 m.
**Weight:** 121 t.                          **Wheel Diameter:** 1067 mm.
**Design Speed:** 60 (* 75) m.p.h.          **Maximum Speed:** 60 (* 75) m.p.h.
**Fuel Capacity:** 4546 litres.             **RA:** 7.
**Train Supply:** Not equipped.             **Multiple Working:** AAR System.

**Class 59/0. Owned by Aggregate Industries.**

| 59001 | **AI** | AI | XYPO | MD | YEOMAN ENDEAVOUR |
| 59002 | **FY** | AI | XYPO | MD | ALAN J DAY |
| 59004 | **FY** | AI | XYPO | MD | PAUL A HAMMOND |
| 59005 | **AI** | AI | XYPO | MD | KENNETH J PAINTER |

**Class 59/1. Owned by Hanson Quarry Products.**

| 59101 | **HA** | HA | XYPA | MD | Village of Whatley |
| 59102 | **HA** | HA | XYPA | MD | Village of Chantry |
| 59103 | **HA** | HA | XYPA | MD | Village of Mells |
| 59104 | **HA** | HA | XYPA | MD | Village of Great Elm |

**Class 59/2. Owned by DB Schenker.**

| 59201 | * | **E** | DB | WDAK | TO | Vale of York |
| 59202 | * | **E** | DB | WDAK | TO | Vale of White Horse |
| 59203 | * | **E** | DB | WDAK | TO | Vale of Pickering |
| 59204 | * | **E** | DB | WDAK | TO | Vale of Glamorgan |
| 59205 | *b | **E** | DB | WDAK | TO | L Keith McNair |
| 59206 | *b | **DB** | DB | WDAK | TO | John F. Yeoman Rail Pioneer |

# CLASS 60          BRUSH/MIRRLEES          Co-Co

**Built:** 1989–1993 by Brush Traction at Loughborough.
**Engine:** Mirrlees 8MB275T of 2310 kW (3100 h.p.) at 1000 r.p.m.
**Main Alternator:** Brush BA1006A.
**Traction Motors:** Brush TM2161A.
**Maximum Tractive Effort:** 500 kN (106500 lbf).
**Continuous Tractive Effort:** 336 kN (71570 lbf) at 17.4 m.p.h.
**Power At Rail:** 1800 kW (2415 h.p.).          **Train Brakes:** Air.
**Brake Force:** 74 (+ 62) t.                   **Dimensions:** 21.34 x 2.64 m.
**Weight:** 129 (+ 131) t.                      **Wheel Diameter:** 1118 mm.
**Design Speed:** 62 m.p.h.                     **Maximum Speed:** 60 m.p.h.
**Fuel Capacity:** 4546 (+ 5225) litres.        **RA:** 8.
**Train Supply:** Not equipped.                 **Multiple Working:** Within class.

**IMPORTANT NOTE: DB Schenker Fleet Management Unit:** As all operational
Class 60s are effectively now treated as "common user" by DB Schenker, and
allocated to operational pools depending on which duties they are on at the
time (sometimes changing between different business units several times per
month), all operational locos are shown in the WFMU Fleet Management pool
here. Details of the other individual pools can be found in the codes section of
this book.

**Notes:** All equipped with Slow Speed Control.

60034, 60061, 60064, 60066, 60072, 60073, 60077, 60079, 60082, 60084, 60088
and 60090 carry their names on one side only.

60500 used to carry the number 60016.

60007, 60044 and 60078 carry EWS logos on their **LH** or **ML** liveries.

**Advertising liveries:**

60040 Territorial Army Centenary (maroon).
60074 Teenage Cancer Trust (light blue).

| | | | | | |
|---|---|---|---|---|---|
| 60001 | **E** | DB | WNTS | TO | The Railway Observer |
| 60002 + | **E** | DB | WNTR | TO | High Peak |
| 60003 + | **E** | DB | WNTS | TO | FREIGHT TRANSPORT ASSOCIATION |
| 60004 + | **E** | DB | WFMU | TO | |
| 60005 + | **E** | DB | WNTS | TO | BP Gas Avonmouth |
| 60006 | **CU** | DB | WNTS | TO | Scunthorpe Ironmaster |
| 60007 + | **LH** | DB | WNTS | CD | |
| 60008 | **E** | DB | WNTS | TO | Sir William McAlpine |
| 60009 + | **E** | DB | WFMU | TO | |
| 60010 + | **E** | DB | WFMU | TO | |
| 60011 | **M** | DB | WNTS | TO | |
| 60012 + | **E** | DB | WFMU | TO | |
| 60013 | **EG** | DB | WFMU | TO | Robert Boyle |
| 60014 | **EG** | DB | WNTS | TO | Alexander Fleming |
| 60015 + | **EG** | DB | WNTS | TO | Bow Fell |
| 60017 + | **E** | DB | WNTS | TO | Shotton Works Centenary Year 1996 |
| 60018 | **E** | DB | WFMU | TO | |

| | | | | | |
|---|---|---|---|---|---|
| 60019 | E | DB | WFMU | TO | PATHFINDER TOURS 30 YEARS OF RAILTOURING 1973–2003 |
| 60020 + | E | DB | WFMU | TO | |
| 60021 + | E | DB | WFMU | TO | Star of the East |
| 60022 + | E | DB | WFMU | TO | |
| 60023 + | E | DB | WNTS | TO | |
| 60024 | E | DB | WFMU | TO | |
| 60025 + | E | DB | WNTS | TO | Caledonian Paper |
| 60026 + | E | DB | WFMU | TO | |
| 60027 + | E | DB | WFMU | TO | |
| 60028 + | EG | DB | WNTS | CE | John Flamsteed |
| 60029 | E | DB | WNTS | TO | Clitheroe Castle |
| 60030 + | E | DB | WNTS | TO | |
| 60031 | E | DB | WFMU | TO | ABP Connect |
| 60032 | F | DB | WNTS | TO | William Booth |
| 60033 + | CU | DB | WNTS | TO | Tees Steel Express |
| 60034 | EG | DB | WNTS | TO | Carnedd Llewelyn |
| 60035 | E | DB | WNTS | CD | |
| 60036 | E | DB | WNTS | TO | GEFCO |
| 60037 + | E | DB | WNTS | TO | Aberddawan/Aberthaw |
| 60038 + | E | DB | WNTR | CD | AvestaPolarit |
| 60039 | E | DB | WNTR | TO | |
| 60040 | AL | DB | WFMU | TO | The Territorial Army Centenary |
| 60041 + | E | DB | WNTR | CD | |
| 60042 | E | DB | WNTS | TO | The Hundred of Hoo |
| 60043 | E | DB | WNTR | CD | |
| 60044 | ML | DB | WFMU | TO | |
| 60045 | E | DB | WNTR | CD | The Permanent Way Institution |
| 60046 + | EG | DB | WNTR | CD | William Wilberforce |
| 60047 | E | DB | WNTS | CD | |
| 60048 | E | DB | WFMU | TO | EASTERN |
| 60049 | E | DB | WFMU | TO | |
| 60050 | E | DB | WNTS | TO | |
| 60051 + | E | DB | WNTS | TO | |
| 60052 + | E | DB | WNTS | TO | Glofa Twr – The last deep mine in Wales – Tower Colliery |
| 60053 | E | DB | WNTS | TO | NORDIC TERMINAL |
| 60054 + | F | DB | WFMU | TO | Charles Babbage |
| 60055 + | EG | DB | WNTS | TO | Thomas Barnardo |
| 60056 + | EG | DB | WNTR | TO | William Beveridge |
| 60057 | EG | DB | WNTS | TO | Adam Smith |
| 60058 + | E | DB | WNTS | TO | |
| 60059 + | LH | DB | WFMU | TO | Swinden Dalesman |
| 60060 | E | DB | WFMU | TO | James Watt |
| 60061 | F | DB | WFMU | TO | Alexander Graham Bell |
| 60062 | E | DB | WFMU | TO | |
| 60063 | EG | DB | WFMU | TO | James Murray |
| 60064 + | EG | DB | WNTS | TO | Back Tor |
| 60065 | E | DB | WFMU | TO | Spirit of JAGUAR |
| 60066 | EG | DB | WFMU | TO | John Logie Baird |
| 60067 | EG | DB | WNTS | TO | James Clerk-Maxwell |

| 60068 | EG | DB | WFMU | TO | Charles Darwin |
|-------|-----|-----|------|-----|----------------|
| 60069 | E | DB | WNTS | TO | Slioch |
| 60070 + | F | DB | WNTS | TO | John Loudon McAdam |
| 60071 + | E | DB | WNTS | TO | Ribblehead Viaduct |
| 60072 | EG | DB | WFMU | TO | Cairn Toul |
| 60073 | EG | DB | WNTS | TO | Cairn Gorm |
| 60074 | AL | DB | WFMU | TO | Teenage Spirit |
| 60075 | E | DB | WNTS | TO | |
| 60076 | EG | DB | WNTR | CD | |
| 60077 + | EG | DB | WNTS | TO | Canisp |
| 60078 | ML | DB | WNTS | TO | |
| 60079 | EG | DB | WNTS | TO | Foinaven |
| 60080 + | E | DB | WNTS | TO | |
| 60081 + | GW | DB | WNTS | TO | ISAMBARD KINGDOM BRUNEL |
| 60082 | EG | DB | WNTS | TO | Mam Tor |
| 60083 | E | DB | WNTS | TO | Mountsorrel |
| 60084 | EG | DB | WFMU | TO | Cross Fell |
| 60085 | E | DB | WFMU | TO | MINI Pride of Oxford |
| 60086 | EG | DB | WNTS | TO | Schiehallion |
| 60087 | E | DB | WFMU | TO | Barry Needham |
| 60088 | F | DB | WNTS | TO | Buachaille Etive Mor |
| 60089 + | E | DB | WNTS | TO | THE RAILWAY HORSE |
| 60090 + | EG | DB | WNTS | TO | Quinag |
| 60091 + | EG | DB | WFMU | TO | An Teallach |
| 60092 + | EG | DB | WNTR | CD | Reginald Munns |
| 60093 | E | DB | WNTS | TO | |
| 60094 | E | DB | WFMU | TO | Rugby Flyer |
| 60095 | EG | DB | WNTR | TO | |
| 60096 + | E | DB | WFMU | TO | |
| 60097 + | E | DB | WNTS | TO | ABP Port of Grimsby & Immingham |
| 60098 + | E | DB | WNTS | TO | Charles Francis Brush |
| 60099 | EG | DB | WFMU | TO | Ben More Assynt |
| 60100 | E | DB | WFMU | TO | Pride of Acton |
| 60500 | E | DB | WNTS | TO | RAIL Magazine |

# CLASS 66    GENERAL MOTORS/EMD    Co-Co

**Built:** 1998–2008 by General Motors/EMD, London, Ontario, Canada (Model JT42CWR (low emission locos Model JT42CWRM)).
**Engine:** General Motors 12N-710G3B-EC two stroke of 2385 kW (3200 h.p.) at 904 r.p.m.
**Main Alternator:** General Motors AR8/CA6.
**Traction Motors:** General Motors D43TR.
**Maximum Tractive Effort:** 409 kN (92000 lbf).
**Continuous Tractive Effort:** 260 kN (58390 lbf) at 15.9 m.p.h.
**Power At Rail:** 1850 kW (2480 h.p.).      **Train Brakes:** Air.
**Brake Force:** 68 t.                         **Dimensions:** 21.35 x 2.64 m.
**Weight:** 127 t.                              **Wheel Diameter:** 1120 mm.
**Design Speed:** 87.5 m.p.h.                   **Maximum Speed:** 75 m.p.h.
**Fuel Capacity:** 6550 litres.                 **RA:** 7.
**Train Supply:** Not equipped.                 **Multiple Working:** AAR System.

**IMPORTANT NOTE: DB Schenker Fleet Management Unit:** As all DB Schenker Class 66s are effectively now treated as "common user" by DB Schenker, and allocated to operational pools depending on which duties they are on at the time (sometimes changing between different business units several times per month), all operational locos are shown in the WFMU Fleet Management pool here. Details of the other individual pools can be found in the codes section of this book.

**Note:** All equipped with Slow Speed Control.

**Class 66 delivery dates.** The Class 66 design has evolved over more than a ten year period with over 400 of these locos now in use in the UK. For clarity the delivery dates (by year) for each batch of locos delivered to the UK is as follows:

| | |
|---|---|
| 66001–66250 | EWS (now DB Schenker). 1998–2000 |
| 66301–66305 | Fastline. 2008 |
| 66401–66410 | DRS. 2003. Now off lease. |
| 66411–66420 | DRS. 2006 |
| 66421–66430 | DRS. 2007 |
| 66431–66434 | DRS. 2008 |
| 66501–66505 | Freightliner. 1999 |
| 66506–66520 | Freightliner. 2000 |
| 66521–66525 | Freightliner. 2000 (66521 since scrapped). |
| 66526–66531 | Freightliner. 2001 |
| 66532–66537 | Freightliner. 2001 |
| 66538–66543 | Freightliner. 2001 |
| 66544–66553 | Freightliner. 2001 |
| 66554 | Freightliner. 2002* |
| 66555–66566 | Freightliner. 2002 |
| 66567–66574 | Freightliner. 2003 |
| 66575–66577 | Freightliner. 2004 |
| 66578–66581 | Freightliner. 2005 |
| 66582–66594 | Freightliner. 2007 (66586 exported to Poland). |
| 66595–66599 | Freightliner. 2008 |
| 66601–66606 | Freightliner. 2000 |

| 66607–66612 | Freightliner. 2002 |
| 66613–66618 | Freightliner. 2003 |
| 66619–66622 | Freightliner. 2005 |
| 66623–66625 | Freightliner. 2007 |
| 66701–66707 | First GBRf. 2001 |
| 66708–66712 | First GBRf. 2002 |
| 66713–66717 | First GBRf. 2003 |
| 66718–66722 | First GBRf. 2006 |
| 66723–66727 | First GBRf. 2006 |
| 66728–66732 | First GBRf. 2008 |
| 66951–66952 | Freightliner. 2004 |
| 66953–66957 | Freightliner. 2008 |

\* Replacement for 66521, written off in the Great Heck accident in 2001.

**Class 66/0. DB Schenker-operated locomotives.**

All fitted with Swinghead Automatic "Buckeye" Combination Couplers except 66001 and 66002.

† Fitted with additional lights and drawgear for Lickey banking duties.

| | | | | | |
|---|---|---|---|---|---|
| 66001 | E | A | WFMU | TO | |
| 66002 | E | A | WFMU | TO | Lafarge Quorn |
| 66003 | E | A | WFMU | TO | |
| 66004 | E | A | WFMU | TO | |
| 66005 | E | A | WFMU | TO | |
| 66006 | E | A | WFMU | TO | |
| 66007 | E | A | WFMU | TO | |
| 66008 | E | A | WFMU | TO | |
| 66009 | E | A | WFMU | TO | |
| 66010 | E | A | WBEN | FN | |
| 66011 | E | A | WFMU | TO | |
| 66012 | E | A | WFMU | TO | |
| 66013 | E | A | WFMU | TO | |
| 66014 | E | A | WFMU | TO | |
| 66015 | E | A | WFMU | TO | |
| 66016 | E | A | WFMU | TO | |
| 66017 | E | A | WFMU | TO | |
| 66018 | E | A | WFMU | TO | |
| 66019 | E | A | WFMU | TO | |
| 66020 | E | A | WFMU | TO | |
| 66021 | E | A | WFMU | TO | |
| 66022 | E | A | WBEN | FN | |
| 66023 | E | A | WFMU | TO | |
| 66024 | E | A | WFMU | TO | |
| 66025 | E | A | WFMU | TO | |
| 66026 | E | A | WBEN | FN | |
| 66027 | E | A | WFMU | TO | |
| 66028 | E | A | WBEN | FN | |
| 66029 | E | A | WBEN | FN | |
| 66030 | E | A | WFMU | TO | |
| 66031 | E | A | WFMU | TO (S) | |

| 66032 | E | A | WBEN | FN | |
|-------|---|---|------|----|--|
| 66033 | E | A | WBEN | FN | |
| 66034 | E | A | WFMU | TO | |
| 66035 | E | A | WFMU | TO | |
| 66036 | E | A | WBEN | FN | |
| 66037 | E | A | WFMU | TO | |
| 66038 | E | A | WBEN | FN | |
| 66039 | E | A | WFMU | TO | |
| 66040 | E | A | WFMU | TO | |
| 66041 | E | A | WFMU | TO | |
| 66042 | E | A | WBEN | FN | |
| 66043 | E | A | WFMU | TO | |
| 66044 | E | A | WFMU | TO | |
| 66045 | E | A | WBEN | FN | |
| 66046 | E | A | WFMU | TO | |
| 66047 | E | A | WFMU | TO | |
| 66048 | E | A | WFMU | TO | |
| 66049 | E | A | WBEN | FN | |
| 66050 | E | A | WFMU | TO | EWS Energy |
| 66051 | E | A | WFMU | TO | |
| 66052 | E | A | WBEN | FN | |
| 66053 | E | A | WFMU | TO | |
| 66054 | E | A | WFMU | TO | |
| 66055 † | E | A | WFMU | TO | |
| 66056 † | E | A | WFMU | TO | |
| 66057 † | E | A | WFMU | TO | |
| 66058 † | E | A | WFMU | TO | |
| 66059 † | E | A | WFMU | TO | |
| 66060 | E | A | WFMU | TO | |
| 66061 | E | A | WFMU | TO | |
| 66062 | E | A | WBEN | FN | |
| 66063 | E | A | WFMU | TO | |
| 66064 | E | A | WBEN | FN | |
| 66065 | E | A | WFMU | TO | |
| 66066 | E | A | WFMU | TO | |
| 66067 | E | A | WFMU | TO | |
| 66068 | E | A | WFMU | TO | |
| 66069 | E | A | WFMU | TO | |
| 66070 | E | A | WFMU | TO | |
| 66071 | E | A | WBEN | FN | |
| 66072 | E | A | WBEN | FN | |
| 66073 | E | A | WBEN | FN | |
| 66074 | E | A | WFMU | TO | |
| 66075 | E | A | WFMU | TO | |
| 66076 | E | A | WFMU | TO | |
| 66077 | E | A | WFMU | TO | Benjamin Gimbert G.C. |
| 66078 | E | A | WFMU | TO | |
| 66079 | E | A | WFMU | TO | James Nightall G.C. |
| 66080 | E | A | WFMU | TO | |
| 66081 | E | A | WFMU | TO | |
| 66082 | E | A | WFMU | TO | |

| 66083 | | E | A | WFMU | TO |
| 66084 | | E | A | WFMU | TO |
| 66085 | | E | A | WFMU | TO |
| 66086 | | E | A | WFMU | TO |
| 66087 | | E | A | WFMU | TO |
| 66088 | | E | A | WFMU | TO |
| 66089 | | E | A | WFMU | TO |
| 66090 | | E | A | WFMU | TO |
| 66091 | | E | A | WFMU | TO |
| 66092 | | E | A | WFMU | TO |
| 66093 | | E | A | WFMU | TO |
| 66094 | | E | A | WFMU | TO |
| 66095 | | E | A | WFMU | TO |
| 66096 | | E | A | WFMU | TO |
| 66097 | | E | A | WFMU | TO |
| 66098 | | E | A | WFMU | TO |
| 66099 | r | E | A | WFMU | TO |
| 66100 | r | E | A | WFMU | TO |
| 66101 | r | E | A | WFMU | TO |
| 66102 | r | E | A | WFMU | TO |
| 66103 | r | E | A | WFMU | TO |
| 66104 | r | E | A | WFMU | TO |
| 66105 | r | E | A | WFMU | TO |
| 66106 | r | E | A | WFMU | TO |
| 66107 | r | E | A | WFMU | TO |
| 66108 | r | E | A | WFMU | TO |
| 66109 | | E | A | WFMU | TO |
| 66110 | r | E | A | WFMU | TO |
| 66111 | r | E | A | WFMU | TO |
| 66112 | r | E | A | WFMU | TO |
| 66113 | r | E | A | WFMU | TO |
| 66114 | r | E | A | WFMU | TO |
| 66115 | | E | A | WFMU | TO |
| 66116 | | E | A | WFMU | TO |
| 66117 | | E | A | WFMU | TO |
| 66118 | | E | A | WFMU | TO |
| 66119 | | E | A | WFMU | TO |
| 66120 | | E | A | WFMU | TO |
| 66121 | | E | A | WFMU | TO |
| 66122 | | E | A | WFMU | TO |
| 66123 | | E | A | WBEN | FN |
| 66124 | | E | A | WFMU | TO |
| 66125 | | E | A | WFMU | TO |
| 66126 | | E | A | WFMU | TO |
| 66127 | | E | A | WFMU | TO |
| 66128 | | E | A | WFMU | TO |
| 66129 | | E | A | WFMU | TO |
| 66130 | | E | A | WFMU | TO |
| 66131 | | E | A | WFMU | TO |
| 66132 | | E | A | WFMU | TO |
| 66133 | | E | A | WFMU | TO |

| 66134 | E | A | WFMU | TO | |
|--------|---|---|------|-----|---|
| 66135 | E | A | WFMU | TO | |
| 66136 | E | A | WFMU | TO | |
| 66137 | E | A | WFMU | TO | |
| 66138 | E | A | WFMU | TO | |
| 66139 | E | A | WFMU | TO | |
| 66140 | E | A | WFMU | TO | |
| 66141 | E | A | WFMU | TO | |
| 66142 | E | A | WFMU | TO | |
| 66143 | E | A | WFMU | TO | |
| 66144 | E | A | WFMU | TO | |
| 66145 | E | A | WFMU | TO | |
| 66146 | E | A | WFMU | TO | |
| 66147 | E | A | WFMU | TO | |
| 66148 | E | A | WFMU | TO | |
| 66149 | E | A | WFMU | TO | |
| 66150 | E | A | WFMU | TO | |
| 66151 | E | A | WFMU | TO | |
| 66152 | E R | A | WFMU | TO | |
| 66153 | E | A | WFMU | TO | |
| 66154 | E | A | WFMU | TO | |
| 66155 | E | A | WFMU | TO | |
| 66156 | E | A | WFMU | TO | |
| 66157 | E | A | WFMU | TO | |
| 66158 | E | A | WFMU | TO | |
| 66159 | E | A | WFMU | TO | |
| 66160 | E | A | WFMU | TO | |
| 66161 | E | A | WFMU | TO | |
| 66162 | E | A | WFMU | TO | |
| 66163 | E | A | WFMU | TO | |
| 66164 | E | A | WFMU | TO | |
| 66165 | E | A | WFMU | TO | |
| 66166 | E | A | WFMU | TO | |
| 66167 | E | A | WFMU | TO | |
| 66168 | E | A | WFMU | TO | |
| 66169 | E | A | WFMU | TO | |
| 66170 | E | A | WFMU | TO | |
| 66171 | E | A | WFMU | TO | |
| 66172 | E | A | WFMU | TO | PAUL MELLENEY |
| 66173 | E | A | WFMU | TO | |
| 66174 | E | A | WFMU | TO | |
| 66175 | E | A | WFMU | TO | |
| 66176 | E | A | WFMU | TO | |
| 66177 | E | A | WFMU | TO | |
| 66178 | E | A | WFMU | TO | |
| 66179 | E | A | WBEN | FN | |
| 66180 | E | A | WFMU | TO | |
| 66181 | E | A | WFMU | TO | |
| 66182 | E | A | WFMU | TO | |
| 66183 | E | A | WFMU | TO | |
| 66184 | E | A | WFMU | TO | |

| 66185 | E | A | WFMU | TO | |
|--------|---|---|------|----|---|
| 66186 | E | A | WFMU | TO | |
| 66187 | E | A | WFMU | TO | |
| 66188 | E | A | WFMU | TO | |
| 66189 | E | A | WFMU | TO | |
| 66190 | E | A | WBEN | FN France | |
| 66191 | E | A | WBEN | FN | |
| 66192 | E | A | WFMU | TO | |
| 66193 | E | A | WFMU | TO | |
| 66194 | E | A | WFMU | TO | |
| 66195 | E | A | WBEN | FN | |
| 66196 | E | A | WFMU | TO | |
| 66197 | E | A | WFMU | TO | |
| 66198 | E | A | WFMU | TO | |
| 66199 | E | A | WFMU | TO | |
| 66200 | E | A | WFMU | TO | RAILWAY HERITAGE COMMITTEE |
| 66201 | E | A | WFMU | TO | |
| 66202 | E | A | WBEN | FN | |
| 66203 | E | A | WBEN | FN | |
| 66204 | E | A | WFMU | TO | |
| 66205 | E | A | WBEN | FN | |
| 66206 | E | A | WFMU | TO | |
| 66207 | E | A | WFMU | TO | |
| 66208 | E | A | WBEN | FN | |
| 66209 | E | A | WBEN | FN | |
| 66210 | E | A | WBEN | FN | |
| 66211 | E | A | WBEN | FN | |
| 66212 | E | A | WBEN | FN | |
| 66213 | E | A | WFMU | TO | |
| 66214 | E | A | WBEN | FN | |
| 66215 | E | A | WBEN | FN | |
| 66216 | E | A | WBEN | FN | |
| 66217 | E | A | WBEN | FN | |
| 66218 | E | A | WBEN | FN | |
| 66219 | E | A | WBEN | FN | |
| 66220 | E | A | WBEN | FN | |
| 66221 | E | A | WFMU | TO | |
| 66222 | E | A | WBEN | FN | |
| 66223 | E | A | WBEN | FN | |
| 66224 | E | A | WBEN | FN | |
| 66225 | E | A | WBEN | FN | |
| 66226 | E | A | WBEN | FN | |
| 66227 | E | A | WFMU | TO | |
| 66228 | E | A | WBEN | FN | |
| 66229 | E | A | WBEN | FN | |
| 66230 | E | A | WFMU | TO | |
| 66231 | E | A | WBEN | FN | |
| 66232 | E | A | WFMU | TO | |
| 66233 | E | A | WBEN | FN | |
| 66234 | E | A | WBEN | FN | |
| 66235 | E | A | WBEN | FN | |

| 66236 | E | A | WBEN | FN |
| 66237 | E | A | WFMU | TO |
| 66238 | E | A | WFMU | TO |
| 66239 | E | A | WBEN | FN |
| 66240 | E | A | WBEN | FN |
| 66241 | E | A | WBEN | FN |
| 66242 | E | A | WBEN | FN |
| 66243 | E | A | WBEN | FN |
| 66244 | E | A | WBEN | FN |
| 66245 | E | A | WBEN | FN |
| 66246 | E | A | WBEN | FN |
| 66247 | E | A | WBEN | FN |
| 66248 | E | A | WFMU | TO |
| 66249 | E | A | WBEN | FN |
| 66250 | E | A | WFMU | TO |

**Class 66/3. Fastline-operated locomotives. Low emission.** Details as Class 66/0 except:

**Engine:** EMD 12N-710G3B-U2 two stroke of 2420 kW (3245 h.p.) at 904 r.p.m.
**Traction Motors:** General Motors D43TRC.
**Fuel Capacity:** 5150 litres.

| 66301 | FA | BM | RCJB | RR |
| 66302 | FA | BM | RCJB | RR |
| 66303 | FA | BM | RCJB | RR |
| 66304 | FA | BM | RCJB | RR |
| 66305 | FA | BM | RCJB | RR |

**Class 66/4. Direct Rail Services-operated locomotives.**
**66401–66410. Porterbrook locos.** Details as Class 66/0. Off-lease at the time of writing.

**Advertising livery:** 66405 WH Malcolm (DRS Blue with WH Malcolm logos).

| 66401 | DS | P | SBXL | LD |
| 66402 | DS | P | SBXL | LD |
| 66403 | DS | P | SBXL | LD |
| 66404 | DS | P | SBXL | LD |
| 66405 | AL | P | SBXL | LD |
| 66406 | DS | P | SBXL | ZH |
| 66407 | DS | P | SBXL | ZH |
| 66408 | DS | P | SBXL | ZH |
| 66409 | DS | P | SBXL | ZH |
| 66410 | DS | P | SBXL | ZH | RN 66845    Colas |

**66411–66434. Low emission. HBOS-owned.** Details as Class 66/0 except:

**Engine:** EMD 12N-710G3B-U2 two stroke of 2420 kW (3245 h.p.) at 904 r.p.m.
**Traction Motors:** General Motors D43TRC.
**Fuel Capacity:** 5150 litres.

**Advertising liveries:** 66411 Eddie Stobart Rail (two tone blue & white).
66412 Malcolm Rail (black with a red solebar stripe).
66414 Tesco Rail (two tone blue & white).

| 66411 | **AL** | HX | XHIM | KM | Eddie the Engine |
| 66412 | **AL** | HX | XHIM | KM | |
| 66413 | **DS** | HX | XHIM | KM | |
| 66414 | **AL** | HX | XHIM | KM | James the Engine |
| 66415 | **DS** | HX | XHIM | KM | |
| 66416 | **DS** | HX | XHIM | KM | |
| 66417 | **DS** | HX | XHIM | KM | |
| 66418 | **DS** | HX | XHIM | KM | |
| 66419 | **DS** | HX | XHIM | KM | |
| 66420 | **DS** | HX | XHIM | KM | |
| 66421 | **DS** | HX | XHIM | KM | |
| 66422 | **DS** | HX | XHIM | KM | |
| 66423 | **DS** | HX | XHIM | KM | |
| 66424 | **DS** | HX | XHIM | KM | |
| 66425 | **DS** | HX | XHIM | KM | |
| 66426 | **DS** | HX | XHIM | KM | |
| 66427 | **DS** | HX | XHIM | KM | |
| 66428 | **DS** | HX | XHIM | KM | |
| 66429 | **DS** | HX | XHIM | KM | |
| 66430 | **DS** | HX | XHIM | KM | |
| 66431 | **DS** | HX | XHIM | KM | |
| 66432 | **DS** | HX | XHIM | KM | |
| 66433 | **DS** | HX | XHIM | KM | |
| 66434 | **DS** | HX | XHIM | KM | |

**Class 66/5. Freightliner-operated locomotives.** Details as Class 66/0.

**Advertising livery:** 66522 Shanks Waste (one half of loco Freightliner green and one half Shanks' Waste light green).

| 66501 | **FL** | P | DFGM | FD | Japan 2001 |
| 66502 | **FL** | P | DFFT | FD | Basford Hall Centenary 2001 |
| 66503 | **FL** | P | DFGM | FD | The RAILWAY MAGAZINE |
| 66504 | **FL** | P | DFGM | FD | |
| 66505 | **FL** | P | DFGM | FD | |
| 66506 | **FL** | H | DFHH | FD | Crewe Regeneration |
| 66507 | **FL** | H | DFRT | FD | |
| 66508 | **FL** | H | DFRT | FD | |
| 66509 | **FL** | H | DFHH | FD | |
| 66510 | **FL** | H | DFRT | FD | |
| 66511 | **FL** | H | DFRT | FD | |
| 66512 | **FL** | H | DFHH | FD | |
| 66513 | **FL** | H | DFHH | FD | |
| 66514 | **FL** | H | DFRT | FD | |
| 66515 | **FL** | H | DFRT | FD | |
| 66516 | **FL** | H | DFGM | FD | |
| 66517 | **FL** | H | DFGM | FD | |
| 66518 | **FL** | H | DFRT | FD | |
| 66519 | **FL** | H | DFHH | FD | |
| 66520 | **FL** | H | DFRT | FD | |
| 66522 | **AL** | H | DFRT | LD | |
| 66523 | **FL** | H | DFRT | FD | |

| 66524 | **FL** | H | DFHH | LD | |
|---|---|---|---|---|---|
| 66525 | **FL** | H | DFHH | FD | |
| 66526 | **FL** | P | DFRT | LD | Driver Steve Dunn (George) |
| 66527 | **FL** | P | DFRT | LD | Don Raider |
| 66528 | **FL** | P | DFHH | FD | |
| 66529 | **FL** | P | DFHH | FD | |
| 66530 | **FL** | P | DFHH | LD | |
| 66531 | **FL** | P | DFHH | FD | |
| 66532 | **FL** | P | DFGM | FD | P&O Nedlloyd Atlas |
| 66533 | **FL** | P | DFGM | FD | Hanjin Express/Senator Express |
| 66534 | **FL** | P | DFGM | FD | OOCL Express |
| 66535 | **FL** | P | DFGM | FD | |
| 66536 | **FL** | P | DFFT | LD | |
| 66537 | **FL** | P | DFGM | FD | |
| 66538 | **FL** | H | DFIM | FD | |
| 66539 | **FL** | H | DFIM | FD | |
| 66540 | **FL** | H | DFIM | FD | Ruby |
| 66541 | **FL** | H | DFIM | FD | |
| 66542 | **FL** | H | DFIM | FD | |
| 66543 | **FL** | H | DFIM | FD | |
| 66544 | **FL** | P | DFHG | LD | |
| 66545 | **FL** | P | DFHG | FD | |
| 66546 | **FL** | P | DFNR | FD | |
| 66547 | **FL** | P | DFNR | LD | |
| 66548 | **FL** | P | DFHG | LD | |
| 66549 | **FL** | P | DFHG | LD | |
| 66550 | **FL** | P | DFHG | LD | |
| 66551 | **FL** | P | DFHG | LD | |
| 66552 | **FL** | P | DFHG | LD | Maltby Raider |
| 66553 | **FL** | P | DFHG | LD | |
| 66554 | **FL** | H | DFHG | LD | |
| 66555 | **FL** | H | DFHG | LD | |
| 66556 | **FL** | H | DFHG | LD | |
| 66557 | **FL** | H | DFHG | FD | |
| 66558 | **FL** | H | DFHG | FD | |
| 66559 | **FL** | H | DFNR | LD | |
| 66560 | **FL** | H | DFHG | FD | |
| 66561 | **FL** | H | DFHG | FD | |
| 66562 | **FL** | H | DFHG | LD | |
| 66563 | **FL** | H | DFHG | FD | |
| 66564 | **FL** | H | DFHG | LD | |
| 66565 | **FL** | H | DFHG | LD | |
| 66566 | **FL** | H | DFHG | LD | |
| 66567 | **FL** | H | DFIM | FD | |
| 66568 | **FL** | H | DFIM | FD | |
| 66569 | **FL** | H | DFIM | FD | |
| 66570 | **FL** | H | DFIM | FD | |
| 66571 | **FL** | H | DFIM | FD | |
| 66572 | **FL** | H | DFIM | FD | |
| 66573 | **FL** | H | DFIM | FD | |
| 66574 | **FL** | H | DFIM | FD | |

| 66575 | **FL** | H | DFIM | FD | |
| 66576 | **FL** | H | DFIM | FD | Hamburg Sud Advantage |
| 66577 | **FL** | H | DFIM | FD | |
| 66578 | **FL** | H | DFIM | FD | |
| 66579 | **FL** | H | DFIM | FD | |
| 66580 | **FL** | H | DFIM | FD | |
| 66581 | **FL** | H | DFHG | FD | Sophie |

**Class 66/5. Freightliner-operated low emission locos.** Details as Class 66/0 except:

**Engine:** EMD 12N-710G3B-U2 two stroke of 2420 kW (3245 h.p.) at 904 r.p.m.
**Traction Motors:** General Motors D43TRC.
**Fuel Capacity:** 5150 litres.

| 66582 | **FL** | HX | DFHG | FD | |
| 66583 | **FL** | HX | DFHG | FD | |
| 66584 | **FL** | HX | DFHG | FD | |
| 66585 | **FL** | HX | DFHG | FD | The Drax Flyer |
| 66587 | **FL** | HX | DFFT | FD | |
| 66588 | **FL** | HX | DFIN | FD | |
| 66589 | **FL** | HX | DFIN | FD | |
| 66590 | **FL** | HX | DFIN | FD | |
| 66591 | **FL** | LY | DFIN | FD | |
| 66592 | **FL** | LY | DFIN | FD | Johnson Stevens Agencies |
| 66593 | **FL** | LY | DFIN | FD | 3MG MERSEY MULTIMODAL GATEWAY |
| 66594 | **FL** | LY | DFIN | FD | NYK Spirit of Kyoto |
| 66595 | **FL** | BM | DFHG | FD | |
| 66596 | **FL** | BM | DFHG | FD | |
| 66597 | **FL** | BM | DFHG | FD | |
| 66598 | **FL** | BM | DFHG | FD | |
| 66599 | **FL** | BM | DFHG | FD | |

**Class 66/6. Freightliner-operated locomotives with modified gear ratios.** Details as Class 66/0 except:

**Maximum Tractive Effort:** 467 kN (105080 lbf).
**Continuous Tractive Effort:** 296 kN (66630 lbf) at 14.0 m.p.h.
**Design Speed:** 65 m.p.h.          **Maximum Speed:** 65 m.p.h.

| 66601 | **FL** | P | DFHH | FD | The Hope Valley |
| 66602 | **FL** | P | DFRT | FD | |
| 66603 | **FL** | P | DFRT | FD | |
| 66604 | **FL** | P | DFRT | FD | |
| 66605 | **FL** | P | DFRT | FD | |
| 66606 | **FL** | P | DFRT | FD | |
| 66607 | **FL** | P | DFHG | FD | |
| 66608 | **FL** | P | DFHG | FD | |
| 66609 | **FL** | P | DFHG | FD | |
| 66610 | **FL** | P | DFHG | FD | |
| 66611 | **FL** | P | DFHG | FD | |
| 66612 | **FL** | P | DFHG | FD | Forth Raider |
| 66613 | **FL** | H | DFHG | FD | |
| 66614 | **FL** | H | DFHG | FD | |

| 66615 | **FL** | H | DFHG | FD | |
|-------|--------|---|------|----|---|
| 66616 | **FL** | H | DFHG | FD | |
| 66617 | **FL** | H | DFHG | FD | |
| 66618 | **FL** | H | DFHG | FD | Railways Illustrated Annual Photographic Awards Alan Barnes |
| 66619 | **FL** | H | DFHG | FD | Derek W. Johnson MBE |
| 66620 | **FL** | H | DFHG | FD | |
| 66621 | **FL** | H | DFHG | FD | |
| 66622 | **FL** | H | DFHG | FD | |

**Class 66/6. Freightliner-operated low emission locos with modified gear ratios.**
**Fuel Capacity:** 5150 litres.

**Advertising livery:** 66623 Bardon Aggregates (blue).

| 66623 | **AL** | HX | DFHG | FD | Bill Bolsover |
|-------|--------|----|------|----|---------------|
| 66624 | **FL** | HX | DFHG ₽L | FD | |
| 66625 | **FL** | HX | DFHG | FD | |

**Class 66/7. First GBRf-operated locomotives.** Details as Class 66/0.

**Non-standard/Advertising liveries:**

66705 **GB** livery but with the addition of "Union Jack" bodyside vinyls.
66709 Black & orange with MEDITE branding.

| 66701 | **GB** | H | GBRT | WB | Whitemoor |
|-------|--------|---|------|----|-----------|
| 66702 | **GB** | H | GBRT | WB | Blue Lightning |
| 66703 | **GB** | H | GBRT | WB | Doncaster PSB 1981–2002 |
| 66704 | **GB** | H | GBRT | WB | Colchester Power Signalbox |
| 66705 | **GB** | H | GBRT | WB | Golden Jubilee |
| 66706 | **GB** | H | GBRT | WB | Nene Valley |
| 66707 | **GB** | H | GBRT | WB | Sir Sam Fay GREAT CENTRAL RAILWAY |
| 66708 | **GB** | H | GBCM | WB | |
| 66709 | **AL** | H | GBCM | WB | Joseph Arnold Davies |
| 66710 | **GB** | H | GBCM | WB | |
| 66711 | **GB** | H | GBCM | WB | |
| 66712 | **GB** | H | GBCM | WB | Peterborough Power Signalbox |
| 66713 | **GB** | H | GBCM | WB | Forest City |
| 66714 | **GB** | H | GBCM | WB | Cromer Lifeboat |
| 66715 | **GB** | H | GBCM | WB | VALOUR – IN MEMORY OF ALL RAILWAY EMPLOYEES WHO GAVE THEIR LIVES FOR THEIR COUNTRY |
| 66716 | **GB** | H | GBCM | WB | Willesden Traincare Centre |
| 66717 | **GB** | H | GBCM | WB | Good Old Boy |

**66718–66732. Low emission.** Details as Class 66/0 except:

**Engine:** EMD 12N-710G3B-U2 two stroke of 2420 kW (3245 h.p.) at 904 r.p.m.
**Traction Motors:** General Motors D43TRC.
**Fuel Capacity:** 5546 litres (66718–722) or 5150 litres (66723–732).

| 66718 | **MT** | H | GBCM | WB | Gwyneth Dunwoody |
|-------|--------|---|------|----|------------------|
| 66719 | **MT** | H | GBCM | WB | METRO-LAND |
| 66720 | **MT** | H | GBCM | WB | Metronet Pathfinder |
| 66721 | **MT** | H | GBCM | WB | Harry Beck |

| 66722 | **MT** | H | GBCM | WB | Sir Edward Watkin |
| 66723 | **FS** | H | GBCM | WB | Chinook |
| 66724 | **FS** | H | GBCM | WB | Drax Power Station |
| 66725 | **FS** | H | GBCM | WB | SUNDERLAND |
| 66726 | **FS** | H | GBCM | WB | |
| 66727 | **FS** | H | GBCM | WB | |
| 66728 | **FS** | P | GBCM | WB | Institution of Railway Operators |
| 66729 | **FS** | P | GBCM | WB | |
| 66730 | **FS** | P | GBCM | WB | |
| 66731 | **FS** | P | GBCM | WB | |
| 66732 | **FS** | P | GBCM | WB | |

**Class 66/9. Freightliner locos. Low emission "demonstrator" locos.** Details as Class 66/0 except:

**Engine:** EMD 12N-710G3B-U2 two stroke of 2420 kW (3245 h.p.) at 904 r.p.m.
**Traction Motors:** General Motors D43TRC.
**Fuel Capacity:** 5905/5150 litres.

| 66951 | **FL** | H | DFHG | FD |
| 66952 | **FL** | H | DFHG | FD |

**Class 66/9. Freightliner-operated low emission locos.** Due to the 665xx number range being full further orders of 66/5s are to be numbered from 66953 onwards. Details as Class 66/5 (low emission):

| 66953 | **FL** | BM | DFHG | FD |
| 66954 | **FL** | BM | DFIN | FD |
| 66955 | **FL** | BM | DFIN | FD |
| 66956 | **FL** | BM | DFIN | FD |
| 66957 | **FL** | BM | DFHG | FD |

*Colas*

*66842*

*66845 (66410)*

# CLASS 67 ALSTOM/GENERAL MOTORS EMD Bo-Bo

**Built:** 1999–2000 by Alstom at Valencia, Spain, as sub-contractors for General Motors (General Motors model JT42 HW-HS).
**Engine:** GM 12N-710G3B-EC two stroke of 2385 kW (3200 h.p.) at 904 r.p.m.
**Main Alternator:** General Motors AR9A/HEP7/CA6C.
**Traction Motors:** General Motors D43FM.
**Maximum Tractive Effort:** 141 kN (31770 lbf).
**Continuous Tractive Effort:** 90 kN (20200 lbf) at 46.5 m.p.h.
**Power At Rail:** 1860 kW.                    **Train Brakes:** Air.
**Brake Force:** 78 t.                         **Dimensions:** 19.74 x 2.72 m.
**Weight:** 90 t.                              **Wheel Diameter:** 965 mm.
**Design Speed:** 125 m.p.h.
**Maximum Speed:** 125 m.p.h. (but only currently authorised for 110 m.p.h.)
**Fuel Capacity:** 4927 litres.               **RA:** 8.
**Train Supply:** Electric, index 66.         **Multiple Working:** AAR System.

**Note:** All equipped with Slow Speed Control and Swinghead Automatic "Buckeye" Combination Couplers.

**Non-standard livery:** 67029 All over silver with EWS logos (EWS "Special Train").

| | | | | | |
|---|---|---|---|---|---|
| 67001 | E | A | WAAN | CE | |
| 67002 | E | A | WAAN | CE | Special Delivery |
| 67003 | E | A | WAAN | CE | |
| 67004 r | E | A | WABN | CE | Post Haste |
| 67005 | RZ | A | WAAN | CE | Queen's Messenger |
| 67006 | RZ | A | WAAN | CE | Royal Sovereign |
| 67007 r | E | A | WABN | CE | |
| 67008 | E | A | WAAN | CE | |
| 67009 r | E | A | WABN | CE | |
| 67010 | WES | A | WNTS | TO | Unicorn |
| 67011 r | E | A | WABN | CE | |
| 67012 | WS | A | WAWN | CE | A Shropshire Lad |
| 67013 | WS | A | WAWN | CE | Dyfrbont Pontcysyllte |
| 67014 | WS | A | WAWN | CE | Thomas Telford |
| 67015 | WS | A | WAWN | CE | David J. Lloyd |
| 67016 | E | A | WAFN | CE | |
| 67017 | E | A | WAFN | CE | Arrow |
| 67018 | E | A | WNTS | TO | Rapid |
| 67019 | E | A | WAAN | CE | |
| 67020 | E | A | WAAN | CE | |
| 67021 | E | A | WAAN | CE | |
| 67022 | E | A | WAAN | CE | |
| 67023 | E | A | WAAN | CE | |
| 67024 | E | A | WAAN | CE | |
| 67025 | E | A | WAAN | CE | Western Star |
| 67026 | E | A | WAAN | CE | |
| 67027 | E | A | WAAN | CE | Rising Star |
| 67028 | E | A | WAAN | CE | |
| 67029 | 0 | A | WAAN | CE | Royal Diamond |
| 67030 r | E | A | WABN | CE | |

## CLASS 68 70    GENERAL ELECTRIC        Co-Co

30 new General Electric "PowerHaul" locos on order for Freightliner. The first is due to arrive in the UK in late 2009. Full details awaited, those below are provisional.

**Built:** 2009–2010 by General Electric, Erie, Pennsylvania, USA.
**Engine:** General Electric PowerHaul P616 of 2750 kW (3686 h.p.) at 904 r.p.m.
**Main Alternator:** General Electric GTA series.
**Traction Motors:** General Electric AC 5GEB30.
**Maximum Tractive Effort:** 544 kN (122 000 lbf).
**Continuous Tractive Effort:** 427 kN (96000 lbf) at ?? m.p.h.

| | |
|---|---|
| **Power At Rail:** | **Train Brakes:** Air. |
| **Brake Force:** | **Dimensions:** 21.71 x 2.64 m. |
| **Weight:** 129 t. | **Wheel Diameter:** 1007 mm. |
| **Design Speed:** 75 m.p.h. | **Maximum Speed:** 75 m.p.h. |
| **Fuel Capacity:** 6000 litres. | **RA:** 7. |
| **Train Supply:** Not equipped. | **Multiple Working:** |

**IMPORTANT NOTE:** These new locomotives have been provisionally allocated the Class 68 number series. Confirmation was expected in early 2009.

68001
68002
68003
68004
68005
68006
68007
68008
68009
68010
68011
68012
68013
68014
68015
68016
68017
68018
68019
68020
68021
68022
68023
68024
68025
68026
68027
68028
68029
68030

▲ Still in Wessex Trains pink livery, 31601 works a 5Z14 07.30 Derby–Mossend test train past Lanark Junction on 20/06/08. 31105 was on the rear. **Robert Brown**

▼ West Coast Railway Company's 33029 "Glen Loy" stands at Stirling with the Royal Scotsman from Bridge of Orchy on 29/07/07. **Ian Lothian**

▲ Carrying the new DRS "Compass" livery, 37423 passes Kegworth with saloon 999506 working from Derby to Ferme Park on 31/05/08. **Phil Chilton**

▼ BR Revised blue-liveried 40145 was a railtour favourite throughout 2008. On 12/04/08 it passes Haddiscoe with a 15.29 Lowestoft–Didcot Parkway charter.
**Paul Higgins**

The first Cross-Country-liveried HST power car entered service in summer 2008, albeit still with old Midland Mainline-liveried stock. On 28/07/08, 43301 leads the 08.30 Penzance–Dundee (with 43178 on the rear) at Wearde Quay, near Saltash. **Ron Westwater**

▲ Grand Central's 43068 and 43123 work the 06.46 Sunderland–London King's Cross past Eaton Lane, south of Retford on 11/04/08. **Andrew Wills**

▼ National Express-liveried 43317 leads the 09.55 Aberdeen–London King's Cross at Bishopwood on 07/05/08. **Gavin Morrison**

BR two-tone green-liveried Riviera Trains Class 47s 47812 (D1916) and 47815 "GREAT WESTERN" pass Penmaenmawr on the North Wales Coast with Compass Tours' Carlisle–Holyhead charter on 24/03/07.
**Robert Pritchard**

▲ Colas Rail-liveried 47727 "Rebecca" at Eastleigh Works on 08/08/08.
**Carl Watson/Arlington Fleet Services**

▼ Fastline's 56303 is seen at Stenson Bubble with 4O90 10.44 Doncaster–Thamesport Intermodal on 08/05/08. **Phil Chilton**

First Group blue-liveried 57605 "Totnes Castle" heads west past Respryn, near Bodmin Parkway, with a 5Z40 Plymouth–Penzance e.c.s. on 23/06/08 following a relaunch special from Penzance to Plymouth for the FGW Sleeper service.

Sam Felce

▲ Advenza Freight-liveried 57006 is seen near Bromsgrove with 6Z72 10.15 Stockton–Cardiff Tidal loaded scrap on 13/05/08. **Dave Gommersall**

▼ Carrying the new Aggregate Industries livery, 59001 "YEOMAN ENDEAVOUR" is seen near Chippenham with 7C77 12.40 Acton–Merehead on 22/08/08.
**Peter Foster**

Painted into a special maroon livery to celebrate the centenary of the Territorial Army, 60040 passes Clink Road Junction near Frome with 6V18 12.43 Hither Green–Whatley stone train on 15/07/08. **Kevin Poole**

▲ DRS-liveried 66414 is seen at Auchengray with 4Z50 08.40 Daventry–Grangemouth Intermodal on 02/08/08. **Ian Lothian**

▼ First GBRf Metronet-liveried 66720 "Metronet Pathfinder" passes Bletchley with the 14.15 Hams Hall–Felixstowe Intermodal on 07/09/07. **Mark Beal**

Before being named, Wrexham & Shropshire-liveried 67015 and 67013 top-and-tail the 16.10 London Marylebone–Wrexham General at Kings Sutton on 02/05/08.
**Paul Higgins**

▲ The Class 73 Locomotive Preservation Society's 73136 "Perseverance" propels Class 442 2410 through Basingstoke on 17/03/08 with 5B42 10.10 Brighton–Eastleigh Works. **Chris Wilson**

▼ Freightliner's 86639 and 86610 power 4M74 13.00 Coatbridge–Crewe Intermodal near Shap Beck on 16/06/08. **Dave McAlone**

▲ National Express-liveried 90008 leads a rake of Nat-Ex Mark 3s through Pudding Mill Lane (DLR) with the 09.00 Norwich–London Liverpool Street on 01/07/08. **Brian Morrison**

▼ Still in old Railfreight grey livery with Freightliner logos, 90049 passes Millmeece on 10/06/08 with 4M88 08.49 Felixstowe–Crewe Freightliner. **Andrew Mist**

▲ The first Class 91 to receive National Express livery was 91111. On 05/06/08 it passes Claypole leading the 17.35 London King's Cross–Bradford Forster Square.
**Lindsay Atkinson**

▼ In two-tone grey livery with EWS logos, 92009 "Elgar" rumbles through Tame Bridge Parkway with 6A42 12.33 Warrington–Bescot–Wembley Enterprise service on 18/09/07. **Cliff Beeton**

▲ **Locos classed as in "industrial service":** 07007 (D2991) is based at Knights Rail Services, Eastleigh Works, where it is seen resting between duties on 20/09/07.
**Robert Pritchard**

▼ West Coast Railway Company's 08678 "ARTILA" is seen between duties at the company's Carnforth depot on 27/07/08. **Robert Pritchard**

▲ Two Harry Needle Class 20s are based at Scunthorpe Steelworks for use on internal shunting movements. On 11/05/08 No. 81 (20056) works a special charter service around the site with the resident DMU. **Gavin Morrison**

▼ Ex-works in new Lafarge Aggregates white/green livery, 20168 "SIR GEORGE EARLE" is seen at Earles Sidings on 26/07/08. **Andrew Wills**

# 1.2. ELECTRO-DIESEL & ELECTRIC LOCOMOTIVES

## CLASS 73          BR/ENGLISH ELECTRIC          Bo-Bo

Electro-diesel locomotives which can operate either from a DC supply or using power from a diesel engine.

**Built:** 1965–1967 by English Electric Co. at Vulcan Foundry, Newton-le-Willows.
**Engine:** English Electric 4SRKT of 447 kW (600 h.p.) at 850 r.p.m.
**Main Generator:** English Electric 824/5D.
**Electric Supply System:** 750 V DC from third rail.
**Traction Motors:** English Electric 546/1B.
**Maximum Tractive Effort (Electric):** 179 kN (40000 lbf).
**Maximum Tractive Effort (Diesel):** 160 kN (36000 lbf).
**Continuous Rating (Electric):** 1060 kW (1420 h.p.) giving a tractive effort of 35 kN (7800 lbf) at 68 m.p.h.
**Continuous Tractive Effort (Diesel):** 60 kN (13600 lbf) at 11.5 m.p.h.
**Maximum Rail Power (Electric):** 2350 kW (3150 h.p.) at 42 m.p.h.
**Train Brakes:** Air, vacuum & electro-pneumatic († Air & electro-pneumatic).
**Brake Force:** 31 t.                          **Dimensions:** 16.36 x 2.64 m.
**Weight:** 77 t.                                **Wheel Diameter:** 1016 mm.
**Design Speed:** 90 m.p.h.                      **Maximum Speed:** 90 m.p.h.
**Fuel Capacity:** 1409 litres.                  **RA:** 6.
**Train Supply:** Electric, index 66 (on electric power only).
**Multiple Working:** SR 27-way System & Blue Star.

Formerly numbered E6001–E6020/E6022–E6026/E6028–E6049 (not in order).

**Note:** Locomotives numbered in the 732xx series are classed as 73/2 and were originally dedicated to Gatwick Express services.

**Non-standard livery:**

73107 Non-standard two-tone grey.

| 73107 | O | 20 | MBED | SE | SPITFIRE |
| 73109 | SD | SW | HYWD | WD | Battle of Britain 50th Anniversary |
| 73130 †c | EP | EU | GPSN | SL | |
| 73141 | Y | NR | QAED | DF | |
| 73201 † | SD | P | MBED | SE | |
| 73202 † | GV | P | IVGA | SL | Dave Berry |
| 73203 † | GX | GB | GBZZ *Sc* | SE | |
| 73204 † | GB | GB | GBED | DF | Janice |
| 73205 † | GB | GB | GBED | DF | Jeanette |
| 73206 † | GB | GB | GBED | DF | Lisa |
| 73207 † | GX | GB | GBZZ | SE | |
| 73208 † | B | GB | GBED | DF | Kirsten |
| 73209 † | GB | GB | GBED | DF | Alison |
| 73212 † | Y | NR | QAED | DF | |

| 73213 † | **Y** | NR | QAED | DF |
|---|---|---|---|---|
| 73235 † | **SD** | P | HYWD | WD |

# CLASS 86    BR/ENGLISH ELECTRIC    Bo-Bo

**Built:** 1965–1966 by English Electric Co. at Vulcan Foundry, Newton-le-Willows or by BR at Doncaster Works.
**Electric Supply System:** 25 kV AC 50 Hz overhead.
**Train Brakes:** Air.                        **Brake Force:** 40 t.
**Dimensions:** 17.83 x 2.65 m.                **Weight:** 83–86.8 t.
**RA:** 6.                                     **Multiple Working:** TDM system.
**Train Supply:** Electric, index 66.
Formerly numbered E3101–E3200 (not in order).

**Class 86/1. Class 87-type bogies & motors.**

Details as above except:
**Traction Motors:** GEC 412AZ frame mounted.
**Maximum Tractive Effort:** 258 kN (58000 lbf).
**Continuous Rating:** 3730 kW (5000 h.p.) giving a tractive effort of 95 kN (21300 lbf) at 87 m.p.h.
**Maximum Rail Power:** 5860 kW (7860 h.p.) at 50.8 m.p.h.
**Wheel Diameter:** 1150 mm.                   **Weight:** 86.8 t.
**Design Speed:** 110 m.p.h.                   **Maximum Speed:** 110 m.p.h.

| 86101 | **B** | AC | ACAC | CP | Sir William A Stanier FRS |
|---|---|---|---|---|---|

**Class 86/2. Standard design rebuilt with resilient wheels and Flexicoil suspension.**

**Traction Motors:** AEI 282BZ axle hung.
**Maximum Tractive Effort:** 207 kN (46500 lbf).
**Continuous Rating:** 3010 kW (4040 h.p.) giving a tractive effort of 85 kN (19200 lbf) at 77.5 m.p.h.
**Maximum Rail Power:** 4550 kW (6100 h.p.) at 49.5 m.p.h.
**Wheel Diameter:** 1156 mm.                   **Weight:** 85–86.2 t.
**Design Speed:** 125 m.p.h.                   **Maximum Speed:** 100 m.p.h.

**Non-standard livery/numbering:** 86233 & 86259 BR "Electric blue" livery.
86233 Also carries number E3172.

| 86205 | **V** | H | SAXL | LM | |
|---|---|---|---|---|---|
| 86212 | **V** | H | SAXL | LM | |
| 86215 | **AR** | H | SAXL | LM | The Round Tabler |
| 86217 | **AR** | H | SAXL | LM | |
| 86218 | **AR** | H | SAXL | LM | |
| 86223 | **AR** | H | SAXL | LM | Norwich Union |
| 86226 | **V** | H | SAXL | LM | |
| 86228 | **IC** | H | SAXL | LM | Vulcan Heritage |
| 86229 | **V** | H | SAXL | LM | |
| 86230 | **AR** | H | SAXL | LM | |
| 86231 | **V** | H | SAXL | LM | |
| 86232 | **AR** | H | SAXL | LM | |
| 86233 | **O** | SR | SRLO | CE | |

| 86234 | AR | H | SAXL | | LM |
|--------|-----|-----|------|----|-----|
| 86235 | AR | H | SAXL | | LM |
| 86242 | AR | H | SAXL | | LM |
| 86245 | V | H | SAXL | Sc | LM |
| 86246 | AR | H | SAXL | | LM |
| 86247 | V | H | SAXL | | LM |
| 86248 | V | EP | EPXX | | LM |
| 86250 | AR | EP | EPXX | | LM |
| 86251 | V | H | SAXL | | LM |
| 86258 | V | H | SAXL | | LM |
| 86259 | 0 | LR | MBEL | | TM | Les Ross |
| 86260 | AR | H | SAXL | | LM |

**Class 86/4.**

**Traction Motors:** AEI 282AZ axle hung.
**Maximum Tractive Effort:** 258 kN (58000 lbf).
**Continuous Rating:** 2680 kW (3600 h.p.) giving a tractive effort of 89 kN (20000 lbf) at 67 m.p.h.
**Maximum Rail Power:** 4400 kW (5900 h.p.) at 38 m.p.h.
**Wheel Diameter:** 1156 mm.     **Weight:** 83–83.9 t.
**Design Speed:** 100 m.p.h.     **Maximum Speed:** 100 m.p.h.

| 86424 | Y | NR | QSTR | CP |
|--------|----|-----|------|----|

**Class 86/5. Regeared locomotive operated by Freightliner.**

Details as Class 86/4 except:

**Continuous Rating:** 2680 kW (3600 h.p.) giving a tractive effort of 117 kN (26300 lbf) at 67 m.p.h.
**Maximum Speed:** 75 m.p.h.     **Train Supply:** Electric, isolated.

| 86501 (86608) | FL | FL | DFGC | FE |
|----------------|------|------|------|----|

**Class 86/6. Freightliner-operated locomotives.**

Details as Class 86/4 except:

**Maximum Speed:** 75 m.p.h.     **Train Supply:** Electric, isolated.

| 86602 | FL | FL | DHLT | CP |
|--------|------|------|------|----|
| 86604 | FL | FL | DFNC | FE |
| 86605 | FL | FL | DFNC | FE |
| 86607 | FL | FL | DFNC | FE |
| 86609 | FL | FL | DFNC | FE |
| 86610 | FL | FL | DFNC | FE |
| 86612 | FL | P | DFNC | FE |
| 86613 | FL | P | DFNC | FE |
| 86614 | FL | P | DFNC | FE |
| 86621 | FL | P | DFNC | FE |
| 86622 | FF | P | DFNC | FE |
| 86623 | FF | P | DHLT | CP |
| 86627 | FL | P | DFNC | FE |
| 86628 | FL | P | DFNC | FE |
| 86632 | FL | P | DFNC | FE |

| 86633 | **FF** | P | DHLT | CP |
| 86635 | **FL** | P | DHLT | BA |
| 86637 | **FF** | P | DFNC | FE |
| 86638 | **FL** | P | DFNC | FE |
| 86639 | **FL** | P | DFNC | FE |

**Class 86/9. Network Rail-owned locomotives.** Rebuilt for use as Mobile Load Bank test locos to test Overhead Line Equipment, initially on the WCML. No. 1 end Traction Motors isolated. Can still move under own power.

**Maximum Speed:** 60 m.p.h.      **Train Supply:** Electric, isolated.

| 86901 | **Y** | NR | QACL | RU | CHIEF ENGINEER |
| 86902 | **Y** | NR | QACL | RU | RAIL VEHICLE ENGINEERING |

# CLASS 87                    BREL/GEC                    Bo-Bo

**Built:** 1973–1975 by BREL at Crewe Works.
**Electric Supply System:** 25 kV AC 50 Hz overhead.
**Traction Motors:** GEC G412AZ frame mounted.
**Maximum Tractive Effort:** 258 kN (58000 lbf).
**Continuous Rating:** 3730 kW (5000 h.p.) giving a tractive effort of 95 kN (21300 lbf) at 87 m.p.h.
**Maximum Rail Power:** 5860 kW (7860 h.p.) at 50.8 m.p.h.
**Train Brakes:** Air.                      **Brake Force:** 40 t.
**Dimensions:** 17.83 x 2.65 m.            **Weight:** 83.3 t.
**Wheel Diameter:** 1150 mm.               **Design Speed:** 110 m.p.h.
**Maximum Speed:** 110 m.p.h.             **Train Supply:** Electric, index 95.
**RA:** 6.                                 **Multiple Working:** TDM system.

**Note:** Apart from 87002, this class have now finished work in the UK and all locos listed below except 87002 and 87027 (the latter being used for spares only) are due to be exported to Bulgaria during 2009/10.

| 87002 | **B** | AC | ACAC | CP | Royal Sovereign |
| 87004 | **V** | BU | SBXL | LM | |
| 87009 | **V** | BU | SBXL | LM | |
| 87011 | **V** | BU | SBXL | LM | |
| 87013 | **V** | BU | SBXL | LM | |
| 87014 | **V** | BU | SBXL | LM | |
| 87017 | **V** | BU | SBXL | LM | |
| 87018 | **V** | BU | SBXL | LM | |
| 87020 | **V** | BU | SBXL | LM | |
| 87021 | **V** | BU | SBXL | LM | |
| 87023 | **V** | BU | SBXL | LM | |
| 87025 | **V** | BU | SBXL | LM | |
| 87027 | **V** | P | SBXL | LM | |
| 87029 | **V** | BU | SBXL | LM | |
| 87030 | **V** | BU | SBXL | LM | |
| 87032 | **V** | BU | SBXL | LM | |
| 87033 | **V** | BU | SBXL | LM | |

# CLASS 90        GEC        Bo-Bo

**Built:** 1987–1990 by BREL at Crewe Works (as sub contractors for GEC).
**Electric Supply System:** 25 kV AC 50 Hz overhead.
**Traction Motors:** GEC G412CY frame mounted.
**Maximum Tractive Effort:** 258 kN (58000 lbf).
**Continuous Rating:** 3730 kW (5000 h.p.) giving a tractive effort of 95 kN (21300 lbf) at 87 m.p.h.
**Maximum Rail Power:** 5860 kW (7860 h.p.) at 68.3 m.p.h.
**Train Brakes:** Air.
**Brake Force:** 40 t.
**Weight:** 84.5 t.
**Design Speed:** 110 m.p.h.
**Train Supply:** Electric, index 95.
**Multiple Working:** TDM system.
**Dimensions:** 18.80 x 2.74 m.
**Wheel Diameter:** 1150 mm.
**Maximum Speed:** 110 m.p.h.
**RA:** 7.

**Non-standard livery:** 90036 As **FE** but with a yellow roof. EWS stickers.

| 90001 b | 1  | P  | IANA | NC |                                  |
|---------|----|----|------|----|----------------------------------|
| 90002 b | 1  | P  | IANA | NC |                                  |
| 90003 b | NX | P  | IANA | NC | Raedwald of East Anglia          |
| 90004 b | 1  | P  | IANA | NC |                                  |
| 90005 b | 1  | P  | IANA | NC | Vice-Admiral Lord Nelson         |
| 90006 b | 1  | P  | IANA | NC | Modern Railways Magazine/        |
|         |    |    |      |    | Roger Ford                       |
| 90007 b | 1  | P  | IANA | NC | Sir John Betjeman                |
| 90008 b | NX | P  | IANA | NC |                                  |
| 90009 b | 1  | P  | IANA | NC |                                  |
| 90010 b | 1  | P  | IANA | NC |                                  |
| 90011 b | 1  | P  | IANA | NC | Let's Go East of England         |
| 90012 b | 1  | P  | IANA | NC | Royal Anglian Regiment           |
| 90013 b | 1  | P  | IANA | NC |                                  |
| 90014 b | 1  | P  | IANA | NC | Norfolk and Norwich Festival     |
| 90015 b | NX | P  | IANA | NC | Colchester Castle                |
| 90016   | FL | P  | DFLC | FE |                                  |
| 90017 b | E  | DB | WNTR | CE |                                  |
| 90018 b | E  | DB | WEFE | CE |                                  |
| 90019 b | FS | DB | WEFE | CE |                                  |
| 90020 b | E  | DB | WEFE | CE | Collingwood                      |
| 90021   | FS | DB | WNTS | CE |                                  |
| 90022   | EG | DB | WNTR | CE | Freightconnection                |
| 90023   | E  | DB | WNTR | CE |                                  |
| 90024   | FS | DB | WEFE | CE |                                  |
| 90025   | F  | DB | WNTR | CE |                                  |
| 90026   | E  | DB | WEFE | CE |                                  |
| 90027   | F  | DB | WNTR | CE | Allerton T&RS Depot              |
| 90028   | E  | DB | WEFE | CE |                                  |
| 90029   | E  | DB | WEFE | CE | The Institution of Civil Engineers |
| 90030   | E  | DB | WNTR | CE | Crewe Locomotive Works           |
| 90031   | E  | DB | WNTS | CE | The Railway Children Partnership |
|         |    |    |      |    | Working For Street Children Worldwide |

| 90032 | E  | DB | WNTR | CE |                       |
|-------|----|----|------|----|-----------------------|
| 90033 | FE | DB | WNTR | CE |                       |
| 90034 | E  | DB | WNTR | CE |                       |
| 90035 | E  | DB | WEFE | CE |                       |
| 90036 | O  | DB | WEFE | CE |                       |
| 90037 | E  | DB | WNTR | CE | Spirit of Dagenham    |
| 90038 | FE | DB | WNTR | CE |                       |
| 90039 | E  | DB | WEFE | CE |                       |
| 90040 | E  | DB | WNTR | CE | The Railway Mission   |
| 90041 | FL | P  | DFLC | FE |                       |
| 90042 | FF | P  | DFLC | FE |                       |
| 90043 | FF | P  | DFLC | FE | Freightliner Coatbridge |
| 90044 | FF | P  | DFLC | FE |                       |
| 90045 | FF | P  | DFLC | FE |                       |
| 90046 | FL | P  | DFLC | FE |                       |
| 90047 | FF | P  | DFLC | FE |                       |
| 90048 | FF | P  | DFLC | FE |                       |
| 90049 | FF | P  | DFLC | FE |                       |
| 90050 | FF | DB | WNTS | CE |                       |

## CLASS 91                    GEC                    Bo-Bo

**Built:** 1988–1991 by BREL at Crewe Works (as sub contractors for GEC).
**Electric Supply System:** 25 kV AC 50 Hz overhead.
**Traction Motors:** GEC G426AZ.
**Maximum Tractive Effort:** 190 kN (43 000 lbf).
**Continuous Rating:** 4540 kW (6090 h.p.) giving a tractive effort of 170 kN at 96 m.p.h.
**Maximum Rail Power:** 4700 kW (6300 h.p.) at ?? m.p.h.
**Train Brakes:** Air.
**Brake Force:** 45 t.
**Weight:** 84 t.
**Design Speed:** 140 m.p.h.
**Train Supply:** Electric, index 95.
**Multiple Working:** TDM system.

**Dimensions:** 19.41 x 2.74 m.
**Wheel Diameter:** 1000 mm.
**Maximum Speed:** 125 m.p.h.
**RA:** 7.

**Note:** Locos originally numbered in the 910xx series, but renumbered upon completion of overhauls at Bombardier, Doncaster by the addition of 100 to their original number. The exception to this rule was 91023 which was renumbered 91132.

| 91101 | GN | H | IECA | BN |
|-------|----|---|------|----|
| 91102 | GN | H | IECA | BN |
| 91103 | GN | H | IECA | BN |
| 91104 | GN | H | IECA | BN |
| 91105 | GN | H | IECA | BN |
| 91106 | GN | H | IECA | BN |
| 91107 | GN | H | IECA | BN |
| 91108 | GN | H | IECA | BN |
| 91109 | GN | H | IECA | BN |
| 91110 | GN | H | IECA | BN |

| 91111 | NX | H | IECA | BN |
| 91112 | GN | H | IECA | BN |
| 91113 | GN | H | IECA | BN |
| 91114 | GN | H | IECA | BN |
| 91115 | GN | H | IECA | BN |
| 91116 | GN | H | IECA | BN |
| 91117 | GN | H | IECA | BN |
| 91118 | GN | H | IECA | BN |
| 91119 | GN | H | IECA | BN |
| 91120 | GN | H | IECA | BN |
| 91121 | GN | H | IECA | BN |
| 91122 | GN | H | IECA | BN |
| 91124 | GN | H | IECA | BN |
| 91125 | GN | H | IECA | BN |
| 91126 | GN | H | IECA | BN |
| 91127 | GN | H | IECA | BN |
| 91128 | GN | H | IECA | BN |
| 91129 | GN | H | IECA | BN |
| 91130 | GN | H | IECA | BN |
| 91131 | GN | H | IECA | BN |
| 91132 | GN | H | IECA | BN |

# CLASS 92            BRUSH            Co-Co

**Built:** 1993–1996 by Brush Traction at Loughborough.
**Electric Supply System:** 25 kV AC 50 Hz overhead or 750 V DC third rail.
**Traction Motors:** Asea Brown Boveri design. Model 6FRA 7059B (Asynchronous 3-phase induction motors).
**Maximum Tractive Effort:** 400 kN (90 000 lbf).
**Continuous Rating:** 5040 kW (6760 h.p.) on AC, 4000 kW (5360 h.p.) on DC.
**Maximum Rail Power:**                    **Train Brakes:** Air.
**Brake Force:** 63 t.                      **Dimensions:** 21.34 x 2.67 m.
**Weight:** 126 t.                          **Wheel Diameter:** 1070 mm.
**Design Speed:** 140 km/h (87 m.p.h.).    **Maximum Speed:** 140 km/h (87 m.p.h.).
**Train Supply:** Electric, index 108 (AC), 70 (DC).
**RA:** 7.

| 92001 | E  | HX | WTAE | CE | Victor Hugo |
| 92002 | EG | HX | WNTS | CE | H.G. Wells |
| 92003 | EG | HX | WTAE | CE | Beethoven |
| 92004 | EG | HX | WTAE | CE | Jane Austen |
| 92005 | EG | HX | WTAE | CE | Mozart |
| 92006 | EP | SF |      | FN | Louis Armand |
| 92007 | EG | HX | WTAE | CE | Schubert |
| 92008 | EG | HX | WNTR | CE | Jules Verne |
| 92009 | EG | HX | WTAE | CE | Elgar |
| 92010 | EP | ET | PTXX | CO | Molière |
| 92011 | EG | HX | WNTS | CE | Handel |
| 92012 | EG | HX | WTAE | CE | Thomas Hardy |
| 92013 | EG | HX | WNTS | CE | Puccini |
| 92014 | EP | SF |      | FN | Emile Zola |

| 92015 | EG | HX | WTAE | CE | D.H. Lawrence |
|-------|-----|-----|------|-------|---------------|
| 92016 | EG | HX | WTAE | CE | Brahms |
| 92017 | EG | HX | WTAE | CE | Shakespeare |
| 92018 | EP | SF | | FN | Stendhal |
| 92019 | EG | HX | WTAE | CE | Wagner |
| 92020 | EP | ET | PTXX | LB (S) | Milton |
| 92021 | EP | ET | PTXX | LB (S) | Purcell |
| 92022 | EG | HX | WTAE | CE | Charles Dickens |
| 92023 | EP | SF | | FN | Ravel |
| 92024 | EG | HX | WNTS | CE | J.S. Bach |
| 92025 | EG | HX | WNTR | CE | Oscar Wilde |
| 92026 | EG | HX | WTAE | CE | Britten |
| 92027 | EG | HX | WNTS | CE | George Eliot |
| 92028 | EP | ET | PTXX | CO | Saint Saëns |
| 92029 | EG | HX | WNTS | CE | Dante |
| 92030 | EG | HX | WTAE | CE | Ashford |
| 92031 | E | HX | WNTR | CE | The Institute of Logistics and Transport |
| 92032 | EP | ET | PTXX | LB (S) | César Franck |
| 92033 | EP | SF | | FN | Berlioz |
| 92034 | EG | HX | WTAE | CE | Kipling |
| 92035 | EP | HX | WNTR | CE | Mendelssohn |
| 92036 | EG | HX | WTAE | CE | Bertolt Brecht |
| 92037 | EG | HX | WTAE | CE | Sullivan |
| 92038 | EP | ET | PTXX | CO | Voltaire |
| 92039 | EG | HX | WTAE | CE | Johann Strauss |
| 92040 | EP | ET | PTXX | LB (S) | Goethe |
| 92041 | EG | HX | WTAE | CE | Vaughan Williams |
| 92042 | EG | HX | WTAE | CE | Honegger |
| 92043 | EP | ET | PTXX | CO | Debussy |
| 92044 | EP | ET | PTXX | CO | Couperin |
| 92045 | EP | ET | PTXX | LB (S) | Chaucer |
| 92046 | EP | ET | PTXX | LB (S) | Sweelinck |

# 1.3. EUROTUNNEL LOCOMOTIVES

## DIESEL LOCOMOTIVES

### 0001–0005                 MaK                Bo-Bo

**Built:** 1992–1993 by MaK at Kiel, Germany (Model DE1004).
**Engine:** MTU 12V 396 TC13 of 940 kW (1260 h.p.) at 1800 rpm.
**Main Alternator:** BBC.            **Traction Motors:** BBC.
**Maximum Tractive Effort:** 305 kN (68600 lbf).
**Continuous Tractive Effort:** 140 kN (31500 lbf) at 20 mph.
**Power At Rail:** 750 kW (1012 h.p.).  **Dimensions:** 14.40 x ?? m.
**Brake Force:** 120 kN.            **Wheel Diameter:** 1000 mm.
**Weight:** 84 t.                 **Maximum Speed:** 120 km/h.
**Design Speed:** 120 km/h.       **Train Brakes:** Air.
**Fuel Capacity:** 3500 litres.      **Multiple Working:** Within class.
**Train Supply:** Not equipped.    **Signalling System:** TVM430 cab signalling.

| | | |
|---|---|---|
| 0001 | **GY** ET | CO |
| 0002 | **GY** ET | CO |
| 0003 | **GY** ET | CO |
| 0004 | **GY** ET | CO |
| 0005 | **GY** ET | CO |

### 0031–0042     HUNSLET/SCHÖMA     0–4–0

**Built:** 1989–1990 by Hunslet Engine Company at Leeds as 900 mm gauge.
**Rebuilt:** 1993–1994 by Schöma in Germany to 1435 mm. gauge.
**Engine:** Deutz of 270 kW (200 h.p.) at ???? rpm.
**Transmission:** Mechanical.       **Maximum Tractive Effort:**
**Cont. Tractive Effort:**           **Power At Rail:**
**Brake Force:**                 **Dimensions:**
**Weight:**                   **Wheel Diameter:**
**Design Speed:** 50 km/h.        **Maximum Speed:** 50 km/h.
**Fuel Capacity:**             **Train Brakes:** Air.
**Train Supply:** Not equipped.    **Multiple Working:** Not equipped.

| | | | |
|---|---|---|---|
| 0031 | **GY** ET | CO | FRANCES |
| 0032 | **GY** ET | CO | ELISABETH |
| 0033 | **GY** ET | CO | SILKE |
| 0034 | **GY** ET | CO | AMANDA |
| 0035 | **GY** ET | CO | MARY |
| 0036 | **GY** ET | CO | LAWRENCE |
| 0037 | **GY** ET | CO | LYDIE |
| 0038 | **GY** ET | CO | JENNY |
| 0039 | **GY** ET | CO | PACITA |
| 0040 | **GY** ET | CO | JILL |
| 0041 | **GY** ET | CO | KIM |
| 0042 | **GY** ET | CO | NICOLE |

# ELECTRIC LOCOMOTIVES

## 9001–9838          BRUSH/ABB          Bo-Bo-Bo

**Built:** 1993–2002 by Brush Traction at Loughborough.
**Supply System:** 25 kV AC 50 Hz overhead.
**Traction Motors:** Asea Brown Boveri design. Asynchronous 3-phase motors.
Model 6FHA 7059 (as built). Model 6FHA 7059C (7000 kW rated locos).
**Maximum Tractive Effort:** 400kN (90 000lbf).
**Continuous Rating:** Class 9/0 and 9/1: 5760 kW (7725 h.p.). Class 9/7 and 9/8: 7000 kW (9387 h.p.).

| | |
|---|---|
| **Maximum Rail Power:** | **Multiple Working:** TDM system. |
| **Brake Force:** 50 t. | **Dimensions:** 22.01 x 2.97 x 4.20 m. |
| **Weight:** 132 t. | **Wheel Diameter:** 1250 mm. |
| **Design Speed:** 100 m.p.h. | **Maximum Speed:** 87 m.p.h. |
| **Train Supply:** Electric. | **Train Brakes:** Air. |

**CLASS 9/0 Original build mixed traffic locos.**

| | | | | |
|---|---|---|---|---|
| 9005 | **EB** | ET | CO | JESSYE NORMAN |
| 9006 | **EB** | ET | CO | REGINE CRESPIN |
| 9007 | **EB** | ET | CO | DAME JOAN SUTHERLAND |
| 9011 | **EB** | ET | CO | JOSÉ VAN DAM |
| 9013 | **EB** | ET | CO | MARIA CALLAS |
| 9015 | **EB** | ET | CO | LÖTSCHBERG 1913 |
| 9018 | **EB** | ET | CO | WILHELMENA FERNANDEZ |
| 9022 | **EB** | ET | CO | DAME JANET BAKER |
| 9023 | **EB** | ET | CO | DAME ELISABETH LEGGE-SCHWARZKOPF |
| 9024 | **EB** | ET | CO | GOTTHARD 1882 |
| 9026 | **EB** | ET | CO | FURKATUNNEL 1982 |
| 9027 | **EB** | ET | CO | BARBARA HENDRICKS |
| 9029 | **EB** | ET | CO | THOMAS ALLEN |
| 9031 | **EB** | ET | CO | |
| 9033 | **EB** | ET | CO | MONTSERRAT CABALLE |
| 9036 | **EB** | ET | CO | ALAIN FONDARY |
| 9037 | **EB** | ET | CO | GABRIEL BACQUIER |
| 9040 | **EB** | ET | CO | |

**CLASS 9/1. Freight Shuttle dedicated locos.**

| | | | |
|---|---|---|---|
| 9101 | **EB** | ET | CO |
| 9102 | **EB** | ET | CO |
| 9103 | **EB** | ET | CO |
| 9104 | **EB** | ET | CO |
| 9105 | **EB** | ET | CO |
| 9106 | **EB** | ET | CO |
| 9107 | **EB** | ET | CO |
| 9108 | **EB** | ET | CO |
| 9109 | **EB** | ET | CO |
| 9110 | **EB** | ET | CO |
| 9111 | **EB** | ET | CO |

| 9112 | **EB** | ET | CO |
| 9113 | **EB** | ET | CO |

**CLASS 9/7. Later build (2001–2002) increased power freight shuttle locos.**

| 9701 | **EB** | ET | CO |
| 9702 | **EB** | ET | CO |
| 9703 | **EB** | ET | CO |
| 9704 | **EB** | ET | CO |
| 9705 | **EB** | ET | CO |
| 9706 | **EB** | ET | CO |
| 9707 | **EB** | ET | CO |

**CLASS 9/8 Locos rebuilt from Class 9/0 by adding 800 to the loco number. Uprated to 7000 kW. Generally used on freight duties.**

| 9801 | **EB** | ET | CO | LESLEY GARRETT |
| 9802 | **EB** | ET | CO | STUART BURROWS |
| 9803 | **EB** | ET | CO | BENJAMIN LUXON |
| 9804 | **EB** | ET | CO | VICTORIA DE LOS ANGELES |
| 9808 | **EB** | ET | CO | ELISABETH SODERSTROM |
| 9809 | **EB** | ET | CO | FRANÇOIS POLLET |
| 9810 | **EB** | ET | CO | JEAN-PHILIPPE COURTIS |
| 9812 | **EB** | ET | CO | LUCIANO PAVAROTTI |
| 9814 | **EB** | ET | CO (S) | LUCIA POPP |
| 9816 | **EB** | ET | CO | WILLARD WHITE |
| 9817 | **EB** | ET | CO (S) | JOSÉ CARRERAS |
| 9819 | **EB** | ET | CO | MARIA EWING |
| 9820 | **EB** | ET | CO | NICOLAI GHIAUROV |
| 9821 | **EB** | ET | CO | TERESA BERGANZA |
| 9825 | **EB** | ET | CO | |
| 9828 | **EB** | ET | CO | DAME KIRI TE KANAWA |
| 9832 | **EB** | ET | CO | RENATA TEBALDI |
| 9834 | **EB** | ET | CO | MIRELLA FRENI |
| 9835 | **EB** | ET | CO | NICOLAI GEDDA |
| 9838 | **EB** | ET | CO | HILDEGARD BEHRENS |

# 1.4. FORMER BR MAIN LINE LOCOS IN INDUSTRIAL SERVICE

Former British Rail main line locomotives considered to be in "industrial use" are listed here. These locomotives do not currently have Network Rail engineering acceptance for operation on the National Rail network.

*Number    Other no./name  Location*

**Class 11**

| | | |
|---|---|---|
| 12082 | 01553 | Deanside Transit, Hillington, Glasgow |
| 12088 | | Johnson's (Chopwell), Widdrington Disposal Point |

**Class 03**

| | | |
|---|---|---|
| 03112 | D2112 | Port of Boston, Boston Docks |
| 03179 | CLIVE | First Capital Connect, Hornsey Depot, London |
| 03196 | JOYCE/GLYNIS | West Coast Railway Company, Carnforth |
| D2381 | | West Coast Railway Company, Carnforth |

**Class 07**

| | | |
|---|---|---|
| 07001 | | Creative Logistics, Salford, Manchester |
| D2991 | 07007 | Knights Rail Services, Old Railway Workshop, Eastleigh |

**Class 08**

| | | |
|---|---|---|
| 08202 | | The Potter Group, Knowsley, Merseyside |
| 08320 | 400D/SUSAN | Imerys Clay Company, Rocks Works, Bugle |
| 08331 | H001 | Midland Railway-Butterley, Derbyshire |
| 08345 | | St. Modwen Properties, Long Marston |
| 08375 | | Prologis Park, Coventry |
| 08398 | 402D/ANNABEL | Imerys Clay Company, Rocks Works, Bugle |
| 08411 | | Colne Valley Railway |
| 08423 | H011  14 | PD Ports, Teesport |
| 08441 | | Colne Valley Railway |
| 08447 | | Deanside Transit, Hillington, Glasgow |
| 08460 | | Colne Valley Railway |
| 08484 | CAPTAIN NATHANIEL DARELL | Felixstowe Dock & Railway Company, Felixstowe |
| 08492 | | Barrow Hill Roundhouse, Chesterfield |
| 08503 | | Rye Farm, Wishaw (Sutton Coldfield) |
| 08517 | | St. Modwen Properties, Long Marston |
| 08523 | | Celtic Energy, Onllwyn Washery, West Glamorgan |
| 08535 | | Corus, Shotton Works, Flintshire |
| 08568 | St. Rollox | Railcare, Springburn Works, Glasgow |
| 08573 | | Bombardier Transportation, Ilford Works, London |
| 08588 | 17 | PD Ports, Teesport |
| 08598 | H016 | The Potter Group, Knowsley, Merseyside |
| 08600 | | LH Group Services, Barton-under-Needwood |
| 08602 | 004 | Bombardier Transportation, Derby Works |
| 08613 | | Corus, Shotton Works, Flintshire |
| 08622 | H028  7 | Corus, Trostre Works, Llanelli, Carmarthenshire |

| 08629 | | Railcare, Wolverton Works |
|---|---|---|
| 08643 | | Aggregate Industries UK, Merehead Stone Terminal |
| 08648 | OLD GEOFF | Wabtec Rail, Doncaster |
| 08649 | G.H. Stratton | Railcare, Wolverton Works |
| 08650 | ISLE OF GRAIN | Aggregate Industries UK, Isle of Grain |
| 08652 | | Hanson Aggregates, Whatley Quarry, near Frome |
| 08668 | | St. Modwen Properties, Long Marston |
| 08678 | ARTILA | West Coast Railway Company, Carnforth |
| 08682 | Lionheart | Bombardier Transportation, Derby Works |
| 08683 | | Rye Farm, Wishaw (Sutton Coldfield) |
| 08695 | | Barrow Hill Roundhouse, Chesterfield |
| 08699 | | Alley's, Studley (Warwickshire) |
| 08704 | D3871 | Port of Boston, Boston Docks |
| 08728 | | St. Modwen Properties, Long Marston |
| 08730 | The Caley | Railcare, Springburn Works, Glasgow |
| 08731[1] | | Aggregate Industries UK, Merehead Stone Terminal |
| 08736 | | St. Modwen Properties, Long Marston |
| 08743 | Bryan Turner | SembCorp Utilities Teesside, Wilton, Middlesbrough |
| 08754 | | Wabtec Rail, Doncaster |
| 08756 | | First GBRf, March Whitemoor Yard |
| 08762 | | Wabtec Rail, Doncaster |
| 08764 | 003 FLORENCE | Transfesa, Tilbury Riverside Terminal, Tilbury |
| 08774 | ARTHUR VERNON DAWSON | AV Dawson, Middlesbrough |
| 08787 | 08296 | Hanson Aggregates, Machen Quarry, near Newport |
| 08807 | | AV Dawson, Middlesbrough |
| 08809 | | Alley's, Studley (Warwickshire) |
| 08813 | | St. Modwen Properties, Long Marston |
| 08818 | MOLLY | Faber Prest Ports, Flixborough Wharf, Scunthorpe |
| 08823 | D3991 | Manchester Ship Canal Company, Trafford Park, Manchester |
| 08827 | | St. Modwen Properties, Long Marston |
| 08846 | 003 | Bombardier Transportation, Derby Works |
| 08869 | | St. Modwen Properties, Long Marston |
| 08870 | H024 | Castle Cement, Ketton, Stamford |
| 08871 | | Wabtec Rail, Doncaster |
| 08873 | | Felixstowe Dock & Railway Company, Felixstowe |
| 08881 | D4095 | Lafarge Aggregates UK, Mountsorrel, Leicestershire |
| 08885 | H042 | First GBRf, March Whitemoor Yard |
| 08896 | | Rye Farm, Wishaw (Sutton Coldfield) |
| 08903 | JOHN W. ANTILL | SembCorp Utilities Teesside, Wilton, Middlesbrough |
| 08912 | | AV Dawson, Middlesbrough |
| 08913 | | Manchester Ship Canal Co., Trafford Park, Manchester |
| 08915 | | Colne Valley Railway |
| 08928 | | St. Modwen Properties, Long Marston |
| 08936 | | Corus, Shotton Works, Flintshire |
| 08937 | BLUEBELL MEL | Aggregate Industries UK, Meldon Quarry, Okehampton |
| 08943 | PET II | Bombardier Transportation, Crewe Works |
| 08947 | | Hanson Aggregates, Whatley Quarry, near Frome |

[1]  Although this locomotive has carried the identity 08731 since 1983 it is in fact a rebuild of 08572, using a number of components from 08731.

### Class 14

| | | |
|---|---|---|
| D9504 | | Aggregate Industries UK, Bardon Hill Quarry, Coalville |
| D9529 | 14029 | Kent & East Sussex Railway |

### Class 20

| | | |
|---|---|---|
| 20056 | 81 | Corus, Appleby-Frodingham Works, Scunthorpe |
| 20066 | 82 | Corus, Appleby-Frodingham Works, Scunthorpe |
| 20168 | SIR GEORGE EARLE | Lafarge Blue Circle Cement Works, Hope |

### Class 56

| | | |
|---|---|---|
| 56009 | 56201 | Brush Traction, Loughborough Works |

### Class 73

| | |
|---|---|
| 73119 | Knights Rail Services, Old Railway Workshop, Eastleigh |
| 73133 | First Swieteisky, Fairwater Yard, Taunton |

# 1.5. LOCOMOTIVES AWAITING DISPOSAL

Locomotives that are still extant but at scrapyards or considered to be awaiting disposal are listed here. It should be noted that some of the locos listed here may see further use on the main line if they are resold by scrap merchants.

| Number | Livery | Location |
|---|---|---|

### Class 08

| | | |
|---|---|---|
| 08694 | E | CF Booth, Rotherham |
| 08715 | 0 | TJ Thomson, Stockton-on-Tees |
| 08775 | E | CF Booth, Rotherham |
| 08900 | DG | TJ Thomson, Stockton-on-Tees |
| 08919 | RX | CF Booth, Rotherham |

### Class 20

| | | |
|---|---|---|
| 20145 | 0 | European Metal Recycling, Kingsbury |

### Class 37

| | | |
|---|---|---|
| 37023 | ML | Alley's, Studley (Warwickshire) |
| 37704 | E | TJ Thomson, Stockton-on-Tees |

### Class 47

| | | |
|---|---|---|
| 47309 | FF | TJ Thomson, Stockton-on-Tees |
| 47358 | FF | TJ Thomson, Stockton-on-Tees |
| 47550 | IM | Rye Farm, Wishaw (Sutton Coldfield) |

# 2. LOCO-HAULED COACHING STOCK

# INTRODUCTION

## NUMBERING SYSTEMS

Seven different numbering systems were in use on BR. These were the BR series, the four pre-nationalisation companies' series', the Pullman Car Company's series and the UIC (International Union of Railways) series. BR number series coaches and former Pullman Car Company series are listed separately. There are also separate listings of "Saloon" type vehicles and locomotive support coaches which are registered to run on the national railway system. Please note the Mark 2 Pullman vehicles were ordered after the Pullman Car Company had been nationalised and are therefore numbered in the BR series.

Also listed separately are the BR number series coaches used on North Yorkshire Moors Railway services on the National Railway system. This is due to their very restricted sphere of operation.

## LAYOUT OF INFORMATION

Coaches are listed in numerical order of painted number in batches according to type.

Each coach entry is laid out as in the following example (previous number(s) column may be omitted where not applicable):

| No. | Prev. No. | Notes | Livery | Owner | Operator | Depot/Location |
|-----|-----------|-------|--------|-------|----------|----------------|
| 42346 | (41053) | *h | **FD** | A | *GW* | OO |

**Notes:**

The owner is the responsible custodian of the coach and this may not always be the legal owner.

The operator is the organisation which facilitates the use of the coach and may not be the actual train operating company which runs the train.

The depot is the facility primarily responsible for the coaches maintenance. Light maintenance and heavy overhauls in particular may be carried out elsewhere.

The location is where coaches not in use are currently being kept/stored.

# DETAILED INFORMATION & CODES

Under each type heading, the following details are shown:

- "Mark" of coach (see below).
- Descriptive text.
- Number of first class seats, standard class seats, lavatory compartments and wheelchair spaces shown as F/S nT nW respectively.
- Bogie type (see below).
- Additional features.
- ETH Index.

# TOPS TYPE CODES

TOPS type codes are allocated to all coaching stock. For vehicles numbered in the passenger stock number series the code consists of:

(1) Two letters denoting the layout of the vehicle as follows:

AA  Gangwayed Corridor
AB  Gangwayed Corridor Brake
AC  Gangwayed Open (2+2 seating)
AD  Gangwayed Open (2+1 seating)
AE  Gangwayed Open Brake
AF  Gangwayed Driving Open Brake
AG  Micro-Buffet
AH  Brake Micro-Buffet
AI  As "AC" but with drop-head buckeye and gangway at one end only
AJ  Kitchen or Buffet Car with seating
AK  Kitchen Car
AL  As "AC" but with disabled person's toilet (Mark 4 only)
AN  Open Second with Miniature Buffet
AP  Pullman Kitchen with Servery
AQ  Pullman Parlour First
AR  Pullman Brake First
AS  Sleeping Car
AT  Royal Train Coach
AU  Sleeping Car with Pantry
AX  Generator Van
AZ  Special Saloon
NE  Gangwayed brake van (100 m.p.h.)
NW  Desiro Barrier Vehicle
NZ  Driving Brake Van ("Driving Van Trailer")

(2) A digit denoting the class of passenger accommodation:

1  First
2  Standard (formerly second)
3  Composite (first & standard)
4  Unclassified
5  None

(3) A suffix relating to the build of coach.

| | |
|---|---|
| 1 | Mark 1 |
| Z | Mark 2 |
| A | Mark 2A |
| B | Mark 2B |
| C | Mark 2C |
| D | Mark 2D |
| E | Mark 2E |
| F | Mark 2F |
| G | Mark 3 or 3A |
| H | Mark 3B |
| J | Mark 4 |

# OPERATING CODES

Operating codes used by train company operating staff (and others) to denote vehicle types in general. These are shown in parentheses adjacent to TOPS type codes. Letters used are:

| | | | |
|---|---|---|---|
| B | Brake | K | Side corridor with lavatory |
| C | Composite | O | Open |
| F | First Class | S | Standard Class (formerly second) |

Various other letters are in use and the meaning of these can be ascertained by referring to the titles at the head of each type.

Readers should note the distinction between an SO (Open Standard) and a TSO (Tourist Open Standard) The former has 2+1 seating layout, whilst the latter has 2+2.

# BOGIE TYPES

**BR Mark 1 (BR1).** Double bolster leaf spring bogie. Generally 90 m.p.h., but Mark 1 bogies may be permitted to run at 100 m.p.h. with special maintenance. Weight: 6.1 t.

**BR Mark 2 (BR2).** Single bolster leaf-spring bogie used on certain types of non-passenger stock and suburban stock (all now withdrawn). Weight: 5.3 t.

**COMMONWEALTH (C).** Heavy, cast steel coil spring bogie. 100 m.p.h. Weight: 6.75 t.

**B4.** Coil spring fabricated bogie. Generally 100 m.p.h., but B4 bogies may be permitted to run at 110 m.p.h. with special maintenance. Weight: 5.2 t.

**B5.** Heavy duty version of B4. 100 m.p.h. Weight: 5.3 t.

**B5 (SR).** A bogie originally used on Southern Region EMUs, similar in design to B5. Now also used on locomotive hauled coaches. 100 m.p.h.

**BT10.** A fabricated bogie designed for 125 m.p.h. Air suspension.

**T4.** A 125 m.p.h. bogie designed by BREL (now Bombardier Transportation).

**BT41.** Fitted to Mark 4 vehicles, designed by SIG in Switzerland. At present limited to 125 m.p.h., but designed for 140 m.p.h.

## BRAKES

Air braking is now standard on British main line trains. Vehicles with other equipment are denoted:

v    Vacuum braked.
x    Dual braked (air and vacuum).

## HEATING & VENTILATION

Electric heating and ventilation is now standard on British main-line trains. Certain coaches for use on charter services may also have steam heating facilities, or be steam heated only.

## PUBLIC ADDRESS

It is assumed all coaches are now fitted with public address equipment, although certain stored vehicles may not have this feature. In addition, it is assumed all vehicles with a conductor's compartment have public address transmission facilities, as have catering vehicles.

## COOKING EQUIPMENT

It is assumed that Mark 1 catering vehicles have gas powered cooking equipment, whilst Mark 2, 3 and 4 catering vehicles have electric powered cooking equipment unless stated otherwise.

## ADDITIONAL FEATURE CODES

| | |
|---|---|
| d | Secondary door locking. |
| dg | Driver–Guard communication equipment. |
| f | Facelifted or fluorescent lighting. |
| h | "High density" seating |
| k | Composition brake blocks (instead of cast iron). |
| n | Day/night lighting. |
| pg | Public address transmission and driver-guard communication. |
| pt | Public address transmission facility. |
| q | Catering staff to shore telephone. |
| T | Toilet. |
| TD | Universal access toilet suitable for use by a disabled person. |
| W | Wheelchair space. |
| ★ | Blue star multiple working cables fitted. |

# NOTES ON ETH INDICES

The sum of ETH indices in a train must not be more than the ETH index of the locomotive. The normal voltage on British trains is 1000 V. Suffix "X" denotes 600 amp wiring instead of 400 amp. Trains whose ETH index is higher than 66 must be formed completely of 600 amp wired stock. Class 33 and 73 locomotives cannot provide a suitable electric train supply for Mark 2D, Mark 2E, Mark 2F, Mark 3, Mark 3A, Mark 3B or Mark 4 coaches. Class 55 locomotives provide an e.t.s. directly from one of their traction generators into the train line. Consequently voltage fluctuations can result in motor-alternator flashover. Thus these locomotives are not suitable for use with Mark 2D, Mark 2E, Mark 2F, Mark 3, Mark 3A, Mark 3B or Mark 4 coaches unless modified motor-alternators are fitted. Such motor alternators were fitted to Mark 2D and 2F coaches used on the East Coast main line, but few remain fitted.

# BUILD DETAILS

### Lot Numbers
Vehicles ordered under the auspices of BR were allocated a lot (batch) number when ordered and these are quoted in class headings and sub-headings.

### Builders
These are shown for each lot. Abbreviations used are shown in Section 6.7.

Information on sub-contracting works which built parts of vehicles e.g. the underframes etc. is not shown.
In addition to the above, certain vintage Pullman cars were built or rebuilt at the following works:

Metropolitan Carriage & Wagon Company, Birmingham
Midland Carriage & Wagon Company, Birmingham
Pullman Car Company, Preston Park, Brighton
Conversions have also been carried out at the Railway Technical Centre, Derby, LNWR, Crewe and Blakes Fabrications, Edinburgh.

### Vehicle Numbers
Where a coach has been renumbered, the former number is shown in parentheses. If a coach has been renumbered more than once, the original number is shown first in parentheses, followed by the most recent previous number.

# THE DEVELOPMENT OF BR STANDARD COACHES

### Mark 1

The standard BR coach built from 1951 to 1963 was the Mark 1. This type features a separate underframe and body. The underframe is normally 64 ft. 6 in. long, but certain vehicles were built on shorter (57 ft.) frames. Tungsten lighting was standard and until 1961, BR Mark 1 bogies were generally provided. In 1959 Lot No. 30525 (TSO) appeared with fluorescent lighting and melamine interior panels, and from 1961 onwards Commonwealth bogies were fitted in an attempt to improve the quality of ride which became very poor when the tyre profiles on the wheels of the BR1 bogies became worn. Later batches of TSO and BSO retained the features of Lot No. 30525, but compartment vehicles – whilst utilising melamine panelling in standard class – still retained tungsten lighting. Wooden interior finish was retained in first class vehicles where the only change was to fluorescent lighting in open vehicles (except Lot No. 30648, which had tungsten lighting). In later years many Mark 1 coaches had BR 1 bogies replaced by B4.

### XP64

In 1964, a new prototype train was introduced. Known as 'XP64', it featured new seat designs, pressure heating & ventilation, aluminium compartment doors and corridor partitions, foot pedal operated toilets and B4 bogies. The vehicles were built on standard Mark 1 underframes. Folding exterior doors were fitted, but these proved troublesome and were later replaced with hinged doors. All XP64 coaches have been withdrawn, but some have been preserved.

### Mark 2

The prototype Mark 2 vehicle (W 13252) was produced in 1963. This was an FK of semi-integral construction and had pressure heating & ventilation, tungsten lighting, and was mounted on B4 bogies. This vehicle had been preserved by the National Railway Museum and is currently stored awaiting disposal at MoD Kineton DM. The production build was similar, but wider windows were used. The TSO and SO vehicles used a new seat design similar to that used in the XP64 and fluorescent lighting was provided. Interior finish reverted to wood. Mark 2 vehicles were built from 1964–66.

### Mark 2A–2C

The Mark 2A design, built 1967–68, incorporated the remainder of the features first used in the XP64 coaches, i.e. foot pedal operated toilets (except BSO), new first class seat design, aluminium compartment doors and partitions together with fluorescent lighting in first class compartments. Folding gangway doors (lime green coloured) were used instead of the traditional one-piece variety.

Mark 2B coaches had wide wrap around doors at vehicle ends, no centre doors and a slightly longer body. In standard class there was one toilet at each end instead of two at one end as previously. The folding gangway doors were red.

Mark 2C coaches had a lowered ceiling with twin strips of fluorescent lighting and ducting for air conditioning, but air conditioning was never fitted.

## Mark 2D–2F

These vehicles were fitted with air conditioning. They had no opening top-lights in saloon windows, which were shallower than previous ones.

Mark 2E vehicles had smaller toilets with luggage racks opposite. The folding gangway doors were fawn coloured.

Mark 2F vehicles had a modified air conditioning system, plastic interior panels and Inter-City 70 type seats.

## Mark 3

The Mark 3 design has BT10 bogies, is 75 ft. (23 m.) long and is of fully integral construction with Inter-City 70 type seats. Gangway doors were yellow (red in RFB) when new, although these were changed on refurbishment. Loco-hauled coaches are classified Mark 3A, Mark 3 being reserved for HST trailers. A new batch of FO and BFO, classified Mark 3B, was built in 1985 with Advanced Passenger Train-style seating and revised lighting. These are now in use on First Great Western sleeping car trains. The last vehicles in the Mark 3 series were the driving brake vans ("Driving Van Trailers") built for West Coast Main Line services.

A number of Mark 3 vehicles have recently been converted for use as HST trailers with Grand Central and Cross-Country.

## Mark 4

The Mark 4 design was built by Metro-Cammell for use on the East Coast Main Line after electrification and featured a body profile suitable for tilting trains, although tilt is not fitted, and is not intended to be. This design is suitable for 140 m.p.h. running, although is restricted to 125 m.p.h. because the signalling system on the route is not suitable for the higher speed. The bogies for these coaches were built by SIG in Switzerland and are designated BT41. Power operated sliding plug exterior doors are standard. All Mark 4s were rebuilt with completely new interiors in 2003–05 for GNER and referred to as "Mallard" stock. These rakes generally run in fixed formations and are now operated by National Express East Coast.

# 2.1. BR NUMBER SERIES COACHING STOCK

## AJ11 (RF)                                 KITCHEN FIRST

Mark 1. Spent most of its life as a Royal Train vehicle and was numbered 2907 for a time. Built with Commonwealth bogies, but B5 bogies substituted. 24/–. ETH 2.

Lot No. 30633 Swindon 1961. 41 t.

| 325 | **PC** | VS | *VS* | SL | |

## AP1Z (PFK) PULLMAN KITCHEN WITH SERVERY

Mark 2. Pressure Ventilated. Seating removed and replaced with servery. 2T. B5 bogies. ETH 6.

Lot No. 30755 Derby 1966. 40 t.

| 504 | **PC** | WC | *WC* | CS | ULLSWATER |
| 506 | **PC** | WC | *WC* | CS | WINDERMERE |

## AQ1Z (PFP)                    PULLMAN PARLOUR FIRST

Mark 2. Pressure Ventilated. 36/– 2T. B4 bogies. ETH 5.

**Non-standard livery:** 546 Maroon & beige.

Lot No. 30754 Derby 1966. 35 t.

| 546 | **0** | WC | | CS | CITY OF MANCHESTER |
| 548 | **PC** | WC | *WC* | CS | GRASMERE |
| 549 | **PC** | WC | *WC* | CS | BASSENTHWAITE |
| 550 | **PC** | WC | *WC* | CS | RYDAL WATER |
| 551 | **PC** | WC | *WC* | CS | BUTTERMERE |
| 552 | **PC** | WC | *WC* | CS | ENNERDALE WATER |
| 553 | **PC** | WC | *WC* | CS | CRUMMOCK WATER |

## AR1Z (PFB)                       PULLMAN BRAKE FIRST

Mark 2. Pressure Ventilated. 30/– 2T. B4 bogies. ETH 4.

Lot No. 30753 Derby 1966. 35 t.

| 586 | **PC** | WC | *WC* | CS | DERWENTWATER |

## AJ1F (RFB)                                          BUFFET FIRST

Mark 2F. Air conditioned. Converted 1988–9/91 at BREL, Derby from Mark 2F
FOs. 1200/1/3/11/14/20/21/50/2/6 have Stones equipment, others have
Temperature Ltd. 25/– 1T 1W (except 1253 which is 26/– 1T). B4 bogies. d.
ETH 6X.

**1200/3/11/14/20/52/6.** Lot No. 30845 Derby 1973. 33 t.
**1201/4/7/10/12/13/21/50/4/8/60.** Lot No. 30859 Derby 1973–74. 33 t.
**1253.** Lot No. 30873 Derby 1974–75. 33 t.

| | | | | | |
|------|-------------|-----|-----|-----|-----|
| 1200 | (3287, 6459) | **RV** | H  | *RV* | OM |
| 1201 | (3361, 6445) | **CH** | H  | *VT* | TM |
| 1203 | (3291)      |     | H   |      | CD |
| 1204 | (3401)      | **V** | H  |      | SN |
| 1207 | (3328, 6422) | **V** | H  |      | ZG |
| 1210 | (3405, 6462) | **FS** | H | *SR* | IS |
| 1211 | (3305)      |     | H   |      | LM |
| 1212 | (3427, 6453) | **V** | H  | *RV* | OM |
| 1213 | (3419)      | **V** | DM |      | MQ |
| 1214 | (3317, 6433) | **AR** | H |      | KT |
| 1220 | (3315, 6432) | **FS** | H | *SR* | IS |
| 1221 | (3371)      |     | H   |      | ZG |
| 1250 | (3372)      | **V** | H  | *RV* | OM |
| 1252 | (3280)      | **V** | H  |      | LM |
| 1253 | (3432)      | **V** | H  |      | KT |
| 1254 | (3391)      | **BG** | CG | *CG* | BH |
| 1256 | (3296)      |     | H   |      | LM |
| 1258 | (3322)      | **V** | H  |      | KT |
| 1260 | (3378)      | **V** | H  |      | CD |

## AK51 (RKB)                              KITCHEN WITH BAR

Mark 1. Built with no seats but three Pullman-style seats now fitted in bar area.
B5 bogies. ETH 1.

Lot No. 30624 Cravens 1960–61. 41 t.

| | | | | |
|------|------|-----|-----|-----|
| 1566 | **VN** | VS | *VS* | CP |

## AJ41 (RBR)   UNCLASSIFIED KITCHEN BUFFET

Mark 1. Built with 23 loose chairs. All remaining vehicles refurbished with 23
fixed polypropylene chairs and fluorescent lighting. ETH 2 (* 2X). 1683/91/92/
99 were further refurbished with 21 chairs, wheelchair space and carpets.

s   Modified for use as servery vehicle with some or all seating removed.
t   Modified with 11 chairs with a food preparation area replacing the former
    seating area.

**1651–1699.** Lot No. 30628 Pressed Steel 1960–61. Commonwealth bogies. 39 t.
**1730.** Lot No. 30512 BRCW 1960–61. B5 bogies. 37 t.

**Non-standard liveries:** 1683 and 1699 Oxford Blue.
1679, 1680 & 1698 British racing green & cream lined out in gold.

| | | | | | | | | | | |
|---|---|---|---|---|---|---|---|---|---|---|
| 1651 | t | **CC** | RV | | OM | 1683 | | **O** | RV | *RV* | OM |
| 1657 | s | **DR** | DR | *DR* | CP | 1691 | t | **CC** | RV | *RV* | OM |
| 1658 | t | **BG** | DB | | OM | 1692 | t | **CH** | RV | *RV* | OM |
| 1659 | s | **PC** | RA | *WT* | OM | 1696 | t | **G** | DB | | OM |
| 1671 | x*t | **M** | RV | *RV* | OM | 1698 | s | **O** | RV | | OM |
| 1679 | t | **O** | DB | | OM | 1699 | t | **O** | RV | *RV* | OM |
| 1680 | *t | **O** | DB | *DB* | OM | 1730 | x | **M** | BK | *BK* | BT |

# AN2F (RSS)                    SELF-SERVICE BUFFET

Mark 2F. Air conditioned. Temperature Ltd. equipment. Inter-City 70 seats. Converted 1974 from Mark 2F TSO 5970 as a prototype self-service buffet for APT-P. Sold to Northern Ireland Railways 1983, regauged to 5′3″ and numbered 546. Since withdrawn, repatriated to Great Britain and converted back to standard gauge. –/24. B5 bogies. ETH 12X.

Lot No. 30860 Derby 1973–74. 33 t.

| | | | | | | |
|---|---|---|---|---|---|---|
| 1800 | | **PC** | WT | *WT* | CS | TINTAGEL |

# AN21 (RMB)
# OPEN STANDARD WITH MINIATURE BUFFET

Mark 1. –/44 2T. These vehicles are basically an open standard with two full window spaces removed to accommodate a buffet counter, and four seats removed to allow for a stock cupboard. All remaining vehicles now have fluorescent lighting. Commonwealth bogies. ETH 3.

**1813–1832.** Lot No. 30520 Wolverton 1960. 38 t.
**1840–1842.** Lot No. 30507 Wolverton 1960. 37 t.
**1859–1863.** Lot No. 30670 Wolverton 1961–62. 38 t.
**1882.** Lot No. 30702 Wolverton 1962. 38 t.

**Notes:**

1842 is refurbished and fitted with a microwave oven.
1861 has had its toilets replaced with store cupboards.

| | | | | | | | | | | |
|---|---|---|---|---|---|---|---|---|---|---|
| 1813 | x | **M** | RV | *RV* | OM | 1860 | x | **M** | WC | *WC* | CS |
| 1832 | x | **CC** | RV | | OM | 1861 | x | **M** | WC | *WC* | CS |
| 1840 | v | **G** | WC | *WC* | CS | 1863 | x | **CH** | RV | *RV* | OM |
| 1842 | | **CH** | RV | *RV* | OM | 1882 | x | **M** | WC | *WC* | CS |
| 1859 | x | **M** | BK | *BK* | BT | | | | | | |

## AJ41 (RBR)    UNCLASSIFIED KITCHEN BUFFET

Mark 1. These vehicles were built as unclassified restaurant (RU). They were rebuilt with buffet counters and 23 fixed polypropylene chairs (RBS), then further refurbished by fitting fluorescent lighting and reclassified RBR. ETH 2X.

s Modified for use as servery vehicle with seating removed.

**1953**. Lot No. 30575 Swindon 1960. B4/B5 bogies. 36.5 t.
**1961**. Lot No. 30632 Swindon 1961. Commonwealth bogies. 39 t.

1953  s    **VN**  VS  *VS*  CP        | 1961  x    **G**  WC *WC*  CS

## AU51        CHARTER TRAIN STAFF COACHES

Mark 1. Converted from BCKs in 1988. Commonwealth bogies. ETH 2.

Lot No. 30732 Derby 1964. 37 t.

**Non-standard livery:** 2834 British racing green & cream lined out in gold.

| 2833 | (21270) | **BG** | DB | | OM |
| 2834 | (21267) | **0** | RV | *RV* | OM |

## AT5G                HM THE QUEEN'S SALOON

Mark 3. Converted from a FO built 1972. Consists of a lounge, bedroom and bathroom for HM The Queen, and a combined bedroom and bathroom for the Queen's dresser. One entrance vestibule has double doors. Air conditioned. BT10 bogies. ETH 9X.

Lot No. 30886 Wolverton 1977. 36 t.

2903  (11001)    **RP**  NR  *RP*        ZN

## AT5G  HRH THE DUKE OF EDINBURGH'S SALOON

Mark 3. Converted from a TSO built 1972. Consists of a combined lounge/dining room, a bedroom and a shower room for the Duke, a kitchen and a valet's bedroom and bathroom. Air conditioned. BT10 bogies. ETH 15X.

Lot No. 30887 Wolverton 1977. 36 t.

2904  (12001)    **RP**  NR  *RP*        ZN

## AT5G        ROYAL HOUSEHOLD SLEEPING CAR

Mark 3A. Built to similar specification as SLE 10647–729. 12 sleeping compartments for use of Royal Household with a fixed lower berth and a hinged upper berth. 2T plus shower room. Air conditioned. BT10 bogies. ETH 11X. Lot No. 31002 Derby/Wolverton 1985. 44 t.

2915            **RP**  NR  *RP*        ZN

## AT5G  HRH THE PRINCE OF WALES'S DINING CAR

Mark 3. Converted from HST TRUK built 1976. Large kitchen retained, but dining area modified for Royal use seating up to 14 at central table(s). Air conditioned. BT10 bogies. ETH 13X.

Lot No. 31059 Wolverton 1988. 43 t.

2916   (40512)        **RP**   NR   *RP*        ZN

## AT5G  ROYAL KITCHEN/HOUSEHOLD DINING CAR

Mark 3. Converted from HST TRUK built 1977. Large kitchen retained and dining area slightly modified with seating for 22 Royal Household members. Air conditioned. BT10 bogies. ETH 13X.

Lot No. 31084 Wolverton 1990. 43 t.

2917   (40514)        **RP**   NR   *RP*        ZN

## AT5G                        ROYAL HOUSEHOLD CARS

Mark 3. Converted from HST TRUKs built 1976/7. Air conditioned. BT10 bogies. ETH 10X.

Lot Nos. 31083 (31085*) Wolverton 1989. 41.05 t.

2918   (40515)        **RP**   NR            ZN
2919   (40518)   *    **RP**   NR            ZN

## AT5B          ROYAL HOUSEHOLD COUCHETTES

Mark 2B. Converted from BFK built 1969. Consists of luggage accommodation, guard's compartment, workshop area, 350 kW diesel generator and staff sleeping accommodation. B5 bogies. ETH2X.

Lot No. 31044 Wolverton 1986. 48 t.

2920   (14109, 17109)    **RP**   NR   *RP*   ZN

Mark 2B. Converted from BFK built 1969. Consists of luggage accommodation, kitchen, brake control equipment and staff accommodation. B5 bogies. ETH7X.

Lot No. 31086 Wolverton 1990. 41.5 t.

2921   (14107, 17107)    **RP**   NR   *RP*   ZN

## AT5H HRH THE PRINCE OF WALES'S SLEEPING CAR

Mark 3B. BT10 bogies. Air conditioned. ETH 7X.

Lot No. 31035 Derby/Wolverton 1987.

| | | | | |
|---|---|---|---|---|
| 2922 | **RP** | NR | *RP* | ZN |

## AT5H ROYAL SALOON

Mark 3B. BT10 bogies. Air conditioned. ETH 6X.

Lot No. 31036 Derby/Wolverton 1987.

| | | | | |
|---|---|---|---|---|
| 2923 | **RP** | NR | *RP* | ZN |

## AD11 (FO) OPEN FIRST

Mark 1. 42/– 2T. ETH 3. Many now fitted with table lamps.

**Non-standard livery:** British racing green & cream lined out in gold.

**3066–3069.** Lot No. 30169 Doncaster 1955. B4 bogies. 33 t.
**3096–3098.** Lot No. 30576 BRCW 1959. B4 bogies. 33 t.

3068 was numbered DB 975606 for a time when in departmental service for British Railways.

| | | | | | | | | | | |
|---|---|---|---|---|---|---|---|---|---|---|
| 3066 | **CC** | RV | *RV* | OM | | 3096 | x **M** | BK | *BK* | BT |
| 3068 | **CC** | RV | *RV* | OM | | 3097 | **CC** | RV | *RV* | OM |
| 3069 | **CC** | RV | *RV* | OM | | 3098 | x **CH** | RV | *RV* | OM |

Later design with fluorescent lighting, aluminium window frames and Commonwealth bogies.

**3105–3128.** Lot No. 30697 Swindon 1962–63. 36 t.
**3130–3150.** Lot No. 30717 Swindon 1963. 36 t.

3128/36/41/3/4/6/7/8 were renumbered 1058/60/3/5/6/8/9/70 when reclassified RUO, then 3600/5/8/9/2/6/4/10 when declassified to SO, but have since regained their original numbers. 3136 was numbered DB977970 for a time when in use with Serco Railtest as a Brake Force Runner.

**Note:** 3105 has had its luggage racks removed and has tungsten lighting.

| | | | | | | | | | | |
|---|---|---|---|---|---|---|---|---|---|---|
| 3105 | x **M** | WC | *WC* | CS | | 3119 | **CC** | RV | *RV* | OM |
| 3107 | x **CH** | RV | *RV* | OM | | 3120 | **CC** | RV | *RV* | OM |
| 3110 | x **CH** | RV | *RV* | OM | | 3121 | **O** | RV | *RV* | OM |
| 3112 | x **CH** | RV | *RV* | OM | | 3122 | x **CH** | RV | *RV* | OM |
| 3113 | x **M** | WC | *WC* | CS | | 3123 | **O** | RV | *RV* | OM |
| 3114 | **G** | RV | | OM | | 3124 | **G** | RV | | OM |
| 3115 | x **M** | BK | *BK* | BT | | 3125 | x **CH** | JH | *VT* | TM |
| 3117 | x **M** | WC | *WC* | CS | | 3127 | **G** | RV | | OM |

| 3128 | x | **M** | WC | *WC* | CS |
|------|---|-------|----|------|----|
| 3130 | v | **M** | WC | *WC* | CS |
| 3131 | x | **M** | RV | | OM |
| 3132 | x | **M** | RV | | OM |
| 3133 | x | **M** | RV | | OM |
| 3136 | | **M** | WC | *WC* | CS |
| 3140 | x | **CH** | RV | *RV* | OM |
| 3141 | | **M** | RV | *RV* | OM |

| 3143 | | **M** | WC | *WC* | CS |
|------|---|-------|----|------|----|
| 3144 | x | **M** | RV | *RV* | OM |
| 3146 | | **M** | RV | *RV* | OM |
| 3147 | | **0** | RV | *RV* | OM |
| 3148 | | **M** | JH | *WC* | CS |
| 3149 | | **CC** | RV | *RV* | OM |
| 3150 | | **G** | BK | | BT |

**Names:**

| 3105 | JULIA |
|------|-------|
| 3113 | JESSICA |
| 3117 | CHRISTINA |
| 3128 | VICTORIA |

| 3130 | PAMELA |
|------|--------|
| 3136 | DIANA |
| 3143 | PATRICIA |

## AD1D (FO) OPEN FIRST

Mark 2D. Air conditioned. Stones equipment. 42/– 2T. B4 bogies. ETH 5.

† Interior modified to Pullman Car standards with new seating, new panelling, tungsten lighting and table lights for VSOE "Northern Belle".

Lot No. 30821 Derby 1971–72. 34 t.

| 3174 | † | **VN** | VS | *VS* | CP | GLAMIS |
|------|---|--------|----|------|----|--------|
| 3182 | † | **VN** | VS | *VS* | CP | WARWICK |
| 3188 | | **PC** | RA | *WT* | OM | SOVEREIGN |

## AD1E (FO) OPEN FIRST

Mark 2E. Air conditioned. Stones equipment. 42/– 2T (w 41/– 2T 1W, p 36/– 2T). B4 bogies. ETH 5.

r Refurbished with new seats.
u Fitted with power supply for Mk. 1 RBR.
† Interior modified to Pullman Car standards with new seating, new panelling, tungsten lighting and table lights for VSOE "Northern Belle".

3255 was numbered 3525 for a time when fitted with a pantry.

Lot No. 30843 Derby 1972–73. 32.5 t. (35.8 t. †).

| 3223 | | **RV** | RV | | OM | DIAMOND |
|------|----|--------|----|------|----|---------|
| 3228 | du | **RV** | RV | | CD | AMETHYST |
| 3229 | d | **RV** | H | | KT | JADE |
| 3231 | p | **PC** | RA | *WT* | OM | APOLLO |
| 3232 | dr | **G** | VS | *VS* | CP | |
| 3240 | | **RV** | RV | | OM | SAPPHIRE |
| 3241 | dr | **FP** | H | | LM | |
| 3244 | d | **RV** | RV | | CD | EMERALD |
| 3247 | † | **VN** | VS | *VS* | CP | CHATSWORTH |
| 3255 | dr | **M** | DB | | OM | |

| 3261 | dw | **FP** | H | | OM | |
| 3267 | † | **VN** | VS | *VS* | CP | BELVOIR |
| 3269 | dr | **M** | DB | | OM | |
| 3273 | † | **VN** | VS | *VS* | CP | ALNWICK |
| 3275 | † | **VN** | VS | *VS* | CP | HARLECH |

# AD1F (FO)       OPEN FIRST

Mark 2F. Air conditioned. 3277–3318/58–79 have Stones equipment, others have Temperature Ltd. 42/– 2T. All now refurbished with power-operated vestibule doors, new panels and new seat trim. B4 bogies. d. ETH 5X.

**3277–3318**. Lot No. 30845 Derby 1973. 33.5 t.
**3325–3426**. Lot No. 30859 Derby 1973–74. 33.5 t.
**3431–3438**. Lot No. 30873 Derby 1974–75. 33.5 t.

r Further refurbished with table lamps and modified seats with burgundy seat trim.
u Fitted with power supply for Mark 1 RBR.

| 3277 | | **AR** | H | *RV* | OM | | 3359 | r | **M** | WC | *WC* | CS |
| 3278 | r | **BP** | DR | | KM | | 3360 | r | | WC | *WC* | CS |
| 3279 | u | **M** | DB | *DB* | OM | | 3362 | r | | WC | *WC* | CS |
| 3292 | | **M** | DB | *DB* | OM | | 3364 | r | **RV** | RV | *RV* | OM |
| 3295 | | **AR** | H | *RV* | OM | | 3366 | r | **V** | H | | BH |
| 3303 | | **AR** | H | | OM | | 3368 | | **M** | DB | | OM |
| 3304 | r | **V** | H | *RV* | OM | | 3374 | | **BG** | CG | *CG* | BH |
| 3309 | | | H | *VT* | TM | | 3375 | | **M** | DB | | OM |
| 3312 | | | H | | LM | | 3379 | u | **AR** | H | | OM |
| 3313 | r | **BP** | CD | | EM | | 3384 | r | **RV** | RV | *RV* | OM |
| 3314 | r | **V** | H | *RV* | OM | | 3385 | r | **BP** | DR | | OY |
| 3318 | | **M** | DB | *DB* | OM | | 3386 | r | **V** | RV | *RV* | OM |
| 3325 | r | **V** | H | *RV* | OM | | 3387 | r | **V** | DM | | MQ |
| 3326 | r | **BP** | CD | | EM | | 3388 | | **M** | DB | | OM |
| 3330 | r | **RV** | RV | *RV* | OM | | 3390 | r | **RV** | RV | *RV* | OM |
| 3331 | | **M** | DB | *DB* | OM | | 3392 | r | **BP** | CD | | EM |
| 3333 | r | **V** | H | | OM | | 3395 | r | **BP** | CD | | EM |
| 3334 | | **AR** | H | *RV* | OM | | 3397 | r | **RV** | RV | *RV* | OM |
| 3336 | u | **AR** | H | *RV* | OM | | 3399 | u | **M** | DB | | OM |
| 3338 | u | **M** | DB | | OM | | 3400 | | **M** | DB | *DB* | OM |
| 3340 | r | **V** | H | *RV* | OM | | 3402 | r | **V** | DM | | Y.I |
| 3344 | r | **V** | RV | *RV* | OM | | 3408 | r | **M** | WC | *WC* | C |
| 3345 | r | **V** | H | *RV* | OM | | 3411 | r | **V** | DM | | I. |
| 3348 | r | **RV** | RV | *RV* | OM | | 3414 | | **M** | DB | | O |
| 3350 | r | **BP** | CD | | EM | | 3416 | | | H | | TM |
| 3351 | | **CH** | H | *VT* | TM | | 3417 | | **AR** | H | *RV* | OM. |
| 3352 | | **BP** | CD | | EM | | 3424 | | **M** | DB | *DB* | CM |
| 3353 | r | **B** | DM | | MQ | | 3425 | r | **V** | DM | | Y.. |
| 3354 | r | **V** | DM | | YJ | | 3426 | r | **RV** | RV | *RV* | OI 4 |
| 3356 | r | **RV** | RV | *RV* | OM | | 3431 | r | **BP** | CD | | EM |
| 3358 | | **M** | DB | *DB* | OM | | 3438 | r | **V** | H | | LM |

**Names:**

| | | | |
|---|---|---|---|
| 3330 | BRUNEL | 3384 | DICKENS |
| 3348 | GAINSBOROUGH | 3390 | CONSTABLE |
| 3356 | TENNYSON | 3397 | WORDSWORTH |
| 3364 | SHAKESPEARE | 3426 | ELGAR |

## AC21 (TSO)         OPEN STANDARD

Mark 1. This coach has narrower seats than later vehicles. Built with BR Mark 1 bogies. –/64 2T. ETH 4.
Lot No. 30079 York 1953. Commonwealth bogies. 36 t.

| 3766 | x | **M** | WC | *WC* | CS | | |

## AC21 (TSO)         OPEN STANDARD

Mark 1. These vehicles are a development of the above with fluorescent lighting and modified design of seat headrest. Built with BR Mark 1 bogies. –/64 2T. ETH 4.

**4831–4836.** Lot No. 30506 Wolverton 1959. Commonwealth bogies. 33 t.
**4856.** Lot No. 30525 Wolverton 1959–60. B4 bogies. 33 t.

| 4831 | x | **M** | BK | *BK* | BT | | 4836 | x | **M** | BK | *BK* | BT |
| 4832 | x | **M** | BK | *BK* | BT | | 4856 | x | **M** | BK | *BK* | BT |

## AC21 (TSO)         OPEN STANDARD

Mark 1. Later vehicles built with Commonwealth bogies. –/64 2T. ETH4.

**4902–4912.** Lot No. 30646 Wolverton 1961. BR Mark 1 bogies substituted by the SR. All now re-rebogied. 34 t B4, 36 t C.
**4925–5044.** Lot No. 30690 Wolverton 1961–62. Aluminium window frames. 37 t.

| 4902 | x B4 | **CH** | RV | *RV* | OM | | 4991 | | **BG** | RV | | OM |
| 4905 | x C | **M** | WC | *WC* | CS | | 4994 | x | **M** | WC | *WC* | CS |
| 4912 | x C | **M** | WC | *WC* | CS | | 4996 | x | **M** | RV | | OM |
| 4925 | | **G** | DB | | OM | | 4998 | | **M** | RV | *RV* | OM |
| 4927 | x | **CH** | RV | *RV* | OM | | 4999 | | **BG** | RV | | OM |
| 4931 | v | **M** | WC | *WC* | CS | | 5005 | | **BG** | DB | | OM |
| 4940 | x | **M** | WC | *WC* | CS | | 5007 | | **G** | RV | | OM |
| 4946 | x | **M** | RV | | OM | | 5008 | x | **M** | RV | *RV* | OM |
| 4949 | x | **M** | RV | *RV* | OM | | 5009 | x | **CH** | RV | *RV* | OM |
| 4951 | x | **M** | WC | *WC* | CS | | 5023 | | **G** | RV | *RV* | OM |
| 4954 | v | **M** | WC | *WC* | CS | | 5027 | | **G** | RV | | OM |
| 4956 | | **BG** | DB | | OM | | 5028 | x | **CC** | BK | *BK* | BT |
| 4958 | v | **M** | WC | *WC* | CS | | 5032 | x | **M** | WC | *WC* | CS |
| 4959 | | **BG** | RV | | OM | | 5033 | x | **M** | WC | *WC* | CS |
| 4960 | x | **M** | WC | *WC* | CS | | 5035 | x | **M** | WC | *WC* | CS |
| 4973 | x | **M** | WC | *WC* | CS | | 5037 | | **G** | DB | | OM |
| 4984 | x | **M** | WC | *WC* | CS | | 5040 | x | **CH** | RV | *RV* | OM |
| 4986 | | **G** | RV | *RV* | OM | | 5044 | x | **M** | WC | *WC* | CS |

## AC2Z (TSO)                    OPEN STANDARD

Mark 2. Pressure ventilated. –/64 2T. B4 bogies. ETH 4.

Lot No. 30751 Derby 1965–67. 32 t.

| | | | | | | | | | | |
|---|---|---|---|---|---|---|---|---|---|---|
| 5148 | v | **RR** | H | | TM | 5193 | v | **LN** | H | | TM |
| 5157 | v | **CH** | H | *VT* | TM | 5194 | v | **RR** | H | | TM |
| 5171 | v | **G** | WC | *WC* | CS | 5198 | v | **CH** | H | *VT* | TM |
| 5177 | v | **CH** | H | *VT* | TM | 5200 | v | **G** | WC | *WC* | CS |
| 5179 | v | **RR** | H | | TM | 5212 | v | **LN** | H | | TM |
| 5183 | v | **RR** | H | | TM | 5216 | v | **G** | WC | *WC* | CS |
| 5186 | v | **RR** | H | | TM | 5221 | v | **RR** | H | | TM |
| 5191 | v | **CH** | H | *VT* | TM | 5222 | v | **G** | WC | *WC* | CS |

**Names:**

| | | | | |
|---|---|---|---|---|
| 5193 | CLAN MACLEOD | | 5212 | CAPERKAILZIE |

## AD2Z (SO)                    OPEN STANDARD

Mark 2. Pressure ventilated. –/48 2T. B4 bogies. ETH 4.

Lot No. 30752 Derby 1966. 32 t.

| | | | | | | |
|---|---|---|---|---|---|---|
| 5229 | | **PC** | WT | *WT* | CS | THE GREEN KNIGHT |
| 5236 | v | **G** | WC | *WC* | CS | |
| 5237 | v | **G** | WC | *WC* | CS | |
| 5239 | | **PC** | WT | *WT* | CS | THE RED KNIGHT |
| 5249 | v | **G** | WC | *WC* | CS | |

## AC2A (TSO)                    OPEN STANDARD

Mark 2A. Pressure ventilated. –/64 2T (–/62 2T w). B4 bogies. ETH 4.

**5276–5341.** Lot No. 30776 Derby 1967–68. 32 t.
**5350–5419.** Lot No. 30787 Derby 1968. 32 t.

f Facelifted vehicles.

| | | | | | | | | | | | |
|---|---|---|---|---|---|---|---|---|---|---|---|
| 5276 | f | **RV** | RV | *RV* | OM | 5350 | | **CH** | RV | *RV* | OM |
| 5278 | | **PC** | WT | *WT* | CS | 5365 | | **RV** | RV | | OM |
| 5292 | f | **RV** | RV | *RV* | OM | 5366 | f | **RV** | RV | *RV* | OM |
| 5309 | | **CH** | DB | | OM | 5376 | | **RV** | RV | | OM |
| 5322 | f | **RV** | RV | *RV* | OM | 5386 | w | **M** | DB | | OM |
| 5331 | | **M** | DB | | OM | 5412 | w | **M** | BK | *BK* | BT |
| 5341 | f | **CC** | RV | *RV* | OM | 5419 | w | **PC** | WT | *WT* | CS |

**Names:**

| | | | | |
|---|---|---|---|---|
| 5278 | MELISANDE | | 5376 | Michaela |
| 5365 | Deborah | | 5419 | SIR. LANCELOT |

## AC2B (TSO)                                      OPEN STANDARD

Mark 2B. Pressure ventilated. –/62 2T. B4 bogies. ETH 4.

**Note:** 5482 was numbered DB977936 for a time when in departmental service for British Railways.

Lot No. 30791 Derby 1969. 32 t.

| | | | | | | | | | | |
|---|---|---|---|---|---|---|---|---|---|---|
| 5453 | d | **M** | WC | *WC* | CS | | 5482 | **M** | RP | OM |
| 5463 | d | **M** | WC | | CS | | 5487 | d | **M** | WC | *WC* | CS |
| 5478 | d | **M** | WC | *WC* | CS | | 5491 | d | **M** | WC | *WC* | CS |

## AC2C (TSO)                                      OPEN STANDARD

Mark 2C. Pressure ventilated. –/62 2T. B4 bogies. d. ETH 4.

Lot No. 30795 Derby 1969–70. 32 t.

5569    **M**  WC  *WC*  CS

## AC2D (TSO)                                      OPEN STANDARD

Mark 2D. Air conditioned. Stones equipment. Refurbished with new seats and end luggage stacks. –/58 2T. B4 bogies. d. ETH 5.

**Note:** 5700 and 5710 are currently in use as barrier vehicles.

Lot No. 30822 Derby 1971. 33 t.

| | | | | | | | | | | |
|---|---|---|---|---|---|---|---|---|---|---|
| 5631 | | **M** | DB | | OM | | 5700 | | **FP** | H | *CD* | GL |
| 5632 | | **M** | DB | | OM | | 5710 | | **FP** | H | *CD* | GL |
| 5657 | | **M** | DB | | OM | | 5737 | | **FP** | H | | KT |
| 5669 | | **BP** | H | | EM | | 5740 | | **FP** | H | | KT |
| 5679 | | **FP** | H | | KT | | | | | | | |

## AC2E (TSO)                                      OPEN STANDARD

Mark 2E. Air conditioned. Stones equipment. –/64 2T (w –/62 2T 1W). B4 bogies. d. ETH 5.

**5745–5797.** Lot No. 30837 Derby 1972. 33.5 t.
**5810–5906.** Lot No. 30844 Derby 1972–73. 33.5 t.

r Refurbished with new interior panelling.
s Refurbished with new interior panelling, modified design of seat headrest and centre luggage stack. –/60 2T (w –/58 2T 1W).
t Refurbished with new interior panelling and new seats.

| | | | | | | | | | | | |
|---|---|---|---|---|---|---|---|---|---|---|---|
| 5745 | s | | **V** | H | | KT | | 5750 | s | | **V** | H | | KT |
| 5748 | r | pt | | H | *RV* | OM | | 5754 | ws | | **V** | H | | KT |

| 5769 | r | | H | RV | OM |
| 5787 | s | V | H | | LM |
| 5788 | r | | H | | KT |
| 5789 | r pt | | H | | LM |
| 5792 | r | | H | RV | OM |
| 5793 | wspt | V | H | | KT |
| 5797 | r★ | | H | | LM |
| 5810 | s | V | H | | BH |
| 5815 | ws | V | H | | LM |
| 5821 | r pt | V | H | | KT |
| 5853 | t | AV | AW | | ZG |
| 5866 | r pt★ | | H | | BH |
| 5869 | t | AV | AW | | ZG |
| 5874 | t | | M | WC | CS |
| 5876 | s pt | V | H | | LM |
| 5881 | ws | V | H | | KT |
| 5886 | s | V | H | | KT |
| 5888 | wr | | H | | KT |
| 5899 | s | V | H | | KT |
| 5900 | wspt | V | H | | KT |
| 5901 | s | V | H | | BH |
| 5903 | s | V | H | | KT |
| 5905 | s | V | H | | KT |
| 5906 | wspt★ | | H | | BH |

# AC2F (TSO)                                    OPEN STANDARD

Mark 2F. Air conditioned. Temperature Ltd. equipment. Inter-City 70 seats. All were refurbished in the 1980s with power-operated vestibule doors, new panels and new seat trim. –/64 2T. (w –/62 2T 1W) B4 bogies. d. ETH 5X.

**5908–5958.** Lot No. 30846 Derby 1973. 33 t.
**5959–6170.** Lot No. 30860 Derby 1973–74. 33 t.
**6173–6183.** Lot No. 30874 Derby 1974–75. 33 t.

* Early Mark 2 style seats.

These vehicles have undergone a second refurbishment with carpets and new seat trim.

q   Fitted with two wheelchair spaces. –/60 2T 2W.
s   Fitted with centre luggage stack. –/60 2T.
t   Fitted with centre luggage stack and wheelchair space. –/58 2T 1W.

| 5908 | | V | H | | ZG |
| 5910 | q | V | H | RV | OM |
| 5911 | s | V | RV | | CD |
| 5912 | s | V | H | | KT |
| 5913 | s | AV | AW | | ZG |
| 5917 | s | V | WC | | CS |
| 5919 | s pt | V | H | | BH |
| 5920 | | V | DM | | YJ |
| 5921 | | AR | H | RV | OM |
| 5922 | | M | DB | SR | OM |
| 5924 | | M | DB | SR | OM |
| 5925 | s pt★ | | H | | LM |
| 5928 | | CH | H | VT | TM |
| 5929 | | AR | H | RV | OM |
| 5930 | t | V | H | | KT |
| 5932 | | V | H | | OM |
| 5933 | | V | H | | ZG |
| 5934 | | V | RV | | OM |
| 5936 | | AR | H | | LM |
| 5937 | | V | RV | RV | OM |
| 5940 | q | V | H | | ZG |
| 5941 | | V | H | | KT |
| 5943 | w | V | H | | ZG |
| 5944 | | AR | H | | ZG |
| 5945 | | V | H | RV | OM |
| 5946 | | V | H | RV | OM |
| 5948 | q | V | H | | KT |
| 5949 | q | V | H | | ZG |
| 5950 | | AR | H | RV | OM |
| 5952 | | V | RV | RV | OM |
| 5954 | | M | DB | | OM |
| 5955 | | V | RV | RV | OM |
| 5957 | | V | H | | ZG |
| 5958 | s★ | | H | | BH |
| 5959 | n | M | DB | SR | OM |
| 5960 | s | | H | | KT |
| 5961 | s pt | V | RV | RV | OM |
| 5962 | s pt | V | H | | KT |
| 5963 | | V | H | | OM |
| 5964 | | AR | H | RV | OM |

| No. | | Bold | | Italic | Code |
|---|---|---|---|---|---|
| 5965 | t | **AB** AW | *AW* | | CF |
| 5969 | q | **V** H | | | ZG |
| 5971 | s | **BG** CG | *CG* | | BH |
| 5976 | t | **AB** AW | *AW* | | CF |
| 5977 | | **V** H | | | ZG |
| 5978 | | **V** H | | | ZG |
| 5980 | | **V** H | | | ZG |
| 5981 | s★ | H | | | LM |
| 5983 | s | **V** H | | | KT |
| 5984 | | **V** H | *RV* | | OM |
| 5985 | | **AR** H | *RV* | | OM |
| 5986 | | **V** H | | | OM |
| 5987 | | **V** H | *RV* | | OM |
| 5989 | t | **V** DR | | | OY |
| 5991 | s | **V** H | | | KT |
| 5995 | s | **V** H | | | BH |
| 5997 | | **V** H | *RV* | | OM |
| 5998 | | **AR** H | *RV* | | OM |
| 6000 | t | **M** WC | *WC* | | CS |
| 6001 | q | **V** CG | | | BH |
| 6002 | | **V** DM | | | YJ |
| 6006 | | **AR** H | *RV* | | OM |
| 6008 | s | **BG** CG | *GW* | | BK |
| 6009 | | **V** H | | | ZG |
| 6012 | | **V** H | | | ZG |
| 6013 | s | **AV** AW | | | ZG |
| 6014 | s pt | WC | | | CS |
| 6016 | | **V** H | | | ZG |
| 6021 | | **V** H | | | ZG |
| 6022 | s | **M** WC | *WC* | | CS |
| 6024 | s | **V** RV | *RV* | | OM |
| 6027 | q | **V** RV | *RV* | | OM |
| 6028 | | **AR** H | | | ZG |
| 6029 | | **V** H | | | ZG |
| 6031 | | **V** H | | | ZG |
| 6035 | t★ | **AV** AW | | | ZG |
| 6036 | * | **M** DB | *SR* | | OM |
| 6037 | | **AR** H | | | ZG |
| 6038 | s | **V** RV | | | CD |
| 6041 | s | **M** WC | *WC* | | CS |
| 6042 | | **AR** H | *RV* | | OM |
| 6045 | w | **V** CG | | | KT |
| 6046 | s | **BG** CG | *GW* | | BK |
| 6049 | | **V** H | | | KT |
| 6050 | s | H | | | ZG |
| 6051 | | **V** RV | *RV* | | OM |
| 6052 | tw | H | | | KT |
| 6053 | * | **AR** H | | | KT |
| 6054 | | **V** H | *RV* | | OM |
| 6056 | | **V** RV | | | OM |
| 6059 | s | **V** H | | | KT |
| 6064 | s | **BG** CG | *GW* | | BK |
| 6065 | | **V** DM | | | KT |
| 6066 | s★ | **AV** AW | | | CF |
| 6067 | s pt | **V** RV | *RV* | | OM |
| 6073 | s | **V** H | | | KT |
| 6101 | | **V** H | | | ZG |
| 6103 | | **M** WC | *WC* | | CS |
| 6104 | | **V** H | *RV* | | OM |
| 6107 | | **V** H | *RV* | | OM |
| 6110 | | **M** DB | | | OM |
| 6115 | s | **M** WC | *WC* | | CS |
| 6117 | t★ | **BG** CG | *GW* | | BK |
| 6119 | s | **AV** AW | | | ZG |
| 6120 | s | **V** H | | | KT |
| 6122 | s★ | **BG** CG | *CG* | | BH |
| 6124 | s pt★ | **AV** AW | | | LM |
| 6134 | | **V** CG | | | KT |
| 6135 | s | WC | | | CS |
| 6136 | | **V** H | | | ZG |
| 6137 | s pt | **AV** AW | | | ZG |
| 6138 | | **V** RV | *RV* | | OM |
| 6139 | n* | **M** DB | *SR* | | OM |
| 6141 | q | **V** RV | *RV* | | OM |
| 6148 | s | WC | | | CS |
| 6150 | s | H | | | ZG |
| 6151 | * | **V** CG | | | KT |
| 6152 | * | **M** DB | *SR* | | OM |
| 6153 | | **V** H | | | ZG |
| 6154 | pt | H | | | LM |
| 6158 | | **V** H | *RV* | | OM |
| 6160 | * | **AR** H | | | LM |
| 6162 | s pt | **AV** AW | | | ZG |
| 6165 | | **V** DM | | | KT |
| 6168 | s★ | H | | | BH |
| 6170 | s★ | **AV** AW | | | ZG |
| 6173 | s★ | **BG** CG | *CG* | | BH |
| 6174 | | **AR** H | | | ZG |
| 6175 | | **V** H | | | ZG |
| 6176 | t | **V** RV | *RV* | | OM |
| 6177 | s | **V** RV | *RV* | | OM |
| 6179 | | **V** H | | | ZG |
| 6181 | wn | **V** DM | | | YJ |
| 6183 | s | **AV** AW | | | ZG |

## AX51                                                BRAKE GENERATOR VAN

Mark 1. Renumbered 1989 from BR departmental series. Converted from NDA in 1973 to three-phase supply brake generator van for use with HST trailers. Modified 1999 for use with loco-hauled stock. B5 bogies.

Lot No. 30400 Pressed Steel 1958.

| 6310 | (81448, 975325) | **CH** | RV | *RV* | OM |

## AX51                                                      GENERATOR VAN

Mark 1. Converted from NDA in 1992 to generator vans for use on Anglo-Scottish sleeping car services. Now normally used on trains hauled by steam locomotives. B4 bogies. ETH75.

**6311.** Lot No. 30162 Pressed Steel 1958. 37.25 t.
**6312.** Lot No. 30224 Cravens 1956. 37.25 t.
**6313.** Lot No. 30484 Pressed Steel 1958. 37.25 t.

| 6311 | (80903, 92911) | **B** | DB | | OM |
| 6312 | (81023, 92925) | **PC** | WC | *WC* | CS |
| 6313 | (81553, 92167) | **PC** | VS | *VS* | SL |

## AG2C (TSOT)        OPEN STANDARD (TROLLEY)

Mark 2C. Converted from TSO by removal of one seating bay and replacing this by a counter with a space for a trolley. Adjacent toilet removed and converted to steward's washing area/store. Pressure ventilated. –/55 1T. B4 bogies. ETH 4.

Lot No. 30795 Derby 1969–70. 32.5 t.

| 6528 | (5592) | **M** | WC | *WC* | CS |

## AN1F (RLO)                    SLEEPER RECEPTION CAR

Mark 2F. Converted from FO, these vehicles consist of pantry, microwave cooking facilities, seating area for passengers (with loose chairs, staff toilet plus two bars). Now refurbished again with new "sofa" seating as well as the loose chairs. Converted at RTC, Derby (6700), Ilford (6701–5) and Derby (6706–8). Air conditioned. 6700/1/3/5–8 have Stones equipment and 6702/4 have Temperature Ltd. equipment. The number of seats per coach can vary but typically is 25/– 1T (12 seats as "sofa" seating and 13 loose chairs). B4 bogies. d. ETH 5X.

**6700–2/4/8.** Lot No. 30859 Derby 1973–74. 33.5 t.
**6703/5–7.** Lot No. 30845 Derby 1973. 33.5 t.

| | | | | | |
|---|---|---|---|---|---|
| 6700 | (3347) | **FB** | H | *SR* | IS |
| 6701 | (3346) | **FS** | H | *SR* | IS |
| 6702 | (3421) | **FS** | H | *SR* | IS |
| 6703 | (3308) | **FS** | H | *SR* | IS |
| 6704 | (3341) | **FS** | H | *SR* | IS |
| 6705 | (3310, 6430) | **FS** | H | *SR* | IS |
| 6706 | (3283, 6421) | **FS** | H | *SR* | IS |
| 6707 | (3276, 6418) | **FS** | H | *SR* | IS |
| 6708 | (3370) | **FS** | H | *SR* | IS |

## AN1D (RFB)                                              BUFFET FIRST

Mark 2D. Converted from TSOT by the removal of another seating bay and fitting a proper buffet counter with boiler and microwave oven. Now converted to first class with new seating and end luggage stacks. Air conditioned. Stones equipment. 30/– 1T. B4 bogies. d. ETH 5.

Lot No. 30822 Derby 1971. 33 t.

| | | | | | |
|---|---|---|---|---|---|
| 6720 | (5622, 6652) | **M** | DB | *DB* | OM |
| 6721 | (5627, 6660) | **FP** | H | | KT |
| 6722 | (5736, 6661) | **FP** | H | | LM |
| 6723 | (5641, 6662) | **FP** | H | | EM |
| 6724 | (5721, 6665) | **FP** | H | | ZD |

## AH2Z (BSOT) OPEN BRAKE STANDARD (TROLLEY)

Mark 2. These vehicles use the same body shell as the Mark 2 BFK. Converted from BSO by removal of one seating bay and replacing this with a counter with a space for a trolley. Adjacent toilet removed and converted to a steward's washing area/store. –/23 0T. B4 bogies. ETH 4.

Lot No. 30757 Derby 1966. 31 t.

| | | | | | | |
|---|---|---|---|---|---|---|
| 9101 | (9398) | v | **CH** | H | *VT* | TM |
| 9104 | (9401) | v | **G** | WC | | CS |

## AE2Z (BSO)                                OPEN BRAKE STANDARD

Mark 2. These vehicles use the same body shell as the Mark 2 BFK and have First Class seat spacing and wider tables. Pressure ventilated. –/31 1T. B4 bogies. ETH 4.

Lot No. 30757 Derby 1966. 31.5 t.

| | | | | | | |
|---|---|---|---|---|---|---|
| 9391 | | **PC** | WT | *WT* | CS | PENDRAGON |
| 9392 | v | **G** | WC | *WC* | CS | |

## AE2A (BSO)                          OPEN BRAKE STANDARD

Mark 2A. These vehicles use the same body shell as the Mark 2A BFK and have
First Class seat spacing and wider tables. Pressure ventilated. –/31 1T. B4 bogies.
ETH 4. Modified for use as Escort Coaches.

**9419.** Lot No. 30777 Derby 1970. 31.5 t.
**9428.** Lot No. 30820 Derby 1970. 31.5 t.

| 9419 | **DR** DR *DR* | KM | | 9428 | **DR** DR *DR* | KM |

## AE2C (BSO)                          OPEN BRAKE STANDARD

Mark 2C. Pressure ventilated. –/31 1T. B4 bogies. ETH 4.

Lot No. 30798 Derby 1970. 32 t.

| 9440 d | **M** WC *WC* | CS | | 9448 d | **M** WC | CS |

## AE2D (BSO)                          OPEN BRAKE STANDARD

Mark 2D. Air conditioned (Stones). –/31 1T. B4 bogies. d. pg. ETH 5.

r Refurbished with new interior panelling.
s Refurbished with new seating –/22 1TD.
w Facelifted –/28 1W 1T.

Lot No. 30824 Derby 1971. 33 t.

| 9479 r | | DR | OY | | 9490 s | **FP** | H | KT |
| 9480 w | **FP** | H | KT | | 9492 w | **FP** | DM | YJ |
| 9481 s | **FP** | H | KT | | 9493 s | **BP** | H | EM |
| 9488 s | **FP** | H | LW | | 9494 s | **M** | DB *DB* | OM |
| 9489 r | **V** | H | KT | | | | | |

## AE2E (BSO)                          OPEN BRAKE STANDARD

Mark 2E. Air conditioned (Stones). –/32 1T. B4 bogies. d. pg. ETH 5.

Lot No. 30838 Derby 1972. 33 t.

**Non-standard livery:** 9502 Pullman umber.

r Refurbished with new interior panelling.
s Refurbished with modified design of seat headrest and new interior panelling.
w Facelifted –/28 1W 1T.

| 9496 r | | H | *VT* | TM | | 9501 w | **FP** | DM | | MQ |
| 9497 r★ | | H | | BH | | 9502 s | **0** | H | *VS* | SL |
| 9498 r | **V** | H | | KT | | 9503 s | **AV** | AW | | ZG |
| 9500 r | | H | | LM | | 9504 s | **V** | H | *RV* | OM |

| | | | | | | | | | |
|---|---|---|---|---|---|---|---|---|---|
| 9505 | s★ | H | | | LM | 9508 | s | **BG** | CG *CG* | BH |
| 9506 | s★ **WX** | H | | | BH | 9509 | s | **AV** | AW | ZG |
| 9507 | s **V** | H | *RV* | | OM | | | | | |

## AE2F (BSO)                  OPEN BRAKE STANDARD

Mark 2F. Air conditioned (Temperature Ltd.). All now refurbished with power-operated vestibule doors, new panels and seat trim. All now further refurbished with carpets. –/32 1T. B4 bogies. d. pg. ETH5X.

Lot No. 30861 Derby 1974. 34 t.

| 9513 | | **BP** | DR | | OY | 9526 | n★ | | H | *RV* | OM |
|---|---|---|---|---|---|---|---|---|---|---|---|
| 9516 | n | **V** | H | | KT | 9527 | n | **V** | RV | *RV* | OM |
| 9520 | n | **V** | RV | *RV* | OM | 9529 | n | **M** | DB | *SR* | OM |
| 9521 | ★ | **AB** | AW | *AW* | CF | 9531 | | **M** | DB | *SR* | OM |
| 9522 | | **V** | H | | KT | 9537 | n | **V** | H | *RV* | OM |
| 9523 | | **V** | H | | KT | 9538 | | **V** | H | | KT |
| 9524 | n★ | **AV** | AW | | ZG | 9539 | | **AV** | AW | | ZG |
| 9525 | | **WX** | H | | BH | | | | | | |

## AF2F (DBSO) DRIVING OPEN BRAKE STANDARD

Mark 2F. Air conditioned (Temperature Ltd.). Push & pull (t.d.m. system). Converted from BSO, these vehicles originally had half cabs at the brake end. They have since been refurbished and have had their cabs widened and the cab-end gangways removed. Five vehicles (9701–03/08/14) have been converted for use in Network Rail test trains and can be found in the Service Stock section of this book. –/30 1W 1T. B4 bogies. d. pg. Cowcatchers. ETH 5X.

**9704–9710**. Lot No. 30861 Derby 1974. Converted Glasgow 1979. Disc brakes. 34 t.
**9711/9713**. Lot No. 30861 Derby 1974. Converted Glasgow 1985. 34 t.

| 9704 | (9512) | **AR** | H | ZG | 9710 | (9518) | **1** | H | ZG |
|---|---|---|---|---|---|---|---|---|---|
| 9705 | (9519) | **AR** | H | ZG | 9711 | (9532) | **AR** | H | TS |
| 9707 | (9511) | **AR** | H | ZG | 9713 | (9535) | **AR** | H | CD |
| 9709 | (9515) | **AR** | H | ZG | | | | | |

## AE4E (BUO)          UNCLASSIFIED OPEN BRAKE

Mark 2E. Converted from TSO with new seating for use on Anglo-Scottish overnight services by Railcare, Wolverton. Air conditioned. Stones equipment. B4 bogies. d. –/31 2T. B4 bogies. ETH 4X.

**9801–9803**. Lot No. 30837 Derby 1972. 33.5 t.
**9804–9810**. Lot No. 30844 Derby 1972–73. 33.5 t.

| 9800 | (5751) | **FS** | H | *SR* | IS | 9803 | (5799) | **FS** | H | *SR* | IS |
|---|---|---|---|---|---|---|---|---|---|---|---|
| 9801 | (5760) | **FS** | H *SR* | | IS | 9804 | (5826) | **FS** | H | *SR* | IS |
| 9802 | (5772) | **FS** | H *SR* | | IS | 9805 | (5833) | **FS** | H | *SR* | IS |

| 9806 | (5840) | **FS** | H *SR* | IS | | 9809 | (5890) | **FS** | H *SR* | IS |
|------|--------|--------|--------|-----|--|------|--------|--------|--------|-----|
| 9807 | (5851) | **FB** | H *SR* | IS | | 9810 | (5892) | **FS** | H *SR* | IS |
| 9808 | (5871) | **FB** | H *SR* | IS | | | | | | |

## AJ1G (RFB)                    KITCHEN BUFFET FIRST

Mark 3A. Air conditioned. Converted from HST TRFKs, RFBs and FOs. Refurbished with table lamps and burgundy seat trim (except *). 18/– plus two seats for staff use (* 24/–, † 24/–, § 24/–). BT10 bogies. d. ETH 14X.

**10200–10211**. Lot No. 30884 Derby 1977. 39.8 t.
**10212–10229**. Lot No. 30878 Derby 1975–76. 39.8 t.
**10230–10260**. Lot No. 30890 Derby 1979. 39.8 t.

§ First Great Western Sleeper "day coaches" that have been fitted with former HST First Class seats to a 2+1 layout.

**Non-standard livery:** 10211 EWS dark maroon.

| 10200 | (40519) | * **1** | P | *EA* | NC | | 10231 | (10016) | **V** | P | | LM |
|-------|---------|---------|------|------|-----|--|-------|---------|--------|-------|-------|-----|
| 10202 | (40504) | † **BG** | CG *CG* | | CE | | 10232 | (10027) | § **FD** | P | *GW* | PZ |
| 10203 | (40506) | * **1** | P | *EA* | NC | | 10233 | (10013) | **V** | DB | | LM |
| 10206 | (40507) | **V** | P | | NC | | 10235 | (10015) | **BG** | DB *WS* | | CE |
| 10208 | (40517) | **V** | DB | | ZJ | | 10236 | (10018) | **V** | DB | | ZJ |
| 10211 | (40510) | **0** | DB *DB* | | TO | | 10237 | (10022) | **DR** | DR | | WB |
| 10212 | (11049) | **V** | P | | ZB | | 10240 | (10003) | **V** | P | | LM |
| 10213 | (11050) | **V** | CG | | HT | | 10241 | (10009) | * **1** | P | *EA* | NC |
| 10214 | (11034) | * **1** | P | *EA* | NC | | 10242 | (10002) | **BG** | CG *CG* | | CE |
| 10215 | (11032) | **BG** | DB *WS* | | CE | | 10245 | (10019) | **V** | NX | | ZB |
| 10216 | (11041) | * **1** | P | *EA* | NC | | 10246 | (10014) | **BG** | CG *WS* | | CE |
| 10217 | (11051) | **V** | P | | ZB | | 10247 | (10011) | * **NX** | P | *EA* | NC |
| 10219 | (11047) | § **FD** | P | *GW* | PZ | | 10249 | (10012) | **AB** | CG *AW* | | CF |
| 10223 | (11043) | * **1** | P | *EA* | NC | | 10250 | (10020) | **V** | DB | | LM |
| 10225 | (11014) | § **FD** | P | *GW* | PZ | | 10253 | (10026) | **V** | P | | LM |
| 10226 | (11015) | **V** | DB | | LM | | 10255 | (10010) | **V** | DB | | ZJ |
| 10228 | (11035) | * **1** | P | *EA* | NC | | 10257 | (10007) | **BG** | DB *WS* | | CE |
| 10229 | (11059) | * **1** | P | *EA* | NC | | 10259 | (10025) | **V** | P | | LM |
| 10230 | (10021) | **1** | DB | | ZJ | | | | | | | |

## AG2J (RSB)                 KITCHEN BUFFET STANDARD

Mark 4. Air conditioned. BT41 bogies. ETH 6X. Rebuilt from First to Standard Class with bar adjacent to seating area instead of adjacent to end of coach. –/30 1T.

Lot No. 31045 Metro-Cammell 1989–1992. 43.2 t.

| 10300 | **GN** | H *EC* | BN | | 10305 | **GN** | H *EC* | BN |
|-------|--------|--------|-----|--|-------|--------|--------|-----|
| 10301 | **GN** | H *EC* | BN | | 10306 | **GN** | H *EC* | BN |
| 10302 | **GN** | H *EC* | BN | | 10307 | **GN** | H *EC* | BN |
| 10303 | **GN** | H *EC* | BN | | 10308 | **GN** | H *EC* | BN |
| 10304 | **GN** | H *EC* | BN | | 10309 | **GN** | H *EC* | BN |

| 10310 | **GN** | H *EC* | BN | | 10323 | **GN** | H *EC* | BN |
|-------|--------|--------|-----|---|-------|--------|--------|-----|
| 10311 | **GN** | H *EC* | BN | | 10324 | **GN** | H *EC* | BN |
| 10312 | **GN** | H *EC* | BN | | 10325 | **GN** | H *EC* | BN |
| 10313 | **GN** | H *EC* | BN | | 10326 | **GN** | H *EC* | BN |
| 10315 | **GN** | H *EC* | BN | | 10328 | **GN** | H *EC* | BN |
| 10317 | **GN** | H *EC* | BN | | 10329 | **GN** | H *EC* | BN |
| 10318 | **GN** | H *EC* | BN | | 10330 | **GN** | H *EC* | BN |
| 10319 | **GN** | H *EC* | BN | | 10331 | **GN** | H *EC* | BN |
| 10320 | **GN** | H *EC* | BN | | 10332 | **GN** | H *EC* | BN |
| 10321 | **GN** | H *EC* | BN | | 10333 | **GN** | H *EC* | BN |

## AN2G (RMB)
## OPEN STANDARD WITH MINIATURE BUFFET

Mark 3A. Air conditioned. Converted from Mark 3 TSOs at Derby 2006. –/52 1T (including 6 Compin Pegasus seats for "priority" use).

Lot No. 30877 Derby 1975–77. 37.8 t.

| 10401 | (12168) | **NX** | P *EA* | NC | | 10404 | (12068) | **1** | P *EA* | NC |
|-------|---------|--------|--------|-----|---|-------|---------|-------|--------|-----|
| 10402 | (12010) | **1** | P *EA* | NC | | 10405 | (12157) | **1** | P *EA* | NC |
| 10403 | (12135) | **1** | P *EA* | NC | | 10406 | (12020) | **1** | P *EA* | NC |

## AU4G (SLEP)          SLEEPING CAR WITH PANTRY

Mark 3A. Air conditioned. Retention toilets. 12 compartments with a fixed lower berth and a hinged upper berth, plus an attendants compartment. 2T. BT10 bogies. ETH 7X.

**Non-standard livery:** 10546 EWS dark maroon.

Lot No. 30960 Derby 1981–83. 41 t.

| 10501 | d | **FS** | P | *SR* | IS | | 10531 | d | **FS** | P | *SR* | IS |
|-------|---|--------|---|------|-----|---|-------|---|--------|---|------|-----|
| 10502 | d | **FS** | P | *SR* | IS | | 10532 | d | **FD** | P | *GW* | PZ |
| 10504 | d | **FS** | P | *SR* | IS | | 10534 | d | **FD** | P | *GW* | PZ |
| 10506 | d | **FS** | P | *SR* | IS | | 10542 | d | **FS** | P | *SR* | IS |
| 10507 | d | **FS** | P | *SR* | IS | | 10543 | d | **FS** | P | *SR* | IS |
| 10508 | d | **FS** | P | *SR* | IS | | 10544 | d | **FS** | P | *SR* | IS |
| 10513 | d | **FS** | P | *SR* | IS | | 10546 | d | **0** | DB*DB* | | TO |
| 10516 | d | **FB** | P | *SR* | IS | | 10548 | d | **FS** | P | *SR* | IS |
| 10519 | d | **FS** | P | *SR* | IS | | 10551 | d | **FS** | P | *SR* | IS |
| 10520 | d | **FS** | P | *SR* | IS | | 10553 | d | **FS** | P | *SR* | IS |
| 10522 | d | **FS** | P | *SR* | IS | | 10561 | d | **FS** | P | *SR* | IS |
| 10523 | d | **FS** | P | *SR* | IS | | 10562 | d | **FB** | P | *SR* | IS |
| 10526 | d | **FS** | P | *SR* | IS | | 10563 | d | **FD** | P | *GW* | PZ |
| 10527 | d | **FS** | P | *SR* | IS | | 10565 | d | **FS** | P | *SR* | IS |
| 10529 | d | **FS** | P | *SR* | IS | | 10580 | d | **FS** | P | *SR* | IS |

| 10584 | d | **FD** | P | *GW* | PZ |
|-------|---|--------|---|------|-----|
| 10588 | d | **BG** | CG | *CG* | CE |
| 10589 | d | **FD** | P | *GW* | PZ |
| 10590 | d | **FD** | P | *GW* | PZ |
| 10594 | d | **FD** | P | *GW* | PZ |
| 10596 | d |  | P |  | LM |
| 10597 | d | **FS** | P | *SR* | IS |
| 10598 | d | **FS** | P | *SR* | IS |
| 10600 | d | **FS** | P | *SR* | IS |

| 10601 | d | **FD** | P | *GW* | PZ |
|-------|---|--------|---|------|-----|
| 10605 | d | **FS** | P | *SR* | IS |
| 10607 | d | **FS** | P | *SR* | IS |
| 10610 | d | **FS** | P | *SR* | IS |
| 10612 | d | **FD** | P | *GW* | PZ |
| 10613 | d | **FS** | P | *SR* | IS |
| 10614 | d | **FS** | P | *SR* | IS |
| 10616 | d | **FD** | P | *GW* | PZ |
| 10617 | d | **FS** | P | *SR* | IS |

# AS4G/AQ4G* (SLE/SLED*)          SLEEPING CAR

Mark 3A. Air conditioned. Retention toilets. 13 compartments with a fixed lower berth and a hinged upper berth (* 11 compartments with a fixed lower berth and a hinged upper berth + one compartment for a disabled person. 1TD). 2T. BT10 bogies. ETH 6X.

**Note:** 10734 was originally 2914 and used as a Royal Train staff sleeping car. It has 12 berths and a shower room and is ETH11X.

**10647–10729.** Lot No. 30961 Derby 1980–84. 43.5 t.
**10734.** Lot No. 31002 Derby/Wolverton 1985. 42.5 t.

| 10647 | d |  | DB |  | LM |
|-------|---|--------|-----|------|-----|
| 10648 | d* | **FS** | P | *SR* | IS |
| 10650 | d* | **FS** | P | *SR* | IS |
| 10666 | d* | **FS** | P | *SR* | IS |
| 10675 | d | **FS** | P | *SR* | IS |
| 10680 | d* | **FS** | P | *SR* | IS |
| 10683 | d | **FS** | P | *SR* | IS |
| 10688 | d | **FS** | P | *SR* | IS |
| 10689 | d* | **FG** | P | *SR* | IS |
| 10690 | d | **FS** | P | *SR* | IS |
| 10693 | d | **FS** | P | *SR* | IS |

| 10699 | d* | **FS** | P | *SR* | IS |
|-------|---|--------|-----|------|-----|
| 10701 | d |  | DB |  | LM |
| 10703 | d | **FS** | P | *SR* | IS |
| 10706 | d* | **FS** | P | *SR* | IS |
| 10714 | d* | **FS** | P | *SR* | IS |
| 10718 | d* | **FS** | P | *SR* | IS |
| 10719 | d* | **FS** | P | *SR* | IS |
| 10722 | d* | **FS** | P | *SR* | IS |
| 10723 | d* | **FS** | P | *SR* | IS |
| 10729 |  | **VN** | VS | *VS* | CP |
| 10734 |  | **VN** | VS | *VS* | CP |

**Names:**

| 10729 | CREWE | | 10734 | BALMORAL |
|-------|-------|---|-------|----------|

# AD1G (FO)                                    OPEN FIRST

Mark 3A. Air conditioned. All refurbished with table lamps and new seat cushions and trim. 48/– 2T (* 48/– 1T 1TD, † 47/– 2T 1W). BT10 bogies. d. ETH 6X.

11005–7 were open composites 11905–7 for a time.

**Non-standard livery:** 11039 EWS dark maroon.

Lot No. 30878 Derby 1975–76. 34.3 t.

| 11005 |  | **V** | DB |  | LM |
|-------|---|-------|-----|------|-----|
| 11006 |  | **V** | P |  | LM |
| 11007 |  | **V** | P |  | ZB |

| 11011 | * | **V** | P |  | LM |
|-------|---|-------|-----|------|-----|
| 11013 |  | **DR** | DR | *DR* | CP |
| 11018 |  | **V** | P |  | ZB |

| 11019 † | **DR** | DR | *DR* | CP |
|---------|--------|-----|------|-----|
| 11021 | **V** | P | | NC |
| 11026 | **V** | P | | LM |
| 11027 | **V** | DB | | CE |
| 11028 | **V** | DR | | OY |
| 11029 | **BG** | DB | | CP |
| 11030 † | **DR** | DR | *DR* | CP |
| 11031 † | **BG** | DB | *WS* | CE |
| 11033 | **DR** | DR | | WB |

| 11039 | **O** | DB | *DB* | TO |
|-------|-------|-----|------|-----|
| 11040 | **V** | DB | | ZG |
| 11042 | **V** | DB | | LM |
| 11044 † | **DR** | DR | *DR* | CP |
| 11046 † | **DR** | DR | *DR* | CP |
| 11048 | **V** | P | | ZB |
| 11052 | **V** | DB | | LM |
| 11054 † | **DR** | DR | *DR* | CP |
| 11058 | **V** | DB | | LM |

## AD1H (FO)                                           OPEN FIRST

Mark 3B. Air conditioned. Inter-City 80 seats. All refurbished with table lamps and new seat cushions and trim. 48/– 2T. BT10 bogies. d. ETH 6X.

† National Express East Anglia vehicles fitted with disabled toilet and reduced seating including three Compin "Pegasus" seats of the same type as used in Standard Class (but regarded as First Class!). 34/3 1T 1TD 2W.

Lot No. 30982 Derby 1985. 36.5 t.

| 11064 | **BG** | CG | *CG* | CE |
|-------|--------|-----|------|-----|
| 11065 | **BG** | CG | *CG* | CE |
| 11066 | **1** | P | *EA* | NC |
| 11067 | **1** | P | *EA* | NC |
| 11068 | **1** | P | *EA* | NC |
| 11069 | **1** | P | *EA* | NC |
| 11070 | **1** | P | *EA* | NC |
| 11071 | **BG** | CG | *WS* | CE |
| 11072 | **1** | P | *EA* | NC |
| 11073 | **1** | P | *EA* | NC |
| 11074 | **V** | P | | NC |
| 11075 | **1** | P | *EA* | NC |
| 11076 | **1** | P | *EA* | NC |
| 11077 | **1** | P | *EA* | NC |
| 11078 † | **1** | P | *EA* | NC |
| 11079 | **V** | CG | | CE |
| 11080 | **1** | P | *EA* | NC |
| 11081 | **1** | P | *EA* | NC |
| 11082 | **1** | P | *EA* | NC |

| 11083 | **BG** | CG | *WS* | CE |
|-------|--------|-----|------|-----|
| 11084 | **BG** | CG | *CG* | CE |
| 11085 † | **1** | P | *EA* | NC |
| 11086 | **BG** | CG | *CG* | CE |
| 11087 † | **NX** | P | *EA* | NC |
| 11088 † | **1** | P | *EA* | NC |
| 11089 | **BG** | CG | *CG* | CE |
| 11090 † | **1** | P | *EA* | NC |
| 11091 | **NX** | P | *EA* | NC |
| 11092 † | **1** | P | *EA* | NC |
| 11093 † | **1** | P | *EA* | NC |
| 11094 † | **1** | P | *EA* | NC |
| 11095 † | **1** | P | *EA* | NC |
| 11096 † | **1** | P | *EA* | NC |
| 11097 | **V** | DB | | LM |
| 11098 † | **1** | P | *EA* | NC |
| 11099 † | **1** | P | *EA* | NC |
| 11100 † | **1** | P | *EA* | NC |
| 11101 † | **1** | P | *EA* | NC |

## AD1J (FO)                                           OPEN FIRST

Mark 4. Air conditioned. Rebuilt with new interior by Bombardier Wakefield 2003–05 (some converted from Standard Class vehicles) 46/– 1T. BT41 bogies. ETH 6X.

**11201–11273**. Lot No. 31046 Metro-Cammell 1989–92. 41.3 t .
**11277–11299**. Lot No. 31049 Metro-Cammell 1989–92. 41.3 t .

| 11201 (11201) | **GN** H *EC* BN | | 11219 (11219) | **GN** H *EC* BN |
|---------------|------------------|---|---------------|------------------|

| | | | | | |
|---|---|---|---|---|---|
| 11229 (11229) | **GN** H *EC* BN | 11285 (12537) | **GN** H *EC* BN |
| 11237 (11237) | **GN** H *EC* BN | 11286 (12482) | **GN** H *EC* BN |
| 11241 (11241) | **GN** H *EC* BN | 11287 (12527) | **GN** H *EC* BN |
| 11244 (11244) | **GN** H *EC* BN | 11288 (12517) | **GN** H *EC* BN |
| 11273 (11273) | **GN** H *EC* BN | 11289 (12528) | **GN** H *EC* BN |
| 11277 (12408) | **GN** H *EC* BN | 11290 (12530) | **GN** H *EC* BN |
| 11278 (12479) | **GN** H *EC* BN | 11291 (12535) | **GN** H *EC* BN |
| 11279 (12521) | **GN** H *EC* BN | 11292 (12451) | **GN** H *EC* BN |
| 11280 (12523) | **GN** H *EC* BN | 11293 (12536) | **GN** H *EC* BN |
| 11281 (12418) | **GN** H *EC* BN | 11294 (12529) | **GN** H *EC* BN |
| 11282 (12524) | **GN** H *EC* BN | 11295 (12475) | **GN** H *EC* BN |
| 11283 (12435) | **GN** H *EC* BN | 11298 (12416) | **GN** H *EC* BN |
| 11284 (12487) | **GN** H *EC* BN | 11299 (12532) | **GN** H *EC* BN |

## AD1J (FOD)                    OPEN FIRST (DISABLED)

Mark 4. Air conditioned. Rebuilt from FO by Bombardier Wakefield 2003–05. 42/– 1W 1TD. BT41 bogies. ETH 6X.

Lot No. 31046 Metro-Cammell 1989–92. 40.7 t.

| | | | | | |
|---|---|---|---|---|---|
| 11301 (11215) | **GN** H *EC* BN | 11316 (11227) | **GN** H *EC* BN |
| 11302 (11203) | **GN** H *EC* BN | 11317 (11223) | **GN** H *EC* BN |
| 11303 (11211) | **GN** H *EC* BN | 11318 (11251) | **GN** H *EC* BN |
| 11304 (11257) | **GN** H *EC* BN | 11319 (11247) | **GN** H *EC* BN |
| 11305 (11261) | **GN** H *EC* BN | 11320 (11255) | **GN** H *EC* BN |
| 11306 (11276) | **GN** H *EC* BN | 11321 (11245) | **GN** H *EC* BN |
| 11307 (11217) | **GN** H *EC* BN | 11322 (11228) | **GN** H *EC* BN |
| 11308 (11263) | **GN** H *EC* BN | 11323 (11235) | **GN** H *EC* BN |
| 11309 (11259) | **GN** H *EC* BN | 11324 (11253) | **GN** H *EC* BN |
| 11310 (11272) | **GN** H *EC* BN | 11325 (11231) | **GN** H *EC* BN |
| 11311 (11221) | **GN** H *EC* BN | 11326 (11206) | **GN** H *EC* BN |
| 11312 (11225) | **GN** H *EC* BN | 11327 (11236) | **GN** H *EC* BN |
| 11313 (11210) | **GN** H *EC* BN | 11328 (11274) | **GN** H *EC* BN |
| 11314 (11207) | **GN** H *EC* BN | 11329 (11243) | **GN** H *EC* BN |
| 11315 (11238) | **GN** H *EC* BN | 11330 (11249) | **GN** H *EC* BN |

## AD1J (FO)                                    OPEN FIRST

Mark 4. Air conditioned. Rebuilt from FO by Bombardier Wakefield 2003–05. Separate area for 7 smokers, although smoking is no longer allowed. 46/– 1W 1TD. BT41 bogies. ETH 6X.

Lot No. 31046 Metro-Cammell 1989–92. 42.1 t.

| | | | | | |
|---|---|---|---|---|---|
| 11401 (11214) | **GN** H *EC* BN | 11407 (11256) | **GN** H *EC* BN |
| 11402 (11216) | **GN** H *EC* BN | 11408 (11218) | **GN** H *EC* BN |
| 11403 (11258) | **GN** H *EC* BN | 11409 (11262) | **GN** H *EC* BN |
| 11404 (11202) | **GN** H *EC* BN | 11410 (11260) | **GN** H *EC* BN |
| 11405 (11204) | **GN** H *EC* BN | 11411 (11240) | **GN** H *EC* BN |
| 11406 (11205) | **GN** H *EC* BN | 11412 (11209) | **GN** H *EC* BN |

| | | | | | | | | |
|---|---|---|---|---|---|---|---|---|
| 11413 (11212) | **GN** H *EC* | BN | | 11422 (11232) | **GN** H *EC* | BN |
| 11414 (11246) | **GN** H *EC* | BN | | 11423 (11230) | **GN** H *EC* | BN |
| 11415 (11208) | **GN** H *EC* | BN | | 11424 (11239) | **GN** H *EC* | BN |
| 11416 (11254) | **GN** H *EC* | BN | | 11425 (11234) | **GN** H *EC* | BN |
| 11417 (11226) | **GN** H *EC* | BN | | 11426 (11252) | **GN** H *EC* | BN |
| 11418 (11222) | **GN** H *EC* | BN | | 11427 (11200) | **GN** H *EC* | BN |
| 11419 (11250) | **GN** H *EC* | BN | | 11428 (11233) | **GN** H *EC* | BN |
| 11420 (11242) | **GN** H *EC* | BN | | 11429 (11275) | **GN** H *EC* | BN |
| 11421 (11220) | **GN** H *EC* | BN | | 11430 (11248) | **GN** H *EC* | BN |

## AD1J (FO)                                     OPEN FIRST

Mark 4. Air conditioned. Converted from TFRB with new interior by Bombardier Wakefield 2005. 46/– 1T. BT41 bogies. ETH 6X.

Lot No. 31046 Metro-Cammell 1989–92. 41.3 t.

| | | | | | | |
|---|---|---|---|---|---|---|
| 11998 (10314) | **GN** H *EC* | BN | | 11999 (10316) | **GN** H *EC* | BN |

## AC2G (TSO)                               OPEN STANDARD

Mark 3A. Air conditioned. All refurbished with modified seat backs and new layout and further refurbished with new seat trim. –/76 2T (s –/70 2T 2W, t –/72 2T, z –/70 1TD 1T 2W, § –/45(2) 2T 1W). BT10 bogies. d. ETH 6X.

h National Express East Anglia modified coaches with eight Compin Pegasus seats at saloon ends for "priority" use and a high density layout with more unidirectional seating. –/80 2T.

§ First Great Western Sleeper "day coaches" that have been fitted with former HST First Class seats to a 2+1 layout and are effectively unclassified.

**Note:** 12169–171 were converted from open composites 11908–10, formerly FOs 11008–10.

**12005–12167.** Lot No. 30877 Derby 1975–77. 34.3 t.
**12169–12171.** Lot No. 30878 Derby 1975–76. 34.3 t.

| | | | | | | | | | | | |
|---|---|---|---|---|---|---|---|---|---|---|---|
| 12005 h | **1** | P | *EA* | NC | | 12026 h | **1** | P | *EA* | NC |
| 12008 | **V** | P | | LM | | 12027 h | **1** | P | *EA* | NC |
| 12009 h | **1** | P | *EA* | NC | | 12029 | **V** | P | | LM |
| 12011 | **V** | P | | ZB | | 12030 h | **1** | P | *EA* | NC |
| 12012 h | **1** | P | *EA* | NC | | 12031 | **1** | P | *EA* | NC |
| 12013 h | **1** | P | *EA* | NC | | 12032 h | **1** | P | *EA* | NC |
| 12014 t | **BG** | CG | *WS* | CE | | 12034 | **1** | P | *EA* | NC |
| 12015 h | **1** | P | *EA* | NC | | 12035 h | **NX** | P | *EA* | NC |
| 12016 | **1** | P | *EA* | NC | | 12036 s | **V** | P | | LM |
| 12017 | **V** | DB | | ZG | | 12037 h | **1** | P | *EA* | NC |
| 12019 h | **1** | P | *EA* | NC | | 12038 t | **BG** | CG | *WS* | CE |
| 12021 | **NX** | P | *EA* | NC | | 12040 h | **1** | P | *EA* | NC |
| 12022 | **V** | P | | LM | | 12041 h | **1** | P | *EA* | NC |
| 12024 h | **1** | P | *EA* | NC | | 12042 h | **1** | P | *EA* | NC |

| | | | | |
|---|---|---|---|---|
| 12043 t | **BG** CG *WS* | CE |
| 12045 | **V** P | LM |
| 12046 h | **1** P *EA* | NC |
| 12047 z | **V** P | LM |
| 12048 | **V** DB | ZJ |
| 12049 | **1** P *EA* | NC |
| 12051 h | **NX** P *EA* | NC |
| 12053 t | **BG** CG *WS* | CE |
| 12054 s | **V** DB | BH |
| 12056 h | **1** P *EA* | NC |
| 12057 h | **1** P *EA* | NC |
| 12058 | **V** ST | LM |
| 12059 s | **V** DB | ZG |
| 12060 h | **1** P *EA* | NC |
| 12061 h | **1** P *EA* | NC |
| 12062 h | **1** P *EA* | NC |
| 12063 | **V** P | BN |
| 12064 | **1** P *EA* | NC |
| 12065 | **V** P | BN |
| 12066 h | **1** P *EA* | NC |
| 12067 | **1** P *EA* | NC |
| 12069 | **V** DB | ZJ |
| 12072 | **V** DB | ZJ |
| 12073 h | **1** P *EA* | NC |
| 12078 | **V** P | ZB |
| 12079 | **1** P *EA* | NC |
| 12081 | **1** P *EA* | NC |
| 12082 h | **1** P *EA* | NC |
| 12083 | **V** P | LM |
| 12084 h | **1** P *EA* | NC |
| 12087 s | **V** P | LM |
| 12089 | **1** P *EA* | NC |
| 12090 h | **1** P *EA* | NC |
| 12091 h | **1** P *EA* | NC |
| 12092 | **V** P | BN |
| 12093 h | **1** P *EA* | NC |
| 12094 | **V** DB | ZG |
| 12095 | **V** P | LM |
| 12097 h | **1** P *EA* | NC |
| 12098 | **1** P *EA* | NC |
| 12099 h | **1** P *EA* | NC |
| 12100 § | **FD** P *GW* | PZ |
| 12101 s | **V** P | LM |
| 12103 | **1** P *EA* | NC |
| 12104 | **V** ST | LM |
| 12105 h | **1** P *EA* | NC |
| 12107 h | **1** P *EA* | NC |
| 12108 | **1** P *EA* | NC |
| 12109 h | **1** P *EA* | NC |

| | | | | |
|---|---|---|---|---|
| 12110 h | **1** P *EA* | NC |
| 12111 | **1** P *EA* | NC |
| 12114 h | **1** P *EA* | NC |
| 12115 h | **1** P *EA* | NC |
| 12116 h | **1** P *EA* | NC |
| 12117 | **V** DB | ZJ |
| 12118 | **1** P *EA* | NC |
| 12119 t | **BG** CG *WS* | CE |
| 12120 h | **1** P *EA* | NC |
| 12122 z | **V** P | ZB |
| 12124 | **V** DB | BH |
| 12125 | **1** P *EA* | NC |
| 12126 h | **1** P *EA* | NC |
| 12127 | **V** DB | ZJ |
| 12129 h | **NX** P *EA* | NC |
| 12130 h | **1** P *EA* | NC |
| 12131 | **V** DB | ZJ |
| 12132 | **NX** P | NC |
| 12133 | **V** P | ZB |
| 12134 | **V** P | LM |
| 12137 h | **1** P *EA* | NC |
| 12138 | **V** P | ZB |
| 12139 | **V** P | BN |
| 12141 | **1** P *EA* | NC |
| 12142 z | **V** P | LM |
| 12143 | **1** P *EA* | NC |
| 12144 s | **V** P | LM |
| 12145 | **V** DB | ZJ |
| 12146 | **1** P *EA* | NC |
| 12147 | **1** P *EA* | NC |
| 12148 | **1** P *EA* | NC |
| 12150 h | **1** P *EA* | NC |
| 12151 | **1** P *EA* | NC |
| 12153 | **1** P *EA* | NC |
| 12154 h | **1** P *EA* | NC |
| 12156 | **V** P | LM |
| 12158 | **V** P | LM |
| 12159 | **1** P *EA* | NC |
| 12160 s | **V** P | LM |
| 12161 § | **FD** P *GW* | PZ |
| 12163 | **V** P | LM |
| 12164 | **1** P *EA* | NC |
| 12165 | **V** ST | LM |
| 12166 | **1** P *EA* | NC |
| 12167 h | **1** P *EA* | NC |
| 12169 | **V** DB | ZJ |
| 12170 | **1** P *EA* | NC |
| 12171 | **1** P *EA* | NC |

## AI2J (TSOE)                    OPEN STANDARD (END)

Mark 4. Air conditioned. Rebuilt with new interior by Bombardier Wakefield 2003–05. Separate area for 26 smokers, although smoking is no longer allowed. –/76 1T. BT41 bogies. ETH 6X.

**Note:** 12232 was converted from the original 12405.

**12200–12231.** Lot No. 31047 Metro-Cammell 1989–91. 39.5 t.
**12232.** Lot No. 31049 Metro-Cammell 1989–92. 39.5 t.

| | | | | | | | | |
|---|---|---|---|---|---|---|---|---|
| 12200 | **GN** | H *EC* | BN | | 12217 | **GN** | H *EC* | BN |
| 12201 | **GN** | H *EC* | BN | | 12218 | **GN** | H *EC* | BN |
| 12202 | **GN** | H *EC* | BN | | 12219 | **GN** | H *EC* | BN |
| 12203 | **GN** | H *EC* | BN | | 12220 | **GN** | H *EC* | BN |
| 12204 | **GN** | H *EC* | BN | | 12222 | **GN** | H *EC* | BN |
| 12205 | **GN** | H *EC* | BN | | 12223 | **GN** | H *EC* | BN |
| 12207 | **GN** | H *EC* | BN | | 12224 | **GN** | H *EC* | BN |
| 12208 | **GN** | H *EC* | BN | | 12225 | **GN** | H *EC* | BN |
| 12209 | **GN** | H *EC* | BN | | 12226 | **GN** | H *EC* | BN |
| 12210 | **GN** | H *EC* | BN | | 12227 | **GN** | H *EC* | BN |
| 12211 | **GN** | H *EC* | BN | | 12228 | **GN** | H *EC* | BN |
| 12212 | **GN** | H *EC* | BN | | 12229 | **GN** | H *EC* | BN |
| 12213 | **GN** | H *EC* | BN | | 12230 | **GN** | H *EC* | BN |
| 12214 | **GN** | H *EC* | BN | | 12231 | **GN** | H *EC* | BN |
| 12215 | **GN** | H *EC* | BN | | 12232 | **GN** | H *EC* | BN |
| 12216 | **GN** | H *EC* | BN | | | | | |

## AL2J (TSOD) OPEN STANDARD (DISABLED ACCESS)

Mark 4. Air conditioned. Rebuilt with new interior by Bombardier Wakefield 2003–05. –/68 2W 1TD. BT41 bogies. ETH 6X.

**Note:** 12331 has been converted from TSO 12531.

**12300–12330.** Lot No. 31048 Metro-Cammell 1989–91. 39.4 t.
**12331.** Lot No. 31049 Metro-Cammell 1989–92. 39.4 t.

| | | | | | | | | |
|---|---|---|---|---|---|---|---|---|
| 12300 | **GN** | H *EC* | BN | | 12310 | **GN** | H *EC* | BN |
| 12301 | **GN** | H *EC* | BN | | 12311 | **GN** | H *EC* | BN |
| 12302 | **GN** | H *EC* | BN | | 12312 | **GN** | H *EC* | BN |
| 12303 | **GN** | H *EC* | BN | | 12313 | **GN** | H *EC* | BN |
| 12304 | **GN** | H *EC* | BN | | 12315 | **GN** | H *EC* | BN |
| 12305 | **GN** | H *EC* | BN | | 12316 | **GN** | H *EC* | BN |
| 12307 | **GN** | H *EC* | BN | | 12317 | **GN** | H *EC* | BN |
| 12308 | **GN** | H *EC* | BN | | 12318 | **GN** | H *EC* | BN |
| 12309 | **GN** | H *EC* | BN | | 12319 | **GN** | H *EC* | BN |

| | | | | | | | | |
|---|---|---|---|---|---|---|---|---|
| 12320 | **GN** | H *EC* | BN | | 12326 | **GN** | H *EC* | BN |
| 12321 | **GN** | H *EC* | BN | | 12327 | **GN** | H *EC* | BN |
| 12322 | **GN** | H *EC* | BN | | 12328 | **GN** | H *EC* | BN |
| 12323 | **GN** | H *EC* | BN | | 12329 | **GN** | H *EC* | BN |
| 12324 | **GN** | H *EC* | BN | | 12330 | **GN** | H *EC* | BN |
| 12325 | **GN** | H *EC* | BN | | 12331 | **GN** | H *EC* | BN |

# AC2J (TSO)                                    OPEN STANDARD

Mark 4. Air conditioned. Rebuilt with new interior by Bombardier Wakefield 2003–05. –/76 1T. BT41 bogies. ETH 6X.

Lot No. 31049 Metro-Cammell 1989–92. 40.8 t.

**Note:** 12405 is the second coach to carry that number. It was built from the bodyshell originally intended for 12221. The original 12405 is now 12232.

| | | | | | | | | |
|---|---|---|---|---|---|---|---|---|
| 12400 | **GN** | H *EC* | BN | | 12440 | **GN** | H *EC* | BN |
| 12401 | **GN** | H *EC* | BN | | 12441 | **GN** | H *EC* | BN |
| 12402 | **GN** | H *EC* | BN | | 12442 | **GN** | H *EC* | BN |
| 12403 | **GN** | H *EC* | BN | | 12443 | **GN** | H *EC* | BN |
| 12404 | **GN** | H *EC* | BN | | 12444 | **GN** | H *EC* | BN |
| 12405 | **GN** | H *EC* | BN | | 12445 | **GN** | H *EC* | BN |
| 12406 | **GN** | H *EC* | BN | | 12446 | **GN** | H *EC* | BN |
| 12407 | **GN** | H *EC* | BN | | 12447 | **GN** | H *EC* | BN |
| 12409 | **GN** | H *EC* | BN | | 12448 | **GN** | H *EC* | BN |
| 12410 | **GN** | H *EC* | BN | | 12449 | **GN** | H *EC* | BN |
| 12411 | **GN** | H *EC* | BN | | 12450 | **GN** | H *EC* | BN |
| 12414 | **GN** | H *EC* | BN | | 12452 | **GN** | H *EC* | BN |
| 12415 | **GN** | H *EC* | BN | | 12453 | **GN** | H *EC* | BN |
| 12417 | **GN** | H *EC* | BN | | 12454 | **GN** | H *EC* | BN |
| 12419 | **GN** | H *EC* | BN | | 12455 | **GN** | H *EC* | BN |
| 12420 | **GN** | H *EC* | BN | | 12456 | **GN** | H *EC* | BN |
| 12421 | **GN** | H *EC* | BN | | 12457 | **GN** | H *EC* | BN |
| 12422 | **GN** | H *EC* | BN | | 12458 | **GN** | H *EC* | BN |
| 12423 | **GN** | H *EC* | BN | | 12459 | **GN** | H *EC* | BN |
| 12424 | **GN** | H *EC* | BN | | 12460 | **GN** | H *EC* | BN |
| 12425 | **GN** | H *EC* | BN | | 12461 | **GN** | H *EC* | BN |
| 12426 | **GN** | H *EC* | BN | | 12462 | **GN** | H *EC* | BN |
| 12427 | **GN** | H *EC* | BN | | 12463 | **GN** | H *EC* | BN |
| 12428 | **GN** | H *EC* | BN | | 12464 | **GN** | H *EC* | BN |
| 12429 | **GN** | H *EC* | BN | | 12465 | **GN** | H *EC* | BN |
| 12430 | **GN** | H *EC* | BN | | 12466 | **GN** | H *EC* | BN |
| 12431 | **GN** | H *EC* | BN | | 12467 | **GN** | H *EC* | BN |
| 12432 | **GN** | H *EC* | BN | | 12468 | **GN** | H *EC* | BN |
| 12433 | **GN** | H *EC* | BN | | 12469 | **GN** | H *EC* | BN |
| 12434 | **GN** | H *EC* | BN | | 12470 | **GN** | H *EC* | BN |
| 12436 | **GN** | H *EC* | BN | | 12471 | **GN** | H *EC* | BN |
| 12437 | **GN** | H *EC* | BN | | 12472 | **GN** | H *EC* | BN |
| 12438 | **GN** | H *EC* | BN | | 12473 | **GN** | H *EC* | BN |
| 12439 | **GN** | H *EC* | BN | | 12474 | **GN** | H *EC* | BN |

| 12476 | **GN** | H *EC* | BN | | 12513 | **GN** | H *EC* | BN |
| 12477 | **GN** | H *EC* | BN | | 12514 | **GN** | H *EC* | BN |
| 12478 | **GN** | H *EC* | BN | | 12515 | **GN** | H *EC* | BN |
| 12480 | **GN** | H *EC* | BN | | 12518 | **GN** | H *EC* | BN |
| 12481 | **GN** | H *EC* | BN | | 12519 | **GN** | H *EC* | BN |
| 12483 | **GN** | H *EC* | BN | | 12520 | **GN** | H *EC* | BN |
| 12484 | **GN** | H *EC* | BN | | 12522 | **GN** | H *EC* | BN |
| 12485 | **GN** | H *EC* | BN | | 12526 | **GN** | H *EC* | BN |
| 12486 | **GN** | H *EC* | BN | | 12533 | **GN** | H *EC* | BN |
| 12488 | **GN** | H *EC* | BN | | 12534 | **GN** | H *EC* | BN |
| 12489 | **GN** | H *EC* | BN | | 12538 | **GN** | H *EC* | BN |

## AA11 (FK)                                    CORRIDOR FIRST

Mark 1. 42/– 2T. ETH 3.

Lot No. 30381 Swindon 1959. B4 bogies. 33 t.

| 13229 | xk | **M** | BK *BK* | BT | | 13230 | xk | **M** | BK *BK* | BT |

Lot No. 30667 Swindon 1961. Commonwealth bogies. This coach was converted in 2008 to a kitchen car with staff accommodation. 37 t.

| 13321 | x | **M** | WC *WC* | CS | |

## AA1A (FK)                                    CORRIDOR FIRST

Mark 2A. Pressure ventilated. 42/– 2T. B4 bogies. ETH 4.

Lot No. 30774 Derby 1968. 33 t.

| 13440 | v | **G** | WC *WC* | CS | |

## AB11 (BFK)                          CORRIDOR BRAKE FIRST

Mark 1. 24/– 1T. Commonwealth bogies. ETH 2.

Lot No. 30668 Swindon 1961. 36 t.

Originally numbered in 14xxx series and then renumbered in 17xxx series.

| 17015 | x | **CC** | RV *RV* | OM | | 17018 | v | **CH** | VT *VT* | TM |

## AB1A (BFK)                          CORRIDOR BRAKE FIRST

Mark 2A. Pressure ventilated. 24/– 1T. B4 bogies. ETH 4.

**17056–17077.** Lot No. 30775 Derby 1967–8. 32 t.
**17090–17102.** Lot No. 30786 Derby 1968. 32 t.

Originally numbered 14056–102. 17090 was numbered 35503 for a time when declassified.

| 17056 | | **M** | RV | OM | | 17090 | v | **CH** | H | TM |
| 17077 | | **RV** | RV *RV* | OM | | 17102 | | **M** | WC *WC* | CS |

## AX5B                    COUCHETTE/GENERATOR COACH

Mark 2B. Formerly part of Royal Train. Converted from a BFK built 1969. Consists of luggage accommodation, guard's compartment, 350 kW diesel generator and staff sleeping accommodation. Pressure ventilated. B5 bogies. ETH 5X.

**Non-standard livery**: 17105 Oxford blue.

Lot No. 30888 Wolverton 1977. 46 t.

| 17105 | (14105, 2905) | **0** | RV | *RV* | OM |
|-------|---------------|-------|----|----|----|

## AB1D (BFK)                    CORRIDOR BRAKE FIRST

Mark 2D. Air conditioned (Stones equipment). 24/– 1T. B4 Bogies. ETH 5.

Lot No. 30823 Derby 1971–72. 33.5 t.

Originally numbered 14159–68.

| 17159 | **DR** DR | | WB | | 17168 | d **M** | WC | | CS |
|-------|-----------|--|----|--|-------|---------|----|--|----|
| 17167 | **VN** VS | *VS* | CP | | | | | | |

## AE1H (BUO)              UNCLASSIFIED OPEN BRAKE

Mark 3B. Air conditioned. Fitted with hydraulic handbrake. Used by First Great Western as Sleeper "day coaches" that have been fitted with former HST First Class seats to a 2+1 layout and are effectively unclassified. 36/– 1T. BT10 bogies. pg. d. ETH 5X.

Lot No. 30990 Derby 1986. 35.81 t.

| 17173 | **FD** P | *GW* | PZ | | 17175 | **FD** P | *GW* | PZ |
|-------|----------|------|----|--|-------|----------|------|----|
| 17174 | **FD** P | *GW* | PZ | | | | | |

## AA21 (SK)                      CORRIDOR STANDARD

Mark 1. Each vehicle has eight compartments. All remaining vehicles have metal window frames and melamine interior panelling. Commonwealth bogies. –/48 2T. ETH 4.

Lot No. 30685 Derby 1961–62. 36 t.

t Rebuilt internally as TSO using components from 4936. –/64 2T.

Originally numbered 25756–25862.

| 18756 | x **M** | WC | *WC* | CS | | 18808 | x | **M** WC | *WC* | CS |
|-------|---------|----|------|----|--|-------|---|----------|------|----|
| 18767 | x **M** | WC | *WC* | CS | | 18862 | x | **M** WC | *WC* | CS |
| 18806 | xt **M** | WC | *WC* | CS | | | | | | |

## AB31 (BCK)       CORRIDOR BRAKE COMPOSITE

Mark 1. There are two variants depending upon whether the Standard Class compartments have armrests. Each vehicle has two First Class and three Standard Class compartments. 12/18 2T (* 12/24 2T). Commonwealth bogies. ETH 2.

**Non-standard livery:** 21269 British racing green & cream lined out in gold.

**21241–21246.** Lot No. 30669 Swindon 1961–62. Commonwealth bogies. 36 t.
**21256.** Lot No. 30731 Derby 1963. Commonwealth bogies. 37 t.
**21266–21272.** Lot No. 30732 Derby 1964. Commonwealth bogies. 37 t.

| | | | | | | | | | | | |
|---|---|---|---|---|---|---|---|---|---|---|---|
| 21241 | x | **M** | BK | *BK* | BT | | 21266 | x* | **M** | WC | *WC* | CS |
| 21245 | x | **M** | RV | *RV* | OM | | 21269 | * | **0** | RV | *RV* | OM |
| 21246 | | **BG** | DB | | OM | | 21272 | x* | **CH** | RV | *RV* | OM |
| 21256 | x | **M** | WC | *WC* | CS | | | | | | |

## AB21 (BSK)       CORRIDOR BRAKE STANDARD

Mark 1. Four compartments. Lot 30721 has metal window frames and melamine interior panelling. –/24 1T. ETH2.

g Fitted with an e.t.s. generator. Weight unknown.

**35185.** Lot No. 30427 Wolverton 1959. B4 bogies. 33 t.
**35459/35469.** Lot No. 30721 Wolverton 1963. Commonwealth bogies. 37 t.

| | | | | | | | | | | | |
|---|---|---|---|---|---|---|---|---|---|---|---|
| 35185 | x | **M** | BK | *BK* | BT | | 35469 | xg | **CC** | RV | *RV* | OM |
| 35459 | x | **M** | WC | *WC* | CS | | | | | | |

## AB5C                       BRAKE/POWER KITCHEN

Mark 2C. Pressure ventilated. Converted from BFK (declassified to BSK) built 1970. Converted at West Coast Railway Company 2000–01. Consists of 60 kVA generator, guard's compartment and electric kitchen. B5 bogies. ETH 4.

**Non-standard livery:** British Racing Green with gold lining.

Lot No. 30796 Derby 1969–70. 32.5 t.

| | | | | | |
|---|---|---|---|---|---|
| 35511 | (14130, 17130) | **0** | RA | | CP |

## AK51 (RK)                       KITCHEN CAR

Mark 1. Converted 1989/2006 from RBR. Buffet and seating area replaced with additional kitchen and food preparation area. Fluorescent lighting. Commonwealth bogies. ETH 2X.

Lot No. 30628 Pressed Steel 1960–61. 39 t.

| | | | | | | |
|---|---|---|---|---|---|---|
| 80041 | (1690) | x | **M** | RV | *RV* | OM |
| 80042 | (1646) | | **DR** | DR | | WB |

# NZ (DLV)     DRIVING BRAKE VAN (110 m.p.h.)

Mark 3B. Air conditioned. T4 bogies. dg. ETH 5X.

Lot No. 31042 Derby 1988. 45.18 t.

**Non-standard livery:** 82146 EWS silver.

| | | | | | | | | | |
|---|---|---|---|---|---|---|---|---|---|
| 82101 | V | P | | CE | 82127 | 1 | P | *EA* | NC |
| 82102 | 1 | P | *EA* | NC | 82128 | V | P | | LM |
| 82103 | 1 | P | *EA* | NC | 82129 | V | P | | LM |
| 82104 | V | P | | NC | 82131 | V | DB | | LM |
| 82105 | 1 | P | *EA* | NC | 82132 | 1 | P | *EA* | NC |
| 82106 | V | P | | ZB | 82133 | 1 | P | *EA* | NC |
| 82107 | NX | P | *EA* | NC | 82136 | 1 | P | *EA* | NC |
| 82108 | V | DB | | LM | 82137 | V | DB | | LM |
| 82109 | V | P | | ZB | 82138 | V | DB | | CE |
| 82110 | V | P | | LM | 82139 | 1 | P | *EA* | NC |
| 82111 | V | P | | LM | 82140 | V | P | | LM |
| 82112 | 1 | P | *EA* | NC | 82141 | V | P | | LM |
| 82113 | V | DB | | CE | 82142 | V | P | | LM |
| 82114 | 1 | P | *EA* | NC | 82143 | 1 | P | *EA* | NC |
| 82115 | B | P | | ZN | 82144 | V | DB | | LM |
| 82116 | V | DB | | LM | 82145 | V | P | | CE |
| 82118 | 1 | P | *EA* | NC | 82146 | 0 | DB | *DB* | TO |
| 82120 | V | DB | | CE | 82147 | V | P | | LM |
| 82121 | 1 | P | *EA* | NC | 82148 | V | DB | | CE |
| 82122 | V | DB | | LM | 82149 | V | P | | LM |
| 82123 | V | DB | | LM | 82150 | V | DB | | CE |
| 82124 | V | P | | LM | 82151 | V | DB | | CE |
| 82125 | V | P | | LM | 82152 | 1 | P | *EA* | NC |
| 82126 | V | P | | ZB | | | | | |

**Name:** 82126 Wembley Traincare Centre

# NZ (DLV)     DRIVING BRAKE VAN (140 m.p.h.)

Mark 4. Air conditioned. Swiss-built (SIG) bogies. dg. ETH 6X.

Fitted with transceiver "domes" for wi-fi.

Lot No. 31043 Metro-Cammell 1988. 45.18 t.

| | | | | | | | | | |
|---|---|---|---|---|---|---|---|---|---|
| 82200 | GN | H | *EC* | BN | 82207 | GN | H | *EC* | BN |
| 82201 | GN | H | *EC* | BN | 82208 | GN | H | *EC* | BN |
| 82202 | GN | H | *EC* | BN | 82209 | GN | H | *EC* | BN |
| 82203 | GN | H | *EC* | BN | 82210 | GN | H | *EC* | BN |
| 82204 | GN | H | *EC* | BN | 82211 | GN | H | *EC* | BN |
| 82205 | GN | H | *EC* | BN | 82212 | GN | H | *EC* | BN |
| 82206 | GN | H | *EC* | BN | 82213 | GN | H | *EC* | BN |

| 82214 | **GN** | H | *EC* | BN |  | 82224 | **GN** | H | *EC* | BN |
|--------|--------|---|------|----|--|-------|--------|---|------|----|
| 82215 | **GN** | H | *EC* | BN |  | 82225 | **GN** | H | *EC* | BN |
| 82216 | **GN** | H | *EC* | BN |  | 82226 | **GN** | H | *EC* | BN |
| 82217 | **GN** | H | *EC* | BN |  | 82227 | **GN** | H | *EC* | BN |
| 82218 | **GN** | H | *EC* | BN |  | 82228 | **GN** | H | *EC* | BN |
| 82219 | **GN** | H | *EC* | BN |  | 82229 | **GN** | H | *EC* | BN |
| 82220 | **GN** | H | *EC* | BN |  | 82230 | **GN** | H | *EC* | BN |
| 82222 | **GN** | H | *EC* | BN |  | 82231 | **GN** | H | *EC* | BN |
| 82223 | **GN** | H | *EC* | BN |  |       |        |   |      |    |

**Name:** 82219 Duke of Edinburgh

# NZ (DLV)    DRIVING BRAKE VAN (110 m.p.h.)

Mark 3B. Air conditioned. T4 bogies. dg. ETH 5X.

Lot No. 31042 Derby 1988. 45.18 t.

These vehicles have been converted for use on Wrexham, Shropshire & Marylebone services. Converted to operate in push-pull mode with 67012–015/029.

| 82301 | (82117) |  | **WS** | DB | *WS* | CE |
|-------|---------|--|--------|----|------|----|
| 82302 | (          ) |  |        |    |      |    |
| 82303 | (82135) |  | **WS** | DB | *WS* | CE |
| 82304 | (82130) |  | **WS** | DB | *WS* | CE |
| 82305 | (82134) |  | **WS** | DB | *WS* | CE |

# NE (BG) GANGWAYED BRAKE VAN (100 m.p.h.)

Mark 1. Short frame. Load 10 t. Adapted 199? for use as Brake Luggage Van. Guard's compartment retained and former baggage area adapted for secure stowage of passengers' luggage. B4 bogies. 100 m.p.h. ETH1X.

Lot No. 30162 Pressed Steel 1956–57. 30.5 t.

| 92904 | (80867, 99554) |  | **VN** | VS | *VS* | CP |
|-------|----------------|--|--------|----|------|----|

# NYMR COACHES FOR PASSENGER USE BETWEEN MIDDLESBROUGH & WHITBY ONLY

These coaches are permitted to operate on the National Rail system but may only be used to convey fare-paying passengers between Middlesbrough and Whitby on the Esk Valley branch line. Only those coaches currently used on the National Rail system are listed here.

## AN21 (RMB)
# OPEN STANDARD WITH MINIATURE BUFFET

Mark 1. –/44 2T. BR Mark 1 bogies. For details see page 106.

Lot No. 30520 Wolverton 1960. 38 t.

| 1823 | v | **M** | NY *NY* | NY | |

## AC21 (TSO)      OPEN STANDARD

Mark 1. –/64 2T (* –/60 2W 2T, † –/60 3W 1T). BR Mark 1 bogies. ETH 4.

**3860/3872.** Lot No. 30080 York 1954. 33 t.
**3948.** Lot No. 30086 Eastleigh 1954–55. 33 t.
**4198/4252.** Lot No. 30172 York 1956. 33 t.
**4290.** Lot No. 30207 BRCW 1956. 33 t.
**4455.** Lot No. 30226 BRCW 1957. 33 t.

| 3860 | v* | **M** | NY *NY* | NY | | 4252 | v* | **CC** | NY *NY* | NY |
| 3872 | v† | **BG** | NY *NY* | NY | | 4290 | v | **M** | NY *NY* | NY |
| 3948 | v | **CC** | NY *NY* | NY | | 4455 | v | **CC** | NY *NY* | NY |
| 4198 | v | **CC** | NY *NY* | NY | | | | | | |

## AD21 (TSO)      OPEN STANDARD

Mark 1. –/48 2T. BR Mark 1 bogies. ETH 4.

**4786.** Lot No. 30376 York 1957. 33 t.
**4817.** Lot No. 30473 BRCW 1959. 33 t.

| 4786 | v | **M** | NY *NY* | NY | | 4817 | v | **M** | NY *NY* | NY |

## AC21 (TSO)      OPEN STANDARD

Mark 1. Later vehicles built with Commonwealth bogies. –/64 2T. ETH 4.

Lot No. 30690 Wolverton 1961–62. Aluminium window frames. 37 t.

| 5000 | v | **M** | NY *NY* | NY | | 5029 | v | **CH** | NY *NY* | NY |

## AE21 (BSO)      OPEN BRAKE STANDARD

Mark 1. –/39 1T. BR Mark 1 bogies. ETH 4.

Lot No. 30170 Doncaster 1956. 34 t.

| 9267 | v | **BG** | NY *NY* | NY | | 9274 | v | **M** | NY *NY* | NY |

## AA31 (CK)      CORRIDOR COMPOSITE

Mark 1. 24/18 1T. BR Mark 1 bogies. ETH 2.

Lot No. 30665 Derby 1961. 36 t.

| 16156 | v | **CC** | NY *NY* | NY | |

# 2.2. HIGH SPEED TRAIN TRAILER CARS

HSTs consist of a number of trailer cars (usually seven to nine) with a power car at each end. All trailer cars are classified Mark 3 and have BT10 bogies with disc brakes and central door locking. Heating is by a 415 V three-phase supply and vehicles have air conditioning. Maximum speed is 125 m.p.h.

All vehicles underwent a mid-life refurbishment in the 1980s, and a further refurbishment programme was completed in November 2000, with each train operating company having a different scheme as follows:

**First Great Western.** Green seat covers and extra partitions between seat bays.

**Great North Eastern Railway.** New ceiling lighting panels and brown seat covers. First Class vehicles have table lamps and imitation walnut plastic end panels.

**Virgin Cross-Country.** Green seat covers. Standard Class vehicles had four seats in the centre of each carriage replaced with a luggage stack. All have now passed to other operators or are in store.

**Midland Mainline.** Grey seat covers, redesigned seat squabs, side carpeting and two seats in the centre of each standard class carriage and one in First Class carriages replaced with a luggage stack.

Since then the remaining three operators of HSTs have embarked on separate, and very different, refurbishment projects:

**Midland Mainline** was first to refurbish its vehicles a second time during 2003/04. This involved fitting new fluorescent and halogen ceiling lighting, although the original seats were retained in First and Standard Class, but with blue upholstery. London St. Pancras and Sheffield/Leeds and Nottingham services are now operated by **East Midlands Trains.**

**First Great Western** started a major rebuild of its HST sets in late 2006, with the programme completed in spring 2008. With an increased fleet of 53 sets the new interiors feature new lighting and seating throughout. First Class seats have leather upholstery, and are made by Primarius UK. Standard Class seats are of high-back design by Grammer. A small number of sets have been reduced to 7-cars without a buffet car but FGW plans to convert 18 vehicles to TSB "mini buffet" vehicles during 2009 (numbered in the 401xx series), and these will be used on shorter distance services within 7-car sets. Two of these will be converted from loco-hauled stock.

**GNER** modernised its buffet cars with new corner bars in 2004 and at the same time each HST set was made up to 9-cars with an extra Standard Class vehicle added with a disabled person's toilet.

At the end of 2006 **GNER** embarked on a major rebuild of its sets, with the work being carried out at Wabtec, Doncaster. All vehicles will have similar interiors to the Mark 4 "Mallard" fleet, with new Primarius seats throughout. 13 sets are to be refurbished (with the work continuing under new operator **National Express East Coast**) with all due to be completed by late 2009.

Ten sets ex-Virgin Cross-Country, and some spare vehicles, were temporarily allocated to Midland Mainline for the interim service to Manchester during 2003/

04 and had a facelift. Buffet cars were converted from TRSB to TRFB and renumbered in the 408xx series. These vehicles are now in use with First Great Western or National Express East Coast.

Open access operator **Grand Central** started operation in December 2007 with a new service from Sunderland to London King's Cross. This operator has three sets mostly using stock converted from loco-hauled Mark 3s.

**Cross-Country** reintroduced HSTs to the Cross-Country network from summer 2008 using ex-Midland Mainline sets. Five sets have been refurbished at Wabtec, Doncaster for regular use on the Plymouth–Edinburgh corridor. Three of these sets use stock mostly converted from loco-hauled Mark 3s and two are sets ex-Midland Mainline. The interiors are similar to refurbished NXEC sets, although the seating layout is different and one toilet per coach has been removed for a luggage stack.

### TOPS Type Codes

TOPS type codes for HST trailer cars are made up as follows:

(1) Two letters denoting the layout of the vehicle as follows:

| | |
|---|---|
| GH Open | GL Kitchen |
| GJ Open with Guard's compartment | GN Buffet |

(2) A digit for the class of passenger accommodation

| | |
|---|---|
| 1 First | 3 Composite |
| 2 Standard (formerly second) | |

(3) A suffix relating to the build of coach.

G Mark 3

### Operator Codes

The normal operator codes are given in brackets after the TOPS codes. These are as follows:

| | | | |
|---|---|---|---|
| TCC | Trailer Composite Catering | TRSB | Trailer Buffet Standard |
| TF | Trailer First | TS | Trailer Standard |
| TGS | Trailer Guard's Standard | TSRMB | Trailer Standard with |
| TRB | Trailer Buffet First | | Miniature Buffet |
| TRFB | Trailer Kitchen Buffet First | | |

## GN2G (TSRMB)
## TRAILER STANDARD WITH MINIATURE BUFFET

18 vehicles being converted from TSs or loco-hauled TSOs for First Great Western. Full details awaited.

**40101–40116.** Lot No. Derby   . t.
**40117/40118.** Lot No. 30877/8 Derby   . t.

| | | |
|---|---|---|
| 40101 | ( | ) |
| 40102 | ( | ) |
| 40103 | ( | ) |
| 40104 | ( | ) |

| | | | | |
|---|---|---|---|---|
| 40105 | ( ) | | | |
| 40106 | ( ) | | | |
| 40107 | ( ) | | | |
| 40108 | ( ) | | | |
| 40109 | ( ) | | | |
| 40110 | ( ) | | | |
| 40111 | ( ) | | | |
| 40112 | ( ) | | | |
| 40113 | ( ) | | | |
| 40114 | (42086) | | P | |
| 40115 | ( ) | | | |
| 40116 | ( ) | | | |
| 40117 | (12128) | | P | |
| 40118 | (12172) | | P | |

## GN1G (TRFB)              TRAILER BUFFET FIRST

Converted from TRSB by fitting First Class seats. Renumbered from 404xx series by subtracting 200. 23/–.

**40204–40228.** Lot No. 30883 Derby 1976–77. 36.12 t.
**40231.** Lot No. 30899 Derby 1978–79. 36.12 t.

* Refurbished First Great Western vehicles. Primarius leather seating.

| | | | | | | | | | | |
|---|---|---|---|---|---|---|---|---|---|---|
| 40204 | * | **FD** | A | *GW* | LA | 40210 | * | **FD** | A | *GW* | LA |
| 40205 | * | **FD** | A | *GW* | LA | 40221 | * | **FD** | A | *GW* | LA |
| 40207 | * | **FD** | A | *GW* | LA | 40228 | | **FG** | A | *GW* | OO |
| 40208 | | **FG** | A | *GW* | OO | 40231 | * | **FD** | A | *GW* | LA |
| 40209 | | **FG** | A | *GW* | OO | | | | | | |

## GK2G (TRSB)           TRAILER BUFFET STANDARD

Renumbered from 400xx series by adding 400. –/33 1W.

**40402–40426.** Lot No. 30883 Derby 1976–77. 36.12 t.
**40433/40434.** Lot No. 30899 Derby 1978–79. 36.12 t.

**Note:** 40433/40434 were numbered 40233/40234 for a time when fitted with 23 first class seats.

† Fitted with transceiver "dome" for wi-fi.

| | | | | | | | | | |
|---|---|---|---|---|---|---|---|---|---|
| 40402 | **V** | P | | LM | 40424 | † | **GC** | ST *GC* | HT |
| 40403 | **V** | P | | LM | 40426 | † | **GC** | ST *GC* | HT |
| 40416 | **V** | P | | LM | 40433 | † | **GC** | ST *GC* | HT |
| 40419 | **V** | P | | LM | 40434 | | **V** | P | LM |

## GK1G (TRFB)              TRAILER BUFFET FIRST

These vehicles have larger kitchens than the 402xx and 404xx series vehicles, and are used in trains where full meal service is required. They were renumbered from the 403xx series (in which the seats were unclassified) by adding 400 to the previous number. 17/–.

**40700–40721.** Lot No. 30921 Derby 1978–79. 38.16 t.
**40722–40735.** Lot No. 30940 Derby 1979–80. 38.16 t.
**40736–40753.** Lot No. 30948 Derby 1980–81. 38.16 t.
**40754–40757.** Lot No. 30966 Derby 1982. 38.16 t.

\*   Refurbished First Great Western vehicles. Primarius leather seating.
m   Refurbished National Express East Coast vehicles with Primarius seating.
†   Fitted with transceiver "dome" for wi-fi.

| | | | | | | | | | |
|---|---|---|---|---|---|---|---|---|---|
| 40700 | | **MN** | P | *EM* | NL | 40730 | **MN** | P | *EM* | NL |
| 40701 | m† | **NX** | P | *EC* | EC | 40731 | **FD** | A | *GW* | OO |
| 40702 | m† | **NX** | P | *EC* | EC | 40732 | **MN** | A | | LM |
| 40703 | \* | **FD** | A | *GW* | LA | 40733 \* | **FD** | A | *GW* | LA |
| 40704 | m† | **GN** | A | *EC* | EC | 40734 \* | **FD** | A | *GW* | LA |
| 40705 | † | **GN** | A | *EC* | EC | 40735 m† | **GN** | A | *EC* | EC |
| 40706 | † | **GN** | A | *EC* | EC | 40736 | **FD** | A | *GW* | OO |
| 40707 | \* | **FD** | A | *GW* | LA | 40737 m† | **NX** | A | *EC* | EC |
| 40708 | m† | **NX** | P | *EC* | EC | 40738 | **FD** | A | *GW* | OO |
| 40709 | | **FG** | A | *GW* | OO | 40739 \* | **FD** | A | *GW* | LA |
| 40710 | \* | **FD** | A | *GW* | LA | 40740 † | **GN** | A | *EC* | EC |
| 40711 | m† | **NX** | A | *EC* | EC | 40741 | **MN** | P | *EM* | NL |
| 40712 | | **FD** | A | *GW* | OO | 40742 † | **GN** | A | *EC* | EC |
| 40713 | \* | **FD** | A | *GW* | LA | 40743 \* | **FD** | A | *GW* | LA |
| 40714 | | **FD** | A | *GW* | OO | 40744 | **FD** | A | *GW* | OO |
| 40715 | \* | **FD** | A | *GW* | LA | 40745 | **FG** | A | *GW* | OO |
| 40716 | \* | **FD** | A | *GW* | LA | 40746 | **MN** | P | *EM* | NL |
| 40717 | | **FD** | A | *GW* | OO | 40747 | **FD** | A | *GW* | OO |
| 40718 | \* | **FD** | A | *GW* | OO | 40748 † | **GN** | A | *EC* | EC |
| 40720 | m† | **NX** | A | *EC* | EC | 40749 | **ST** | P | *EM* | NL |
| 40721 | \* | **FD** | A | *GW* | LA | 40750 m† | **NX** | A | *EC* | EC |
| 40722 | \* | **FD** | A | *GW* | LA | 40751 | **MN** | P | *EM* | NL |
| 40723 | | **MN** | A | | LM | 40752 \* | **FD** | A | *GW* | LA |
| 40724 | | **FD** | A | *GW* | OO | 40753 | **MN** | P | *EM* | NL |
| 40725 | | **FD** | A | *GW* | OO | 40754 | **MN** | P | *EM* | NL |
| 40726 | | **FD** | A | *GW* | OO | 40755 \* | **FD** | A | *GW* | LA |
| 40727 | \* | **FD** | A | *GW* | LA | 40756 | **MN** | P | *EM* | NL |
| 40728 | | **MN** | P | *EM* | NL | 40757 \* | **FD** | A | *GW* | LA |
| 40729 | | **MN** | P | *EM* | NL | | | | | |

# GL1G (TRFB)      TRAILER BUFFET FIRST

These vehicles have been converted from TRSBs in the 404xx series to be similar
to the 407xx series vehicles. 17/–.

**40801–40803/40805/40808/40809/40811.** Lot No. 30883 Derby 1976–77. 38.16 t.
**40804/40806/40807/40810.** Lot No. 30899 Derby 1978–79. 38.16 t.

**Note:** 40802/40804/40811 were numbered 40212/40232/40211 for a time when
fitted with 23 first class seats.

m   Refurbished National Express East Coast vehicle with Primarius seating.
†   Fitted with transceiver "dome" for wi-fi.

| 40801 | (40027, 40427) | **FG** | P | *GW* | OO |
|---|---|---|---|---|---|
| 40802 | (40012, 40412) | **FG** | P | *GW* | OO |
| 40803 | (40018, 40418) | **FG** | P | *GW* | OO |
| 40804 | (40032, 40432) | **GN** | P | | ZK |
| 40805 | (40020, 40420) | m† **GN** | P | *EC* | EC |
| 40806 | (40029, 40429) | **FG** | P | *GW* | OO |
| 40807 | (40035, 40435) | **FG** | P | *GW* | LA |
| 40808 | (40015, 40415) | **FG** | P | *GW* | OO |
| 40809 | (40014, 40414) | **FD** | P | *GW* | LA |
| 40810 | (40030, 40430) | **FD** | P | *GW* | LA |
| 40811 | (40011, 40411) | **FD** | P | *GW* | LA |

## GN1G (TRB)                                    TRAILER BUFFET FIRST

Vehicles owned by First Group. Converted from TRSB by First Great Western. 23/–.

**40900/40902/40904**. Lot No. 30883 Derby 1976–77. 36.12 t.
**40901/40903**. Lot No. 30899 Derby 1978–79. 36.12 t.

* Refurbished First Great Western vehicles. Primarius leather seating.

| 40900 | (40022, 40422) | * | **FD** | FG | *GW* | LA |
|---|---|---|---|---|---|---|
| 40901 | (40036, 40436) | * | **FD** | FG | *GW* | LA |
| 40902 | (40023, 40423) | * | **FD** | FG | *GW* | LA |
| 40903 | (40037, 40437) | * | **FD** | FG | *GW* | LA |
| 40904 | (40001, 40401) | * | **FD** | FG | *GW* | LA |

## GH1G (TF)                                              TRAILER FIRST

**41003–41056**. Lot No. 30881 Derby 1976–77. 33.66 t.
**41057–41120**. Lot No. 30896 Derby 1977–78. 33.66 t.
**41121–41148**. Lot No. 30938 Derby 1979–80. 33.66 t.
**41149–41166**. Lot No. 30947 Derby 1980. 33.66 t.
**41167–41169**. Lot No. 30963 Derby 1982. 33.66 t.
**41170**. Lot No. 30967 Derby 1982. Former prototype vehicle. 33.66 t.
**41176**. Lot No. 30897 Derby 1977. 33.66 t.
**41179/41180**. Lot No. 30884 Derby 1976–77. 33.66 t.
**41181–41184/41189**. Lot No. 30939 Derby 1979–80. 33.66 t.
**41185–41187/41191**. Lot No. 30969 Derby 1982. 33.66 t.
**41190**. Lot No. 30882 Derby 1976–77. 33.60 t.
**41192**. Lot No. 30897 Derby 1977–79. 33.60 t.
**41193–41195/41201–41206**. Lot No. 30878 Derby 1975–76. 34.3 t. Converted from Mark 3A FO.

As built and m 48/– 2T.
* Refurbished First Great Western vehicles. Primarius leather seating.
c Refurbished Cross-Country vehicles with Primarius seating and 2 tip-up seats.            One toilet removed. 40/– 1TD 1W.
m Refurbished National Express East Coast vehicles with Primarius seating.
s Fitted with centre luggage stack, disabled toilet and wheelchair space. 46/– 1T 1TD 1W.
w Wheelchair space. 47/– 2T 1W.

x   Toilet removed for trolley space (FGW). 48/– 1T.

| | | | | | | | | | | |
|---|---|---|---|---|---|---|---|---|---|---|
| 41003 | *x | **FD** | A | *GW* | LA | 41066 | | **GN** | A | *EC* | EC |
| 41004 | *x | **FD** | A | *GW* | OO | 41067 | s | **MN** | P | *EM* | NL |
| 41005 | *x | **FD** | A | *GW* | OO | 41068 | s | **MN** | P | *EM* | NL |
| 41006 | *w | **FD** | A | *GW* | OO | 41069 | s | **MN** | P | *EM* | NL |
| 41007 | *x | **FD** | A | *GW* | OO | 41070 | s | **MN** | P | *EM* | NL |
| 41008 | *w | **FD** | A | *GW* | OO | 41071 | | **MN** | P | *EM* | NL |
| 41009 | *x | **FD** | A | *GW* | LA | 41072 | s | **MN** | P | *EM* | NL |
| 41010 | *w | **FD** | A | *GW* | LA | 41075 | | **MN** | P | *EM* | NL |
| 41011 | *x | **FD** | A | *GW* | LA | 41076 | s | **MN** | P | *EM* | NL |
| 41012 | *w | **FD** | A | *GW* | LA | 41077 | | **ST** | P | *EM* | NL |
| 41015 | *x | **FD** | A | *GW* | LA | 41078 | | **MN** | P | *EM* | NL |
| 41016 | *w | **FD** | A | *GW* | LA | 41079 | | **MN** | P | *EM* | NL |
| 41017 | *x | **FD** | A | *GW* | OO | 41081 | *x | **FD** | P | *GW* | OO |
| 41018 | *w | **FD** | A | *GW* | OO | 41083 | mw | **NX** | P | *EC* | EC |
| 41019 | *x | **FD** | A | *GW* | OO | 41084 | s | **MN** | P | *EM* | NL |
| 41020 | *w | **FD** | A | *GW* | LA | 41085 | *x | **FD** | FG | *GW* | LA |
| 41021 | *x | **FD** | A | *GW* | LA | 41086 | *x | **FD** | FG | *GW* | LA |
| 41022 | *w | **FD** | A | *GW* | LA | 41087 | | **GN** | A | *EC* | EC |
| 41023 | *x | **FD** | A | *GW* | LA | 41088 | w | **GN** | A | *EC* | EC |
| 41024 | *w | **FD** | A | *GW* | LA | 41089 | *w | **FD** | A | *GW* | OO |
| 41026 | c | **XC** | A | *XC* | EC | 41090 | m | **NX** | A | *EC* | EC |
| 41027 | *x | **FD** | A | *GW* | OO | 41091 | m | **GN** | A | *EC* | EC |
| 41028 | *w | **FD** | A | *GW* | OO | 41092 | mw | **GN** | A | *EC* | EC |
| 41029 | *x | **FD** | A | *GW* | OO | 41093 | *x | **FD** | A | *GW* | LA |
| 41030 | *w | **FD** | A | *GW* | OO | 41094 | *w | **FD** | A | *GW* | LA |
| 41031 | *x | **FD** | A | *GW* | LA | 41095 | mw | **NX** | P | *EC* | EC |
| 41032 | *w | **FD** | A | *GW* | OO | 41096 | *x | **FD** | P | *GW* | OO |
| 41033 | *x | **FD** | A | *GW* | OO | 41097 | m | **NX** | A | *EC* | EC |
| 41034 | *w | **FD** | A | *GW* | LA | 41098 | mw | **NX** | A | *EC* | EC |
| 41035 | c | **XC** | A | *XC* | EC | 41099 | m | **NX** | A | *EC* | EC |
| 41037 | *x | **FD** | A | *GW* | LA | 41100 | mw | **NX** | A | *EC* | EC |
| 41038 | *w | **FD** | A | *GW* | LA | 41101 | *x | **FD** | A | *GW* | OO |
| 41039 | m | **GN** | A | *EC* | EC | 41102 | *w | **FD** | A | *GW* | OO |
| 41040 | mw | **GN** | A | *EC* | EC | 41103 | *x | **FD** | A | *GW* | LA |
| 41041 | s | **MN** | P | *EM* | NL | 41104 | *w | **FD** | A | *GW* | LA |
| 41044 | mw | **NX** | A | *EC* | EC | 41105 | *x | **FD** | A | *GW* | OO |
| 41045 | *x | **FD** | FG | *GW* | LA | 41106 | *w | **FD** | A | *GW* | OO |
| 41046 | s | **MN** | P | *EM* | NL | 41108 | *w | **FD** | P | *GW* | OO |
| 41051 | *x | **FD** | A | *GW* | LA | 41109 | *x | **FD** | P | *GW* | OO |
| 41052 | *w | **FD** | A | *GW* | LA | 41110 | *w | **FD** | A | *GW* | OO |
| 41055 | *x | **FD** | A | *GW* | OO | 41111 | | **MN** | P | *EM* | NL |
| 41056 | *w | **FD** | A | *GW* | OO | 41112 | | **MN** | P | *EM* | NL |
| 41057 | | **MN** | P | *EM* | NL | 41113 | s | **MN** | P | *EM* | NL |
| 41059 | *w | **FD** | FG | *GW* | LA | 41114 | *x | **FD** | FG | *GW* | LA |
| 41061 | | **MN** | P | *EM* | NL | 41115 | m | **NX** | P | *EC* | EC |
| 41062 | w | **MN** | P | *EM* | NL | 41116 | *x | **FD** | A | *GW* | LA |
| 41063 | | **MN** | P | *EM* | NL | 41117 | | **MN** | P | *EM* | NL |
| 41064 | s | **ST** | P | *EM* | NL | 41118 | mw | **NX** | A | *EC* | EC |
| 41065 | *x | **FD** | A | *GW* | OO | 41119 | *x | **FD** | P | *GW* | OO |

| | | | | | | | | | | | | |
|---|---|---|---|---|---|---|---|---|---|---|---|---|
| 41120 | | **GN** | A | *EC* | EC | | 41145 | *x | **FD** | A | *GW* | LA |
| 41121 | *x | **FD** | A | *GW* | LA | | 41146 | *w | **FD** | A | *GW* | LA |
| 41122 | *w | **FD** | A | *GW* | LA | | 41147 | *w | **FD** | P | *GW* | OO |
| 41123 | *x | **FD** | A | *GW* | LA | | 41148 | *x | **FD** | P | *GW* | OO |
| 41124 | *w | **FD** | A | *GW* | LA | | 41149 | *w | **FD** | P | *GW* | OO |
| 41125 | *x | **FD** | A | *GW* | OO | | 41150 | w | **GN** | A | *EC* | EC |
| 41126 | *w | **FD** | A | *GW* | OO | | 41151 | | **GN** | A | *EC* | EC |
| 41127 | *x | **FD** | A | *GW* | OO | | 41152 | w | **GN** | A | *EC* | EC |
| 41128 | *w | **FD** | A | *GW* | OO | | 41153 | | **GN** | P | | ZK |
| 41129 | *x | **FD** | A | *GW* | LA | | 41154 | s | **MN** | P | *EM* | NL |
| 41130 | *w | **FD** | A | *GW* | LA | | 41155 | *x | **FD** | P | *GW* | OO |
| 41131 | *x | **FD** | A | *GW* | OO | | 41156 | | **MN** | P | *EM* | NL |
| 41132 | *w | **FD** | A | *GW* | OO | | 41157 | *x | **FD** | A | *GW* | LA |
| 41133 | *x | **FD** | A | *GW* | LA | | 41158 | *w | **FD** | A | *GW* | LA |
| 41134 | *w | **FD** | A | *GW* | LA | | 41159 | m | **NX** | P | *EC* | EC |
| 41135 | *w | **FD** | A | *GW* | LA | | 41160 | *w | **FD** | FG | *GW* | LA |
| 41136 | *w | **FD** | A | *GW* | LA | | 41161 | *w | **FD** | P | *GW* | OO |
| 41137 | *x | **FD** | A | *GW* | OO | | 41162 | *w | **FD** | FG | *GW* | LA |
| 41138 | *w | **FD** | A | *GW* | OO | | 41163 | *x | **FD** | FG | *GW* | LA |
| 41139 | *x | **FD** | A | *GW* | OO | | 41164 | w | **GN** | A | *EC* | EC |
| 41140 | *w | **FD** | A | *GW* | OO | | 41165 | mw | **NX** | P | *EC* | EC |
| 41141 | *x | **FD** | A | *GW* | LA | | 41166 | *w | **FD** | FG | *GW* | LA |
| 41142 | *w | **FD** | A | *GW* | LA | | 41167 | *w | **FD** | FG | *GW* | LA |
| 41143 | *x | **FD** | A | *GW* | LA | | 41168 | *x | **FD** | P | *GW* | OO |
| 41144 | *w | **FD** | A | *GW* | LA | | 41169 | *w | **FD** | P | *GW* | OO |

| | | | | | | |
|---|---|---|---|---|---|---|
| 41170 | (41001) | m | **NX** | A | *EC* | EC |
| 41176 | (42142, 42352) | | **GN** | P | | ZK |
| 41179 | (40505) | *x | **FD** | A | *GW* | OO |
| 41180 | (40511) | *w | **FD** | A | *GW* | OO |
| 41181 | (42282) | *x | **FD** | P | *GW* | OO |
| 41182 | (42278) | *w | **FD** | P | *GW* | OO |
| 41183 | (42274) | *w | **FD** | P | *GW* | OO |
| 41184 | (42270) | *x | **FD** | P | *GW* | OO |
| 41185 | (42313) | m | **NX** | P | *EC* | EC |
| 41186 | (42312) | *x | **FD** | P | *GW* | OO |
| 41187 | (42311) | *w | **FD** | P | *GW* | OO |
| 41189 | (42298) | *w | **FD** | P | *GW* | OO |
| 41190 | (42088) | mw | **GN** | P | *EC* | EC |
| 41191 | (42318) | *x | **FD** | P | *GW* | OO |
| 41192 | (42246) | *w | **FD** | P | *GW* | OO |

The following coaches have been converted from loco-hauled Mark 3 vehicles for Cross-Country.

| | | | | | | |
|---|---|---|---|---|---|---|
| 41193 | (11060) | c | **XC** | P | *XC* | EC |
| 41194 | (11016) | c | **XC** | P | *XC* | EC |
| 41195 | (11020) | c | **XC** | P | *XC* | EC |

The following coaches have been converted from loco-hauled Mark 3 vehicles for Grand Central. 48/– 2T.

| | | | | | | |
|---|---|---|---|---|---|---|
| 41201 | (11045) | | **GC** | ST | *GC* | HT |

| 41202 | (11017) | **GC** | ST *GC* | HT |
| 41203 | (11038) | **GC** | ST | ZJ |
| 41204 | (11023) | **GC** | ST *GC* | HT |
| 41205 | (11036) | **GC** | ST *GC* | HT |
| 41206 | (11055) | **GC** | ST *GC* | HT |

# GH2G (TS)                        TRAILER STANDARD

**42003–42090/42362.** Lot No. 30882 Derby 1976–77. 33.60 t.
**42091–42250.** Lot No. 30897 Derby 1977–79. 33.60 t.
**42251–42305.** Lot No. 30939 Derby 1979–80. 33.60 t.
**42306–42322.** Lot No. 30969 Derby 1982. 33.60 t.
**42323–42341.** Lot No. 30983 Derby 1984–85. 33.60 t.
**42242–42360.** Lot No. 30949 Derby 1982. 33.47 t. Converted from TGS.
**42343–42345.** Lot No. 30970 Derby 1982. 33.47 t. Converted from TGS.
**42344/42361.** Lot No. 30964 Derby 1982. 33.47 t. Converted from TGS.
**42346/42347/42350/42351/42379/42380.** Lot No. 30881 Derby 1976–77. 33.66 t. Converted from TF.
**42348/42349/42363–42365/42381.** Lot No. 30896 Derby 1977–78. 33.66 t. Converted from TF.
**42354.** Lot No. 30897 Derby 1977. Was TF from 1983 to 1992. 33.66 t.
**42353/42355–42357.** Lot No. 30967 Derby 1982. Ex-prototype vehicles. 33.66 t.
**42366–42378/42401–42409.** Lot No. 30877 Derby 1975–77. 34.3 t. Converted from Mark 3A TSO.

**Notes:** 42158 was numbered 41177 for a time when fitted with First Class seats. 42310 was numbered 41188 for a time when fitted with First Class seats.

Standard seating and m –/76 2T.
* Refurbished First Great Western vehicles. Grammer seating. –/80 2T (unless h – high density).
c Refurbished Cross-Country vehicles with Primarius seating. One toilet removed –/82 1T.
§c Refurbished Cross-Country vehicles with Primarius seating and 2 tip-up seats One toilet removed. –/66 1TD 2W. Note 42379/380 are –/71 1TD 1T 2W.
d FGW vehicles with disabled persons toilet and 5, 6 or 7 tip-up seats. –/68 1T 1TD 2W.
h "High density" FGW vehicles. –/84 2T.
k "High density" FGW refurbished vehicle with disabled persons toilet and 6 or 7 tip-up seats. –/72 1T 1TD 2W.
m Refurbished National Express East Coast vehicles with Primarius seating.
u Centre luggage stack (EMT) –/74 2T.
w Centre luggage stack and wheelchair space (EMT) –72 2T 1W.
† Disabled persons toilet (NXEC) –/62 1T 1TD 1W.

| 42003 | *h | **FD** | A | *GW* | OO | | 42010 | *h | **FD** | A | *GW* | LA |
| 42004 | *d | **FD** | A | *GW* | LA | | 42012 | *k | **FD** | A | *GW* | LA |
| 42005 | *h | **FD** | A | *GW* | LA | | 42013 | *h | **FD** | A | *GW* | LA |
| 42006 | *h | **FD** | A | *GW* | LA | | 42014 | *h | **FD** | A | *GW* | LA |
| 42007 | *d | **FD** | A | *GW* | LA | | 42015 | *k | **FD** | A | *GW* | LA |
| 42008 | *k | **FD** | A | *GW* | OO | | 42016 | *h | **FD** | A | *GW* | LA |
| 42009 | *h | **FD** | A | *GW* | LA | | 42019 | * | **FD** | A | *GW* | LA |

| | | | | | | | | | | | |
|---|---|---|---|---|---|---|---|---|---|---|---|
| 42021 | *k | **FD** | A | *GW* | LA | 42073 | *h | **FD** | A | *GW* | OO |
| 42023 | *h | **FD** | A | *GW* | LA | 42074 | *h | **FD** | A | *GW* | OO |
| 42024 | *k | **FD** | A | *GW* | OO | 42075 | * | **FD** | A | *GW* | LA |
| 42025 | *h | **FD** | A | *GW* | OO | 42076 | * | **FD** | A | *GW* | LA |
| 42026 | *h | **FD** | A | *GW* | OO | 42077 | * | **FD** | A | *GW* | LA |
| 42027 | *h | **FD** | A | *GW* | OO | 42078 | * | **FD** | A | *GW* | LA |
| 42028 | *h | **FD** | A | *GW* | LA | 42079 | *h | **FD** | A | *GW* | OO |
| 42029 | *h | **FD** | A | *GW* | LA | 42080 | *h | **FD** | A | *GW* | OO |
| 42030 | *k | **FD** | A | *GW* | LA | 42081 | *k | **FD** | A | *GW* | OO |
| 42031 | *h | **FD** | A | *GW* | LA | 42083 | *h | **FD** | A | *GW* | OO |
| 42032 | *h | **FD** | A | *GW* | LA | 42084 | *h | **FD** | P | *GW* | OO |
| 42033 | * | **FD** | A | *GW* | LA | 42085 | *h | **FD** | P | *GW* | OO |
| 42034 | * | **FD** | A | *GW* | LA | 42087 | *h | **FD** | P | *GW* | OO |
| 42035 | * | **FD** | A | *GW* | LA | 42089 | *h | **FD** | A | *GW* | OO |
| 42036 | c | **XC** | A | *XC* | EC | 42090 | *h | **FD** | P | *GW* | OO |
| 42037 | c | **XC** | A | *XC* | EC | 42091 | † | **GN** | A | *EC* | EC |
| 42038 | c | **XC** | A | *XC* | EC | 42092 | *d | **FD** | FG | *GW* | LA |
| 42039 | *h | **FD** | A | *GW* | OO | 42093 | *h | **FD** | FG | *GW* | LA |
| 42040 | *h | **FD** | A | *GW* | OO | 42094 | *h | **FD** | FG | *GW* | LA |
| 42041 | *h | **FD** | A | *GW* | OO | 42095 | * | **FD** | FG | *GW* | LA |
| 42042 | *h | **FD** | A | *GW* | OO | 42096 | *h | **FD** | A | *GW* | LA |
| 42043 | *h | **FD** | A | *GW* | OO | 42097 | c | **XC** | A | *XC* | EC |
| 42044 | *h | **FD** | A | *GW* | OO | 42098 | *h | **FD** | A | *GW* | OO |
| 42045 | * | **FD** | A | *GW* | LA | 42099 | *h | **FD** | A | *GW* | OO |
| 42046 | * | **FD** | A | *GW* | LA | 42100 | u | **MN** | P | *EM* | NL |
| 42047 | * | **FD** | A | *GW* | LA | 42101 | | **GN** | P | | ZK |
| 42048 | *h | **FD** | A | *GW* | OO | 42102 | | **GN** | P | | ZK |
| 42049 | *h | **FD** | A | *GW* | OO | 42103 | *k | **FD** | FG | *GW* | LA |
| 42050 | *h | **FD** | A | *GW* | OO | 42104 | | **GN** | A | *EC* | EC |
| 42051 | c | **XC** | A | *XC* | EC | 42105 | *d | **FD** | FG | *GW* | LA |
| 42052 | c | **XC** | A | *XC* | EC | 42106 | m | **GN** | A | *EC* | EC |
| 42053 | c | **XC** | A | *XC* | EC | 42107 | * | **FD** | A | *GW* | LA |
| 42054 | * | **FD** | A | *GW* | LA | 42108 | *h | **FD** | FG | *GW* | LA |
| 42055 | * | **FD** | A | *GW* | LA | 42109 | m | **NX** | P | *EC* | EC |
| 42056 | * | **FD** | A | *GW* | LA | 42110 | m | **NX** | P | *EC* | EC |
| 42057 | m | **GN** | A | *EC* | EC | 42111 | u | **MN** | P | *EM* | NL |
| 42058 | m | **GN** | A | *EC* | EC | 42112 | u | **MN** | P | *EM* | NL |
| 42059 | m | **GN** | A | *EC* | EC | 42113 | u | **MN** | P | *EM* | NL |
| 42060 | *h | **FD** | A | *GW* | OO | 42115 | *h | **FD** | P | *GW* | OO |
| 42061 | *h | **FD** | A | *GW* | OO | 42116 | † | **GN** | A | *EC* | EC |
| 42062 | *k | **FD** | A | *GW* | OO | 42117 | m | **NX** | P | *EC* | EC |
| 42063 | m | **NX** | A | *EC* | EC | 42118 | *h | **FD** | A | *GW* | OO |
| 42064 | m | **NX** | A | *EC* | EC | 42119 | u | **MN** | P | *EM* | NL |
| 42065 | m | **NX** | A | *EC* | EC | 42120 | u | **MN** | P | *EM* | NL |
| 42066 | *k | **FD** | A | *GW* | OO | 42121 | u | **MN** | P | *EM* | NL |
| 42067 | *h | **FD** | A | *GW* | OO | 42122 | | **GN** | A | *EC* | EC |
| 42068 | *h | **FD** | A | *GW* | OO | 42123 | u | **MN** | P | *EM* | NL |
| 42069 | *k | **FD** | A | *GW* | OO | 42124 | u | **MN** | P | *EM* | NL |
| 42070 | *h | **FD** | A | *GW* | OO | 42125 | u | **MN** | P | *EM* | NL |
| 42071 | *h | **FD** | A | *GW* | OO | 42126 | *h | **FD** | A | *GW* | OO |
| 42072 | * | **FD** | A | *GW* | LA | 42127 | m† | **NX** | A | *EC* | EC |

▲ **Mark 1s:** In all over Oxford Blue livery Mark 1 RBR 1699 (with Commonwealth bogies) is seen near Rhyl on 16/02/08.                    **Robert Pritchard**

▼ Chocolate & Cream-liveried Mark 1 FO 3112 is seen at Rhyl on 16/02/08.
**Robert Pritchard**

▲ Pullman Car umber & cream-liveried Mark 1 RBR 1659 is seen at Oxford on 09/05/08. **Andrew Mason**

▲ BR Carmine & Cream-liveried Mark 1 BFK 17015 is seen near Dawlish on 21/06/08. **Mark Beal**

▶ The SRPS's BR Maroon-liveried Mark 1 FK 13229 (with B4 bogies) at Doncaster on 20/04/07. **Mark Beal**

▲ BR Maroon-liveried Mark 1 BSK 99723 (35459) is seen near Dove Holes behind 40145 on 15/09/07.  **Robert Pritchard**

▼ **Mark 2s:** Pullman PFB 586 "DERWENTWATER" is seen at Carnforth on 27/07/08.  **Robert Pritchard**

▲ Riviera Trains blue & cream-liveried Mark 2F FO 3330 "BRUNEL" at Doncaster on 28/04/07. **Mark Beal**

▲ Freshly painted maroon-liveried Mark 2F FO 3408 is seen at Carnforth on 27/07/08.
**Robert Pritchard**

▶ Vintage Trains' Chocolate & Cream-liveried Mark 2F FO 3351 at Carnforth on 27/07/08.
**Robert Pritchard**

▲ Pullman Car-liveried Mark 2D FO 3188 "SOVEREIGN" at Didcot Parkway on 12/04/08. **Mark Beal**

▼ In maroon livery with EWS logos, Mark 2F FO 3358 stands at York (in a loco-hauled rake in temporary use with Grand Central between York and Sunderland) on 16/06/08. **Robert Pritchard**

▲ Many Mark 2Fs still carry Virgin Trains livery (but without branding). On 14/06/08 TSO 6141 is seen at Bristol Temple Meads in the formation of a First Great Western service to Weymouth. **Robert Pritchard**

▼ DRS owns two Mark 2s for use as escort vehicles. Here Mark 2A BSO 9419 is seen at Grangemouth on 14/07/08. **Ian Lothian**

▲ First ScotRail-liveried Mark 2E Unclassified Open Brake 9801 is seen stabled between duties at Polmadie depot, Glasgow on 09/02/08. **Robin Ralston**

▼ **Mark 3s:** Carrying "One" livery with a National Express white stripe, Mark 3A RMB 10403 is seen at Stratford on 19/03/08. **Robert Pritchard**

▲ National Express-liveried Mark 3A TSO 12051 at Stratford on 27/02/08.
**Robert Pritchard**

▼ In BR Blue & Grey livery with Wrexham & Shropshire Railway brandings, Mark 3A
TSO 12053 stands at London Marylebone on 15/06/08.　　**Robert Pritchard**

▲ **Mark 3 Sleeping cars:** First Group-liveried Mark 3A SLEP 10529 is seen stabled at Polmadie depot on 09/02/08 between ScotRail "Caledonian Sleeper" duties.
**Robin Ralston**

▼ First Great Western "Dynamic Lines"-liveried Mark 3A SLEP 10532 is seen at Bodmin Parkway on 12/06/08.　　**Robert Pritchard**

▲ **Mark 3 HST vehicles:** Grand Central-liveried HST TRSB 40424 is seen at Peterborough on 01/03/08. **Stephen Widdowson**

▼ Carrying the new Stagecoach/East Midlands Trains HST livery is TRFB 40749 at Dore & Totley on 19/07/08. **Robert Pritchard**

▲ National Express-liveried TS 42238 at Hexham on 27/09/08. **Robert Pritchard**

▼ First Great Western TGS 44043 at Plymouth on 09/06/08. **Robert Pritchard**

▲ **Mark 4s:** In GNER livery with a white stripe applied by National Express, Mark 4 FO 11298 is seen at Retford on 10/02/08. **Robert Pritchard**

▼ **Pullman Cars and Saloons:** Pullman First Bar 310 "PEGASUS" (also carrying "THE TRIANON BAR" branding) is seen at Oxford on 09/05/08. **Andrew Mason**

▲ Maroon-liveried Metro-Cammell Pullman Parlour Second 348 (numbered 99348 and now used as an open first) is seen at Carlisle on 24/05/08. **Robin Ralston**

▼ Converted from a Mark 1 TSO, BR Maroon-liveried "LMS Club Car" 99993 is also seen at Carlisle on 24/05/08. **Robin Ralston**

▲ **DVTs:** GNER-liveried Mark 4 DVT 82207 (with white National Express stripe) leads the 12.40 Leeds–London King's Cross at Retford on 10/02/08.

**Robert Pritchard**

▼ **Service Stock:** Network Rail yellow-liveried Mark 1 Generator Van 6263 is seen at Tyseley depot on 28/06/08.

**Robert Pritchard**

▲ Network Rail yellow-liveried Driving Trailer Coach (former DBSO) 9703 arrives at Derby, being propelled by 31233 and 31601, on 27/02/08, whilst under test. **Paul Biggs**

▼ Most of the Network Rail Service Stock is now in yellow livery, but Green-liveried Inspection Saloon 975025 has managed to escape the yellow paint so far. On 01/07/08 37423 propels "CAROLINE" at Spetchley near Worcester with an 08.51 London Paddington–Bristol Temple Meads. **Stephen Widdowson**

► Network Rail yellow-liveried Generator Van 975482 is seen at Derby on 07/06/08 in use as a temporary buffer stop during station rebuilding works. **Robert Pritchard**

▼ Network Rail Breakdown Train Coach 975612 is seen at Margam on 12/08/07. **Mark Beal**

▼ Track Recording Coach 999508 is seen at Stratford on 19/03/08 as part of a test train top-and-tailed by 31602 and 31233. **Robert Pritchard**

| | | | | | | | | | | | |
|---|---|---|---|---|---|---|---|---|---|---|---|
| 42128 | † | GN | A | *EC* | EC | | 42180 | m | GN | A | *EC* | EC |
| 42129 | * | FD | A | *GW* | LA | | 42181 | m | GN | A | *EC* | EC |
| 42130 | m | NX | P | *EC* | EC | | 42182 | | GN | A | *EC* | EC |
| 42131 | u | MN | P | *EM* | NL | | 42183 | *d | FD | A | *GW* | LA |
| 42132 | * | MN | P | *EM* | NL | | 42184 | * | FD | A | *GW* | LA |
| 42133 | u | MN | P | *EM* | NL | | 42185 | * | FD | A | *GW* | LA |
| 42134 | | GN | A | *EC* | EC | | 42186 | | GN | A | *EC* | EC |
| 42135 | u | MN | P | *EM* | NL | | 42187 | *h | FD | P | *GW* | OO |
| 42136 | u | MN | P | *EM* | NL | | 42188 | m† | GN | A | *EC* | EC |
| 42137 | u | MN | P | *EM* | NL | | 42189 | m† | GN | A | *EC* | EC |
| 42138 | *k | FD | A | *GW* | OO | | 42190 | | GN | A | *EC* | EC |
| 42139 | u | MN | P | *EM* | NL | | 42191 | m | NX | A | *EC* | EC |
| 42140 | u | MN | P | *EM* | NL | | 42192 | m | NX | A | *EC* | EC |
| 42141 | u | MN | P | *EM* | NL | | 42193 | m | NX | A | *EC* | EC |
| 42143 | * | FD | A | *GW* | LA | | 42194 | w | MN | P | *EM* | NL |
| 42144 | * | FD | A | *GW* | LA | | 42195 | *k | FD | P | *GW* | OO |
| 42145 | * | FD | A | *GW* | LA | | 42196 | *h | FD | A | *GW* | OO |
| 42146 | | GN | A | *EC* | EC | | 42197 | *h | FD | A | *GW* | OO |
| 42147 | | GN | P | | ZK | | 42198 | m | NX | A | *EC* | EC |
| 42148 | u | MN | P | *EM* | NL | | 42199 | m | NX | A | *EC* | EC |
| 42149 | u | MN | P | *EM* | NL | | 42200 | *d | FD | A | *GW* | LA |
| 42150 | | GN | A | *EC* | EC | | 42201 | *k | FD | A | *GW* | OO |
| 42151 | w | ST | P | *EM* | NL | | 42202 | *k | FD | A | *GW* | OO |
| 42152 | u | MN | P | *EM* | NL | | 42203 | *h | FD | A | *GW* | OO |
| 42153 | u | ST | P | *EM* | NL | | 42204 | *h | FD | A | *GW* | OO |
| 42154 | | GN | A | *EC* | EC | | 42205 | u | MN | P | *EM* | NL |
| 42155 | w | MN | P | *EM* | NL | | 42206 | *d | FD | A | *GW* | LA |
| 42156 | u | MN | P | *EM* | NL | | 42207 | *d | FD | A | *GW* | LA |
| 42157 | u | MN | P | *EM* | NL | | 42208 | * | FD | A | *GW* | LA |
| 42158 | m | NX | A | *EC* | EC | | 42209 | * | FD | A | *GW* | LA |
| 42159 | m† | NX | P | *EC* | EC | | 42210 | u | MN | P | *EM* | NL |
| 42160 | m | NX | P | *EC* | EC | | 42211 | *k | FD | A | *GW* | OO |
| 42161 | † | GN | A | *EC* | EC | | 42212 | *h | FD | A | *GW* | OO |
| 42162 | *h | FD | P | *GW* | OO | | 42213 | *h | FD | A | *GW* | OO |
| 42163 | m | NX | P | *EC* | EC | | 42214 | *h | FD | A | *GW* | OO |
| 42164 | | ST | P | *EM* | NL | | 42215 | | GN | A | *EC* | EC |
| 42165 | | ST | P | *EM* | NL | | 42216 | *h | FD | A | *GW* | OO |
| 42166 | *h | FD | P | *GW* | OO | | 42217 | *k | FD | P | *GW* | OO |
| 42167 | *h | FD | FG | *GW* | LA | | 42218 | *d | FD | P | *GW* | OO |
| 42168 | *h | FD | FG | *GW* | LA | | 42219 | | GN | A | *EC* | EC |
| 42169 | *h | FD | FG | *GW* | LA | | 42220 | w | MN | P | *EM* | NL |
| 42170 | *h | FD | P | *GW* | OO | | 42221 | *h | FD | A | *GW* | OO |
| 42171 | | GN | A | *EC* | EC | | 42222 | *h | FD | P | *GW* | OO |
| 42172 | | GN | A | *EC* | EC | | 42223 | *h | FD | P | *GW* | OO |
| 42173 | *k | FD | P | *GW* | OO | | 42224 | *k | FD | P | *GW* | OO |
| 42174 | *k | FD | P | *GW* | OO | | 42225 | u | MN | P | *EM* | NL |
| 42175 | *h | FD | FG | *GW* | LA | | 42226 | | GN | A | *EC* | EC |
| 42176 | *h | FD | FG | *GW* | LA | | 42227 | u | MN | P | *EM* | NL |
| 42177 | *h | FD | FG | *GW* | LA | | 42228 | m | NX | P | *EC* | EC |
| 42178 | *h | FD | P | *GW* | OO | | 42229 | u | MN | P | *EM* | NL |
| 42179 | m | GN | A | *EC* | EC | | 42230 | u | MN | P | *EM* | NL |

| ID | | | | | | ID | | | | | |
|---|---|---|---|---|---|---|---|---|---|---|---|
| 42231 | *h | **FD** | FG | *GW* | LA | 42287 | *k | **FD** | A | *GW* | OO |
| 42232 | *h | **FD** | FG | *GW* | LA | 42288 | *h | **FD** | A | *GW* | OO |
| 42233 | *h | **FD** | FG | *GW* | LA | 42289 | *h | **FD** | A | *GW* | OO |
| 42234 | c | **XC** | P | *XC* | EC | 42290 | c | **XC** | P | *XC* | EC |
| 42235 | m | **NX** | A | *EC* | EC | 42291 | *d | **FD** | A | *GW* | LA |
| 42236 | *h | **FD** | A | *GW* | OO | 42292 | *d | **FD** | A | *GW* | LA |
| 42237 | m | **NX** | P | *EC* | EC | 42293 | * | **FD** | A | *GW* | LA |
| 42238 | m† | **NX** | A | *EC* | EC | 42294 | | **GN** | P | | ZK |
| 42239 | m† | **NX** | A | *EC* | EC | 42295 | *d | **FD** | A | *GW* | LA |
| 42240 | m | **NX** | A | *EC* | EC | 42296 | * | **FD** | A | *GW* | LA |
| 42241 | m | **NX** | A | *EC* | EC | 42297 | * | **FD** | A | *GW* | LA |
| 42242 | m | **NX** | A | *EC* | EC | 42299 | *d | **FD** | A | *GW* | LA |
| 42243 | m | **NX** | A | *EC* | EC | 42300 | * | **FD** | A | *GW* | LA |
| 42244 | m | **NX** | A | *EC* | EC | 42301 | * | **FD** | A | *GW* | LA |
| 42245 | * | **FD** | A | *GW* | LA | 42302 | *k | **FD** | FG | *GW* | LA |
| 42247 | *h | **FD** | P | *GW* | OO | 42303 | *h | **FD** | FG | *GW* | LA |
| 42248 | *h | **FD** | P | *GW* | OO | 42304 | *h | **FD** | FG | *GW* | LA |
| 42249 | *h | **FD** | P | *GW* | OO | 42305 | *h | **FD** | FG | *GW* | LA |
| 42250 | * | **FD** | A | *GW* | LA | 42306 | m | **NX** | P | *EC* | EC |
| 42251 | *k | **FD** | A | *GW* | OO | 42307 | m | **NX** | P | *EC* | EC |
| 42252 | * | **FD** | A | *GW* | LA | 42308 | *h | **FD** | P | *GW* | OO |
| 42253 | * | **FD** | A | *GW* | LA | 42309 | *h | **FD** | P | *GW* | OO |
| 42254 | *h | **FD** | P | *GW* | OO | 42310 | *k | **FD** | P | *GW* | OO |
| 42255 | *d | **FD** | A | *GW* | LA | 42314 | *h | **FD** | P | *GW* | OO |
| 42256 | * | **FD** | A | *GW* | LA | 42315 | *h | **FD** | P | *GW* | OO |
| 42257 | * | **FD** | A | *GW* | LA | 42316 | *h | **FD** | P | *GW* | OO |
| 42258 | *h | **FD** | P | *GW* | OO | 42317 | *k | **FD** | P | *GW* | OO |
| 42259 | *k | **FD** | A | *GW* | LA | 42319 | *h | **FD** | P | *GW* | OO |
| 42260 | *h | **FD** | A | *GW* | OO | 42320 | *h | **FD** | P | *GW* | OO |
| 42261 | *h | **FD** | A | *GW* | OO | 42321 | *h | **FD** | P | *GW* | OO |
| 42262 | *h | **FD** | P | *GW* | OO | 42322 | m | **NX** | P | *EC* | EC |
| 42263 | * | **FD** | A | *GW* | LA | 42323 | m | **GN** | A | *EC* | EC |
| 42264 | *k | **FD** | A | *GW* | OO | 42324 | w | **MN** | P | *EM* | NL |
| 42265 | * | **FD** | A | *GW* | LA | 42325 | * | **FD** | A | *GW* | LA |
| 42266 | *k | **FD** | P | *GW* | OO | 42326 | m | **NX** | P | *EC* | EC |
| 42267 | *d | **FD** | A | *GW* | LA | 42327 | w | **MN** | P | *EM* | NL |
| 42268 | *d | **FD** | A | *GW* | LA | 42328 | w | **MN** | P | *EM* | NL |
| 42269 | * | **FD** | A | *GW* | LA | 42329 | w | **MN** | P | *EM* | NL |
| 42271 | *k | **FD** | A | *GW* | OO | 42330 | m | **NX** | P | *EC* | EC |
| 42272 | *h | **FD** | A | *GW* | OO | 42331 | w | **MN** | P | *EM* | NL |
| 42273 | *h | **FD** | A | *GW* | OO | 42332 | * | **FD** | A | *GW* | LA |
| 42275 | *d | **FD** | A | *GW* | LA | 42333 | * | **FD** | A | *GW* | LA |
| 42276 | * | **FD** | A | *GW* | LA | 42334 | *h | **FD** | P | *GW* | OO |
| 42277 | * | **FD** | A | *GW* | LA | 42335 | u | **MN** | P | *EM* | NL |
| 42279 | *d | **FD** | A | *GW* | LA | 42336 | *h | **FD** | P | *GW* | OO |
| 42280 | * | **FD** | A | *GW* | LA | 42337 | w | **MN** | P | *EM* | NL |
| 42281 | * | **FD** | A | *GW* | LA | 42338 | *h | **FD** | P | *GW* | OO |
| 42283 | *h | **FD** | A | *GW* | OO | 42339 | w | **MN** | P | *EM* | NL |
| 42284 | *h | **FD** | A | *GW* | OO | 42340 | m | **NX** | A | *EC* | EC |
| 42285 | *h | **FD** | A | *GW* | OO | 42341 | u | **MN** | P | *EM* | NL |
| 42286 | m† | **NX** | P | *EC* | EC | | | | | | |

| 42342 | (44082) | c | **XC** | A | *XC* | EC |
| 42343 | (44095) | * | **FD** | A | *GW* | LA |
| 42344 | (44092) | *k | **FD** | A | *GW* | OO |
| 42345 | (44096) | *d | **FD** | A | *GW* | LA |
| 42346 | (41053) | *h | **FD** | A | *GW* | OO |
| 42347 | (41054) | *k | **FD** | A | *GW* | OO |
| 42348 | (41073) | *k | **FD** | A | *GW* | OO |
| 42349 | (41074) | *h | **FD** | A | *GW* | OO |
| 42350 | (41047) | * | **FD** | A | *GW* | LA |
| 42351 | (41048) | * | **FD** | A | *GW* | LA |
| 42353 | (42001, 41171) | *k | **FD** | FG | *GW* | LA |
| 42354 | (42114, 41175) | | **GN** | A | *EC* | EC |
| 42355 | (42000, 41172) | | **GN** | A | *EC* | EC |
| 42356 | (42002, 41173) | *k | **FD** | A | *GW* | OO |
| 42357 | (41002, 41174) | | **GN** | A | *EC* | EC |
| 42360 | (44084, 45084) | *h | **FD** | A | *GW* | LA |
| 42361 | (44099, 42000) | *h | **FD** | A | *GW* | LA |
| 42362 | (42011, 41178) | *h | **FD** | A | *GW* | OO |
| 42363 | (41082) | m† | **NX** | A | *EC* | EC |
| 42364 | (41080) | * | **FD** | P | *GW* | OO |
| 42365 | (41107) | *h | **FD** | P | *GW* | OO |

42366–378 have been converted from loco-hauled Mark 3 vehicles for Cross-Country.

| 42367 | (12025) | c | **XC** | P | *XC* | EC |
| 42368 | (12028) | c | **XC** | P | *XC* | EC |
| 42369 | (12050) | c | **XC** | P | *XC* | EC |
| 42370 | (12086) | c | **XC** | P | *XC* | EC |
| 42371 | (12052) | §c | **XC** | P | *XC* | EC |
| 42372 | (12055) | c | **XC** | P | *XC* | EC |
| 42373 | (12071) | c | **XC** | P | *XC* | EC |
| 42374 | (12075) | c | **XC** | P | *XC* | EC |
| 42375 | (12113) | c | **XC** | P | *XC* | EC |
| 42376 | (12085) | §c | **XC** | P | *XC* | EC |
| 42377 | (12102) | c | **XC** | P | *XC* | EC |
| 42378 | (12123) | c | **XC** | P | *XC* | EC |
| 42379 | (41036) | §c | **XC** | A | *XC* | EC |
| 42380 | (41025) | §c | **XC** | A | *XC* | EC |
| 42381 | (41058) | | **GN** | P | | ZK |

The following coaches have been converted from loco-hauled Mark 3 vehicles for Grand Central. They have a lower density seating layout (most seats arranged around tables). Seating layouts were being altered in early 2009 and the final planned seating details are shown here. –/64 2T († –/60 1TD 1T 2W).

| 42401 | (12149) | | **GC** | ST | *GC* | HT |
| 42402 | (12155) | | **GC** | ST | *GC* | HT |
| 42403 | (12033) | † | **GC** | ST | *GC* | HT |
| 42404 | (12152) | | **GC** | ST | *GC* | HT |
| 42405 | (12136) | | **GC** | ST | *GC* | HT |
| 42406 | (12112) | † | **GC** | ST | *GC* | HT |
| 42407 | (12044) | | **GC** | ST | | ZJ |

| | | | | | | |
|---|---|---|---|---|---|---|
| 42408 | (12121) | | **GC** | ST | *GC* | HT |
| 42409 | (12088) | † | **GC** | ST | | ZJ |

# GJ2G (TGS)   TRAILER GUARD'S STANDARD

**44000.** Lot No. 30953 Derby 1980. 33.47 t.
**44001–44090.** Lot No. 30949 Derby 1980–82. 33.47 t.
**44091–44094.** Lot No. 30964 Derby 1982. 33.47 t.
**44097–44101.** Lot No. 30970 Derby 1982. 33.47 t.

As built and m –/65 1T (w –/63 1T 1W).
* Refurbished First Great Western vehicles. Grammer seating and toilet removed for trolley store. –/67 (unless h).
c Refurbished Cross-Country vehicles with Primarius seating. –/67 1T.
h "High density" FGW vehicles. –/71.
m Refurbished National Express East Coast vehicles with Primarius seating.
s Fitted with centre luggage stack –/63 1T.
t Fitted with centre luggage stack –/61 1T.

| | | | | | | | | | | | |
|---|---|---|---|---|---|---|---|---|---|---|---|
| 44000 | *h | **FD** | P | *GW* | OO | | 44033 | *h | **FD** | A | *GW* | OO |
| 44001 | * | **FD** | A | *GW* | LA | | 44034 | * | **FD** | A | *GW* | LA |
| 44002 | *h | **FD** | A | *GW* | OO | | 44035 | * | **FD** | A | *GW* | LA |
| 44003 | *h | **FD** | A | *GW* | OO | | 44036 | *h | **FD** | A | *GW* | OO |
| 44004 | *h | **FD** | A | *GW* | LA | | 44037 | *h | **FD** | A | *GW* | OO |
| 44005 | *h | **FD** | A | *GW* | LA | | 44038 | * | **FD** | A | *GW* | LA |
| 44007 | *h | **FD** | A | *GW* | LA | | 44039 | * | **FD** | A | *GW* | LA |
| 44008 | *h | **FD** | A | *GW* | OO | | 44040 | * | **FD** | A | *GW* | LA |
| 44009 | *h | **FD** | A | *GW* | LA | | 44041 | s | **MN** | P | *EM* | NL |
| 44010 | *h | **FD** | A | *GW* | LA | | 44042 | *h | **FD** | P | *GW* | OO |
| 44011 | * | **FD** | A | *GW* | LA | | 44043 | *h | **FD** | A | *GW* | OO |
| 44012 | c | **XC** | A | *XC* | EC | | 44044 | s | **MN** | P | *EM* | NL |
| 44013 | *h | **FD** | A | *GW* | OO | | 44045 | m | **NX** | A | *EC* | EC |
| 44014 | *h | **FD** | A | *GW* | OO | | 44046 | s | **MN** | P | *EM* | NL |
| 44015 | * | **FD** | A | *GW* | LA | | 44047 | s | **ST** | P | *EM* | NL |
| 44016 | *h | **FD** | A | *GW* | OO | | 44048 | s | **MN** | P | *EM* | NL |
| 44017 | c | **XC** | A | *XC* | EC | | 44049 | * | **FD** | A | *GW* | LA |
| 44018 | * | **FD** | A | *GW* | LA | | 44050 | m | **NX** | P | *EC* | EC |
| 44019 | m | **GN** | A | *EC* | EC | | 44051 | s | **MN** | P | *EM* | NL |
| 44020 | *h | **FD** | A | *GW* | OO | | 44052 | c | **XC** | P | *XC* | EC |
| 44021 | c | **XC** | P | *XC* | EC | | 44054 | s | **MN** | P | *EM* | NL |
| 44022 | *h | **FD** | A | *GW* | OO | | 44055 | *h | **FD** | FG | *GW* | LA |
| 44023 | *h | **FD** | A | *GW* | OO | | 44056 | w | **GN** | A | *EC* | EC |
| 44024 | *h | **FD** | A | *GW* | OO | | 44057 | m | **NX** | P | *EC* | EC |
| 44025 | * | **FD** | A | *GW* | LA | | 44058 | m | **GN** | A | *EC* | EC |
| 44026 | *h | **FD** | A | *GW* | OO | | 44059 | * | **FD** | A | *GW* | LA |
| 44027 | s | **MN** | P | *EM* | NL | | 44060 | *h | **FD** | P | *GW* | OO |
| 44028 | * | **FD** | A | *GW* | LA | | 44061 | m | **NX** | A | *EC* | EC |
| 44029 | * | **FD** | A | *GW* | LA | | 44063 | m | **NX** | A | *EC* | EC |
| 44030 | *h | **FD** | A | *GW* | OO | | 44064 | *h | **FD** | A | *GW* | OO |
| 44031 | w | **GN** | A | *EC* | EC | | 44065 | t | **V** | ST | | LM |
| 44032 | * | **FD** | A | *GW* | LA | | 44066 | * | **FD** | A | *GW* | LA |

| | | | | | | | | | | |
|---|---|---|---|---|---|---|---|---|---|---|
| 44067 | *h | **FD** | A | *GW* | OO | 44081 | *h | **FD** | FG | *GW* | LA |

| 44067 | *h | **FD** | A | *GW* | OO |
|---|---|---|---|---|---|
| 44068 | *h | **FD** | FG | *GW* | LA |
| 44069 | *h | **FD** | P | *GW* | OO |
| 44070 | s | **MN** | P | *EM* | NL |
| 44071 | s | **MN** | P | *EM* | NL |
| 44072 | c | **XC** | P | *XC* | EC |
| 44073 | s | **MN** | P | *EM* | NL |
| 44074 | *h | **FD** | FG | *GW* | LA |
| 44075 | m | **NX** | P | *EC* | EC |
| 44076 | *h | **FD** | FG | *GW* | LA |
| 44077 | w | **GN** | A | *EC* | EC |
| 44078 | *h | **FD** | P | *GW* | OO |
| 44079 | *h | **FD** | P | *GW* | OO |
| 44080 | w | **GN** | A | *EC* | EC |
| 44081 | *h | **FD** | FG | *GW* | LA |
| 44083 | | **GN** | P | | ZK |
| 44085 | s | **MN** | P | *EM* | NL |
| 44086 | * | **FD** | A | *GW* | LA |
| 44088 | t | **V** | ST | | LM |
| 44089 | t | **V** | ST | | LM |
| 44090 | *h | **FD** | P | *GW* | OO |
| 44091 | *h | **FD** | P | *GW* | OO |
| 44093 | *h | **FD** | A | *GW* | OO |
| 44094 | w | **GN** | A | *EC* | EC |
| 44097 | *h | **FD** | P | *GW* | OO |
| 44098 | m | **NX** | A | *EC* | EC |
| 44100 | *h | **FD** | FG | *GW* | PM |
| 44101 | *h | **FD** | P | *GW* | OO |

## GH3G (TCC)      TRAILER COMPOSITE CATERING

**45001–45005.** Lot No. 30877 Derby 1975–77. 34.3 t. Converted from Mark 3A TSO. Refurbished Cross-Country vehicles with Primarius seating. Galley for the preparation of hot food and stowage space for two trolleys between First and Standard Class sections. One toilet removed. 30/10 1T.

| 45001 | (12004) | c | **XC** | P | *XC* | EC |
|---|---|---|---|---|---|---|
| 45002 | (12106) | c | **XC** | P | *XC* | EC |
| 45003 | (12076) | c | **XC** | P | *XC* | EC |
| 45004 | (12077) | c | **XC** | P | *XC* | EC |
| 45005 | (12080) | c | **XC** | P | *XC* | EC |

# 2.3. HST SET FORMATIONS

## FIRST GREAT WESTERN

The largest operator of HSTs is First Great Western with 53 sets to cover 48 diagrams (plus two standby sets, one at Old Oak Common and one at Bristol St Philip's Marsh). There are 16 "low density" sets, designed for working longer distance West Country services. The rest of the sets are "high density" for other services. A small number of sets have had their buffet cars removed for Paddington–Oxford services, spare buffets are often used in sets OC45–OC49. 18 vehicles are under conversion to Trailer Standard Buffets and these will be formed into high density sets throughout 2009 in place of full buffet vehicles.

**Number of sets:** 53. OC50 (ex-EC64) is currently being refurbished.
**Maximum number of daily diagrams:** 50.
**Formations:** Mostly 8-cars plus a small number of 7-cars (no buffet).
**Allocation:** Laira (Plymouth) or Old Oak Common (London).
**Other maintenance and servicing depots:** Landore (Swansea), St. Philip's Marsh (Bristol), Long Rock (Penzance).
**Operation:** London Paddington–Exeter/Plymouth/Penzance, Bristol, Cardiff/Swansea/West Wales, Oxford/Hereford/Malvern/Gloucester.

| Set | H | G | F | E | D | C | B | A | density |
|-----|-----|-----|-----|-----|-----|-----|-----|-----|---------|
| LA01 | 41023 | 41024 | 40755 | 42007 | 42033 | 42034 | 42035 | 44011 | L |
| LA02 | 41031 | 41032 | 40727 | 42207 | 42045 | 42046 | 42047 | 44015 | L |
| LA03 | 41037 | 41038 | 40757 | 42292 | 42343 | 42055 | 42056 | 44018 | L |
| LA04 | 41051 | 41052 | 40710 | 42004 | 42076 | 42077 | 42078 | 44025 | L |
| LA05 | 41093 | 41094 | 40707 | 42183 | 42184 | 42185 | 42107 | 44001 | L |
| LA06 | 41103 | 41104 | 40713 | 42206 | 42054 | 42208 | 42209 | 44066 | L |
| LA07 | 41121 | 41122 | 40722 | 42345 | 42019 | 42252 | 42253 | 44028 | L |
| LA08 | 41123 | 41124 | 40739 | 42255 | 42263 | 42256 | 42257 | 44029 | L |
| LA09 | 41129 | 41130 | 40716 | 42267 | 42325 | 42072 | 42269 | 44032 | L |
| LA10 | 41133 | 41134 | 40721 | 42275 | 42332 | 42276 | 42277 | 44034 | L |
| LA11 | 41116 | 41135 | 40703 | 42279 | 42265 | 42280 | 42281 | 44035 | L |
| LA12 | 41003 | 41136 | 40752 | 42268 | 42143 | 42144 | 42145 | 44049 | L |
| LA13 | 41141 | 41142 | 40734 | 42291 | 42075 | 42333 | 42293 | 44038 | L |
| LA14 | 41143 | 41144 | 40733 | 42295 | 42350 | 42296 | 42297 | 44039 | L |
| LA15 | 41145 | 41146 | 40715 | 42299 | 42351 | 42300 | 42301 | 44040 | L |
| LA16 | 41157 | 41158 | 40743 | 42200 | 42129 | 42245 | 42250 | 44086 | L |
| OC30 | 41007 | 41008 | 40747 | 42264 | 42236 | 42079 | 42080 | 44026 | H |
| OC31 | 41127 | 41128 | 40717 | 42347 | 42197 | 42060 | 42061 | 44020 | H |
| OC32 | 41017 | 41018 | 40208 | 42024 | 42362 | 42025 | 42026 | 44008 | H |
| OC33 | 41027 | 41028 | 40725 | 42348 | 42039 | 42040 | 42041 | 44013 | H |
| OC34 | 41101 | 41102 | 40712 | 42201 | 42027 | 42203 | 42204 | 44064 | H |
| OC35 | 41105 | 41106 | 40714 | 42211 | 42212 | 42213 | 42214 | 44067 | H |
| OC36 | 41004 | 41110 | 40209 | 42138 | 42349 | 42346 | 42089 | 44003 | H |
| OC37 | 41131 | 41132 | 40736 | 42271 | 42073 | 42272 | 42273 | 44033 | H |
| OC38 | 41137 | 41138 | 40228 | 42202 | 42003 | 42284 | 42285 | 44036 | H |

| | | | | | | | | | |
|---|---|---|---|---|---|---|---|---|---|
| OC39 | 41179 | 41180 | 40745 | 42251 | 42098 | 42196 | 42283 | 44093 | H |
| OC40 | 41181 | 41149 | 40801 | 42174 | 42170 | 42162 | 42166 | 44079 | H |
| OC41 | 41109 | 41182 | 40802 | 42224 | 42223 | 42334 | 42222 | 44101 | H |
| OC42 | 41168 | 41183 | 40803 | 42317 | 42315 | 42314 | 42316 | 44090 | H |
| OC43 | 41186 | 41147 | 40806 | 42266 | 42262 | 42254 | 42258 | 44000 | H |
| OC44 | 41191 | 41192 | 40808 | 42218 | 42115 | 42187 | 42084 | 44097 | H |
| OC45 | 41114 | 41187 | | 42173 | 42247 | 42248 | 42249 | 44078 | H |
| OC46 | 41096 | 41161 | | 42195 | 42178 | 42336 | 42338 | 44042 | H |
| OC47 | 41081 | 41108 | | 42217 | 42308 | 42309 | 42090 | 44060 | H |
| OC48 | 41184 | 41189 | | 42310 | 42285 | 42086 | 42087 | 44069 | H |
| OC49 | 41148 | 41169 | | 42356 | 42319 | 42320 | 42321 | 44091 | H |
| OC50 | 41153 | 41176 | 40116 | | 42102 | 42381 | 42101 | 44083 | H* |
| OC51 | 41005 | 41006 | 40744 | 42069 | 42070 | 42071 | 42118 | 44023 | H |
| OC52 | 41029 | 41030 | 40726 | 42008 | 42042 | 42043 | 42044 | 44014 | H |
| OC53 | 41033 | 41034 | 40731 | 42066 | 42048 | 42049 | 42050 | 44016 | H |
| OC54 | 41055 | 41056 | 40709 | 42081 | 42074 | 42083 | 42126 | 44043 | H |
| OC55 | 41065 | 41089 | 40738 | 42062 | 42221 | 42067 | 42068 | 44022 | H |
| OC56 | 41125 | 41126 | 40724 | 42344 | 42216 | 42260 | 42261 | 44030 | H |
| OC57 | 41139 | 41140 | 40718 | 42287 | 42099 | 42288 | 42289 | 44037 | H |
| LA60 | 41114 | 41162 | 40900 | 42353 | 42232 | 42231 | 42233 | 44074 | H |
| LA61 | 41086 | 41160 | 40901 | 42302 | 42303 | 42304 | 42305 | 44068 | H |
| LA62 | 41085 | 41167 | 40902 | 42103 | 42167 | 42168 | 42169 | 44055 | H |
| LA63 | 41045 | 41059 | 40903 | 42105 | 42175 | 42176 | 42177 | 44081 | H |
| LA64 | 41163 | 41166 | 40904 | 42092 | 42093 | 42094 | 42108 | 44076 | H |
| LA71 | 41009 | 41010 | 40204 | 42012 | 42360 | 42013 | 42014 | 44004 | H |
| LA72 | 41011 | 41012 | 40205 | 42015 | 42005 | 42016 | 42361 | 44005 | H |
| LA73 | 41015 | 41016 | 40207 | 42021 | 42096 | 42006 | 42023 | 44007 | H |
| LA74 | 41019 | 41020 | 40221 | 42259 | 42009 | 42028 | 42029 | 44009 | H |
| LA75 | 41021 | 41022 | 40210 | 42030 | 42010 | 42031 | 42032 | 44010 | H |

* Being refurbished at Brush-Barclay, Kilmarnock. Due into traffic in May 2009.

Spares:

OO:   41155   42294   42364   42365   44002   44024
LA:   40231   40809   40810   40811   42095   44059
PM:   44100

**Note:** 18 coaches will be converted to Trailer Standard Buffets numbered in the 40101–40118 series during 2009. These will run in 7-car OC rakes with 16 unrefurbished 402xx and 407xx buffets going off-lease.

# NETWORK RAIL: NEW MEASUREMENT TRAIN

The Network Rail "New Measurement Train" is used to test and evaluate Britain's main railway lines.

977984   977994   977993   975814   975984

**Spare:** 977995

## NATIONAL EXPRESS EAST COAST

National Express East Coast took over operation of the GNER HST fleet in December 2007. As well as serving non-electrified destinations such as Hull and Inverness the NXEC HSTs also work alongside Class 91s and Mark 4 sets on services to Leeds and Newcastle. Sets are continuing to be refurbished at Wabtec, Doncaster to "Mallard" standard. Those refurbished are shown below (i.e. M1 was the first refurbished Mallard set).

**Number of sets:** 13.
**Maximum number of daily diagrams:** 11.
**Formations:** 9-cars.
**Allocation:** Craigentinny (Edinburgh).
**Other maintenance depot:** Neville Hill (Leeds).
**Operation:** London King's Cross–Leeds/Harrogate/Skipton/Hull/Newcastle/Edinburgh/Aberdeen/Inverness.

| Set | M | L | J | G | F | E | D | C | B | Ref |
|-----|-----|-----|-----|-----|-----|-----|-----|-----|-----|-----|
| EC51 | 41120 | 41150 | 40748 | 42215 | 42091 | 42146 | 42150 | 42154 | 44094 | |
| EC52 | 41039 | 41040 | 40735 | 42323 | 42189 | 42057 | 42058 | 42059 | 44019 | M3 |
| EC53 | 41090 | 41044 | 40737 | 42340 | 42127 | 42063 | 42064 | 42065 | 44045 | M9 |
| EC54 | 41087 | 41088 | 40706 | 42104 | 42161 | 42171 | 42172 | 42219 | 44056 | |
| EC55 | 41091 | 41092 | 40704 | 42179 | 42188 | 42180 | 42181 | 42106 | 44058 | M4 |
| EC56 | 41170 | 41118 | 40720 | 42241 | 42363 | 42242 | 42243 | 42244 | 44098 | M8 |
| EC57 | 41151 | 41152 | 40740 | 42226 | 42128 | 42182 | 42186 | 42190 | 44080 | |
| EC58 | 41097 | 41098 | 40750 | 42158 | 42238 | 42191 | 42192 | 42193 | 44061 | M2 |
| EC59 | 41099 | 41100 | 40711 | 42235 | 42239 | 42240 | 42198 | 42199 | 44063 | M5 |
| EC60 | 41066 | 41164 | 40742 | 42122 | 42116 | 42357 | 42134 | 42355 | 44031 | |
| EC61 | 41115 | 41165 | 40702 | 42117 | 42159 | 42160 | 42109 | 42110 | 44057 | M1 |
| EC62 | 41185 | 41095 | 40701 | 42306 | 42326 | 42330 | 42237 | 42307 | 44075 | M7 |
| EC63 | 41159 | 41083 | 40708 | 42163 | 42286 | 42228 | 42130 | 42322 | 44050 | M6 |

Spares:
EC:   40705 40805 41190 42354 44077

## GRAND CENTRAL

Grand Central started running services from Sunderland to London in December 2007 and by summer 2008 all three sets were available for use, although three coaches were still awaiting delivery following refurbishment at Marcroft (41203, 42407 and 42409).

**Number of sets:** 3.
**Maximum number of daily diagrams:** 2.
**Formations:** 5-cars.
**Allocation:** Heaton (Newcastle).
**Operation:** London King's Cross–Sunderland

| Set | TF | TRSB | TS(D) | TS | TS |
|-----|-----|-----|-----|-----|-----|
| GC01 | 41204 | 40424 | 42403 | 42402 | 42401 |
| GC02 | 41205 | 40426 | 42406 | 42405 | 42404 |
| GC03 | 41206 | 40433 | 42408 | 41202* | 41201* * declassified |

# EAST MIDLANDS TRAINS

From the December 2008 timetable East Midlands Trains HSTs are concentrated on the Nottingham corridor during the day, with early morning and evening services to Leeds for servicing at Neville Hill.

**Number of sets:** 11.
**Maximum number of daily diagrams:** 9.
**Formations:** 8-cars and one 6-car to act as a "hot spare".
**Allocation:** Neville Hill (Leeds).
**Other maintenance depot:** Derby Etches Park.
**Operation:** London St. Pancras–Nottingham, Sheffield/Leeds.

| Set | J | G | F | E | D | C | B | A |
|-----|------|------|------|------|------|------|------|------|
| NL01 | 41057 | 41084 | 40746 | 42335 | 42111 | 42112 | 42113 | 44041 |
| NL02 | 41112 | 41067 | 40754 | 42194 | 42229 | 42227 | 42225 | 44027 |
| NL03 | 41061 | 41068 | | 42337 | 42119 | 42120 | | 44054 |
| NL04 | 41077 | 41064 | 40749 | 42151 | 42164 | 42165 | 42153 | 44047 |
| NL05 | 41062 | 41154 | 40741 | 42327 | 42123 | 42205 | 42210 | 44073 |
| NL06 | 41156 | 41041 | 40730 | 42331 | 42131 | 42132 | 42133 | 44046 |
| NL07 | 41111 | 41070 | 40751 | 42339 | 42135 | 42136 | 42137 | 44044 |
| NL08 | 41071 | 41072 | 40728 | 42329 | 42139 | 42140 | 42141 | 44042 |
| NL10 | 41075 | 41076 | 40756 | 42328 | 42341 | 42148 | 42149 | 44085 |
| NL11 | 41117 | 41046 | 40753 | 42220 | 42152 | 42230 | 42124 | 44051 |
| NL12 | 41079 | 41069 | 40700 | 42155 | 42156 | 42157 | 42100 | 44070 |

Spares:
NL: 40729 41063 41078 41113 42121 42125 42324 44071

# CROSS-COUNTRY

Cross-Country reintroduced regular HST diagrams on its services from the December 2008 timetable. XC05 was due for release in February 2009 and its formation was to be confirmed at the time of writing.

**Number of sets:** 5.
**Maximum number of daily diagrams:** 4 or 5.
**Formations:** 8-cars.
**Allocation:** Craigentinny (Edinburgh).
**Other maintenance depots:** Laira (Plymouth) or Neville Hill (Leeds).
**Operation:** Edinburgh–Leeds–Plymouth is the core route with some services extending to Dundee or Penzance.

| Set | A | B | C | D | E | F | G | H |
|-----|------|------|------|------|------|------|------|------|
| XC01 | 41193 | 45001 | 42368 | 42369 | 42370 | 42367 | 42366 | 44021 |
| XC02 | 41194 | 45002 | 42375 | 42374 | 42373 | 42372 | 42371 | 44072 |
| XC03 | 41195 | 45003 | 42290 | 42234 | 42377 | 42376 | 42376 | 44052 |
| XC04 | 41026 | 45004 | 42038 | 42097 | 42037 | 42036 | 42380 | 44012 |
| XC05 | 41035 | 45005 | *42051* | *42052* | *42053* | *42342* | 42379 | 44017 |

# 2.4. SALOONS

Several specialist passenger carrying vehicles, normally referred to as saloons are permitted to run on the National Rail system. Many of these are to pre-nationalisation designs.

## WCJS FIRST SALOON

Built 1892 by LNWR, Wolverton. Originally dining saloon mounted on six-wheel bogies. Rebuilt with new underframe with four-wheel bogies in 1927. Rebuilt 1960 as observation saloon with DMU end. Gangwayed at other end. The interior has a saloon, kitchen, guards vestibule and observation lounge. Gresley bogies. 19/– 1T. 28.5 t. 75 m.p.h.

**Non-standard livery:** London & North Western Railway.

41      (484, 45018)      x   **0**     WC  *WC*    CJ

## LNWR DINING SALOON

Built 1890 by LNWR, Wolverton. Mounted on the underframe of LMS GUV 37908 in the 1980s. Contains kitchen and dining area seating 12 at tables for two. Gresley bogies. 10/–. 75 m.p.h. 25.4 t.

**Non-standard livery:** London & North Western Railway.

159     (5159)           x   **0**     WC  *WC*    CJ

## GNR FIRST CLASS SALOON

Built 1912 by GNR, Doncaster. Contains entrance vestibule, lavatory, two separate saloons, library and luggage space. Gresley bogies. 19/– 1T. 75 m.p.h. 29.4 t.

**Non-standard livery:** Teak.

807     (4807)           x   **0**     WC  *WC*    CJ

## LNER GENERAL MANAGERS SALOON

Built 1945 by LNER, York. Gangwayed at one end with a veranda at the other. The interior has a dining saloon seating 12, kitchen, toilet, office and nine seat lounge. 21/– 1T. B4 bogies. 75 m.p.h. ETH3. 35.7 t.

1999    (902260)         **M**   GS  *GS*    CS        DINING CAR No. 2

## GENERAL MANAGER'S SALOON

Renumbered 1989 from London Midland Region departmental series. Formerly the LMR General Manager's saloon. Rebuilt from LMS period 1 BFK M 5033 M to dia. 1654 and mounted on the underframe of BR suburban BS M 43232. Screw couplings have been removed. B4 bogies. 100 m.p.h. ETH2X.

LMS Lot No. 326 Derby 1927. 27.5 t.

6320   (5033, DM 395707) x   **M**   62   *62*   SK

## GWR FIRST CLASS SALOON

Built 1930 by GWR, Swindon. Contains saloons at either end with body end observation windows, staff compartment, central kitchen and pantry/bar. Numbered DE321011 when in departmental service with British Railways. 20/– 1T. GWR bogies. 75 m.p.h. 34 t.

GWR Lot No. 1431 1930.

9004      **CH**   RA   *WC*   CJ

## LMS INSPECTION SALOON

Built as engineers' inspection saloon. Non-gangwayed. Observation windows at each end. The interior layout consists of two saloons interspersed by a central lavatory/kitchen/guards section. B5 bogies. 80 m.p.h. 31.5 t.

**Non-standard livery:** EWS dark maroon.

LMS Lot No. 1356 Wolverton 1944.

45020           **0**   DB   *DB*   TO

## "QUEEN OF SCOTS" SERVICE CARS

Converted from BR Mark 1 BSKs. Commonwealth bogies. 100 m.p.h. ETH2.

**Non-standard livery:** London & North Western Railway.

**99035.** Lot No. 30699 Wolverton 1962–63.
**99886.** Lot No. 30721 Wolverton 1963.

99035 (35322)   x   **0**   WC   *WC*   CJ          SERVICE CAR No. 2
99886 (35407)   x   **0**   WC   *WC*   CJ          SERVICE CAR No. 1

# VSOE SUPPORT CAR

Converted 199? from Courier vehicle converted from Mark 1 BSK 1986–87. Toilet retained and former compartment area replaced with train manager's office, crew locker room, linen store and dry goods store. The former luggage area has been adapted for use as an engineers' compartment and workshop. Commonwealth bogies. 100 m.p.h. ETH2.

Lot No. 30721 Wolverton 1963. 37 t.

| | | | | | |
|---|---|---|---|---|---|
| 99545 (35466, 80207) | **PC** | VS | *VS* | SL | BAGGAGE CAR No. 11 |

# ROYAL SCOTSMAN SALOONS

Built 1960 by Metro-Cammell as Pullman Parlour First (§ Pullman Kitchen First) for East Coast Main Line services. Rebuilt 1990 as sleeping cars with four twin sleeping rooms (*§ three twin sleeping rooms and two single sleeping rooms at each end). Commonwealth bogies. 38.5 t.

| | | | | | |
|---|---|---|---|---|---|
| 99961 (324 AMBER) * | **M** | GS | *GS* | CS | STATE CAR 1 |
| 99962 (329 PEARL) | **M** | GS | *GS* | CS | STATE CAR 2 |
| 99963 (331 TOPAZ) | **M** | GS | *GS* | CS | STATE CAR 3 |
| 99964 (313 FINCH) § | **M** | GS | *GS* | CS | STATE CAR 4 |

Built 1960 by Metro-Cammell as Pullman Kitchen First for East Coast Main Line services. Rebuilt 1990 as observation car with open verandah seating 32. Commonwealth bogies. 38.5 t.

| | | | | | |
|---|---|---|---|---|---|
| 99965 (319 SNIPE) | **M** | GS | *GS* | CS | OBSERVATION CAR |

Built 1960 by Metro-Cammell as Pullman Kitchen First for East Coast Main Line services. Rebuilt 1993 as dining car. Commonwealth bogies. 38.5 t.

| | | | | | |
|---|---|---|---|---|---|
| 99967 (317 RAVEN) | **M** | GS | *GS* | CS | DINING CAR |

Mark 3A. Converted from SLEP at Carnforth Railway Restoration and Engineering Services in 1997. BT10 bogies. Attendant's and adjacent two sleeping compartments converted to generator room containing a 160 kW Volvo unit. In 99968 four sleeping compartments remain for staff use with another converted for use as a staff shower and toilet. The remaining five sleeping compartments have been replaced by two passenger cabins. In 99969 seven sleeping compartments remain for staff use. A further sleeping compartment, along with one toilet, have been converted to store rooms. The other two sleeping compartments have been combined to form a crew mess. ETH7X. 41.5 t.

Lot. No. 30960 Derby 1981–3.

| | | | | | |
|---|---|---|---|---|---|
| 99968 (10541) | **M** | GS | *GS* | CS | STATE CAR 5 |
| 99969 (10556) | **M** | GS | *GS* | CS | SERVICE CAR |

## RAILFILMS "LMS CLUB CAR"

Converted from BR Mark 1 TSO at Carnforth Railway Restoration and Engineering Services in 1994. Contains kitchen, pantry and two dining saloons. 20/– 1T. Commonwealth bogies. 100 m.p.h. ETH 4.

Lot. No. 30724 York 1963. 37 t.

99993 (5067)           **M**    RA   *WC*    CS              LMS CLUB CAR

## BR INSPECTION SALOON

Mark 1. Short frames. Non-gangwayed. Observation windows at each end. The interior layout consists of two saloons interspersed by a central lavatory/kitchen/guards/luggage section. 90 m.p.h.

BR Wagon Lot No.  3095 Swindon 1957. B4 bogies. 30.5 t.

999506                 **M**    WC   *WC*    CS

# 2.5. PULLMAN CAR COMPANY SERIES

Pullman cars have never generally been numbered as such, although many have carried numbers, instead they have carried titles. However, a scheme of schedule numbers exists which generally lists cars in chronological order. In this section those numbers are shown followed by the car's title. Cars described as "kitchen" contain a kitchen in addition to passenger accommodation and have gas cooking unless otherwise stated. Cars described as "parlour" consist entirely of passenger accommodation. Cars described as "brake" contain a compartment for the use of the guard and a luggage compartment in addition to passenger accommodation.

## PULLMAN PARLOUR FIRST

Built 1927 by Midland Carriage & Wagon Company. Gresley bogies. 26/– 2T. ETH 2. 41 t.

| 213 | MINERVA | **PC** | VS | *VS* | SL |

## PULLMAN PARLOUR FIRST

Built 1928 by Metropolitan Carriage & Wagon Company. Gresley bogies. 24/– 2T. ETH 4. 40 t.

| 239 | AGATHA | **PC** | VS | | SL |
| 243 | LUCILLE | **PC** | VS | *VS* | SL |

## PULLMAN KITCHEN FIRST

Built 1925 by BRCW. Rebuilt by Midland Carriage & Wagon Company in 1928. Gresley bogies. 20/– 1T. ETH 4. 41 t.

| 245 | IBIS | **PC** | VS | *VS* | SL |

## PULLMAN PARLOUR FIRST

Built 1928 by Metropolitan Carriage & Wagon Company. Gresley bogies. 24/– 2T. ETH 4.

| 254 | ZENA | **PC** | VS | *VS* | SL |

## PULLMAN KITCHEN FIRST

Built 1928 by Metropolitan Carriage & Wagon Company. Gresley bogies. 20/– 1T. ETH 4. 42 t.

| 255 | IONE | **PC** | VS | *VS* | SL |

## PULLMAN KITCHEN COMPOSITE

Built 1932 by Metropolitan Carriage & Wagon Company. Originally included in 6-Pul EMU. Electric cooking. EMU bogies. 12/16 1T.

| 264 | RUTH | | **PC** | VS | | SL |
|-----|------|---|--------|----|----|----|

## PULLMAN KITCHEN FIRST

Built 1932 by Metropolitan Carriage & Wagon Company. Originally included in "Brighton Belle" EMUs but now used as hauled stock. Electric cooking. B5 (SR) bogies (§ EMU bogies). 20/– 1T. ETH 2. 44 t.

| 280 | AUDREY | | **PC** | VS | *VS* | SL |
|-----|--------|---|--------|----|----|----|
| 281 | GWEN | | **PC** | VS | *VS* | SL |
| 283 | MONA | § | **PC** | VS | | SL |
| 284 | VERA | | **PC** | VS | *VS* | SL |

## PULLMAN PARLOUR THIRD

Built 1932 by Metropolitan Carriage & Wagon Company. Originally included in "Brighton Belle" EMUs. EMU bogies. –/56 2T.

| 286 | CAR No. 86 | **PC** | VS | | SL |
|-----|-----------|--------|----|----|----|

## PULLMAN BRAKE THIRD

Built 1932 by Metropolitan Carriage & Wagon Company. Originally driving motor cars in "Brighton Belle" EMUs. Traction and control equipment removed for use as hauled stock. EMU bogies. –/48 1T.

| 288 | CAR No. 88 | **PC** | VS | | SL |
|-----|-----------|--------|----|----|----|
| 292 | CAR No. 92 | **PC** | VS | | SL |
| 293 | CAR No. 93 | **PC** | VS | | SL |

## PULLMAN PARLOUR FIRST

Built 1951 by Birmingham Railway Carriage & Wagon Company. Gresley bogies. 32/– 2T. ETH 3. 39 t.

| 301 | PERSEUS | **PC** | VS | *VS* | SL |
|-----|---------|--------|----|----|----|

Built 1952 by Pullman Car Company, Preston Park using underframe and bogies from 176 RAINBOW, the body of which had been destroyed by fire. Gresley bogies. 26/– 2T. ETH 4. 38 t.

| 302 | PHOENIX | **PC** | VS | *VS* | SL |
|-----|---------|--------|----|----|----|

## PULLMAN PARLOUR FIRST

Built 1951 by Birmingham Railway Carriage & Wagon Company. Gresley
bogies. 32/– 2T. ETH 3. 39 t.

308  CYGNUS              **PC**  VS  *VS*  SL

## PULLMAN FIRST BAR

Built 1951 by Birmingham Railway Carriage & Wagon Company. Rebuilt 1999
by Blake Fabrications, Edinburgh with original timber-framed body replaced
by a new fabricated steel body. Contains kitchen, bar, dining saloon and coupé.
Electric cooking. Gresley bogies. 14/– 1T. ETH 3.

310  PEGASUS            **PC**  RA  *WT*  OM

Also carries "THE TRIANON BAR" branding.

## PULLMAN KITCHEN SECOND

Built 1960–1961 by Metro-Cammell for East Coast Main Line services.
Commonwealth bogies. –/30 1T. 40 t.

335  CAR No. 335     x  **PC**  VT  *VT*  TM

## PULLMAN PARLOUR SECOND

Built 1960–1961 by Metro-Cammell for East Coast Main Line services.
Commonwealth bogies. 348 and 350 are used as FOs. –/42 2T. 38.5 t.

| 348 | CAR No. 348 | x | **M**  | WC | *WC* | CS |
|-----|-------------|---|--------|----|------|----|
| 349 | CAR No. 349 | x | **PC** | VT | *VT* | TM |
| 350 | CAR No. 350 | x | **M**  | WC | *WC* | CS |
| 353 | CAR No. 353 | x | **PC** | VT | *VT* | TM |

## PULLMAN SECOND BAR

Built 1960–1961 by Metro-Cammell for East Coast Main Line services.
Commonwealth bogies. –/24 + 17 bar seats. 38.5 t.

354  THE HADRIAN BAR  x  **PC**  WC  *WC*  CS

# 2.6. LOCOMOTIVE SUPPORT COACHES

These carriages have been adapted from Mark 1 BCK, BFK, BSK, NNX and Mark 2 BFK for use as support carriages for heritage steam locomotives. Some seating is retained for the use of personnel supporting the locomotives operation with the remainder of the carriage adapted for storage, workshop, dormitory and catering purposes. These carriages can spend considerable periods of time off the national railway system when the locomotives they support are not being used on that system. After the depot code, the locomotive(s) each carriage is usually used to support is given. Operator codes are not included in this section. Seating capacities refer to the original vehicle as running in normal service.

## AB11 (BFK)                      CORRIDOR BRAKE FIRST

Mark 1. 24/– 1T. Commonwealth bogies. ETH 2.

**14007.** Lot No. 30382 Swindon 1959. 35 t.
**17013–17019.** Lot No. 30668 Swindon 1961. 36 t.
**17025.** Lot No. 30718 Swindon 1963. Metal window frames. 36 t.

| | | | | | | |
|---|---|---|---|---|---|---|
| 14007 | (14007, 17007) | x | **M** | B1 | BH | LNER 61264/New build 60163 |
| 17013 | (14013) | x | **PC** | JH | SO | LNER 60019      BUTARUS |
| 17019 | (14019) | x | **M** | 92 | CS | BR 70013/SR 30777 |
| 17025 | (14025) | v | **M** | PO | BQ | LMS 45690 |

## AB1Z (BFK)                      CORRIDOR BRAKE FIRST

Mark 2. Pressure ventilated. 24/– 1T. B4 bogies. ETH 4.

Lot No. 30756 Derby 1966. 31.5 t.

| | | | | | |
|---|---|---|---|---|---|
| 17041 | (14041) | **M** | DG | BQ | BR 71000 |

## AB1A (BFK)                      CORRIDOR BRAKE FIRST

Mark 2A. Pressure ventilated. 24/– 1T. B4 bogies. ETH 4.

Lot No. 30786 Derby 1968. 32 t.

| | | | | | | |
|---|---|---|---|---|---|---|
| 17096 | (14096) | **PC** | MN | SL | SR 35028 | MERCATOR |

## AB31 (BCK)          CORRIDOR BRAKE COMPOSITE

Mark 1. Two First Class and three standard class compartments. 12/18 2T (* 12/24 2T). ETH 2.

**21096.** Lot No. 30185 Metro-Cammell 1956. BR Mark 1 bogies. 32.5 t.
**21232.** Lot No. 30574 GRCW 1960. B4 bogies. 34 t.
**21268.** Lot No. 30732 Derby 1964. Commonwealth bogies. 37 t.

| | | | | | |
|---|---|---|---|---|---|
| 21096 | | x | **M** | A4 | NY | LNER 60007 |
| 21232 | | x | **CC** | 62 | SK | LMS 46233 |

| | | | | | |
|---|---|---|---|---|---|
| 21268 | * | | BS | SO | LMS 46100 |

## AB21 (BSK)  CORRIDOR BRAKE STANDARD

Mark 1. Four compartments. Metal window frames and melamine interior panelling. –/24 1T. ETH2.

**35333.** Lot No. 30699 Wolverton 1962–63. Commonwealth bogies. 37 t.
**35449.** Lot No. 30728 Wolverton 1963. Commonwealth bogies. 37 t.
**35453–35486.** Lot No. 30721 Wolverton 1963. Commonwealth bogies. 37 t.

| | | | | | |
|---|---|---|---|---|---|
| 35333 | x | **CH** | 24 | DI | GWR 6024 |
| 35449 | x | **M** | BE | BQ | LMS 45231 |
| 35453 | x | **CH** | GW | DI | GWR 5051 |
| 35461 | x | **CH** | JH | TM | GWR 5029 |
| 35463 | v | **M** | WC | CS | GWR 5972/LMS 46115/LMS 48151 |
| 35465 | v | **CC** | LW | BQ | LMS 46201 |
| 35468 | v | **M** | NM | YK | National Railway Museum locomotives |
| 35470 | v | **CH** | VT | TM | Tyseley Locomotive Works-based locomotives |
| 35476 | v | **M** | 62 | SK | LMS 46233 |
| 35479 | v | **CH** | SV | KR | Severn Valley Railway-based locomotives |
| 35486 | x | **M** | JC | TN | LNER 60009/61994 |

## AB1C (BFK)  CORRIDOR BRAKE FIRST

Mark 2C. Pressure ventilated. Renumbered when declassified. –/24 1T. B4 bogies. ETH 4.

Lot No. 30796 Derby 1969–70. 32.5 t.

| | | | | | |
|---|---|---|---|---|---|
| 35508 | (14128, 17128) | **M** | IR | BQ | LMS 45407/BR 76079 |

## AB1A (BFK)  CORRIDOR BRAKE FIRST

Mark 2A. Pressure ventilated. Renumbered when declassified. –/24 1T. B4 bogies. Cage removed from brake compartment. ETH 4.

Lot No. 30786 Derby 1968. 32 t.

| | | | | | |
|---|---|---|---|---|---|
| 35517 | (14088, 17088) | **M** | IR | BQ | LMS 45407/BR 76079 |
| 35518 | (14097, 17097) | **G** | 67 | SO | SR 34067 |

## NNX  COURIER VEHICLE

Mark 1. Converted 1986–7 from BSKs. One compartment and toilet retained for courier use. One set of roller shutter doors inserted on each side. ETH 2.

**80204/17.** Lot No. 30699 Wolverton 1962. Commonwealth bogies. 37 t.
**80220.** Lot No. 30573 Gloucester 1960. B4 bogies. 33 t.

| | | | | | |
|---|---|---|---|---|---|
| 80204 | (35297) | **M** | WC | CS | GWR 5972/LMS46115/LMS 48151 |
| 80217 | (35299) | **M** | WC | CS | GWR 5972/LMS46115/LMS 48151 |
| 80220 | (35276) | **M** | NE | NY | LNER 62005 |

# 2.7. 99xxx RANGE NUMBER CONVERSION TABLE

The following table is presented to help readers identify vehicles which may carry numbers in the 99xxx range, the former private owner number series which is no longer in general use.

| 99xxx | BR No. | 99xxx | BR No. | 99xxx | BR No. |
|-------|--------|-------|--------|-------|--------|
| 99040 | 21232 | 99348 | Pullman 348 | 99671 | 548 |
| 99041 | 35476 | 99349 | Pullman 349 | 99672 | 549 |
| 99052 | Saloon 41 | 99350 | Pullman 350 | 99673 | 550 |
| 99121 | 3105 | 99353 | Pullman 353 | 99674 | 551 |
| 99125 | 3113 | 99354 | Pullman 354 | 99675 | 552 |
| 99127 | 3117 | 99361 | Pullman 335 | 99676 | 553 |
| 99128 | 3130 | 99371 | 3128 | 99677 | 586 |
| 99131 | 1999 | 99530 | Pullman 301 | 99678 | 504 |
| 99141 | 17041 | 99531 | Pullman 302 | 99679 | 506 |
| 99241 | 35449 | 99532 | Pullman 308 | 99680 | 17102 |
| 99304 | 21256 | 99534 | Pullman 245 | 99710 | 18767 |
| 99311 | 1882 | 99535 | Pullman 213 | 99716 | 18808 |
| 99312 | 35463 | 99536 | Pullman 254 | 99718 | 18862 |
| 99316 | 13321 | 99537 | Pullman 280 | 99721 | 18756 |
| 99317 | 3766 | 99539 | Pullman 255 | 99722 | 18806 |
| 99318 | 4912 | 99541 | Pullman 243 | 99723 | 35459 |
| 99319 | 17168 | 99543 | Pullman 284 | 99792 | 17019 |
| 99326 | 4954 | 99546 | Pullman 281 | 99880 | 159 |
| 99327 | 5044 | 99547 | Pullman 292 | 99881 | 807 |
| 99328 | 5033 | 99548 | Pullman 293 | 99953 | 35468 |
| 99329 | 4931 | 99670 | 546 | | |

# 2.8. MARK 4 SET FORMATIONS

The National Express East Coast Mark 4 sets generally run in fixed formations since their refurbishment at Bombardier, Wakefield (2003–05). These rakes are listed below. Class 91 locomotives are positioned next to Coach B.

| Set | B | C | D | E | F | H | K | L | M | DVT |
|-----|---|---|---|---|---|---|---|---|---|-----|
| BN01 | 12207 | 12417 | 12415 | 12414 | 12307 | 10307 | 11298 | 11301 | 11401 | 82207 |
| BN02 | 12232 | 12402 | 12450 | 12448 | 12302 | 10302 | 11299 | 11302 | 11402 | 82202 |
| BN03 | 12201 | 12401 | 12459 | 12478 | 12301 | 10320 | 11277 | 11303 | 11403 | 82219 |
| BN04 | 12202 | 12480 | 12421 | 12518 | 12327 | 10303 | 11278 | 11304 | 11404 | 82209 |
| BN05 | 12209 | 12486 | 12520 | 12522 | 12300 | 10326 | 11219 | 11305 | 11405 | 82210 |
| BN06 | 12208 | 12406 | 12420 | 12422 | 12313 | 10309 | 11279 | 11306 | 11406 | 82208 |
| BN07 | 12231 | 12411 | 12405 | 12489 | 12329 | 10323 | 11280 | 11307 | 11407 | 82204 |
| BN08 | 12205 | 12481 | 12485 | 12407 | 12328 | 10300 | 11229 | 11308 | 11408 | 82211 |
| BN09 | 12230 | 12513 | 12483 | 12514 | 12308 | 10331 | 11281 | 11309 | 11409 | 82215 |
| BN10 | 12214 | 12419 | 12488 | 12443 | 12305 | 10304 | 11282 | 11310 | 11410 | 82205 |
| BN11 | 12203 | 12437 | 12436 | 12484 | 12315 | 10308 | 11283 | 11311 | 11411 | 82218 |
| BN12 | 12212 | 12431 | 12404 | 12426 | 12330 | 10333 | 11284 | 11312 | 11412 | 82212 |
| BN13 | 12228 | 12469 | 12430 | 12424 | 12311 | 10313 | 11285 | 11313 | 11413 | 82213 |
| BN14 | 12229 | 12410 | 12526 | 12423 | 12312 | 10332 | 11201 | 11314 | 11414 | 82206 |
| BN15 | 12226 | 12442 | 12409 | 12515 | 12309 | 10306 | 11286 | 11315 | 11415 | 82214 |
| BN16 | 12213 | 12428 | 12445 | 12433 | 12304 | 10315 | 11287 | 11316 | 11416 | 82225 |
| BN17 | 12223 | 12444 | 12427 | 12432 | 12303 | 10324 | 11288 | 11317 | 11417 | 82222 |
| BN18 | 12215 | 12453 | 12468 | 12467 | 12324 | 10305 | 11289 | 11318 | 11418 | 82220 |
| BN19 | 12211 | 12434 | 12400 | 12470 | 12310 | 10318 | 11290 | 11319 | 11419 | 82201 |
| BN20 | 12224 | 12477 | 12439 | 12440 | 12326 | 10321 | 11241 | 11320 | 11420 | 82200 |
| BN21 | 12222 | 12461 | 12441 | 12476 | 12323 | 10330 | 11244 | 11321 | 11421 | 82227 |
| BN22 | 12210 | 12452 | 12460 | 12473 | 12316 | 10301 | 11291 | 11322 | 11422 | 82230 |
| BN23 | 12225 | 12454 | 12456 | 12455 | 12318 | 10325 | 11292 | 11323 | 11423 | 82226 |
| BN24 | 12219 | 12447 | 12425 | 12403 | 12319 | 10328 | 11293 | 11324 | 11424 | 82229 |
| BN25 | 12217 | 12446 | 12519 | 12464 | 12322 | 10312 | 11294 | 11325 | 11425 | 82216 |
| BN26 | 12220 | 12474 | 12465 | 12429 | 12325 | 10311 | 11295 | 11326 | 11426 | 82223 |
| BN27 | 12216 | 12449 | 12466 | 12538 | 12317 | 10319 | 11237 | 11327 | 11427 | 82228 |
| BN28 | 12218 | 12458 | 12463 | 12533 | 12320 | 10310 | 11273 | 11328 | 11428 | 82217 |
| BN29 | 12204 | 12462 | 12457 | 12438 | 12321 | 10317 | 11998 | 11329 | 11429 | 82231 |
| BN30 | 12227 | 12471 | 12534 | 12472 | 12331 | 10329 | 11999 | 11330 | 11430 | 82203 |
| Spare | 12200 | | | | | | | | | 82224 |

# 2.9. SERVICE STOCK

Most vehicles in this section are numbered in the former BR departmental number series. They are used for internal purposes within the railway industry, i.e. they do not generate revenue from outside the industry.

## BARRIER & TRANSLATOR VEHICLES

These vehicles are used to move multiple unit and HST vehicles around the National Rail system.

**Desiro EMU Barrier Vehicles.** Mark 1. Converted from GUVs with bodies removed and B4 bogies for use as Eurostar barrier vehicles but modified in 2003 by LNWR Co., Crewe for current use.

**6321.** Lot No. 30343 York 1957. 40 t.
**6322/23.** Lot No. 30616 Pressed Steel 1959–60. 40 t.
**6324.** Lot No. 30403 Glasgow 1958–60. 40 t.
**6325.** Lot No. 30417 Pressed Steel 1958–59. 40 t.

| 6321 | (86515, 96385) | | **B** | SM | *FL* | NN |
| 6322 | (86859, 96386) | | **B** | SM | *FL* | NN |
| 6323 | (86973, 96387) | | **B** | SM | *FL* | NN |
| 6324 | (86562, 96388) | | **B** | SM | *FL* | NN |
| 6325 | (86135, 96389) | | **B** | SM | *FL* | NN |

**HST Barrier Vehicles.** Mark 1/2A. Renumbered from BR departmental series, or converted from various types. B4 bogies (* Commonwealth bogies).

**6330.** Mark 2A. Lot No. 30786 Derby 1968. 32 t.
**6336/38/44.** Mark 1. Lot No. 30715 Gloucester 1962. 31 t.
**6340.** Mark 1. Lot No. 30669 Swindon 1962. 36 t.
**6346.** Mark 2A. Lot No. 30777 Derby 1967. 31.5 t.
**6348.** Mark 1. Lot No. 30163 Pressed Steel 1957. 31.5 t.

**Non-standard livery:** 6340, 6344, 6346 All over dark blue.

| 6330 | (14084, 975629) | | **FB** | A | *GW* | LA |
| 6336 | (81591, 92185) | | **FB** | A | *GW* | LA |
| 6338 | (81581, 92180) | | **FB** | A | *GW* | LA |
| 6340 | (21251, 975678) | * | **0** | A | *EC* | EC |
| 6344 | (81263, 92080) | | **0** | A | *EC* | EC |
| 6346 | (9422) | | **0** | A | *EC* | EC |
| 6348 | (81233, 92963) | | **FB** | A | *GW* | LA |

**Mark 4 Barrier Vehicles.** Mark 2A/2C. Converted from FK* or BSO. B4 bogies.

**6352/3.** Mark 2A. Lot No. 30774 Derby 1968. 33 t.
**6354/5.** Mark 2C. Lot No. 30820 Derby 1970. 32 t.
**6358/9.** Mark 2A. Lot No. 30788 Derby 1968. 31.5 t.

| 6352 | (13465, 19465) | * | **GN** | H | *EC* | BN |
| 6353 | (13478, 19478) | * | **GN** | H | *EC* | BN |
| 6354 | (9459) | | **GN** | H | *EC* | BN |

| 6355 | (9477) | **GN** | H | *EC* | BN |
| 6358 | (9432) | **GN** | H | *EC* | BN |
| 6359 | (9429) | **GN** | H | *EC* | BN |

**EMU Translator Vehicles**. Mark 1. Converted 1992 from BG. BR Mark 1 bogies.

**6364**. Mark 1. Lot No. 30039 Derby 1954. 32 t.
**6365**. Mark 1. Lot No. 30323 Pressed Steel 1957. 32 t.

| 6364 | (80565) | **RR** | LM | *LM* | SI |
| 6365 | (81296, 84296) | **RR** | LM | *LM* | SI |

**EMU Translator Vehicles**. Mark 1. Converted 1980 from RUO. Commonwealth bogies.

Lot No. 30647 Wolverton 1959–61. 36 t.

| 6376 | (1021, 975973) | **P** | P | *GB* | WB |
| 6377 | (1042, 975975) | **P** | P | *GB* | WB |
| 6378 | (1054, 975971) | **P** | P | *GB* | WB |
| 6379 | (1059, 975972) | **P** | P | *GB* | WB |

**HST Barrier Vehicles**. Mark 1. Converted from BG in 1994–95. B4 bogies.

**6392**. Lot No. 30715 Gloucester 1962. 29.5 t.
**6393/97**. Lot No. 30716 Gloucester 1962. 29.5 t.
**6394**. Lot No. 30162 Pressed Steel 1956–57. 30.5 t.
**6395**. Lot No. 30484 Pressed Steel 1958. 30.5 t.
**6398/99**. Lot No. 30400 Pressed Steel 1957–58. 30.5 t.

| 6392 | (81588, 92183) | **P** | P | *EM* | NL |
| 6393 | (81609, 92196) | **P** | P | *EC* | EC |
| 6394 | (80878, 92906) | **P** | P | *EC* | EC |
| 6395 | (81506, 92148) | **P** | EM | *EM* | NL |
| 6397 | (81600, 92190) | **P** | P | *EM* | NL |
| 6398 | (81471, 92126) | **MA** | EM | *EM* | NL |
| 6399 | (81367, 92994) | **MA** | EM | *EM* | NL |

**Eurostar Barrier Vehicles**. Mark 1. Converted from GUVs. Bodies removed. B4 bogies.

**96380–96382**. Lot No. 30417 Pressed Steel 1958–59. 40 t.
**96383**. Lot No. 30565 Pressed Steel 1959. 40 t.
**96384**. Lot No. 30616 Pressed Steel 1959–60. 40 t.

| 96380 | (86386, 6380) | **B** | EU | *EU* | TI |
| 96381 | (86187, 6381) | **B** | EU | *EU* | TI |
| 96382 | (86295, 6382) | **B** | EU | *EU* | TI |
| 96383 | (86664, 6383) | **B** | EU | *EU* | TI |
| 96384 | (86955, 6384) | **B** | EU | *EU* | TI |

**EMU Translator Vehicles**. Converted from Mark 1 TSO, RSOs, RUOs, BSKs and GUVs (NP/NL).

**975864**. Lot No. 30054 Eastleigh 1951–54. Commonwealth bogies.
**975867**. Lot No. 30014 York 1950–51. Commonwealth bogies.
**975875**. Lot No. 30143 Charles Roberts 1954–55. Commonwealth bogies.
**975974/975978**. Lot No. 30647 Wolverton 1959–61. Commonwealth bogies.

**977087**. Lot No. 30229 Metro–Cammell 1955–57. Commonwealth bogies.
**977942/948**. Lot No. 30417 Pressed Steel 1958–59. B5 bogies.
**977943/949**. Lot No. 30565 Pressed Steel 1959. B5 bogies.

**Non-standard livery:** 975974 and 975978 Plain grey.

| | | | | | |
|---|---|---|---|---|---|
| 975864 | (3849) | **HB** | H | *FL* | LD |
| 975867 | (1006) | **HB** | H | *FL* | LD |
| 975875 | (34643) | **HB** | H | *FL* | LD |
| 975974 | (1030) | **O** | A | *ME* | BD |
| 975978 | (1025) | **O** | A | *ME* | BD |
| 977087 | (34971) | **HB** | H | *FL* | LD |
| 977942 | (86467, 80251) | **E** | DB | *DB* | TO |
| 977943 | (86718, 80252) | **E** | DB | *DB* | TO |
| 977948 | (86733, 94028) | **E** | DB | *DB* | TO |
| 977949 | (86377, 94025) | **E** | DB | *DB* | TO |

# LABORATORY, TESTING & INSPECTION COACHES

These coaches are used for research, development, testing and inspection on the National Rail system. Many are fitted with sophisticated technical equipment.

**Generator Vans.** Mark 1. Converted from BR Mark 1 BGs. B5 bogies.

**6260**. Lot No. 30400 Pressed Steel 1957–58.
**6261**. Lot No. 30323 Pressed Steel 1957.
**6262**. Lot No. 30228 Metro-Cammell 1957–58.
**6263**. Lot No. 30163 Pressed Steel 1957.
**6264**. Lot No. 30173 York 1956.

| | | | | | |
|---|---|---|---|---|---|
| 6260 | (81450, 92116) | **NR** | NR | | ZG |
| 6261 | (81284, 92988) | **Y** | NR | *SO* | ZA |
| 6262 | (81064, 92928) | **Y** | NR | *SO* | ZA |
| 6263 | (81231, 92961) | **Y** | NR | *SO* | ZA |
| 6264 | (80971, 92923) | **Y** | NR | *SO* | ZA |

**Driving Trailer Coaches.** Converted 2008 at Serco, Derby from Mark 2F DBSOs. Disc brakes. B4 bogies.

**9701–08**. Lot No. 30861 Derby 1974. Converted to DBSO Glasgow 1974.
**9714**. Lot No. 30861 Derby 1974. Converted to DBSO Glasgow 1986.

| | | | | | |
|---|---|---|---|---|---|
| 9701 | (9528) | **Y** | NR | *SO* | ZA |
| 9702 | (9510) | **Y** | NR | *SO* | ZA |
| 9703 | (9517) | **Y** | NR | *SO* | ZA |
| 9708 | (9530) | **Y** | NR | *SO* | ZA |
| 9714 | (9536) | **Y** | NR | *SO* | ZA |

**Ultrasonic Test Coach.** Converted from BR Mark 2E FO then converted to exhibition van. Lot No. 30843 Derby 1972–73. B4 bogies.

| | | | | | |
|---|---|---|---|---|---|
| 99666 | (3250) | **Y** | NR | *SO* | ZA |

**Inspection Saloon**. Converted from Class 202 DEMU TRB at Stewarts Lane for use as a BR Southern Region General Manager's Saloon. Overhauled at FM Rail, Derby in 2004/05 for use as a New Trains Project Saloon. Can be used in push-pull mode with suitably equipped locomotives. Eastleigh 1958. SR Mk. 4 bogies.

| | | | | | |
|---|---|---|---|---|---|
| 975025 (60755) | **G** | NR | *SO* | ZA | CAROLINE |

**Structure Gauging Train Coach**. Originally used as a Driving Trailer. Converted from BR Mark 1 BSK. Lot No. 30699 Wolverton 1961–63. B4 bogies.

| | | | | |
|---|---|---|---|---|
| 975081 (35313) | **Y** | NR | *SO* | ZA |

**Overhead Line Equipment Test Coach ("MENTOR")**. Converted from BR Mark 1 BSK Lot No. 30142 Gloucester 1954–5. Fitted with pantograph. B4 bogies.

| | | | | |
|---|---|---|---|---|
| 975091 (34615) | **Y** | NR | *SO* | ZA |

**Structure Gauging Train Dormitory and Generator Coach**. Converted from BR Mark 1 BCK Lot No. 30732 Derby 1962–4. B4 bogies.

| | | | | |
|---|---|---|---|---|
| 975280 (21263) | **Y** | NR | *SO* | ZA |

**Test Coach**. Converted from BR Mark 1 BSK Lot No. 30699 Wolverton 1961–63. Commonwealth bogies.

| | | | | |
|---|---|---|---|---|
| 975397 (35386) | **SO** | SO | *SO* | ZA |

**New Measurement Train Conference Coach**. Converted from prototype HST TF Lot No. 30848 Derby 1972. BT10 bogies.

| | | | | |
|---|---|---|---|---|
| 975814 (11000,41000) | **Y** | NR | *SO* | EC |

**New Measurement Train Lecture Coach**. Converted from prototype HST TRUB Lot No. 30849 Derby 1972–3. BT10 bogies.

| | | | | |
|---|---|---|---|---|
| 975984 (10000, 40000) | **Y** | NR | *SO* | EC |

**Track Recording Train Dormitory Coach**. Converted from BR Mark 2 BSO. Lot No 30757 Derby 1965–66. B4 bogies.

| | | | | |
|---|---|---|---|---|
| 977337 (9395) | **Y** | NR | *SO* | ZA |

**Radio Equipment Survey Coaches**. Converted from BR Mark 2E TSO. Lot No. 30844 Derby 1972–73. B4 bogies.

| | | | | |
|---|---|---|---|---|
| 977868 (5846) | **Y** | NR | *SO* | ZA |
| 977869 (5858) | **Y** | NR | *SO* | ZA |

**Test Train Staff Coach**. Converted from Royal Household couchette Lot No. 30889, which in turn had been converted from BR Mark 2B BFK Lot No. 30790 Derby 1969. B5 bogies.

| | | | | |
|---|---|---|---|---|
| 977969 (14112, 2906) | **Y** | NR | *SO* | ZA |

**Hot Box Detection Coach**. Converted from BR Mark 2F FO converted to Class 488/2 EMU TFOH. Lot No. 30859 Derby 1973–74. B4 bogies.

| | | | | |
|---|---|---|---|---|
| 977983 (3407, 72503) | **Y** | NR | *SO* | ZA |

**New Measurement Train Staff Coach.** Converted from HST TRFK. Lot No. 30884 Derby 1976–77.  BT10 bogies.

977984  (40501)                    Y      P      *SO*      EC

**Test Train Coach.** Converted from BR Mark 2F TSO converted to Class 488/3 EMU TSO. Lot No. 30860 Derby 1973–74.  B4 bogies.

977985  (6019, 72715)              Y      NR     *SO*      ZA

**Track Recording Train Coach.** Converted from BR Mark 2D FO subsequently declassified to SO and then converted to exhibition van. Lot No. 30821 Derby 1971.

977986  (3189, 99664)              Y      NR     *SO*      ZA

**New Measurement Train Overhead Line Equipment Test Coach.** Converted from HST TGS. Lot No. 30949 Derby 1982. Fitted with pantograph. BT10 bogies.

977993  (44053)                    Y      P      *SO*      EC

**New Measurement Train Track Recording Coach.** Converted from HST TGS. Lot No. 30949 Derby 1982.  BT10 bogies.

977994  (44087)                    Y      P      *SO*      EC

**New Measurement Train Coach.** Converted from HST TRFM. Lot No. 30921 Derby 1978–79.  BT10 bogies. Fitted with generator.

977995  (40719, 40619)             Y      P      *SO*      EC

**New Measurement Train Coach.** Converted from HST TGS for Hitachi. Lot No. 30949 Derby 1982. BT10 bogies.

977996  (44062)                    Y      P              LM

**Track Recording Coach.** Converted from BR Inspection Saloon.  BR Wagon Lot No. 3379. Swindon 1960. B4 bogies.

999508                             Y      SO     *SO*      ZA

**Track Recording Coach.** Purpose built Mark 2. B4 bogies.

999550                             Y      NR     *SO*      ZA

**Ultrasonic Test Coaches.** Converted from Class 421 EMU MBSO and Class 432 EMU MSO.

**999602/605.** Lot No. 30862 York 1974. 55.5 t. SR Mk. 6 bogies.
**999606.** Lot No. 30816. York 1970. ? bogies.

999602  (62483)                    Y      NR     *SO*      ZA
999605  (62482)                    Y      NR     *SO*      ZA
999606  (62356)                    Y      NR     *SO*      ZA

# TEST TRAIN BRAKE FORCE RUNNERS

Converted from Class 488/3 ex-Gatwick Express locomotive-hauled stock (formerly Mark 2 coaches). These vehicles are included in test trains to provide brake force and are not used for any other purposes.

**72612–72639.** Lot No. 30860 Derby 1973–74. 33.5 t.
**72708.** Lot No. 30860 Derby 1973–74. 33.5 t.

| | | | | | |
|---|---|---|---|---|---|
| 72612 | (6156) | **RK** | NR | *SO* | ZA |
| 72613 | (6126) | **RK** | NR | *SO* | ZA |
| 72616 | (6007) | **Y** | NR | *SO* | ZA |
| 72630 | (6094) | **Y** | NR | *SO* | ZA |
| 72631 | (6096) | **Y** | NR | *SO* | ZA |
| 72639 | (6070) | **Y** | NR | *SO* | ZA |

# BREAKDOWN TRAIN COACHES

These coaches are formed in trains used for the recovery of derailed railway vehicles and were converted from BR Mark 1 BCK, BG and BSK. The current use of each vehicle is given. 975611–613 were previously converted to trailer luggage vans in 1968. BR Mark 1 bogies.

**975087.** Lot No. 30032 Wolverton 1951–52.
**975477/494.** Lot No. 30233 GRCW 1955–57.
**975471.** Lot No. 30095 Wolverton 1953–55.
**975481/574.** Lot No. 30141 GRCW 1954–55.
**975573.** Lot No. 30156 Wolverton 1954–55.
**975611–613.** Lot No. 30162 Pressed Steel 1954–57.
**977088/235.** Lot No. 30229 Metro-Cammell 1955–57.
**977107.** Lot No. 30425 Metro-Cammell 1956–58.

r refurbished

| | | | | | | | |
|---|---|---|---|---|---|---|---|
| 975087 | (34289) | r | **NR** | NR | | SP | Generator Van |
| 975471 | (34543) | r | **NR** | NR | | SP | Staff & Tool Coach |
| 975477 | (35108) | r | **NR** | NR | | SP | Staff Coach |
| 975481 | (34606) | r | **Y** | NR | | ZA | Generator Van |
| 975494 | (35082) | r | **Y** | NR | *DB* | MG | Generator Van |
| 975573 | (34729) | r | **Y** | NR | *DB* | MG | Staff Coach |
| 975574 | (34599) | r | **Y** | NR | *DB* | TO | Staff Coach |
| 975611 | (80915, 68201) | r | **Y** | NR | *DB* | TO | Generator Van |
| 975612 | (80922, 68203) | r | **Y** | NR | *DB* | MG | Tool Van |
| 975613 | (80918, 68202) | r | **Y** | NR | *DB* | TO | Tool Van |
| 977088 | (34990) | | **Y** | NR | *DB* | SP | Generator Van |
| 977107 | (21202) | | **Y** | NR | *DB* | SP | Staff Coach |
| 977235 | (34989, 083172) | | **Y** | NR | *DB* | SP | Tool Van |

# INFRASTRUCTURE MAINTENANCE COACHES

### Snowblower Train Coaches

These coaches worked with Snowblower ADB 968501. They were converted from BR Mark 1 BSK. The former use of each vehicle is given. Commonwealth bogies.

**975464**. Lot No. 30386 Charles Roberts 1956–58.
**975486**. Lot No. 30025 Wolverton 1950–52.

| | | | | | |
|---|---|---|---|---|---|
| 975464 | (35171) | **Y** | NR | SP | Staff & dormitory coach |
| 975486 | (34100) | **Y** | NR | SP | Tool van |

### De-Icing Coaches

These coaches are used for removing ice from the conductor rail of DC lines. They were converted from Class 489 DMLVs that had originally been Class 414/3 DMBSOs.

Lot No. 30452 Ashford/Eastleigh 1959. Mk. 4 bogies.

| | | | | | |
|---|---|---|---|---|---|
| 68501 | (61281) | **Y** | NR | *GB* | TW |
| 68504 | (61286) | **Y** | NR | *GB* | TW |
| 68505 | (61299) | **Y** | NR | *GB* | TW |
| 68508 | (61272) | **Y** | NR | *GB* | TW |

### Miscellaneous Infrastructure Coaches

These coaches are used for various infrastructure projects on the National Rail network. They were converted from BR Mark 1 BSK & BG and BR Mark 3 SLEP. The current use of each vehicle is given.

**80211**. Lot No. 30699 Wolverton 1961–63. Commonwealth bogies.
**975463**. Lot No. 30156 Wolverton 1954–55. BR Mark 1 bogies.
**975482**. Lot No. 30141 GRCW 1954–55. BR Mark 1 bogies.
**975498**. Lot No. 30074 Wolverton 1953–54. BR Mark 1 bogies.
**977989**. Lot No. 30960 Derby 1981–83. BT 10 bogies.
**977990**. Lot No. 30228 Metro-Cammell 1957-58. B4 bogies.
**977991**. Lot No. 30323 Pressed steel 1957. B4 bogies.

| | | | | | |
|---|---|---|---|---|---|
| 80211 | (35296) | **Y** | NR | *SO* ZA | Staff & Tool Van |
| 975463 | (34721) | **Y** | NR | *SO* ZA | Staff Coach |
| 975482 | (34602) | **Y** | NR | *SO* ZA | Generator Van |
| 975498 | (34367) | **Y** | NR | *SO* ZA | Tool Van |
| 977989 | (10536) | **M** | NR | ZA | Staff & Dormitory Coach |
| 977990 | (81165, 92937) | **NR** | NR | SP | Tool Van |
| 977991 | (81308, 92991) | **NR** | NR | SP | Tool Van |

## INTERNAL USER VEHICLES

These vehicles are confined to yards and depots or do not normally move at all.
Details are given of the internal user number (if allocated), type, former identity,
current use and location. Many of those listed no longer see regular use.

| | | | |
|---|---|---|---|
| 024877 | BR CCT 94698 | Stores van | Wavertree Yard, Edge Hill |
| 024909 | BR BSOT 9106 | Staff accommodation | Preston Station |
| 025000 | BR BSO 9423 | Staff accommodation | Preston Station |
| 025026 | BR TSO 5259 | Staff accommodation | Wavertree Yard, Edge Hill |
| 041379 | LMS CCT 35527 | Stores van | Leeman Road EY, York |
| 041898 | BR BG 84608 | Stores van | Leeman Road EY, York |
| 041947 | BR GUV 93425 | Stores van | IL |
| 041963 | LMS milk tank 44047 | Storage tank | DR |
| 042154 | BR GUV 93975 | Stores van | Ipswich Upper Yard |
| 061061 | BR CCT 94135 | Stores van | Oxford station |
| 061223 | BR GUV 93714 | Stores van | Oxford station |
| 083439 | BR CCT 94752 | Stores van | WD |
| 083602 | BR CCT 94494 | Stores van | Three Bridges station |
| 083637 | BR NW 99203 | Stores van | SL |
| 083644 | BR Ferry Van 889201 | Stores van | EH |
| 083664 | BR Ferry Van 889203 | Stores van | EH |
| 095020 | LNER BG 70170 | Stores van | Inverness Yard |
| 095030 | BR GUV 96140 | Stores van | EC |
| - | BR FO 3186 | Instruction Coach | DY |
| - | BR FO 3381 | Instruction Coach | HE |
| - | BR TSO 5636 | Instruction Coach | PM |
| - | BR HSBV 6396 | Stores van | MA |
| - | BR RFB 10256 | Instruction Coach | GW |
| - | BR RFB 10260 | Instruction Coach | GW |
| - | BR BFK 17156 | Instruction Coach | DY |
| - | BR TSOLH 72614 | Instruction Coach | DY |
| - | BR TSOLH 72615 | Instruction Coach | DY |
| - | BR TSOL 72707 | Instruction Coach | DY |
| - | BR BG 92901 | Stores van | WB |
| - | BR NL 94003 | Stores van | OO |
| - | BR NL 94006 | Stores van | OO |
| - | BR NK 94101 | Stores van | GL |
| - | BR NK 94121 | Stores van | TO |
| - | BR CCT 94181 | Stores van | SL |
| - | BR NB 94438 | Stores van | TO |
| - | BR GUV 96139 | Stores van | MA |
| - | BR Ferry Van 889017 | Stores van | SL |
| - | BR Ferry Van 889200 | Stores van | SL |
| - | BR Ferry Van 889202 | Stores van | SL |
| - | BR TSO 975403 | Cinema Coach | PM |

**Notes:**  CCT = Covered Carriage Truck (a 4-wheeled van similar to a GUV)
GUV = General Utility Van
NB = High Security Brake Van (converted from BG)
NK= High Security General Utility Van
NL = Newspaper Van (converted from a GUV)
NW = Bullion Van (converted from a BSK)

# 2.10. COACHING STOCK AWAITING DISPOSAL

This list contains the last known locations of coaching stock awaiting disposal. The definition of which vehicles are "awaiting disposal" is somewhat vague, but generally speaking these are vehicles of types not now in normal service or vehicles which have been damaged by fire, vandalism or collision.

| | | | | | | | |
|---|---|---|---|---|---|---|---|
| 1205 | ZA | 10547 | IS | 92939 | ZA | 94306 | TY |
| 1644 | CS | 10554 | TO | 93723 | BY | 94307 | ** |
| 1650 | CS | 10682 | TO | 94103 | ** | 94308 | ML |
| 1652 | CS | 10709 | ZN | 94104 | OM | 94310 | WE |
| 1655 | CS | 10710 | LM | 94106 | ML | 94311 | WE |
| 1663 | CS | 12096 | ZN | 94113 | OM | 94313 | WE |
| 1670 | CS | 13306 | CS | 94116 | TY | 94316 | SM |
| 2127 | CS | 13320 | CS | 94137 | ME | 94317 | OM |
| 3181 | CD | 13323 | CS | 94147 | ME | 94318 | ** |
| 4860 | CS | 13508 | CS | 94150 | BS | 94322 | ML |
| 4932 | CS | 17144 | LM | 94153 | WE | 94323 | TY |
| 4997 | CS | 17161 | OM | 94155 | BS | 94326 | TY |
| 5299 | CS | 17170 | LM | 94160 | ML | 94331 | ** |
| 5389 | OM | 18837 | CS | 94166 | BS | 94332 | TY |
| 5480 | KT | 18893 | CS | 94168 | BS | 94333 | TY |
| 5600 | CS | 19013 | CS | 94170 | ML | 94334 | CD |
| 5647 | CD | 34525 | CS | 94176 | BS | 94335 | TY |
| 5727 | CS | 35452 | CP | 94177 | SM | 94336 | TY |
| 5756 | CS | 35516 | ** | 94190 | SP | 94337 | WE |
| 5779 | IS | 40417 | ZK | 94191 | SP | 94338 | WE |
| 5812 | IS | 40425 | ZK | 94192 | ME | 94340 | CD |
| 5897 | IS | 41043 | ZB | 94195 | BS | 94343 | ML |
| 6178 | HM | 45029 | ML | 94196 | ME | 94344 | SM |
| 6335 | LA | 80403 | CS | 94197 | BS | 94400 | ** |
| 6339 | EC | 80404 | CS | 94199 | ME | 94401 | ME |
| 6345 | EC | 84364 | DW | 94203 | SP | 94406 | ML |
| 6356 | LM | 84519 | CD | 94207 | OM | 94408 | TY |
| 6357 | LM | 92111 | CD | 94208 | SM | 94410 | WE |
| 6360 | NL | 92114 | ZA | 94209 | ** | 94411 | ** |
| 6361 | NL | 92159 | KT | 94213 | ME | 94412 | ME |
| 6523 | CS | 92174 | SN | 94214 | ML | 94413 | ME |
| 6805 | ZG | 92193 | ** | 94217 | ML | 94416 | ME |
| 6808 | ZG | 92303 | OM | 94221 | ME | 94420 | ML |
| 6811 | ZG | 92350 | OM | 94222 | ML | 94422 | OM |
| 6817 | ZG | 92384 | OM | 94224 | CD | 94423 | BS |
| 6828 | ZG | 92400 | CD | 94225 | ML | 94427 | WE |
| 6829 | ZG | 92908 | CS | 94227 | TE | 94428 | ME |
| 9482 | NL | 92929 | CD | 94229 | ML | 94429 | TE |
| 9712 | ZJ | 92931 | SN | 94302 | TY | 94431 | ML |
| 10201 | LM | 92936 | OM | 94303 | TY | 94432 | ME |
| 10540 | OM | 92938 | SN | 94304 | ML | 94433 | ML |

| | | | | | | | |
|---|---|---|---|---|---|---|---|
| 94434 | TY | 94531 | TY | 96192 | CS | 975700 | Preston |
| 94435 | OM | 94532 | OM | 96210 | CS | 975714 | Preston |
| 94440 | ME | 94534 | ME | 96218 | CS | 975724 | Preston |
| 94445 | WE | 94536 | ME | 96371 | WB | 975734 | Preston |
| 94450 | WE | 94538 | ML | 96372 | WB | 975744 | Preston |
| 94451 | WE | 94539 | ML | 96373 | WB | 975976 | KT |
| 94458 | ** | 94540 | TJ | 96374 | WB | 975977 | KT |
| 94462 | CD | 94541 | ME | 96375 | WB | 975991 | CD |
| 94463 | TY | 94542 | TY | 96602 | LM | 977077 | ** |
| 94470 | OM | 94543 | ME | 96603 | LM | 977085 | BH |
| 94476 | CD | 94544 | ML | 96604 | LM | 977095 | CS |
| 94479 | OM | 94545 | TE | 96605 | LM | 977111 | ** |
| 94481 | ** | 94546 | TY | 96606 | LM | 977112 | ** |
| 94482 | ML | 94547 | ML | 96607 | LM | 977163 | AP |
| 94488 | CD | 94548 | TY | 96608 | LM | 977165 | AP |
| 94490 | ML | 95300 | ML | 96609 | LM | 977166 | AP |
| 94492 | WE | 95301 | ML | 99014 | ** | 977167 | AP |
| 94495 | TY | 95400 | ML | 99015 | ** | 977193 | BH |
| 94497 | ME | 95410 | ML | 99019 | ZR | 977359 | ZN |
| 94498 | ML | 95727 | WE | 200715 | IS | 977390 | CD |
| 94499 | CD | 95754 | TY | 787395 | IS | 977399 | NL |
| 94501 | OM | 95758 | SP | 889400 | ZA | 977442 | CP |
| 94504 | TY | 95761 | WE | 975000 | ZA | 977595 | CD |
| 94512 | TY | 95763 | BS | 975290 | ZA | 977618 | BY |
| 94514 | ME | 96100 | TM | 975336 | CP | 977789 | LU |
| 94515 | ML | 96101 | LM | 975379 | ** | 977790 | LU |
| 94517 | CD | 96110 | CS | 975454 | TO | 977791 | LU |
| 94518 | ME | 96132 | CS | 975484 | CS | 977793 | LU |
| 94519 | ME | 96135 | CS | 975497 | Sudbrook | 977794 | LU |
| 94520 | TY | 96164 | CS | 975639 | CS | 977855 | ZA |
| 94521 | CD | 96165 | CS | 975681 | Portobello | 977905 | EH |
| 94522 | TY | 96170 | CS | 975682 | Portobello | 977974 | ZA |
| 94525 | TY | 96175 | CS | 975685 | Portobello | | |
| 94526 | TY | 96177 | CP | 975686 | Portobello | 150359 | CP |
| 94527 | TY | 96178 | CS | 975687 | Portobello | 150395 | CP |
| 94528 | ME | 96181 | LM | 975688 | Portobello | 024529 | CP |
| 94529 | CD | 96182 | CS | 975699 | Preston | DS 70220 | ** |
| 94530 | ME | 96191 | CS | | | | |

** Other locations:

| | |
|---|---|
| 35516 | Railway Restorations North East, Shildon |
| 92193 | Preston Carriage Sidings |
| 94103 | Cardiff Tidal Yard |
| 94209 | Cardiff Tidal Yard |
| 94307 | Cardiff Tidal Yard |
| 94318 | Cardiff Tidal Yard |
| 94331 | Cardiff Tidal Yard |
| 94400 | Cardiff Tidal Yard |
| 94411 | Cardiff Tidal Yard |
| 94458 | Cardiff Tidal Yard |
| 94481 | Cardiff Tidal Yard |

| 99014 | Horsham Yard |
| 99015 | Horsham Yard |
| 975379 | Leeman Road, EY York |
| 977077 | Ripple Lane Yard |
| 977111 | Ripple Lane Yard |
| 977112 | Ripple Lane Yard |
| DS70220 | Western Trading Estate Siding, North Acton |

**Former Gatwick Express stock awaiting disposal:**

**Advertising livery:** As **GX** but with a deep blue instead of a white lower bodyside, advertising Continental Airlines.

| 8208 | **AL** | GB | PB | 72507 (3412) | 72643 (6040) | |
| 8312 | **GX** | GB | SN | 72622 (6004) | 72711 (6109) | 72623 (6118) |
| 8315 | **GX** | GB | SN | 72636 (6071) | 72714 (6092) | 72645 (5942) |

▲ The first completed bodyshell of two Parry People Movers for London Midland, numbered 139 001, was displayed on a low loader at Tyseley on 28/06/08. These will enter service on the Stourbridge branch from December 2008. **Robert Pritchard**

▼ Arriva Trains-liveried 142 072 and 143 610 pass Cardiff Queen Street North Junction with the 15.17 Bargoed–Penarth on 17/10/07. **Andrew Mist**

▲ 143 616 and 143 601 arrive at Radyr with the 12.39 Pontypridd–Cardiff Central on 06/08/07. **John Binch**

▼ 3-car Class 144 No. 144 020, in West Yorkshire PTE-livery, arrives at Sheffield on 26/09/07 forming the 14.34 from Leeds via Barnsley. **Peter Fox**

First Group "Dynamic Lines"-liveried 150 261 pauses at Saltash with the 17.06 Plymouth–Liskeard on 09/06/08.
**Robert Pritchard**

Arriva Trains-liveried 150 259 and 150 227 are seen south of Cwm on the newly reopened Ebbw Vale branch with the 13.40 Ebbw Vale Parkway–Cardiff Central on 18/02/08.

**Andrew Mist**

▲ Northern-liveried 153 316 waits departure from Sheffield with the 10.44 to Gainsborough Lea Road on 25/07/08. **Robert Pritchard**

▼ East Midlands Trains blue 153 374 and 153 313 (still in North Western Trains blue) pass Barrow-on-Soar with the 15.35 Leicester–Lincoln on 30 July. **Paul Biggs**

▲ Just the rear vehicle of Northern-liveried 155 345 carrys promotional vinyls, as it passes Eastwood, Caldervale with the 09.37 Leeds–Manchester Victoria on 19/05/08. **Gavin Morrison**

▼ Strathclyde PTE-liveried 156 513 passes Magiscroft with the 07.52 Glasgow Queen Street–Cumbernauld on 21/07/08. **Ian Lothian**

▲ 3-car Northern-liveried 158 758 arrives at Preston with the 15.52 York–Blackpool North on 29/06/08. **Robin Ralston**

▼ First Group-liveried 158 736 leaves Helmsdale with the 07.14 Inverness–Wick on 31/05/08. **Adrian Sumner**

▲ A 9-car Class 159/0 formation – 159 002/004/006 – passes Vauxhall on 24/05/08 shortly after departure from London Waterloo with the 09.20 to Plymouth/Bristol Temple Meads. **Alex Dasi-Sutton**

▼ First Great Western "Dynamic Lines"-liveried 166 216 passes Buckland on the North Downs Line with the 11.04 Reading–Redhill on 03/05/08.
**Alex Dasi-Sutton**

Chiltern Railways-liveried 165 031 passes Denham Golf Club with the 09.41 Stratford-upon-Avon–London Marylebone on 08/05/08.
**Robert Pritchard**

▲ One of the original Chiltern Railways Class 168/0s, 168 002, passes Neasden shortly after departure from London Marylebone with the 17.00 to Kidderminster on 08/05/08. **Robert Pritchard**

▼ Cross-Country-liveried 170 521 leaves Gloucester with the 12.45 Cardiff Central–Nottingham on 10/06/08. **Robert Pritchard**

▲ London Midland-liveried 170 507, coupled to a Central 153, pauses at Tame Bridge Parkway with the 14.35 Stafford–Birmingham New Street via Rugeley on 06/05/08. **Cliff Beeton**

▼ Southern-liveried 171 804 is seen near Hurst Green with the 11.08 London Bridge–Uckfield on 02/02/08 **Alex Dasi-Sutton**

▲ Arriva Trains-liveried 175 005 is seen at Tyndall Street, Cardiff with the 08.35 Manchester Piccadilly–Milford Haven on 24/05/08. **Andrew Mist**

▼ First Hull Trains now uses 180s on some services. On 180 111 passes Eaton Lane crossing, south of Retford on 24/05/08 with the 08.02 Hull–London King's Cross. **Andrew Wills**

First Trans-Pennine Express "Dynamic Lines"-liveried 185 145 passes Grindleford in the Hope Valley with the 09.52 Manchester Airport–Cleethorpes South Trans-Pennine service on 09/11/07.
**Robert Pritchard**

▲ All 220s are now in Cross-Country livery. On 15/06/08 220 001 passes Longport with the 17.36 Birmingham New Street–Manchester Piccadilly.　**Cliff Beeton**

▼ Virgin Trains-liveried 221 107 "Sir Martin Frobisher" passes Llanfairyneubwll as it crosses Anglesey with the 14.15 Holyhead–Crewe on 14/06/08.　**Phil Chilton**

▲ Stagecoach-liveried 222 015 and 222 023, still in Midland Mainline livery at the time of this photograph, pass Cossington with the 08.07 Nottingham–London St. Pancras East Midlands Trains service on 11/08/08.                 **Paul Biggs**

▼ Network Rail Track Assessment Unit 950 001, which is similar to the Class 150 design, is seen near Wellingborough with a test train from Derby to Bletchley on 06/05/08.                                                          **Richard Gennis**

▲ South West Trains-liveried Route Learning Unit 960 012 "John Cameron" (converted from a Class 121) is seen at Clapham Junction sidings on 29/05/08.
**William Turvill**

▼ Chiltern's Water-Jetting unit 960 301 (converted from a Class 117) passes West Ruislip on leaf clearing duties on 19/10/07. **Alex Dasi-Sutton**

# 3. DIESEL MULTIPLE UNITS

# INTRODUCTION

## DMU CLASSES

DMU Classes are listed in class number order. Principal details and dimensions are quoted for each class in metric and/or imperial units as considered appropriate bearing in mind common usage in the UK.

All dimensions and weights are quoted for vehicles in an "as new" condition with all necessary supplies (e.g. oil, water, sand) on board. Dimensions are quoted in the order Length – Width. All lengths quoted are over buffers or couplers as appropriate. Where two lengths are quoted, the first refers to outer vehicles in a set and the second to inner vehicles. All width dimensions quoted are maxima.

## NUMERICAL LISTINGS

DMUs are listed in numerical order of set – using current numbers as allocated by the RSL. Individual "loose" vehicles are listed in numerical order after vehicles formed into fixed formations. Where sets or vehicles have been renumbered in recent years, former numbering detail is shown in parentheses. Each entry is laid out as in the following example:

| Set No. | Detail | Livery | Owner | Operator | Depot | Formation | Name |
|---------|--------|--------|-------|----------|-------|-----------|------|
| 142 073 | v | **AV** | A | *AW* | CF | 55723 55769 | Myfanwy |

**Detail Differences**. Detail differences which currently affect the areas and types of train which vehicles may work are shown, plus differences in interior layout. Where such differences occur within a class, these are shown either in the heading information or alongside the individual set or vehicle number. The following standard abbreviation is used:

r  Radio Electronic Token Block (RETB) equipment fitted.

In all cases use of the above abbreviation indicates the equipment indicated is normally operable. Meaning of non-standard abbreviations is detailed in individual class headings.

**Set Formations**. Regular set formations are shown where these are normally maintained. Readers should note set formations might be temporarily varied from time to time to suit maintenance and/or operational requirements. Vehicles shown as "spare" are not formed in any regular set formation.

**Codes**. Codes are used to denote the livery, owner, operator and depot of each unit. Details of these will be found in section 6 of this book. Where a unit or spare car is off-lease, the operator column will be left blank.

**Names**. Only names carried with official sanction are listed. As far as possible names are shown in UPPER/lower case characters as actually shown on the name carried on the vehicle(s). Unless otherwise shown, complete units are regarded as named rather than just the individual car(s) which carry the name.

# GENERAL INFORMATION

## CLASSIFICATION AND NUMBERING

First generation ("Heritage") DMUs are classified in the series 100–138.
Parry People Mover Gas/flywheel hybrid drive units are classified 139.
Second generation DMUs are classified in the series 140–199.
Diesel Electric Multiple Units are classified in the series 200–249.
Service units are classified in the series 930–999.

Parry People Mover individual cars are numbered in the series 39001–002.

First and second generation individual cars are numbered in the series 50000–59999 and 79000–79999.

DEMU individual cars are numbered in the series 60000–60999, except for a few former EMU vehicles which retain their EMU numbers.

Service stock individual cars are numbered in the series 975000–975999 and 977000–999601, although this series is not exclusively used for DMU vehicles.

## OPERATING CODES

These codes are used by train operating company staff to describe the various different types of vehicles and normally appear on data panels on the inner (i.e. non driving) ends of vehicles.

The first part of the code describes whether or not the car has a motor or a driving cab as follows:

DM  Driving motor.
M   Motor
DT  Driving trailer
T   Trailer

The next letter is a "B" for cars with a brake compartment.

This is followed by the saloon details:

F   First
S   Standard
C   Composite

L denotes a vehicle with a lavatory compartment.

Finally vehicles with a buffet are suffixed RB or RMB for a miniature buffet.

Where two vehicles of the same type are formed within the same unit, the above codes may be suffixed by (A) and (B) to differentiate between the vehicles.

A composite is a vehicle containing both First and Standard Class accommodation, whilst a brake vehicle is a vehicle containing separate specific accommodation for the conductor.

**Special Note:** Where vehicles have been declassified, the correct operating code which describes the actual vehicle layout is quoted in this publication.

# BUILD DETAILS

**Lot Numbers**
Vehicles ordered under the auspices of BR were allocated a lot (batch) number when ordered and these are quoted in class headings and sub-headings.

**Builders**
These are shown in class headings. Abbreviations used are found in section 6.7.

Information on sub-contracting works which built parts of vehicles e.g. the underframes etc. is not shown.

# ACCOMMODATION

The information given in class headings and sub-headings is in the form F/S nT (or TD) nW. For example 12/54 1T 1W denotes 12 First Class and 54 Standard Class seats, one toilet and one wheelchair space. A number in brackets (i.e. (2)) denotes tip-up seats (in addition to the fixed seats). Tip-up seats in vestibules do not count. The seating layout of open saloons is shown as 2+1, 2+2 or 3+2 as the case may be. Where units have First Class accommodation as well as Standard and the layout is different for each class then these are shown separately prefixed by "1:" and "2:". TD denotes a toilet suitable for use by a disabled person.

# 3.1. DIESEL MECHANICAL & DIESEL HYDRAULIC UNITS

## 3.1.1. FIRST GENERATION UNITS

## CLASS 121                PRESSED STEEL SUBURBAN

First generation units used by Chiltern Railways on selected Aylesbury–Princes Risborough services (121 020) and by Arriva Trains Wales on Cardiff Queen Street–Cardiff Bay shuttles (121 032).
**Construction:** Steel.
**Engines:** Two Leyland 1595 of 112 kW (150 h.p.) at 1800 r.p.m.
**Transmission:** Mechanical. Cardan shaft and freewheel to a four-speed epicyclic gearbox and final drive.
**Bogies:** DD10.
**Brakes:** Vacuum.
**Couplers:** Screw.
**Dimensions:** 20.45 x 2.82 m.
**Gangways:** Non gangwayed single cars with cabs at each end.
**Wheel arrangement:** 1-A + A-1.
**Doors:** Manually-operated slam.
**Maximum Speed:** 70 m.p.h.
**Seating Layout:** 3+2 facing.
**Multiple Working:** "Blue Square" coupling code. First Generation vehicles cannot be coupled to Second Generation units.

**55020/55032. DMBS.** Lot No. 30518 1960/1961. –/65. 38.0 t.

**Non-standard livery:** 121 020 All over Chiltern blue with a silver stripe.

**Notes:** Fitted with central door locking.

121 020 formerly in departmental use as unit 960 002 (977722).

121 032 formerly in departmental use as 977842, and more recently in preservation at The Railway Age, Crewe.

| | | | | | |
|---|---|---|---|---|---|
| 121 020 | **0** | CR | *CR* | AL | 55020 |
| 121 032 | **AV** | AW | *AW* | CF | 55032 |

## 3.1.2 PARRY PEOPLE MOVERS

## CLASS 139                                                   PPM-60

Gas/flywheel hybrid drive Railcars for use on the Stourbridge Junction–
Stourbridge Town branch from early 2009.
**Body construction:** Stainless steel framework.
**Chassis construction:** Welded mild steel box section.
**Primary Drive:** Ford MVH420 2.0 litre LPG fuel engine driving through Newage
marine gearbox, Tandler bevel box and 4 "V" belt driver to flywheel.
**Flywheel Energy Store:** 500 kg, 1 m diameter, normal operational speed range
1000–1500 r.p.m.
**Final transmission:** 4 "V" belt driver from flywheel to Tandler bevel box, Linde
hydrostatic transmission and spiral bevel gearbox at No. 2 end axle.
**Braking:** Normal service braking by regeneration to flywheel (1 m/s/s);
emergency/parking braking by sprung-on, air-off disc brakes (3 m/s/s).
**Maximum Speed:** 40 m.p.h.
**Dimensions:** 8.7 x 2.4 m.
**Doors:** Deans powered doors, double-leaf folding (one per side).
**Seating Layout:**
**Multiple Working:** Not applicable.

**39001–39002. DMS.** Main Road Sheet Metal, Leyland 2007–08. –/23 1W. 12.5 t.

| 139 001 | **LM** | P | 39001 |
|---------|--------|---|-------|
| 139 002 | **LM** | P | 39002 |

## 3.1.3. SECOND GENERATION UNITS

All units in this section have air brakes and are equipped with public address,
with transmission equipment on driving vehicles and flexible diaphragm
gangways. Except where otherwise stated, transmission is Voith 211r hydraulic
with a cardan shaft to a Gmeinder GM190 final drive.

## CLASS 142    PACER    BREL DERBY/LEYLAND

DMS–DMSL.

**Construction:** Steel underframe, aluminium alloy body and roof. Built from
Leyland National bus parts on four-wheeled underframes.
**Engines:** One Cummins LTA10-R of 172 kW (230 h.p.) at 2100 r.p.m.
**Couplers:** BSI at outer ends, bar within unit.
**Dimensions:** 15.45 x 2.80 m.
**Gangways:** Within unit only.          **Wheel Arrangement:** 1-A + A-1.
**Doors:** Twin-leaf inward pivoting.    **Maximum Speed:** 75 m.p.h.
**Seating Layout:** 3+2 mainly unidirectional bus/bench style unless stated.
**Multiple Working:** Within class and with Classes 143, 144, 150, 153, 155, 156,
158 and 159.

**55542–55591. DMS.** Lot No. 31003 1985–1986. –/62 (c –/46(6) 2W, s –/56, t –/53
or 55 1W, u –/52 or 54 1W). 24.5 t.

**55592–55641. DMSL.** Lot No. 31004 1985–1986. –/59 1T (c –/44(6) 1T 2W, s –/50 1T, u –/60 1T). 25.0 t.
**55701–55746. DMS.** Lot No. 31013 1986–1987. –/62 (c –/46(6) 2W, s –/56, t –/53 or 55 1W, u –/52 or 54 1W). 24.5 t.
**55747–55792. DMSL.** Lot No. 31014 1986–1987. –/59 1T (c –/44(6) 1T 2W, s –/50 1T, u –/60 1T). 25.0 t.

**Notes:**

c Refurbished Arriva Trains Wales units. Fitted with 2+2 individual Chapman seating.
s Fitted with 2+2 individual high-back seating.
t Former First North Western facelifted units – DMS fitted with a luggage/bicycle rack and wheelchair space.
u Merseytravel units – Fitted with 3+2 individual low-back seating.

The following units are on sub-lease from Northern to First Great Western until 30 June 2010: 142 001/009/029/030/063/064/068.

| | | | | | | | |
|---|---|---|---|---|---|---|---|
| 142 001 | t | **NW** | A | *GW* | EX | 55542 | 55592 |
| 142 002 | c | **AV** | A | *AW* | CF | 55543 | 55593 |
| 142 003 | | **NO** | A | *NO* | NH | 55544 | 55594 |
| 142 004 | t | **NW** | A | *NO* | NH | 55545 | 55595 |
| 142 005 | t | **NO** | A | *NO* | NH | 55546 | 55596 |
| 142 006 | c | **AV** | A | *AW* | CF | 55547 | 55597 |
| 142 007 | t | **NO** | A | *NO* | NH | 55548 | 55598 |
| 142 009 | t | **NW** | A | *GW* | EX | 55550 | 55600 |
| 142 010 | c | **AV** | A | *AW* | CF | 55551 | 55601 |
| 142 011 | t | **NO** | A | *NO* | NH | 55552 | 55602 |
| 142 012 | t | **NO** | A | *NO* | NH | 55553 | 55603 |
| 142 013 | | **NO** | A | *NO* | NH | 55554 | 55604 |
| 142 014 | t | **NO** | A | *NO* | NH | 55555 | 55605 |
| 142 015 | s | **NO** | A | *NO* | HT | 55556 | 55606 |
| 142 016 | s | **NO** | A | *NO* | HT | 55557 | 55607 |
| 142 017 | s | **NO** | A | *NO* | HT | 55558 | 55608 |
| 142 018 | s | **NO** | A | *NO* | HT | 55559 | 55609 |
| 142 019 | s | **NO** | A | *NO* | HT | 55560 | 55610 |
| 142 020 | s | **NO** | A | *NO* | HT | 55561 | 55611 |
| 142 021 | s | **NO** | A | *NO* | HT | 55562 | 55612 |
| 142 022 | s | **NO** | A | *NO* | HT | 55563 | 55613 |
| 142 023 | t | **NO** | A | *NO* | HT | 55564 | 55614 |
| 142 024 | s | **NO** | A | *NO* | HT | 55565 | 55615 |
| 142 025 | s | **NO** | A | *NO* | HT | 55566 | 55616 |
| 142 026 | s | **NO** | A | *NO* | HT | 55567 | 55617 |
| 142 027 | t | **NO** | A | *NO* | HT | 55568 | 55618 |
| 142 028 | t | **NW** | A | *NO* | NH | 55569 | 55619 |
| 142 029 | | **NW** | A | *GW* | EX | 55570 | 55620 |
| 142 030 | | **NW** | A | *GW* | EX | 55571 | 55621 |
| 142 031 | t | **NO** | A | *NO* | NH | 55572 | 55622 |
| 142 032 | t | **NO** | A | *NO* | NH | 55573 | 55623 |
| 142 033 | t | **NO** | A | *NO* | NH | 55574 | 55624 |
| 142 034 | t | **NO** | A | *NO* | NH | 55575 | 55625 |
| 142 035 | t | **NO** | A | *NO* | NH | 55576 | 55626 |

| | | | | | | | | |
|---|---|---|---|---|---|---|---|---|
| 142 036 | t | **NO** | A | *NO* | NH | 55577 | 55627 | |
| 142 037 | t | **NO** | A | *NO* | NH | 55578 | 55628 | |
| 142 038 | t | **NO** | A | *NO* | NH | 55579 | 55629 | |
| 142 039 | t | **NO** | A | *NO* | NH | 55580 | 55630 | |
| 142 040 | t | **NO** | A | *NO* | NH | 55581 | 55631 | |
| 142 041 | u | **NO** | A | *NO* | NH | 55582 | 55632 | |
| 142 042 | u | **NO** | A | *NO* | NH | 55583 | 55633 | |
| 142 043 | u | **NO** | A | *NO* | NH | 55584 | 55634 | |
| 142 044 | u | **NO** | A | *NO* | NH | 55585 | 55635 | |
| 142 045 | u | **NO** | A | *NO* | NH | 55586 | 55636 | |
| 142 046 | u | **NO** | A | *NO* | NH | 55587 | 55637 | |
| 142 047 | u | **NO** | A | *NO* | NH | 55588 | 55638 | |
| 142 048 | u | **NO** | A | *NO* | NH | 55589 | 55639 | |
| 142 049 | u | **NO** | A | *NO* | NH | 55590 | 55640 | |
| 142 050 | s | **NO** | A | *NO* | HT | 55591 | 55641 | |
| 142 051 | u | **NO** | A | *NO* | NH | 55701 | 55747 | |
| 142 052 | u | **NO** | A | *NO* | NH | 55702 | 55748 | |
| 142 053 | u | **NO** | A | *NO* | NH | 55703 | 55749 | |
| 142 054 | u | **NO** | A | *NO* | NH | 55704 | 55750 | |
| 142 055 | u | **NO** | A | *NO* | NH | 55705 | 55751 | |
| 142 056 | u | **NO** | A | *NO* | NH | 55706 | 55752 | |
| 142 057 | u | **NO** | A | *NO* | NH | 55707 | 55753 | |
| 142 058 | u | **NO** | A | *NO* | NH | 55708 | 55754 | |
| 142 060 | t | **NO** | A | *NO* | NH | 55710 | 55756 | |
| 142 061 | t | **NO** | A | *NO* | NH | 55711 | 55757 | |
| 142 062 | t | **NW** | A | *NO* | NH | 55712 | 55758 | |
| 142 063 | t | **NW** | A | *GW* | EX | 55713 | 55759 | |
| 142 064 | t | **NW** | A | *GW* | EX | 55714 | 55760 | |
| 142 065 | s | **NO** | A | *NO* | HT | 55715 | 55761 | |
| 142 066 | s | **NO** | A | *NO* | HT | 55716 | 55762 | |
| 142 067 | | **NW** | A | *NO* | NH | 55717 | 55763 | |
| 142 068 | t | **NW** | A | *GW* | EX | 55718 | 55764 | |
| 142 069 | c | **AV** | A | *AW* | CF | 55719 | 55765 | |
| 142 070 | t | **NO** | A | *NO* | HT | 55720 | 55766 | |
| 142 071 | s | **NO** | A | *NO* | HT | 55721 | 55767 | |
| 142 072 | c | **AV** | A | *AW* | CF | 55722 | 55768 | |
| 142 073 | c | **AV** | A | *AW* | CF | 55723 | 55769 | Myfanwy |
| 142 074 | c | **AV** | A | *AW* | CF | 55724 | 55770 | |
| 142 075 | c | **AV** | A | *AW* | CF | 55725 | 55771 | |
| 142 076 | c | **AV** | A | *AW* | CF | 55726 | 55772 | |
| 142 077 | c | **AV** | A | *AW* | CF | 55727 | 55773 | |
| 142 078 | s | **NO** | A | *NO* | HT | 55728 | 55774 | |
| 142 079 | s | **AV** | A | *NO* | HT | 55729 | 55775 | |
| 142 080 | c | **AV** | A | *AW* | CF | 55730 | 55776 | |
| 142 081 | c | **AV** | A | *AW* | CF | 55731 | 55777 | |
| 142 082 | c | **AV** | A | *AW* | CF | 55732 | 55778 | |
| 142 083 | c | **AV** | A | *AW* | CF | 55733 | 55779 | |
| 142 084 | s | **NO** | A | *NO* | HT | 55734 | 55780 | |
| 142 085 | c | **AV** | A | *AW* | CF | 55735 | 55781 | |
| 142 086 | s | **NO** | A | *NO* | HT | 55736 | 55782 | |
| 142 087 | s | **AV** | A | *NO* | HT | 55737 | 55783 | |

| | | | | | | |
|---|---|---|---|---|---|---|
| 142 088 | s | AV | A | NO | HT | 55738 55784 |
| 142 089 | s | NO | A | NO | HT | 55739 55785 |
| 142 090 | s | NO | A | NO | HT | 55740 55786 |
| 142 091 | s | AV | A | NO | HT | 55741 55787 |
| 142 092 | s | AV | A | NO | HT | 55742 55788 |
| 142 093 | s | AV | A | NO | HT | 55743 55789 |
| 142 094 | s | AV | A | NO | HT | 55744 55790 |
| 142 095 | s | AV | A | NO | HT | 55745 55791 |
| 142 096 | s | AV | A | NO | HT | 55746 55792 |

## CLASS 143    PACER    ALEXANDER/BARCLAY

DMS–DMSL. Similar design to Class 142, but bodies built by W. Alexander with Barclay underframes.

**Construction:** Steel underframe, aluminium alloy body and roof. Alexander bus bodywork on four-wheeled underframes.
**Engines:** One Cummins LTA10-R of 172 kW (230 h.p.) at 2100 r.p.m.
**Couplers:** BSI at outer ends, bar within unit.
**Dimensions:** 15.45 x 2.80 m.
**Gangways:** Within unit only.          **Wheel Arrangement:** 1-A + A-1.
**Doors:** Twin-leaf inward pivoting.     **Maximum Speed:** 75 m.p.h.
**Seating Layout:** 2+2 high-back Chapman seating, mainly unidirectional.
**Multiple Working:** Within class and with Classes 142, 144, 150, 153, 155, 156, 158 and 159.

**DMS.** Lot No. 31005 Andrew Barclay 1985–1986. –/48(6) 2W. 24.0 t.
**DMSL.** Lot No. 31006 Andrew Barclay 1985–1986. –/44(6) 1T 2W. 24.5 t.

| | | | | | | |
|---|---|---|---|---|---|---|
| 143 601 | AV | BC | AW | CF | 55642 55667 | |
| 143 602 | AV | P | AW | CF | 55661 55668 | |
| 143 603 | FI | P | GW | EX | 55658 55669 | |
| 143 604 | AV | P | AW | CF | 55645 55670 | |
| 143 605 | AV | P | AW | CF | 55646 55671 | |
| 143 606 | AV | P | AW | CF | 55647 55672 | |
| 143 607 | AV | P | AW | CF | 55648 55673 | |
| 143 608 | AV | P | AW | CF | 55649 55674 | |
| 143 609 | AV | CC | AW | CF | 55650 55675 | Sir Tom Jones |
| 143 610 | AV | BC | AW | CF | 55643 55676 | |
| 143 611 | BI | P | GW | EX | 55652 55677 | |
| 143 612 | FI | P | GW | EX | 55653 55678 | |
| 143 614 | AV | BC | AW | CF | 55655 55680 | |
| 143 616 | AV | P | AW | CF | 55657 55682 | |
| 143 617 | FI | RI | GW | EX | 55644 55683 | |
| 143 618 | FI | RI | GW | EX | 55659 55684 | |
| 143 619 | BI | RI | GW | EX | 55660 55685 | |
| 143 620 | BI | P | GW | EX | 55661 55686 | |
| 143 621 | BI | P | GW | EX | 55662 55687 | |
| 143 622 | AV | P | AW | CF | 55663 55688 | |
| 143 623 | AV | P | AW | CF | 55664 55689 | |
| 143 624 | AV | P | AW | CF | 55665 55690 | |
| 143 625 | AV | P | AW | CF | 55666 55691 | |

# CLASS 144 PACER ALEXANDER/BREL DERBY

DMS–DMSL or DMS–MS–DMSL. As Class 143, but underframes built by BREL.

**Construction:** Steel underframe, aluminium alloy body and roof. Alexander bus bodywork on four-wheeled underframes.
**Engines:** One Cummins LTA10-R of 172 kW (230 h.p.) at 2100 r.p.m.
**Couplers:** BSI at outer ends, bar within unit.
**Dimensions:** 15.45/15.43 x 2.80 m.
**Gangways:** Within unit only. **Wheel Arrangement:** 1-A + A-1.
**Doors:** Twin-leaf inward pivoting. **Maximum Speed:** 75 m.p.h.
**Seating Layout:** 2+2 high-back Richmond seating, mainly unidirectional.
**Multiple Working:** Within class and with Classes 142, 143, 150, 153, 155, 156, 158 and 159.

**DMS.** Lot No. 31015 BREL Derby 1986–1987. –/45(3) 1W 24.0 t.
**MS.** Lot No. BREL Derby 31037 1987. –/58. 23.5 t.
**DMSL.** Lot No. BREL Derby 31016 1986–1987. –/42(3) 1T. 24.5 t.

**Note:** The centre cars of the 3-car units are owned by West Yorkshire PTE, although managed by Porterbrook Leasing Company.

| | | | | | | |
|---|---|---|---|---|---|---|
| 144 001 | **YP** | P | *NO* | NL | 55801 | | 55824 |
| 144 002 | **YP** | P | *NO* | NL | 55802 | | 55825 |
| 144 003 | **YP** | P | *NO* | NL | 55803 | | 55826 |
| 144 004 | **YP** | P | *NO* | NL | 55804 | | 55827 |
| 144 005 | **YP** | P | *NO* | NL | 55805 | | 55828 |
| 144 006 | **YP** | P | *NO* | NL | 55806 | | 55829 |
| 144 007 | **YP** | P | *NO* | NL | 55807 | | 55830 |
| 144 008 | **YP** | P | *NO* | NL | 55808 | | 55831 |
| 144 009 | **YP** | P | *NO* | NL | 55809 | | 55832 |
| 144 010 | **YP** | P | *NO* | NL | 55810 | | 55833 |
| 144 011 | **YP** | P | *NO* | NL | 55811 | | 55834 |
| 144 012 | **YP** | P | *NO* | NL | 55812 | | 55835 |
| 144 013 | **YP** | P | *NO* | NL | 55813 | | 55836 |
| 144 014 | **YP** | P | *NO* | NL | 55814 | 55850 | 55837 |
| 144 015 | **YP** | P | *NO* | NL | 55815 | 55851 | 55838 |
| 144 016 | **YP** | P | *NO* | NL | 55816 | 55852 | 55839 |
| 144 017 | **YP** | P | *NO* | NL | 55817 | 55853 | 55840 |
| 144 018 | **YP** | P | *NO* | NL | 55818 | 55854 | 55841 |
| 144 019 | **YP** | P | *NO* | NL | 55819 | 55855 | 55842 |
| 144 020 | **YP** | P | *NO* | NL | 55820 | 55856 | 55843 |
| 144 021 | **YP** | P | *NO* | NL | 55821 | 55857 | 55844 |
| 144 022 | **YP** | P | *NO* | NL | 55822 | 55858 | 55845 |
| 144 023 | **YP** | P | *NO* | NL | 55823 | 55859 | 55846 |

**Name (carried on DMSL):**

144 001 THE PENISTONE LINE PARTNERSHIP

## CLASS 150/0          SPRINTER          BREL YORK

DMSL–MS–DMS. Prototype Sprinter.

**Construction:** Steel.
**Engines:** One Cummins NT-855-R4 of 213 kW (285 h.p.) at 2100 r.p.m.
**Bogies:** BX8P (powered), BX8T (non-powered).
**Couplers:** BSI at outer end of driving vehicles, bar non-driving ends.
**Dimensions:** 20.06/20.18 x 2.82 m.
**Gangways:** Within unit only.          **Wheel Arrangement:** 2-B + 2-B + B-2.
**Doors:** Twin-leaf sliding.          **Maximum Speed:** 75 m.p.h.
**Seating Layout:** 3+2 (mainly unidirectional).
**Multiple Working:** Within class and with Classes 142, 143, 144, 153, 155, 156, 158, 159, 170 and 172.

**DMSL.** Lot No. 30984 1984. –/72 1T. 35.4 t.
**MS.** Lot No. 30986 1984. –/92. 34.1 t.
**DMS.** Lot No. 30985 1984. –/76. 29.5 t.

| | | | | | | | |
|---|---|---|---|---|---|---|---|
| 150 001 | | CI | A | *LM* | TS | 55200 55400 55300 |
| 150 002 | | CI | A | *LM* | TS | 55201 55401 55301 |

## CLASS 150/1          SPRINTER          BREL YORK

DMSL–DMS or DMSL–DMSL–DMS or DMSL–DMS–DMS.

**Construction:** Steel.
**Engines:** One Cummins NT855R5 of 213 kW (285 h.p.) at 2100 r.p.m.
**Bogies:** BP38 (powered), BT38 (non-powered).
**Couplers:** BSI.
**Dimensions:** 19.74 x 2.82 m.
**Gangways:** Within unit only.          **Wheel Arrangement:** 2-B (+ 2–B) + B-2.
**Doors:** Twin-leaf sliding.          **Maximum Speed:** 75 m.p.h.
**Seating Layout:** 3+2 facing as built but Centro units were reseated with mainly unidirectional seating.
**Multiple Working:** Within class and with Classes 142, 143, 144, 153, 155, 156, 158, 159, 170 and 172.

**DMSL.** Lot No. 31011 1985–1986. –/72 1T (c –/59 1TD (except 52144 which is –/62 1TD), t –/71 1T, u –/71 1T). 38.3 t.
**DMS.** Lot No. 31012 1985–1986. –/76 (c –/65, t –/73, u –/70). 38.1 t.

**Northern promotional vinyls:** 150 146 & 150 147 Liverpool: European Capital of Culture.

**Notes:** The centre cars of 3-car units are Class 150/2 vehicles. For details see Class 150/2.

c 3+2 Chapman seating.

| | | | | | | | | |
|---|---|---|---|---|---|---|---|---|
| 150 003 | u | **WM** | A | *LM* | TS | 52103 | 57210 | 57103 |
| 150 005 | u | **CI** | A | *LM* | TS | 52105 | 52210 | 57105 |
| 150 007 | u | **CI** | A | *LM* | TS | 52107 | 52202 | 57107 |
| 150 009 | u | **CI** | A | *LM* | TS | 52109 | 57202 | 57109 |

| | | | | | | | | |
|---|---|---|---|---|---|---|---|---|
| 150 010 | u | **WM** | A | *LM* | TS | 52110 | 57226 | 57110 | |
| 150 011 | u | **CI** | A | *LM* | TS | 52111 | 52204 | 57111 | |
| 150 012 | u | **CI** | A | *LM* | TS | 52112 | 57206 | 57112 | |
| 150 013 | u | **CI** | A | *LM* | TS | 52113 | 52226 | 57113 | |
| 150 014 | u | **CI** | A | *LM* | TS | 52114 | 57204 | 57114 | |
| 150 015 | u | **CI** | A | *LM* | TS | 52115 | 52206 | 57115 | |
| 150 016 | u | **CI** | A | *LM* | TS | 52116 | 57212 | 57116 | |
| 150 017 | u | **CI** | A | *LM* | TS | 52117 | 57209 | 57117 | |
| 150 018 | u | **WM** | A | *LM* | TS | 52118 | 52220 | 57118 | |
| 150 019 | u | **CI** | A | *LM* | TS | 52119 | 57220 | 57119 | |
| | | | | | | | | | |
| 150 101 | u | **CI** | A | *LM* | TS | 52101 | 57101 | |
| 150 102 | u | **CI** | A | *LM* | TS | 52102 | 57102 | |
| 150 104 | u | **CI** | A | *LM* | TS | 52104 | 57104 | |
| 150 106 | u | **CI** | A | *LM* | TS | 52106 | 57106 | |
| 150 108 | u | **CI** | A | *LM* | TS | 52108 | 57108 | |
| 150 120 | t | **SL** | A | *LO* | WN | 52120 | 57120 | Gospel Oak–Barking 2000 |
| 150 121 | u | **SL** | A | *GW* | PM | 52121 | 57121 | |
| 150 122 | u | **CI** | A | *LM* | TS | 52122 | 57122 | |
| 150 123 | t | **SL** | A | *LO* | WN | 52123 | 57123 | Willesden TMD |
| 150 124 | u | **CI** | A | *LM* | TS | 52124 | 57124 | |
| 150 125 | u | **CI** | A | *LM* | TS | 52125 | 57125 | |
| 150 126 | u | **WM** | A | *LM* | TS | 52126 | 57126 | |
| 150 127 | t | **SL** | A | *GW* | PM | 52127 | 57127 | |
| 150 128 | t | **SL** | A | *LO* | WN | 52128 | 57128 | Bedford-Bamberg 30 |
| 150 129 | t | **SL** | A | *LO* | WN | 52129 | 57129 | ~~MARSTON VALE~~ |
| 150 130 | t | **SL** | A | *LO* | WN | 52130 | 57130 | ~~Bedford–Bletchley 150~~ |
| 150 131 | t | **SL** | A | *LO* | WN | 52131 | 57131 | LESLIE CRABBE |
| 150 132 | u | **WM** | A | *LM* | TS | 52132 | 57132 | |
| 150 133 | c | **NO** | A | *NO* | NH | 52133 | 57133 | |
| 150 134 | c | **NO** | A | *NO* | NH | 52134 | 57134 | |
| 150 135 | c | **NO** | A | *NO* | NH | 52135 | 57135 | |
| 150 136 | c | **NO** | A | *NO* | NH | 52136 | 57136 | |
| 150 137 | c | **NO** | A | *NO* | NH | 52137 | 57137 | |
| 150 138 | c | **NO** | A | *NO* | NH | 52138 | 57138 | |
| 150 139 | c | **NO** | A | *NO* | NH | 52139 | 57139 | |
| 150 140 | c | **NO** | A | *NO* | NH | 52140 | 57140 | |
| 150 141 | c | **NO** | A | *NO* | NH | 52141 | 57141 | |
| 150 142 | c | **NO** | A | *NO* | NH | 52142 | 57142 | |
| 150 143 | c | **NO** | A | *NO* | NH | 52143 | 57143 | |
| 150 144 | c | **NO** | A | *NO* | NH | 52144 | 57144 | |
| 150 145 | c | **NO** | A | *NO* | NH | 52145 | 57145 | |
| 150 146 | c | **NO** | A | *NO* | NH | 52146 | 57146 | |
| 150 147 | c | **NO** | A | *NO* | NH | 52147 | 57147 | |
| 150 148 | c | **NO** | A | *NO* | NH | 52148 | 57148 | |
| 150 149 | c | **NO** | A | *NO* | NH | 52149 | 57149 | |
| 150 150 | c | **NO** | A | *NO* | NH | 52150 | 57150 | |

# CLASS 150/2          SPRINTER          BREL YORK

DMSL–DMS.

**Construction:** Steel.
**Engines:** One Cummins NT855R5 of 213 kW (285 h.p.) at 2100 r.p.m.
**Bogies:** BP38 (powered), BT38 (non-powered).
**Couplers:** BSI.
**Dimensions:** 19.74 x 2.82 m.
**Gangways:** Throughout.                **Wheel Arrangement:** 2-B + B-2.
**Doors:** Twin-leaf sliding.            **Maximum Speed:** 75 m.p.h.
**Seating Layout:** 3+2 mainly unidirectional seating as built, but most units have now been refurbished with new 2+2 seating (see notes below).
**Multiple Working:** Within class and with Classes 142, 143, 144, 153, 155, 156, 158, 159, 170 and 172.

**DMSL.** Lot No. 31017 1986–1987. –/73 1T (c –/62 1TD, p –/60(4) 1T, u –/71 1T), v –/60(8) 1T, w –/60(8) 1T). 37.5 t.
**DMS.** Lot No. 31018 1986–1987. –/76 (c –/70, p –/56(10) 1W, u –/70), v –/56(15) 2W, w –/56(17) 2W, z –/68). 36.5 t.

**Northern promotional vinyls:** 150 271 Rugby League (Northern Rail Cup).
150 272 R&B Festival week, Colne.

**Notes:**

c   3+2 Chapman seating (former First North Western units).
p   Refurbished Arriva Trains Wales units with 2+2 Primarius seating.
v   Units refurbished for Valley Lines with 2+2 Chapman seating.
w   Units refurbished for First Great Western with 2+2 Chapman seating.

The following units are on short-term sub-lease from Arriva Trains Wales to First Great Western: 150 267/278–281.

| 150 201 | c | **NO** | A | *NO* | NH | 52201 | 57201 |
| 150 203 | c | **NO** | A | *NO* | NH | 52203 | 57203 |
| 150 205 | c | **NO** | A | *NO* | NH | 52205 | 57205 |
| 150 207 | c | **NO** | A | *NO* | NH | 52207 | 57207 |
| 150 208 | p | **AV** | P | *AW* | CF | 52208 | 57208 |
| 150 211 | c | **NO** | A | *NO* | NH | 52211 | 57211 |
| 150 213 | p | **AV** | P | *AW* | CF | 52213 | 57213 |
| 150 214 | u | **CI** | A | *LM* | TS | 52214 | 57214 |
| 150 215 | c | **NO** | A | *NO* | NH | 52215 | 57215 |
| 150 216 | u | **CI** | A | *LM* | TS | 52216 | 57216 |
| 150 217 | p | **AV** | P | *AW* | CF | 52217 | 57217 |
| 150 218 | c | **NO** | A | *NO* | NH | 52218 | 57218 |
| 150 219 | w | **FI** | P | *GW* | PM | 52219 | 57219 |
| 150 221 | w | **FI** | P | *GW* | PM | 52221 | 57221 |
| 150 222 | c | **NO** | A | *NO* | NH | 52222 | 57222 |
| 150 223 | c | **NO** | A | *NO* | NH | 52223 | 57223 |
| 150 224 | c | **NO** | A | *NO* | NH | 52224 | 57224 |
| 150 225 | c | **NO** | A | *NO* | NH | 52225 | 57225 |
| 150 227 | p | **AV** | P | *AW* | CF | 52227 | 57227 |

| | | | | | | | |
|---|---|---|---|---|---|---|---|
| 150 228 | | NO | P | NO | NH | 52228 | 57228 | |
| 150 229 | p | AV | P | AW | CF | 52229 | 57229 | |
| 150 230 | w | AV | P | AW | CF | 52230 | 57230 | |
| 150 231 | p | AV | P | AW | CF | 52231 | 57231 | |
| 150 232 | w | FI | P | GW | PM | 52232 | 57232 | |
| 150 233 | w | FI | P | GW | PM | 52233 | 57233 | |
| 150 234 | w | FI | P | GW | PM | 52234 | 57234 | |
| 150 235 | p | AV | P | AW | CF | 52235 | 57235 | |
| 150 236 | w | AV | P | AW | CF | 52236 | 57236 | |
| 150 237 | p | AV | P | AW | CF | 52237 | 57237 | |
| 150 238 | w | FI | P | GW | PM | 52238 | 57238 | |
| 150 239 | w | FI | P | GW | PM | 52239 | 57239 | |
| 150 240 | w | AV | P | AW | CF | 52240 | 57240 | |
| 150 241 | w | AV | P | AW | CF | 52241 | 57241 | |
| 150 242 | w | AV | P | AW | CF | 52242 | 57242 | |
| 150 243 | w | FI | P | GW | PM | 52243 | 57243 | |
| 150 244 | w | FI | P | GW | PM | 52244 | 57244 | |
| 150 245 | p | AV | P | AW | CF | 52245 | 57245 | |
| 150 246 | w | FI | P | GW | PM | 52246 | 57246 | |
| 150 247 | w | FI | P | GW | PM | 52247 | 57247 | |
| 150 248 | w | FI | P | GW | PM | 52248 | 57248 | |
| 150 249 | w | FI | P | GW | PM | 52249 | 57249 | |
| 150 250 | p | AV | P | AW | CF | 52250 | 57250 | |
| 150 251 | w | AV | P | AW | CF | 52251 | 57251 | |
| 150 252 | p | AV | P | AW | CF | 52252 | 57252 | |
| 150 253 | w | AV | P | AW | CF | 52253 | 57253 | |
| 150 254 | w | AV | P | AW | CF | 52254 | 57254 | |
| 150 255 | p | AV | P | AW | CF | 52255 | 57255 | |
| 150 256 | p | AV | P | AW | CF | 52256 | 57256 | |
| 150 257 | p | AV | P | AW | CF | 52257 | 57257 | |
| 150 258 | p | AV | P | AW | CF | 52258 | 57258 | |
| 150 259 | p | AV | P | AW | CF | 52259 | 57259 | |
| 150 260 | p | AV | P | AW | CF | 52260 | 57260 | |
| 150 261 | w | FI | P | GW | PM | 52261 | 57261 | |
| 150 262 | p | AV | P | AW | CF | 52262 | 57262 | |
| 150 263 | w | FI | P | GW | PM | 52263 | 57263 | |
| 150 264 | p | AV | P | AW | CF | 52264 | 57264 | |
| 150 265 | w | WZ | P | GW | PM | 52265 | 57265 | The Falmouth Flyer |
| 150 266 | w | FI | P | GW | PM | 52266 | 57266 | |
| 150 267 | v | AV | P | GW | PM | 52267 | 57267 | |
| 150 268 | | NO | P | NO | NH | 52268 | 57268 | Benny Rothman – The Manchester Rambler |
| 150 269 | | NO | P | NO | NH | 52269 | 57269 | |
| 150 270 | | NO | P | NO | NH | 52270 | 57270 | |
| 150 271 | | NO | P | NO | NH | 52271 | 57271 | |
| 150 272 | | NO | P | NO | NH | 52272 | 57272 | |
| 150 273 | | NO | P | NO | NH | 52273 | 57273 | Driver John Axon G.C. |
| 150 274 | | NO | P | NO | NH | 52274 | 57274 | |
| 150 275 | | NO | P | NO | NH | 52275 | 57275 | |
| 150 276 | | NO | P | NO | NH | 52276 | 57276 | |
| 150 277 | | NO | P | NO | NH | 52277 | 57277 | |

| | | | | | | |
|---|---|---|---|---|---|---|
| 150 278 | v | **AV** | P | *GW* | PM | 52278 | 57278 |
| 150 279 | v | **AV** | P | *GW* | PM | 52279 | 57279 |
| 150 280 | v | **AV** | P | *GW* | PM | 52280 | 57280 |
| 150 281 | v | **AV** | P | *GW* | PM | 52281 | 57281 |
| 150 282 | v | **AV** | P | *AW* | CF | 52282 | 57282 |
| 150 283 | p | **AV** | P | *AW* | CF | 52283 | 57283 |
| 150 284 | p | **AV** | P | *AW* | CF | 52284 | 57284 |
| 150 285 | p | **AV** | P | *AW* | CF | 52285 | 57285 |

# CLASS 153   SUPER SPRINTER   LEYLAND BUS

DMSL. Converted by Hunslet-Barclay, Kilmarnock from Class 155 2-car units.

**Construction:** Steel underframe, aluminium alloy body and roof. Built from Leyland National bus parts on bogied underframes.
**Engine:** One Cummins NT855R5 of 213 kW (285 h.p.) at 2100 r.p.m.
**Bogies:** One P3-10 (powered) and one BT38 (non-powered).
**Couplers:** BSI.
**Dimensions:** 23.21 x 2.70 m.
**Gangways:** Throughout.                    **Wheel Arrangement:** 2-B.
**Doors:** Single-leaf sliding plug.          **Maximum Speed:** 75 m.p.h.
**Seating Layout:** 2+2 facing/unidirectional.
**Multiple Working:** Within class and with Classes 142, 143, 144, 150, 155, 156, 158, 159, 170 and 172.

**52301–52335. DMSL.** Lot No. 31026 1987–1988. Converted under Lot No. 31115 1991–1992. –/72(3) 1T 1W. (* –/66(3) 1T 1W, s –/72 1T 1W, t –/72(2) 1T 1W). 41.2 t.
**57301–57335. DMSL.** Lot No. 31027 1987–1988. Converted under Lot No. 31115 1991–1992. –/72(3) 1T 1W. (* –/66(3) 1T 1W). 41.2 t.

**Notes:** Cars numbered in the 573xx series were renumbered by adding 50 to their original number so that the last two digits correspond with the set number.

*   Refurbished East Anglia area units with a bicycle rack.
c   Chapman seating.
d   Richmond seating.
Units not shown as c or d were reseated using original Class 158 seats.

| | | | | | | | |
|---|---|---|---|---|---|---|---|
| 153 301 | d | **NO** | A | *NO* | NL | 52301 | |
| 153 302 | | **DC** | A | *EM* | NM | 52302 | |
| 153 303 | | **AV** | A | *AW* | CF | 52303 | |
| 153 304 | d | **NO** | A | *NO* | NL | 52304 | |
| 153 305 | d | **FI** | A | *GW* | EX | 52305 | |
| 153 306 | cr | **1** | P | *EA* | NC | 52306 | |
| 153 307 | d | **NO** | A | *NO* | NL | 52307 | |
| 153 308 | | **DC** | A | *EM* | NM | 52308 | |
| 153 309 | cr | **AR** | P | *EA* | NC | 52309 | GERARD FIENNES |
| 153 310 | c | **EM** | P | *EM* | NM | 52310 | |
| 153 311 | c* | **EM** | P | *EM* | NM | 52311 | |
| 153 312 | s | **AV** | A | *AW* | CF | 52312 | |
| 153 313 | cs | **NW** | P | *EM* | NM | 52313 | |
| 153 314 | cr | **1** | P | *EA* | NC | 52314 | |
| 153 315 | ds | **NO** | A | *NO* | NL | 52315 | |

| | | | | | | | |
|---|---|---|---|---|---|---|---|
| 153 316 | c | **NO** | P | *NO* | NL | 52316 | |
| 153 317 | d | **NO** | A | *NO* | NL | 52317 | |
| 153 318 | d | **FI** | A | *GW* | EX | 52318 | |
| 153 319 | d | **EM** | A | *EM* | NM | 52319 | |
| 153 320 | | **AV** | P | *AW* | CF | 52320 | |
| 153 321 | c | **EM** | P | *EM* | NM | 52321 | |
| 153 322 | cr | **AR** | P | *EA* | NC | 52322 | BENJAMIN BRITTEN |
| 153 323 | | **AV** | P | *AW* | CF | 52323 | |
| 153 324 | c | **NO** | P | *NO* | NL | 52324 | |
| 153 325 | c | **LM** | P | *LM* | TS | 52325 | |
| 153 326 | c* | **EM** | P | *EM* | NM | 52326 | |
| 153 327 | | **AV** | A | *AW* | CF | 52327 | |
| 153 328 | d | **NO** | A | *NO* | NL | 52328 | |
| 153 329 | c | **FI** | P | *GW* | EX | 52329 | |
| 153 330 | cs | **NO** | P | *NO* | NL | 52330 | |
| 153 331 | d | **NO** | A | *NO* | NL | 52331 | |
| 153 332 | c | **NW** | P | *NO* | NL | 52332 | |
| 153 333 | cs | **CT** | P | *LM* | TS | 52333 | |
| 153 334 | ct | **LM** | P | *LM* | TS | 52334 | |
| 153 335 | cr | **AR** | P | *EA* | NC | 52335 | MICHAEL PALIN |
| 153 351 | d | **NO** | A | *NO* | NL | 57351 | |
| 153 352 | d | **NO** | A | *NO* | NL | 57352 | |
| 153 353 | | **AV** | A | *AW* | CF | 57353 | |
| 153 354 | c | **LM** | P | *LM* | TS | 57354 | |
| 153 355 | | **EM** | A | *EM* | NM | 57355 | |
| 153 356 | c | **LM** | P | *LM* | TS | 57356 | |
| 153 357 | d | **EM** | A | *EM* | NM | 57357 | |
| 153 358 | c | **NW** | P | *NO* | NL | 57358 | |
| 153 359 | c | **NW** | P | *NO* | NL | 57359 | |
| 153 360 | c | **NW** | P | *NO* | NL | 57360 | |
| 153 361 | cs | **FI** | P | *GW* | EX | 57361 | |
| 153 362 | | **AV** | A | *AW* | CF | 57362 | Dylan Thomas 1914–1953 |
| 153 363 | cs | **NW** | P | *NO* | NL | 57363 | |
| 153 364 | c | **CT** | P | *LM* | TS | 57364 | |
| 153 365 | c | **LM** | P | *LM* | TS | 57365 | |
| 153 366 | c | **CT** | P | *LM* | TS | 57366 | |
| 153 367 | c | **AV** | P | *AW* | CF | 57367 | |
| 153 368 | d | **FI** | A | *GW* | EX | 57368 | |
| 153 369 | c | **FI** | P | *GW* | EX | 57369 | |
| 153 370 | d | **FI** | A | *GW* | EX | 57370 | |
| 153 371 | c | **CT** | P | *LM* | TS | 57371 | |
| 153 372 | d | **FI** | A | *GW* | EX | 57372 | |
| 153 373 | d | **FI** | A | *GW* | EX | 57373 | |
| 153 374 | | **EM** | A | *EM* | NM | 57374 | |
| 153 375 | c | **CT** | P | *LM* | TS | 57375 | |
| 153 376 | c | **CT** | P | *EM* | NM | 57376 | |
| 153 377 | d | **FI** | A | *GW* | EX | 57377 | |
| 153 378 | d | **NO** | A | *NO* | NL | 57378 | |
| 153 379 | c | **CT** | P | *EM* | NM | 57379 | |
| 153 380 | d | **FI** | A | *GW* | EX | 57380 | |
| 153 381 | c | **EM** | P | *EM* | NM | 57381 | |

| 153 382 | d | **FI** | A | *GW* | EX | 57382 |
|---------|---|--------|---|------|-----|-------|
| 153 383 | c | **CT** | P | *EM* | NM | 57383 |
| 153 384 | c | **CT** | P | *EM* | NM | 57384 |
| 153 385 | c | **CT** | P | *EM* | NM | 57385 |

# CLASS 155   SUPER SPRINTER   LEYLAND BUS

DMSL–DMS.

**Construction:** Steel underframe, aluminium alloy body and roof. Built from Leyland National bus parts on bogied underframes.
**Engines:** One Cummins NT855R5 of 213 kW (285 h.p.) at 2100 r.p.m.
**Bogies:** One P3-10 (powered) and one BT38 (non-powered).
**Couplers:** BSI.
**Dimensions:** 23.21 x 2.70 m.
**Gangways:** Throughout.                 **Wheel Arrangement:** 2-B + B-2.
**Doors:** Single-leaf sliding plug.       **Maximum Speed:** 75 m.p.h.
**Seating Layout:** 2+2 facing/unidirectional Chapman seating.
**Multiple Working:** Within class and with Classes 142, 143, 144, 150, 153, 156, 158, 159, 170 and 172.

**DMSL.** Lot No. 31057 1988. –/76 1TD 1W. 39.0 t.
**DMS.** Lot No. 31058 1988. –/80. 38.6 t.

**Northern promotional vinyls:** 155 341–347 Leeds–Bradford–Manchester route (the "Calder Valley").

**Note:** These units are owned by West Yorkshire PTE, although managed by Porterbrook Leasing Company.

| 155 341 | **NO** | P | *NO* | NL | 52341 | 57341 |
|---------|--------|---|------|-----|-------|-------|
| 155 342 | **NO** | P | *NO* | NL | 52342 | 57342 |
| 155 343 | **NO** | P | *NO* | NL | 52343 | 57343 |
| 155 344 | **NO** | P | *NO* | NL | 52344 | 57344 |
| 155 345 | **NO** | P | *NO* | NL | 52345 | 57345 |
| 155 346 | **NO** | P | *NO* | NL | 52346 | 57346 |
| 155 347 | **NO** | P | *NO* | NL | 52347 | 57347 |

# CLASS 156 SUPER SPRINTER METRO-CAMMELL

DMSL–DMS.

**Construction:** Steel.
**Engines:** One Cummins NT855R5 of 213 kW (285 h.p.) at 2100 r.p.m.
**Bogies:** One P3-10 (powered) and one BT38 (non-powered).
**Couplers:** BSI.
**Dimensions:** 23.03 x 2.73 m.
**Gangways:** Throughout.                 **Wheel Arrangement:** 2-B + B-2.
**Doors:** Single-leaf sliding.            **Maximum Speed:** 75 m.p.h.
**Seating Layout:** 2+2 facing/unidirectional.
**Multiple Working:** Within class and with Classes 142, 143, 144, 150, 153, 155, 158, 159, 170 and 172.

**DMSL.** Lot No. 31028 1988–1989. –/74 (†* –/72, c, t –/70, u –/68) 1TD 1W. 38.6 t.
**DMS.** Lot No. 31029 1987–1989. –/76 (d –/78, † –/74, t, u –/72) 37.9 t.

**Non-standard livery:** 156 425, 156 460 & 156 464 Northern experimental. White with two-tone lilac swooshe.

**Advertising livery:** 156 402 Chapelfield Shopping Centre (white & blue).

**Northern promotional vinyls:**

156 448 Hadrians Wall Country (Newcastle–Carlisle line).
156 461 Ravenglass & Eskdale Railway.
156 469 Bishop Auckland branch.
156 484 Settle & Carlisle line.
156 490 National Railway Museum.

**Notes:**

c  Chapman seating.
d  Richmond seating.

| | | | | | | |
|---|---|---|---|---|---|---|
| 156 401 | c* | **EM** | P | *EM* | DY | 52401 57401 |
| 156 402 | cr | **AL** | P | *EA* | NC | 52402 57402 |
| 156 403 | c* | **EM** | P | *EM* | DY | 52403 57403 |
| 156 404 | c* | **EM** | P | *EM* | DY | 52404 57404 |
| 156 405 | c* | **EM** | P | *EM* | DY | 52405 57405 |
| 156 406 | c* | **EM** | P | *EM* | DY | 52406 57406 |
| 156 407 | cr | **1** | P | *EA* | NC | 52407 57407 |
| 156 408 | c* | **EM** | P | *EM* | DY | 52408 57408 |
| 156 409 | cr | **1** | P | *EA* | NC | 52409 57409 |
| 156 410 | c* | **EM** | P | *EM* | DY | 52410 57410 |
| 156 411 | c* | **EM** | P | *EM* | DY | 52411 57411 |
| 156 412 | cr | **CT** | P | *EA* | NC | 52412 57412 |
| 156 413 | c* | **EM** | P | *EM* | DY | 52413 57413 |
| 156 414 | c* | **EM** | P | *EM* | DY | 52414 57414 |
| 156 415 | c* | **EM** | P | *EM* | DY | 52415 57415 |
| 156 416 | cr | **1** | P | *EA* | NC | 52416 57416 |
| 156 417 | cr | **1** | P | *EA* | NC | 52417 57417 |
| 156 418 | cr | **CT** | P | *EA* | NC | 52418 57418 |
| 156 419 | cr | **NX** | P | *EA* | NC | 52419 57419 |
| 156 420 | c | **FS** | P | *NO* | NH | 52420 57420 |
| 156 421 | c | **NO** | P | *NO* | NH | 52421 57421 |
| 156 422 | cr | **1** | P | *EA* | NC | 52422 57422 |
| 156 423 | c | **FS** | P | *NO* | NH | 52423 57423 |
| 156 424 | c | **FS** | P | *NO* | NH | 52424 57424 |
| 156 425 | c | **0** | P | *NO* | NH | 52425 57425 |
| 156 426 | c | **FB** | P | *NO* | NH | 52426 57426 |
| 156 427 | c | **FS** | P | *NO* | NH | 52427 57427 |
| 156 428 | c | **FS** | P | *NO* | NH | 52428 57428 |
| 156 429 | c | **FB** | P | *NO* | NH | 52429 57429 |
| 156 430 | t | **SC** | A | *SR* | CK | 52430 57430 |
| 156 431 | t | **SC** | A | *SR* | CK | 52431 57431 |
| 156 432 | t | **SC** | A | *SR* | CK | 52432 57432 |
| 156 433 | t | **SC** | A | *SR* | CK | 52433 57433 |

| | | | | | | | |
|---|---|---|---|---|---|---|---|
| 156 434 | t | **SC** | A | *SR* | CK | 52434 | 57434 |
| 156 435 | t | **SC** | A | *SR* | CK | 52435 | 57435 |
| 156 436 | † | **SC** | A | *SR* | CK | 52436 | 57436 |
| 156 437 | t | **SC** | A | *SR* | CK | 52437 | 57437 |
| 156 438 | d | **NO** | A | *NO* | HT | 52438 | 57438 |
| 156 439 | t | **SC** | A | *SR* | CK | 52439 | 57439 |
| 156 440 | c | **FS** | P | *NO* | NH | 52440 | 57440 |
| 156 441 | c | **FS** | P | *NO* | NH | 52441 | 57441 |
| 156 442 | t | **SC** | A | *SR* | CK | 52442 | 57442 |
| 156 443 | d | **NO** | A | *NO* | HT | 52443 | 57443 |
| 156 444 | d | **NO** | A | *NO* | HT | 52444 | 57444 |
| 156 445 | u | **SC** | A | *SR* | CK | 52445 | 57445 |
| 156 446 | rt | **FS** | A | *SR* | CK | 52446 | 57446 |
| 156 447 | ru | **FS** | A | *SR* | CK | 52447 | 57447 |
| 156 448 | d | **NO** | A | *NO* | HT | 52448 | 57448 |
| 156 449 | u | **FS** | A | *SR* | CK | 52449 | 57449 |
| 156 450 | ru | **FS** | A | *SR* | CK | 52450 | 57450 |
| 156 451 | d | **NO** | A | *NO* | HT | 52451 | 57451 |
| 156 452 | c | **FS** | P | *NO* | NH | 52452 | 57452 |
| 156 453 | ru | **FS** | A | *SR* | CK | 52453 | 57453 |
| 156 454 | d | **NO** | A | *NO* | HT | 52454 | 57454 |
| 156 455 | c | **FB** | P | *NO* | NH | 52455 | 57455 |
| 156 456 | rt | **FS** | A | *SR* | CK | 52456 | 57456 |
| 156 457 | rt | **FS** | A | *SR* | CK | 52457 | 57457 |
| 156 458 | rt | **FS** | A | *SR* | CK | 52458 | 57458 |
| 156 459 | c | **FB** | P | *NO* | NH | 52459 | 57459 |
| 156 460 | c | **0** | P | *NO* | NH | 52460 | 57460 |
| 156 461 | c | **NO** | P | *NO* | NH | 52461 | 57461 |
| 156 462 | | **FS** | A | *SR* | CK | 52462 | 57462 |
| 156 463 | d | **NO** | A | *NO* | HT | 52463 | 57463 |
| 156 464 | c | **0** | P | *NO* | NH | 52464 | 57464 |
| 156 465 | ru | **FS** | A | *SR* | CK | 52465 | 57465 |
| 156 466 | c | **FS** | P | *NO* | NH | 52466 | 57466 |
| 156 467 | | **FS** | A | *SR* | CK | 52467 | 57467 |
| 156 468 | d | **NO** | A | *NO* | NH | 52468 | 57468 |
| 156 469 | d | **NO** | A | *NO* | HT | 52469 | 57469 |
| 156 470 | d | **NO** | A | *NO* | NH | 52470 | 57470 |
| 156 471 | d | **NO** | A | *NO* | NH | 52471 | 57471 |
| 156 472 | d | **NO** | A | *NO* | NH | 52472 | 57472 |
| 156 473 | d | **NO** | A | *NO* | NH | 52473 | 57473 |
| 156 474 | rt | **FS** | A | *SR* | CK | 52474 | 57474 |
| 156 475 | d | **NO** | A | *NO* | HT | 52475 | 57475 |
| 156 476 | rt | **FS** | A | *SR* | CK | 52476 | 57476 |
| 156 477 | t | **FS** | A | *SR* | CK | 52477 | 57477 |
| 156 478 | rt | **FS** | A | *SR* | CK | 52478 | 57478 |
| 156 479 | d | **NO** | A | *NO* | HT | 52479 | 57479 |
| 156 480 | d | **NO** | A | *NO* | HT | 52480 | 57480 |
| 156 481 | d | **NO** | A | *NO* | HT | 52481 | 57481 |
| 156 482 | d | **NO** | A | *NO* | NH | 52482 | 57482 |
| 156 483 | d | **NO** | A | *NO* | NH | 52483 | 57483 |
| 156 484 | d | **NO** | A | *NO* | HT | 52484 | 57484 |

| | | | | | | |
|---|---|---|---|---|---|---|
| 156 485 | ru | **FS** | A | *SR* | CK | 52485 | 57485 |
| 156 486 | d | **NO** | A | *NO* | NH | 52486 | 57486 |
| 156 487 | d | **NO** | A | *NO* | NH | 52487 | 57487 |
| 156 488 | d | **NS** | A | *NO* | NH | 52488 | 57488 |
| 156 489 | d | **NS** | A | *NO* | NH | 52489 | 57489 |
| 156 490 | d | **NO** | A | *NO* | HT | 52490 | 57490 |
| 156 491 | d | **NO** | A | *NO* | NH | 52491 | 57491 |
| 156 492 | rt† | **FS** | A | *SR* | CK | 52492 | 57492 |
| 156 493 | rt | **FS** | A | *SR* | CK | 52493 | 57493 |
| 156 494 | u | **SC** | A | *SR* | CK | 52494 | 57494 |
| 156 495 | u | **SC** | A | *SR* | CK | 52495 | 57495 |
| 156 496 | ru | **FS** | A | *SR* | CK | 52496 | 57496 |
| 156 497 | d | **NS** | A | *NO* | NH | 52497 | 57497 |
| 156 498 | d | **NS** | A | *NO* | NH | 52498 | 57498 |
| 156 499 | rt | **FS** | A | *SR* | CK | 52499 | 57499 |
| 156 500 | u | **SC** | A | *SR* | CK | 52500 | 57500 |
| 156 501 | | **SC** | A | *SR* | CK | 52501 | 57501 |
| 156 502 | | **SC** | A | *SR* | CK | 52502 | 57502 |
| 156 503 | | **SC** | A | *SR* | CK | 52503 | 57503 |
| 156 504 | | **SC** | A | *SR* | CK | 52504 | 57504 |
| 156 505 | | **SC** | A | *SR* | CK | 52505 | 57505 |
| 156 506 | | **SC** | A | *SR* | CK | 52506 | 57506 |
| 156 507 | | **SC** | A | *SR* | CK | 52507 | 57507 |
| 156 508 | | **SC** | A | *SR* | CK | 52508 | 57508 |
| 156 509 | | **SC** | A | *SR* | CK | 52509 | 57509 |
| 156 510 | | **SC** | A | *SR* | CK | 52510 | 57510 |
| 156 511 | | **SC** | A | *SR* | CK | 52511 | 57511 |
| 156 512 | | **SC** | A | *SR* | CK | 52512 | 57512 |
| 156 513 | | **SC** | A | *SR* | CK | 52513 | 57513 |
| 156 514 | | **SC** | A | *SR* | CK | 52514 | 57514 |

**Names:**

| | |
|---|---|
| 156 416 | Saint Edmund |
| 156 420 | LA' AL RATTY Ravenglass & Eskdale Railway |
| 156 433 | The Kilmarnock Edition |

---

# CLASS 158/0                                                    BREL

DMSL(B)–DMSL(A) or DMCL–DMSL or DMSL–MSL–DMSL.

**Construction:** Welded aluminium.
**Engines:** 158 701–158 813/158 880–158 890/158 950–158 959: One Cummins NTA855R of 260 kW (350 h.p.) at 1900 r.p.m.
158 815–158 862: One Perkins 2006-TWH of 260 kW (350 h.p.) at 1900 r.p.m.
158 863–158 872: One Cummins NTA855R of 300 kW (400 h.p.) at 2100 r.p.m.
**Bogies:** One BREL P4 (powered) and one BREL T4 (non-powered) per car.
**Couplers:** BSI.
**Dimensions:** 23.21 x 2.70 m.
**Gangways:** Throughout.
**Doors:** Twin-leaf swing plug.
**Wheel Arrangement:** 2-B + B-2.
**Maximum Speed:** 90 m.p.h.

**Seating Layout:** 2+2 facing/unidirectional in all Standard and First Class except 2+1 in South West Trains First Class.
**Multiple Working:** Within class and with Classes 142, 143, 144, 150, 153, 155, 156, 159, 170 and 172.

**DMSL(B).** Lot No. 31051 BREL Derby 1989–1992. –/68 1TD 1W. († –/72 1TD 1W, c, w –/66 1TD 1W, t –/64 1TD 1W). 38.5 t.
**MSL.** Lot No. 31050 BREL Derby 1991. –/66(3) 1T. 38.5 t.
**DMSL(A).** Lot No. 31052 BREL Derby 1989–1992. –/70 1T († –/74, c, w –/68 1T, * –/64(2) 1T plus cycle stowage area, t –/66 1T). 38.5 t.

The above details refer to the "as built" condition. The following DMSL(B) have now been converted to DMCL as follows:

**52701–52736/52738–52741 (First ScotRail).** 15/53 1TD 1W (* refurbished sets 14/46(6) 1TD 1W plus cycle stowage area).
**52773/774/777. (Former Trans-Pennine Express 2-car units).** 16/48 1TD 1W.
**52786/52789 (Former South West Trains units).** 13/44 1TD 1W.
**52799/806/810/812/813 (vehicles from former Trans-Pennine Express 3-car units).** 32/32 1TD 1W.

**Non-standard livery:** 158 782, 158 786 & 158 789 Unbranded Northern dark blue.

**Northern promotional vinyls:** 158 784 PTEG: 40 years.
158 787, 158 792–796 Sheffield–Leeds fast service.
158 790 Rugby League (Northern Rail Cup).
158 902, 158 904, 158 905, 158 908 & 158 909 Leeds–Bradford–Manchester route (the "Calder Valley").

**Notes:**

* Refurbished First ScotRail units fitted with Grammer seating, additional luggage stacks and cycle stowage areas.
  First ScotRail units 158 726–741 are fitted with Richmond seating.
† Refurbished East Midlands Trains units with Primarius seating.
c Chapman seating.
s Former Trans-Pennine and Central Trains units refurbished with new shape seat cushions.
t Arriva Trains Wales and Northern units with some seats removed for additional luggage space.
u Refurbished former South West Trains units with Class 159-style interiors, including First Class seating.
w Refurbished First Great Western units. Units 158 745–751 & 158 762 (most formed into 3-car sets) have been fitted with Richmond seating.

The following units are on sub-lease from Northern to First ScotRail until 30 June 2010: 158 782/786/789/867–871.

All First ScotRail 158s are "fitted" for RETB. When a unit arrives at Inverness the cab display unit is clipped on and plugged in. Similarly Arriva Trains Wales units have RETB plugged in at Shrewsbury for working the Cambrian Lines.

| | | | | | | |
|---|---|---|---|---|---|---|
| 158 701 | * | **FS** | P | *SR* | IS | 52701 57701 |
| 158 702 | * | **FS** | P | *SR* | IS | 52702 57702 |
| 158 703 | * | **FS** | P | *SR* | IS | 52703 57703 |
| 158 704 | * | **FS** | P | *SR* | IS | 52704 57704 |

| | | | | | | | | |
|---|---|---|---|---|---|---|---|---|
| 158 705 | * | **FS** | P | *SR* | IS | 52705 | 57705 | |
| 158 706 | * | **FS** | P | *SR* | IS | 52706 | 57706 | |
| 158 707 | * | **FS** | P | *SR* | IS | 52707 | 57707 | |
| 158 708 | * | **FS** | P | *SR* | IS | 52708 | 57708 | |
| 158 709 | * | **FS** | P | *SR* | IS | 52709 | 57709 | |
| 158 710 | * | **FS** | P | *SR* | IS | 52710 | 57710 | |
| 158 711 | * | **FS** | P | *SR* | IS | 52711 | 57711 | |
| 158 712 | * | **FS** | P | *SR* | IS | 52712 | 57712 | |
| 158 713 | * | **FS** | P | *SR* | IS | 52713 | 57713 | |
| 158 714 | * | **FS** | P | *SR* | IS | 52714 | 57714 | |
| 158 715 | * | **FS** | P | *SR* | IS | 52715 | 57715 | |
| 158 716 | * | **FS** | P | *SR* | IS | 52716 | 57716 | |
| 158 717 | * | **FS** | P | *SR* | IS | 52717 | 57717 | |
| 158 718 | * | **FS** | P | *SR* | IS | 52718 | 57718 | |
| 158 719 | * | **FS** | P | *SR* | IS | 52719 | 57719 | |
| 158 720 | * | **FS** | P | *SR* | IS | 52720 | 57720 | |
| 158 721 | * | **FS** | P | *SR* | IS | 52721 | 57721 | |
| 158 722 | * | **FS** | P | *SR* | IS | 52722 | 57722 | |
| 158 723 | * | **FS** | P | *SR* | IS | 52723 | 57723 | |
| 158 724 | * | **FS** | P | *SR* | IS | 52724 | 57724 | |
| 158 725 | * | **FS** | P | *SR* | IS | 52725 | 57725 | |
| 158 726 | | **FS** | P | *SR* | HA | 52726 | 57726 | |
| 158 727 | | **FS** | P | *SR* | HA | 52727 | 57727 | |
| 158 728 | | **FS** | P | *SR* | HA | 52728 | 57728 | |
| 158 729 | | **FS** | P | *SR* | HA | 52729 | 57729 | |
| 158 730 | | **FS** | P | *SR* | HA | 52730 | 57730 | |
| 158 731 | | **FS** | P | *SR* | HA | 52731 | 57731 | |
| 158 732 | | **FS** | P | *SR* | HA | 52732 | 57732 | |
| 158 733 | | **FS** | P | *SR* | HA | 52733 | 57733 | |
| 158 734 | | **FS** | P | *SR* | HA | 52734 | 57734 | |
| 158 735 | | **FS** | P | *SR* | HA | 52735 | 57735 | |
| 158 736 | | **FS** | P | *SR* | HA | 52736 | 57736 | |
| 158 738 | | **FS** | P | *SR* | HA | 52738 | 57738 | |
| 158 739 | | **FS** | P | *SR* | HA | 52739 | 57739 | |
| 158 740 | | **FS** | P | *SR* | HA | 52740 | 57740 | |
| 158 741 | | **FS** | P | *SR* | HA | 52741 | 57741 | |
| 158 745 | w | **FI** | P | *GW* | PM | 52745 | 57745 | |
| 158 752 | | **NO** | P | *NO* | NL | 52752 | 58716 | 57752 |
| 158 753 | | **NO** | P | *NO* | NL | 52753 | 58710 | 57753 |
| 158 754 | | **NO** | P | *NO* | NL | 52754 | 58708 | 57754 |
| 158 755 | | **NO** | P | *NO* | NL | 52755 | 58702 | 57755 |
| 158 756 | | **NO** | P | *NO* | NL | 52756 | 58712 | 57756 |
| 158 757 | | **NO** | P | *NO* | NL | 52757 | 58706 | 57757 |
| 158 758 | | **NO** | P | *NO* | NL | 52758 | 58714 | 57758 |
| 158 759 | | **NO** | P | *NO* | NL | 52759 | 58713 | 57759 |
| 158 763 | w | **FI** | P | *GW* | PM | 52763 | 57763 | |
| 158 766 | w | **FI** | P | *GW* | PM | 52766 | 57766 | |
| 158 767 | w | **FI** | P | *GW* | PM | 52767 | 57767 | |
| 158 769 | w | **FI** | P | *GW* | PM | 52769 | 57769 | |
| 158 770 | s | **TC** | P | *EM* | NM | 52770 | 57770 | |
| 158 773 | s | **TC** | P | *EM* | NM | 52773 | 57773 | |

| | | | | | | | |
|---|---|---|---|---|---|---|---|
| 158 774 | s | TC | P | EM | NM | 52774 | 57774 |
| 158 777 | s | TC | P | EM | NM | 52777 | 57777 |
| 158 780 | s | CT | A | EM | NM | 52780 | 57780 |
| 158 782 | s | O | A | SR | HA | 52782 | 57782 |
| 158 783 | † | ST | A | EM | NM | 52783 | 57783 |
| 158 784 | st | NO | A | NO | NL | 52784 | 57784 |
| 158 785 | † | ST | A | EM | NM | 52785 | 57785 |
| 158 786 | u | O | A | SR | HA | 52786 | 57786 |
| 158 787 | s | NO | A | NO | NL | 52787 | 57787 |
| 158 788 | s | CT | A | EM | NM | 52788 | 57788 |
| 158 789 | u | O | A | SR | HA | 52789 | 57789 |
| 158 790 | st | NO | A | NO | NL | 52790 | 57790 |
| 158 791 | st | NO | A | NO | NL | 52791 | 57791 |
| 158 792 | s | NO | A | NO | NL | 52792 | 57792 |
| 158 793 | s | NO | A | NO | NL | 52793 | 57793 |
| 158 794 | s | NO | A | NO | NL | 52794 | 57794 |
| 158 795 | s | NO | A | NO | NL | 52795 | 57795 |
| 158 796 | s | NO | A | NO | NL | 52796 | 57796 |
| 158 797 | st | NO | A | NO | NL | 52797 | 57797 |
| 158 798 | w | FI | P | GW | PM | 52798 | 58715 | 57798 |
| 158 799 | s | TC | P | EM | NM | 52799 | 57799 |
| 158 806 | s | TC | P | EM | NM | 52806 | 57806 |
| 158 810 | s | TC | P | EM | NM | 52810 | 57810 |
| 158 812 | s | TC | P | EM | NM | 52812 | 57812 |
| 158 813 | s | TC | P | EM | NM | 52813 | 57813 |
| 158 815 | c | NO | A | NO | NL | 52815 | 57815 |
| 158 816 | c | NO | A | NO | NL | 52816 | 57816 |
| 158 817 | c | NO | A | NO | NL | 52817 | 57817 |
| 158 818 | c | AV | A | AW | MN | 52818 | 57818 |
| 158 819 | c | WB | A | AW | MN | 52819 | 57819 |
| 158 820 | c | AV | A | AW | MN | 52820 | 57820 |
| 158 821 | c | WB | A | AW | MN | 52821 | 57821 |
| 158 822 | c | WB | A | AW | MN | 52822 | 57822 |
| 158 823 | c | AV | A | AW | MN | 52823 | 57823 |
| 158 824 | c | WB | A | AW | MN | 52824 | 57824 |
| 158 825 | c | WB | A | AW | MN | 52825 | 57825 |
| 158 826 | c | WB | A | AW | MN | 52826 | 57826 |
| 158 827 | c | WB | A | AW | MN | 52827 | 57827 |
| 158 828 | c | AV | A | AW | MN | 52828 | 57828 |
| 158 829 | c | AV | A | AW | MN | 52829 | 57829 |
| 158 830 | c | WB | A | AW | MN | 52830 | 57830 |
| 158 831 | c | WB | A | AW | MN | 52831 | 57831 |
| 158 832 | c | WB | A | AW | MN | 52832 | 57832 |
| 158 833 | c | WB | A | AW | MN | 52833 | 57833 |
| 158 834 | c | WB | A | AW | MN | 52834 | 57834 |
| 158 835 | c | WB | A | AW | MN | 52835 | 57835 |
| 158 836 | c | WB | A | AW | MN | 52836 | 57836 |
| 158 837 | c | AV | A | AW | CF | 52837 | 57837 |
| 158 838 | c | WB | A | AW | CF | 52838 | 57838 |
| 158 839 | c | WB | A | AW | CF | 52839 | 57839 |
| 158 840 | c | AV | A | AW | CF | 52840 | 57840 |

| | | | | | | | |
|---|---|---|---|---|---|---|---|
| 158 841 | c | **WB** | A | *AW* | CF | 52841 | 57841 |
| 158 842 | c | **NO** | A | *NO* | NL | 52842 | 57842 |
| 158 843 | c | **NO** | A | *NO* | NL | 52843 | 57843 |
| 158 844 | t | **NO** | A | *NO* | NL | 52844 | 57844 |
| 158 845 | t | **NO** | A | *NO* | NL | 52845 | 57845 |
| 158 846 | t | **CT** | A | *EM* | NM | 52846 | 57846 |
| 158 847 | t | **CT** | A | *EM* | NM | 52847 | 57847 |
| 158 848 | t | **NO** | A | *NO* | NL | 52848 | 57848 |
| 158 849 | t | **NO** | A | *NO* | NL | 52849 | 57849 |
| 158 850 | t | **NO** | A | *NO* | NL | 52850 | 57850 |
| 158 851 | t | **NO** | A | *NO* | NL | 52851 | 57851 |
| 158 852 | t | **CT** | A | *EM* | NM | 52852 | 57852 |
| 158 853 | t | **NO** | A | *NO* | NL | 52853 | 57853 |
| 158 854 | t | **CT** | A | *EM* | NM | 52854 | 57854 |
| 158 855 | s | **NO** | A | *NO* | NL | 52855 | 57855 |
| 158 856 | s | **CT** | A | *EM* | NM | 52856 | 57856 |
| 158 857 | s | **CT** | A | *EM* | NM | 52857 | 57857 |
| 158 858 | s | **CT** | A | *EM* | NM | 52858 | 57858 |
| 158 859 | s | **NO** | A | *NO* | NL | 52859 | 57859 |
| 158 860 | s | **NO** | A | *NO* | NL | 52860 | 57860 |
| 158 861 | s | **NO** | A | *NO* | NL | 52861 | 57861 |
| 158 862 | s | **CT** | A | *EM* | NM | 52862 | 57862 |
| 158 863 | c | **WT** | A | *EM* | NM | 52863 | 57863 |
| 158 864 | c | **WT** | A | *EM* | NM | 52864 | 57864 |
| 158 865 | c | **WT** | A | *EM* | NM | 52865 | 57865 |
| 158 866 | c | **WT** | A | *EM* | NM | 52866 | 57866 |
| 158 867 | c | **WT** | A | *SR* | HA | 52867 | 57867 |
| 158 868 | c | **WT** | A | *SR* | HA | 52868 | 57868 |
| 158 869 | c | **WT** | A | *SR* | HA | 52869 | 57869 |
| 158 870 | c | **WT** | A | *SR* | HA | 52870 | 57870 |
| 158 871 | c | **WT** | A | *SR* | HA | 52871 | 57871 |
| 158 872 | c | **NO** | A | *NO* | NL | 52872 | 57872 |

**Names:**

| | |
|---|---|
| 158 702 | BBC Scotland – 75 years |
| 158 707 | Far North Line 125th ANNIVERSARY |
| 158 715 | Haymarket |
| 158 720 | Inverness & Nairn Railway – 150 years |
| 158 784 | Barbara Castle |
| 158 791 | County of Nottinghamshire |
| 158 796 | Fred Trueman Cricketing Legend |

**Class 158/8. Refurbished South West Trains units.** Converted from former Trans-Pennine Express units at Wabtec, Doncaster in 2007. 2+1 seating in First Class. Details as Class 158/0 except:

**DMCL.** Lot No. 31051 BREL Derby 1989–1992. 13/44 1TD 1W. 38.5 t.
**DMSL.** Lot No. 31052 BREL Derby 1989–1992. –/70 1T. 38.5 t.

| | | | | | | | |
|---|---|---|---|---|---|---|---|
| 158 880 | (158 737) | **ST** | P | *SW* | SA | 52737 | 57737 |
| 158 881 | (158 742) | **ST** | P | *EM* | NM | 52742 | 57742 |
| 158 882 | (158 743) | **ST** | P | *EM* | NM | 52743 | 57743 |

| | | | | | | | |
|---|---|---|---|---|---|---|---|
| 158 883 | (158 744) | **ST** | P | *SW* | SA | 52744 | 57744 |
| 158 884 | (158 772) | **ST** | P | *SW* | SA | 52772 | 57772 |
| 158 885 | (158 775) | **ST** | P | *SW* | SA | 52775 | 57775 |
| 158 886 | (158 779) | **ST** | P | *SW* | SA | 52779 | 57779 |
| 158 887 | (158 781) | **ST** | P | *SW* | SA | 52781 | 57781 |
| 158 888 | (158 802) | **ST** | P | *SW* | SA | 52802 | 57802 |
| 158 889 | (158 808) | **ST** | P | *SW* | SA | 52808 | 57808 |
| 158 890 | (158 814) | **ST** | P | *SW* | SA | 52814 | 57814 |

## CLASS 158/9                                                    BREL

DMSL–DMS. Units leased by West Yorkshire PTE but managed by HSBC Rail.
Details as Class 158/0 except for seating and toilets.

**DMSL.** Lot No. 31051 BREL Derby 1990–1992. –/70 1TD 1W. 38.5 t.
**DMS.** Lot No. 31052 BREL Derby 1990–1992. –/72 and parcels area. 38.5 t.

| | | | | | | | |
|---|---|---|---|---|---|---|---|
| 158 901 | **NO** | H | *NO* | NL | 52901 | 57901 | |
| 158 902 | **NO** | H | *NO* | NL | 52902 | 57902 | |
| 158 903 | **NO** | H | *NO* | NL | 52903 | 57903 | |
| 158 904 | **NO** | H | *NO* | NL | 52904 | 57904 | |
| 158 905 | **NO** | H | *NO* | NL | 52905 | 57905 | |
| 158 906 | **NO** | H | *NO* | NL | 52906 | 57906 | |
| 158 907 | **NO** | H | *NO* | NL | 52907 | 57907 | |
| 158 908 | **NO** | H | *NO* | NL | 52908 | 57908 | |
| 158 909 | **NO** | H | *NO* | NL | 52909 | 57909 | |
| 158 910 | **NO** | H | *NO* | NL | 52910 | 57910 | William Wilberforce |

## CLASS 158/0                                                    BREL

DMSL–DMSL–DMSL. Refurbished units reformed in 2008 for First Great Western.
For vehicle details see above.

| | | | | | | | | |
|---|---|---|---|---|---|---|---|---|
| 158 950 | w | **FI** | P | *GW* | PM | 57751 | 52761 | 57761 |
| 158 951 | w | **FI** | P | *GW* | PM | 57751 | 52764 | 57764 |
| 158 952 | w | **FI** | P | *GW* | PM | 57748 | 52762 | 57762 |
| 158 953 | w | **FI** | P | *GW* | PM | 52748 | 52750 | 57750 |
| 158 954 | w | **FI** | P | *GW* | PM | 57747 | 52760 | 57760 |
| 158 955 | w | **FI** | P | *GW* | PM | 52747 | 52765 | 57765 |
| 158 956 | w | **FI** | P | *GW* | PM | 57749 | 52768 | 57768 |
| 158 957 | w | **FI** | P | *GW* | PM | 52749 | 52771 | 57771 |
| 158 958 | w | **FI** | P | *GW* | PM | 57746 | 52776 | 57776 |
| 158 959 | w | **FI** | P | *GW* | PM | 52746 | 52778 | 57778 |

## CLASS 159/0                                                  BREL

DMCL–MSL–DMSL. Built as Class 158. Converted before entering passenger service to Class 159 by Rosyth Dockyard.

**Construction:** Welded aluminium.
**Engines:** One Cummins NTA855R of 300 kW (400 h.p.) at 2100 r.p.m.
**Bogies:** One BREL P4 (powered) and one BREL T4 (non-powered) per car.
**Couplers:** BSI.
**Dimensions:** 22.16 x 2.70 m.
**Gangways:** Throughout.         **Wheel Arrangement:** 2-B + B-2 + B-2.
**Doors:** Twin-leaf swing plug.     **Maximum Speed:** 90 m.p.h.
**Seating Layout:** 1: 2+1 facing, 2: 2+2 facing/unidirectional.
**Multiple Working:** Within class and with Classes 142, 143, 144, 150, 153, 155, 156, 158 and 170.

**DMCL.** Lot No. 31051 BREL Derby 1992–1993. 24/28 1TD 1W. 38.5 t.
**MSL.** Lot No. 31050 BREL Derby 1992–1993. –/70(6) 1T. 38.5 t.
**DMSL.** Lot No. 31052 BREL Derby 1992–1993. –/72 1T. 38.5 t.

| | | | | | | | |
|---|---|---|---|---|---|---|---|
| 159 001 | **ST** | P | *SW* | SA | 52873 | 58718 | 57873 | CITY OF EXETER |
| 159 002 | **ST** | P | *SW* | SA | 52874 | 58719 | 57874 | CITY OF SALISBURY |
| 159 003 | **ST** | P | *SW* | SA | 52875 | 58720 | 57875 | TEMPLECOMBE |
| 159 004 | **ST** | P | *SW* | SA | 52876 | 58721 | 57876 | BASINGSTOKE AND DEANE |
| 159 005 | **ST** | P | *SW* | SA | 52877 | 58722 | 57877 | |
| 159 006 | **ST** | P | *SW* | SA | 52878 | 58723 | 57878 | |
| 159 007 | **ST** | P | *SW* | SA | 52879 | 58724 | 57879 | |
| 159 008 | **ST** | P | *SW* | SA | 52880 | 58725 | 57880 | |
| 159 009 | **ST** | P | *SW* | SA | 52881 | 58726 | 57881 | |
| 159 010 | **ST** | P | *SW* | SA | 52882 | 58727 | 57882 | |
| 159 011 | **ST** | P | *SW* | SA | 52883 | 58728 | 57883 | |
| 159 012 | **ST** | P | *SW* | SA | 52884 | 58729 | 57884 | |
| 159 013 | **ST** | P | *SW* | SA | 52885 | 58730 | 57885 | |
| 159 014 | **ST** | P | *SW* | SA | 52886 | 58731 | 57886 | |
| 159 015 | **ST** | P | *SW* | SA | 52887 | 58732 | 57887 | |
| 159 016 | **ST** | P | *SW* | SA | 52888 | 58733 | 57888 | |
| 159 017 | **ST** | P | *SW* | SA | 52889 | 58734 | 57889 | |
| 159 018 | **ST** | P | *SW* | SA | 52890 | 58735 | 57890 | |
| 159 019 | **ST** | P | *SW* | SA | 52891 | 58736 | 57891 | |
| 159 020 | **ST** | P | *SW* | SA | 52892 | 58737 | 57892 | |
| 159 021 | **ST** | P | *SW* | SA | 52893 | 58738 | 57893 | |
| 159 022 | **ST** | P | *SW* | SA | 52894 | 58739 | 57894 | |

## CLASS 159/1                                          BREL

DMCL–MSL–DMSL. Units converted from Class 158s at Wabtec, Doncaster in 2006–07 for South West Trains.

Details as Class 158/0 except:
**Seating Layout:** 1: 2+1 facing, 2: 2+2 facing/unidirectional.

**DMCL.** Lot No. 31051 BREL Derby 1989–1992. 24/28 1TD 1W. 38.5 t.
**MSL.** Lot No. 31050 BREL Derby 1989–1992. –/70 1T. 38.5 t.
**DMSL.** Lot No. 31052 BREL Derby 1989–1992. –/72 1T.38.5 t.

| 159 101 | (158 800) | **ST** | P | *SW* | SA | 52800 | 58717 | 57800 |
|---------|-----------|--------|---|------|----|-------|-------|-------|
| 159 102 | (158 803) | **ST** | P | *SW* | SA | 52803 | 58703 | 57803 |
| 159 103 | (158 804) | **ST** | P | *SW* | SA | 52804 | 58704 | 57804 |
| 159 104 | (158 805) | **ST** | P | *SW* | SA | 52805 | 58705 | 57805 |
| 159 105 | (158 807) | **ST** | P | *SW* | SA | 52807 | 58707 | 57807 |
| 159 106 | (158 809) | **ST** | P | *SW* | SA | 52809 | 58709 | 57809 |
| 159 107 | (158 811) | **ST** | P | *SW* | SA | 52811 | 58711 | 57811 |
| 159 108 | (158 801) | **ST** | P | *SW* | SA | 52801 | 58701 | 57801 |

## CLASS 165/0          NETWORK TURBO          BREL

DMSL–DMS and DMSL–MS–DMS. Chiltern Railways units. Refurbished 2003–2005 with First Class seats removed and air conditioning fitted.

**Construction:** Welded aluminium.
**Engines:** One Perkins 2006-TWH of 260 kW (350 h.p.) at 1900 r.p.m.
**Bogies:** BREL P3-17 (powered), BREL T3-17 (non-powered).
**Couplers:** BSI.
**Dimensions:** 23.50/23.25 x 2.81 m.
**Gangways:** Within unit only.          **Wheel Arrangement:** 2-B (+ B-2) + B-2.
**Doors:** Twin-leaf swing plug.          **Maximum Speed:** 75 m.p.h.
**Seating Layout:** 2+2/3+2 facing/unidirectional.
**Multiple Working:** Within class and with Classes 166 and 168.

Fitted with tripcocks for working over London Underground tracks between Harrow-on-the-Hill and Amersham.

**58801–58822/58873–58878. DMSL.** Lot No. 31087 BREL York 1990. –/82(7) 1T 2W. 40.1 t.
**58823–58833. DMSL.** Lot No. 31089 BREL York 1991–1992. –/82(7) 1T 2W. 40.1 t.
**MS.** Lot No. 31090 BREL York 1991–1992. –/106. 37.0 t.
**DMS.** Lot No. 31088 BREL York 1991–1992. –/94. 39.4 t.

| 165 001 | **CR** | A | *CR* | AL | 58801 | 58834 |
|---------|--------|---|------|----|-------|-------|
| 165 002 | **CR** | A | *CR* | AL | 58802 | 58835 |
| 165 003 | **CR** | A | *CR* | AL | 58803 | 58836 |
| 165 004 | **CR** | A | *CR* | AL | 58804 | 58837 |
| 165 005 | **CR** | A | *CR* | AL | 58805 | 58838 |
| 165 006 | **CR** | A | *CR* | AL | 58806 | 58839 |
| 165 007 | **CR** | A | *CR* | AL | 58807 | 58840 |
| 165 008 | **CR** | A | *CR* | AL | 58808 | 58841 |

| 165 009 | CR | A | CR | AL | 58809 |       | 58842 |
|---------|----|---|----|----|-------|-------|-------|
| 165 010 | CR | A | CR | AL | 58810 |       | 58843 |
| 165 011 | CR | A | CR | AL | 58811 |       | 58844 |
| 165 012 | CR | A | CR | AL | 58812 |       | 58845 |
| 165 013 | CR | A | CR | AL | 58813 |       | 58846 |
| 165 014 | CR | A | CR | AL | 58814 |       | 58847 |
| 165 015 | CR | A | CR | AL | 58815 |       | 58848 |
| 165 016 | CR | A | CR | AL | 58816 |       | 58849 |
| 165 017 | CR | A | CR | AL | 58817 |       | 58850 |
| 165 018 | CR | A | CR | AL | 58818 |       | 58851 |
| 165 019 | CR | A | CR | AL | 58819 |       | 58852 |
| 165 020 | CR | A | CR | AL | 58820 |       | 58853 |
| 165 021 | CR | A | CR | AL | 58821 |       | 58854 |
| 165 022 | CR | A | CR | AL | 58822 |       | 58855 |
| 165 023 | CR | A | CR | AL | 58873 |       | 58867 |
| 165 024 | CR | A | CR | AL | 58874 |       | 58868 |
| 165 025 | CR | A | CR | AL | 58875 |       | 58869 |
| 165 026 | CR | A | CR | AL | 58876 |       | 58870 |
| 165 027 | CR | A | CR | AL | 58877 |       | 58871 |
| 165 028 | CR | A | CR | AL | 58878 |       | 58872 |
| 165 029 | CR | A | CR | AL | 58823 | 55404 | 58856 |
| 165 030 | CR | A | CR | AL | 58824 | 55405 | 58857 |
| 165 031 | CR | A | CR | AL | 58825 | 55406 | 58858 |
| 165 032 | CR | A | CR | AL | 58826 | 55407 | 58859 |
| 165 033 | CR | A | CR | AL | 58827 | 55408 | 58860 |
| 165 034 | CR | A | CR | AL | 58828 | 55409 | 58861 |
| 165 035 | CR | A | CR | AL | 58829 | 55410 | 58862 |
| 165 036 | CR | A | CR | AL | 58830 | 55411 | 58863 |
| 165 037 | CR | A | CR | AL | 58831 | 55412 | 58864 |
| 165 038 | CR | A | CR | AL | 58832 | 55413 | 58865 |
| 165 039 | CR | A | CR | AL | 58833 | 55414 | 58866 |

## CLASS 165/1          NETWORK TURBO          BREL

First Great Western units. DMCL–MS–DMS or DMCL–DMS.

**Construction:** Welded aluminium.
**Engines:** One Perkins 2006-TWH of 260 kW (350 h.p.) at 1900 r.p.m.
**Bogies:** BREL P3-17 (powered), BREL T3-17 (non-powered).
**Couplers:** BSI.
**Dimensions:** 23.50/23.25 x 2.81 m.
**Gangways:** Within unit only.          **Wheel Arrangement:** 2-B (+ B-2) + B-2.
**Doors:** Twin-leaf swing plug.          **Maximum Speed:** 90 m.p.h.
**Seating Layout:** 1: 2+2 facing, 2: 3+2 facing/unidirectional.
**Multiple Working:** Within class and with Classes 166 and 168.

**58953–58969. DMCL.** Lot No. 31098 BREL York 1992. 16/66 1T. 38.0 t.
**58879–58898. DMCL.** Lot No. 31096 BREL York 1992. 16/72 1T. 38.0 t.
**MS.** Lot No. 31099 BREL 1992. –/106. 37.0 t.
**DMS.** Lot No. 31097 BREL 1992. –/98. 37.0 t.

| 165 101 | FD | A | *GW* | RG | 58953 | 55415 | 58916 |
| 165 102 | FD | A | *GW* | RG | 58954 | 55416 | 58917 |
| 165 103 | FD | A | *GW* | RG | 58955 | 55417 | 58918 |
| 165 104 | FD | A | *GW* | RG | 58956 | 55418 | 58919 |
| 165 105 | FD | A | *GW* | RG | 58957 | 55419 | 58920 |
| 165 106 | FD | A | *GW* | RG | 58958 | 55420 | 58921 |
| 165 107 | FD | A | *GW* | RG | 58959 | 55421 | 58922 |
| 165 108 | FD | A | *GW* | RG | 58960 | 55422 | 58923 |
| 165 109 | FD | A | *GW* | RG | 58961 | 55423 | 58924 |
| 165 110 | FD | A | *GW* | RG | 58962 | 55424 | 58925 |
| 165 111 | FD | A | *GW* | RG | 58963 | 55425 | 58926 |
| 165 112 | FD | A | *GW* | RG | 58964 | 55426 | 58927 |
| 165 113 | FD | A | *GW* | RG | 58965 | 55427 | 58928 |
| 165 114 | FD | A | *GW* | RG | 58966 | 55428 | 58929 |
| 165 116 | FD | A | *GW* | RG | 58968 | 55430 | 58931 |
| 165 117 | FD | A | *GW* | RG | 58969 | 55431 | 58932 |
| 165 118 | FD | A | *GW* | RG | 58879 |       | 58933 |
| 165 119 | FD | A | *GW* | RG | 58880 |       | 58934 |
| 165 120 | FD | A | *GW* | RG | 58881 |       | 58935 |
| 165 121 | FD | A | *GW* | RG | 58882 |       | 58936 |
| 165 122 | FD | A | *GW* | RG | 58883 |       | 58937 |
| 165 123 | FD | A | *GW* | RG | 58884 |       | 58938 |
| 165 124 | FD | A | *GW* | RG | 58885 |       | 58939 |
| 165 125 | FD | A | *GW* | RG | 58886 |       | 58940 |
| 165 126 | FD | A | *GW* | RG | 58887 |       | 58941 |
| 165 127 | FD | A | *GW* | RG | 58888 |       | 58942 |
| 165 128 | FD | A | *GW* | RG | 58889 |       | 58943 |
| 165 129 | FD | A | *GW* | RG | 58890 |       | 58944 |
| 165 130 | FD | A | *GW* | RG | 58891 |       | 58945 |
| 165 131 | FD | A | *GW* | RG | 58892 |       | 58946 |
| 165 132 | FD | A | *GW* | RG | 58893 |       | 58947 |
| 165 133 | FD | A | *GW* | RG | 58894 |       | 58948 |
| 165 134 | FD | A | *GW* | RG | 58895 |       | 58949 |
| 165 135 | FD | A | *GW* | RG | 58896 |       | 58950 |
| 165 136 | FD | A | *GW* | RG | 58897 |       | 58951 |
| 165 137 | FD | A | *GW* | RG | 58898 |       | 58952 |

# CLASS 166   NETWORK EXPRESS TURBO   ABB

DMCL(A)–MS–DMCL(B). First Great Western units, built for Paddington–Oxford/
Newbury services. Air conditioned and with additional luggage space compared
to the Class 165s.

**Construction:** Welded aluminium.
**Engines:** One Perkins 2006-TWH of 260 kW (350 h.p.) at 1900 r.p.m.
**Bogies:** BREL P3-17 (powered), BREL T3-17 (non-powered).
**Couplers:** BSI.
**Dimensions:** 23.50 x 2.81 m.
**Gangways:** Within unit only.                 **Wheel Arrangement:** 2-B + B-2 + B-2.
**Doors:** Twin-leaf swing plug.               **Maximum Speed:** 90 m.p.h.
**Seating Layout:** 1: 2+2 facing, 2: 2+2/3+2 facing/unidirectional.

**Multiple Working:** Within class and with Classes 165 and 168.

**DMCL (A).** Lot No. 31116 ABB York 1992–1993. 16/68 1T. 39.6 t.
**MS.** Lot No. 31117 ABB York 1992–1993. –/91. 38.0 t.
**DMCL (B).** Lot No. 31116 ABB York 1992–1993. 16/68 1T. 39.6 t.

| | | | | | | | |
|---|---|---|---|---|---|---|---|
| 166 201 | FD | A | GW | RG | 58101 | 58601 | 58122 |
| 166 202 | FD | A | GW | RG | 58102 | 58602 | 58123 |
| 166 203 | FD | A | GW | RG | 58103 | 58603 | 58124 |
| 166 204 | FD | A | GW | RG | 58104 | 58604 | 58125 |
| 166 205 | FD | A | GW | RG | 58105 | 58605 | 58126 |
| 166 206 | FD | A | GW | RG | 58106 | 58606 | 58127 |
| 166 207 | FD | A | GW | RG | 58107 | 58607 | 58128 |
| 166 208 | FD | A | GW | RG | 58108 | 58608 | 58129 |
| 166 209 | FD | A | GW | RG | 58109 | 58609 | 58130 |
| 166 210 | FD | A | GW | RG | 58110 | 58610 | 58131 |
| 166 211 | FD | A | GW | RG | 58111 | 58611 | 58132 |
| 166 212 | FD | A | GW | RG | 58112 | 58612 | 58133 |
| 166 213 | FD | A | GW | RG | 58113 | 58613 | 58134 |
| 166 214 | FD | A | GW | RG | 58114 | 58614 | 58135 |
| 166 215 | FD | A | GW | RG | 58115 | 58615 | 58136 |
| 166 216 | FD | A | GW | RG | 58116 | 58616 | 58137 |
| 166 217 | FD | A | GW | RG | 58117 | 58617 | 58138 |
| 166 218 | FD | A | GW | RG | 58118 | 58618 | 58139 |
| 166 219 | FD | A | GW | RG | 58119 | 58619 | 58140 |
| 166 220 | FD | A | GW | RG | 58120 | 58620 | 58141 |
| 166 221 | FD | A | GW | RG | 58121 | 58621 | 58142 |

# CLASS 168   CLUBMAN   ADTRANZ/BOMBARDIER

Air conditioned.

**Construction:** Welded aluminium bodies with bolt-on steel ends.
**Engines:** One MTU 6R183TD13H of 315 kW (422 h.p.) at 1900 r.p.m.
**Transmission:** Hydraulic. Voith T211rzze to ZF final drive.
**Bogies:** One Adtranz P3–23 and one BREL T3–23 per car.
**Couplers:** BSI at outer ends, bar within unit.
**Dimensions:** Class 168/0: 24.10/23.61 x 2.75 m. Others: 23.62/23.61 x 2.75 m.
**Gangways:** Within unit only.   **Wheel Arrangement:** 2-B (+ B-2 + B-2) + B-2.
**Doors:** Twin-leaf swing plug.   **Maximum Speed:** 100 m.p.h.
**Seating Layout:** 2+2 facing/unidirectional.
**Multiple Working:** Within class and with Classes 165 and 166.

Fitted with tripcocks for working over London Underground tracks between Harrow-on-the-Hill and Amersham.

**Class 168/0.** Original Design. DMSL(A)–MS–MSL–DMSL(B) or DMSL(A)–MSL–MS–DMSL(B).

**58151–58155. DMSL(A).** Adtranz Derby 1997–1998. –/57 1TD 1W. 43.7 t.
**58651–58655. MSL.** Adtranz Derby 1998. –/73 1T. 41.0 t.
**58451–58455. MS.** Adtranz Derby 1998. –/77. 40.5 t.
**58251–58255. DMSL(B).** Adtranz Derby 1998. –/68 1T. 43.6 t.

**Note:** 58451–58455 were numbered 58656–58660 for a time when used in 168 106–168 110.

| 168 001 | **CR** | P | *CR* | AL | 58151 | 58451 | 58651 | 58251 |
|---------|--------|---|------|----|-------|-------|-------|-------|
| 168 002 | **CR** | P | *CR* | AL | 58152 | 58652 | 58452 | 58252 |
| 168 003 | **CR** | P | *CR* | AL | 58153 | 58653 | 58453 | 58253 |
| 168 004 | **CR** | P | *CR* | AL | 58154 | 58654 | 58454 | 58254 |
| 168 005 | **CR** | P | *CR* | AL | 58155 | 58655 | 58455 | 58255 |

**Class 168/1.** These units are effectively Class 170s. DMSL(A)–MSL–MS–DMSL(B), DMSL(A)–MS–MSL–DMSL(B) or DMSL(A)–MS–DMSL(B).

**58156–58163. DMSL(A).** Adtranz Derby 2000. –/57 1TD 2W. 45.2 t.
**58456–58460. MS.** Bombardier Derby 2002. –/76. 41.8 t.
**58756–58757. MSL.** Bombardier Derby 2002. –/73 1T. 42.9 t.
**58461–58463. MS.** Adtranz Derby 2000. –/76. 42.4 t.
**58256–58263. DMSL(B).** Adtranz Derby 2000. –/69 1T. 45.2 t.

**Notes:** 58461–58463 have been renumbered from 58661–58663.

| 168 106 | **CR** | P | *CR* | AL | 58156 | 58756 | 58456 | 58256 |
|---------|--------|---|------|----|-------|-------|-------|-------|
| 168 107 | **CR** | P | *CR* | AL | 58157 | 58457 | 58757 | 58257 |
| 168 108 | **CR** | P | *CR* | AL | 58158 |       | 58458 | 58258 |
| 168 109 | **CR** | P | *CR* | AL | 58159 |       | 58459 | 58259 |
| 168 110 | **CR** | P | *CR* | AL | 58160 |       | 58460 | 58260 |
| 168 111 | **CR** | H | *CR* | AL | 58161 |       | 58461 | 58261 |
| 168 112 | **CR** | H | *CR* | AL | 58162 |       | 58462 | 58262 |
| 168 113 | **CR** | H | *CR* | AL | 58163 |       | 58463 | 58263 |

**Class 168/2.** These units are effectively Class 170s. DMSL(A)–(MS)–MS–DMSL(B).

**58164–58169. DMSL(A).** Bombardier Derby 2003–2004. –/57 1TD 2W. 45.4 t.
**58365–58367. MS.** Bombardier Derby 2006. –/76. 43.3 t.
**58464/58468/58469. MS.** Bombardier Derby 2003–2004. –/76. 44.0 t.
**58465–58467. MS.** Bombardier Derby 2006. –/76. 43.3 t.
**58264–58269. DMSL(B).** Bombardier Derby 2003–2004. –/69 1T. 45.5 t.

| 168 214 | **CR** | P | *CR* | AL | 58164 |       | 58464 | 58264 |
|---------|--------|---|------|----|-------|-------|-------|-------|
| 168 215 | **CR** | P | *CR* | AL | 58165 | 58365 | 58465 | 58265 |
| 168 216 | **CR** | P | *CR* | AL | 58166 | 58366 | 58466 | 58266 |
| 168 217 | **CR** | P | *CR* | AL | 58167 | 58367 | 58467 | 58267 |
| 168 218 | **CR** | P | *CR* | AL | 58168 |       | 58468 | 58268 |
| 168 219 | **CR** | P | *CR* | AL | 58169 |       | 58469 | 58269 |

# CLASS 170   TURBOSTAR   ADTRANZ/BOMBARDIER

Various formations. Air conditioned.

**Construction:** Welded aluminium bodies with bolt-on steel ends.
**Engines:** One MTU 6R183TD13H of 315 kW (422 h.p.) at 1900 r.p.m.
**Transmission:** Hydraulic. Voith T211rzze to ZF final drive.
**Bogies:** One Adtranz P3–23 and one BREL T3–23 per car.
**Couplers:** BSI at outer ends, bar within later build units.
**Dimensions:** 23.62/23.61 x 2.75 m.
**Gangways:** Within unit only.           **Wheel Arrangement:** 2-B (+ B-2) + B-2.
**Doors:** Twin-leaf sliding plug.          **Maximum Speed:** 100 m.p.h.
**Seating Layout:** 1: 2+1 facing/unidirectional. 2: 2+2 unidirectional/facing.
**Multiple Working:** Within class and with Classes 150, 153, 155, 156, 158, 159
and 172.

**Class 170/1. Cross-Country units (former Midland Mainline sets).** Lazareni
seating. DMSL–MS–DMCL/DMSL–DMCL.

**DMSL.** Adtranz Derby 1998–1999. –/59 1TD 2W. 45.0 t.
**MS.** Adtranz Derby 2001. –/80. 43.0 t.
**DMCL.** Adtranz Derby 1998–1999. 9/52 1T. 44.8 t

| 170 101 | CM | P | XC | TS | 50101 | 55101 | 79101 |
|---------|----|----|----|----|-------|-------|-------|
| 170 102 | XC | P | XC | TS | 50102 | 55102 | 79102 |
| 170 103 | CM | P | XC | TS | 50103 | 55103 | 79103 |
| 170 104 | CM | P | XC | TS | 50104 | 55104 | 79104 |
| 170 105 | XC | P | XC | TS | 50105 | 55105 | 79105 |
| 170 106 | CM | P | XC | TS | 50106 | 55106 | 79106 |
| 170 107 | CM | P | XC | TS | 50107 | 55107 | 79107 |
| 170 108 | CM | P | XC | TS | 50108 | 55108 | 79108 |
| 170 109 | CM | P | XC | TS | 50109 | 55109 | 79109 |
| 170 110 | CM | P | XC | TS | 50110 | 55110 | 79110 |
| 170 111 | XC | P | XC | TS | 50111 |       | 79111 |
| 170 112 | XC | P | XC | TS | 50112 |       | 79112 |
| 170 113 | XC | P | XC | TS | 50113 |       | 79113 |
| 170 114 | XC | P | XC | TS | 50114 |       | 79114 |
| 170 115 | CM | P | XC | TS | 50115 |       | 79115 |
| 170 116 | XC | P | XC | TS | 50116 |       | 79116 |
| 170 117 | CM | P | XC | TS | 50117 |       | 79117 |

**Class 170/2. National Express East Anglia 3-car units.** Chapman seating. DMCL–
MSL–DMSL.

**DMCL.** Adtranz Derby 1999. 7/39 1TD 2W. 45.0 t.
**MSL.** Adtranz Derby 1999. –/68 1T. Guard's office. 45.3 t.
**DMSL.** Adtranz Derby 1999. –/66 1T. 43.4 t.

| 170 201 | r | 1 | P | EA | NC | 50201 | 56201 | 79201 |
|---------|---|---|---|----|----|-------|-------|-------|
| 170 202 | r | 1 | P | EA | NC | 50202 | 56202 | 79202 |
| 170 203 | r | 1 | P | EA | NC | 50203 | 56203 | 79203 |
| 170 204 | r | 1 | P | EA | NC | 50204 | 56204 | 79204 |
| 170 205 | r | 1 | P | EA | NC | 50205 | 56205 | 79205 |

| 170 206 | r | 1 | P | *EA* | NC | 50206 | 56206 | 79206 |
| 170 207 | r | 1 | P | *EA* | NC | 50207 | 56207 | 79207 |
| 170 208 | r | 1 | P | *EA* | NC | 50208 | 56208 | 79208 |

**Class 170/2. National Express East Anglia 2-car units.** Chapman seating. DMSL–DMCL.

**DMSL.** Bombardier Derby 2002. –/57 1TD 2W. 45.7 t.
**DMCL.** Bombardier Derby 2002. 9/53 1T. 45.7 t.

| 170 270 | r | 1 | P | *EA* | NC | 50270 | 79270 |
| 170 271 | r | AN | P | *EA* | NC | 50271 | 79271 |
| 170 272 | r | AN | P | *EA* | NC | 50272 | 79272 |
| 170 273 | r | AN | P | *EA* | NC | 50273 | 79273 |

**Class 170/3. First Trans-Pennine Express units.** Chapman seating. DMCL–DMSL. 170 309 renumbered from 170 399.

**50301–50308/50399. DMCL.** Adtranz Derby 2000–2001. 8/43 1TD 2W. 45.8 t.
**79301–79308/79399. DMSL.** Adtranz Derby 2000–2001. –/65 1T. 45.8 t.

| 170 301 | FT | P | *TP* | XW | 50301 | 79301 |
| 170 302 | FT | P | *TP* | XW | 50302 | 79302 |
| 170 303 | FT | P | *TP* | XW | 50303 | 79303 |
| 170 304 | FT | P | *TP* | XW | 50304 | 79304 |
| 170 305 | FT | P | *TP* | XW | 50305 | 79305 |
| 170 306 | FT | P | *TP* | XW | 50306 | 79306 |
| 170 307 | FT | P | *TP* | XW | 50307 | 79307 |
| 170 308 | FT | P | *TP* | XW | 50308 | 79308 |
| 170 309 | FT | P | *TP* | XW | 50399 | 79399 |

**Class 170/3. Units built for Hull Trains. Now in use with First ScotRail and dedicated to Edinburgh/Glasgow–Inverness services.** Chapman seating. DMCL–MSLRB–DMSL.

**DMCL.** Bombardier Derby 2004. 7/41 1TD 2W. 46.5 t.
**MSLRB.** Bombardier Derby 2004. –/60 1T. Buffet and guard's office 44.7 t.
**DMSL.** Bombardier Derby 2004. –/71 1T. 46.3 t.

| 170 393 | FS | P | *SR* | HA | 50393 | 56393 | 79393 |
| 170 394 | FS | P | *SR* | HA | 50394 | 56394 | 79394 |
| 170 395 | FS | P | *SR* | HA | 50395 | 56395 | 79395 |
| 170 396 | FS | P | *SR* | HA | 50396 | 56396 | 79396 |

**Class 170/3. Cross-Country units.** Lazareni seating. DMSL–MS–DMCL.

**DMSL.** Bombardier Derby 2002. –/59 1TD 2W. 45.4 t.
**MS.** Bombardier Derby 2002. –/80. 43.0 t.
**DMCL.** Bombardier Derby 2002. 9/52 1T. 45.8 t.

| 170 397 | XC | P | *XC* | TS | 50397 | 56397 | 79397 |
| 170 398 | XC | P | *XC* | TS | 50398 | 56398 | 79398 |

**Class 170/4. First ScotRail "express" units.** Chapman seating. DMCL–MS–DMCL.

**DMCL(A).** Adtranz Derby 1999–2001. 9/43 1TD 2W. 45.2 t.
**MS.** Adtranz Derby 1999–2001. –/76. 42.5 t.
**DMCL(B).** Adtranz Derby 1999–2001. 9/49 1T. 45.2 t.

| 170 401 | **FS** | P | *SR* | HA | 50401 | 56401 | 79401 |
| 170 402 | **FS** | P | *SR* | HA | 50402 | 56402 | 79402 |
| 170 403 | **FS** | P | *SR* | HA | 50403 | 56403 | 79403 |
| 170 404 | **FS** | P | *SR* | HA | 50404 | 56404 | 79404 |
| 170 405 | **FS** | P | *SR* | HA | 50405 | 56405 | 79405 |
| 170 406 | **FS** | P | *SR* | HA | 50406 | 56406 | 79406 |
| 170 407 | **FS** | P | *SR* | HA | 50407 | 56407 | 79407 |
| 170 408 | **FS** | P | *SR* | HA | 50408 | 56408 | 79408 |
| 170 409 | **FS** | P | *SR* | HA | 50409 | 56409 | 79409 |
| 170 410 | **FS** | P | *SR* | HA | 50410 | 56410 | 79410 |
| 170 411 | **FS** | P | *SR* | HA | 50411 | 56411 | 79411 |
| 170 412 | **FS** | P | *SR* | HA | 50412 | 56412 | 79412 |
| 170 413 | **FS** | P | *SR* | HA | 50413 | 56413 | 79413 |
| 170 414 | **FS** | P | *SR* | HA | 50414 | 56414 | 79414 |
| 170 415 | **FS** | P | *SR* | HA | 50415 | 56415 | 79415 |
| 170 416 | **FS** | H | *SR* | HA | 50416 | 56416 | 79416 |
| 170 417 | **FS** | H | *SR* | HA | 50417 | 56417 | 79417 |
| 170 418 | **FS** | H | *SR* | HA | 50418 | 56418 | 79418 |
| 170 419 | **FS** | H | *SR* | HA | 50419 | 56419 | 79419 |
| 170 420 | **FS** | H | *SR* | HA | 50420 | 56420 | 79420 |
| 170 421 | **FS** | H | *SR* | HA | 50421 | 56421 | 79421 |
| 170 422 | **FS** | H | *SR* | HA | 50422 | 56422 | 79422 |
| 170 423 | **FS** | H | *SR* | HA | 50423 | 56423 | 79423 |
| 170 424 | **FS** | H | *SR* | HA | 50424 | 56424 | 79424 |

**Class 170/4. First ScotRail "express" units.** Chapman seating. DMCL–MS–DMCL.

**DMCL.** Bombardier Derby 2003–2005. 9/43 1TD 2W. 46.8 t.
**MS.** Bombardier Derby 2003–2005. –/76. 43.7 t.
**DMCL.** Bombardier Derby 2003–2005. 9/49 1T. 46.5 t.

**Note:** 170 431 & 170 432 have new uprated engines fitted: MTU 6H1800R83 of 360 kW (483 h.p.) at 1800 r.p.m.

| 170 425 | | **FS** | P | *SR* | HA | 50425 | 56425 | 79425 | |
| 170 426 | | **FS** | P | *SR* | HA | 50426 | 56426 | 79426 | |
| 170 427 | | **FS** | P | *SR* | HA | 50427 | 56427 | 79427 | |
| 170 428 | | **FS** | P | *SR* | HA | 50428 | 56428 | 79428 | |
| 170 429 | | **FS** | P | *SR* | HA | 50429 | 56429 | 79429 | |
| 170 430 | | **FS** | P | *SR* | HA | 50430 | 56430 | 79430 | |
| 170 431 | * | **FS** | P | *SR* | HA | 50431 | 56431 | 79431 | |
| 170 432 | * | **FS** | P | *SR* | HA | 50432 | 56432 | 79432 | |
| 170 433 | | **FS** | P | *SR* | HA | 50433 | 56433 | 79433 | Investor in People |
| 170 434 | | **SR** | P | *SR* | HA | 50434 | 56434 | 79434 | |

**Class 170/4. First ScotRail units.** Originally built as Standard Class only units. 170 450–455 retro-fitted with First Class in 2008. Chapman seating. DMSL–MS–DMSL or † DMCL–MS–DMCL.

**DMSL.** Bombardier Derby 2004–2005. –/55 1TD 2W († 9/47 1TD 2W). 46.3 t.
**MS.** Bombardier Derby 2004–2005. –/76. 43.4 t.
**DMSL.** Bombardier Derby 2004–2005. –/67 1T († 9/53 1T). 46.4 t.

| 170 450 | † | **FS** | P | *SR* | HA | 50450 | 56450 | 79450 |

| 170 451 | † | **FS** | P | *SR* | HA | 50451 | 56451 | 79451 |
| 170 452 | † | **FS** | P | *SR* | HA | 50452 | 56452 | 79452 |
| 170 453 | † | **FS** | P | *SR* | HA | 50453 | 56453 | 79453 |
| 170 454 | † | **FS** | P | *SR* | HA | 50454 | 56454 | 79454 |
| 170 455 | † | **FS** | P | *SR* | HA | 50455 | 56455 | 79455 |
| 170 456 | | **FS** | P | *SR* | HA | 50456 | 56456 | 79456 |
| 170 457 | | **FS** | P | *SR* | HA | 50457 | 56457 | 79457 |
| 170 458 | | **FS** | P | *SR* | HA | 50458 | 56458 | 79458 |
| 170 459 | | **FS** | P | *SR* | HA | 50459 | 56459 | 79459 |
| 170 460 | | **FS** | P | *SR* | HA | 50460 | 56460 | 79460 |
| 170 461 | | **FS** | P | *SR* | HA | 50461 | 56461 | 79461 |

**Class 170/4. First ScotRail units.** Standard Class only units. Chapman seating. DMSL–MS–DMSL.

**50470–50471. DMSL(A).** Adtranz Derby 2001. –/55 1TD 2W. 45.1 t.
**50472–50478. DMSL(A).** Bombardier Derby 2004–2005. –/57 1TD 2W. 46.3 t.
**56470–56471. MS.** Adtranz Derby 2001. –/76. 42.4 t.
**56472–56478. MS.** Bombardier Derby 2004–2005. –/76. 43.4 t.
**79470–79471. DMSL(B).** Adtranz Derby 2001. –/67 1T. 45.1 t.
**79472–79478. DMSL(B).** Bombardier Derby 2004–2005. –/67 1T. 46.4 t.

| 170 470 | **SC** | P | *SR* | HA | 50470 | 56470 | 79470 |
| 170 471 | **SC** | P | *SR* | HA | 50471 | 56471 | 79471 |
| 170 472 | **SP** | P | *SR* | HA | 50472 | 56472 | 79472 |
| 170 473 | **SP** | P | *SR* | HA | 50473 | 56473 | 79473 |
| 170 474 | **SP** | P | *SR* | HA | 50474 | 56474 | 79474 |
| 170 475 | **SP** | P | *SR* | HA | 50475 | 56475 | 79475 |
| 170 476 | **SP** | P | *SR* | HA | 50476 | 56476 | 79476 |
| 170 477 | **SP** | P | *SR* | HA | 50477 | 56477 | 79477 |
| 170 478 | **SP** | P | *SR* | HA | 50478 | 56478 | 79478 |

**Class 170/5. London Midland and Cross-Country 2-car units.** Lazareni seating. DMSL–DMSL or * DMSL–DMCL (Cross-Country).

**DMSL(A).** Adtranz Derby 1999–2000. –/55 1TD 2W (* –/59 1TD 2W). 45.8 t.
**DMSL(B).** Adtranz Derby 1999–2000. –/67 1T (* DMCL 9/52 1T). 45.9 t.

| 170 501 | **LM** | P | *LM* | TS | 50501 | 79501 |
| 170 502 | **LM** | P | *LM* | TS | 50502 | 79502 |
| 170 503 | **LM** | P | *LM* | TS | 50503 | 79503 |
| 170 504 | **LM** | P | *LM* | TS | 50504 | 79504 |
| 170 505 | **LM** | P | *LM* | TS | 50505 | 79505 |
| 170 506 | **LM** | P | *LM* | TS | 50506 | 79506 |
| 170 507 | **LM** | P | *LM* | TS | 50507 | 79507 |
| 170 508 | **LM** | P | *LM* | TS | 50508 | 79508 |
| 170 509 | **LM** | P | *LM* | TS | 50509 | 79509 |
| 170 510 | **LM** | P | *LM* | TS | 50510 | 79510 |
| 170 511 | **LM** | P | *LM* | TS | 50511 | 79511 |
| 170 512 | **LM** | P | *LM* | TS | 50512 | 79512 |
| 170 513 | **LM** | P | *LM* | TS | 50513 | 79513 |
| 170 514 | **LM** | P | *LM* | TS | 50514 | 79514 |
| 170 515 | **LM** | P | *LM* | TS | 50515 | 79515 |
| 170 516 | **LM** | P | *LM* | TS | 50516 | 79516 |

| 170 517 | | LM | P | LM | TS | 50517 | | 79517 |
|---------|---|----|---|----|----|----|---|----|
| 170 518 | * | XC | P | XC | TS | 50518 | | 79518 |
| 170 519 | * | XC | P | XC | TS | 50519 | | 79519 |
| 170 520 | * | XC | P | XC | TS | 50520 | | 79520 |
| 170 521 | * | XC | P | XC | TS | 50521 | | 79521 |
| 170 522 | * | XC | P | XC | TS | 50522 | | 79522 |
| 170 523 | * | CT | P | XC | TS | 50523 | | 79523 |

**Class 170/6. London Midland and Cross-Country 3-car units.** Lazareni seating. DMSL–MS–DMSL or * DMSL–MS–DMCL (Cross-Country).

**DMSL(A).** Adtranz Derby 2000. –/55 1TD 2W (* –/59 1TD 2W). 45.8 t.
**MS.** Adtranz Derby 2000. –/74 (* –/80). 42.4 t.
**DMSL(B).** Adtranz Derby 2000. –/67 1T (* DMCL 9/52 1T). 45.9 t.

| 170 630 | | LM | P | LM | TS | 50630 | 56630 | 79630 |
|---------|---|----|---|----|----|----|----|----|
| 170 631 | | LM | P | LM | TS | 50631 | 56631 | 79631 |
| 170 632 | | LM | P | LM | TS | 50632 | 56632 | 79632 |
| 170 633 | | LM | P | LM | TS | 50633 | 56633 | 79633 |
| 170 634 | | LM | P | LM | TS | 50634 | 56634 | 79634 |
| 170 635 | | LM | P | LM | TS | 50635 | 56635 | 79635 |
| 170 636 | * | XC | P | XC | TS | 50636 | 56636 | 79636 |
| 170 637 | * | XC | P | XC | TS | 50637 | 56637 | 79637 |
| 170 638 | * | XC | P | XC | TS | 50638 | 56638 | 79638 |
| 170 639 | * | CT | P | XC | TS | 50639 | 56639 | 79639 |

# CLASS 171    TURBOSTAR    BOMBARDIER

DMCL–DMSL or DMCL–MS–MS–DMCL. Southern units. Air conditioned. Chapman seating.

**Construction:** Welded aluminium bodies with bolt-on steel ends.
**Engines:** One MTU 6R183TD13H of 315 kW (422 h.p.) at 1900 r.p.m.
**Transmission:** Hydraulic. Voith T211rzze to ZF final drive.
**Bogies:** One Adtranz P3–23 and one BREL P3–23 per car.
**Couplers:** Dellner 12 at outer ends, bar within unit (Class 171/8s).
**Dimensions:** 23.62/23.61 x 2.75 m.
**Gangways:** Within unit only.    **Wheel Arrangement:** 2-B (+ B-2 + B-2) + B-2.
**Doors:** Twin-leaf swing plug.    **Maximum Speed:** 100 m.p.h.
**Seating Layout:** 1: 2+1 facing/unidirectional. 2: 2+2 facing/unidirectional.
**Multiple Working:** Within class and with EMU Classes 375 and 377 in an emergency.

**Class 171/7. 2-car units.** DMCL–DMSL.

**50721–50726. DMCL.** Bombardier Derby 2003. 9/43 1TD 2W. 47.6 t.
**50727–50729. DMCL.** Bombardier Derby 2005. 9/43 1TD 2W. 46.3 t.
**50392. DMCL.** Bombardier Derby 2003. 9/43 1TD 2W. 46.6 t.
**79721–79726. DMSL.** Bombardier Derby 2003. –/64 1T. 47.8 t.
**79727–79729. DMSL.** Bombardier Derby 2005. –/64 1T. 46.2 t.
**79392. DMSL.** Bombardier Derby 2003. –/64 1T. 46.5 t.

**Notes:** 171 721–171 726 were built as Class 170s (170 721–170 726), but renumbered as 171s on fitting with Dellner couplers.

171 730 was formerly South West Trains unit 170 392, before transferring to Southern in 2007.

| 171 721 | **SN** | P | *SN* | SU | 50721 | 79721 |
| 171 722 | **SN** | P | *SN* | SU | 50722 | 79722 |
| 171 723 | **SN** | P | *SN* | SU | 50723 | 79723 |
| 171 724 | **SN** | P | *SN* | SU | 50724 | 79724 |
| 171 725 | **SN** | P | *SN* | SU | 50725 | 79725 |
| 171 726 | **SN** | P | *SN* | SU | 50726 | 79726 |
| 171 727 | **SN** | P | *SN* | SU | 50727 | 79727 |
| 171 728 | **SN** | P | *SN* | SU | 50728 | 79728 |
| 171 729 | **SN** | P | *SN* | SU | 50729 | 79729 |
| 171 730 | **SN** | P | *SN* | SU | 50392 | 79392 |

**Class 171/8. 4-car units.** DMCL(A)–MS–MS–DMCL(B).

**DMCL(A).** Bombardier Derby 2004. 9/43 1TD 2W. 46.5 t.
**MS.** Bombardier Derby 2004. –/74. 43.7 t.
**DMCL(B).** Bombardier Derby 2004. 9/50 1T. 46.5 t.

| 171 801 | **SN** | P | *SN* | SU | 50801 | 54801 | 56801 | 79801 |
| 171 802 | **SN** | P | *SN* | SU | 50802 | 54802 | 56802 | 79802 |
| 171 803 | **SN** | P | *SN* | SU | 50803 | 54803 | 56803 | 79803 |
| 171 804 | **SN** | P | *SN* | SU | 50804 | 54804 | 56804 | 79804 |
| 171 805 | **SN** | P | *SN* | SU | 50805 | 54805 | 56805 | 79805 |
| 171 806 | **SN** | P | *SN* | SU | 50806 | 54806 | 56806 | 79806 |

# CLASS 172        TURBOSTAR        BOMBARDIER

New generation Turbostars on order for London Overground, Chiltern and London Midland. Full details awaited.

**Construction:** Welded aluminium bodies with bolt-on steel ends.
**Engines:** One MTU 6H1800R83 of 360 kW (483 h.p.) at 1800 r.p.m.
**Transmission:** Mechanical. Supplied by ZG, Germany.
**Bogies:** B5000 type "lightweight" bogies.
**Couplers:** BSI
**Dimensions:** 23.27/23.36 x 2.75 m.
**Gangways:** London Overground & Chiltern units: Within unit only. London Midland units: Throughout.
**Wheel Arrangement:**
**Doors:** Twin-leaf swing plug.
**Maximum Speed:** 75 m.p.h. (London Midland units 100 m.p.h.)
**Seating Layout:** 2+2 facing/unidirectional.
**Multiple Working:** Within class and with Classes 150, 153, 155, 156, 158, 159 and 170.

**Class 172/0. London Overground units.** DMS–DMS. On order for use on the Gospel Oak–Barking line. Due for delivery early 2010.

**59311–59318. DMS.** Bombardier Derby 2009–2010.     2W.    . t.
**59411–59418. DMS.** Bombardier Derby 2009–2010.     .    . t.

| 172 001 | A | 59311 | 59411 |
| 172 002 | A | 59312 | 59412 |

| 172 003 | A | 59313 | 59413 |
|---------|---|-------|-------|
| 172 004 | A | 59314 | 59414 |
| 172 005 | A | 59315 | 59415 |
| 172 006 | A | 59316 | 59416 |
| 172 007 | A | 59317 | 59417 |
| 172 008 | A | 59318 | 59418 |

**Class 172/1. Chiltern Railways units.** DMSL–DMS. On order. Due for delivery summer 2010.

**59111–59114. DMSL.** Bombardier Derby 2009–2010.    1TD 2W.    . t.
**59211–59214. DMS.** Bombardier Derby 2009–2010.    . t.

| 172 101 | A | 59111 | 59211 |
|---------|---|-------|-------|
| 172 102 | A | 59112 | 59212 |
| 172 103 | A | 59113 | 59213 |
| 172 104 | A | 59114 | 59214 |

**Class 172/2. London Midland 2-car units.** DMSL–DMS. On order for use on West Midlands suburban services. Due for delivery from spring 2010.

**50211–50222. DMSL.** Bombardier Derby 2009–2010. –/53(4) 1TD 2W.    . t.
**79211–79222. DMS.** Bombardier Derby 2009–2010. –/68(3).    . t.

| 172 211 | P | 50211 | 79211 |
|---------|---|-------|-------|
| 172 212 | P | 50212 | 79212 |
| 172 213 | P | 50213 | 79213 |
| 172 214 | P | 50214 | 79214 |
| 172 215 | P | 50215 | 79215 |
| 172 216 | P | 50216 | 79216 |
| 172 217 | P | 50217 | 79217 |
| 172 218 | P | 50218 | 79218 |
| 172 219 | P | 50219 | 79219 |
| 172 220 | P | 50220 | 79220 |
| 172 221 | P | 50221 | 79221 |
| 172 222 | P | 50222 | 79222 |

**Class 172/3. London Midland 3-car units.** DMSL–MS–DMS. On order for use on West Midlands suburban services. Due for delivery from spring 2010.

**50331–50345. DMSL.** Bombardier Derby 2009–2010. –/53(4) 1TD 2W.    . t.
**56331–56345. MS.** Bombardier Derby 2009–2010. –/72.    . t.
**79331–79345. DMS.** Bombardier Derby 2009–2010. –/68(3).    . t.

| 172 331 | P | 50331 | 56331 | 79331 |
|---------|---|-------|-------|-------|
| 172 332 | P | 50332 | 56332 | 79332 |
| 172 333 | P | 50333 | 56333 | 79333 |
| 172 334 | P | 50334 | 56334 | 79334 |
| 172 335 | P | 50335 | 56335 | 79335 |
| 172 336 | P | 50336 | 56336 | 79336 |
| 172 337 | P | 50337 | 56337 | 79337 |
| 172 338 | P | 50338 | 56338 | 79338 |
| 172 339 | P | 50339 | 56339 | 79339 |
| 172 340 | P | 50340 | 56340 | 79340 |
| 172 341 | P | 50341 | 56341 | 79341 |

| 172 342 | P | | 50342 | 56342 | 79342 |
| 172 343 | P | | 50343 | 56343 | 79343 |
| 172 344 | P | | 50344 | 56344 | 79344 |
| 172 345 | P | | 50345 | 56345 | 79345 |

## CLASS 175          CORADIA 1000          ALSTOM

Air conditioned.

**Construction:** Steel.
**Engines:** One Cummins N14 of 335 kW (450 h.p.).
**Transmission:** Hydraulic. Voith T211rzze to ZF Voith final drive.
**Bogies:** ACR (Alstom FBO) – LTB-MBS1, TB-MB1, MBS1-LTB.
**Couplers:** Scharfenberg outer ends and bar within unit (Class 175/1).
**Dimensions:** 23.06/23.93 x 2.80 m.
**Gangways:** Within unit only.          **Wheel Arrangement:** 2-B (+ B-2) + B-2.
**Doors:** Single-leaf swing plug.          **Maximum Speed:** 100 m.p.h.
**Seating Layout:** 2+2 facing/unidirectional.
**Multiple Working:** Within class and with Class 180.

**Class 175/0.** DMSL–DMSL. 2-car units.

**DMSL(A).** Alstom Birmingham 1999–2000. –/54 1TD 2W. 50.7 t.
**DMSL(B).** Alstom Birmingham 1999–2000. –/64 1T. 50.7 t.

| 175 001 | **AV** | A | *AW* | CH | 50701 | 79701 |
| 175 002 | **AV** | A | *AW* | CH | 50702 | 79702 |
| 175 003 | **AV** | A | *AW* | CH | 50703 | 79703 |
| 175 004 | **AV** | A | *AW* | CH | 50704 | 79704 |
| 175 005 | **AV** | A | *AW* | CH | 50705 | 79705 |
| 175 006 | **AV** | A | *AW* | CH | 50706 | 79706 |
| 175 007 | **AV** | A | *AW* | CH | 50707 | 79707 |
| 175 008 | **AV** | A | *AW* | CH | 50708 | 79708 |
| 175 009 | **AV** | A | *AW* | CH | 50709 | 79709 |
| 175 010 | **AV** | A | *AW* | CH | 50710 | 79710 |
| 175 011 | **AV** | A | *AW* | CH | 50711 | 79711 |

**Class 175/1.** DMSL–MSL–DMSL. 3-car units.

**DMSL(A).** Alstom Birmingham 1999–2001. –/54 1TD 2W. 50.7 t.
**MSL.** Alstom Birmingham 1999–2001. –/68 1T. 47.5 t.
**DMSL(B).** Alstom Birmingham 1999–2001. –/64 1T. 50.7 t.

| 175 101 | **AV** | A | *AW* | CH | 50751 | 56751 | 79751 |
| 175 102 | **AV** | A | *AW* | CH | 50752 | 56752 | 79752 |
| 175 103 | **FS** | A | *AW* | CH | 50753 | 56753 | 79753 |
| 175 104 | **FS** | A | *AW* | CH | 50754 | 56754 | 79754 |
| 175 105 | **AV** | A | *AW* | CH | 50755 | 56755 | 79755 |
| 175 106 | **FS** | A | *AW* | CH | 50756 | 56756 | 79756 |
| 175 107 | **FS** | A | *AW* | CH | 50757 | 56757 | 79757 |
| 175 108 | **AV** | A | *AW* | CH | 50758 | 56758 | 79758 |
| 175 109 | **AV** | A | *AW* | CH | 50759 | 56759 | 79759 |
| 175 110 | **AW** | A | *AW* | CH | 50760 | 56760 | 79760 |
| 175 111 | **FS** | A | *AW* | CH | 50761 | 56761 | 79761 |
| 175 112 | **FS** | A | *AW* | CH | 50762 | 56762 | 79762 |

| 175 113 | **FS** | A | *AW* | CH | 50763 | 56763 | 79763 |
| 175 114 | **FS** | A | *AW* | CH | 50764 | 56764 | 79764 |
| 175 115 | **FS** | A | *AW* | CH | 50765 | 56765 | 79765 |
| 175 116 | **FS** | A | *AW* | CH | 50766 | 56766 | 79766 |

**Names (carried on one side of each DMSL):**

| 175 103 | Mum |
| 175 107 | CORONATION ST. ROVERS RETURN |
| 175 111 | Brief Encounter |
| 175 112 | South Lakes Wild Animal Park SUMATRAN TIGER |
| 175 114 | Commonwealth Cruiser |
| 175 116 | PETER VL JONES Community Rail Officer – Conwy Valley Line |

# CLASS 180     CORADIA 1000     ALSTOM

Air conditioned. This fleet is in a state of flux at the time of writing, with three units in use with First Great Western (until May 2009 – 180 102/104/105), two with First Hull Trains (180 110/111, with 180 109/113 also set to move to this operator), and three units on short-term lease to Northern for use on Manchester/ Hazel Grove–Blackpool services (180 103/106/108).

**Construction:** Steel.
**Engines:** One Cummins QSK19 of 560 kW (750 h.p.) at 2100 r.p.m.
**Transmission:** Hydraulic. Voith T312br to Voith final drive.
**Bogies:** ACR (Alstom FBO): LTB1-MBS2, TB1-MB2, TB1-MB2, TB2-MB2, MBS2-LTB1.
**Couplers:** Scharfenberg outer ends, bar within unit.
**Dimensions:** 23.71/23.03 x 2.80 m.
**Gangways:** Within unit only.
**Wheel Arrangement:** 2-B + B-2 + B-2 + B-2 + B-2.
**Doors:** Single-leaf swing plug.     **Maximum Speed:** 125 m.p.h.
**Seating Layout:** 1: 2+1 facing/unidirectional, 2: 2+2 facing/unidirectional.
**Multiple Working:** Within class and with Class 175.

**DMSL(A).** Alstom Birmingham 2000–2001. –/46 2W 1TD. 51.7 t.
**MFL.** Alstom Birmingham 2000–2001. 42/– 1T 1W + catering point. 49.6 t.
**MSL.** Alstom Birmingham 2000–2001. –/68 1T. 49.5 t.
**MSLRB.** Alstom Birmingham 2000–2001. –/56 1T. 50.3 t.
**DMSL(B).** Alstom Birmingham 2000–2001. –/56 1T. 51.4 t.

| 180 101 | **FG** | A | | OY | 50901 | 54901 | 55901 | 56901 | 59901 |
| 180 102 | **FG** | A | *GW* | OO | 50902 | 54902 | 55902 | 56902 | 59902 |
| 180 103 | **FB** | A | *NO* | NH | 50903 | 54903 | 55903 | 56903 | 59903 |
| 180 104 | **FG** | A | *GW* | OO | 50904 | 54904 | 55904 | 56904 | 59904 |
| 180 105 | **FG** | A | *GW* | OO | 50905 | 54905 | 55905 | 56905 | 59905 |
| 180 106 | **FB** | A | *NO* | NH | 50906 | 54906 | 55906 | 56906 | 59906 |
| 180 107 | **FG** | A | | ZN | 50907 | 54907 | 55907 | 56907 | 59907 |
| 180 108 | **FB** | A | *NO* | NH | 50908 | 54908 | 55908 | 56908 | 59908 |
| 180 109 | **FG** | A | | XW | 50909 | 54909 | 55909 | 56909 | 59909 |
| 180 110 | **FG** | A | *HT* | XW | 50910 | 54910 | 55910 | 56910 | 59910 |
| 180 111 | **FG** | A | *HT* | XW | 50911 | 54911 | 55911 | 56911 | 59911 |
| 180 112 | **FG** | A | | OY | 50912 | 54912 | 55912 | 56912 | 59912 |
| 180 113 | **FG** | A | | ZN | 50913 | 54913 | 55913 | 56913 | 59913 |
| 180 114 | **FG** | A | | OY | 50914 | 54914 | 55914 | 56914 | 59914 |

# CLASS 185        DESIRO UK        SIEMENS

Air conditioned. Grammer seating.

**Construction:** Aluminium.
**Engines:** One Cummins QSK19 of 560 kW (750 h.p.) at 2100 r.p.m.
**Transmission:** Voith.
**Bogies:** Siemens.
**Couplers:** Dellner 12.
**Dimensions:** 23.76/23.75 x 2.66 m.
**Gangways:** Within unit only.          **Wheel Arrangement:** 2-B + 2-B + B-2.
**Doors:** Double-leaf sliding plug.     **Maximum Speed:** 100 m.p.h.
**Seating Layout:** 1: 2+1 facing/unidirectional, 2: 2+2 facing/unidirectional.
**Multiple Working:** Within class only.

**DMCL.** Siemens Uerdingen 2005–2006. 15/18(8) 2W 1TD + catering point. 55.4 t.
**MSL.** Siemens Uerdingen 2005–2006. –/72 1T. 52.7 t.
**DMS.** Siemens Uerdingen 2005–2006. –/64(4). 54.9 t.

| | | | | | | | |
|---|---|---|---|---|---|---|---|
| 185 101 | **FT** | H | *TP* | AK | 51101 | 53101 | 54101 |
| 185 102 | **FT** | H | *TP* | AK | 51102 | 53102 | 54102 |
| 185 103 | **FT** | H | *TP* | AK | 51103 | 53103 | 54103 |
| 185 104 | **FT** | H | *TP* | AK | 51104 | 53104 | 54104 |
| 185 105 | **FT** | H | *TP* | AK | 51105 | 53105 | 54105 |
| 185 106 | **FT** | H | *TP* | AK | 51106 | 53106 | 54106 |
| 185 107 | **FT** | H | *TP* | AK | 51107 | 53107 | 54107 |
| 185 108 | **FT** | H | *TP* | AK | 51108 | 53108 | 54108 |
| 185 109 | **FT** | H | *TP* | AK | 51109 | 53109 | 54109 |
| 185 110 | **FT** | H | *TP* | AK | 51110 | 53110 | 54110 |
| 185 111 | **FT** | H | *TP* | AK | 51111 | 53111 | 54111 |
| 185 112 | **FT** | H | *TP* | AK | 51112 | 53112 | 54112 |
| 185 113 | **FT** | H | *TP* | AK | 51113 | 53113 | 54113 |
| 185 114 | **FT** | H | *TP* | AK | 51114 | 53114 | 54114 |
| 185 115 | **FT** | H | *TP* | AK | 51115 | 53115 | 54115 |
| 185 116 | **FT** | H | *TP* | AK | 51116 | 53116 | 54116 |
| 185 117 | **FT** | H | *TP* | AK | 51117 | 53117 | 54117 |
| 185 118 | **FT** | H | *TP* | AK | 51118 | 53118 | 54118 |
| 185 119 | **FT** | H | *TP* | AK | 51119 | 53119 | 54119 |
| 185 120 | **FT** | H | *TP* | AK | 51120 | 53120 | 54120 |
| 185 121 | **FT** | H | *TP* | AK | 51121 | 53121 | 54121 |
| 185 122 | **FT** | H | *TP* | AK | 51122 | 53122 | 54122 |
| 185 123 | **FT** | H | *TP* | AK | 51123 | 53123 | 54123 |
| 185 124 | **FT** | H | *TP* | AK | 51124 | 53124 | 54124 |
| 185 125 | **FT** | H | *TP* | AK | 51125 | 53125 | 54125 |
| 185 126 | **FT** | H | *TP* | AK | 51126 | 53126 | 54126 |
| 185 127 | **FT** | H | *TP* | AK | 51127 | 53127 | 54127 |
| 185 128 | **FT** | H | *TP* | AK | 51128 | 53128 | 54128 |
| 185 129 | **FT** | H | *TP* | AK | 51129 | 53129 | 54129 |
| 185 130 | **FT** | H | *TP* | AK | 51130 | 53130 | 54130 |
| 185 131 | **FT** | H | *TP* | AK | 51131 | 53131 | 54131 |
| 185 132 | **FT** | H | *TP* | AK | 51132 | 53132 | 54132 |

| 185 133 | **FT** | H | *TP* | AK | 51133 | 53133 | 54133 |
| 185 134 | **FT** | H | *TP* | AK | 51134 | 53134 | 54134 |
| 185 135 | **FT** | H | *TP* | AK | 51135 | 53135 | 54135 |
| 185 136 | **FT** | H | *TP* | AK | 51136 | 53136 | 54136 |
| 185 137 | **FT** | H | *TP* | AK | 51137 | 53137 | 54137 |
| 185 138 | **FT** | H | *TP* | AK | 51138 | 53138 | 54138 |
| 185 139 | **FT** | H | *TP* | AK | 51139 | 53139 | 54139 |
| 185 140 | **FT** | H | *TP* | AK | 51140 | 53140 | 54140 |
| 185 141 | **FT** | H | *TP* | AK | 51141 | 53141 | 54141 |
| 185 142 | **FT** | H | *TP* | AK | 51142 | 53142 | 54142 |
| 185 143 | **FT** | H | *TP* | AK | 51143 | 53143 | 54143 |
| 185 144 | **FT** | H | *TP* | AK | 51144 | 53144 | 54144 |
| 185 145 | **FT** | H | *TP* | AK | 51145 | 53145 | 54145 |
| 185 146 | **FT** | H | *TP* | AK | 51146 | 53146 | 54146 |
| 185 147 | **FT** | H | *TP* | AK | 51147 | 53147 | 54147 |
| 185 148 | **FT** | H | *TP* | AK | 51148 | 53148 | 54148 |
| 185 149 | **FT** | H | *TP* | AK | 51149 | 53149 | 54149 |
| 185 150 | **FT** | H | *TP* | AK | 51150 | 53150 | 54150 |
| 185 151 | **FT** | H | *TP* | AK | 51151 | 53151 | 54151 |

# 3.2. DIESEL ELECTRIC UNITS

## CLASS 201/202 PRESERVED "HASTINGS" UNIT BR

DMBS–TSL–TSL–TSRB–TSL–DMBS.

Preserved unit made up from two Class 201 short-frame cars and three Class 202 long-frame cars. The "Hastings" units were made with narrow body-profiles for use on the section between Tonbridge and Battle which had tunnels of restricted loading gauge. These tunnels were converted to single track operation in the 1980s thus allowing standard loading gauge stock to be used. The set also contains a Class 411 EMU trailer (not Hastings line gauge) and a Class 422 EMU buffet car.

**Construction:** Steel.
**Engine:** One English Electric 4SRKT Mk. 2 of 450 kW (600 h.p.) at 850 r.p.m.
**Main Generator:** English Electric EE824.
**Traction Motors:** Two English Electric EE507 mounted on the inner bogie.
**Bogies:** SR Mk. 4. (Former EMU TSL vehicles have Commonwealth bogies).
**Couplers:** Drophead buckeye.
**Dimensions:** 18.40 x 2.50 m (60000), 20.35 x 2.50 m (60116/60118/60529), 18.36 x 2.50 m (60501), 20.35 x 2.82 m (69337), 20.30 x 2.82 m (70262).
**Gangways:** Within unit only.
**Doors:** Manually operated slam.
**Brakes:** Electro-pneumatic and automatic air.
**Maximum Speed:** 75 m.p.h.
**Seating Layout:** 2+2 facing.
**Multiple Working:** Other ex-BR Southern Region DEMU vehicles.

**60000. DMBS.** Lot No. 30329 Eastleigh 1957. –/22. 55.0 t.
**60116. DMBS.** Lot No. 30395 Eastleigh 1957. –/31. 56.0 t.
**60118. DMBS.** Lot No. 30395 Eastleigh 1957. –/30. 56.0 t.
**60501. TSL.** Lot No. 30331 Eastleigh 1957. –/52 2T. 29.5 t.
**60529. TSL.** Lot No. 30397 Eastleigh 1957. –/60 2T. 30.5 t.
**69337. TSRB (ex-Class 422 EMU).** Lot No. 30805 York 1970. –/40. 35.0 t.
**70262. TSL (ex-Class 411/5 EMU).** Lot No. 30455 Eastleigh 1958. –/64 2T. 31.5 t.

| | | | | | | | | | |
|---|---|---|---|---|---|---|---|---|---|
| 201 001 | **G** | HD *HD* | SE | 60116 | 60529 | 70262 | 69337 | 60501 | 60118 |
| Spare | **G** | HD *HD* | SE | 60000 | | | | | |

**Names:**

60000 Hastings
60116 Mountfield
60118 Tunbridge Wells

# CLASS 220      VOYAGER      BOMBARDIER

DMS–MSRMB–MS–DMF or † DMS–MS–MS–DMF.

**Construction:** Steel.
**Engine:** Cummins QSK19 of 560 kW (750 h.p.) at 1800 r.p.m.
**Transmission:** Two Alstom Onix 800 three-phase traction motors of 275 kW.
**Braking:** Rheostatic and electro-pneumatic.
**Bogies:** Bombardier B5005.
**Couplers:** Dellner 12 at outer ends, bar within unit.
**Dimensions:** 23.67/23.00(602xx) x 2.73 m.
**Gangways:** Within unit only.
**Wheel Arrangement:** 1A-A1 + 1A-A1 + 1A-A1 + 1A-A1.
**Doors:** Single-leaf swing plug.
**Maximum Speed:** 125 m.p.h.
**Seating Layout:** 1: 2+1 facing/unidirectional, 2: 2+2 mainly unidirectional.
**Multiple Working:** Within class and with Classes 221 and 222 (in an emergency).
Also can be controlled from Class 57/3 locomotives.

**DMS.** Bombardier Brugge/Wakefield 2000–2001. –/42 1TD 1W. 48.0 t (†   . t).
**MSRMB († MS).** Bombardier Brugge/Wakefield 2000–2001. –/58 († –/66) 45.0 t
(†   . t).
**MS.** Bombardier Brugge/Wakefield 2000–2001. –/60 1TD († –/66 1TD). 44.5 t
(†   . t).
**DMF.** Bombardier Brugge/Wakefield 2000–2001. 26/– 1TD 1W. 48.1 t (†   . t).

**Note:** † Modified Cross-Country units. Shop removed from MSRMB and flexible
space for bicycles and luggage fitted in its place.

| | | | | | | | | |
|---|---|---|---|---|---|---|---|---|
| 220 001 | † | **XC** | HX | *XC* | CZ | 60301 | 60701 | 60201 | 60401 |
| 220 002 | | **XC** | HX | *XC* | CZ | 60302 | 60702 | 60202 | 60402 |
| 220 003 | | **XC** | HX | *XC* | CZ | 60303 | 60703 | 60203 | 60403 |
| 220 004 | | **XC** | HX | *XC* | CZ | 60304 | 60704 | 60204 | 60404 |
| 220 005 | | **XC** | HX | *XC* | CZ | 60305 | 60705 | 60205 | 60405 |
| 220 006 | | **XC** | HX | *XC* | CZ | 60306 | 60706 | 60206 | 60406 |
| 220 007 | | **XC** | HX | *XC* | CZ | 60307 | 60707 | 60207 | 60407 |
| 220 008 | | **XC** | HX | *XC* | CZ | 60308 | 60708 | 60208 | 60408 |
| 220 009 | | **XC** | HX | *XC* | CZ | 60309 | 60709 | 60209 | 60409 |
| 220 010 | | **XC** | HX | *XC* | CZ | 60310 | 60710 | 60210 | 60410 |
| 220 011 | | **XC** | HX | *XC* | CZ | 60311 | 60711 | 60211 | 60411 |
| 220 012 | | **XC** | HX | *XC* | CZ | 60312 | 60712 | 60212 | 60412 |
| 220 013 | | **XC** | HX | *XC* | CZ | 60313 | 60713 | 60213 | 60413 |
| 220 014 | | **XC** | HX | *XC* | CZ | 60314 | 60714 | 60214 | 60414 |
| 220 015 | | **XC** | HX | *XC* | CZ | 60315 | 60715 | 60215 | 60415 |
| 220 016 | | **XC** | HX | *XC* | CZ | 60316 | 60716 | 60216 | 60416 |
| 220 017 | | **XC** | HX | *XC* | CZ | 60317 | 60717 | 60217 | 60417 |
| 220 018 | | **XC** | HX | *XC* | CZ | 60318 | 60718 | 60218 | 60418 |
| 220 019 | | **XC** | HX | *XC* | CZ | 60319 | 60719 | 60219 | 60419 |
| 220 020 | | **XC** | HX | *XC* | CZ | 60320 | 60720 | 60220 | 60420 |
| 220 021 | | **XC** | HX | *XC* | CZ | 60321 | 60721 | 60221 | 60421 |
| 220 022 | | **XC** | HX | *XC* | CZ | 60322 | 60722 | 60222 | 60422 |
| 220 023 | | **XC** | HX | *XC* | CZ | 60323 | 60723 | 60223 | 60423 |

| 220 024 | XC | HX | XC | CZ | 60324 | 60724 | 60224 | 60424 |
| 220 025 | XC | HX | XC | CZ | 60325 | 60725 | 60225 | 60425 |
| 220 026 | XC | HX | XC | CZ | 60326 | 60726 | 60226 | 60426 |
| 220 027 | XC | HX | XC | CZ | 60327 | 60727 | 60227 | 60427 |
| 220 028 | XC | HX | XC | CZ | 60328 | 60728 | 60228 | 60428 |
| 220 029 | XC | HX | XC | CZ | 60329 | 60729 | 60229 | 60429 |
| 220 030 | XC | HX | XC | CZ | 60330 | 60730 | 60230 | 60430 |
| 220 031 | XC | HX | XC | CZ | 60331 | 60731 | 60231 | 60431 |
| 220 032 | XC | HX | XC | CZ | 60332 | 60732 | 60232 | 60432 |
| 220 033 | XC | HX | XC | CZ | 60333 | 60733 | 60233 | 60433 |
| 220 034 | XC | HX | XC | CZ | 60334 | 60734 | 60234 | 60434 |

# CLASS 221    SUPER VOYAGER    BOMBARDIER

DMS–MSRMB–MS(–MS)–DMF or * DMS–MS–MS–MSRMB–DMF (modified Virgin West Coast 5-car sets) or † DMS–MS–MS–MS–DMF (modified Cross-Country units). Built as tilting units but tilt now isolated on Cross-Country sets.

**Construction:** Steel.
**Engine:** Cummins QSK19 of 560 kW (750 h.p.) at 1800 r.p.m.
**Transmission:** Two Alstom Onix 800 three-phase traction motors of 275 kW.
**Braking:** Rheostatic and electro-pneumatic.
**Bogies:** Bombardier HVP.
**Couplers:** Dellner 12 at outer ends, bar within unit.
**Dimensions:** 23.67 x 2.73 m.
**Gangways:** Within unit only.
**Wheel Arrangement:** 1A-A1 + 1A-A1 + 1A-A1 (+ 1A-A1) + 1A-A1.
**Doors:** Single-leaf swing plug.
**Maximum Speed:** 125 m.p.h.
**Seating Layout:** 1: 2+1 facing/unidirectional, 2: 2+2 mainly unidirectional.
**Multiple Working:** Within class and with Classes 220 and 222 (in an emergency). Also can be controlled from Class 57/3 locomotives.

**DMS.** Bombardier Brugge/Wakefield 2001–2002. –/42 1TD 1W. 56.6 t (* 58.9 t, † 58.5 t.)
**MSRMB († MS).** Bombardier Brugge/Wakefield 2001–2002. –/58 (* –/52, † –/66). 53.1 t (* 55.9 t, † 54.1 t.)
**60951–994. MS.** Bombardier Brugge/Wakefield 2001–2002. –/60 1TD (* –/68 1TD, † –/66 1TD). 56.6 t (* 54.3 t, † 54.8 t.)
**60851–890. MS.** Bombardier Brugge/Wakefield 2001–2002. –/60 1TD (* –/68 1TD, † –/62 1TD). 53.1 t (* 55.0 t, † 54.4 t.)
**DMF.** Bombardier Brugge/Wakefield 2001–2002. 26/– 1TD 1W. 56.6 t (* 59.1 t, † 58.9 t.)

**Notes:** * Modified Virgin West Coast units. MSRMB moved adjacent to the DMF. The seating in this vehicle (2+2 facing) can be used by First or Standard Class passengers depending on demand.

† Modified Cross-Country units. Shop removed from MSRMB and flexible space for bicycles and luggage fitted in its place.

| 221 101 | * | VT | HX | VW | CZ | 60351 | 60951 | 60851 | 60751 | 60451 |
| 221 102 | * | VT | HX | VW | CZ | 60352 | 60952 | 60852 | 60752 | 60452 |
| 221 103 | * | VT | HX | VW | CZ | 60353 | 60953 | 60853 | 60753 | 60453 |

| | | | | | | | | | | |
|---|---|---|---|---|---|---|---|---|---|---|
| 221 104 | * | **VT** | HX | *VW* | CZ | 60354 | 60954 | 60854 | 60754 | 60454 |
| 221 105 | * | **VT** | HX | *VW* | CZ | 60355 | 60955 | 60855 | 60755 | 60455 |
| 221 106 | * | **VT** | HX | *VW* | CZ | 60356 | 60956 | 60856 | 60756 | 60456 |
| 221 107 | * | **VT** | HX | *VW* | CZ | 60357 | 60957 | 60857 | 60757 | 60457 |
| 221 108 | * | **VT** | HX | *VW* | CZ | 60358 | 60958 | 60858 | 60758 | 60458 |
| 221 109 | * | **VT** | HX | *VW* | CZ | 60359 | 60959 | 60859 | 60759 | 60459 |
| 221 110 | * | **VT** | HX | *VW* | CZ | 60360 | 60960 | 60860 | 60760 | 60460 |
| 221 111 | * | **VT** | HX | *VW* | CZ | 60361 | 60961 | 60861 | 60761 | 60461 |
| 221 112 | * | **VT** | HX | *VW* | CZ | 60362 | 60962 | 60862 | 60762 | 60462 |
| 221 113 | * | **VT** | HX | *VW* | CZ | 60363 | 60963 | 60863 | 60763 | 60463 |
| 221 114 | | **VT** | HX | *VW* | CZ | 60364 | 60764 | 60964 | 60864 | 60464 |
| 221 115 | | **VT** | HX | *VW* | CZ | 60365 | 60765 | 60965 | 60865 | 60465 |
| 221 116 | | **VT** | HX | *VW* | CZ | 60366 | 60766 | 60966 | 60866 | 60466 |
| 221 117 | | **VT** | HX | *VW* | CZ | 60367 | 60767 | 60967 | 60867 | 60467 |
| 221 118 | | **VT** | HX | *VW* | CZ | 60368 | 60768 | 60968 | 60868 | 60468 |
| 221 119 | † | **XC** | HX | *XC* | CZ | 60369 | 60769 | 60969 | 60869 | 60469 |
| 221 120 | † | **XC** | HX | *XC* | CZ | 60370 | 60770 | 60970 | 60870 | 60470 |
| 221 121 | | **XC** | HX | *XC* | CZ | 60371 | 60771 | 60971 | 60871 | 60471 |
| 221 122 | | **XC** | HX | *XC* | CZ | 60372 | 60772 | 60972 | 60872 | 60472 |
| 221 123 | | **XC** | HX | *XC* | CZ | 60373 | 60773 | 60973 | 60873 | 60473 |
| 221 124 | | **XC** | HX | *XC* | CZ | 60374 | 60774 | 60974 | 60874 | 60474 |
| 221 125 | | **XC** | HX | *XC* | CZ | 60375 | 60775 | 60975 | 60875 | 60475 |
| 221 126 | † | **XC** | HX | *XC* | CZ | 60376 | 60776 | 60976 | 60876 | 60476 |
| 221 127 | | **XC** | HX | *XC* | CZ | 60377 | 60777 | 60977 | 60877 | 60477 |
| 221 128 | | **XC** | HX | *XC* | CZ | 60378 | 60778 | 60978 | 60878 | 60478 |
| 221 129 | | **XC** | HX | *XC* | CZ | 60379 | 60779 | 60979 | 60879 | 60479 |
| 221 130 | | **XC** | HX | *XC* | CZ | 60380 | 60780 | 60980 | 60880 | 60480 |
| 221 131 | | **XC** | HX | *XC* | CZ | 60381 | 60781 | 60981 | 60881 | 60481 |
| 221 132 | | **XC** | HX | *XC* | CZ | 60382 | 60782 | 60982 | 60882 | 60482 |
| 221 133 | | **XC** | HX | *XC* | CZ | 60383 | 60783 | 60983 | 60883 | 60483 |
| 221 134 | | **XC** | HX | *XC* | CZ | 60384 | 60784 | 60984 | 60884 | 60484 |
| 221 135 | | **XC** | HX | *XC* | CZ | 60385 | 60785 | 60985 | 60885 | 60485 |
| 221 136 | | **XC** | HX | *XC* | CZ | 60386 | 60786 | 60986 | 60886 | 60486 |
| 221 137 | | **XC** | HX | *XC* | CZ | 60387 | 60787 | 60987 | 60887 | 60487 |
| 221 138 | | **XC** | HX | *XC* | CZ | 60388 | 60788 | 60988 | 60888 | 60488 |
| 221 139 | | **XC** | HX | *XC* | CZ | 60389 | 60789 | 60989 | 60889 | 60489 |
| 221 140 | | **XC** | HX | *XC* | CZ | 60390 | 60790 | 60990 | 60890 | 60490 |
| 221 141 | | **XC** | HX | *XC* | CZ | 60391 | 60791 | 60991 | | 60491 |
| 221 142 | | **VT** | HX | *VW* | CZ | 60392 | 60992 | 60792 | | 60492 |
| 221 143 | | **VT** | HX | *VW* | CZ | 60393 | 60993 | 60793 | | 60493 |
| 221 144 | | **VT** | HX | *VW* | CZ | 60394 | 60994 | 60794 | | 60494 |

**Names (carried on MS No. 609xx):**

| | | | | |
|---|---|---|---|---|
| 221 101 | Louis Bleriot | | 221 109 | Marco Polo |
| 221 102 | John Cabot | | 221 110 | James Cook |
| 221 103 | Christopher Columbus | | 221 111 | Roald Amundsen |
| 221 104 | Sir John Franklin | | 221 112 | Ferdinand Magellan |
| 221 105 | William Baffin | | 221 113 | Sir Walter Raleigh |
| 221 106 | Willem Barents | | 221 142 | Matthew Flinders |
| 221 107 | Sir Martin Frobisher | | 221 143 | Auguste Picard |
| 221 108 | Sir Ernest Shackleton | | 221 144 | Prince Madoc |

# CLASS 222   MERIDIAN/PIONEER   BOMBARDIER

**Construction:** Steel.
**Engine:** Cummins QSK19 of 560 kW (750 h.p.) at 1800 r.p.m.
**Transmission:** Two Alstom Onix 800 three-phase traction motors of 275 kW.
**Braking:** Rheostatic and electro-pneumatic.
**Bogies:** Bombardier B5005.
**Couplers:** Dellner at outer ends, bar within unit.
**Dimensions:** 23.85/23.00 x 2.73 m.
**Gangways:** Within unit only.            **Wheel Arrangement:** All cars 1A-A1.
**Doors:** Single-leaf swing plug.          **Maximum Speed:** 125 m.p.h.
**Seating Layout:** 1: 2+1, 2: 2+2 facing/unidirectional.
**Multiple Working:** Within class and with Classes 220 and 221 (in an emergency).

**222 001–222 006. East Midlands Trains Meridian.** 7-car units. DMF–MF–MF–
MSRMB–MS–MS–DMS.

**Note:** The 7-car units were built as 9-car units, before being reduced to 8-car
sets and then later to 7-car sets to strengthen all 4-car units to 5-cars. 222 007
was built as a 9-car unit but has now been reduced to a 5-car unit.

**DMF.** Bombardier Brugge 2004–2005. 22/– 1TD 1W. 52.8 t.
**MF.** Bombardier Brugge 2004–2005. 42/– 1T. 46.8 t.
**MSRMB.** Bombardier Brugge 2004–2005. –/62. 48.0 t.
**MS.** Bombardier Brugge 2004–2005. –/68 1T. 47.0 t.
**DMS.** Bombardier Brugge 2004–2005. –/38 1TD 1W. 49.4 t.

| 222 001 | **ST** | H | *EM* | DY | 60241 | 60445 | 60341 | 60621 |
|         |        |   |      |    | 60561 | 60551 | 60161 |       |
| 222 002 | **ST** | H | *EM* | DY | 60242 | 60346 | 60342 | 60622 |
|         |        |   |      |    | 60562 | 60544 | 60162 |       |
| 222 003 | **ST** | H | *EM* | DY | 60243 | 60446 | 60343 | 60623 |
|         |        |   |      |    | 60563 | 60553 | 60163 |       |
| 222 004 | **ST** | H | *EM* | DY | 60244 | 60345 | 60344 | 60624 |
|         |        |   |      |    | 60564 | 60554 | 60164 |       |
| 222 005 | **ST** | H | *EM* | DY | 60245 | 60347 | 60443 | 60625 |
|         |        |   |      |    | 60565 | 60555 | 60165 |       |
| 222 006 | **ST** | H | *EM* | DY | 60246 | 60447 | 60441 | 60626 |
|         |        |   |      |    | 60566 | 60556 | 60166 |       |

**222 007–222 023. East Midlands Trains Meridian.** 5-car units. DMF–MC–
MSRMB–MS–DMS.

**DMF.** Bombardier Brugge 2003–2004. 22/– 1TD 1W. 52.8 t.
**MC.** Bombardier Brugge 2003–2004. 28/22 1T. 48.6 t.
**MSRMB.** Bombardier Brugge 2003–2004. –/62. 49.6 t.
**MS.** Bombardier Brugge 2004–2005. –/68 1T. 47.0 t.
**DMS.** Bombardier Brugge 2003–2004. –/40 1TD 1W. 51.0 t.

| 222 007 | **ST** | H | *EM* | DY | 60247 | 60442 | 60627 | 60567 | 60167 |
| 222 008 | **ST** | H | *EM* | DY | 60248 | 60918 | 60628 | 60545 | 60168 |
| 222 009 | **ST** | H | *EM* | DY | 60249 | 60919 | 60629 | 60557 | 60169 |
| 222 010 | **ST** | H | *EM* | DY | 60250 | 60920 | 60630 | 60546 | 60170 |

| 222 011 | **ST** | H | *EM* | DY | 60251 | 60921 | 60631 | 60531 | 60171 |
| 222 012 | **ST** | H | *EM* | DY | 60252 | 60922 | 60632 | 60532 | 60172 |
| 222 013 | **ST** | H | *EM* | DY | 60253 | 60923 | 60633 | 60533 | 60173 |
| 222 014 | **ST** | H | *EM* | DY | 60254 | 60924 | 60634 | 60534 | 60174 |
| 222 015 | **ST** | H | *EM* | DY | 60255 | 60925 | 60635 | 60535 | 60175 |
| 222 016 | **ST** | H | *EM* | DY | 60256 | 60926 | 60636 | 60536 | 60176 |
| 222 017 | **ST** | H | *EM* | DY | 60257 | 60927 | 60637 | 60537 | 60177 |
| 222 018 | **ST** | H | *EM* | DY | 60258 | 60928 | 60638 | 60444 | 60178 |
| 222 019 | **ST** | H | *EM* | DY | 60259 | 60929 | 60639 | 60547 | 60179 |
| 222 020 | **ST** | H | *EM* | DY | 60260 | 60930 | 60640 | 60543 | 60180 |
| 222 021 | **ST** | H | *EM* | DY | 60261 | 60931 | 60641 | 60552 | 60181 |
| 222 022 | **ST** | H | *EM* | DY | 60262 | 60932 | 60642 | 60542 | 60182 |
| 222 023 | **ST** | H | *EM* | DY | 60263 | 60933 | 60643 | 60541 | 60183 |

**222 101–222 104. Hull Trains Pioneer.** DMF–MC–MSRMB–DMS.

**Notes:** 222 103 is currently out of traffic following accident damage.

These units are due to transfer to East Midlands Trains in 2009.

**DMF.** Bombardier Brugge 2005. 22/– 1TD 1W. 52.8 t.
**MC.** Bombardier Brugge 2005. 11/46 1T. 48.6 t.
**MSRMB.** Bombardier Brugge 2005. –/62. 49.6 t.
**DMS.** Bombardier Brugge 2005. –/40 1TD 1W. 51.0 t.

| 222 101 | **HT** | H | *HT* | XW | 60271 | 60571 | 60681 | 60191 |
| 222 102 | **HT** | H | *HT* | XW | 60272 | 60572 | 60682 | 60192 |
| 222 103 | **HT** | H |   | ZC | 60273 | 60573 | 60683 | 60193 |
| 222 104 | **HT** | H | *HT* | XW. | 60274 | 60574 | 60684 | 60194 |

**Names (carried on end cars):**

| 222 101 | Professor GEORGE GRAY |
| 222 102 | Professor STUART PALMER |
| 222 103 | Dr JOHN GODBER |
| 222 104 | Sir TERRY FARRELL |

# 3.3. SERVICE DMUS

This section lists vehicles not used for passenger-carrying purposes. Some vehicles are numbered in the special service stock number series. The Plasser type Universal Track Recording Units are now classed as "On Track Plant" vehicles.

## CLASS 950                      TRACK ASSESSMENT UNIT

DM–DM. Purpose built service unit based on the Class 150/1 design. Gangwayed within unit.

**Construction:** Steel.
**Engine:** One Cummins NT-855-RT5 of 213 kW (285 h.p.) at 2100 r.p.m. per power car.
**Transmission:** Hydraulic. Voith T211r with cardan shafts to Gmeinder GM190 final drive.
**Maximum Speed:** 75 m.p.h.                 **Couplers:** BSI automatic.
**Bogies:** BP38 (powered), BT38 (non-powered).
**Brakes:** Electro-pneumatic.                **Dimensions:** 20.06 x 2.82 m.
**Doors:** Manually operated slam & power operated sliding.
**Multiple Working:** Classes 142, 143, 144, 150, 153, 155, 156, 158, 159 and 170.

**999600. DM.** Lot No. 4060 BREL York 1987. 35.0 t.
**999601. DM.** Lot No. 4061 BREL York 1987. 35.0 t.

| 950 001 | Y | NR | SO | ZA | 999600 999601 |
|---|---|---|---|---|---|

## CLASS 960                SANDITE & SERVICE UNITS

DMB. Converted from Class 121s. Non gangwayed.

**For details see Page 212.**

960 012 is a South West Trains Route Learning Unit.
960 014 is a Chiltern Route Learning Unit and is also hired to other operators.

**977723. DMB.** Lot No. 30518 Pressed Steel 1960. 38.0 t.
**977858–60/66/73. DMB.** Lot No. 30518 Pressed Steel 1960. 38.0 t.

| 960 010 | M | NR | CR | AL | 977858 | (55024) | |
| 960 012 | SD | SW | SW | BM | 977860 | (55028) | John Cameron |
| 960 013 | N | NR | | AL | 977866 | (55030) | |
| 960 014 | BG | CR | CR | AL | 977873 | (55022) | |
| 960 021 | RO | NR | | AL | 977723 | (55021) | |

## CLASS 960                                    SANDITE UNIT

DMB. Converted 1991 from Class 122. Non gangwayed.

**Construction:** Steel.
**Engines:** Two Leyland 1595 of 112 kW (150 h.p.) at 1800 r.p.m.
**Transmission:** Mechanical. Cardan shaft and freewheel to a four-speed epicyclic gearbox with a further cardan shaft to the final drive, each engine driving the inner axle of one bogie.
**Maximum Speed:** 70 m.p.h.
**Bogies:** DD10.                              **Couplings:** Screw.
**Brakes:** Twin pipe vacuum.                  **Multiple Working:** Blue Square.
**Doors:** Manually operated slam.             **Dimensions:** 20.45 x 2.82  m.

**975042. DMB.** Lot No. 30419 Gloucester 1958. 36.5 t.

960 015      **Y**     NR          AL      975042    (55019)

## CLASS 960                              WATER-JETTING UNIT

DMB–MS–DMB. Converted 2003/04 from Class 117. Non gangwayed.

**Construction:** Steel.
**Engines:** Two Leyland 1595 of 112 kW (150 h.p.) at 1800 r.p.m.
**Transmission:** Mechanical. Cardan shaft and freewheel to a four-speed epicyclic gearbox with a further cardan shaft to the final drive, each engine driving the inner axle of one bogie.
**Maximum Speed:** 70 m.p.h.
**Bogies:** DD10.                              **Couplings:** Screw.
**Brakes:** Twin pipe vacuum.                  **Multiple Working:** Blue Square.
**Doors:** Manually operated slam.             **Dimensions:** 20.45 x 2.84 m.

**977987/977988. DMB.** Lot No. 30546/30548 Pressed Steel 1959–1960. 36.5 t.
**977992. MS.** Lot No. 30548 Pressed Steel 1959–1960. 36.5 t.

960 301      **G**     CR  *CR*     AL      977987    (51371)    977992 (51375)
                                           977988    (51413)

## CLASS 960                              DRIVER TRAINING UNIT

Converted from a Class 121.

**For details see Page 212.**

**977968. DMB.** Lot No. 30518 Pressed Steel 1960. 38.0 t.

-            **Y**     CS  *CS*     RU      977968    (55029)

# 3.4. DMUS AWAITING DISPOSAL

The list below comprises vehicles awaiting disposal which are stored on the National Railway network.

**IMPORTANT NOTE**: DMUs still intact but already at scrapyards, unless specifically there for storage purposes, are not included in this list.

**Class 101**

| Spare | **S** | X | ZA | 51231 | |
|-------|-------|---|----|-------|--|
| Spare | **RR** | X | SN | 51432 | 51498 |

**Class 117**

| Spare | **N** | CR | LM | 51350 | 51383 | 51408 |
|-------|-------|----|----|-------|-------|-------|
| Spare | **RR** | CR | AL | 51411 | | |

**Class 122**

| - | **LH** | X | TE | 977941 (55012) |
|---|--------|---|----|-----------------|

**Class 901**

Converted from Class 205. For sale.

| 930 301 | **RO** | NR | SE | 977939 (60145) | 977870 (60660) |
|---------|--------|----|----|-----------------|-----------------|
| | | | | 977940 (60149) | |

**Class 960**

Converted from Class 121. 960 302/303 converted for use as Severn Tunnel Emergency Train units, but not actually used as such.

| 960 011 | **RK** | NR | ZA | 977859 (55025) |
|---------|--------|----|----|-----------------|
| 960 302 | **Y** | AW | CF | 977975 (55027) |
| 960 303 | **Y** | AW | CF | 977976 (55031) |

# 4. ELECTRIC MULTIPLE UNITS

# INTRODUCTION

## EMU CLASSES

Principal details and dimensions are quoted for each class in metric and/or imperial units as considered appropriate bearing in mind common UK usage.

All dimensions and weights are quoted for vehicles in an "as new" condition with all necessary supplies on board. Dimensions are quoted in the order length x overall width. All lengths quoted are over buffers or couplers as appropriate. Where two lengths are quoted, the first refers to outer vehicles in a set and the second to inner vehicles.

Bogie Types are quoted in the format motored/non-motored (e.g BP20/BT13 denotes BP20 motored bogies and BT non-motored bogies).

Unless noted to the contrary, all vehicles listed have bar couplers at non-driving ends.

Vehicles ordered under the auspices of BR were allocated a Lot (batch) number when ordered and these are quoted in class headings and sub-headings. Vehicles ordered since 1995 have no Lot Numbers, but the manufacturer and location that they were built is given.

## NUMERICAL LISTINGS

25 kV AC 50 Hz overhead Electric Multiple Units (EMUs) and dual voltage EMUs are listed in numerical order of set numbers. Individual "loose" vehicles are listed in numerical order after vehicles formed into fixed formations.

750 V DC third rail EMUs are listed in numerical order of class number, then in numerical order of set number. Some of these use the former Southern Region four-digit set numbers. These are derived from theoretical six digit set numbers which are the four-digit set number prefixed by the first two numbers of the class.

Where sets or vehicles have been renumbered in recent years, former numbering detail is shown alongside current detail. Each entry is laid out as in the following example:

| Set No. | Detail | Livery | Owner | Operator | Allocation | Formation | | | |
|---------|--------|--------|-------|----------|------------|-----------|------|------|------|
| 59˙2    | †      | **SS** | P     | *SW*     | WD         | 77835     | 62837| 67400| 77836|

**Detail Differences**. Only detail differences which currently affect the areas and types of train which vehicles may work are shown. All other detail differences are specifically excluded. Where such differences occur within a class or part class, these are shown alongside the individual set or vehicle number. Meaning of abbreviations are detailed in individual class headings.

**Set Formations**. Set formations shown are those normally maintained. Readers should note some set formations might be temporarily varied from time to time to suit maintenance and/or operational requirements. Vehicles shown as "Spare" are not formed in any regular set formation.

**Codes**. Codes are used to denote the livery, owner, operator and depot of each unit. Details of these will be found in section 6 of this book. Where a unit or spare car is off-lease, the operator column will be left blank.

**Names**. Only names carried with official sanction are listed. As far as possible names are shown in UPPER/lower case characters as actually shown on the name carried on the vehicle(s). Unless otherwise shown, complete units are regarded as named rather than just the individual car(s) which carry the name.

# GENERAL INFORMATION

## CLASSIFICATION AND NUMBERING

25 kV AC 50 Hz overhead and "Versatile" EMUs are classified in the series 300–399.

750 V DC third rail EMUs are classified in the series 400–599.

Service units are classified in the series 900–949.

EMU individual cars are numbered in the series 61000–78999, except for vehicles used on the Isle of Wight – which are numbered in a separate series, and for the Class 378s and 395s, which take up new 38xxx and 39xxx series'.

Any vehicle constructed or converted to replace another vehicle following accident damage and carrying the same number as the original vehicle is denoted by the suffix[II] in this publication.

## OPERATING CODES

These codes are used by train operating company staff to describe the various different types of vehicles and normally appear on data panels on the inner (i.e. non driving) ends of vehicles.

A "B" prefix indicates a battery vehicle.
A "P" prefix indicates a trailer vehicle on which is mounted the pantograph, instead of the default case where the pantograph is mounted on a motor vehicle.

The first part of the code describes whether or not the car has a motor or a driving cab as follows:

DM Driving motor.
M Motor
DT Driving trailer
T Trailer

The next letter is a "B" for cars with a brake compartment.
This is followed by the saloon details:

F   First
S   Standard
C   Composite

The next letter denotes the style of accommodation as follows:

O   Open
K   Side compartment with lavatory
so  Semi-open  (part compartments, part open). All other vehicles are
assumed                                          to consist solely of open saloons.

Finally vehicles with a buffet are suffixed RB or RMB for a miniature buffet.

Where two vehicles of the same type are formed within the same unit, the above codes may be suffixed by (A) and (B) to differentiate between the vehicles.

A composite is a vehicle containing both First and Standard Class accommodation, whilst a brake vehicle is a vehicle containing separate specific accommodation for the conductor.

# BUILD DETAILS

### Lot Numbers

Vehicles ordered under the auspices of BR were allocated a Lot (batch) number when ordered and these are quoted in class headings and sub-headings.

### Builders

These are shown in class headings. Abbreviations used are found in section 6.7.

Information on sub-contracting works which built parts of vehicles e.g. the underframes etc. is not shown.

# ACCOMMODATION

The information given in class headings and sub-headings is in the form F/S nT (or TD) nW. For example 12/54 1T 1W denotes 12 First Class and 54 Standard Class seats, one toilet and one space for a wheelchair. A number in brackets (i.e. (2)) denotes tip-up seats (in addition to the fixed seats). Tip-up seats in vestibules do not count. The seating layout of open saloons is shown as 2+1, 2+2 or 3+2 as the case may be. Where units have first class accommodation as well as standard and the layout is different for each class then these are shown separately prefixed by "1:" and "2:". Compartments are three seats a side in First Class and mostly four a side in Standard Class in EMUs. TD denotes a toilet suitable for use by a disabled person.

# 4.1. 25 kV AC 50 Hz OVERHEAD & DUAL VOLTAGE UNITS

**Note:** Except where otherwise stated, all units in this section operate on 25 kV AC 50 Hz overhead only.

## CLASS 313                                    BREL YORK

Inner suburban units.

**Formation:** DMSO–PTSO–BDMSO.
**Systems:** 25 kV AC overhead/750 V DC third rail.
**Construction:** Steel underframe, aluminium alloy body and roof.
**Traction Motors:** Four GEC G310AZ of 82.125 kW.
**Wheel Arrangement:** Bo-Bo + 2-2 + Bo-Bo.
**Braking:** Disc & rheostatic.          **Dimensions:** 20.33/20.18 x 2.82 m.
**Bogies:** BX1.                          **Couplers:** Tightlock.
**Gangways:** Within unit + end doors.    **Control System:** Camshaft.
**Doors:** Sliding.                       **Maximum Speed:** 75 m.p.h.
**Seating Layout:** 313/0: Refurbished with high back seats (3+2 facing layout).
313/1 Low back seats, mainly 2+2 facing.
**Multiple Working:** Within class.

**DMSO.** Lot No. 30879 1976–1977. –/74 (313/1 –/66). 36.0 t.
**PTSO.** Lot No. 30880 1976–1977. –/83 (313/1 –/70 1W). 31.0 t.
**BDMSO.** Lot No. 30885 1976–1977. –/74 (313/1 –/66). 37.5 t.

**Class 313/0. Standard Design.**

| | | | | | | | |
|---|---|---|---|---|---|---|---|
| 313 018 | **FU** | H | *FC* | HE | 62546 | 71230 | 62610 |
| 313 024 | **FU** | H | *FC* | HE | 62552 | 71236 | 62616 |
| 313 025 | **FU** | H | *FC* | HE | 62553 | 71237 | 62617 |
| 313 026 | **FU** | H | *FC* | HE | 62554 | 71238 | 62618 |
| 313 027 | **FU** | H | *FC* | HE | 62555 | 71239 | 62619 |
| 313 028 | **FU** | H | *FC* | HE | 62556 | 71240 | 62620 |
| 313 029 | **FU** | H | *FC* | HE | 62557 | 71241 | 62621 |
| 313 030 | **FU** | H | *FC* | HE | 62558 | 71242 | 62622 |
| 313 031 | **FU** | H | *FC* | HE | 62559 | 71243 | 62623 |
| 313 032 | **FU** | H | *FC* | HE | 62560 | 71244 | 62643 |
| 313 033 | **FU** | H | *FC* | HE | 62561 | 71245 | 62625 |
| 313 035 | **FU** | H | *FC* | HE | 62563 | 71247 | 62627 |
| 313 036 | **FU** | H | *FC* | HE | 62564 | 71248 | 62628 |
| 313 037 | **FU** | H | *FC* | HE | 62565 | 71249 | 62629 |
| 313 038 | **FU** | H | *FC* | HE | 62566 | 71250 | 62630 |
| 313 039 | **FU** | H | *FC* | HE | 62567 | 71251 | 62631 |
| 313 040 | **FU** | H | *FC* | HE | 62568 | 71252 | 62632 |
| 313 041 | **FU** | H | *FC* | HE | 62569 | 71253 | 62633 |
| 313 042 | **FU** | H | *FC* | HE | 62570 | 71254 | 62634 |
| 313 043 | **FU** | H | *FC* | HE | 62571 | 71255 | 62635 |
| 313 044 | **FU** | H | *FC* | HE | 62572 | 71256 | 62636 |

| 313 045 | **FU** | H | *FC* | HE | 62573 | 71257 | 62637 |
|---------|--------|---|------|----|-------|-------|-------|
| 313 046 | **FU** | H | *FC* | HE | 62574 | 71258 | 62638 |
| 313 047 | **FU** | H | *FC* | HE | 62575 | 71259 | 62639 |
| 313 048 | **FU** | H | *FC* | HE | 62576 | 71260 | 62640 |
| 313 049 | **FU** | H | *FC* | HE | 62577 | 71261 | 62641 |
| 313 050 | **FU** | H | *FC* | HE | 62578 | 71262 | 62649 |
| 313 051 | **FU** | H | *FC* | HE | 62579 | 71263 | 62624 |
| 313 052 | **FU** | H | *FC* | HE | 62580 | 71264 | 62644 |
| 313 053 | **FU** | H | *FC* | HE | 62581 | 71265 | 62645 |
| 313 054 | **FU** | H | *FC* | HE | 62582 | 71266 | 62646 |
| 313 055 | **FU** | H | *FC* | HE | 62583 | 71267 | 62647 |
| 313 056 | **FU** | H | *FC* | HE | 62584 | 71268 | 62648 |
| 313 057 | **FU** | H | *FC* | HE | 62585 | 71269 | 62642 |
| 313 058 | **FU** | H | *FC* | HE | 62586 | 71270 | 62650 |
| 313 059 | **FU** | H | *FC* | HE | 62587 | 71271 | 62651 |
| 313 060 | **FU** | H | *FC* | HE | 62588 | 71272 | 62652 |
| 313 061 | **FU** | H | *FC* | HE | 62589 | 71273 | 62653 |
| 313 062 | **FU** | H | *FC* | HE | 62590 | 71274 | 62654 |
| 313 063 | **FU** | H | *FC* | HE | 62591 | 71275 | 62655 |
| 313 064 | **FU** | H | *FC* | HE | 62592 | 71276 | 62656 |

**Class 313/1. Extra shoegear for London Overground services.**

| 313 101 | **SL** | H | *LO* | WN | 62529 | 71213 | 62593 |
|---------|--------|---|------|----|-------|-------|-------|
| 313 102 | **SL** | H | *LO* | WN | 62530 | 71214 | 62594 |
| 313 103 | **SL** | H | *LO* | WN | 62531 | 71215 | 62595 |
| 313 104 | **SL** | H | *LO* | WN | 62532 | 71216 | 62596 |
| 313 105 | **SL** | H | *LO* | WN | 62533 | 71217 | 62597 |
| 313 106 | **SL** | H | *LO* | WN | 62534 | 71218 | 62598 |
| 313 107 | **SL** | H | *LO* | WN | 62535 | 71219 | 62599 |
| 313 108 | **SL** | H | *LO* | WN | 62536 | 71220 | 62600 |
| 313 109 | **SL** | H | *LO* | WN | 62537 | 71221 | 62601 |
| 313 110 | **SL** | H | *LO* | WN | 62538 | 71222 | 62602 |
| 313 111 | **SL** | H | *LO* | WN | 62539 | 71223 | 62603 |
| 313 112 | **SL** | H | *LO* | WN | 62540 | 71224 | 62604 |
| 313 113 | **SL** | H | *LO* | WN | 62541 | 71225 | 62605 |
| 313 114 | **SL** | H | *LO* | WN | 62542 | 71226 | 62606 |
| 313 115 | **SL** | H | *LO* | WN | 62543 | 71227 | 62607 |
| 313 116 | **SL** | H | *LO* | WN | 62544 | 71228 | 62608 |
| 313 117 | **SL** | H | *LO* | WN | 62545 | 71229 | 62609 |
| 313 119 | **SL** | H | *LO* | WN | 62547 | 71231 | 62611 |
| 313 120 | **SL** | H | *LO* | WN | 62548 | 71232 | 62612 |
| 313 121 | **SL** | H | *LO* | WN | 62549 | 71233 | 62613 |
| 313 122 | **SL** | H | *LO* | WN | 62550 | 71234 | 62614 |
| 313 123 | **SL** | H | *LO* | WN | 62551 | 71235 | 62615 |
| 313 134 | **SL** | H | *LO* | WN | 62562 | 71246 | 62626 |

**Names (carried on PTSO):**

| 313 101 | Silvertown | | 313 109 | Arnold Leah |
|---------|------------|---|---------|-------------|
| 313 111 | London TravelWatch | | 313 116 | Nikola Tesla |
| 313 120 | PARLIAMENT HILL | | 313 134 | The Hackney Empire |

# CLASS 314                                          BREL YORK

Inner suburban units.

**Formation:** DMSO–PTSO–DMSO.
**Construction:** Steel underframe, aluminium alloy body and roof.
**Traction Motors:** Four GEC G310AZ (* Brush TM61-53) of 82.125 kW.
**Wheel Arrangement:** Bo-Bo + 2-2 + Bo-Bo.
**Braking:** Disc & rheostatic.             **Dimensions:** 20.33/20.18 x 2.82 m.
**Bogies:** BX1.                            **Couplers:** Tightlock.
**Gangways:** Within unit + end doors.      **Control System:** Thyristor.
**Doors:** Sliding.                         **Maximum Speed:** 70 m.p.h.
**Seating Layout:** 3+2 low-back facing.
**Multiple Working:** Within class and with Class 315.

**DMSO.** Lot No. 30912 1979. –/68. 34.5 t.
**64588**[II]. **DMSO.** Lot No. 30908 1978–1980. Rebuilt Railcare Glasgow 1996 from Class 507 No. 64426. The original 64588 has been scrapped. –/74. 34.5 t.
**PTSO.** Lot No. 30913 1979. –/76. 33.0 t.

| | | | | | | | |
|---|---|---|---|---|---|---|---|
| 314 201 | * | **SC** | A | *SR* | GW | 64583 71450 64584 | |
| 314 202 | * | **SC** | A | *SR* | GW | 64585 71451 64586 | |
| 314 203 | * | **SC** | A | *SR* | GW | 64587 71452 64588[II] | European Union |
| 314 204 | * | **SC** | A | *SR* | GW | 64589 71453 64590 | |
| 314 205 | * | **SC** | A | *SR* | GW | 64591 71454 64592 | |
| 314 206 | * | **SC** | A | *SR* | GW | 64593 71455 64594 | |
| 314 207 | | **SC** | A | *SR* | GW | 64595 71456 64596 | |
| 314 208 | | **SC** | A | *SR* | GW | 64597 71457 64598 | |
| 314 209 | | **SC** | A | *SR* | GW | 64599 71458 64600 | |
| 314 210 | | **SC** | A | *SR* | GW | 64601 71459 64602 | |
| 314 211 | | **SC** | A | *SR* | GW | 64603 71460 64604 | |
| 314 212 | | **SC** | A | *SR* | GW | 64605 71461 64606 | |
| 314 213 | | **SC** | A | *SR* | GW | 64607 71462 64608 | |
| 314 214 | | **SC** | A | *SR* | GW | 64609 71463 64610 | |
| 314 215 | | **SC** | A | *SR* | GW | 64611 71464 64612 | |
| 314 216 | | **SC** | A | *SR* | GW | 64613 71465 64614 | |

# CLASS 315                                          BREL YORK

Inner suburban units.

**Formation:** DMSO–TSO–PTSO–DMSO.
**Construction:** Steel underframe, aluminium alloy body and roof.
**Traction Motors:** Four Brush TM61-53 (* GEC G310AZ) of 82.125 kW.
**Wheel Arrangement:** Bo-Bo + 2-2 + 2-2 + Bo-Bo.
**Braking:** Disc & rheostatic.             **Dimensions:** 20.33/20.18 x 2.82 m.
**Bogies:** BX1.                            **Couplers:** Tightlock.
**Gangways:** Within unit + end doors.      **Control System:** Thyristor.
**Doors:** Sliding.                         **Maximum Speed:** 75 m.p.h.
**Seating Layout:** 3+2 low-back facing.
**Multiple Working:** Within class and with Class 314.

**DMSO.** Lot No. 30902 1980–1981. –/74. 35.0 t.
**TSO.** Lot No. 30904 1980–1981. –/86. 25.5 t.
**PTSO.** Lot No. 30903 1980–1981. /84. 32.0 t.

| | | | | | | | | |
|---|---|---|---|---|---|---|---|---|
| 315 801 | 1 | H | EA | IL | 64461 | 71281 | 71389 | 64462 |
| 315 802 | 1 | H | EA | IL | 64463 | 71282 | 71390 | 64464 |
| 315 803 | 1 | H | EA | IL | 64465 | 71283 | 71391 | 64466 |
| 315 804 | 1 | H | EA | IL | 64467 | 71284 | 71392 | 64468 |
| 315 805 | 1 | H | EA | IL | 64469 | 71285 | 71393 | 64470 |
| 315 806 | 1 | H | EA | IL | 64471 | 71286 | 71394 | 64472 |
| 315 807 | 1 | H | EA | IL | 64473 | 71287 | 71395 | 64474 |
| 315 808 | 1 | H | EA | IL | 64475 | 71288 | 71396 | 64476 |
| 315 809 | 1 | H | EA | IL | 64477 | 71289 | 71397 | 64478 |
| 315 810 | 1 | H | EA | IL | 64479 | 71290 | 71398 | 64480 |
| 315 811 | 1 | H | EA | IL | 64481 | 71291 | 71399 | 64482 |
| 315 812 | 1 | H | EA | IL | 64483 | 71292 | 71400 | 64484 |
| 315 813 | 1 | H | EA | IL | 64485 | 71293 | 71401 | 64486 |
| 315 814 | 1 | H | EA | IL | 64487 | 71294 | 71402 | 64488 |
| 315 815 | 1 | H | EA | IL | 64489 | 71295 | 71403 | 64490 |
| 315 816 | 1 | H | EA | IL | 64491 | 71296 | 71404 | 64492 |
| 315 817 | 1 | H | EA | IL | 64493 | 71297 | 71405 | 64494 |
| 315 818 | 1 | H | EA | IL | 64495 | 71298 | 71406 | 64496 |
| 315 819 | 1 | H | EA | IL | 64497 | 71299 | 71407 | 64498 |
| 315 820 | 1 | H | EA | IL | 64499 | 71300 | 71408 | 64500 |
| 315 821 | 1 | H | EA | IL | 64501 | 71301 | 71409 | 64502 |
| 315 822 | 1 | H | EA | IL | 64503 | 71302 | 71410 | 64504 |
| 315 823 | 1 | H | EA | IL | 64505 | 71303 | 71411 | 64506 |
| 315 824 | 1 | H | EA | IL | 64507 | 71304 | 71412 | 64508 |
| 315 825 | 1 | H | EA | IL | 64509 | 71305 | 71413 | 64510 |
| 315 826 | 1 | H | EA | IL | 64511 | 71306 | 71414 | 64512 |
| 315 827 | 1 | H | EA | IL | 64513 | 71307 | 71415 | 64514 |
| 315 828 | 1 | H | EA | IL | 64515 | 71308 | 71416 | 64516 |
| 315 829 | 1 | H | EA | IL | 64517 | 71309 | 71417 | 64518 |
| 315 830 | 1 | H | EA | IL | 64519 | 71310 | 71418 | 64520 |
| 315 831 | 1 | H | EA | IL | 64521 | 71311 | 71419 | 64522 |
| 315 832 | 1 | H | EA | IL | 64523 | 71312 | 71420 | 64524 |
| 315 833 | 1 | H | EA | IL | 64525 | 71313 | 71421 | 64526 |
| 315 834 | 1 | H | EA | IL | 64527 | 71314 | 71422 | 64528 |
| 315 835 | 1 | H | EA | IL | 64529 | 71315 | 71423 | 64530 |
| 315 836 | 1 | H | EA | IL | 64531 | 71316 | 71424 | 64532 |
| 315 837 | 1 | H | EA | IL | 64533 | 71317 | 71425 | 64534 |
| 315 838 | 1 | H | EA | IL | 64535 | 71318 | 71426 | 64536 |
| 315 839 | 1 | H | EA | IL | 64537 | 71319 | 71427 | 64538 |
| 315 840 | 1 | H | EA | IL | 64539 | 71320 | 71428 | 64540 |
| 315 841 | 1 | H | EA | IL | 64541 | 71321 | 71429 | 64542 |
| 315 842 | * 1 | H | EA | IL | 64543 | 71322 | 71430 | 64544 |
| 315 843 | * 1 | H | EA | IL | 64545 | 71323 | 71431 | 64546 |
| 315 844 | * 1 | H | EA | IL | 64547 | 71324 | 71432 | 64548 |
| 315 845 | * 1 | H | EA | IL | 64549 | 71325 | 71433 | 64550 |
| 315 846 | * 1 | H | EA | IL | 64551 | 71326 | 71434 | 64552 |
| 315 847 | * 1 | H | EA | IL | 64553 | 71327 | 71435 | 64554 |

| 315 848 | * | 1 | H | EA | IL | 64555 | 71328 | 71436 | 64556 |
| 315 849 | * | 1 | H | EA | IL | 64557 | 71329 | 71437 | 64558 |
| 315 850 | * | 1 | H | EA | IL | 64559 | 71330 | 71438 | 64560 |
| 315 851 | * | 1 | H | EA | IL | 64561 | 71331 | 71439 | 64562 |
| 315 852 | * | 1 | H | EA | IL | 64563 | 71332 | 71440 | 64564 |
| 315 853 | * | 1 | H | EA | IL | 64565 | 71333 | 71441 | 64566 |
| 315 854 | * | 1 | H | EA | IL | 64567 | 71334 | 71442 | 64568 |
| 315 855 | * | 1 | H | EA | IL | 64569 | 71335 | 71443 | 64570 |
| 315 856 | * | 1 | H | EA | IL | 64571 | 71336 | 71444 | 64572 |
| 315 857 | * | 1 | H | EA | IL | 64573 | 71337 | 71445 | 64574 |
| 315 858 | * | 1 | H | EA | IL | 64575 | 71338 | 71446 | 64576 |
| 315 859 | * | 1 | H | EA | IL | 64577 | 71339 | 71447 | 64578 |
| 315 860 | * | 1 | H | EA | IL | 64579 | 71340 | 71448 | 64580 |
| 315 861 | * | 1 | H | EA | IL | 64581 | 71341 | 71449 | 64582 |

**Names (carried on DMSO):**

| 315 817 | Transport for London |
| 315 829 | London Borough of Havering Celebrating 40 years |
| 315 845 | Herbie Woodward |
| 315 857 | Stratford Connections |

# CLASS 317 BREL YORK/DERBY

Outer suburban units.

**Formation:** Various, see sub-class headings.
**Construction:** Steel.
**Traction Motors:** Four GEC G315BZ of 247.5 kW.
**Wheel Arrangement:** 2-2 + Bo-Bo + 2-2 + 2-2.
**Braking:** Disc.     **Dimensions:** 20.13/20.18 x 2.82 m.
**Bogies:** BP20 (MSO), BT13 (others).     **Couplers:** Tightlock.
**Gangways:** Throughout     **Control System:** Thyristor.
**Doors:** Sliding.     **Maximum Speed:** 100 m.p.h.
**Seating Layout:** Various, see sub-class headings.
**Multiple Working:** Within class & with Classes 318, 319, 320, 321, 322 and 323.

**Class 317/1.** Pressure ventilated.

**Formation:** DTSO–MSO–TCO–DTSO.
**Seating Layout:** 1: 2+2 facing, 2: 3+2 facing.

**DTSO(A)** Lot No. 30955 York 1981–1982. –/74. 29.5 t.
**MSO.** Lot No. 30958 York 1981–1982. –/79. 49.0 t.
**TCO.** Lot No. 30957 Derby 1981–1982. 22/46 2T. 29.0 t.
**DTSO(B)** Lot No. 30956 York 1981–1982. –/71. 29.5 t.

| 317 337 | FU | A | FC | HE | 77036 | 62671 | 71613 | 77084 |
| 317 338 | FU | A | FC | HE | 77037 | 62698 | 71614 | 77085 |
| 317 339 | FU | A | FC | HE | 77038 | 62699 | 71615 | 77086 |
| 317 340 | FU | A | FC | HE | 77039 | 62700 | 71616 | 77087 |
| 317 341 | WP | A | FC | HE | 77040 | 62701 | 71617 | 77088 |
| 317 342 | FU | A | FC | HE | 77041 | 62702 | 71618 | 77089 |
| 317 343 | FU | A | FC | HE | 77042 | 62703 | 71619 | 77090 |

| | | | | | | | | |
|---|---|---|---|---|---|---|---|---|
| 317 344 | WP | A | *FC* | HE | 77029 | 62690 | 71620 | 77091 |
| 317 345 | FU | A | *FC* | HE | 77044 | 62705 | 71621 | 77092 |
| 317 346 | WP | A | *FC* | HE | 77045 | 62706 | 71622 | 77093 |
| 317 347 | WP | A | *FC* | HE | 77046 | 62707 | 71623 | 77094 |
| 317 348 | WP | A | *FC* | HE | 77047 | 62708 | 71624 | 77095 |

**Names (carried on TCO):**

| | | | |
|---|---|---|---|
| 317 345 | Driver John Webb | 317 348 | Richard A Jenner |

**Class 317/5.** Pressure ventilated. Units renumbered from Class 317/1 in 2005 for West Anglia Metro services. Refurbished with new upholstery and Passenger Information Systems. Details as Class 317/1.

| | | | | | | | | |
|---|---|---|---|---|---|---|---|---|
| 317 501 | (317 301) | NX | A | *EA* | IL | 77024 | 62661 | 71577 | 77048 |
| 317 502 | (317 302) | NX | A | *EA* | IL | 77001 | 62662 | 71578 | 77049 |
| 317 503 | (317 303) | NX | A | *EA* | IL | 77002 | 62663 | 71579 | 77050 |
| 317 504 | (317 304) | NX | A | *EA* | IL | 77003 | 62664 | 71580 | 77051 |
| 317 505 | (317 305) | NX | A | *EA* | IL | 77004 | 62665 | 71581 | 77052 |
| 317 506 | (317 306) | NX | A | *EA* | IL | 77005 | 62666 | 71582 | 77053 |
| 317 507 | (317 307) | NX | A | *EA* | IL | 77006 | 62667 | 71583 | 77054 |
| 317 508 | (317 311) | NX | A | *EA* | IL | 77010 | 62697 | 71587 | 77058 |
| 317 509 | (317 312) | NX | A | *EA* | IL | 77011 | 62672 | 71588 | 77059 |
| 317 510 | (317 313) | NX | A | *EA* | IL | 77012 | 62673 | 71589 | 77060 |
| 317 511 | (317 315) | 1 | A | *EA* | IL | 77014 | 62675 | 71591 | 77062 |
| 317 512 | (317 316) | 1 | A | *EA* | IL | 77015 | 62676 | 71592 | 77063 |
| 317 513 | (317 317) | 1 | A | *EA* | IL | 77016 | 62677 | 71593 | 77064 |
| 317 514 | (317 318) | 1 | A | *EA* | IL | 77017 | 62678 | 71594 | 77065 |
| 317 515 | (317 320) | 1 | A | *EA* | IL | 77019 | 62680 | 71596 | 77067 |

**Class 317/6.** Convection heating. Units converted from Class 317/2 by Railcare Wolverton 1998–99 with new seating layouts.

**Formation:** DTSO–MSO–TSO–DTCO.

**Seating Layout:** 2+2 facing.

**77200–77219. DTSO.** Lot No. 30994 York 1985–1986. –/64. 29.5 t.
**77280–77283. DTSO.** Lot No. 31007 York 1987. –/64. 29.5 t.
**62846–62865. MSO.** Lot No. 30996 York 1985–1986. –/70. 49.0 t.
**62886–62889. MSO.** Lot No. 31009 York 1987. –/70. 49.0 t.
**71734–71753. TSO.** Lot No. 30997 York 1985–1986. –/62 2T. 29.0 t.
**71762–71765. TSO.** Lot No. 31010 York 1987. –/62 2T. 29.0 t.
**77220–77239. DTCO.** Lot No. 30995 York 1985–1986. 24/48. 29.5 t.
**77284–77287. DTCO.** Lot No. 31008 York 1987. 24/48. 29.5 t.

| | | | | | | | | |
|---|---|---|---|---|---|---|---|---|
| 317 649 | WN | A | *EA* | IL | 77200 | 62846 | 71734 | 77220 |
| 317 650 | WN | A | *EA* | IL | 77201 | 62847 | 71735 | 77221 |
| 317 651 | WN | A | *EA* | IL | 77202 | 62848 | 71736 | 77222 |
| 317 652 | 1 | A | *EA* | IL | 77203 | 62849 | 71739 | 77223 |
| 317 653 | 1 | A | *EA* | IL | 77204 | 62850 | 71738 | 77224 |
| 317 654 | 1 | A | *EA* | IL | 77205 | 62851 | 71737 | 77225 |
| 317 655 | 1 | A | *EA* | IL | 77206 | 62852 | 71740 | 77226 |
| 317 656 | 1 | A | *EA* | IL | 77207 | 62853 | 71742 | 77227 |
| 317 657 | 1 | A | *EA* | IL | 77208 | 62854 | 71741 | 77228 |
| 317 658 | 1 | A | *EA* | IL | 77209 | 62855 | 71743 | 77229 |

| 317 659 | 1 | A | EA | IL | 77210 | 62856 | 71744 | 77230 |
| 317 660 | 1 | A | EA | IL | 77211 | 62857 | 71745 | 77231 |
| 317 661 | 1 | A | EA | IL | 77212 | 62858 | 71746 | 77232 |
| 317 662 | 1 | A | EA | IL | 77213 | 62859 | 71747 | 77233 |
| 317 663 | 1 | A | EA | IL | 77214 | 62860 | 71748 | 77234 |
| 317 664 | 1 | A | EA | IL | 77215 | 62861 | 71749 | 77235 |
| 317 665 | 1 | A | EA | IL | 77216 | 62862 | 71750 | 77236 |
| 317 666 | 1 | A | EA | IL | 77217 | 62863 | 71752 | 77237 |
| 317 667 | 1 | A | EA | IL | 77218 | 62864 | 71751 | 77238 |
| 317 668 | 1 | A | EA | IL | 77219 | 62865 | 71753 | 77239 |
| 317 669 | 1 | A | EA | IL | 77280 | 62886 | 71762 | 77284 |
| 317 670 | 1 | A | EA | IL | 77281 | 62887 | 71763 | 77285 |
| 317 671 | 1 | A | EA | IL | 77282 | 62888 | 71764 | 77286 |
| 317 672 | 1 | A | EA | IL | 77283 | 62889 | 71765 | 77287 |

**Name (carried on TCO):**

317 654    Richard Wells

**Class 317/7.** Units converted from Class 317/1 by Railcare Wolverton 2000 for Stansted Express services between London Liverpool Street and Stansted. Air conditioning. Fitted with luggage stacks.

**Formation:** DTSO–MSO–TSO–DTCO.
**Seating Layout:** 1: 2+1 facing, 2: 2+2 facing.

**DTSO** Lot No. 30955 York 1981–1982. –/52 + catering point. 31.4 t.
**MSO.** Lot No. 30958 York 1981–1982. –/62. 51.3 t.
**TSO.** Lot No. 30957 Derby 1981–1982. –/42 1W 1T 1TD. 30.2 t.
**DTCO** Lot No. 30956 York 1981–1982. 22/16 + catering point. 31.6 t.

| 317 708 | (317 308) | NX | A | EA | IL | 77007 | 62668 | 71584 | 77055 |
| 317 709 | (317 309) | NX | A | EA | IL | 77008 | 62669 | 71585 | 77056 |
| 317 710 | (317 310) | NX | A | EA | IL | 77009 | 62670 | 71586 | 77057 |
| 317 714 | (317 314) | NX | A | EA | IL | 77013 | 62674 | 71590 | 77061 |
| 317 719 | (317 319) | SX | A | EA | IL | 77018 | 62679 | 71595 | 77066 |
| 317 722 | (317 392) | SX | A | EA | IL | 77021 | 62682 | 71598 | 77069 |
| 317 723 | (317 393) | SX | A | EA | IL | 77022 | 62683 | 71599 | 77070 |
| 317 729 | (317 329) | 1 | A | EA | IL | 77028 | 62689 | 71605 | 77076 |
| 317 732 | (317 332) | SX | A | EA | IL | 77031 | 62692 | 71608 | 77079 |

**Names (carried on DTCO):**

| 317 709 | Len Camp | | 317 723 | The Tottenham Flyer |

**Class 317/8.** Pressure Ventilated. Units refurbished and renumbered from Class 317/1 in 2005–2006 at Wabtec, Doncaster for use on Stansted Express services. Fitted with luggage stacks.

**Formation:** DTSO–MSO–TCO–DTSO.
**Seating Layout:** 1: 2+2 facing, 2: 3+2 facing.

**DTSO(A)** Lot No. 30955 York 1981–1982. –/66. 29.5 t.
**MSO.** Lot No. 30958 York 1981–1982. –/71. 49.0 t.
**TCO.** Lot No. 30957 Derby 1981–1982. 20/42 2T. 29.0 t.
**DTSO(B)** Lot No. 30956 York 1981–1982. –/66. 29.5 t.

| 317 881 | (317 321) | **SU** | A | *EA* | IL | 77020 | 62681 | 71597 | 77068 |
| 317 882 | (317 324) | **SU** | A | *EA* | IL | 77023 | 62684 | 71600 | 77071 |
| 317 883 | (317 325) | **SU** | A | *EA* | IL | 77000 | 62685 | 71601 | 77072 |
| 317 884 | (317 326) | **SU** | A | *EA* | IL | 77025 | 62686 | 71602 | 77073 |
| 317 885 | (317 327) | **SU** | A | *EA* | IL | 77026 | 62687 | 71603 | 77074 |
| 317 886 | (317 328) | **SU** | A | *EA* | IL | 77027 | 62688 | 71604 | 77075 |
| 317 887 | (317 330) | **SU** | A | *EA* | IL | 77043 | 62704 | 71606 | 77077 |
| 317 888 | (317 331) | **SU** | A | *EA* | IL | 77030 | 62691 | 71607 | 77078 |
| 317 889 | (317 333) | **SU** | A | *EA* | IL | 77032 | 62693 | 71609 | 77080 |
| 317 890 | (317 334) | **SU** | A | *EA* | IL | 77033 | 62694 | 71610 | 77081 |
| 317 891 | (317 335) | **SU** | A | *EA* | IL | 77034 | 62695 | 71611 | 77082 |
| 317 892 | (317 336) | **SU** | A | *EA* | IL | 77035 | 62696 | 71612 | 77083 |

**Name (carried on TCO):**

317 892   Ilford Depot

# CLASS 318                            BREL YORK

Outer suburban units.

**Formation:** DTSO–MSO–DTSO.
**Construction:** Steel.
**Traction Motors:** Four Brush TM 2141 of 268 kW.
**Wheel Arrangement:** 2-2 + Bo-Bo + 2-2.
**Braking:** Disc.                    **Dimensions:** 20.86 x 2.82 m.
**Bogies:** BP20 (MSO), BT13 (others).    **Couplers:** Tightlock.
**Gangways:** Within unit.           **Control System:** Thyristor.
**Doors:** Sliding.                  **Maximum Speed:** 90 m.p.h.
**Seating Layout:** 3+2 facing.
**Multiple Working:** Within class & with Classes 317, 319, 320, 321, 322 and 323.

**77240–77259.** DTSO. Lot No. 30999 1985–1986. –/64 1T. 30.0 t.
**77288.** DTSO. Lot No. 31020 1987. –/64 1T. 30.0 t.
**62866–62885.** MSO. Lot No. 30998 1985–1986. –/77. 50.9 t.
**62890.** MSO. Lot No. 31019 1987. –/77. 50.9 t.
**77260–77279.** DTSO. Lot No. 31000 1985–1986. –/72. 29.6 t.
**77289.** DTSO. Lot No. 31021 1987. –/72. 29.6 t.

| 318 250 | **SC** | H | *SR* | GW | 77240 | 62866 | 77260 |
| 318 251 | **SC** | H | *SR* | GW | 77241 | 62867 | 77261 |
| 318 252 | **SC** | H | *SR* | GW | 77242 | 62868 | 77262 |
| 318 253 | **SC** | H | *SR* | GW | 77243 | 62869 | 77263 |
| 318 254 | **SC** | H | *SR* | GW | 77244 | 62870 | 77264 |
| 318 255 | **SC** | H | *SR* | GW | 77245 | 62871 | 77265 |
| 318 256 | **SC** | H | *SR* | GW | 77246 | 62872 | 77266 |
| 318 257 | **SC** | H | *SR* | GW | 77247 | 62873 | 77267 |
| 318 258 | **SC** | H | *SR* | GW | 77248 | 62874 | 77268 |
| 318 259 | **SC** | H | *SR* | GW | 77249 | 62875 | 77269 |
| 318 260 | **SC** | H | *SR* | GW | 77250 | 62876 | 77270 |
| 318 261 | **SC** | H | *SR* | GW | 77251 | 62877 | 77271 |
| 318 262 | **SC** | H | *SR* | GW | 77252 | 62878 | 77272 |
| 318 263 | **SC** | H | *SR* | GW | 77253 | 62879 | 77273 |

| 318 264 | **SC** | H | *SR* | GW | 77254 | 62880 | 77274 |
| 318 265 | **SC** | H | *SR* | GW | 77255 | 62881 | 77275 |
| 318 266 | **SC** | H | *SR* | GW | 77256 | 62882 | 77276 |
| 318 267 | **SC** | H | *SR* | GW | 77257 | 62883 | 77277 |
| 318 268 | **SC** | H | *SR* | GW | 77258 | 62884 | 77278 |
| 318 269 | **SC** | H | *SR* | GW | 77259 | 62885 | 77279 |
| 318 270 | **SC** | H | *SR* | GW | 77288 | 62890 | 77289 |

**Names (carried on MSO):**

| 318 259 | Citizens' Network | | 318 266 | STRATHCLYDER |

# CLASS 319                                    BREL YORK

Express and outer suburban units.

**Formation:** Various, see sub-class headings.
**Systems:** 25 kV AC overhead/750 V DC third rail.
**Construction:** Steel.
**Traction Motors:** Four GEC G315BZ of 268 kW.
**Wheel Arrangement:** 2-2 + Bo-Bo + 2-2 + 2-2.
**Braking:** Disc.                                    **Dimensions:** 20.17/20.16 x 2.82 m.
**Bogies:** P7-4 (MSO), T3-7 (others).    **Couplers:** Tightlock.
**Gangways:** Within unit + end doors.    **Control System:** GTO chopper.
**Doors:** Sliding.                                    **Maximum Speed:** 100 m.p.h.
**Seating Layout:** Various, see sub-class headings.
**Multiple Working:** Within class & with Classes 317, 318, 320, 321, 322 and 323.

**Class 319/0.** DTSO–MSO–TSO–DTSO.

**Seating Layout:** 3+2 facing.

**DTSO(A).** Lot No. 31022 (odd nos.) 1987–1988. –/82. 28.2 t.
**MSO.** Lot No. 31023 1987–1988. –/82. 49.2 t.
**TSO.** Lot No. 31024 1987–1988. –/77 2T. 31.0 t.
**DTSO(B).** Lot No. 31025 (even nos.) 1987–1988. –/78. 28.1 t.

| 319 001 | **FU** | P | *FC* | BF | 77291 | 62891 | 71772 | 77290 |
| 319 002 | **FU** | P | *FC* | BF | 77293 | 62892 | 71773 | 77292 |
| 319 003 | **SN** | P | *FC* | BF | 77295 | 62893 | 71774 | 77294 |
| 319 004 | **SN** | P | *FC* | BF | 77297 | 62894 | 71775 | 77296 |
| 319 005 | **SN** | P | *FC* | BF | 77299 | 62895 | 71776 | 77298 |
| 319 006 | **FU** | P | *FC* | BF | 77301 | 62896 | 71777 | 77300 |
| 319 007 | **FU** | P | *FC* | BF | 77303 | 62897 | 71778 | 77302 |
| 319 008 | **SN** | P | *FC* | BF | 77305 | 62898 | 71779 | 77304 |
| 319 009 | **SN** | P | *FC* | BF | 77307 | 62899 | 71780 | 77306 |
| 319 010 | **FU** | P | *FC* | BF | 77309 | 62900 | 71781 | 77308 |
| 319 011 | **SN** | P | *FC* | BF | 77311 | 62901 | 71782 | 77310 |
| 319 012 | **SN** | P | *FC* | BF | 77313 | 62902 | 71783 | 77312 |
| 319 013 | **SN** | P | *FC* | BF | 77315 | 62903 | 71784 | 77314 |

**Names (carried on TSO):**

| 319 011 | John Ruskin College | | 319 013 | The Surrey Hills |

**Class 319/2.** DTSO–MSO–TSO–DTCO. Units converted from Class 319/0 for express services from London to Brighton. 319 217–220 still used by Southern on outer suburban services but due to transfer to FCC spring 2009.

**Seating Layout:** 1: 2+1 facing, 2: 2+2 facing.

**DTSO.** Lot No. 31022 (odd nos.) 1987–1988. –/64. 28.2 t.
**MSO.** Lot No. 31023 1987–1988. –/60 2T. (including 12 seats in a "snug" under the pantograph area). External sliding doors sealed adjacent to this area. 49.2 t.
**TSO.** Lot No. 31024 1987–1988. –/52 1T 1TD. 31.0 t.
**DTCO.** Lot No. 31025 (even nos.) 1987–1988. 18/36. 28.1 t.

| | | | | | | | |
|---|---|---|---|---|---|---|---|
| 319 214 | **SN** | P | *FC* | BF | 77317 | 62904 | 71785 | 77316 |
| 319 215 | **SN** | P | *FC* | BF | 77319 | 62905 | 71786 | 77318 |
| 319 216 | **SN** | P | *FC* | BF | 77321 | 62906 | 71787 | 77320 |
| 319 217 | **SN** | P | *SN* | SU | 77323 | 62907 | 71788 | 77322 |
| 319 218 | **SN** | P | *SN* | SU | 77325 | 62908 | 71789 | 77324 |
| 319 219 | **SN** | P | *SN* | SU | 77327 | 62909 | 71790 | 77326 |
| 319 220 | **SN** | P | *SN* | SU | 77329 | 62910 | 71791 | 77328 |

**Names (carried on TSO):**

| | | | |
|---|---|---|---|
| 319 215 | London | 319 218 | Croydon |
| 319 217 | Brighton | | |

**Class 319/3.** DTSO–MSO–TSO–DTSO. Converted from Class 319/1 by replacing first class seats with standard class seats. Used mainly on the Luton–Sutton/Wimbledon routes.

**Seating Layout:** 3+2 facing.
**Dimensions:** 19.33 x 2.82 m.

**Advertising livery:** 319 364 & 319 365 Thameslink Programme (multi-coloured horizontal stripes with pink ends).

\* Sets refurbished by First Capital Connect. This programme is ongoing.

**DTSO(A).** Lot No. 31063 1990. –/70. 29.0 t.
**MSO.** Lot No. 31064 1990. –/78. 50.6 t.
**TSO.** Lot No. 31065 1990. –/74 2T. 31.0 t.
**DTSO(B).** Lot No. 31066 1990. –/78 (\* –/75). 29.7 t.

| | | | | | | | |
|---|---|---|---|---|---|---|---|
| 319 361 | \* **FU** | P | *FC* | BF | 77459 | 63043 | 71929 | 77458 |
| 319 362 | \* **FU** | P | *FC* | BF | 77461 | 63044 | 71930 | 77460 |
| 319 363 | \* **FU** | P | *FC* | BF | 77463 | 63045 | 71931 | 77462 |
| 319 364 | \* **AL** | P | *FC* | BF | 77465 | 63046 | 71932 | 77464 |
| 319 365 | \* **AL** | P | *FC* | BF | 77467 | 63047 | 71933 | 77466 |
| 319 366 | \* **FU** | P | *FC* | BF | 77469 | 63048 | 71934 | 77468 |
| 319 367 | \* **FU** | P | *FC* | BF | 77471 | 63049 | 71935 | 77470 |
| 319 368 | **TW** | P | *FC* | BF | 77473 | 63050 | 71936 | 77472 |
| 319 369 | \* **FU** | P | *FC* | BF | 77475 | 63051 | 71937 | 77474 |
| 319 370 | **TW** | P | *FC* | BF | 77477 | 63052 | 71938 | 77476 |
| 319 371 | **TW** | P | *FC* | BF | 77479 | 63053 | 71939 | 77478 |
| 319 372 | **FU** | P | *FC* | BF | 77481 | 63054 | 71940 | 77480 |
| 319 373 | **FU** | P | *FC* | BF | 77483 | 63055 | 71941 | 77482 |
| 319 374 | **TW** | P | *FC* | BF | 77485 | 63056 | 71942 | 77484 |

| 319 375 | | TW | P | FC | BF | 77487 | 63057 | 71943 | 77486 |
| 319 376 | | TW | P | FC | BF | 77489 | 63058 | 71944 | 77488 |
| 319 377 | * | FU | P | FC | BF | 77491 | 63059 | 71945 | 77490 |
| 319 378 | | TW | P | FC | BF | 77493 | 63060 | 71946 | 77492 |
| 319 379 | | TW | P | FC | BF | 77495 | 63061 | 71947 | 77494 |
| 319 380 | | TW | P | FC | BF | 77497 | 63062 | 71948 | 77496 |
| 319 381 | | TW | P | FC | BF | 77973 | 63093 | 71979 | 77974 |
| 319 382 | | TW | P | FC | BF | 77975 | 63094 | 71980 | 77976 |
| 319 383 | | TW | P | FC | BF | 77977 | 63095 | 71981 | 77978 |
| 319 384 | | TW | P | FC | BF | 77979 | 63096 | 71982 | 77980 |
| 319 385 | | TW | P | FC | BF | 77981 | 63097 | 71983 | 77982 |
| 319 386 | | TW | P | FC | BF | 77983 | 63098 | 71984 | 77984 |

**Names (carried on TSO):**

| 319 364 | Transforming Blackfriars |
| 319 365 | Transforming Farringdon |

**Class 319/4.** DTCO–MSO–TSO–DTSO. Converted from Class 319/0. Refurbished with carpets. DTSO(A) converted to composite. Used mainly on the Bedford–Gatwick–Brighton route.

**Seating Layout:** 1: 2+1 facing 2: 2+2/3+2 facing.

* Sets refurbished by First Capital Connect with some seats removed for additional luggage space. This programme is ongoing.

**77331–77381.** DTCO. Lot No. 31022 (odd nos.) 1987–1988. 12/54 (* 12/51). 28.2 t.
**77431–77457.** DTCO. Lot No. 31038 (odd nos.) 1988. 12/54 (* 12/51). 28.2 t.
**62911–62936.** MSO. Lot No. 31023 1987–1988. –/77 (* –/74). 49.2 t.
**62961–62974.** MSO. Lot No. 31039 1988. –/77 (* –/74). 49.2 t.
**71792–71817.** TSO. Lot No. 31024 1987–1988. –/72 2T (* –/67 2T). 31.0 t.
**71866–71879.** TSO. Lot No. 31040 1988. –/72 2T (* –/67 2T). 31.0 t.
**77330–77380.** DTSO. Lot No. 31025 (even nos.) 1987–1988. –/74 (* –/71 1W). 28.1 t.
**77430–77456.** DTSO. Lot No. 31041 (even nos.) 1988. –/74 (* –/71 1W). 28.1 t.

| 319 421 | * | FU | P | FC | BF | 77331 | 62911 | 71792 | 77330 |
| 319 422 | * | FU | P | FC | BF | 77333 | 62912 | 71793 | 77332 |
| 319 423 | * | FU | P | FC | BF | 77335 | 62913 | 71794 | 77334 |
| 319 424 | * | FU | P | FC | BF | 77337 | 62914 | 71795 | 77336 |
| 319 425 | * | FU | P | FC | BF | 77339 | 62915 | 71796 | 77338 |
| 319 426 | * | FU | P | FC | BF | 77341 | 62916 | 71797 | 77340 |
| 319 427 | * | FU | P | FC | BF | 77343 | 62917 | 71798 | 77342 |
| 319 428 | * | FU | P | FC | BF | 77345 | 62918 | 71799 | 77344 |
| 319 429 | | FU | P | FC | BF | 77347 | 62919 | 71800 | 77346 |
| 319 430 | | TL | P | FC | BF | 77349 | 62920 | 71801 | 77348 |
| 319 431T | | FU | P | FC | BF | 77351 | 62921 | 71802 | 77350 |
| 319 432 | * | FU | P | FC | BF | 77353 | 62922 | 71803 | 77352 |
| 319 433 | * | FU | P | FC | BF | 77355 | 62923 | 71804 | 77354 |
| 319 434 | * | FU | P | FC | BF | 77357 | 62924 | 71805 | 77356 |
| 319 435 | * | FU | P | FC | BF | 77359 | 62925 | 71806 | 77358 |
| 319 436 | * | FU | P | FC | BF | 77361 | 62926 | 71807 | 77360 |
| 319 437 | * | FU | P | FC | BF | 77363 | 62927 | 71808 | 77362 |

| | | | | | | | | |
|---|---|---|---|---|---|---|---|---|
| 319 438 | | **FU** | P | *FC* | BF | 77365 | 62928 | 71809 | 77364 |
| 319 439 | | **FU** | P | *FC* | BF | 77367 | 62929 | 71810 | 77366 |
| 319 440 | * | **FU** | P | *FC* | BF | 77369 | 62930 | 71811 | 77368 |
| 319 441 | * | **FU** | P | *FC* | BF | 77371 | 62931 | 71812 | 77370 |
| 319 442 | * | **FU** | P | *FC* | BF | 77373 | 62932 | 71813 | 77372 |
| 319 443 | | **FU** | P | *FC* | BF | 77375 | 62933 | 71814 | 77374 |
| 319 444 | | **FU** | P | *FC* | BF | 77377 | 62934 | 71815 | 77376 |
| 319 445 | | **FU** | P | *FC* | BF | 77379 | 62935 | 71816 | 77378 |
| 319 446 | * | **FU** | P | *FC* | BF | 77381 | 62936 | 71817 | 77380 |
| 319 447 | | **FU** | P | *FC* | BF | 77431 | 62961 | 71866 | 77430 |
| 319 448 | * | **FU** | P | *FC* | BF | 77433 | 62962 | 71867 | 77432 |
| 319 449 | * | **FU** | P | *FC* | BF | 77435 | 62963 | 71868 | 77434 |
| 319 450 | | **FU** | P | *FC* | BF | 77437 | 62964 | 71869 | 77436 |
| 319 451 | * | **FU** | P | *FC* | BF | 77439 | 62965 | 71870 | 77438 |
| 319 452 | * | **FU** | P | *FC* | BF | 77441 | 62966 | 71871 | 77440 |
| 319 453 | * | **FU** | P | *FC* | BF | 77443 | 62967 | 71872 | 77442 |
| 319 454 | * | **FU** | P | *FC* | BF | 77445 | 62968 | 71873 | 77444 |
| 319 455 | * | **FU** | P | *FC* | BF | 77447 | 62969 | 71874 | 77446 |
| 319 456 | * | **FU** | P | *FC* | BF | 77449 | 62970 | 71875 | 77448 |
| 319 457 | * | **FU** | P | *FC* | BF | 77451 | 62971 | 71876 | 77450 |
| 319 458 | * | **FU** | P | *FC* | BF | 77453 | 62972 | 71877 | 77452 |
| 319 459 | * | **FU** | P | *FC* | BF | 77455 | 62973 | 71878 | 77454 |
| 319 460 | * | **FU** | P | *FC* | BF | 77457 | 62974 | 71879 | 77456 |

**Names (carried on TSO):**

| | |
|---|---|
| 319 425 | Transforming Travel |
| 319 435 | Adrian Jackson-Robbins Chairman 1987–2007 Association of Public Transport Users |
| 319 446 | St. Pancras International |
| 319 449 | King's Cross Thameslink |

# CLASS 320                                               BREL YORK

Suburban units.

**Formation:** DTSO–MSO–DTSO.
**Construction:** Steel
**Traction Motors:** Four Brush TM2141B of 268 kW.
**Wheel Arrangement:** 2-2 + Bo-Bo + 2-2.
**Braking:** Disc.                        **Dimensions:** 19.33 x 2.82 m.
**Bogies:** P7-4 (MSO), T3-7 (others).    **Couplers:** Tightlock.
**Gangways:** Within unit.                **Control System:** Thyristor.
**Doors:** Sliding.                       **Maximum Speed:** 75 m.p.h.
**Seating Layout:** 3+2 facing.
**Multiple Working:** Within class & with Classes 317, 318, 319, 321, 322 and 323.

**DTSO (A).** Lot No. 31060 1990. –/76 1W. 30.7 t.
**MSO.** Lot No. 31062 1990. –/76 1W. 52.1 t.
**DTSO (B).** Lot No. 31061 1990. –/75. 31.7 t.

| | | | | | | | |
|---|---|---|---|---|---|---|---|
| 320 301 | **SC** | H | *SR* | GW | 77899 | 63021 | 77921 |
| 320 302 | **SC** | H | *SR* | GW | 77900 | 63022 | 77922 |

| 320 303 | **SC** | H | *SR* | GW | 77901 | 63023 | 77923 |
| 320 304 | **SC** | H | *SR* | GW | 77902 | 63024 | 77924 |
| 320 305 | **SC** | H | *SR* | GW | 77903 | 63025 | 77925 |
| 320 306 | **SC** | H | *SR* | GW | 77904 | 63026 | 77926 |
| 320 307 | **SC** | H | *SR* | GW | 77905 | 63027 | 77927 |
| 320 308 | **SC** | H | *SR* | GW | 77906 | 63028 | 77928 |
| 320 309 | **SC** | H | *SR* | GW | 77907 | 63029 | 77929 |
| 320 310 | **SC** | H | *SR* | GW | 77908 | 63030 | 77930 |
| 320 311 | **SC** | H | *SR* | GW | 77909 | 63031 | 77931 |
| 320 312 | **SC** | H | *SR* | GW | 77910 | 63032 | 77932 |
| 320 313 | **SC** | H | *SR* | GW | 77911 | 63033 | 77933 |
| 320 314 | **SC** | H | *SR* | GW | 77912 | 63034 | 77934 |
| 320 315 | **SC** | H | *SR* | GW | 77913 | 63035 | 77935 |
| 320 316 | **SC** | H | *SR* | GW | 77914 | 63036 | 77936 |
| 320 317 | **SC** | H | *SR* | GW | 77915 | 63037 | 77937 |
| 320 318 | **SC** | H | *SR* | GW | 77916 | 63038 | 77938 |
| 320 319 | **SC** | H | *SR* | GW | 77917 | 63039 | 77939 |
| 320 320 | **SC** | H | *SR* | GW | 77918 | 63040 | 77940 |
| 320 321 | **SC** | H | *SR* | GW | 77919 | 63041 | 77941 |
| 320 322 | **SC** | H | *SR* | GW | 77920 | 63042 | 77942 |

**Names (carried on MSO):**

| 320 305 | GLASGOW SCHOOL OF ART 1845 150 1995 |
| 320 306 | Model Rail Scotland |
| 320 308 | High Road 20th Anniversary 2000 |
| 320 309 | Radio Clyde 25th Anniversary |
| 320 311 | Royal College of Physicians and Surgeons of Glasgow |
| 320 312 | Sir William A Smith Founder of the Boys' Brigade |
| 320 321 | The Rt. Hon. John Smith, QC, MP |
| 320 322 | Festive Glasgow Orchid |

# CLASS 321                                    BREL YORK

Outer suburban units.

**Formation:** DTCO (DTSO on Class 321/9)–MSO–TSO–DTSO.
**Construction:** Steel.
**Traction Motors:** Four Brush TM2141C (268 kW).
**Wheel Arrangement:** 2-2 + Bo-Bo + 2-2 + 2-2.
**Braking:** Disc.                    **Dimensions:** 19.95 x 2.82 m.
**Bogies:** P7-4 (MSO), T3-7 (others).  **Couplers:** Tightlock.
**Gangways:** Within unit.            **Control System:** Thyristor.
**Doors:** Sliding.                   **Maximum Speed:** 100 m.p.h..
**Seating Layout:** 1: 2+2 facing, 2: 3+2 facing.
**Multiple Working:** Within class & with Classes 317, 318, 319, 320, 322 and 323.

**Class 321/3.**

**DTCO.** Lot No. 31053 1988–1990. 16/57. 29.7 t.
**MSO.** Lot No. 31054 1988–1990. –/82. 51.5 t.
**TSO.** Lot No. 31055 1988–1990. –/75 2T. 29.1 t.
**DTSO.** Lot No. 31056 1988–1990. –/78. 29.7 t.

| | | | | | | | | |
|---|---|---|---|---|---|---|---|---|
| 321 301 | GE | H | *EA* | IL | 78049 | 62975 | 71880 | 77853 |
| 321 302 | GE | H | *EA* | IL | 78050 | 62976 | 71881 | 77854 |
| 321 303 | NX | H | *EA* | IL | 78051 | 62977 | 71882 | 77855 |
| 321 304 | NX | H | *EA* | IL | 78052 | 62978 | 71883 | 77856 |
| 321 305 | GE | H | *EA* | IL | 78053 | 62979 | 71884 | 77857 |
| 321 306 | GE | H | *EA* | IL | 78054 | 62980 | 71885 | 77858 |
| 321 307 | GE | H | *EA* | IL | 78055 | 62981 | 71886 | 77859 |
| 321 308 | GE | H | *EA* | IL | 78056 | 62982 | 71887 | 77860 |
| 321 309 | GE | H | *EA* | IL | 78057 | 62983 | 71888 | 77861 |
| 321 310 | GE | H | *EA* | IL | 78058 | 62984 | 71889 | 77862 |
| 321 311 | GE | H | *EA* | IL | 78059 | 62985 | 71890 | 77863 |
| 321 312 | GE | H | *EA* | IL | 78060 | 62986 | 71891 | 77864 |
| 321 313 | GE | H | *EA* | IL | 78061 | 62987 | 71892 | 77865 |
| 321 314 | GE | H | *EA* | IL | 78062 | 62988 | 71893 | 77866 |
| 321 315 | GE | H | *EA* | IL | 78063 | 62989 | 71894 | 77867 |
| 321 316 | GE | H | *EA* | IL | 78064 | 62990 | 71895 | 77868 |
| 321 317 | GE | H | *EA* | IL | 78065 | 62991 | 71896 | 77869 |
| 321 318 | GE | H | *EA* | IL | 78066 | 62992 | 71897 | 77870 |
| 321 319 | GE | H | *EA* | IL | 78067 | 62993 | 71898 | 77871 |
| 321 320 | GE | H | *EA* | IL | 78068 | 62994 | 71899 | 77872 |
| 321 321 | NX | H | *EA* | IL | 78069 | 62995 | 71900 | 77873 |
| 321 322 | GE | H | *EA* | IL | 78070 | 62996 | 71901 | 77874 |
| 321 323 | GE | H | *EA* | IL | 78071 | 62997 | 71902 | 77875 |
| 321 324 | GE | H | *EA* | IL | 78072 | 62998 | 71903 | 77876 |
| 321 325 | GE | H | *EA* | IL | 78073 | 62999 | 71904 | 77877 |
| 321 326 | GE | H | *EA* | IL | 78074 | 63000 | 71905 | 77878 |
| 321 327 | GE | H | *EA* | IL | 78075 | 63001 | 71906 | 77879 |
| 321 328 | GE | H | *EA* | IL | 78076 | 63002 | 71907 | 77880 |
| 321 329 | GE | H | *EA* | IL | 78077 | 63003 | 71908 | 77881 |
| 321 330 | GE | H | *EA* | IL | 78078 | 63004 | 71909 | 77882 |
| 321 331 | GE | H | *EA* | IL | 78079 | 63005 | 71910 | 77883 |
| 321 332 | GE | H | *EA* | IL | 78080 | 63006 | 71911 | 77884 |
| 321 333 | GE | H | *EA* | IL | 78081 | 63007 | 71912 | 77885 |
| 321 334 | GE | H | *EA* | IL | 78082 | 63008 | 71913 | 77886 |
| 321 335 | GE | H | *EA* | IL | 78083 | 63009 | 71914 | 77887 |
| 321 336 | GE | H | *EA* | IL | 78084 | 63010 | 71915 | 77888 |
| 321 337 | GE | H | *EA* | IL | 78085 | 63011 | 71916 | 77889 |
| 321 338 | GE | H | *EA* | IL | 78086 | 63012 | 71917 | 77890 |
| 321 339 | GE | H | *EA* | IL | 78087 | 63013 | 71918 | 77891 |
| 321 340 | GE | H | *EA* | IL | 78088 | 63014 | 71919 | 77892 |
| 321 341 | GE | H | *EA* | IL | 78089 | 63015 | 71920 | 77893 |
| 321 342 | GE | H | *EA* | IL | 78090 | 63016 | 71921 | 77894 |
| 321 343 | GE | H | *EA* | IL | 78091 | 63017 | 71922 | 77895 |
| 321 344 | GE | H | *EA* | IL | 78092 | 63018 | 71923 | 77896 |
| 321 345 | GE | H | *EA* | IL | 78093 | 63019 | 71924 | 77897 |
| 321 346 | GE | H | *EA* | IL | 78094 | 63020 | 71925 | 77898 |
| 321 347 | GE | H | *EA* | IL | 78131 | 63105 | 71991 | 78280 |
| 321 348 | GE | H | *EA* | IL | 78132 | 63106 | 71992 | 78281 |
| 321 349 | GE | H | *EA* | IL | 78133 | 63107 | 71993 | 78282 |
| 321 350 | GE | H | *EA* | IL | 78134 | 63108 | 71994 | 78283 |
| 321 351 | GE | H | *EA* | IL | 78135 | 63109 | 71995 | 78284 |

| 321 352 | **GE** | H | *EA* | IL | 78136 | 63110 | 71996 | 78285 |
| 321 353 | **GE** | H | *EA* | IL | 78137 | 63111 | 71997 | 78286 |
| 321 354 | **GE** | H | *EA* | IL | 78138 | 63112 | 71998 | 78287 |
| 321 355 | **GE** | H | *EA* | IL | 78139 | 63113 | 71999 | 78288 |
| 321 356 | **GE** | H | *EA* | IL | 78140 | 63114 | 72000 | 78289 |
| 321 357 | **GE** | H | *EA* | IL | 78141 | 63115 | 72001 | 78290 |
| 321 358 | **GE** | H | *EA* | IL | 78142 | 63116 | 72002 | 78291 |
| 321 359 | **GE** | H | *EA* | IL | 78143 | 63117 | 72003 | 78292 |
| 321 360 | **GE** | H | *EA* | IL | 78144 | 63118 | 72004 | 78293 |
| 321 361 | **GE** | H | *EA* | IL | 78145 | 63119 | 72005 | 78294 |
| 321 362 | **GE** | H | *EA* | IL | 78146 | 63120 | 72006 | 78295 |
| 321 363 | **GE** | H | *EA* | IL | 78147 | 63121 | 72007 | 78296 |
| 321 364 | **GE** | H | *EA* | IL | 78148 | 63122 | 72008 | 78297 |
| 321 365 | **GE** | H | *EA* | IL | 78149 | 63123 | 72009 | 78298 |
| 321 366 | **GE** | H | *EA* | IL | 78150 | 63124 | 72010 | 78299 |

**Names (carried on TSO):**

| 321 312 | Southend-on-Sea |
| 321 321 | NSPCC ESSEX FULL STOP |
| 321 334 | Amsterdam |
| 321 336 | GEOFFREY FREEMAN ALLEN |
| 321 343 | RSA RAILWAY STUDY ASSOCIATION |
| 321 351 | GURKHA |
| 321 361 | Phoenix |

**Class 321/4.**

**DTCO.** Lot No. 31067 1989–1990. 28/40. 29.8 t.
**MSO.** Lot No. 31068 1989–1990. –/79. 51.6 t.
**TSO.** Lot No. 31069 1989–1990. –/74 2T. 29.2 t.
**DTSO.** Lot No. 31070 1989–1990. –/78. 29.8 t.

**Note:** The DTCOs of the National Express East Anglia units have had 12 first class seats declassified.

| 321 401 | **SL** | H | *LM* | NN | 78095 | 63063 | 71949 | 77943 |
| 321 402 | **SL** | H | *LM* | NN | 78096 | 63064 | 71950 | 77944 |
| 321 403 | **SL** | H | *LM* | NN | 78097 | 63065 | 71951 | 77945 |
| 321 404 | **SL** | H | *LM* | NN | 78098 | 63066 | 71952 | 77946 |
| 321 405 | **SL** | H | *LM* | NN | 78099 | 63067 | 71953 | 77947 |
| 321 406 | **SL** | H | *LM* | NN | 78100 | 63068 | 71954 | 77948 |
| 321 407 | **SL** | H | *LM* | NN | 78101 | 63069 | 71955 | 77949 |
| 321 408 | **SL** | H | *LM* | NN | 78102 | 63070 | 71956 | 77950 |
| 321 409 | **SL** | H | *LM* | NN | 78103 | 63071 | 71957 | 77951 |
| 321 410 | **SL** | H | *LM* | NN | 78104 | 63072 | 71958 | 77952 |
| 321 411 | **SL** | H | *LM* | NN | 78105 | 63073 | 71959 | 77953 |
| 321 412 | **SL** | H | *LM* | NN | 78106 | 63074 | 71960 | 77954 |
| 321 413 | **SL** | H | *LM* | NN | 78107 | 63075 | 71961 | 77955 |
| 321 414 | **SL** | H | *LM* | NN | 78108 | 63076 | 71962 | 77956 |
| 321 415 | **SL** | H | *LM* | NN | 78109 | 63077 | 71963 | 77957 |
| 321 416 | **SL** | H | *LM* | NN | 78110 | 63078 | 71964 | 77958 |
| 321 417 | **SL** | H | *LM* | NN | 78111 | 63079 | 71965 | 77959 |
| 321 418 | **SL** | H | *LM* | NN | 78112 | 63080 | 71968 | 77962 |

| 321 419 | SL | H | *LM* | NN | 78113 | 63081 | 71967 | 77961 |
|---------|-----|---|------|-----|-------|-------|-------|-------|
| 321 420 | SL | H | *LM* | NN | 78114 | 63082 | 71966 | 77960 |
| 321 421 | SL | H | *LM* | NN | 78115 | 63083 | 71969 | 77963 |
| 321 422 | SL | H | *LM* | NN | 78116 | 63084 | 71970 | 77964 |
| 321 423 | SL | H | *LM* | NN | 78117 | 63085 | 71971 | 77965 |
| 321 424 | SL | H | *LM* | NN | 78118 | 63086 | 71972 | 77966 |
| 321 425 | SL | H | *LM* | NN | 78119 | 63087 | 71973 | 77967 |
| 321 426 | SL | H | *LM* | NN | 78120 | 63088 | 71974 | 77968 |
| 321 427 | SL | H | *LM* | NN | 78121 | 63089 | 71975 | 77969 |
| 321 428 | SL | H | *LM* | NN | 78122 | 63090 | 71976 | 77970 |
| 321 429 | SL | H | *LM* | NN | 78123 | 63091 | 71977 | 77971 |
| 321 430 | SL | H | *LM* | NN | 78124 | 63092 | 71978 | 77972 |
| 321 431 | SL | H | *LM* | NN | 78151 | 63125 | 72011 | 78300 |
| 321 432 | SL | H | *LM* | NN | 78152 | 63126 | 72012 | 78301 |
| 321 433 | SL | H | *LM* | NN | 78153 | 63127 | 72013 | 78302 |
| 321 434 | SL | H | *LM* | NN | 78154 | 63128 | 72014 | 78303 |
| 321 435 | SL | H | *LM* | NN | 78155 | 63129 | 72015 | 78304 |
| 321 436 | SL | H | *LM* | NN | 78156 | 63130 | 72016 | 78305 |
| 321 437 | SL | H | *LM* | NN | 78157 | 63131 | 72017 | 78306 |
| 321 438 | GE | H | *EA* | IL | 78158 | 63132 | 72018 | 78307 |
| 321 439 | GE | H | *EA* | IL | 78159 | 63133 | 72019 | 78308 |
| 321 440 | GE | H | *EA* | IL | 78160 | 63134 | 72020 | 78309 |
| 321 441 | GE | H | *EA* | IL | 78161 | 63135 | 72021 | 78310 |
| 321 442 | GE | H | *EA* | IL | 78162 | 63136 | 72022 | 78311 |
| 321 443 | GE | H | *EA* | IL | 78125 | 63099 | 71985 | 78274 |
| 321 444 | GE | H | *EA* | IL | 78126 | 63100 | 71986 | 78275 |
| 321 445 | GE | H | *EA* | IL | 78127 | 63101 | 71987 | 78276 |
| 321 446 | 1 | H | *EA* | IL | 78128 | 63102 | 71988 | 78277 |
| 321 447 | GE | H | *EA* | IL | 78129 | 63103 | 71989 | 78278 |
| 321 448 | GE | H | *EA* | IL | 78130 | 63104 | 71990 | 78279 |

**Names (carried on TSO):**

| 321 407 | HERTFORDSHIRE WRVS |
|---------|--------------------|
| 321 413 | Bill Green |
| 321 420 | Silver Service |
| 321 425 | Bletchley Pride |
| 321 427 | Major Tim Warr |
| 321 444 | Essex Lifeboats |
| 321 446 | George Mullings |

**Class 321/9.** DTSO(A)–MSO–TSO–DTSO(B).

**DTSO(A).** Lot No. 31108 1991. –/70(8). 29.0 t.
**MSO.** Lot No. 31109 1991. –/79. 51.0 t.
**TSO.** Lot No. 31110 1991. –/74 2T. 29.0 t.
**DTSO(B).** Lot No. 31111 1991. –/70(7) 1W. 29.0 t.

| 321 901 | YR | H | *NO* | NL | 77990 | 63153 | 72128 | 77993 |
|---------|-----|---|------|-----|-------|-------|-------|-------|
| 321 902 | YR | H | *NO* | NL | 77991 | 63154 | 72129 | 77994 |
| 321 903 | YR | H | *NO* | NL | 77992 | 63155 | 72130 | 77995 |

# CLASS 322                                              BREL YORK

Units built for use on Stansted Airport services, now in use with First ScotRail.

**Formation:** DTSO–MSO–TSO–DTSO.
**Construction:** Steel.
**Traction Motors:** Four Brush TM2141C (268 kW).
**Wheel Arrangement:** 2-2 + Bo-Bo + 2-2 + 2-2.
**Braking:** Disc.                          **Dimensions:** 19.95/19.92 x 2.82 m.
**Bogies:** P7-4 (MSO), T3-7 (others).       **Couplers:** Tightlock.
**Gangways:** Within unit.                   **Control System:** Thyristor.
**Doors:** Sliding.                          **Maximum Speed:** 100 m.p.h.
**Seating Layout:** 3+2 facing.
**Multiple Working:** Within class & with Classes 317, 318, 319, 320, 321 and 323.

**DTSO(A).** Lot No. 31094 1990. –/58. 29.3 t.
**MSO.** Lot No. 31092 1990. –/83. 51.5 t.
**TSO.** Lot No. 31093 1990. –/76 2T. 28.8 t.
**DTSO(B).** Lot No. 31091 1990. –/74(2) 1W. 29.1 t.

| 322 481 | FS | H | *SR* | GW | 78163 | 63137 | 72023 | 77985 |
| 322 482 | FS | H | *SR* | GW | 78164 | 63138 | 72024 | 77986 |
| 322 483 | FS | H | *SR* | GW | 78165 | 63139 | 72025 | 77987 |
| 322 484 | FS | H | *SR* | GW | 78166 | 63140 | 72026 | 77988 |
| 322 485 | FS | H | *SR* | GW | 78167 | 63141 | 72027 | 77989 |

**Name (carried on DTSO(A)):**

322 481    North Berwick Flyer 1850–2000

# CLASS 323 HUNSLET TRANSPORTATION PROJECTS

Suburban units.

**Formation:** DMSO–PTSO–DMSO.
**Construction:** Welded aluminium alloy.
**Traction Motors:** Four Holec DMKT 52/24 asynchronous of 146 kW.
**Wheel Arrangement:** Bo-Bo + 2-2 + Bo-Bo.
**Braking:** Disc.                          **Dimensions:** 23.37/23.44 x 2.80 m.
**Bogies:** SRP BP62 (DMSO), BT52 (PTSO).   **Couplers:** Tightlock.
**Gangways:** Within unit.                   **Control System:** GTO Inverter.
**Doors:** Sliding plug.                     **Maximum Speed:** 90 m.p.h.
**Seating Layout:** 3+2 facing/unidirectional.
**Multiple Working:** Within class & with Classes 317, 318, 319, 320, 321 and 322.

**DMSO(A).** Lot No. 31112 Hunslet 1992–1993. –/98 (* –/82). 39.1 t.
**TSO.** Lot No. 31113 Hunslet 1992–1993. –/88(5) 1T 2W. (* –/80 1T 2W). 36.5 t.
**DMSO(B).** Lot No. 31114 Hunslet 1992–1993. –/98 (* –/82). 39.1 t.

| 323 201 | LM | P | *LM* | SI | 64001 | 72201 | 65001 |
| 323 202 | LM | P | *LM* | SI | 64002 | 72202 | 65002 |
| 323 203 | LM | P | *LM* | SI | 64003 | 72203 | 65003 |
| 323 204 | LM | P | *LM* | SI | 64004 | 72204 | 65004 |
| 323 205 | LM | P | *LM* | SI | 64005 | 72205 | 65005 |

| 323 206 | **LM** | P | *LM* | SI | 64006 | 72206 | 65006 |
| 323 207 | **LM** | P | *LM* | SI | 64007 | 72207 | 65007 |
| 323 208 | **LM** | P | *LM* | SI | 64008 | 72208 | 65008 |
| 323 209 | **LM** | P | *LM* | SI | 64009 | 72209 | 65009 |
| 323 210 | **LM** | P | *LM* | SI | 64010 | 72210 | 65010 |
| 323 211 | **LM** | P | *LM* | SI | 64011 | 72211 | 65011 |
| 323 212 | **LM** | P | *LM* | SI | 64012 | 72212 | 65012 |
| 323 213 | **LM** | P | *LM* | SI | 64013 | 72213 | 65013 |
| 323 214 | **LM** | P | *LM* | SI | 64014 | 72214 | 65014 |
| 323 215 | **LM** | P | *LM* | SI | 64015 | 72215 | 65015 |
| 323 216 | **LM** | P | *LM* | SI | 64016 | 72216 | 65016 |
| 323 217 | **LM** | P | *LM* | SI | 64017 | 72217 | 65017 |
| 323 218 | **LM** | P | *LM* | SI | 64018 | 72218 | 65018 |
| 323 219 | **LM** | P | *LM* | SI | 64019 | 72219 | 65019 |
| 323 220 | **LM** | P | *LM* | SI | 64020 | 72220 | 65020 |
| 323 221 | **LM** | P | *LM* | SI | 64021 | 72221 | 65021 |
| 323 222 | **LM** | P | *LM* | SI | 64022 | 72222 | 65022 |
| 323 223 | * **NO** | P | *NO* | LG | 64023 | 72223 | 65023 |
| 323 224 | * **FS** | P | *NO* | LG | 64024 | 72224 | 65024 |
| 323 225 | * **FS** | P | *NO* | LG | 64025 | 72225 | 65025 |
| 323 226 | **FS** | P | *NO* | LG | 64026 | 72226 | 65026 |
| 323 227 | **FS** | P | *NO* | LG | 64027 | 72227 | 65027 |
| 323 228 | **FS** | P | *NO* | LG | 64028 | 72228 | 65028 |
| 323 229 | **FS** | P | *NO* | LG | 64029 | 72229 | 65029 |
| 323 230 | **FS** | P | *NO* | LG | 64030 | 72230 | 65030 |
| 323 231 | **FS** | P | *NO* | LG | 64031 | 72231 | 65031 |
| 323 232 | **FS** | P | *NO* | LG | 64032 | 72232 | 65032 |
| 323 233 | **FS** | P | *NO* | LG | 64033 | 72233 | 65033 |
| 323 234 | **FS** | P | *NO* | LG | 64034 | 72234 | 65034 |
| 323 235 | **FS** | P | *NO* | LG | 64035 | 72235 | 65035 |
| 323 236 | **FS** | P | *NO* | LG | 64036 | 72236 | 65036 |
| 323 237 | **FS** | P | *NO* | LG | 64037 | 72237 | 65037 |
| 323 238 | **FS** | P | *NO* | LG | 64038 | 72238 | 65038 |
| 323 239 | **FS** | P | *NO* | LG | 64039 | 72239 | 65039 |
| 323 240 | **LM** | P | *LM* | SI | 64040 | 72340 | 65040 |
| 323 241 | **LM** | P | *LM* | SI | 64041 | 72341 | 65041 |
| 323 242 | **LM** | P | *LM* | SI | 64042 | 72342 | 65042 |
| 323 243 | **LM** | P | *LM* | SI | 64043 | 72343 | 65043 |

# CLASS 325            ABB DERBY

Postal units based on Class 319s. Compatible with diesel or electric locomotive haulage.

**Formation:** DTPMV–MPMV–TPMV–DTPMV.
**System:** 25 kV AC overhead/750 V DC third rail.
**Construction:** Steel.
**Traction Motors:** Four GEC G315BZ of 268 kW.
**Wheel Arrangement:** 2-2 + Bo-Bo + 2-2 + 2-2.
**Braking:** Disc.      **Dimensions:** 19.33 x 2.82 m.
**Bogies:** P7-4 (MSO), T3-7 (others).      **Couplers:** Drop-head buckeye.

**Gangways:** None.
**Doors:** Roller shutter.
**Multiple Working:** Within class.

**Control System:** GTO Chopper.
**Maximum Speed:** 100 m.p.h.

**DTPMV.** Lot No. 31144 1995. 29.1 t.
**MPMV.** Lot No. 31145 1995. 49.5 t.
**TPMV.** Lot No. 31146 1995. 30.7 t.

| | | | | | | | |
|---|---|---|---|---|---|---|---|
| 325 001 | **RM** | RM *GB* | WB | 68300 | 68340 | 68360 | 68301 |
| 325 002 | **RM** | RM *GB* | WB | 68302 | 68341 | 68361 | 68303 |
| 325 003 | **RM** | RM *GB* | WB | 68304 | 68342 | 68362 | 68305 |
| 325 004 | **RM** | RM *GB* | WB | 68306 | 68343 | 68363 | 68307 |
| 325 005 | **RM** | RM *GB* | WB | 68308 | 68344 | 68364 | 68309 |
| 325 006 | **RM** | RM *GB* | WB | 68310 | 68345 | 68365 | 68311 |
| 325 007 | **RM** | RM *GB* | WB | 68312 | 68346 | 68366 | 68313 |
| 325 008 | **RM** | RM *GB* | WB | 68314 | 68347 | 68367 | 68315 |
| 325 009 | **RM** | RM *GB* | WB | 68316 | 68349 | 68368 | 68317 |
| 325 010 | **RM** | RM *GB* | WB | 68318 | 68348 | 68369 | 68319 |
| 325 011 | **RM** | RM *GB* | WB | 68320 | 68350 | 68370 | 68321 |
| 325 012 | **RM** | RM *GB* | WB | 68322 | 68351 | 68371 | 68323 |
| 325 013 | **RM** | RM *GB* | WB | 68324 | 68352 | 68372 | 68325 |
| 325 014 | **RM** | RM *GB* | WB | 68326 | 68353 | 68373 | 68327 |
| 325 015 | **RM** | RM *GB* | WB | 68328 | 68354 | 68374 | 68329 |
| 325 016 | **RM** | RM *GB* | WB | 68330 | 68355 | 68375 | 68331 |

**Names (carried on one side of each DTPMV):**

| | |
|---|---|
| 325 002 | Royal Mail North Wales & North West |
| 325 006 | John Grierson |
| 325 008 | Peter Howarth CBE |

# CLASS 332   HEATHROW EXPRESS   SIEMENS

Dedicated Heathrow Express units. Five units were increased from 4-car to 5-car in 2002. Usually operate in coupled pairs.

**Formations:** Various.
**Construction:** Steel.
**Traction Motors:** Two Siemens monomotors asynchronous of 350 kW.
**Wheel Arrangement:** B-B + 2-2 + 2-2 (+ 2-2) + B-B.
**Braking:** Disc.
**Bogies:** CAF.
**Gangways:** Within unit.
**Doors:** Sliding plug.
**Dimensions:** 23.63/23.35 x 2.75 m.
**Couplers:** Scharfenberg 10L.
**Control System:** IGBT Inverter.
**Maximum Speed:** 100 m.p.h.
**Heating & ventilation:** Air conditioning.
**Seating Layout:** 1: 2+1 facing, 2: 2+2 mainly unidirectional.
**Multiple Working:** Within class.

**332 001–332 007.** DMFO–TSO–PTSO–(TSO)–DMSO.

**DMFO.** CAF 1997–1998. 26/–. 48.8 t.
**72400–72413. TSO.** CAF 1997–1998. –/56 35.8 t.
**72414–72418. TSO.** CAF 2002. –/56 35.8 t.
**PTSO.** CAF 1997–1998. –/44 1TD 1W. 45.6 t.

**DMSO.** CAF 1997–1998. –/48. 48.8 t.
**DMLFO.** CAF 1997–1998. 14/– 1W. 48.8 t.

**Advertising livery:** Vehicles 78401, 78402, 78405, 78406, 78408, 78410, 78412
Royal Bank of Scotland (deep blue).

| 332 001 | **HE** | HE *HE* | OH | 78400 | 72412 | 63400 |       | 78401 |
|---------|--------|---------|----|-------|-------|-------|-------|-------|
| 332 002 | **HE** | HE *HE* | OH | 78402 | 72409 | 63401 |       | 78403 |
| 332 003 | **HE** | HE *HE* | OH | 78404 | 72407 | 63402 |       | 78405 |
| 332 004 | **HE** | HE *HE* | OH | 78406 | 72405 | 63403 |       | 78407 |
| 332 005 | **HE** | HE *HE* | OH | 78408 | 72411 | 63404 | 72417 | 78409 |
| 332 006 | **HE** | HE *HE* | OH | 78410 | 72410 | 63405 | 72415 | 78411 |
| 332 007 | **HE** | HE *HE* | OH | 78412 | 72401 | 63406 | 72414 | 78413 |

**332 008–332 014.** DMSO–TSO–PTSO–(TSO)–DMLFO.

**Advertising livery:** Vehicles 78414, 78416, 78419, 78421, 78423, 78425, 78427
Royal Bank of Scotland (deep blue).

| 332 008 | **HE** | HE *HE* | OH | 78414 | 72413 | 63407 | 72418 | 78415 |
|---------|--------|---------|----|-------|-------|-------|-------|-------|
| 332 009 | **HE** | HE *HE* | OH | 78416 | 72400 | 63408 | 72416 | 78417 |
| 332 010 | **HE** | HE *HE* | OH | 78418 | 72402 | 63409 |       | 78419 |
| 332 011 | **HE** | HE *HE* | OH | 78420 | 72403 | 63410 |       | 78421 |
| 332 012 | **HE** | HE *HE* | OH | 78422 | 72404 | 63411 |       | 78423 |
| 332 013 | **HE** | HE *HE* | OH | 78424 | 72408 | 63412 |       | 78425 |
| 332 014 | **HE** | HE *HE* | OH | 78426 | 72406 | 63413 |       | 78427 |

# CLASS 333                                                        SIEMENS

West Yorkshire area suburban units.

**Formation:** DMSO–PTSO–TSO–DMSO.
**Construction:** Steel.
**Traction Motors:** Two Siemens monomotors asynchronous of 350 kW.
**Wheel Arrangement:** B-B + 2-2 + 2-2 + B-B.
**Braking:** Disc.
**Dimensions:** 23.74 (outer ends)/23.35 (TSO) x 2.75 m.
**Bogies:** CAF.                              **Couplers:** Dellner 10L.
**Gangways:** Within unit.                    **Control System:** IGBT Inverter.
**Doors:** Sliding plug.                      **Maximum Speed:** 100 m.p.h.
**Heating & ventilation:** Air conditioning.
**Seating Layout:** 3+2 facing/unidirectional.
**Multiple Working:** Within class.

**DMSO(A).** (Odd Nos.) CAF 2001. –/90. 50.6 t.
**PTSO.** CAF 2001. –/73(6) 1TD 2W. 46.7 t.
**TSO.** CAF 2002–2003. –/100. 38.5 t.
**DMSO(B).** (Even Nos.) CAF 2001. –/90. 50.6 t.

**Notes:** 333 001–333 008 were made up to 4-car units from 3-car units in 2002.

333 009–333 016 were made up to 4-car units from 3-car units in 2003.

| 333 001 | **YN** | A | *NO* | NL | 78451 | 74461 | 74477 | 78452 |
|---------|--------|---|------|----|-------|-------|-------|-------|
| 333 002 | **YR** | A | *NO* | NL | 78453 | 74462 | 74478 | 78454 |
| 333 003 | **YN** | A | *NO* | NL | 78455 | 74463 | 74479 | 78456 |

| 333 004 | **YR** | A | *NO* | NL | 78457 | 74464 | 74480 | 78458 |
| 333 005 | **YN** | A | *NO* | NL | 78459 | 74465 | 74481 | 78460 |
| 333 006 | **YN** | A | *NO* | NL | 78461 | 74466 | 74482 | 78462 |
| 333 007 | **YN** | A | *NO* | NL | 78463 | 74467 | 74483 | 78464 |
| 333 008 | **YN** | A | *NO* | NL | 78465 | 74468 | 74484 | 78466 |
| 333 009 | **YN** | A | *NO* | NL | 78467 | 74469 | 74485 | 78468 |
| 333 010 | **YN** | A | *NO* | NL | 78469 | 74470 | 74486 | 78470 |
| 333 011 | **YN** | A | *NO* | NL | 78471 | 74471 | 74487 | 78472 |
| 333 012 | **YN** | A | *NO* | NL | 78473 | 74472 | 74488 | 78474 |
| 333 013 | **YN** | A | *NO* | NL | 78475 | 74473 | 74489 | 78476 |
| 333 014 | **YN** | A | *NO* | NL | 78477 | 74474 | 74490 | 78478 |
| 333 015 | **YN** | A | *NO* | NL | 78479 | 74475 | 74491 | 78480 |
| 333 016 | **YN** | A | *NO* | NL | 78481 | 74476 | 74492 | 78482 |

**Name:**

333 007    Alderman J Arthur Godwin First Lord Mayor of Bradford 1907

# CLASS 334 JUNIPER ALSTOM BIRMINGHAM

First ScotRail outer suburban units.

**Formation:** DMSO–PTSO–DMSO.
**Construction:** Steel.
**Traction Motors:** Two Alstom ONIX 800 asynchronous of 270 kW.
**Wheel Arrangement:** 2-Bo + 2-2 + Bo-2.
**Braking:** Disc.                          **Dimensions:** 21.01/19.94 x 2.80 m.
**Bogies:** Alstom LTB3/TBP3.               **Couplers:** Tightlock.
**Gangways:** Within unit.                  **Control System:** IGBT Inverter.
**Doors:** Sliding plug.                    **Maximum Speed:** 90 m.p.h.
**Heating & ventilation:** Pressure heating and ventilation.
**Seating Layout:** 2+2 facing/unidirectional (3+2 in PTSO).
**Multiple Working:** Within class.

**64101–64140. DMSO.** Alstom Birmingham 1999–2001. –/64. 42.6 t.
**PTSO.** Alstom Birmingham 1999–2001. –/55 1TD 1W. 39.4 t.
**65101–65140. DMSO.** Alstom Birmingham 1999–2001. –/64. 42.6 t.

| 334 001 | **SP** | H | *SR* | GW | 64101 | 74301 | 65101 | Donald Dewar |
| 334 002 | **SP** | H | *SR* | GW | 64102 | 74302 | 65102 | |
| 334 003 | **SP** | H | *SR* | GW | 64103 | 74303 | 65103 | |
| 334 004 | **SP** | H | *SR* | GW | 64104 | 74304 | 65104 | |
| 334 005 | **SP** | H | *SR* | GW | 64105 | 74305 | 65105 | |
| 334 006 | **SP** | H | *SR* | GW | 64106 | 74306 | 65106 | |
| 334 007 | **SP** | H | *SR* | GW | 64107 | 74307 | 65107 | |
| 334 008 | **SP** | H | *SR* | GW | 64108 | 74308 | 65108 | |
| 334 009 | **SP** | H | *SR* | GW | 64109 | 74309 | 65109 | |
| 334 010 | **SP** | H | *SR* | GW | 64110 | 74310 | 65110 | |
| 334 011 | **SP** | H | *SR* | GW | 64111 | 74311 | 65111 | |
| 334 012 | **SP** | H | *SR* | GW | 64112 | 74312 | 65112 | |
| 334 013 | **SP** | H | *SR* | GW | 64113 | 74313 | 65113 | |
| 334 014 | **SP** | H | *SR* | GW | 64114 | 74314 | 65114 | |

| 334 015 | **SP** | H | *SR* | GW | 64115 | 74315 | 65115 |          |
| 334 016 | **SP** | H | *SR* | GW | 64116 | 74316 | 65116 |          |
| 334 017 | **SP** | H | *SR* | GW | 64117 | 74317 | 65117 |          |
| 334 018 | **SP** | H | *SR* | GW | 64118 | 74318 | 65118 |          |
| 334 019 | **SP** | H | *SR* | GW | 64119 | 74319 | 65119 |          |
| 334 020 | **SP** | H | *SR* | GW | 64120 | 74320 | 65120 |          |
| 334 021 | **SP** | H | *SR* | GW | 64121 | 74321 | 65121 | Larkhall |
| 334 022 | **SP** | H | *SR* | GW | 64122 | 74322 | 65122 |          |
| 334 023 | **SP** | H | *SR* | GW | 64123 | 74323 | 65123 |          |
| 334 024 | **SP** | H | *SR* | GW | 64124 | 74324 | 65124 |          |
| 334 025 | **SP** | H | *SR* | GW | 64125 | 74325 | 65125 |          |
| 334 026 | **SP** | H | *SR* | GW | 64126 | 74326 | 65126 |          |
| 334 027 | **SP** | H | *SR* | GW | 64127 | 74327 | 65127 |          |
| 334 028 | **SP** | H | *SR* | GW | 64128 | 74328 | 65128 |          |
| 334 029 | **SP** | H | *SR* | GW | 64129 | 74329 | 65129 |          |
| 334 030 | **SP** | H | *SR* | GW | 64130 | 74330 | 65130 |          |
| 334 031 | **SP** | H | *SR* | GW | 64131 | 74331 | 65131 |          |
| 334 032 | **SP** | H | *SR* | GW | 64132 | 74332 | 65132 |          |
| 334 033 | **SP** | H | *SR* | GW | 64133 | 74333 | 65133 |          |
| 334 034 | **SP** | H | *SR* | GW | 64134 | 74334 | 65134 |          |
| 334 035 | **SP** | H | *SR* | GW | 64135 | 74335 | 65135 |          |
| 334 036 | **SP** | H | *SR* | GW | 64136 | 74336 | 65136 |          |
| 334 037 | **SP** | H | *SR* | GW | 64137 | 74337 | 65137 |          |
| 334 038 | **SP** | H | *SR* | GW | 64138 | 74338 | 65138 |          |
| 334 039 | **SP** | H | *SR* | GW | 64139 | 74339 | 65139 |          |
| 334 040 | **SP** | H | *SR* | GW | 64140 | 74340 | 65140 |          |

# CLASS 350              DESIRO UK              SIEMENS

Outer suburban and long distance units.

**Formation:** DMCO–TCO–PTSO–DMCO.
**Systems:** 25 kV AC overhead (350/1s built with 750 V DC).
**Construction:** Welded aluminium.
**Traction Motors:** 4 Siemens 1TB2016-0GB02 asynchronous of 250 kW.
**Wheel Arrangement:** Bo-Bo + 2-2 + 2-2 + Bo-Bo.
**Braking:** Disc & regenerative.          **Dimensions:** 20.34 x 2.80 m.
**Bogies:** SGP SF5000.                    **Couplers:** Dellner 12.
**Gangways:** Throughout.                  **Control System:** IGBT Inverter.
**Doors:** Sliding plug.                   **Maximum Speed:** 100 m.p.h.
**Heating & ventilation:** Air conditioning.
**Seating Layout:** 1: 2+2 facing, 2: 2+2 facing/unidirectional (3+2 in 350/2s).
**Multiple Working:** Within class.

**Class 350/1.** Original build units owned by Angel Trains. Formerly part of an aborted South West Trains 5-car Class 450/2 order. 2+2 seating.

**DMSO(A).** Siemens Uerdingen 2004–2005. –/60. 48.7 t.
**TCO.** Siemens Uerdingen/Praha 2004–2005. 24/32 1T. 36.2 t.
**PTSO.** Siemens Uerdingen/Praha 2004–2005. –/48(9) 1TD 2W. 45.2 t.
**DMSO(B).** Siemens Uerdingen 2004–2005. –/60. 49.2 t.

| | | | | | | | | |
|---|---|---|---|---|---|---|---|---|
| 350 101 | **LM** | A | *LM* | NN | 63761 | 66811 | 66861 | 63711 |
| 350 102 | **LM** | A | *LM* | NN | 63762 | 66812 | 66862 | 63712 |
| 350 103 | **LM** | A | *LM* | NN | 63765 | 66813 | 66863 | 63713 |
| 350 104 | **LM** | A | *LM* | NN | 63764 | 66814 | 66864 | 63714 |
| 350 105 | **LM** | A | *LM* | NN | 63763 | 66815 | 66868 | 63715 |
| 350 106 | **LM** | A | *LM* | NN | 63766 | 66816 | 66866 | 63716 |
| 350 107 | **LM** | A | *LM* | NN | 63767 | 66817 | 66867 | 63717 |
| 350 108 | **LM** | A | *LM* | NN | 63768 | 66818 | 66865 | 63718 |
| 350 109 | **LM** | A | *LM* | NN | 63769 | 66819 | 66869 | 63719 |
| 350 110 | **LM** | A | *LM* | NN | 63770 | 66820 | 66870 | 63720 |
| 350 111 | **LM** | A | *LM* | NN | 63771 | 66821 | 66871 | 63721 |
| 350 112 | **LM** | A | *LM* | NN | 63772 | 66822 | 66872 | 63722 |
| 350 113 | **LM** | A | *LM* | NN | 63773 | 66823 | 66873 | 63723 |
| 350 114 | **LM** | A | *LM* | NN | 63774 | 66824 | 66874 | 63724 |
| 350 115 | **LM** | A | *LM* | NN | 63775 | 66825 | 66875 | 63725 |
| 350 116 | **LM** | A | *LM* | NN | 63776 | 66826 | 66876 | 63726 |
| 350 117 | **LM** | A | *LM* | NN | 63777 | 66827 | 66877 | 63727 |
| 350 118 | **LM** | A | *LM* | NN | 63778 | 66828 | 66878 | 63728 |
| 350 119 | **LM** | A | *LM* | NN | 63779 | 66829 | 66879 | 63729 |
| 350 120 | **LM** | A | *LM* | NN | 63780 | 66830 | 66880 | 63730 |
| 350 121 | **LM** | A | *LM* | NN | 63781 | 66831 | 66881 | 63731 |
| 350 122 | **LM** | A | *LM* | NN | 63782 | 66832 | 66882 | 63732 |
| 350 123 | **LM** | A | *LM* | NN | 63783 | 66833 | 66883 | 63733 |
| 350 124 | **LM** | A | *LM* | NN | 63784 | 66834 | 66884 | 63734 |
| 350 125 | **LM** | A | *LM* | NN | 63785 | 66835 | 66885 | 63735 |
| 350 126 | **LM** | A | *LM* | NN | 63786 | 66836 | 66886 | 63736 |
| 350 127 | **LM** | A | *LM* | NN | 63787 | 66837 | 66887 | 63737 |
| 350 128 | **LM** | A | *LM* | NN | 63788 | 66838 | 66888 | 63738 |
| 350 129 | **LM** | A | *LM* | NN | 63789 | 66839 | 66889 | 63739 |
| 350 130 | **LM** | A | *LM* | NN | 63790 | 66840 | 66890 | 63740 |

**Class 350/2.** Currently being delivered and all due to be in traffic by summer 2009. Owned by Porterbrook Leasing. 3+2 seating.

**DMSO(A).** Siemens Uerdingen 2008–2009. –/70. 43.8 t.
**TCO.** Siemens Praha 2008–2009. 24/42 1T. 34.9 t.
**PTSO.** Siemens Praha 2008–2009. –/61(9) 1TD 2W. 42.9 t.
**DMSO(B).** Siemens Uerdingen 2008–2009. –/70. 44.2 t.

| | | | | | | | | |
|---|---|---|---|---|---|---|---|---|
| 350 231 | **LM** | P | *LM* | NN | 61431 | 65231 | 67531 | 61531 |
| 350 232 | **LM** | P | *LM* | NN | 61432 | 65232 | 67532 | 61532 |
| 350 233 | **LM** | P | *LM* | NN | 61433 | 65233 | 67533 | 61533 |
| 350 234 | **LM** | P | | | 61434 | 65234 | 67534 | 61534 |
| 350 235 | **LM** | P | *LM* | NN | 61435 | 65235 | 67535 | 61535 |
| 350 236 | **LM** | P | *LM* | NN | 61436 | 65236 | 67536 | 61536 |
| 350 237 | **LM** | P | *LM* | NN | 61437 | 65237 | 67537 | 61537 |
| 350 238 | **LM** | P | *LM* | NN | 61438 | 65238 | 67538 | 61538 |
| 350 239 | **LM** | P | *LM* | NN | 61439 | 65239 | 67539 | 61539 |
| 350 240 | **LM** | P | *LM* | NN | 61440 | 65240 | 67540 | 61540 |
| 350 241 | **LM** | P | *LM* | NN | 61441 | 65241 | 67541 | 61541 |
| 350 242 | **LM** | P | | | 61442 | 65242 | 67542 | 61542 |
| 350 243 | **LM** | P | | | 61443 | 65243 | 67543 | 61543 |

| 350 244 | **LM** | P |  | 61444 | 65244 | 67544 | 61544 |
| 350 245 | **LM** | P |  | 61445 | 65245 | 67545 | 61545 |
| 350 246 | **LM** | P |  | 61446 | 65246 | 67546 | 61546 |
| 350 247 | **LM** | P |  | 61447 | 65247 | 67546 | 61547 |
| 350 248 | **LM** | P |  | 61448 | 65248 | 67548 | 61548 |
| 350 249 | **LM** | P |  | 61449 | 65249 | 67549 | 61549 |
| 350 250 | **LM** | P |  | 61450 | 65250 | 67550 | 61550 |
| 350 251 | **LM** | P |  | 61451 | 65251 | 67551 | 61551 |
| 350 252 | **LM** | P |  | 61452 | 65252 | 67552 | 61552 |
| 350 253 | **LM** | P |  | 61453 | 65253 | 67553 | 61553 |
| 350 254 | **LM** | P |  | 61454 | 65254 | 67554 | 61554 |
| 350 255 | **LM** | P |  | 61455 | 65255 | 67555 | 61555 |
| 350 256 | **LM** | P |  | 61456 | 65256 | 67556 | 61556 |
| 350 257 | **LM** | P |  | 61457 | 65257 | 67557 | 61557 |
| 350 258 | **LM** | P |  | 61458 | 65258 | 67558 | 61558 |
| 350 259 | **LM** | P |  | 61459 | 65259 | 67559 | 61559 |
| 350 260 | **LM** | P |  | 61460 | 65260 | 67560 | 61560 |
| 350 261 | **LM** | P |  | 61461 | 65261 | 67561 | 61561 |
| 350 262 | **LM** | P |  | 61462 | 65262 | 67562 | 61562 |
| 350 263 | **LM** | P |  | 61463 | 65263 | 67563 | 61563 |
| 350 264 | **LM** | P |  | 61464 | 65264 | 67564 | 61564 |
| 350 265 | **LM** | P |  | 61465 | 65265 | 67565 | 61565 |
| 350 266 | **LM** | P |  | 61466 | 65266 | 67566 | 61566 |
| 350 267 | **LM** | P |  | 61467 | 65267 | 67567 | 61567 |

# CLASS 357 ELECTROSTAR
## ADTRANZ/BOMBARDIER DERBY

Provision for 750 V DC supply if required.

**Formation:** DMSO–MSO–PTSO–DMSO.
**Construction:** Welded aluminium alloy underframe, sides and roof with steel ends. All sections bolted together.
**Traction Motors:** Two Adtranz asynchronous of 250 kW.
**Wheel Arrangement:** 2-Bo + 2-Bo + 2-2 + Bo-2.

| | |
|---|---|
| **Braking:** Disc & regenerative. | **Dimensions:** 20.40/19.99 x 2.80 m. |
| **Bogies:** Adtranz P3-25/T3-25. | **Couplers:** Tightlock. |
| **Gangways:** Within unit. | **Control System:** IGBT Inverter. |
| **Doors:** Sliding plug. | **Maximum Speed:** 100 m.p.h. |

**Heating & ventilation:** Air conditioning.
**Seating Layout:** 3+2 facing/unidirectional.
**Multiple Working:** Within class.

Class **357/0**. Owned by Porterbrook Leasing.

**DMSO(A).** Adtranz Derby 1999–2001. –/71. 40.7 t.
**MSO.** Adtranz Derby 1999–2001. –/78. 36.7 t.
**PTSO.** Adtranz Derby 1999–2001. –/58(4) 1TD 2W. 39.5 t.
**DMSO(B).** Adtranz Derby 1999–2001. –/71. 40.7 t.

**Advertising livery:**
357 010 c2c "green train" (green with purple doors).

| | | | | | | | | |
|---|---|---|---|---|---|---|---|---|
| 357 001 | C2 | P | C2 | EM | 67651 | 74151 | 74051 | 67751 |
| 357 002 | C2 | P | C2 | EM | 67652 | 74152 | 74052 | 67752 |
| 357 003 | C2 | P | C2 | EM | 67653 | 74153 | 74053 | 67753 |
| 357 004 | C2 | P | C2 | EM | 67654 | 74154 | 74054 | 67754 |
| 357 005 | C2 | P | C2 | EM | 67655 | 74155 | 74055 | 67755 |
| 357 006 | C2 | P | C2 | EM | 67656 | 74156 | 74056 | 67756 |
| 357 007 | C2 | P | C2 | EM | 67657 | 74157 | 74057 | 67757 |
| 357 008 | C2 | P | C2 | EM | 67658 | 74158 | 74058 | 67758 |
| 357 009 | C2 | P | C2 | EM | 67659 | 74159 | 74059 | 67759 |
| 357 010 | AL | P | C2 | EM | 67660 | 74160 | 74060 | 67760 |
| 357 011 | C2 | P | C2 | EM | 67661 | 74161 | 74061 | 67761 |
| 357 012 | C2 | P | C2 | EM | 67662 | 74162 | 74062 | 67762 |
| 357 013 | C2 | P | C2 | EM | 67663 | 74163 | 74063 | 67763 |
| 357 014 | C2 | P | C2 | EM | 67664 | 74164 | 74064 | 67764 |
| 357 015 | C2 | P | C2 | EM | 67665 | 74165 | 74065 | 67765 |
| 357 016 | C2 | P | C2 | EM | 67666 | 74166 | 74066 | 67766 |
| 357 017 | C2 | P | C2 | EM | 67667 | 74167 | 74067 | 67767 |
| 357 018 | C2 | P | C2 | EM | 67668 | 74168 | 74068 | 67768 |
| 357 019 | C2 | P | C2 | EM | 67669 | 74169 | 74069 | 67769 |
| 357 020 | C2 | P | C2 | EM | 67670 | 74170 | 74070 | 67770 |
| 357 021 | C2 | P | C2 | EM | 67671 | 74171 | 74071 | 67771 |
| 357 022 | C2 | P | C2 | EM | 67672 | 74172 | 74072 | 67772 |
| 357 023 | C2 | P | C2 | EM | 67673 | 74173 | 74073 | 67773 |
| 357 024 | C2 | P | C2 | EM | 67674 | 74174 | 74074 | 67774 |
| 357 025 | C2 | P | C2 | EM | 67675 | 74175 | 74075 | 67775 |
| 357 026 | C2 | P | C2 | EM | 67676 | 74176 | 74076 | 67776 |
| 357 027 | C2 | P | C2 | EM | 67677 | 74177 | 74077 | 67777 |
| 357 028 | C2 | P | C2 | EM | 67678 | 74178 | 74078 | 67778 |
| 357 029 | C2 | P | C2 | EM | 67679 | 74179 | 74079 | 67779 |
| 357 030 | C2 | P | C2 | EM | 67680 | 74180 | 74080 | 67780 |
| 357 031 | C2 | P | C2 | EM | 67681 | 74181 | 74081 | 67781 |
| 357 032 | C2 | P | C2 | EM | 67682 | 74182 | 74082 | 67782 |
| 357 033 | C2 | P | C2 | EM | 67683 | 74183 | 74083 | 67783 |
| 357 034 | C2 | P | C2 | EM | 67684 | 74184 | 74084 | 67784 |
| 357 035 | C2 | P | C2 | EM | 67685 | 74185 | 74085 | 67785 |
| 357 036 | C2 | P | C2 | EM | 67686 | 74186 | 74086 | 67786 |
| 357 037 | C2 | P | C2 | EM | 67687 | 74187 | 74087 | 67787 |
| 357 038 | C2 | P | C2 | EM | 67688 | 74188 | 74088 | 67788 |
| 357 039 | C2 | P | C2 | EM | 67689 | 74189 | 74089 | 67789 |
| 357 040 | C2 | P | C2 | EM | 67690 | 74190 | 74090 | 67790 |
| 357 041 | C2 | P | C2 | EM | 67691 | 74191 | 74091 | 67791 |
| 357 042 | C2 | P | C2 | EM | 67692 | 74192 | 74092 | 67792 |
| 357 043 | C2 | P | C2 | EM | 67693 | 74193 | 74093 | 67793 |
| 357 044 | C2 | P | C2 | EM | 67694 | 74194 | 74094 | 67794 |
| 357 045 | C2 | P | C2 | EM | 67695 | 74195 | 74095 | 67795 |
| 357 046 | C2 | P | C2 | EM | 67696 | 74196 | 74096 | 67796 |

Names (carried on DMSO(A) and DMSO(B) (one plate on each)):

357 001    BARRY FLAXMAN
357 002    ARTHUR LEWIS STRIDE 1841–1922
357 003    JASON LEONARD

| 357 004 | TONY AMOS |
| 357 011 | JOHN LOWING |
| 357 028 | London, Tilbury & Southend Railway 1854–2004 |
| 357 029 | THOMAS WHITELEGG 1840–1922 |
| 357 030 | ROBERT HARBEN WHITELEGG 1871–1957 |

**Class 357/2.** Owned by Angel Trains.

**DMSO(A).** Bombardier Derby 2001–2002. –/71. 40.7 t.
**MSO.** Bombardier Derby 2001–2002. –/78. 36.7 t.
**PTSO.** Bombardier Derby 2001–2002. –/58(4) 1TD 2W. 39.5 t.
**DMSO(B).** Bombardier Derby 2001–2002. –/71. 40.7 t.

| 357 201 | **C2** | A | *C2* | EM | 68601 | 74701 | 74601 | 68701 |
| 357 202 | **C2** | A | *C2* | EM | 68602 | 74702 | 74602 | 68702 |
| 357 203 | **C2** | A | *C2* | EM | 68603 | 74703 | 74603 | 68703 |
| 357 204 | **C2** | A | *C2* | EM | 68604 | 74704 | 74604 | 68704 |
| 357 205 | **C2** | A | *C2* | EM | 68605 | 74705 | 74605 | 68705 |
| 357 206 | **C2** | A | *C2* | EM | 68606 | 74706 | 74606 | 68706 |
| 357 207 | **C2** | A | *C2* | EM | 68607 | 74707 | 74607 | 68707 |
| 357 208 | **C2** | A | *C2* | EM | 68608 | 74708 | 74608 | 68708 |
| 357 209 | **C2** | A | *C2* | EM | 68609 | 74709 | 74609 | 68709 |
| 357 210 | **C2** | A | *C2* | EM | 68610 | 74710 | 74610 | 68710 |
| 357 211 | **C2** | A | *C2* | EM | 68611 | 74711 | 74611 | 68711 |
| 357 212 | **C2** | A | *C2* | EM | 68612 | 74712 | 74612 | 68712 |
| 357 213 | **C2** | A | *C2* | EM | 68613 | 74713 | 74613 | 68713 |
| 357 214 | **C2** | A | *C2* | EM | 68614 | 74714 | 74614 | 68714 |
| 357 215 | **C2** | A | *C2* | EM | 68615 | 74715 | 74615 | 68715 |
| 357 216 | **C2** | A | *C2* | EM | 68616 | 74716 | 74616 | 68716 |
| 357 217 | **C2** | A | *C2* | EM | 68617 | 74717 | 74617 | 68717 |
| 357 218 | **C2** | A | *C2* | EM | 68618 | 74718 | 74618 | 68718 |
| 357 219 | **C2** | A | *C2* | EM | 68619 | 74719 | 74619 | 68719 |
| 357 220 | **C2** | A | *C2* | EM | 68620 | 74720 | 74620 | 68720 |
| 357 221 | **C2** | A | *C2* | EM | 68621 | 74721 | 74621 | 68721 |
| 357 222 | **C2** | A | *C2* | EM | 68622 | 74722 | 74622 | 68722 |
| 357 223 | **C2** | A | *C2* | EM | 68623 | 74723 | 74623 | 68723 |
| 357 224 | **C2** | A | *C2* | EM | 68624 | 74724 | 74624 | 68724 |
| 357 225 | **C2** | A | *C2* | EM | 68625 | 74725 | 74625 | 68725 |
| 357 226 | **C2** | A | *C2* | EM | 68626 | 74726 | 74626 | 68726 |
| 357 227 | **C2** | A | *C2* | EM | 68627 | 74727 | 74627 | 68727 |
| 357 228 | **C2** | A | *C2* | EM | 68628 | 74728 | 74628 | 68728 |

**Names (carried on DMSO(A) and DMSO(B) (one plate on each)):**

| 357 201 | KEN BIRD | 357 202 | KENNY MITCHELL |
| 357 203 | HENRY PUMFRETT | 357 204 | DEREK FOWERS |
| 357 205 | JOHN D'SILVA | 357 206 | MARTIN AUNGIER |
| 357 207 | JOHN PAGE | 357 208 | DAVE DAVIS |
| 357 209 | JAMES SNELLING | 357 213 | UPMINSTER I.E.C.C. |
| 357 217 | ALLAN BURNELL | | |

# CLASS 360/0          DESIRO UK          SIEMENS

Outer suburban/express units.

**Formation:** DMCO–PTSO–TSO–DMCO.
**Construction:** Welded aluminium.
**Traction Motors:** 4 Siemens 1TB2016-0GB02 asynchronous of 250 kW.
**Wheel Arrangement:** Bo-Bo + 2-2 + 2-2 + Bo-Bo.
**Braking:** Disc & regenerative.          **Dimensions:** 20.34 x 2.80 m.
**Bogies:** SGP SF5000.                    **Couplers:** Dellner 12.
**Gangways:** Within unit.                 **Control System:** IGBT Inverter.
**Doors:** Sliding plug.                   **Maximum Speed:** 100 m.p.h.
**Heating & ventilation:** Air conditioning.
**Seating Layout:** 1: 2+2 facing, 2: 3+2 facing/unidirectional.
**Multiple Working:** Within class.

**DMCO(A).** Siemens Uerdingen 2002–2003. 8/59. 45.0 t.
**PTSO.** Siemens Wien (Vienna) 2002–2003. –/60(9) 1TD 2W. 43.0 t.
**TSO.** Siemens Wien (Vienna) 2002–2003. –/78. 35.0 t.
**DMCO(B).** Siemens Uerdingen 2002–2003. 8/59. 45.0 t.

| | | | | | | | | |
|---|---|---|---|---|---|---|---|---|
| 360 101 | FB | A | EA | IL | 65551 | 72551 | 74551 | 68551 |
| 360 102 | FB | A | EA | IL | 65552 | 72552 | 74552 | 68552 |
| 360 103 | FB | A | EA | IL | 65553 | 72553 | 74553 | 68553 |
| 360 104 | FB | A | EA | IL | 65554 | 72554 | 74554 | 68554 |
| 360 105 | FB | A | EA | IL | 65555 | 72555 | 74555 | 68555 |
| 360 106 | FB | A | EA | IL | 65556 | 72556 | 74556 | 68556 |
| 360 107 | FB | A | EA | IL | 65557 | 72557 | 74557 | 68557 |
| 360 108 | FB | A | EA | IL | 65558 | 72558 | 74558 | 68558 |
| 360 109 | FB | A | EA | IL | 65559 | 72559 | 74559 | 68559 |
| 360 110 | FB | A | EA | IL | 65560 | 72560 | 74560 | 68560 |
| 360 111 | FB | A | EA | IL | 65561 | 72561 | 74561 | 68561 |
| 360 112 | FB | A | EA | IL | 65562 | 72562 | 74562 | 68562 |
| 360 113 | FB | A | EA | IL | 65563 | 72563 | 74563 | 68563 |
| 360 114 | FB | A | EA | IL | 65564 | 72564 | 74564 | 68564 |
| 360 115 | NX | A | EA | IL | 65565 | 72565 | 74565 | 68565 |
| 360 116 | FB | A | EA | IL | 65566 | 72566 | 74566 | 68566 |
| 360 117 | FB | A | EA | IL | 65567 | 72567 | 74567 | 68567 |
| 360 118 | FB | A | EA | IL | 65568 | 72568 | 74568 | 68568 |
| 360 119 | FB | A | EA | IL | 65569 | 72569 | 74569 | 68569 |
| 360 120 | FB | A | EA | IL | 65570 | 72570 | 74570 | 68570 |
| 360 121 | FB | A | EA | IL | 65571 | 72571 | 74571 | 68571 |

# CLASS 360/2          DESIRO UK          SIEMENS

Original 4-car Class 350 testbed units rebuilt for use by Heathrow Express on Paddington–Heathrow Airport stopping services ("Heathrow Connect").

Original 4-car sets 360 201–360 204 were made up to 5-cars during 2007 using additional TSOs. A fifth unit (360 205) was delivered in late 2005 as a 5-car set.

**Formation:** DMSO–PTSO–TSO–TSO–DMSO.
**Construction:** Welded aluminium.
**Traction Motors:** 4 Siemens 1TB2016-0GB02 asynchronous of 250 kW.
**Wheel Arrangement:** Bo-Bo + 2-2 + 2-2 + 2-2 + Bo-Bo.
**Braking:** Disc & regenerative.          **Dimensions:** 20.34 x 2.80 m.
**Bogies:** SGP SF5000.                    **Couplers:** Dellner 12.
**Gangways:** Within unit.                 **Control System:** IGBT Inverter.
**Doors:** Sliding plug.                    **Maximum Speed:** 100 m.p.h.
**Heating & ventilation:** Air conditioning.
**Seating Layout:** 3+2 facing/unidirectional.
**Multiple Working:** Within class.

**DMSO(A).** Siemens Uerdingen 2002–2006. –/63. 44.8 t.
**PTSO.** Siemens Uerdingen 2002–2006. –/57(9) 1TD 2W. 44.2 t.
**TSO.** Siemens Uerdingen 2005–2006. –/74. 35.3 t.
**TSO.** Siemens Uerdingen 2002–2006. –/74. 34.1 t.
**DMSO(B).** Siemens Uerdingen 2002–2006. –/63. 44.4 t.

| | | | | | | | | |
|---|---|---|---|---|---|---|---|---|
| 360 201 | **HC** | HE | *HC* | OH | 78431 | 63421 | 72431 | 72421 | 78441 |
| 360 202 | **HC** | HE | *HC* | OH | 78432 | 63422 | 72432 | 72422 | 78442 |
| 360 203 | **HC** | HE | *HC* | OH | 78433 | 63423 | 72433 | 72423 | 78443 |
| 360 204 | **HC** | HE | *HC* | OH | 78434 | 63424 | 72434 | 72424 | 78444 |
| 360 205 | **HC** | HE | *HC* | OH | 78435 | 63425 | 72435 | 72425 | 78445 |

# CLASS 365  NETWORKER EXPRESS  ABB YORK

Outer suburban units.

**Formations:** DMCO–TSO–PTSO–DMCO.
**Systems:** 25 kV AC overhead but with 750 V DC third rail capability (units marked * were formerly used on DC lines in the South-East).
**Construction:** Welded aluminium alloy.
**Traction Motors:** Four GEC-Alsthom G354CX asynchronous of 157 kW.
**Wheel Arrangement:** Bo-Bo + 2-2 + 2-2 + Bo-Bo.
**Braking:** Disc & rheostatic.
**Dimensions:** 20.89/20.06 x 2.81 m.
**Bogies:** ABB P3-16/T3-16.                **Couplers:** Tightlock.
**Gangways:** Within unit.                 **Control System:** GTO Inverter.
**Doors:** Sliding plug.                    **Maximum Speed:** 100 m.p.h.
**Seating Layout:** 1: 2+2 facing, 2: 2+2 facing.
**Multiple Working:** Within class only.

**DMCO(A).** Lot No. 31133 1994–1995. 12/56. 41.7 t.
**TSO.** Lot No. 31134 1994–1995. –/65 1TD (* –/64 1TD) 32.9 t.
**PTSO.** Lot No. 31135 1994–1995. –/68 1T. 34.6 t.
**DMCO(B).** Lot No. 31136 1994–1995. 12/56. 41.7 t.

**Advertising liveries:**

365 510 Cambridge & Ely; Cathedral cities (blue & white with various images).
365 519 Peterborough; environment capital (blue & white with various images).
365 531 Nelson's County; Norfolk (blue & white with various images).
365 540 Garden cities of Hertfordshire (blue & white with various images).

| | | | | | | | | |
|---|---|---|---|---|---|---|---|---|
| 365 501 | * | FU | H | FC | HE | 65894 | 72241 | 72240 | 65935 |
| 365 502 | * | FU | H | FC | HE | 65895 | 72243 | 72242 | 65936 |
| 365 503 | * | FU | H | FC | HE | 65896 | 72245 | 72244 | 65937 |
| 365 504 | * | FU | H | FC | HE | 65897 | 72247 | 72246 | 65938 |
| 365 505 | * | FU | H | FC | HE | 65898 | 72249 | 72248 | 65939 |
| 365 506 | * | FU | H | FC | HE | 65899 | 72251 | 72250 | 65940 |
| 365 507 | * | FU | H | FC | HE | 65900 | 72253 | 72252 | 65941 |
| 365 508 | * | FU | H | FC | HE | 65901 | 72255 | 72254 | 65942 |
| 365 509 | * | FU | H | FC | HE | 65902 | 72257 | 72256 | 65943 |
| 365 510 | * | AL | H | FC | HE | 65903 | 72259 | 72258 | 65944 |
| 365 511 | * | FU | H | FC | HE | 65904 | 72261 | 72260 | 65945 |
| 365 512 | * | FU | H | FC | HE | 65905 | 72263 | 72262 | 65946 |
| 365 513 | * | FU | H | FC | HE | 65906 | 72265 | 72264 | 65947 |
| 365 514 | * | FU | H | FC | HE | 65907 | 72267 | 72266 | 65948 |
| 365 515 | * | FU | H | FC | HE | 65908 | 72269 | 72268 | 65949 |
| 365 516 | * | FU | H | FC | HE | 65909 | 72271 | 72270 | 65950 |
| 365 517 | | FU | H | FC | HE | 65910 | 72273 | 72272 | 65951 |
| 365 518 | | FU | H | FC | HE | 65911 | 72275 | 72274 | 65952 |
| 365 519 | | AL | H | FC | HE | 65912 | 72277 | 72276 | 65953 |
| 365 520 | | FU | H | FC | HE | 65913 | 72279 | 72278 | 65954 |
| 365 521 | | FU | H | FC | HE | 65914 | 72281 | 72280 | 65955 |
| 365 522 | | FU | H | FC | HE | 65915 | 72283 | 72282 | 65956 |
| 365 523 | | FU | H | FC | HE | 65916 | 72285 | 72284 | 65957 |
| 365 524 | | FU | H | FC | HE | 65917 | 72287 | 72286 | 65958 |
| 365 525 | | FU | H | FC | HE | 65918 | 72289 | 72288 | 65959 |
| 365 526 | | N | H | | ZC | 65919 | 72291 | 72290 | 65960 |
| 365 527 | | FU | H | FC | HE | 65920 | 72293 | 72292 | 65961 |
| 365 528 | | FU | H | FC | HE | 65921 | 72295 | 72294 | 65962 |
| 365 529 | | FU | H | FC | HE | 65922 | 72297 | 72296 | 65963 |
| 365 530 | | FU | H | FC | HE | 65923 | 72299 | 72298 | 65964 |
| 365 531 | | AL | H | FC | HE | 65924 | 72301 | 72300 | 65965 |
| 365 532 | | FU | H | FC | HE | 65925 | 72303 | 72302 | 65966 |
| 365 533 | | FU | H | FC | HE | 65926 | 72305 | 72304 | 65967 |
| 365 534 | | FU | H | FC | HE | 65927 | 72307 | 72306 | 65968 |
| 365 535 | | FU | H | FC | HE | 65928 | 72309 | 72308 | 65969 |
| 365 536 | | FU | H | FC | HE | 65929 | 72311 | 72310 | 65970 |
| 365 537 | | FU | H | FC | HE | 65930 | 72313 | 72312 | 65971 |
| 365 538 | | FU | H | FC | HE | 65931 | 72315 | 72314 | 65972 |
| 365 539 | | FU | H | FC | HE | 65932 | 72317 | 72316 | 65973 |
| 365 540 | | AL | H | FC | HE | 65933 | 72319 | 72318 | 65974 |
| 365 541 | | FU | H | FC | HE | 65934 | 72321 | 72320 | 65975 |

**Names (carried on each DMCO):**

| | |
|---|---|
| 365 514 | Captain George Vancouver |
| 365 518 | The Fenman |
| 365 527 | Robert Stripe Passenger's Champion |
| 365 536 | Rufus Barnes Chief Executive of London Travelwatch for 25 years |

# CLASS 375 ELECTROSTAR
## ADTRANZ/BOMBARDIER DERBY

Express and outer suburban units.

**Formations:** Various.
**Systems:** 25 kV AC overhead/750 V DC third rail (some third rail only with provision for retro-fitting of AC equipment).
**Construction:** Welded aluminium alloy underframe, sides and roof with steel ends. All sections bolted together.
**Traction Motors:** Two Adtranz asynchronous of 250 kW.
**Wheel Arrangement:** 2-Bo (+ 2-Bo) + 2-2 + Bo-2.
**Braking:** Disc & regenerative.              **Dimensions:** 20.40/19.99 x 2.80 m.
**Bogies:** Adtranz P3-25/T3-25.                **Couplers:** Dellner 12.
**Gangways:** Throughout.                       **Control System:** IGBT Inverter.
**Doors:** Sliding plug.                        **Maximum Speed:** 100 m.p.h.
**Heating & ventilation:** Air conditioning.
**Seating Layout:** 1: 2+2 facing/unidirectional (seats behind drivers cab in each DMCO). 2: 2+2 facing/unidirectional (except 375/9 – 3+2 facing/unidirectional).
**Multiple Working:** Within class and with Classes 376, 377 and 378.

**Class 375/3.** Express units. 750 V DC only. DMCO–TSO–DMCO.

**DMCO(A).** Bombardier Derby 2001–2002. 12/48. 43.8 t.
**TSO.** Bombardier Derby 2001–2002. –/56 1TD 2W. 35.5 t.
**DMCO(B).** Bombardier Derby 2001–2002. 12/48. 43.8 t.

| | | | | | | |
|---|---|---|---|---|---|---|
| 375 301 | CN | H | SE | RM | 67921 | 74351 | 67931 |
| 375 302 | CN | H | SE | RM | 67922 | 74352 | 67932 |
| 375 303 | CN | H | SE | RM | 67923 | 74353 | 67933 |
| 375 304 | CN | H | SE | RM | 67924 | 74354 | 67934 |
| 375 305 | CN | H | SE | RM | 67925 | 74355 | 67935 |
| 375 306 | CN | H | SE | RM | 67926 | 74356 | 67936 |
| 375 307 | CN | H | SE | RM | 67927 | 74357 | 67937 |
| 375 308 | CN | H | SE | RM | 67928 | 74358 | 67938 |
| 375 309 | CN | H | SE | RM | 67929 | 74359 | 67939 |
| 375 310 | CN | H | SE | RM | 67930 | 74360 | 67940 |

**Name (carried on TSO):**

375 304     Medway Valley Line 1856–2006

**Class 375/6.** Express units. 25 kV AC/750 V DC. DMCO–MSO–PTSO–DMCO.

**DMCO(A).** Adtranz Derby 1999–2001. 12/48. 46.2 t.
**MSO.** Adtranz Derby 1999–2001. –/66 1T. 40.5 t.
**PTSO.** Adtranz Derby 1999–2001. –/56 1TD 2W. 40.7 t.
**DMCO(B).** Adtranz Derby 1999–2001. 12/48. 46.2 t.

| | | | | | | | |
|---|---|---|---|---|---|---|---|
| 375 601 | CN | H | SE | RM | 67801 | 74251 | 74201 | 67851 |
| 375 602 | CN | H | SE | RM | 67802 | 74252 | 74202 | 67852 |
| 375 603 | CN | H | SE | RM | 67803 | 74253 | 74203 | 67853 |
| 375 604 | CN | H | SE | RM | 67804 | 74254 | 74204 | 67854 |
| 375 605 | CN | H | SE | RM | 67805 | 74255 | 74205 | 67855 |

| 375 606 | CN | H | SE | RM | 67806 | 74256 | 74206 | 67856 |
| 375 607 | CN | H | SE | RM | 67807 | 74257 | 74207 | 67857 |
| 375 608 | CN | H | SE | RM | 67808 | 74258 | 74208 | 67858 |
| 375 609 | CN | H | SE | RM | 67809 | 74259 | 74209 | 67859 |
| 375 610 | CN | H | SE | RM | 67810 | 74260 | 74210 | 67860 |
| 375 611 | CN | H | SE | RM | 67811 | 74261 | 74211 | 67861 |
| 375 612 | CN | H | SE | RM | 67812 | 74262 | 74212 | 67862 |
| 375 613 | CN | H | SE | RM | 67813 | 74263 | 74213 | 67863 |
| 375 614 | CN | H | SE | RM | 67814 | 74264 | 74214 | 67864 |
| 375 615 | CN | H | SE | RM | 67815 | 74265 | 74215 | 67865 |
| 375 616 | CN | H | SE | RM | 67816 | 74266 | 74216 | 67866 |
| 375 617 | CN | H | SE | RM | 67817 | 74267 | 74217 | 67867 |
| 375 618 | CN | H | SE | RM | 67818 | 74268 | 74218 | 67868 |
| 375 619 | CN | H | SE | RM | 67819 | 74269 | 74219 | 67869 |
| 375 620 | CN | H | SE | RM | 67820 | 74270 | 74220 | 67870 |
| 375 621 | CN | H | SE | RM | 67821 | 74271 | 74221 | 67871 |
| 375 622 | CN | H | SE | RM | 67822 | 74272 | 74222 | 67872 |
| 375 623 | CN | H | SE | RM | 67823 | 74273 | 74223 | 67873 |
| 375 624 | CN | H | SE | RM | 67824 | 74274 | 74224 | 67874 |
| 375 625 | CN | H | SE | RM | 67825 | 74275 | 74225 | 67875 |
| 375 626 | CN | H | SE | RM | 67826 | 74276 | 74226 | 67876 |
| 375 627 | CN | H | SE | RM | 67827 | 74277 | 74227 | 67877 |
| 375 628 | CN | H | SE | RM | 67828 | 74278 | 74228 | 67878 |
| 375 629 | CN | H | SE | RM | 67829 | 74279 | 74229 | 67879 |
| 375 630 | CN | H | SE | RM | 67830 | 74280 | 74230 | 67880 |

**Names (carried on one side of each MSO or PTSO):**

| 375 608 | Bromley Travelwise | 375 610 | Royal Tunbridge Wells |
| 375 611 | Dr. William Harvey | 375 619 | Driver John Neve |
| 375 623 | Hospice in the Weald | | |

**Class 375/7.** Express units. 750 V DC only. DMCO–MSO–TSO–DMCO.

**DMCO(A).** Bombardier Derby 2001–2002. 12/48. 43.8 t.
**MSO.** Bombardier Derby 2001–2002. –/66 1T. 36.4 t.
**TSO.** Bombardier Derby 2001–2002. –/56 1TD 2W. 34.1 t.
**DMCO(B).** Bombardier Derby 2001–2002. 12/48. 43.8 t.

| 375 701 | CN | H | SE | RM | 67831 | 74281 | 74231 | 67881 |
| 375 702 | CN | H | SE | RM | 67832 | 74282 | 74232 | 67882 |
| 375 703 | CN | H | SE | RM | 67833 | 74283 | 74233 | 67883 |
| 375 704 | CN | H | SE | RM | 67834 | 74284 | 74234 | 67884 |
| 375 705 | CN | H | SE | RM | 67835 | 74285 | 74235 | 67885 |
| 375 706 | CN | H | SE | RM | 67836 | 74286 | 74236 | 67886 |
| 375 707 | CN | H | SE | RM | 67837 | 74287 | 74237 | 67887 |
| 375 708 | CN | H | SE | RM | 67838 | 74288 | 74238 | 67888 |
| 375 709 | CN | H | SE | RM | 67839 | 74289 | 74239 | 67889 |
| 375 710 | CN | H | SE | RM | 67840 | 74290 | 74240 | 67890 |
| 375 711 | CN | H | SE | RM | 67841 | 74291 | 74241 | 67891 |
| 375 712 | CN | H | SE | RM | 67842 | 74292 | 74242 | 67892 |
| 375 713 | CN | H | SE | RM | 67843 | 74293 | 74243 | 67893 |
| 375 714 | CN | H | SE | RM | 67844 | 74294 | 74244 | 67894 |
| 375 715 | CN | H | SE | RM | 67845 | 74295 | 74245 | 67895 |

**Names (carried on one side of each MSO or TSO):**

375 701   Kent Air Ambulance Explorer
375 703   Dickens Traveller

**Class 375/8.** Express units. 750 V DC only. DMCO–MSO–TSO–DMCO.

**DMCO(A).** Bombardier Derby 2004. 12/48. 43.3 t.
**MSO.** Bombardier Derby 2004. –/66 1T. 39.8 t.
**TSO.** Bombardier Derby 2004. –/52 1TD 2W. 35.9 t.
**DMCO(B).** Bombardier Derby 2004. 12/52. 43.3 t.

| | | | | | | | | |
|---|---|---|---|---|---|---|---|---|
| 375 801 | **CN** | H | *SE* | RM | 73301 | 79001 | 78201 | 73701 |
| 375 802 | **CN** | H | *SE* | RM | 73302 | 79002 | 78202 | 73702 |
| 375 803 | **CN** | H | *SE* | RM | 73303 | 79003 | 78203 | 73703 |
| 375 804 | **CN** | H | *SE* | RM | 73304 | 79004 | 78204 | 73704 |
| 375 805 | **CN** | H | *SE* | RM | 73305 | 79005 | 78205 | 73705 |
| 375 806 | **CN** | H | *SE* | RM | 73306 | 79006 | 78206 | 73706 |
| 375 807 | **CN** | H | *SE* | RM | 73307 | 79007 | 78207 | 73707 |
| 375 808 | **CN** | H | *SE* | RM | 73308 | 79008 | 78208 | 73708 |
| 375 809 | **CN** | H | *SE* | RM | 73309 | 79009 | 78209 | 73709 |
| 375 810 | **CN** | H | *SE* | RM | 73310 | 79010 | 78210 | 73710 |
| 375 811 | **CN** | H | *SE* | RM | 73311 | 79011 | 78211 | 73711 |
| 375 812 | **CN** | H | *SE* | RM | 73312 | 79012 | 78212 | 73712 |
| 375 813 | **CN** | H | *SE* | RM | 73313 | 79013 | 78213 | 73713 |
| 375 814 | **CN** | H | *SE* | RM | 73314 | 79014 | 78214 | 73714 |
| 375 815 | **CN** | H | *SE* | RM | 73315 | 79015 | 78215 | 73715 |
| 375 816 | **CN** | H | *SE* | RM | 73316 | 79016 | 78216 | 73716 |
| 375 817 | **CN** | H | *SE* | RM | 73317 | 79017 | 78217 | 73717 |
| 375 818 | **CN** | H | *SE* | RM | 73318 | 79018 | 78218 | 73718 |
| 375 819 | **CN** | H | *SE* | RM | 73319 | 79019 | 78219 | 73719 |
| 375 820 | **CN** | H | *SE* | RM | 73320 | 79020 | 78220 | 73720 |
| 375 821 | **CN** | H | *SE* | RM | 73321 | 79021 | 78221 | 73721 |
| 375 822 | **CN** | H | *SE* | RM | 73322 | 79022 | 78222 | 73722 |
| 375 823 | **CN** | H | *SE* | RM | 73323 | 79023 | 78223 | 73723 |
| 375 824 | **CN** | H | *SE* | RM | 73324 | 79024 | 78224 | 73724 |
| 375 825 | **CN** | H | *SE* | RM | 73325 | 79025 | 78225 | 73725 |
| 375 826 | **CN** | H | *SE* | RM | 73326 | 79026 | 78226 | 73726 |
| 375 827 | **CN** | H | *SE* | RM | 73327 | 79027 | 78227 | 73727 |
| 375 828 | **CN** | H | *SE* | RM | 73328 | 79028 | 78228 | 73728 |
| 375 829 | **CN** | H | *SE* | RM | 73329 | 79029 | 78229 | 73729 |
| 375 830 | **CN** | H | *SE* | RM | 73330 | 79030 | 78230 | 73730 |

**Name (carried on one side of each MSO or TSO):**

375 830   City of London

**Class 375/9.** Outer suburban units. 750 V DC only. DMCO–MSO–TSO–DMCO.

**DMCO(A).** Bombardier Derby 2003–2004. 12/59. 43.4 t.
**MSO.** Bombardier Derby 2003–2004. –/73 1T. 39.3 t.
**TSO.** Bombardier Derby 2003–2004. –/59 1TD 2W. 35.6 t.
**DMCO(B).** Bombardier Derby 2003–2004. 12/59. 43.4 t.

| | | | | | | | | |
|---|---|---|---|---|---|---|---|---|
| 375 901 | **CN** | H | *SE* | RM | 73331 | 79031 | 79061 | 73731 |
| 375 902 | **CN** | H | *SE* | RM | 73332 | 79032 | 79062 | 73732 |

| 375 903 | CN | H | *SE* | RM | 73333 | 79033 | 79063 | 73733 |
| 375 904 | CN | H | *SE* | RM | 73334 | 79034 | 79064 | 73734 |
| 375 905 | CN | H | *SE* | RM | 73335 | 79035 | 79065 | 73735 |
| 375 906 | CN | H | *SE* | RM | 73336 | 79036 | 79066 | 73736 |
| 375 907 | CN | H | *SE* | RM | 73337 | 79037 | 79067 | 73737 |
| 375 908 | CN | H | *SE* | RM | 73338 | 79038 | 79068 | 73738 |
| 375 909 | CN | H | *SE* | RM | 73339 | 79039 | 79069 | 73739 |
| 375 910 | CN | H | *SE* | RM | 73340 | 79040 | 79070 | 73740 |
| 375 911 | CN | H | *SE* | RM | 73341 | 79041 | 79071 | 73741 |
| 375 912 | CN | H | *SE* | RM | 73342 | 79042 | 79072 | 73742 |
| 375 913 | CN | H | *SE* | RM | 73343 | 79043 | 79073 | 73743 |
| 375 914 | CN | H | *SE* | RM | 73344 | 79044 | 79074 | 73744 |
| 375 915 | CN | H | *SE* | RM | 73345 | 79045 | 79075 | 73745 |
| 375 916 | CN | H | *SE* | RM | 73346 | 79046 | 79076 | 73746 |
| 375 917 | CN | H | *SE* | RM | 73347 | 79047 | 79077 | 73747 |
| 375 918 | CN | H | *SE* | RM | 73348 | 79048 | 79078 | 73748 |
| 375 919 | CN | H | *SE* | RM | 73349 | 79049 | 79079 | 73749 |
| 375 920 | CN | H | *SE* | RM | 73350 | 79050 | 79080 | 73750 |
| 375 921 | CN | H | *SE* | RM | 73351 | 79051 | 79081 | 73751 |
| 375 922 | CN | H | *SE* | RM | 73352 | 79052 | 79082 | 73752 |
| 375 923 | CN | H | *SE* | RM | 73353 | 79053 | 79083 | 73753 |
| 375 924 | CN | H | *SE* | RM | 73354 | 79054 | 79084 | 73754 |
| 375 925 | CN | H | *SE* | RM | 73355 | 79055 | 79085 | 73755 |
| 375 926 | CN | H | *SE* | RM | 73356 | 79056 | 79086 | 73756 |
| 375 927 | CN | H | *SE* | RM | 73357 | 79057 | 79087 | 73757 |

## CLASS 376    ELECTROSTAR    BOMBARDIER DERBY

Inner suburban units.

**Formation:** DMSO–MSO–TSO–MSO–DMSO.
**System:** 750 V DC third rail.
**Construction:** Welded aluminium alloy underframe, sides and roof with steel ends. All sections bolted together.
**Traction Motors:** Two Bombardier asynchronous of 250 kW.
**Wheel Arrangement:** 2-Bo + 2-Bo + 2-2 + Bo-2 + Bo-2.
**Braking:** Disc & regenerative.          **Dimensions:** 20.40/19.99 x 2.80 m.
**Bogies:** Bombardier P3-25/T3-25.       **Couplers:** Dellner 12.
**Gangways:** Within unit.                **Control System:** IGBT Inverter.
**Doors:** Sliding.                       **Maximum Speed:** 75 m.p.h.
**Heating & ventilation:** Pressure heating and ventilation.
**Seating Layout:** 2+2 low density facing.
**Multiple Working:** Within class and with Classes 375, 377 and 378.

**DMSO(A).** Bombardier Derby 2004–2005. –/36(6) 1W. 42.1 t.
**MSO.** Bombardier Derby 2004–2005. –/48. 36.2 t.
**TSO.** Bombardier Derby 2004–2005. –/48. 36.3 t.
**DMSO(B).** Bombardier Derby 2004–2005. –/36(6) 1W. 42.1 t.

| 376 001 | CN | H | *SE* | SG | 61101 | 63301 | 64301 | 63501 | 61601 |
| 376 002 | CN | H | *SE* | SG | 61102 | 63302 | 64302 | 63502 | 61602 |
| 376 003 | CN | H | *SE* | SG | 61103 | 63303 | 64303 | 63503 | 61603 |

| | | | | | | | | |
|---|---|---|---|---|---|---|---|---|
| 376 004 | CN | H | *SE* | SG | 61104 | 63304 | 64304 | 63504 | 61604 |
| 376 005 | CN | H | *SE* | SG | 61105 | 63305 | 64305 | 63505 | 61605 |
| 376 006 | CN | H | *SE* | SG | 61106 | 63306 | 64306 | 63506 | 61606 |
| 376 007 | CN | H | *SE* | SG | 61107 | 63307 | 64307 | 63507 | 61607 |
| 376 008 | CN | H | *SE* | SG | 61108 | 63308 | 64308 | 63508 | 61608 |
| 376 009 | CN | H | *SE* | SG | 61109 | 63309 | 64309 | 63509 | 61609 |
| 376 010 | CN | H | *SE* | SG | 61110 | 63310 | 64310 | 63510 | 61610 |
| 376 011 | CN | H | *SE* | SG | 61111 | 63311 | 64311 | 63511 | 61611 |
| 376 012 | CN | H | *SE* | SG | 61112 | 63312 | 64312 | 63512 | 61612 |
| 376 013 | CN | H | *SE* | SG | 61113 | 63313 | 64313 | 63513 | 61613 |
| 376 014 | CN | H | *SE* | SG | 61114 | 63314 | 64314 | 63514 | 61614 |
| 376 015 | CN | H | *SE* | SG | 61115 | 63315 | 64315 | 63515 | 61615 |
| 376 016 | CN | H | *SE* | SG | 61116 | 63316 | 64316 | 63516 | 61616 |
| 376 017 | CN | H | *SE* | SG | 61117 | 63317 | 64317 | 63517 | 61617 |
| 376 018 | CN | H | *SE* | SG | 61118 | 63318 | 64318 | 63518 | 61618 |
| 376 019 | CN | H | *SE* | SG | 61119 | 63319 | 64319 | 63519 | 61619 |
| 376 020 | CN | H | *SE* | SG | 61120 | 63320 | 64320 | 63520 | 61620 |
| 376 021 | CN | H | *SE* | SG | 61121 | 63321 | 64321 | 63521 | 61621 |
| 376 022 | CN | H | *SE* | SG | 61122 | 63322 | 64322 | 63522 | 61622 |
| 376 023 | CN | H | *SE* | SG | 61123 | 63323 | 64323 | 63523 | 61623 |
| 376 024 | CN | H | *SE* | SG | 61124 | 63324 | 64324 | 63524 | 61624 |
| 376 025 | CN | H | *SE* | SG | 61125 | 63325 | 64325 | 63525 | 61625 |
| 376 026 | CN | H | *SE* | SG | 61126 | 63326 | 64326 | 63526 | 61626 |
| 376 027 | CN | H | *SE* | SG | 61127 | 63327 | 64327 | 63527 | 61627 |
| 376 028 | CN | H | *SE* | SG | 61128 | 63328 | 64328 | 63528 | 61628 |
| 376 029 | CN | H | *SE* | SG | 61129 | 63329 | 64329 | 63529 | 61629 |
| 376 030 | CN | H | *SE* | SG | 61130 | 63330 | 64330 | 63530 | 61630 |
| 376 031 | CN | H | *SE* | SG | 61131 | 63331 | 64331 | 63531 | 61631 |
| 376 032 | CN | H | *SE* | SG | 61132 | 63332 | 64332 | 63532 | 61632 |
| 376 033 | CN | H | *SE* | SG | 61133 | 63333 | 64333 | 63533 | 61633 |
| 376 034 | CN | H | *SE* | SG | 61134 | 63334 | 64334 | 63534 | 61634 |
| 376 035 | CN | H | *SE* | SG | 61135 | 63335 | 64335 | 63535 | 61635 |
| 376 036 | CN | H | *SE* | SG | 61136 | 63336 | 64336 | 63536 | 61636 |

## CLASS 377   ELECTROSTAR   BOMBARDIER DERBY

Express and outer suburban units.

**Formations:** Various.
**Systems:** 25 kV AC overhead/750 V DC third rail or third rail only with provision for retro-fitting of AC equipment.
**Construction:** Welded aluminium alloy underframe, sides and roof with steel ends. All sections bolted together.
**Traction Motors:** Two Bombardier asynchronous of 250 kW.
**Wheel Arrangement:** 2-Bo (+ 2-Bo) + 2-2 + Bo-2.
**Braking:** Disc & regenerative.	**Dimensions:** 20.40/19.99 x 2.80 m.
**Bogies:** Bombardier P3-25/T3-25.	**Couplers:** Dellner 12.
**Gangways:** Throughout.	**Control System:** IGBT Inverter.
**Doors:** Sliding plug.	**Maximum Speed:** 100 m.p.h.
**Heating & ventilation:** Air conditioning.
**Seating Layout:** Various.

**Multiple Working:** Within class and with Classes 375, 376 and 378.

**Class 377/1.** 750 V DC only. DMCO–MSO–TSO–DMCO.
**Seating layout:** 1: 2+2 facing/unidirectional, 2: 2+2 facing/unidirectional
(377 101–377 119), 3+2 and 2+2 facing/unidirectional (377 120–377 164) (3+2
seating in middle cars only 377 140–377 164).

**DMCO(A).** Bombardier Derby 2002–2003. 12/48 (s 12/56). 43.4 t.
**MSO.** Bombardier Derby 2002–2003. –/62 (s –/70, t –/69). 1T. 39.0 t.
**TSO.** Bombardier Derby 2002–2003. –/52 (s –/60, t –/57). 1TD 2W. 35.4 t.
**DMCO(B).** Bombardier Derby 2002–2003. 12/48 (s 12/56). 43.4 t.

| | | | | | | | | |
|---|---|---|---|---|---|---|---|---|
| 377 101 | | **SN** | P | *SN* | BI | 78501 | 77101 | 78901 | 78701 |
| 377 102 | | **SN** | P | *SN* | BI | 78502 | 77102 | 78902 | 78702 |
| 377 103 | | **SN** | P | *SN* | BI | 78503 | 77103 | 78903 | 78703 |
| 377 104 | | **SN** | P | *SN* | BI | 78504 | 77104 | 78904 | 78704 |
| 377 105 | | **SN** | P | *SN* | BI | 78505 | 77105 | 78905 | 78705 |
| 377 106 | | **SN** | P | *SN* | BI | 78506 | 77106 | 78906 | 78706 |
| 377 107 | | **SN** | P | *SN* | BI | 78507 | 77107 | 78907 | 78707 |
| 377 108 | | **SN** | P | *SN* | BI | 78508 | 77108 | 78908 | 78708 |
| 377 109 | | **SN** | P | *SN* | BI | 78509 | 77109 | 78909 | 78709 |
| 377 110 | | **SN** | P | *SN* | BI | 78510 | 77110 | 78910 | 78710 |
| 377 111 | | **SN** | P | *SN* | BI | 78511 | 77111 | 78911 | 78711 |
| 377 112 | | **SN** | P | *SN* | BI | 78512 | 77112 | 78912 | 78712 |
| 377 113 | | **SN** | P | *SN* | BI | 78513 | 77113 | 78913 | 78713 |
| 377 114 | | **SN** | P | *SN* | BI | 78514 | 77114 | 78914 | 78714 |
| 377 115 | | **SN** | P | *SN* | BI | 78515 | 77115 | 78915 | 78715 |
| 377 116 | | **SN** | P | *SN* | BI | 78516 | 77116 | 78916 | 78716 |
| 377 117 | | **SN** | P | *SN* | BI | 78517 | 77117 | 78917 | 78717 |
| 377 118 | | **SN** | P | *SN* | BI | 78518 | 77118 | 78918 | 78718 |
| 377 119 | | **SN** | P | *SN* | BI | 78519 | 77119 | 78919 | 78719 |
| 377 120 | s | **SN** | P | *SN* | SU | 78520 | 77120 | 78920 | 78720 |
| 377 121 | s | **SN** | P | *SN* | SU | 78521 | 77121 | 78921 | 78721 |
| 377 122 | s | **SN** | P | *SN* | SU | 78522 | 77122 | 78922 | 78722 |
| 377 123 | s | **SN** | P | *SN* | SU | 78523 | 77123 | 78923 | 78723 |
| 377 124 | s | **SN** | P | *SN* | SU | 78524 | 77124 | 78924 | 78724 |
| 377 125 | s | **SN** | P | *SN* | SU | 78525 | 77125 | 78925 | 78725 |
| 377 126 | s | **SN** | P | *SN* | SU | 78526 | 77126 | 78926 | 78726 |
| 377 127 | s | **SN** | P | *SN* | SU | 78527 | 77127 | 78927 | 78727 |
| 377 128 | s | **SN** | P | *SN* | SU | 78528 | 77128 | 78928 | 78728 |
| 377 129 | s | **SN** | P | *SN* | SU | 78529 | 77129 | 78929 | 78729 |
| 377 130 | s | **SN** | P | *SN* | SU | 78530 | 77130 | 78930 | 78730 |
| 377 131 | s | **SN** | P | *SN* | SU | 78531 | 77131 | 78931 | 78731 |
| 377 132 | s | **SN** | P | *SN* | SU | 78532 | 77132 | 78932 | 78732 |
| 377 133 | s | **SN** | P | *SN* | SU | 78533 | 77133 | 78933 | 78733 |
| 377 134 | s | **SN** | P | *SN* | SU | 78534 | 77134 | 78934 | 78734 |
| 377 135 | s | **SN** | P | *SN* | SU | 78535 | 77135 | 78935 | 78735 |
| 377 136 | s | **SN** | P | *SN* | SU | 78536 | 77136 | 78936 | 78736 |
| 377 137 | s | **SN** | P | *SN* | SU | 78537 | 77137 | 78937 | 78737 |
| 377 138 | s | **SN** | P | *SN* | SU | 78538 | 77138 | 78938 | 78738 |
| 377 139 | s | **SN** | P | *SN* | SU | 78539 | 77139 | 78939 | 78739 |
| 377 140 | t | **SN** | P | *SN* | SU | 78540 | 77140 | 78940 | 78740 |

| | | | | | | | | |
|---|---|---|---|---|---|---|---|---|
| 377 141 | t | **SN** | P | *SN* | SU | 78541 | 77141 | 78941 | 78741 |
| 377 142 | t | **SN** | P | *SN* | SU | 78542 | 77142 | 78942 | 78742 |
| 377 143 | t | **SN** | P | *SN* | SU | 78543 | 77143 | 78943 | 78743 |
| 377 144 | t | **SN** | P | *SN* | SU | 78544 | 77144 | 78944 | 78744 |
| 377 145 | t | **SN** | P | *SN* | SU | 78545 | 77145 | 78945 | 78745 |
| 377 146 | t | **SN** | P | *SN* | SU | 78546 | 77146 | 78946 | 78746 |
| 377 147 | t | **SN** | P | *SN* | SU | 78547 | 77147 | 78947 | 78747 |
| 377 148 | t | **SN** | P | *SN* | SU | 78548 | 77148 | 78948 | 78748 |
| 377 149 | t | **SN** | P | *SN* | SU | 78549 | 77149 | 78949 | 78749 |
| 377 150 | t | **SN** | P | *SN* | SU | 78550 | 77150 | 78950 | 78750 |
| 377 151 | t | **SN** | P | *SN* | SU | 78551 | 77151 | 78951 | 78751 |
| 377 152 | t | **SN** | P | *SN* | SU | 78552 | 77152 | 78952 | 78752 |
| 377 153 | t | **SN** | P | *SN* | SU | 78553 | 77153 | 78953 | 78753 |
| 377 154 | t | **SN** | P | *SN* | SU | 78554 | 77154 | 78954 | 78754 |
| 377 155 | t | **SN** | P | *SN* | SU | 78555 | 77155 | 78955 | 78755 |
| 377 156 | t | **SN** | P | *SN* | SU | 78556 | 77156 | 78956 | 78756 |
| 377 157 | t | **SN** | P | *SN* | SU | 78557 | 77157 | 78957 | 78757 |
| 377 158 | t | **SN** | P | *SN* | BI | 78558 | 77158 | 78958 | 78758 |
| 377 159 | t | **SN** | P | *SN* | BI | 78559 | 77159 | 78959 | 78759 |
| 377 160 | t | **SN** | P | *SN* | BI | 78560 | 77160 | 78960 | 78760 |
| 377 161 | t | **SN** | P | *SN* | BI | 78561 | 77161 | 78961 | 78761 |
| 377 162 | t | **SN** | P | *SN* | BI | 78562 | 77162 | 78962 | 78762 |
| 377 163 | t | **SN** | P | *SN* | BI | 78563 | 77163 | 78963 | 78763 |
| 377 164 | t | **SN** | P | *SN* | BI | 78564 | 77164 | 78964 | 78764 |

**Class 377/2.** 25 kV AC/750 V DC. DMCO–MSO–PTSO–DMCO. These dual-voltage units are used on the East Croydon–Milton Keynes cross-London service.
**Seating layout:** 1: 2+2 facing/unidirectional, 2: 2+2 and 3+2 facing/unidirectional (3+2 seating in middle cars only).

**DMCO(A).** Bombardier Derby 2003–2004. 12/48. 44.2 t.
**MSO.** Bombardier Derby 2003–2004. –/69 1T. 39.8 t.
**PTSO.** Bombardier Derby 2003–2004. –/57 1TD 2W. 40.1 t.
**DMCO(B).** Bombardier Derby 2003–2004. 12/48. 44.2 t.

| | | | | | | | | |
|---|---|---|---|---|---|---|---|---|
| 377 201 | **SN** | P | *SN* | BI | 78571 | 77171 | 78971 | 78771 |
| 377 202 | **SN** | P | *SN* | SU | 78572 | 77172 | 78972 | 78772 |
| 377 203 | **SN** | P | *SN* | BI | 78573 | 77173 | 78973 | 78773 |
| 377 204 | **SN** | P | *SN* | BI | 78574 | 77174 | 78974 | 78774 |
| 377 205 | **SN** | P | *SN* | BI | 78575 | 77175 | 78975 | 78775 |
| 377 206 | **SN** | P | *SN* | BI | 78576 | 77176 | 78976 | 78776 |
| 377 207 | **SN** | P | *SN* | BI | 78577 | 77177 | 78977 | 78777 |
| 377 208 | **SN** | P | *SN* | BI | 78578 | 77178 | 78978 | 78778 |
| 377 209 | **SN** | P | *SN* | SU | 78579 | 77179 | 78979 | 78779 |
| 377 210 | **SN** | P | *SN* | SU | 78580 | 77180 | 78980 | 78780 |
| 377 211 | **SN** | P | *SN* | SU | 78581 | 77181 | 78981 | 78781 |
| 377 212 | **SN** | P | *SN* | SU | 78582 | 77182 | 78982 | 78782 |
| 377 213 | **SN** | P | *SN* | SU | 78583 | 77183 | 78983 | 78783 |
| 377 214 | **SN** | P | *SN* | SU | 78584 | 77184 | 78984 | 78784 |
| 377 215 | **SN** | P | *SN* | SU | 78585 | 77185 | 78985 | 78785 |

**Class 377/3.** 750 V DC only. DMCO–TSO–DMCO.
**Seating Layout:** 1: 2+2 facing/unidirectional, 2: 2+2 facing/unidirectional.

**Notes:** Units built as Class 375, but renumbered in the Class 377/3 range when fitted with Dellner couplers.

† Wi-fi high-speed internet connection equipment fitted. Units generally used on Victoria–Brighton fast services.

**DMCO(A).** Bombardier Derby 2001–2002. 12/48. 43.5 t.
**TSO.** Bombardier Derby 2001–2002. –/56 1TD 2W. 35.4 t.
**DMCO(B).** Bombardier Derby 2001–2002. 12/48. 43.5 t.

| | | | | | | | | |
|---|---|---|---|---|---|---|---|---|
| 377 301 | (375 311) | | **SN** | P | *SN* | BI | 68201 | 74801 | 68401 |
| 377 302 | (375 312) | | **SN** | P | *SN* | BI | 68202 | 74802 | 68402 |
| 377 303 | (375 313) | | **SN** | P | *SN* | BI | 68203 | 74803 | 68403 |
| 377 304 | (375 314) | † | **SN** | P | *SN* | BI | 68204 | 74804 | 68404 |
| 377 305 | (375 315) | † | **SN** | P | *SN* | BI | 68205 | 74805 | 68405 |
| 377 306 | (375 316) | | **SN** | P | *SN* | BI | 68206 | 74806 | 68406 |
| 377 307 | (375 317) | | **SN** | P | *SN* | BI | 68207 | 74807 | 68407 |
| 377 308 | (375 318) | | **SN** | P | *SN* | BI | 68208 | 74808 | 68408 |
| 377 309 | (375 319) | | **SN** | P | *SN* | BI | 68209 | 74809 | 68409 |
| 377 310 | (375 320) | | **SN** | P | *SN* | BI | 68210 | 74810 | 68410 |
| 377 311 | (375 321) | | **SN** | P | *SN* | BI | 68211 | 74811 | 68411 |
| 377 312 | (375 322) | | **SN** | P | *SN* | BI | 68212 | 74812 | 68412 |
| 377 313 | (375 323) | † | **SN** | P | *SN* | BI | 68213 | 74813 | 68413 |
| 377 314 | (375 324) | | **SN** | P | *SN* | BI | 68214 | 74814 | 68414 |
| 377 315 | (375 325) | † | **SN** | P | *SN* | BI | 68215 | 74815 | 68415 |
| 377 316 | (375 326) | † | **SN** | P | *SN* | BI | 68216 | 74816 | 68416 |
| 377 317 | (375 327) | † | **SN** | P | *SN* | BI | 68217 | 74817 | 68417 |
| 377 318 | (375 328) | | **SN** | P | *SN* | BI | 68218 | 74818 | 68418 |
| 377 319 | (375 329) | | **SN** | P | *SN* | BI | 68219 | 74819 | 68419 |
| 377 320 | (375 330) | † | **SN** | P | *SN* | BI | 68220 | 74820 | 68420 |
| 377 321 | (375 331) | † | **SN** | P | *SN* | BI | 68221 | 74821 | 68421 |
| 377 322 | (375 332) | † | **SN** | P | *SN* | BI | 68222 | 74822 | 68422 |
| 377 323 | (375 333) | | **SN** | P | *SN* | BI | 68223 | 74823 | 68423 |
| 377 324 | (375 334) | † | **SN** | P | *SN* | BI | 68224 | 74824 | 68424 |
| 377 325 | (375 335) | † | **SN** | P | *SN* | BI | 68225 | 74825 | 68425 |
| 377 326 | (375 336) | † | **SN** | P | *SN* | BI | 68226 | 74826 | 68426 |
| 377 327 | (375 337) | † | **SN** | P | *SN* | BI | 68227 | 74827 | 68427 |
| 377 328 | (375 338) | † | **SN** | P | *SN* | BI | 68228 | 74828 | 68428 |

**Class 377/4.** 750 V DC only. DMCO–MSO–TSO–DMCO.
**Seating Layout:** 1: 2+2 facing/two seats longitudinal, 2: 2+2 and 3+2 facing/unidirectional (3+2 seating in middle cars only).

**DMCO(A).** Bombardier Derby 2004–2005. 10/48. 43.1 t.
**MSO.** Bombardier Derby 2004–2005. –/69 1T. 39.3 t.
**TSO.** Bombardier Derby 2004–2005. –/56 1TD 2W. 35.3 t.
**DMCO(B).** Bombardier Derby 2004–2005. 10/48. 43.1 t.

| | | | | | | | | |
|---|---|---|---|---|---|---|---|---|
| 377 401 | **SN** | P | *SN* | BI | 73401 | 78801 | 78601 | 73801 |
| 377 402 | **SN** | P | *SN* | BI | 73402 | 78802 | 78602 | 73802 |
| 377 403 | **SN** | P | *SN* | BI | 73403 | 78803 | 78603 | 73803 |

| | | | | | | | | |
|---|---|---|---|---|---|---|---|---|
| 377 404 | SN | P | SN | BI | 73404 | 78804 | 78604 | 73804 |
| 377 405 | SN | P | SN | BI | 73405 | 78805 | 78605 | 73805 |
| 377 406 | SN | P | SN | BI | 73406 | 78806 | 78606 | 73806 |
| 377 407 | SN | P | SN | BI | 73407 | 78807 | 78607 | 73807 |
| 377 408 | SN | P | SN | BI | 73408 | 78808 | 78608 | 73808 |
| 377 409 | SN | P | SN | BI | 73409 | 78809 | 78609 | 73809 |
| 377 410 | SN | P | SN | BI | 73410 | 78810 | 78610 | 73810 |
| 377 411 | SN | P | SN | BI | 73411 | 78811 | 78611 | 73811 |
| 377 412 | SN | P | SN | BI | 73412 | 78812 | 78612 | 73812 |
| 377 413 | SN | P | SN | BI | 73413 | 78813 | 78613 | 73813 |
| 377 414 | SN | P | SN | BI | 73414 | 78814 | 78614 | 73814 |
| 377 415 | SN | P | SN | BI | 73415 | 78815 | 78615 | 73815 |
| 377 416 | SN | P | SN | BI | 73416 | 78816 | 78616 | 73816 |
| 377 417 | SN | P | SN | BI | 73417 | 78817 | 78617 | 73817 |
| 377 418 | SN | P | SN | BI | 73418 | 78818 | 78618 | 73818 |
| 377 419 | SN | P | SN | BI | 73419 | 78819 | 78619 | 73819 |
| 377 420 | SN | P | SN | BI | 73420 | 78820 | 78620 | 73820 |
| 377 421 | SN | P | SN | BI | 73421 | 78821 | 78621 | 73821 |
| 377 422 | SN | P | SN | BI | 73422 | 78822 | 78622 | 73822 |
| 377 423 | SN | P | SN | BI | 73423 | 78823 | 78623 | 73823 |
| 377 424 | SN | P | SN | BI | 73424 | 78824 | 78624 | 73824 |
| 377 425 | SN | P | SN | BI | 73425 | 78825 | 78625 | 73825 |
| 377 426 | SN | P | SN | BI | 73426 | 78826 | 78626 | 73826 |
| 377 427 | SN | P | SN | BI | 73427 | 78827 | 78627 | 73827 |
| 377 428 | SN | P | SN | BI | 73428 | 78828 | 78628 | 73828 |
| 377 429 | SN | P | SN | BI | 73429 | 78829 | 78629 | 73829 |
| 377 430 | SN | P | SN | BI | 73430 | 78830 | 78630 | 73830 |
| 377 431 | SN | P | SN | BI | 73431 | 78831 | 78631 | 73831 |
| 377 432 | SN | P | SN | BI | 73432 | 78832 | 78632 | 73832 |
| 377 433 | SN | P | SN | BI | 73433 | 78833 | 78633 | 73833 |
| 377 434 | SN | P | SN | BI | 73434 | 78834 | 78634 | 73834 |
| 377 435 | SN | P | SN | BI | 73435 | 78835 | 78635 | 73835 |
| 377 436 | SN | P | SN | BI | 73436 | 78836 | 78636 | 73836 |
| 377 437 | SN | P | SN | BI | 73437 | 78837 | 78637 | 73837 |
| 377 438 | SN | P | SN | BI | 73438 | 78838 | 78638 | 73838 |
| 377 439 | SN | P | SN | BI | 73439 | 78839 | 78639 | 73839 |
| 377 440 | SN | P | SN | BI | 73440 | 78840 | 78640 | 73840 |
| 377 441 | SN | P | SN | BI | 73441 | 78841 | 78641 | 73841 |
| 377 442 | SN | P | SN | BI | 73442 | 78842 | 78642 | 73842 |
| 377 443 | SN | P | SN | BI | 73443 | 78843 | 78643 | 73843 |
| 377 444 | SN | P | SN | BI | 73444 | 78844 | 78644 | 73844 |
| 377 445 | SN | P | SN | BI | 73445 | 78845 | 78645 | 73845 |
| 377 446 | SN | P | SN | BI | 73446 | 78846 | 78646 | 73846 |
| 377 447 | SN | P | SN | BI | 73447 | 78847 | 78647 | 73847 |
| 377 448 | SN | P | SN | BI | 73448 | 78848 | 78648 | 73848 |
| 377 449 | SN | P | SN | BI | 73449 | 78849 | 78649 | 73849 |
| 377 450 | SN | P | SN | BI | 73450 | 78850 | 78650 | 73850 |
| 377 451 | SN | P | SN | BI | 73451 | 78851 | 78651 | 73851 |
| 377 452 | SN | P | SN | BI | 73452 | 78852 | 78652 | 73852 |
| 377 453 | SN | P | SN | BI | 73453 | 78853 | 78653 | 73853 |
| 377 454 | SN | P | SN | BI | 73454 | 78854 | 78654 | 73854 |

| 377 455 | SN | P | SN | Bl | 73455 | 78855 | 78655 | 73855 | |
| 377 456 | SN | P | SN | Bl | 73456 | 78856 | 78656 | 73856 | |
| 377 457 | SN | P | SN | Bl | 73457 | 78857 | 78657 | 73857 | |
| 377 458 | SN | P | SN | Bl | 73458 | 78858 | 78658 | 73858 | |
| 377 459 | SN | P | SN | Bl | 73459 | 78859 | 78659 | 73859 | |
| 377 460 | SN | P | SN | Bl | 73460 | 78860 | 78660 | 73860 | |
| 377 461 | SN | P | SN | Bl | 73461 | 78861 | 78661 | 73861 | |
| 377 462 | SN | P | SN | Bl | 73462 | 78862 | 78662 | 73862 | |
| 377 463 | SN | P | SN | Bl | 73463 | 78863 | 78663 | 73863 | |
| 377 464 | SN | P | SN | Bl | 73464 | 78864 | 78664 | 73864 | |
| 377 465 | SN | P | SN | Bl | 73465 | 78865 | 78665 | 73865 | |
| 377 466 | SN | P | SN | Bl | 73466 | 78866 | 78666 | 73866 | |
| 377 467 | SN | P | SN | Bl | 73467 | 78867 | 78667 | 73867 | |
| 377 468 | SN | P | SN | Bl | 73468 | 78868 | 78668 | 73868 | |
| 377 469 | SN | P | SN | Bl | 73469 | 78869 | 78669 | 73869 | |
| 327 470 | SN | P | SN | Bl | 73470 | 78870 | 78670 | 73870 | |
| 377 471 | SN | P | SN | Bl | 73471 | 78871 | 78671 | 73871 | |
| 377 472 | SN | P | SN | Bl | 73472 | 78872 | 78672 | 73872 | |
| 377 473 | SN | P | SN | Bl | 73473 | 78873 | 78673 | 73873 | |
| 377 474 | SN | P | SN | Bl | 73474 | 78874 | 78674 | 73874 | |
| 327 475 | SN | P | SN | Bl | 73475 | 78875 | 78675 | 73875 | |

**Class 377/5.** 25 kV AC/750 V DC. DMCO–MSO–PTSO–DMCO. Under construction. Dual voltage units for First Capital Connect (to be sub-leased from Southern). Full details awaited.

**DMCO(A).** Bombardier Derby 2008–2009.                     .     t.
**MSO.** Bombardier Derby 2008–2009.                     .     t.
**PTSO.** Bombardier Derby 2008–2009.                     .     t.
**DMCO(B).** Bombardier Derby 2008–2009.                     .     t.

| 377 501 | FU | P | | 73501 | 75901 | 74901 | 73601 | |
| 377 502 | FU | P | | 73502 | 75902 | 74902 | 73602 | |
| 377 503 | FU | P | | 73503 | 75903 | 74903 | 73603 | |
| 377 504 | FU | P | | 73504 | 75904 | 74904 | 73604 | |
| 377 505 | FU | P | | 73505 | 75905 | 74905 | 73605 | |
| 377 506 | FU | P | | 73506 | 75906 | 74906 | 73606 | |
| 377 507 | FU | P | | 73507 | 75907 | 74907 | 73607 | |
| 377 508 | FU | P | | 73508 | 75908 | 74908 | 73608 | |
| 377 509 | FU | P | | 73509 | 75909 | 74909 | 73609 | |
| 377 510 | FU | P | | 73510 | 75910 | 74910 | 73610 | |
| 377 511 | FU | P | | 73511 | 75911 | 74911 | 73611 | |
| 377 512 | FU | P | | 73512 | 75912 | 74912 | 73612 | |
| 377 513 | FU | | | 73513 | 75913 | 74913 | 73613 | |
| 377 514 | FU | | | 73514 | 75914 | 74914 | 73614 | |
| 377 515 | FU | | | 73515 | 75915 | 74915 | 73615 | |
| 377 516 | FU | | | 73516 | 75916 | 74916 | 73616 | |
| 377 517 | FU | | | 73517 | 75917 | 74917 | 73617 | |
| 377 518 | FU | | | 73518 | 75918 | 74918 | 73618 | |
| 377 519 | FU | | | 73519 | 75919 | 74919 | 73619 | |
| 377 520 | FU | | | 73520 | 75920 | 74920 | 73620 | |
| 377 521 | FU | | | 73521 | 75921 | 74921 | 73621 | |

| 377 522 | **FU** | 73522 | 75922 | 74922 | 73622 |
|---------|--------|-------|-------|-------|-------|
| 377 523 | **FU** | 73523 | 75923 | 74923 | 73623 |

# CLASS 378 CAPITALSTAR BOMBARDIER DERBY

54 new Class 378 suburban Electrostars (designated "Capitalstars" by TfL) are under construction at Derby for the London Overground network. The first is due to enter traffic in early 2009.

**Formation:** DMSO–(MSO)–PTSO–DMSO or DMSO–MSO–TSO–DMSO.
**System:** Class 378/0 and Class 378/2 25 kV AC overhead and 750 V DC third rail. Class 378/1 750 V DC third rail only.
**Construction:** Welded aluminium alloy underframe, sides and roof with steel ends. All sections bolted together.
**Traction Motors:** Two Bombardier asynchronous of 250 kW.
**Wheel Arrangement:**
**Braking:** Disc & regenerative.              **Dimensions:** 20.46/20.14 x 2.80 m.
**Bogies:** Bombardier P3-25/T3-25.            **Couplers:** Dellner 12.
**Gangways:** Within unit + end doors.         **Control System:** IGBT Inverter.
**Doors:** Sliding.                            **Maximum Speed:** 75 m.p.h.
**Heating & ventilation:** Air conditioning.
**Seating Layout:** Longitudinal ("tube style") low density.
**Multiple Working:** Within class and with Classes 375, 376 and 377.

**DMSO(A).** Bombardier Derby 2008–2010. –/36. 43.2 t.
**MSO.** Bombardier Derby 2008–2010. –/40. 39.0 t.
**PTSO/TSO.** Bombardier Derby 2008–2010. –/34(6) 2W. . t.
**DMSO(B).** Bombardier Derby 2008–2010. –/36. 42.8 t.

**Class 378/0.** 25 kV AC/750 V DC. DMSO–PTSO–DMSO. Initial order of 24 3-car sets for North London Railway services. These units will be renumbered in the 378 2xx series when extra (MSO) vehicles are added in 2010.

| 378 001 | **LO** | QW | 38001 | 38301 | 38101 |
|---------|--------|----|-------|-------|-------|
| 378 002 | **LO** | QW | 38002 | 38302 | 38102 |
| 378 003 | **LO** | QW | 38003 | 38303 | 38103 |
| 378 004 | **LO** | QW | 38004 | 38304 | 38104 |
| 378 005 | **LO** | QW | 38005 | 38305 | 38105 |
| 378 006 | **LO** | QW | 38006 | 38306 | 38106 |
| 378 007 | **LO** | QW | 38007 | 38307 | 38107 |
| 378 008 | **LO** | QW | 38008 | 38308 | 38108 |
| 378 009 | **LO** | QW | 38009 | 38309 | 38109 |
| 378 010 | **LO** | QW | 38010 | 38310 | 38110 |
| 378 011 | **LO** | QW | 38011 | 38311 | 38111 |
| 378 012 | **LO** | QW | 38012 | 38312 | 38112 |
| 378 013 | **LO** | QW | 38013 | 38313 | 38113 |
| 378 014 | **LO** | QW | 38014 | 38314 | 38114 |
| 378 015 | **LO** | QW | 38015 | 38315 | 38115 |
| 378 016 | **LO** | QW | 38016 | 38316 | 38116 |
| 378 017 | **LO** | QW | 38017 | 38317 | 38117 |
| 378 018 | **LO** | QW | 38018 | 38318 | 38118 |
| 378 019 | **LO** | QW | 38019 | 38319 | 38119 |

| 378 020 | LO | QW | 38020 | | 38320 | 38120 |
|---------|----|----|-------|--|-------|-------|
| 378 021 | LO | QW | 38021 | | 38321 | 38121 |
| 378 022 | LO | QW | 38022 | | 38322 | 38122 |
| 378 023 | LO | QW | 38023 | | 38323 | 38123 |
| 378 024 | LO | QW | 38024 | | 38324 | 38124 |

**Class 378/1.** 750 V DC. DMSO–MSO–TSO–DMSO. Third rail only units for East London Railway services from 2010. Provision for retro-fitting as dual voltage if required.

| 378 135 | LO | QW | 38035 | 38235 | 38335 | 38135 |
|---------|----|----|-------|-------|-------|-------|
| 378 136 | LO | QW | 38036 | 38236 | 38336 | 38136 |
| 378 137 | LO | QW | 38037 | 38237 | 38337 | 38137 |
| 378 138 | LO | QW | 38038 | 38238 | 38338 | 38138 |
| 378 139 | LO | QW | 38039 | 38239 | 38339 | 38139 |
| 378 140 | LO | QW | 38040 | 38240 | 38340 | 38140 |
| 378 141 | LO | QW | 38041 | 38241 | 38341 | 38141 |
| 378 142 | LO | QW | 38042 | 38242 | 38342 | 38142 |
| 378 143 | LO | QW | 38043 | 38243 | 38343 | 38143 |
| 378 144 | LO | QW | 38044 | 38244 | 38344 | 38144 |
| 378 145 | LO | QW | 38045 | 38245 | 38345 | 38145 |
| 378 146 | LO | QW | 38046 | 38246 | 38346 | 38146 |
| 378 147 | LO | QW | 38047 | 38247 | 38347 | 38147 |
| 378 148 | LO | QW | 38048 | 38248 | 38348 | 38148 |
| 378 149 | LO | QW | 38049 | 38249 | 38349 | 38149 |
| 378 150 | LO | QW | 38050 | 38250 | 38350 | 38150 |
| 378 151 | LO | QW | 38051 | 38251 | 38351 | 38151 |
| 378 152 | LO | QW | 38052 | 38252 | 38352 | 38152 |
| 378 153 | LO | QW | 38053 | 38253 | 38353 | 38153 |
| 378 154 | LO | QW | 38054 | 38254 | 38354 | 38154 |

**Class 378/2.** 25 kV AC/750 V DC. DMSO–MSO–PTSO–DMSO. Extra ten 4-car dual voltage units for NLL or ELL services. Note that 378 001–024 will be renumbered into the 378 2xx series in 2010 (by addition of 200 to their original numbers) when they receive their extra MSO vehicles.

| 378 225 | LO | QW | 38025 | 38225 | 38325 | 38125 |
|---------|----|----|-------|-------|-------|-------|
| 378 226 | LO | QW | 38026 | 38226 | 38326 | 38126 |
| 378 227 | LO | QW | 38027 | 38227 | 38327 | 38127 |
| 378 228 | LO | QW | 38028 | 38228 | 38328 | 38128 |
| 378 229 | LO | QW | 38029 | 38229 | 38329 | 38129 |
| 378 230 | LO | QW | 38030 | 38230 | 38330 | 38130 |
| 378 231 | LO | QW | 38031 | 38231 | 38331 | 38131 |
| 378 232 | LO | QW | 38032 | 38232 | 38332 | 38132 |
| 378 233 | LO | QW | 38033 | 38233 | 38333 | 38133 |
| 378 234 | LO | QW | 38034 | 38234 | 38334 | 38134 |

## CLASS 380    DESIRO UK    SIEMENS

38 new Class 380 EMUs are on order for the First ScotRail franchise (Strathclyde area services), with the first due to be delivered in spring 2010. There be 22 3-car units (380 001–022) and 16 4-car units (380 101–116) but the vehicle numbers had yet to be confirmed at the time of writing.

## CLASS 390    PENDOLINO    ALSTOM BIRMINGHAM

Tilting WCML units.

**Formation:** DMRFO–MFO–PTFO–MFO–TSO–MSO–PTSRMB–MSO–DMSO.
**Construction:** Welded aluminium alloy.
**Traction Motors:** Two Alstom ONIX 800 of 425 kW.
**Wheel Arrangement:** 1A-A1 + 1A-A1 + 2-2 + 1A-A1 + 2-2 + 1A-A1 + 2-2 + 1A-A1 + 1A-A1.
**Braking:** Disc, rheostatic & regenerative.
**Dimensions:** 24.80/23.90 x 2.73 m.
**Bogies:** Fiat-SIG.                     **Couplers:** Dellner 12.
**Gangways:** Within unit.               **Control System:** IGBT Inverter.
**Doors:** Sliding plug.                 **Maximum Speed:** 125 m.p.h.
**Heating & ventilation:** Air conditioning.
**Seating Layout:** 1: 2+1 facing/unidirectional, 2: 2+2 facing/unidirectional.
**Multiple Working:** Within class. Can also be controlled from Class 57/3 locos.

**DMRFO:** Alstom Birmingham 2001–2005. 18/–. 55.6 t.
**MFO(A):** Alstom Birmingham 2001–2005. 37/–(2) 1TD 1W. 52.0 t.
**PTFO:** Alstom Birmingham 2001–2005. 44/– 1T. 50.1 t.
**MFO(B):** Alstom Birmingham 2001–2005. 46/– 1T. 51.8 t.
**TSO:** Alstom Birmingham 2001–2005. –/76 1T. 45.5 t.
**MSO(A):** Alstom Birmingham 2001–2005. –/62(4) 1TD 1W. 50.0 t.
**PTSRMB:** Alstom Birmingham 2001–2005. –/48. 52.0 t.
**MSO(B):** Alstom Birmingham 2001–2005. –/62(2) 1TD 1W. 51.7 t.
**DMSO:** Alstom Birmingham 2001–2005. –/46 1T. 51.0 t.

**Notes:** Units up to 390 034 were delivered as 8-car sets, without the TSO (688xx). During 2004 and early 2005 these units had their 9th cars added.

390 033 was written off following accident damage in the Lambrigg accident of February 2007. It has been sold to Virgin and is now shown in the "EMUs awaiting disposal" section of this book.

| 390 001 | **VT** | A | *VW* | MA | 69101 | 69401 | 69501 | 69601 | 68801 |
|---------|--------|---|------|----|-------|-------|-------|-------|-------|
|         |        |   |      |    | 69701 | 69801 | 69901 | 69201 |       |
| 390 002 | **VT** | A | *VW* | MA | 69102 | 69402 | 69502 | 69602 | 68802 |
|         |        |   |      |    | 69702 | 69802 | 69902 | 69202 |       |
| 390 003 | **VT** | A | *VW* | MA | 69103 | 69403 | 69503 | 69603 | 68803 |
|         |        |   |      |    | 69703 | 69803 | 69903 | 69203 |       |
| 390 004 | **VT** | A | *VW* | MA | 69104 | 69404 | 69504 | 69604 | 68804 |
|         |        |   |      |    | 69704 | 69804 | 69904 | 69204 |       |
| 390 005 | **VT** | A | *VW* | MA | 69105 | 69405 | 69505 | 69605 | 68805 |
|         |        |   |      |    | 69705 | 69805 | 69905 | 69205 |       |

| | | | | | | | | | |
|---|---|---|---|---|---|---|---|---|---|
| 390 006 | **VT** | A | *VW* | MA | 69106 | 69406 | 69506 | 69606 | 68806 |
| | | | | | 69706 | 69806 | 69906 | 69206 | |
| 390 007 | **VT** | A | *VW* | MA | 69107 | 69407 | 69507 | 69607 | 68807 |
| | | | | | 69707 | 69807 | 69907 | 69207 | |
| 390 008 | **VT** | A | *VW* | MA | 69108 | 69408 | 69508 | 69608 | 68808 |
| | | | | | 69708 | 69808 | 69908 | 69208 | |
| 390 009 | **VT** | A | *VW* | MA | 69109 | 69409 | 69509 | 69609 | 68809 |
| | | | | | 69709 | 69809 | 69909 | 69209 | |
| 390 010 | **VT** | A | *VW* | MA | 69110 | 69410 | 69510 | 69610 | 68810 |
| | | | | | 69710 | 69810 | 69910 | 69210 | |
| 390 011 | **VT** | A | *VW* | MA | 69111 | 69411 | 69511 | 69611 | 68811 |
| | | | | | 69711 | 69811 | 69911 | 69211 | |
| 390 012 | **VT** | A | *VW* | MA | 69112 | 69412 | 69512 | 69612 | 68812 |
| | | | | | 69712 | 69812 | 69912 | 69212 | |
| 390 013 | **VT** | A | *VW* | MA | 69113 | 69413 | 69513 | 69613 | 68813 |
| | | | | | 69713 | 69813 | 69913 | 69213 | |
| 390 014 | **VT** | A | *VW* | MA | 69114 | 69414 | 69514 | 69614 | 68814 |
| | | | | | 69714 | 69814 | 69914 | 69214 | |
| 390 015 | **VT** | A | *VW* | MA | 69115 | 69415 | 69515 | 69615 | 68815 |
| | | | | | 69715 | 69815 | 69915 | 69215 | |
| 390 016 | **VT** | A | *VW* | MA | 69116 | 69416 | 69516 | 69616 | 68816 |
| | | | | | 69716 | 69816 | 69916 | 69216 | |
| 390 017 | **VT** | A | *VW* | MA | 69117 | 69417 | 69517 | 69617 | 68817 |
| | | | | | 69717 | 69817 | 69917 | 69217 | |
| 390 018 | **VT** | A | *VW* | MA | 69118 | 69418 | 69518 | 69618 | 68818 |
| | | | | | 69718 | 69818 | 69918 | 69218 | |
| 390 019 | **VT** | A | *VW* | MA | 69119 | 69419 | 69519 | 69619 | 68819 |
| | | | | | 69719 | 69819 | 69919 | 69219 | |
| 390 020 | **VT** | A | *VW* | MA | 69120 | 69420 | 69520 | 69620 | 68820 |
| | | | | | 69720 | 69820 | 69920 | 69220 | |
| 390 021 | **VT** | A | *VW* | MA | 69121 | 69421 | 69521 | 69621 | 68821 |
| | | | | | 69721 | 69821 | 69921 | 69221 | |
| 390 022 | **VT** | A | *VW* | MA | 69122 | 69422 | 69522 | 69622 | 68822 |
| | | | | | 69722 | 69822 | 69922 | 69222 | |
| 390 023 | **VT** | A | *VW* | MA | 69123 | 69423 | 69523 | 69623 | 68823 |
| | | | | | 69723 | 69823 | 69923 | 69223 | |
| 390 024 | **VT** | A | *VW* | MA | 69124 | 69424 | 69524 | 69624 | 68824 |
| | | | | | 69724 | 69824 | 69924 | 69224 | |
| 390 025 | **VT** | A | *VW* | MA | 69125 | 69425 | 69525 | 69625 | 68825 |
| | | | | | 69725 | 69825 | 69925 | 69225 | |
| 390 026 | **VT** | A | *VW* | MA | 69126 | 69426 | 69526 | 69626 | 68826 |
| | | | | | 69726 | 69826 | 69926 | 69226 | |
| 390 027 | **VT** | A | *VW* | MA | 69127 | 69427 | 69527 | 69627 | 68827 |
| | | | | | 69727 | 69827 | 69927 | 69227 | |
| 390 028 | **VT** | A | *VW* | MA | 69128 | 69428 | 69528 | 69628 | 68828 |
| | | | | | 69728 | 69828 | 69928 | 69228 | |
| 390 029 | **VT** | A | *VW* | MA | 69129 | 69429 | 69529 | 69629 | 68829 |
| | | | | | 69729 | 69829 | 69929 | 69229 | |
| 390 030 | **VT** | A | *VW* | MA | 69130 | 69430 | 69530 | 69630 | 68830 |
| | | | | | 69730 | 69830 | 69930 | 69230 | |

▲ Strathclyde PTE-liveried 314 209 is seen between Neilston and Patterton with the 09.41 Neilston–Glasgow Central on 04/08/08. **Robin Ralston**

▼ National Express-liveried 317 506 passes Pudding Mill Lane (DLR) with an e.c.s. from Ilford to London Liverpool Street on 27/02/08 as part of the relaunch of the franchise as National Express East Anglia (from "One"). **Robert Pritchard**

▲ Strathclyde PTE-liveried 318 262 passes Lanark Junction with the 10.42 Milngavie–Lanark on 10/10/07. **Robin Ralston**

▼ First Group "Urban Lights"-liveried 319 443 leads an 8-car formation near Redhill with the 07.26 Bedford–Brighton on 15/04/08. **Alex Dasi-Sutton**

▲ In the new West Yorkshire PTE/Northern EMU livery, 321 903 arrives at Doncaster with the 16.19 from Leeds on 26/09/07. **Robert Pritchard**

▼ The only Northern-liveried Class 323 at the time of going to press, 323 223, is seen near Longport with the 15.02 (SuO) Manchester Piccadilly–Stoke-on-Trent on 15/06/08. **Cliff Beeton**

▲ Royal Mail-liveried 325 003 leads a 12-car formation on 1M44 15.47 Shieldmuir–Willesden Mail at Shapbeck on 21/07/08.　　**Gavin Morrison**

▼ Carrying the original West Yorkshire Class 333 livery, 333 010 is seen near Keighley with the 09.02 Skipton–Bradford Forster Square on 25/06/08. These units are currently being reliveried in the new (321/9 style) livery.　　**Andrew Wills**

▲ Strathclyde PTE Carmine & Cream-liveried 334 021 "Larkhall" arrives at Wemyss Bay with the 09.50 from Glasgow Central on 05/04/08.　**Ian Lothian**

▼ All Class 350s are now in London Midland livery. On 10/06/08 350 115 passes Millmeece on the WCML with the 15.51 Birmingham NS–Liverpool.　**Andrew Mist**

▲ Carrying a special "green" livery to mark c2c's use of regenerative braking on its Class 357 fleet, 357 010 passes Leigh-on-Sea with a Shoeburyness–London Fenchurch Street service on 07/05/08. **Charlie Robbins**

▼ Most of the NXEA Class 360s carry all over First Group blue livery at the time of writing. On 27/02/08 360 108 and 360 109 leave Stratford with the 09.50 Clacton-on-Sea–London Liverpool Street. **Robert Pritchard**

▲ First Group "Urban Lights"-liveried 365 536 at Hitchin with the 08.52 London King's Cross–Cambridge on 26/04/08.　　**Mark Beal**

▼ Carrying a slightly revised Southeastern livery, with blue instead of yellow doors, 375 624 leads an 8-car formation near Paddock Wood with the 12.14/12.43 Ramsgate–London Charing Cross on 05/07/08.　　**Alex Dasi-Sutton**

▲ Southeastern's 376 004 is seen near Hither Green with the 10.48 London Cannon Street–Cannon Street via Sidcup on 01/03/08.  **Alex Dasi-Sutton**

▼ Southern-liveried 377 472 passes Arundel Junction with the 10.20 Southampton Central–London Victoria on 07/12/07.  **Chris Wilson**

▲ The first London Overground Class 378 "Capitalstar", 378 001, is seen on the Derby Works test track on 16/09/08. This unit will initially enter traffic in early 2009 as a 3-car unit, but will be strengthened to 4-car formation in 2010 and renumbered 378 201. **Robert Pritchard**

▼ Virgin Pendolino 390 010 "A Decade of Progress" passes Cartland with the 09.39 Glasgow Central–London Euston on 24/03/08. **Ian Lothian**

▲ The first of the new Hitachi Class 395s, 395 001, for Southeastern high speed services is seen at the new Ashford depot on 02/10/07. **Robert Pritchard**

▼ BR Green-liveried 3 Cig 1498 is propelled by 73109 on the 08.59 Brockenhurst–Lymington Pier on the Lymington branch on 12/07/08. The 73 was in use as part of the line's 150th anniversary celebrations. **Paul Waring**

▲ Stagecoach-liveried 444 036 passes Eastleigh with the 09.39 London Waterloo–Poole on 12/02/08. **Andrew Mist**

▼ South West Trains blue-liveried 450 106 leads an 8-car formation at Peasmarsh, south of Guildford, forming the 11.30 London Waterloo–Portsmouth Harbour on 03/05/08. **Chris Wilson**

▲ Southern-liveried 455 804 arrives at Streatham Common with the 14.45 London Victoria–Caterham on 31/03/07. **Mark Beal**

▼ Southern-liveried 456 014 and 456 010 arrive at Wandsworth Road with the 11.41 London Victoria–London Bridge on 03/11/07. **Alex Dasi-Sutton**

▲ Stagecoach-liveried Class 458s 8001 and 8024 approach Twickenham with the 09.12 Reading–London Waterloo on 02/02/08. **Chris Wilson**

▼ Gatwick Express services are now operated by Southern. On 04/04/08 460 007 and 460 002 cross at Purley Oaks with Victoria/Gatwick-bound services.
**Alex Dasi-Sutton**

▲ Southeastern-liveried 465 243 approaches Swanley with a London Charing Cross–Sevenoaks service on 06/11/07. **Chris Wilson**

▼ Former London Underground tube stock continues to work services on the Isle of Wight. London Transport Maroon-liveried 008 and 004 pause at Sandown with the 16.49 Ryde Pier Head–Shanklin on 28/07/08. **Jason Cross**

▲ Merseyrail-liveried 508 126 arrives at West Kirby with the 16.40 from Liverpool Central on 06/06/08. **Robert Pritchard**

▼ Southeastern-liveried 508 208 calls at Redhill with the 16.57 London Bridge–Tonbridge on 04/06/08. **Alex Dasi-Sutton**

▲ Carrying the new Midland Metro/Network West Midlands pink/grey livery, 09 "JEFF ASTLE" pauses at Soho Benson Road with a Wolverhampton St. Georges–Birmingham Snow Hill service on 02/08/07. **Mike Miller**

▼ Croydon Tramlink 2550 is seen near the Lebanon Road stop with a West Croydon service on 03/09/06. **Robert Pritchard**

| | | | | | | | | | |
|---|---|---|---|---|---|---|---|---|---|
| 390 031 | **VT** | A | *VW* | MA | 69131 | 69431 | 69531 | 69631 | 68831 |
| | | | | | 69731 | 69831 | 69931 | 69231 | |
| 390 032 | **VT** | A | *VW* | MA | 69132 | 69432 | 69532 | 69632 | 68832 |
| | | | | | 69732 | 69832 | 69932 | 69232 | |
| 390 034 | **VT** | A | *VW* | MA | 69134 | 69434 | 69534 | 69634 | 68834 |
| | | | | | 69734 | 69834 | 69934 | 69234 | |
| 390 035 | **VT** | A | *VW* | MA | 69135 | 69435 | 69535 | 69635 | 68835 |
| | | | | | 69735 | 69835 | 69935 | 69235 | |
| 390 036 | **VT** | A | *VW* | MA | 69136 | 69436 | 69536 | 69636 | 68836 |
| | | | | | 69736 | 69836 | 69936 | 69236 | |
| 390 037 | **VT** | A | *VW* | MA | 69137 | 69437 | 69537 | 69637 | 68837 |
| | | | | | 69737 | 69837 | 69937 | 69237 | |
| 390 038 | **VT** | A | *VW* | MA | 69138 | 69438 | 69538 | 69638 | 68838 |
| | | | | | 69738 | 69838 | 69938 | 69238 | |
| 390 039 | **VT** | A | *VW* | MA | 69139 | 69439 | 69539 | 69639 | 68839 |
| | | | | | 69739 | 69839 | 69939 | 69239 | |
| 390 040 | **VT** | A | *VW* | MA | 69140 | 69440 | 69540 | 69640 | 68840 |
| | | | | | 69740 | 69840 | 69940 | 69240 | |
| 390 041 | **VT** | A | *VW* | MA | 69141 | 69441 | 69541 | 69641 | 68841 |
| | | | | | 69741 | 69841 | 69941 | 69241 | |
| 390 042 | **VT** | A | *VW* | MA | 69142 | 69442 | 69542 | 69642 | 68842 |
| | | | | | 69742 | 69842 | 69942 | 69242 | |
| 390 043 | **VT** | A | *VW* | MA | 69143 | 69443 | 69543 | 69643 | 68843 |
| | | | | | 69743 | 69843 | 69943 | 69243 | |
| 390 044 | **VT** | A | *VW* | MA | 69144 | 69444 | 69544 | 69644 | 68844 |
| | | | | | 69744 | 69844 | 69944 | 69244 | |
| 390 045 | **VT** | A | *VW* | MA | 69145 | 69445 | 69545 | 69645 | 68845 |
| | | | | | 69745 | 69845 | 69945 | 69245 | |
| 390 046 | **VT** | A | *VW* | MA | 69146 | 69446 | 69546 | 69646 | 68846 |
| | | | | | 69746 | 69846 | 69946 | 69246 | |
| 390 047 | **VT** | A | *VW* | MA | 69147 | 69447 | 69547 | 69647 | 68847 |
| | | | | | 69747 | 69847 | 69947 | 69247 | |
| 390 048 | **VT** | A | *VW* | MA | 69148 | 69448 | 69548 | 69648 | 68848 |
| | | | | | 69748 | 69848 | 69948 | 69248 | |
| 390 049 | **VT** | A | *VW* | MA | 69149 | 69449 | 69549 | 69649 | 68849 |
| | | | | | 69749 | 69849 | 69949 | 69249 | |
| 390 050 | **VT** | A | *VW* | MA | 69150 | 69450 | 69550 | 69650 | 68850 |
| | | | | | 69750 | 69850 | 69950 | 69250 | |
| 390 051 | **VT** | A | *VW* | MA | 69151 | 69451 | 69551 | 69651 | 68851 |
| | | | | | 69751 | 69851 | 69951 | 69251 | |
| 390 052 | **VT** | A | *VW* | MA | 69152 | 69452 | 69552 | 69652 | 68852 |
| | | | | | 69752 | 69852 | 69952 | 69252 | |
| 390 053 | **VT** | A | *VW* | MA | 69153 | 69453 | 69553 | 69653 | 68853 |
| | | | | | 69753 | 69853 | 69953 | 69253 | |

**Names (carried on MFO No. 696xx):**

| | | | |
|---|---|---|---|
| 390 001 | Virgin Pioneer | 390 027 | Virgin Buccaneer |
| 390 002 | Virgin Angel | 390 028 | City of Preston |
| 390 003 | Virgin Hero | 390 029 | City of Stoke-on-Trent |
| 390 004 | Virgin Scot | 390 030 | City of Edinburgh |
| 390 005 | City of Wolverhampton | 390 031 | City of Liverpool |
| 390 006 | Tate Liverpool | 390 032 | City of Birmingham |
| 390 007 | Virgin Lady | 390 034 | City of Carlisle |
| 390 008 | Virgin King | 390 035 | City of Lancaster |
| 390 009 | Treaty of Union | 390 036 | City of Coventry |
| 390 010 | A Decade of Progress | 390 037 | Virgin Difference |
| 390 011 | City of Lichfield | 390 038 | City of London |
| 390 012 | Virgin Star | 390 039 | Virgin Quest |
| 390 013 | Virgin Spirit | 390 040 | Virgin Pathfinder |
| 390 014 | City of Manchester | 390 041 | City of Chester |
| 390 015 | Virgin Crusader | 390 042 | City of Bangor/Dinas Bangor |
| 390 016 | Virgin Champion | 390 043 | Virgin Explorer |
| 390 017 | Virgin Prince | 390 044 | Virgin Lionheart |
| 390 018 | Virgin Princess | 390 045 | 101 Squadron |
| 390 019 | Virgin Warrior | 390 046 | Virgin Soldiers |
| 390 020 | Virgin Cavalier | 390 047 | Heaven's Angels |
| 390 021 | Virgin Dream | 390 048 | Virgin Harrier |
| 390 022 | Penny the Pendolino | 390 049 | Virgin Express |
| 390 023 | Virgin Glory | 390 050 | Virgin Invader |
| 390 024 | Virgin Venturer | 390 051 | Virgin Ambassador |
| 390 025 | Virgin Stagecoach | 390 052 | Virgin Knight |
| 390 026 | Virgin Enterprise | 390 053 | Mission Accomplished |

# CLASS 395  HS1 DOMESTIC SETS  HITACHI JAPAN

New 6-car dual-voltage units for domestic services from St. Pancras International to Ashford/Dover/Ramsgate, to be operated by Southeastern. The first unit arrived for testing in August 2007 and the first sets are due into traffic in late 2009.

**Formation:** DTSO–MSO–MSO–MSO–MSO–DTSO.
**Systems:** 25 kV AC overhead/750 V DC third rail.
**Construction:** Aluminium.
**Traction Motors:** Hitachi asynchronous of 210 kW.
**Wheel Arrangement:** 2-2 + Bo-Bo + Bo-Bo + Bo-Bo + Bo-Bo + 2-2.
**Braking:** Disc, rheostatic & capability for regenerative braking.

| | |
|---|---|
| **Dimensions:** 20.00 x 2.81 m. | **Couplers:** Scharfenberg. |
| **Bogies:** Hitachi. | **Control System:** IGBT Inverter. |
| **Gangways:** Within unit. | **Maximum Speed:** 140 m.p.h. |
| **Doors:** Single-leaf sliding. | **Multiple Working:** Within class only.. |

**Heating & ventilation:** Air conditioning.
**Seating Layout:** 2+2 facing/unidirectional (mainly unidirectional).

**DTSO(A):** Hitachi Kasado, Japan 2006–2008. –/28(12) 1TD 2W. 46.7 t.
**MSO:** Hitachi Kasado, Japan 2006–2008. –/66. 45.7 t.
**DTSO(B):** Hitachi Kasado, Japan 2006–2008. –/48 1T. 46.6 t.

| | | | | | | | | | |
|---|---|---|---|---|---|---|---|---|---|
| 395 001 | **SB** | H | | AD | 39011 | 39012 | 39013 | 39014 | 39015 | 39016 |
| 395 002 | **SB** | H | | AD | 39021 | 39022 | 39023 | 39024 | 39025 | 39026 |
| 395 003 | **SB** | H | | AD | 39031 | 39032 | 39033 | 39034 | 39035 | 39036 |
| 395 004 | **SB** | H | | AD | 39041 | 39042 | 39043 | 39044 | 39045 | 39046 |
| 395 005 | | H | | | 39051 | 39052 | 39053 | 39054 | 39055 | 39056 |
| 395 006 | | H | | | 39061 | 39062 | 39063 | 39064 | 39065 | 39066 |
| 395 007 | | H | | | 39071 | 39072 | 39073 | 39074 | 39075 | 39076 |
| 395 008 | | H | | | 39081 | 39082 | 39083 | 39084 | 39085 | 39086 |
| 395 009 | | H | | | 39091 | 39092 | 39093 | 39094 | 39095 | 39096 |
| 395 010 | | H | | | 39101 | 39102 | 39103 | 39104 | 39105 | 39106 |
| 395 011 | | H | | | 39111 | 39112 | 39113 | 39114 | 39115 | 39116 |
| 395 012 | | H | | | 39121 | 39122 | 39123 | 39124 | 39125 | 39126 |
| 395 013 | | H | | | 39131 | 39132 | 39133 | 39134 | 39135 | 39136 |
| 395 014 | | H | | | 39141 | 39142 | 39143 | 39144 | 39145 | 39146 |
| 395 015 | | H | | | 39151 | 39152 | 39153 | 39154 | 39155 | 39156 |
| 395 016 | | H | | | 39161 | 39162 | 39163 | 39164 | 39165 | 39166 |
| 395 017 | | H | | | 39171 | 39172 | 39173 | 39174 | 39175 | 39176 |
| 395 018 | | H | | | 39181 | 39182 | 39183 | 39184 | 39185 | 39186 |
| 395 019 | | H | | | 39191 | 39192 | 39193 | 39194 | 39195 | 39196 |
| 395 020 | | H | | | 39201 | 39202 | 39203 | 39204 | 39205 | 39206 |
| 395 021 | | H | | | 39211 | 39212 | 39213 | 39214 | 39215 | 39216 |
| 395 022 | | H | | | 39221 | 39222 | 39223 | 39224 | 39225 | 39226 |
| 395 023 | | H | | | 39231 | 39232 | 39233 | 39234 | 39235 | 39236 |
| 395 024 | | H | | | 39241 | 39242 | 39243 | 39244 | 39245 | 39246 |
| 395 025 | | H | | | 39251 | 39252 | 39253 | 39254 | 39255 | 39256 |
| 395 026 | | H | | | 39261 | 39262 | 39263 | 39264 | 39265 | 39266 |
| 395 027 | | H | | | 39271 | 39272 | 39273 | 39274 | 39275 | 39276 |
| 395 028 | | H | | | 39281 | 39282 | 39283 | 39284 | 39285 | 39286 |
| 395 029 | | H | | | 39291 | 39292 | 39293 | 39294 | 39295 | 39296 |

# 4.2. 750 V DC THIRD RAIL EMUs

These classes use the third rail system at 750 V DC (unless stated). Outer couplers are buckeyes on units built before 1982 with bar couplers within the units. Newer units generally have Dellner outer couplers.

## CLASS 421                                                    BR YORK

Units built for Portsmouth and Brighton lines. Facelifted with new trim and fluorescent lighting in saloons.

**Formation:** DTCso–MBSO–DTCso.
**Construction:** Steel.
**Traction Motors:** Four EE507 of 185 kW.
**SR designation:** 3 Cig.
**Wheel Arrangement:** 2-2 + Bo-Bo + 2-2.
**Braking:** Tread.                          **Dimensions:** 20.18 x 2.82 m.
**Bogies:** Mark 6 motor bogies (MBSO). B5 (SR) bogies (trailer cars).
**Couplers:** Buckeye.
**Gangways:** Throughout.                     **Control System:** 1963-type.
**Doors:** Slam.                              **Maximum Speed:** 90 m.p.h.
**Seating Layout:** 1: Compartments, 2: 2+2 facing (plus one four-a-side compartment per DTC).
**Multiple Working:** Within class.

**Class 421/7. Phase 2 sets.** Specially converted 3-car units for use on the Lymington branch line. Central Door Locking system fitted and wheelchair space created. Toilets removed.

**76764/76773. DTCso(A).** Lot No. 30814 1971. 18/36. 35.5 t.
**62402/62411. MBSO.** Lot No. 30816 1971. –/56 1W + 3 tip-up seats. 49 t.
**76835/76844. DTCso(B).** Lot No. 30815 1971. 18/36. 35 t.

| | | | | | | | |
|---|---|---|---|---|---|---|---|
| 1497 (1883) | **BG** | SW *SW* | BM | 76764 | 62402 | 76835 | Freshwater |
| 1498 (1888) | **G** | SW *SW* | BM | 76773 | 62411 | 76844 | Farringford |

## CLASS 442     WESSEX EXPRESS     BREL DERBY

Stock built for Waterloo–Bournemouth–Weymouth services. Withdrawn from service with South West Trains in early 2007. 17 sets are being refurbished at Railcare, Wolverton for use by Southern on Victoria–Gatwick Airport–Brighton services (in 10-car formations).

**Formation:** As built: DTFso–TSO–MBRMB–TSO–DTSO * refurbished Southern: DTSO(A)–TSO–MBC–TSO(W)–DTSO(B).
**Construction:** Steel.
**Traction Motors:** Four EE546 of 300 kW recovered from Class 432s.
**SR designation:** 5 Wes.
**Wheel Arrangement:** 2-2 + 2-2 + Bo-Bo + 2-2 + 2-2.
**Braking:** Disc.                    **Dimensions:** 23.15/23.00 x 2.74 m.
**Bogies:** Two BREL P7 motor bogies (MBSO). T4 bogies (trailer cars).

**Couplers:** Buckeye.
**Gangways:** Throughout.
**Doors:** Sliding plug.
**Control System:** 1986-type.
**Maximum Speed:** 100 m.p.h.
**Heating & Ventilation:** Air conditioning.
**Seating Layout (unrefurbished):** 1: 2+2 facing/compartments, 2: 2+2 facing/unidirectional.
**Seating Layout (refurbished):** 1: 2+1 facing, 2: 2+2 mainly unidirectional.
**Multiple Working:** Within class and with locos of Classes 33/1 & 73 in an emergency.

Details of refurbished Southern units (*):

**DTSO(A).** Lot No. 31030 Derby 1988–1989. –/74. 38.5 t.
**TSO.** Lot No. 31032 Derby 1988–1989. –/76 2T. 37.5 t.
**MBC.** Lot No. 31034 Derby 1988–1989. 24/28. 55.0 t.
**TSO(W).** Lot No. 31033 Derby 1988–1989. –/66(4) 1TD 1T 2W. 37.8 t.
**DTSO(B).** Lot No. 31031 Derby 1988–1989. –/74. 37.3 t.

Details of unrefurbished units:

**DTFso.** Lot No. 31030 Derby 1988–1989. 50/– 1T. (36 in six compartments and 14 in one saloon). 39.0 t.
**TSO(A).** Lot No. 31032 Derby 1988–1989. –/80 2T. 35.3 t.
**MBRMB.** Lot No. 31034 Derby 1988–1989. –/30+17 ("snug") 1W. 54.7 t.
**TSO(B).** Lot No. 31033 Derby 1988–1989. –/76(2) 1TD 1T 1W. 35.4 t.
**DTSO.** Lot No. 31031 Derby 1988–1989. –/78 1T. 35.7 t.

| | | | | | | | | | |
|---|---|---|---|---|---|---|---|---|---|
| 442 401 | **ST** | A | | ZN | 77382 | 71818 | 62937 | 71842 | 77406 |
| 442 402 | **GV** | A | *SN* | BI | 77383 | 71819 | 62938 | 71843 | 77407 |
| 442 403 | **ST** | A | | ZN | 77384 | 71820 | 62941 | 71844 | 77408 |
| 442 404 | **ST** | A | | ZN | 77385 | 71821 | 62939 | 71845 | 77409 |
| 442 405 | **ST** | A | *SN* | BI | 77386 | 71822 | 62944 | 71846 | 77410 |
| 442 406 | **ST** | A | | ZN | 77389 | 71823 | 62942 | 71847 | 77411 |
| 442 407 | **ST** | A | | ZN | 77388 | 71824 | 62943 | 71848 | 77412 |
| 442 408 | **ST** | A | | ZN | 77387 | 71825 | 62945 | 71849 | 77413 |
| 2409 | **ST** | A | | AF | 77390 | 71826 | 62946 | 71850 | 77414 |
| 442 410 | **GV** | A | *SN* | BI | 77391 | 71827 | 62948 | 71851 | 77415 |
| 442 411 | **ST** | A | | ZN | 77392 | 71828 | 62940 | 71858 | 77422 |
| 442 412 | **GV** | A | *SN* | SI | 77393 | 71829 | 62947 | 71853 | 77417 |
| 442 413 | **ST** | A | *SN* | BI | 77394 | 71830 | 62949 | 71854 | 77418 |
| 442 414 | **GV** | A | *SN* | BI | 77395 | 71831 | 62950 | 71855 | 77419 |
| 2415 | **ST** | A | | ZG | 77396 | 71832 | 62951 | 71856 | 77420 |
| 2416 | **ST** | A | | ZG | 77397 | 71833 | 62952 | 71857 | 77421 |
| 442 417 | **GV** | A | *SN* | BI | 77398 | 71834 | 62953 | 71852 | 77416 |
| 2418 | **ST** | A | | ZG | 77399 | 71835 | 62954 | 71859 | 77423 |
| 442 419 | **GV** | A | *SN* | BI | 77400 | 71836 | 62955 | 71860 | 77424 |
| 2420 | **ST** | A | | ZG | 77401 | 71837 | 62956 | 71861 | 77425 |
| 442 421 | **GV** | A | *SN* | BI | 77402 | 71838 | 62957 | 71862 | 77426 |
| 2422 | **ST** | A | | ZG | 77403 | 71839 | 62958 | 71863 | 77427 |
| 2423 | **ST** | A | | ZG | 77404 | 71840 | 62959 | 71864 | 77428 |
| 442 424 | **GV** | A | *SN* | BI | 77405 | 71841 | 62960 | 71865 | 77429 |

# CLASS 444          DESIRO UK          SIEMENS

Express units.

**Formation:** DMCO–TSO–TSO–TSORMB–DMSO.
**Construction:** Aluminium.
**Traction Motors:** 4 Siemens 1TB2016-0GB02 asynchronous of 250 kW.
**Wheel Arrangement:** Bo-Bo + 2-2 + 2-2 + 2-2 + Bo-Bo.
**Braking:** Disc & rheostatic.                    **Dimensions:** 23.57 x 2.80 m.
**Bogies:** SGP SF5000.                             **Couplers:** Dellner 12.
**Gangways:** Throughout.                           **Control System:** IGBT Inverter.
**Doors:** Single-leaf sliding plug.                **Maximum Speed:** 100 m.p.h.
**Heating & Ventilation:** Air conditioning.
**Seating Layout:** 1: 2+1 facing/unidirectional, 2: 2+2 facing/unidirectional.
**Multiple Working:** Within class and with Class 450.

**DMSO.** Siemens Wien (Vienna)/Uerdingen 2003–2004. –/76. 51.3 t.
**TSO 67101–67145.** Siemens Wien (Vienna)/Uerdingen 2003–2004. –/76 1T. 40.3 t.
**TSO 67151–67195.** Siemens Wien (Vienna)/Uerdingen 2003–2004. –/76 1T. 36.8 t.
**TSORMB.** Siemens Wien (Vienna)/Uerdingen 2003–2004. –/47 1T 1TD 2W. 42.1 t.
**DMCO.** Siemens Wien (Vienna)/Uerdingen 2003–2004. 35/24. 51.3 t.

| | | | | | | | | | |
|---|---|---|---|---|---|---|---|---|---|
| 444 001 | ST | A | SW | NT | 63801 | 67101 | 67151 | 67201 | 63851 |
| 444 002 | ST | A | SW | NT | 63802 | 67102 | 67152 | 67202 | 63852 |
| 444 003 | ST | A | SW | NT | 63803 | 67103 | 67153 | 67203 | 63853 |
| 444 004 | ST | A | SW | NT | 63804 | 67104 | 67154 | 67204 | 63854 |
| 444 005 | ST | A | SW | NT | 63805 | 67105 | 67155 | 67205 | 63855 |
| 444 006 | ST | A | SW | NT | 63806 | 67106 | 67156 | 67206 | 63856 |
| 444 007 | ST | A | SW | NT | 63807 | 67107 | 67157 | 67207 | 63857 |
| 444 008 | ST | A | SW | NT | 63808 | 67108 | 67158 | 67208 | 63858 |
| 444 009 | ST | A | SW | NT | 63809 | 67109 | 67159 | 67209 | 63859 |
| 444 010 | ST | A | SW | NT | 63810 | 67110 | 67160 | 67210 | 63860 |
| 444 011 | ST | A | SW | NT | 63811 | 67111 | 67161 | 67211 | 63861 |
| 444 012 | ST | A | SW | NT | 63812 | 67112 | 67162 | 67212 | 63862 |
| 444 013 | ST | A | SW | NT | 63813 | 67113 | 67163 | 67213 | 63863 |
| 444 014 | ST | A | SW | NT | 63814 | 67114 | 67164 | 67214 | 63864 |
| 444 015 | ST | A | SW | NT | 63815 | 67115 | 67165 | 67215 | 63865 |
| 444 016 | ST | A | SW | NT | 63816 | 67116 | 67166 | 67216 | 63866 |
| 444 017 | ST | A | SW | NT | 63817 | 67117 | 67167 | 67217 | 63867 |
| 444 018 | ST | A | SW | NT | 63818 | 67118 | 67168 | 67218 | 63868 |
| 444 019 | ST | A | SW | NT | 63819 | 67119 | 67169 | 67219 | 63869 |
| 444 020 | ST | A | SW | NT | 63820 | 67120 | 67170 | 67220 | 63870 |
| 444 021 | ST | A | SW | NT | 63821 | 67121 | 67171 | 67221 | 63871 |
| 444 022 | ST | A | SW | NT | 63822 | 67122 | 67172 | 67222 | 63872 |
| 444 023 | ST | A | SW | NT | 63823 | 67123 | 67173 | 67223 | 63873 |
| 444 024 | ST | A | SW | NT | 63824 | 67124 | 67174 | 67224 | 63874 |
| 444 025 | ST | A | SW | NT | 63825 | 67125 | 67175 | 67225 | 63875 |
| 444 026 | ST | A | SW | NT | 63826 | 67126 | 67176 | 67226 | 63876 |
| 444 027 | ST | A | SW | NT | 63827 | 67127 | 67177 | 67227 | 63877 |
| 444 028 | ST | A | SW | NT | 63828 | 67128 | 67178 | 67228 | 63878 |
| 444 029 | ST | A | SW | NT | 63829 | 67129 | 67179 | 67229 | 63879 |

| 444 030 | ST | A | SW | NT | 63830 | 67130 | 67180 | 67230 | 63880 |
|---------|----|---|----|----|-------|-------|-------|-------|-------|
| 444 031 | ST | A | SW | NT | 63831 | 67131 | 67181 | 67231 | 63881 |
| 444 032 | ST | A | SW | NT | 63832 | 67132 | 67182 | 67232 | 63882 |
| 444 033 | ST | A | SW | NT | 63833 | 67133 | 67183 | 67233 | 63883 |
| 444 034 | ST | A | SW | NT | 63834 | 67134 | 67184 | 67234 | 63884 |
| 444 035 | ST | A | SW | NT | 63835 | 67135 | 67185 | 67235 | 63885 |
| 444 036 | ST | A | SW | NT | 63836 | 67136 | 67186 | 67236 | 63886 |
| 444 037 | ST | A | SW | NT | 63837 | 67137 | 67187 | 67237 | 63887 |
| 444 038 | ST | A | SW | NT | 63838 | 67138 | 67188 | 67238 | 63888 |
| 444 039 | ST | A | SW | NT | 63839 | 67139 | 67189 | 67239 | 63889 |
| 444 040 | ST | A | SW | NT | 63840 | 67140 | 67190 | 67240 | 63890 |
| 444 041 | ST | A | SW | NT | 63841 | 67141 | 67191 | 67241 | 63891 |
| 444 042 | ST | A | SW | NT | 63842 | 67142 | 67192 | 67242 | 63892 |
| 444 043 | ST | A | SW | NT | 63843 | 67143 | 67193 | 67243 | 63893 |
| 444 044 | ST | A | SW | NT | 63844 | 67144 | 67194 | 67244 | 63894 |
| 444 045 | ST | A | SW | NT | 63845 | 67145 | 67195 | 67245 | 63895 |

**Names (carried on TSORMB):**

| 444 001 | NAOMI HOUSE |
|---------|-------------|
| 444 012 | DESTINATION WEYMOUTH |
| 444 018 | THE FAB 444 |

# CLASS 450          DESIRO UK          SIEMENS

Outer suburban units.

**Formation:** DMSO–TCO–TSO–DMSO (DMSO–TSO–TCO–DMSO 450 111–127).
**Construction:** Aluminium.
**Traction Motors:** 4 Siemens 1TB2016-0GB02 asynchronous of 250 kW.
**Wheel Arrangement:** Bo-Bo + 2-2 + 2-2 + Bo-Bo.
**Braking:** Disc & rheostatic.          **Dimensions:** 20.34 x 2.79 m.
**Bogies:** SGP SF5000.          **Couplers:** Dellner 12.
**Gangways:** Throughout.          **Control System:** IGBT Inverter.
**Doors:** Sliding plug.          **Maximum Speed:** 100 m.p.h.
**Heating & Ventilation:** Air conditioning.
**Seating Layout:** 1: 2+2 facing/unidirectional, 2: 3+2 facing/unidirectional.
**Multiple Working:** Within class and with Class 444.

**Class 450/0. Standard units.**

**DMSO(A).** Siemens Uerdingen/Wien (Vienna) 2002–2006. –/70. 48.0 t.
**TCO.** Siemens Uerdingen/Wien (Vienna) 2002–2006. 24/32(4) 1T. 35.8 t.
**TSO.** Siemens Uerdingen/Wien (Vienna) 2002–2006. –/61(9) 1TD 2W. 39.8 t.
**DMSO(B).** Siemens Uerdingen/Wien (Vienna) 2002–2006. –/70. 48.6 t.

| 450 001 | SD | A | SW | NT | 63201 | 64201 | 68101 | 63601 |
|---------|----|---|----|----|-------|-------|-------|-------|
| 450 002 | SD | A | SW | NT | 63202 | 64202 | 68102 | 63602 |
| 450 003 | SD | A | SW | NT | 63203 | 64203 | 68103 | 63603 |
| 450 004 | SD | A | SW | NT | 63204 | 64204 | 68104 | 63604 |
| 450 005 | SD | A | SW | NT | 63205 | 64205 | 68105 | 63605 |
| 450 006 | SD | A | SW | NT | 63206 | 64206 | 68106 | 63606 |
| 450 007 | SD | A | SW | NT | 63207 | 64207 | 68107 | 63607 |

| | | | | | | | | |
|---|---|---|---|---|---|---|---|---|
| 450 008 | **SD** | A | *SW* | NT | 63208 | 64208 | 68108 | 63608 |
| 450 009 | **SD** | A | *SW* | NT | 63209 | 64209 | 68109 | 63609 |
| 450 010 | **SD** | A | *SW* | NT | 63210 | 64210 | 68110 | 63610 |
| 450 011 | **SD** | A | *SW* | NT | 63211 | 64211 | 68111 | 63611 |
| 450 012 | **SD** | A | *SW* | NT | 63212 | 64212 | 68112 | 63612 |
| 450 013 | **SD** | A | *SW* | NT | 63213 | 64213 | 68113 | 63613 |
| 450 014 | **SD** | A | *SW* | NT | 63214 | 64214 | 68114 | 63614 |
| 450 015 | **SD** | A | *SW* | NT | 63215 | 64215 | 68115 | 63615 |
| 450 016 | **SD** | A | *SW* | NT | 63216 | 64216 | 68116 | 63616 |
| 450 017 | **SD** | A | *SW* | NT | 63217 | 64217 | 68117 | 63617 |
| 450 018 | **SD** | A | *SW* | NT | 63218 | 64218 | 68118 | 63618 |
| 450 019 | **SD** | A | *SW* | NT | 63219 | 64219 | 68119 | 63619 |
| 450 020 | **SD** | A | *SW* | NT | 63220 | 64220 | 68120 | 63620 |
| 450 021 | **SD** | A | *SW* | NT | 63221 | 64221 | 68121 | 63621 |
| 450 022 | **SD** | A | *SW* | NT | 63222 | 64222 | 68122 | 63622 |
| 450 023 | **SD** | A | *SW* | NT | 63223 | 64223 | 68123 | 63623 |
| 450 024 | **SD** | A | *SW* | NT | 63224 | 64224 | 68124 | 63624 |
| 450 025 | **SD** | A | *SW* | NT | 63225 | 64225 | 68125 | 63625 |
| 450 026 | **SD** | A | *SW* | NT | 63226 | 64226 | 68126 | 63626 |
| 450 027 | **SD** | A | *SW* | NT | 63227 | 64227 | 68127 | 63627 |
| 450 028 | **SD** | A | *SW* | NT | 63228 | 64228 | 68128 | 63628 |
| 450 029 | **SD** | A | *SW* | NT | 63229 | 64229 | 68129 | 63629 |
| 450 030 | **SD** | A | *SW* | NT | 63230 | 64230 | 68130 | 63630 |
| 450 031 | **SD** | A | *SW* | NT | 63231 | 64231 | 68131 | 63631 |
| 450 032 | **SD** | A | *SW* | NT | 63232 | 64232 | 68132 | 63632 |
| 450 033 | **SD** | A | *SW* | NT | 63233 | 64233 | 68133 | 63633 |
| 450 034 | **SD** | A | *SW* | NT | 63234 | 64234 | 68134 | 63634 |
| 450 035 | **SD** | A | *SW* | NT | 63235 | 64235 | 68135 | 63635 |
| 450 036 | **SD** | A | *SW* | NT | 63236 | 64236 | 68136 | 63636 |
| 450 037 | **SD** | A | *SW* | NT | 63237 | 64237 | 68137 | 63637 |
| 450 038 | **SD** | A | *SW* | NT | 63238 | 64238 | 68138 | 63638 |
| 450 039 | **SD** | A | *SW* | NT | 63239 | 64239 | 68139 | 63639 |
| 450 040 | **SD** | A | *SW* | NT | 63240 | 64240 | 68140 | 63640 |
| 450 041 | **SD** | A | *SW* | NT | 63241 | 64241 | 68141 | 63641 |
| 450 042 | **SD** | A | *SW* | NT | 63242 | 64242 | 68142 | 63642 |
| 450 071 | **SD** | A | *SW* | NT | 63271 | 64271 | 68171 | 63671 |
| 450 072 | **SD** | A | *SW* | NT | 63272 | 64272 | 68172 | 63672 |
| 450 073 | **SD** | A | *SW* | NT | 63273 | 64273 | 68173 | 63673 |
| 450 074 | **SD** | A | *SW* | NT | 63274 | 64274 | 68174 | 63674 |
| 450 075 | **SD** | A | *SW* | NT | 63275 | 64275 | 68175 | 63675 |
| 450 076 | **SD** | A | *SW* | NT | 63276 | 64276 | 68176 | 63676 |
| 450 077 | **SD** | A | *SW* | NT | 63277 | 64277 | 68177 | 63677 |
| 450 078 | **SD** | A | *SW* | NT | 63278 | 64278 | 68178 | 63678 |
| 450 079 | **SD** | A | *SW* | NT | 63279 | 64279 | 68179 | 63679 |
| 450 080 | **SD** | A | *SW* | NT | 63280 | 64280 | 68180 | 63680 |
| 450 081 | **SD** | A | *SW* | NT | 63281 | 64281 | 68181 | 63681 |
| 450 082 | **SD** | A | *SW* | NT | 63282 | 64282 | 68182 | 63682 |
| 450 083 | **SD** | A | *SW* | NT | 63283 | 64283 | 68183 | 63683 |
| 450 084 | **SD** | A | *SW* | NT | 63284 | 64284 | 68184 | 63684 |
| 450 085 | **SD** | A | *SW* | NT | 63285 | 64285 | 68185 | 63685 |
| 450 086 | **SD** | A | *SW* | NT | 63286 | 64286 | 68186 | 63686 |

| | | | | | | | | |
|---|---|---|---|---|---|---|---|---|
| 450 087 | **SD** | A | *SW* | NT | 63287 | 64287 | 68187 | 63687 |
| 450 088 | **SD** | A | *SW* | NT | 63288 | 64288 | 68188 | 63688 |
| 450 089 | **SD** | A | *SW* | NT | 63289 | 64289 | 68189 | 63689 |
| 450 090 | **SD** | A | *SW* | NT | 63290 | 64290 | 68190 | 63690 |
| 450 091 | **SD** | A | *SW* | NT | 63291 | 64291 | 68191 | 63691 |
| 450 092 | **SD** | A | *SW* | NT | 63292 | 64292 | 68192 | 63692 |
| 450 093 | **SD** | A | *SW* | NT | 63293 | 64293 | 68193 | 63693 |
| 450 094 | **SD** | A | *SW* | NT | 63294 | 64294 | 68194 | 63694 |
| 450 095 | **SD** | A | *SW* | NT | 63295 | 64295 | 68195 | 63695 |
| 450 096 | **SD** | A | *SW* | NT | 63296 | 64296 | 68196 | 63696 |
| 450 097 | **SD** | A | *SW* | NT | 63297 | 64297 | 68197 | 63697 |
| 450 098 | **SD** | A | *SW* | NT | 63298 | 64298 | 68198 | 63698 |
| 450 099 | **SD** | A | *SW* | NT | 63299 | 64299 | 68199 | 63699 |
| 450 100 | **SD** | A | *SW* | NT | 63300 | 64300 | 68200 | 63700 |
| 450 101 | **SD** | A | *SW* | NT | 63701 | 66851 | 66801 | 63751 |
| 450 102 | **SD** | A | *SW* | NT | 63702 | 66852 | 66802 | 63752 |
| 450 103 | **SD** | A | *SW* | NT | 63703 | 66853 | 66803 | 63753 |
| 450 104 | **SD** | A | *SW* | NT | 63704 | 66854 | 66804 | 63754 |
| 450 105 | **SD** | A | *SW* | NT | 63705 | 66855 | 66805 | 63755 |
| 450 106 | **SD** | A | *SW* | NT | 63706 | 66856 | 66806 | 63756 |
| 450 107 | **SD** | A | *SW* | NT | 63707 | 66857 | 66807 | 63757 |
| 450 108 | **SD** | A | *SW* | NT | 63708 | 66858 | 66808 | 63758 |
| 450 109 | **SD** | A | *SW* | NT | 63709 | 66859 | 66809 | 63759 |
| 450 110 | **SD** | A | *SW* | NT | 63710 | 66860 | 66810 | 63760 |
| 450 111 | **SD** | A | *SW* | NT | 63901 | 66921 | 66901 | 63921 |
| 450 112 | **SD** | A | *SW* | NT | 63902 | 66922 | 66902 | 63922 |
| 450 113 | **SD** | A | *SW* | NT | 63903 | 66923 | 66903 | 63923 |
| 450 114 | **SD** | A | *SW* | NT | 63904 | 66924 | 66904 | 63924 |
| 450 115 | **SD** | A | *SW* | NT | 63905 | 66925 | 66905 | 63925 |
| 450 116 | **SD** | A | *SW* | NT | 63906 | 66926 | 66906 | 63926 |
| 450 117 | **SD** | A | *SW* | NT | 63907 | 66927 | 66907 | 63927 |
| 450 118 | **SD** | A | *SW* | NT | 63908 | 66928 | 66908 | 63928 |
| 450 119 | **SD** | A | *SW* | NT | 63909 | 66929 | 66909 | 63929 |
| 450 120 | **SD** | A | *SW* | NT | 63910 | 66930 | 66910 | 63930 |
| 450 121 | **SD** | A | *SW* | NT | 63911 | 66931 | 66911 | 63931 |
| 450 122 | **SD** | A | *SW* | NT | 63912 | 66932 | 66912 | 63932 |
| 450 123 | **SD** | A | *SW* | NT | 63913 | 66933 | 66913 | 63933 |
| 450 124 | **SD** | A | *SW* | NT | 63914 | 66934 | 66914 | 63934 |
| 450 125 | **SD** | A | *SW* | NT | 63915 | 66935 | 66915 | 63935 |
| 450 126 | **SD** | A | *SW* | NT | 63916 | 66936 | 66916 | 63936 |
| 450 127 | **SD** | A | *SW* | NT | 63917 | 66937 | 66917 | 63937 |

**Names (carried on DMSO(B)):**

450 015   DESIRO
450 042   TRELOAR COLLEGE
450 114   FAIRBRIDGE investing in the future

**Class 450/5. "High density" units.** 28 units converted at Bournemouth for Waterloo–Windsor/Weybridge/Hounslow services. First Class removed and modified seating layout with more standing room. Details as Class 450/0 except:

**Formation:** DMSO–TSO–TSO–DMSO.

**DMSO(A).** Siemens Uerdingen/Wien (Vienna) 2002–2004. –/64. 48.0 t.
**TSO(A).** Siemens Uerdingen/Wien (Vienna) 2002–2004. –/56(4) 1T. 35.8 t.
**TSO(B).** Siemens Uerdingen/Wien (Vienna) 2002–2004. –/56(9) 1TD 2W. 39.8 t.
**DMSO(B).** Siemens Uerdingen/Wien (Vienna) 2002–2004. –/64. 48.6 t.

| | | | | | | | | | |
|---|---|---|---|---|---|---|---|---|---|
| 450 543 | (450 043) | **SD** | A | *SW* | NT | 63243 | 64243 | 68143 | 63643 |
| 450 544 | (450 044) | **SD** | A | *SW* | NT | 63244 | 64244 | 68144 | 63644 |
| 450 545 | (450 045) | **SD** | A | *SW* | NT | 63245 | 64245 | 68145 | 63645 |
| 450 546 | (450 046) | **SD** | A | *SW* | NT | 63246 | 64246 | 68146 | 63646 |
| 450 547 | (450 047) | **SD** | A | *SW* | NT | 63247 | 64247 | 68147 | 63647 |
| 450 548 | (450 048) | **SD** | A | *SW* | NT | 63248 | 64248 | 68148 | 63648 |
| 450 549 | (450 049) | **SD** | A | *SW* | NT | 63249 | 64249 | 68149 | 63649 |
| 450 550 | (450 050) | **SD** | A | *SW* | NT | 63250 | 64250 | 68150 | 63650 |
| 450 551 | (450 051) | **SD** | A | *SW* | NT | 63251 | 64251 | 68151 | 63651 |
| 450 552 | (450 052) | **SD** | A | *SW* | NT | 63252 | 64252 | 68152 | 63652 |
| 450 553 | (450 053) | **SD** | A | *SW* | NT | 63253 | 64253 | 68153 | 63653 |
| 450 554 | (450 054) | **SD** | A | *SW* | NT | 63254 | 64254 | 68154 | 63654 |
| 450 555 | (450 055) | **SD** | A | *SW* | NT | 63255 | 64255 | 68155 | 63655 |
| 450 556 | (450 056) | **SD** | A | *SW* | NT | 63256 | 64256 | 68156 | 63656 |
| 450 557 | (450 057) | **SD** | A | *SW* | NT | 63257 | 64257 | 68157 | 63657 |
| 450 558 | (450 058) | **SD** | A | *SW* | NT | 63258 | 64258 | 68158 | 63658 |
| 450 559 | (450 059) | **SD** | A | *SW* | NT | 63259 | 64259 | 68159 | 63659 |
| 450 560 | (450 060) | **SD** | A | *SW* | NT | 63260 | 64260 | 68160 | 63660 |
| 450 561 | (450 061) | **SD** | A | *SW* | NT | 63261 | 64261 | 68161 | 63661 |
| 450 562 | (450 062) | **SD** | A | *SW* | NT | 63262 | 64262 | 68162 | 63662 |
| 450 563 | (450 063) | **SD** | A | *SW* | NT | 63263 | 64263 | 68163 | 63663 |
| 450 564 | (450 064) | **SD** | A | *SW* | NT | 63264 | 64264 | 68164 | 63664 |
| 450 565 | (450 065) | **SD** | A | *SW* | NT | 63265 | 64265 | 68165 | 63665 |
| 450 566 | (450 066) | **SD** | A | *SW* | NT | 63266 | 64266 | 68166 | 63666 |
| 450 567 | (450 067) | **SD** | A | *SW* | NT | 63267 | 64267 | 68167 | 63667 |
| 450 568 | (450 068) | **SD** | A | *SW* | NT | 63268 | 64268 | 68168 | 63668 |
| 450 569 | (450 069) | **SD** | A | *SW* | NT | 63269 | 64269 | 68169 | 63669 |
| 450 570 | (450 070) | **SD** | A | *SW* | NT | 63270 | 64270 | 68170 | 63670 |

# CLASS 455                                                              BR YORK

Inner suburban units.

**Formation:** DTSO–MSO–TSO–DTSO.
**Construction:** Steel. Class 455/7 TSO have a steel underframe and an aluminium alloy body & roof.
**Traction Motors:** Four GEC507-20J of 185 kW, some recovered from Class 405s.
**Wheel Arrangement:** 2-2 + Bo-Bo + 2-2 + 2-2.
**Braking:** Disc.                                    **Dimensions:** 20.28/20.18 x 2.82 m.
**Bogies:** P7 (motor) and T3 (455/8 & 455/9) BX1 (455/7) trailer.
**Gangways:** Within unit + end doors (sealed on Southern units).
**Couplers:** Tightlock.                              **Control System:** 1982-type, camshaft.

**Doors**: Sliding.                    **Maximum Speed**: 75 m.p.h.
**Heating & Ventilation**: Various.
**Seating Layout**: All units refurbished. SWT units: 2+2 high-back unidirectional/facing seating. Southern units: 3+2 high back mainly facing seating.
**Multiple Working**: Within class and with Class 456.

**Class 455/7. South West Trains units.** Second series with TSOs originally in Class 508s. Pressure heating & ventilation.

**DTSO**. Lot No. 30976 1984–1985. –/50(4) 1W. 30.3 t.
**MSO**. Lot No. 30975 1984–1985. –/68. 45.7 t.
**TSO**. Lot No. 30944 1979–1980. –/68. 26.1 t.

| | | | | | | | | |
|---|---|---|---|---|---|---|---|---|
| 5701 | **SS** | P | *SW* | WD | 77727 | 62783 | 71545 | 77728 |
| 5702 | **SS** | P | *SW* | WD | 77729 | 62784 | 71547 | 77730 |
| 5703 | **SS** | P | *SW* | WD | 77731 | 62785 | 71540 | 77732 |
| 5704 | **SS** | P | *SW* | WD | 77733 | 62786 | 71548 | 77734 |
| 5705 | **SS** | P | *SW* | WD | 77735 | 62787 | 71565 | 77736 |
| 5706 | **SS** | P | *SW* | WD | 77737 | 62788 | 71534 | 77738 |
| 5707 | **SS** | P | *SW* | WD | 77739 | 62789 | 71536 | 77740 |
| 5708 | **SS** | P | *SW* | WD | 77741 | 62790 | 71560 | 77742 |
| 5709 | **SS** | P | *SW* | WD | 77743 | 62791 | 71532 | 77744 |
| 5710 | **SS** | P | *SW* | WD | 77745 | 62792 | 71566 | 77746 |
| 5711 | **SS** | P | *SW* | WD | 77747 | 62793 | 71542 | 77748 |
| 5712 | **SS** | P | *SW* | WD | 77749 | 62794 | 71546 | 77750 |
| 5713 | **SS** | P | *SW* | WD | 77751 | 62795 | 71567 | 77752 |
| 5714 | **SS** | P | *SW* | WD | 77753 | 62796 | 71539 | 77754 |
| 5715 | **SS** | P | *SW* | WD | 77755 | 62797 | 71535 | 77756 |
| 5716 | **SS** | P | *SW* | WD | 77757 | 62798 | 71564 | 77758 |
| 5717 | **SS** | P | *SW* | WD | 77759 | 62799 | 71528 | 77760 |
| 5718 | **SS** | P | *SW* | WD | 77761 | 62800 | 71557 | 77762 |
| 5719 | **SS** | P | *SW* | WD | 77763 | 62801 | 71558 | 77764 |
| 5720 | **SS** | P | *SW* | WD | 77765 | 62802 | 71568 | 77766 |
| 5721 | **SS** | P | *SW* | WD | 77767 | 62803 | 71553 | 77768 |
| 5722 | **SS** | P | *SW* | WD | 77769 | 62804 | 71533 | 77770 |
| 5723 | **SS** | P | *SW* | WD | 77771 | 62805 | 71526 | 77772 |
| 5724 | **SS** | P | *SW* | WD | 77773 | 62806 | 71561 | 77774 |
| 5725 | **SS** | P | *SW* | WD | 77775 | 62807 | 71541 | 77776 |
| 5726 | **SS** | P | *SW* | WD | 77777 | 62808 | 71556 | 77778 |
| 5727 | **SS** | P | *SW* | WD | 77779 | 62809 | 71562 | 77780 |
| 5728 | **SS** | P | *SW* | WD | 77781 | 62810 | 71527 | 77782 |
| 5729 | **SS** | P | *SW* | WD | 77783 | 62811 | 71550 | 77784 |
| 5730 | **SS** | P | *SW* | WD | 77785 | 62812 | 71551 | 77786 |
| 5731 | **SS** | P | *SW* | WD | 77787 | 62813 | 71555 | 77788 |
| 5732 | **SS** | P | *SW* | WD | 77789 | 62814 | 71552 | 77790 |
| 5733 | **SS** | P | *SW* | WD | 77791 | 62815 | 71549 | 77792 |
| 5734 | **SS** | P | *SW* | WD | 77793 | 62816 | 71531 | 77794 |
| 5735 | **SS** | P | *SW* | WD | 77795 | 62817 | 71563 | 77796 |
| 5736 | **SS** | P | *SW* | WD | 77797 | 62818 | 71554 | 77798 |
| 5737 | **SS** | P | *SW* | WD | 77799 | 62819 | 71544 | 77800 |
| 5738 | **SS** | P | *SW* | WD | 77801 | 62820 | 71529 | 77802 |
| 5739 | **SS** | P | *SW* | WD | 77803 | 62821 | 71537 | 77804 |

| 5740 | SS | P | SW | WD | 77805 | 62822 | 71530 | 77806 |
| 5741 | SS | P | SW | WD | 77807 | 62823 | 71559 | 77808 |
| 5742 | SS | P | SW | WD | 77809 | 62824 | 71543 | 77810 |
| 5750 | SS | P | SW | WD | 77811 | 62825 | 71538 | 77812 |

**Class 455/8. Southern units.** First series. Pressure heating & ventilation. Fitted with in-cab air conditioning systems meaning that the end door has been sealed.

**DTSO.** Lot No. 30972 York 1982–1984. –/74. 33.6 t.
**MSO.** Lot No. 30973 York 1982–1984. –/84. 37.9 t.
**TSO.** Lot No. 30974 York 1982–1984. –/75(3) 2W. 34.0 t.

| 455 801 | SN | H | SN | SU | 77627 | 62709 | 71657 | 77580 |
| 455 802 | SN | H | SN | SU | 77581 | 62710 | 71664 | 77582 |
| 455 803 | SN | H | SN | SU | 77583 | 62711 | 71639 | 77584 |
| 455 804 | SN | H | SN | SU | 77585 | 62712 | 71640 | 77586 |
| 455 805 | SN | H | SN | SU | 77587 | 62713 | 71641 | 77588 |
| 455 806 | SN | H | SN | SU | 77589 | 62714 | 71642 | 77590 |
| 455 807 | SN | H | SN | SU | 77591 | 62715 | 71643 | 77592 |
| 455 808 | SN | H | SN | SU | 77637 | 62716 | 71644 | 77594 |
| 455 809 | SN | H | SN | SU | 77623 | 62717 | 71648 | 77602 |
| 455 810 | SN | H | SN | SU | 77597 | 62718 | 71646 | 77598 |
| 455 811 | SN | H | SN | SU | 77599 | 62719 | 71647 | 77600 |
| 455 812 | SN | H | SN | SU | 77595 | 62720 | 71645 | 77626 |
| 455 813 | SN | H | SN | SU | 77603 | 62721 | 71649 | 77604 |
| 455 814 | SN | H | SN | SU | 77605 | 62722 | 71650 | 77606 |
| 455 815 | SN | H | SN | SU | 77607 | 62723 | 71651 | 77608 |
| 455 816 | SN | H | SN | SU | 77609 | 62724 | 71652 | 77633 |
| 455 817 | SN | H | SN | SU | 77611 | 62725 | 71653 | 77612 |
| 455 818 | SN | H | SN | SU | 77613 | 62726 | 71654 | 77632 |
| 455 819 | SN | H | SN | SU | 77615 | 62727 | 71637 | 77616 |
| 455 820 | SN | H | SN | SU | 77617 | 62728 | 71656 | 77618 |
| 455 821 | SN | H | SN | SU | 77619 | 62729 | 71655 | 77620 |
| 455 822 | SN | H | SN | SU | 77621 | 62730 | 71658 | 77622 |
| 455 823 | SN | H | SN | SU | 77601 | 62731 | 71659 | 77596 |
| 455 824 | SN | H | SN | SU | 77593 | 62732 | 71660 | 77624 |
| 455 825 | SN | H | SN | SU | 77579 | 62733 | 71661 | 77628 |
| 455 826 | SN | H | SN | SU | 77630 | 62734 | 71662 | 77629 |
| 455 827 | SN | H | SN | SU | 77610 | 62735 | 71663 | 77614 |
| 455 828 | SN | H | SN | SU | 77631 | 62736 | 71638 | 77634 |
| 455 829 | SN | H | SN | SU | 77635 | 62737 | 71665 | 77636 |
| 455 830 | SN | H | SN | SU | 77625 | 62743 | 71666 | 77638 |
| 455 831 | SN | H | SN | SU | 77639 | 62739 | 71667 | 77640 |
| 455 832 | SN | H | SN | SU | 77641 | 62740 | 71668 | 77642 |
| 455 833 | SN | H | SN | SU | 77643 | 62741 | 71669 | 77644 |
| 455 834 | SN | H | SN | SU | 77645 | 62742 | 71670 | 77646 |
| 455 835 | SN | H | SN | SU | 77647 | 62738 | 71671 | 77648 |
| 455 836 | SN | H | SN | SU | 77649 | 62744 | 71672 | 77650 |
| 455 837 | SN | H | SN | SU | 77651 | 62745 | 71673 | 77652 |
| 455 838 | SN | H | SN | SU | 77653 | 62746 | 71674 | 77654 |
| 455 839 | SN | H | SN | SU | 77655 | 62747 | 71675 | 77656 |
| 455 840 | SN | H | SN | SU | 77657 | 62748 | 71676 | 77658 |

| 455 841 | SN | H | SN | SU | 77659 | 62749 | 71677 | 77660 |
| 455 842 | SN | H | SN | SU | 77661 | 62750 | 71678 | 77662 |
| 455 843 | SN | H | SN | SU | 77663 | 62751 | 71679 | 77664 |
| 455 844 | SN | H | SN | SU | 77665 | 62752 | 71680 | 77666 |
| 455 845 | SN | H | SN | SU | 77667 | 62753 | 71681 | 77668 |
| 455 846 | SN | H | SN | SU | 77669 | 62754 | 71682 | 77670 |

**Class 455/8. South West Trains units.** First series. Pressure heating & ventilation.

**DTSO.** Lot No. 30972 York 1982–1984. –50(4) 1W. 29.5 t.
**MSO.** Lot No. 30973 York 1982–1984. –/84 –/68. 45.6 t.
**TSO.** Lot No. 30974 York 1982–1984. –/84 –/68. 27.1 t.

| 5847 | SS | P | SW | WD | 77671 | 62755 | 71683 | 77672 |
| 5848 | SS | P | SW | WD | 77673 | 62756 | 71684 | 77674 |
| 5849 | SS | P | SW | WD | 77675 | 62757 | 71685 | 77676 |
| 5850 | SS | P | SW | WD | 77677 | 62758 | 71686 | 77678 |
| 5851 | SS | P | SW | WD | 77679 | 62759 | 71687 | 77680 |
| 5852 | SS | P | SW | WD | 77681 | 62760 | 71688 | 77682 |
| 5853 | SS | P | SW | WD | 77683 | 62761 | 71689 | 77684 |
| 5854 | SS | P | SW | WD | 77685 | 62762 | 71690 | 77686 |
| 5855 | SS | P | SW | WD | 77687 | 62763 | 71691 | 77688 |
| 5856 | SS | P | SW | WD | 77689 | 62764 | 71692 | 77690 |
| 5857 | SS | P | SW | WD | 77691 | 62765 | 71693 | 77692 |
| 5858 | SS | P | SW | WD | 77693 | 62766 | 71694 | 77694 |
| 5859 | SS | P | SW | WD | 77695 | 62767 | 71695 | 77696 |
| 5860 | SS | P | SW | WD | 77697 | 62768 | 71696 | 77698 |
| 5861 | SS | P | SW | WD | 77699 | 62769 | 71697 | 77700 |
| 5862 | SS | P | SW | WD | 77701 | 62770 | 71698 | 77702 |
| 5863 | SS | P | SW | WD | 77703 | 62771 | 71699 | 77704 |
| 5864 | SS | P | SW | WD | 77705 | 62772 | 71700 | 77706 |
| 5865 | SS | P | SW | WD | 77707 | 62773 | 71701 | 77708 |
| 5866 | SS | P | SW | WD | 77709 | 62774 | 71702 | 77710 |
| 5867 | SS | P | SW | WD | 77711 | 62775 | 71703 | 77712 |
| 5868 | SS | P | SW | WD | 77713 | 62776 | 71704 | 77714 |
| 5869 | SS | P | SW | WD | 77715 | 62777 | 71705 | 77716 |
| 5870 | SS | P | SW | WD | 77717 | 62778 | 71706 | 77718 |
| 5871 | SS | P | SW | WD | 77719 | 62779 | 71707 | 77720 |
| 5872 | SS | P | SW | WD | 77721 | 62780 | 71708 | 77722 |
| 5873 | SS | P | SW | WD | 77723 | 62781 | 71709 | 77724 |
| 5874 | SS | P | SW | WD | 77725 | 62782 | 71710 | 77726 |

**Class 455/9. South West Trains units.** Third series. Convection heating.
**Dimensions:** 19.96/20.18 x 2.82 m.

**DTSO.** Lot No. 30991 York 1985. –/50(4) 1W. 29.0 t.
**MSO.** Lot No. 30992 York 1985. –/68. 46.3 t.
**TSO.** Lot No. 30993 York 1985. –/68. 28.3 t.
**TSO†.** Lot No. 30932 Derby 1981. –/68. 26.5 t.

**Note:** † Prototype vehicle 67400 converted from a Class 210 DEMU.

| 5901 | SS | P | SW | WD | 77813 | 62826 | 71714 | 77814 |
| 5902 | SS | P | SW | WD | 77815 | 62827 | 71715 | 77816 |

| 5903 | | SS | P | *SW* | WD | 77817 | 62828 | 71716 | 77818 |
| 5904 | | SS | P | *SW* | WD | 77819 | 62829 | 71717 | 77820 |
| 5905 | | SS | P | *SW* | WD | 77821 | 62830 | 71725 | 77822 |
| 5906 | | SS | P | *SW* | WD | 77823 | 62831 | 71719 | 77824 |
| 5907 | | SS | P | *SW* | WD | 77825 | 62832 | 71720 | 77826 |
| 5908 | | SS | P | *SW* | WD | 77827 | 62833 | 71721 | 77828 |
| 5909 | | SS | P | *SW* | WD | 77829 | 62834 | 71722 | 77830 |
| 5910 | | SS | P | *SW* | WD | 77831 | 62835 | 71723 | 77832 |
| 5911 | | SS | P | *SW* | WD | 77833 | 62836 | 71724 | 77834 |
| 5912 | † | SS | P | *SW* | WD | 77835 | 62837 | 67400 | 77836 |
| 5913 | | SS | P | *SW* | WD | 77837 | 62838 | 71726 | 77838 |
| 5914 | | SS | P | *SW* | WD | 77839 | 62839 | 71727 | 77840 |
| 5915 | | SS | P | *SW* | WD | 77841 | 62840 | 71728 | 77842 |
| 5916 | | SS | P | *SW* | WD | 77843 | 62841 | 71729 | 77844 |
| 5917 | | SS | P | *SW* | WD | 77845 | 62842 | 71730 | 77846 |
| 5918 | | SS | P | *SW* | WD | 77847 | 62843 | 71732 | 77848 |
| 5919 | | SS | P | *SW* | WD | 77849 | 62844 | 71718 | 77850 |
| 5920 | | SS | P | *SW* | WD | 77851 | 62845 | 71733 | 77852 |

# CLASS 456        BREL YORK

Inner suburban units.

**Formation:** DMSO–DTSO.
**Construction:** Steel underframe, aluminium alloy body & roof.
**Traction Motors:** Two GEC507-20J of 185 kW, some recovered from Class 405s.
**Wheel Arrangement:** 2-Bo + 2-2.
**Braking:** Disc.      **Dimensions:** 20.61 x 2.82 m.
**Bogies:** P7 (motor) and T3 (trailer).      **Couplers:** Tightlock.
**Gangways:** Within unit.      **Control System:** GTO Chopper.
**Doors:** Sliding.      **Maximum Speed:** 75 m.p.h.
**Heating & Ventilation:** Convection heating.
**Seating Layout:** 3+2 facing.
**Multiple Working:** Within class and with Class 455.

**DMSO.** Lot No. 31073 1990–1991. –/79. 41.1 t.
**DTSO.** Lot No. 31074 1990–1991. –/73. 31.4 t.

**Advertising livery:**
456 006 TfL/City of London (blue & green with various images).

| 456 001 | SN | P | *SN* | SU | 64735 | 78250 |
| 456 002 | SN | P | *SN* | SU | 64736 | 78251 |
| 456 003 | SN | P | *SN* | SU | 64737 | 78252 |
| 456 004 | SN | P | *SN* | SU | 64738 | 78253 |
| 456 005 | SN | P | *SN* | SU | 64739 | 78254 |
| 456 006 | AL | P | *SN* | SU | 64740 | 78255 |
| 456 007 | SN | P | *SN* | SU | 64741 | 78256 |
| 456 008 | SN | P | *SN* | SU | 64742 | 78257 |
| 456 009 | SN | P | *SN* | SU | 64743 | 78258 |
| 456 010 | SN | P | *SN* | SU | 64744 | 78259 |
| 456 011 | SN | P | *SN* | SU | 64745 | 78260 |
| 456 012 | SN | P | *SN* | SU | 64746 | 78261 |

| 456 013 | SN | P | SN | SU | 64747 | 78262 | |
| 456 014 | SN | P | SN | SU | 64748 | 78263 | |
| 456 015 | SN | P | SN | SU | 64749 | 78264 | |
| 456 016 | SN | P | SN | SU | 64750 | 78265 | |
| 456 017 | SN | P | SN | SU | 64751 | 78266 | |
| 456 018 | SN | P | SN | SU | 64752 | 78267 | |
| 456 019 | SN | P | SN | SU | 64753 | 78268 | |
| 456 020 | SN | P | SN | SU | 64754 | 78269 | |
| 456 021 | SN | P | SN | SU | 64755 | 78270 | |
| 456 022 | SN | P | SN | SU | 64756 | 78271 | |
| 456 023 | SN | P | SN | SU | 64757 | 78272 | |
| 456 024 | SN | P | SN | SU | 64758 | 78273 | Sir Cosmo Bonsor |

## CLASS 458   JUNIPER   ALSTOM BIRMINGHAM

Outer suburban units.

**Formation:** DMCO–TSO–MSO–DMCO.
**Construction:** Steel.
**Traction Motors:** Two Alstom ONIX 800 asynchronous of 270 kW.
**Wheel Arrangement:** 2-Bo + 2-2 + Bo-2 + Bo-2.
**Braking:** Disc & regenerative.           **Dimensions:** 21.16/19.94 x 2.80 m.
**Bogies:** ACR.                             **Couplers:** Scharfenberg AAR.
**Gangways:** Throughout (not in use).       **Control System:** IGBT Inverter.
**Doors:** Sliding plug.                     **Maximum Speed:** 100 m.p.h.
**Heating & Ventilation:** Air conditioning.
**Seating Layout:** 1: 2+2 facing, 2: 3+2 facing/unidirectional.
**Multiple Working:** Within class.

**DMCO(A).** Alstom 1998–2000. 12/63. 46.4 t.
**TSO.** Alstom 1998–2000. –/54(6) 1TD 2W. 34.6 t.
**MSO.** Alstom 1998–2000. –/75 1T. 42.1 t.
**DMCO(B).** Alstom 1998–2000. 12/63. 46.4 t.

| 8001 | ST | P | SW | WD | 67601 | 74001 | 74101 | 67701 |
| 8002 | ST | P | SW | WD | 67602 | 74002 | 74102 | 67702 |
| 8003 | ST | P | SW | WD | 67603 | 74003 | 74103 | 67703 |
| 8004 | ST | P | SW | WD | 67604 | 74004 | 74104 | 67704 |
| 8005 | ST | P | SW | WD | 67605 | 74005 | 74105 | 67705 |
| 8006 | ST | P | SW | WD | 67606 | 74006 | 74106 | 67706 |
| 8007 | ST | P | SW | WD | 67607 | 74007 | 74107 | 67707 |
| 8008 | ST | P | SW | WD | 67608 | 74008 | 74108 | 67708 |
| 8009 | ST | P | SW | WD | 67609 | 74009 | 74109 | 67709 |
| 8010 | ST | P | SW | WD | 67610 | 74010 | 74110 | 67710 |
| 8011 | ST | P | SW | WD | 67611 | 74011 | 74111 | 67711 |
| 8012 | ST | P | SW | WD | 67612 | 74012 | 74112 | 67712 |
| 8013 | ST | P | SW | WD | 67613 | 74013 | 74113 | 67713 |
| 8014 | ST | P | SW | WD | 67614 | 74014 | 74114 | 67714 |
| 8015 | ST | P | SW | WD | 67615 | 74015 | 74115 | 67715 |
| 8016 | ST | P | SW | WD | 67616 | 74016 | 74116 | 67716 |
| 8017 | ST | P | SW | WD | 67617 | 74017 | 74117 | 67717 |
| 8018 | ST | P | SW | WD | 67618 | 74018 | 74118 | 67718 |

| 8019 | ST | P | *SW* | WD | 67619 | 74019 | 74119 | 67719 |
| 8020 | ST | P | *SW* | WD | 67620 | 74020 | 74120 | 67720 |
| 8021 | ST | P | *SW* | WD | 67621 | 74021 | 74121 | 67721 |
| 8022 | ST | P | *SW* | WD | 67622 | 74022 | 74122 | 67722 |
| 8023 | ST | P | *SW* | WD | 67623 | 74023 | 74123 | 67723 |
| 8024 | ST | P | *SW* | WD | 67624 | 74024 | 74124 | 67724 |
| 8025 | ST | P | *SW* | WD | 67625 | 74025 | 74125 | 67725 |
| 8026 | ST | P | *SW* | WD | 67626 | 74026 | 74126 | 67726 |
| 8027 | ST | P | *SW* | WD | 67627 | 74027 | 74127 | 67727 |
| 8028 | ST | P | *SW* | WD | 67628 | 74028 | 74128 | 67728 |
| 8029 | ST | P | *SW* | WD | 67629 | 74029 | 74129 | 67729 |
| 8030 | ST | P | *SW* | WD | 67630 | 74030 | 74130 | 67730 |

# CLASS 460                              GEC-ALSTHOM JUNIPER

Only the last two digits of the unit number are carried on the front ends of these units.

**Formation:** DMLFO–TFO–TCO–MSO–MSO–TSO–MSO–DMSO.
**Construction:** Steel.
**Traction Motors:** Two Alstom ONIX 800 asynchronous of 270 kW.
**Wheel Arrangement:** 2-Bo + 2-2 + 2-2 +Bo-2 + 2-Bo + 2-2 + Bo-2 + Bo-2.
**Braking:** Disc & regenerative.          **Dimensions:** 21.01/19.94 x 2.80 m.
**Bogies:** ACR.
**Couplers:** Scharfenberg 330 at outer ends and between cars 4 and 5.
**Gangways:** Within unit.                **Control System:** IGBT Inverter.
**Doors:** Sliding plug.                  **Maximum Speed:** 100 m.p.h.
**Heating & Ventilation:** Air conditioning.
**Seating Layout:** 1: 2+1 facing, 2: 2+2 facing/unidirectional.
**Multiple Working:** Within class.

**DMLFO.** Alstom 1998–1999. 10/– 42.6 t.
**TFO.** Alstom 1998–1999. 28/– 1TD 1W. 33.5 t.
**TCO.** Alstom 1998–1999. 9/42 1T. 34.9 t.
**MSO(A).** Alstom 1998–1999. –/60. 42.5 t.
**MSO(B).** Alstom 1998–1999. –/60. 42.5 t.
**TSO.** Alstom 1998–1999. –/38 1TD 1W. 35.2 t.
**MSO(C).** Alstom 1998–1999. –/60. 40.5 t.
**DMSO.** Alstom 1998–1999. –/56. 45.3 t.

**Advertising liveries:**
460 002 Emirates Airlines (Australia)
460 003 Emirates Airlines (China)
460 004 Emirates Airlines (General)
460 006 Emirates Airlines (Africa)

| 460 001 | GV | P | *SN* | SL | 67901 | 74401 | 74411 | 74421 |
|         |    |   |      |    | 74431 | 74441 | 74451 | 67911 |
| 460 002 | AL | P | *SN* | SL | 67902 | 74402 | 74412 | 74422 |
|         |    |   |      |    | 74432 | 74442 | 74452 | 67912 |
| 460 003 | AL | P | *SN* | SL | 67903 | 74403 | 74413 | 74423 |
|         |    |   |      |    | 74433 | 74443 | 74453 | 67913 |

| 460 004 | **AL** | P | *SN* | SL | 67904 | 74404 | 74414 | 74424 |
|         |        |   |      |    | 74434 | 74444 | 74454 | 67914 |
| 460 005 | **GV** | P | *SN* | SL | 67905 | 74405 | 74415 | 74425 |
|         |        |   |      |    | 74435 | 74445 | 74455 | 67915 |
| 460 006 | **AL** | P | *SN* | SL | 67906 | 74406 | 74416 | 74426 |
|         |        |   |      |    | 74436 | 74446 | 74456 | 67916 |
| 460 007 | **GV** | P | *SN* | SL | 67907 | 74407 | 74417 | 74427 |
|         |        |   |      |    | 74437 | 74447 | 74457 | 67917 |
| 460 008 | **GV** | P | *SN* | SL | 67908 | 74408 | 74418 | 74428 |
|         |        |   |      |    | 74438 | 74448 | 74458 | 67918 |

# CLASS 465                                                    NETWORKER

Inner/outer suburban units.

**Formation:** DMSO–TSO–TSO–DMSO.
**Construction:** Welded aluminium alloy.
**Traction Motors:** Four Brush TIM970 (Classes 465/0 and 465/1) or GEC-Alsthom G352BY (Classes 465/2 and 465/9) asynchronous of 280 kW.
**Wheel Arrangement:** Bo-Bo + 2-2 + 2-2 + Bo-Bo.
**Braking:** Disc, rheostatic & regenerative.
**Dimensions:** 20.89/20.06 x 2.81 m.
**Bogies:** BREL P3/T3 (Classes 465/0 and 465/1), SRP BP62/BT52 (Classes 465/2 and 465/9).
**Couplers:** Tightlock.
**Gangways:** Within unit.                  **Control System:** 1992-type GTO Inverter.
**Doors:** Sliding plug.                      **Maximum Speed:** 75 m.p.h.
**Seating Layout:** 3+2 facing/unidirectional.
**Multiple Working:** Within class and with Class 466.

**64759–64808. DMSO(A).** Lot No. 31100 BREL York 1991–1993. –/86. 39.2 t.
**64809–64858. DMSO(B).** Lot No. 31100 BREL York 1991–1993. –/86. 39.2 t.
**65734–65749. DMSO(A).** Lot No. 31103 Metro-Cammell 1991–1993. –/86. 39.2 t.
**65784–65799. DMSO(B).** Lot No. 31103 Metro-Cammell 1991–1993. –/86. 39.2 t.
**65800–65846. DMSO(A).** Lot No. 31130 ABB York 1993–1994. –/86. 39.2 t.
**65847–65893. DMSO(B).** Lot No. 31130 ABB York 1993–1994. –/86. 39.2 t.
**72028–72126 (even nos.) TSO.** Lot No. 31102 BREL York 1991–1993. –/90. 27.2 t.
**72029–72127 (odd nos.) TSO.** Lot No. 31101 BREL York 1991–1993. –/86 1T. 28.0 t.
**72787–72817 (odd nos.) TSO.** Lot No. 31104 Metro-Cammell 1991–1992. –/86 1T. 28.0 t.
**72788–72818 (even nos.) TSO.** Lot No. 31105 Metro-Cammell 1991–1992. –/90. 27.2 t.
**72900–72992 (even nos.) TSO.** Lot No. 31102 ABB York 1993–1994. –/90. 27.2 t.
**72901–72993 (odd nos.) TSO.** Lot No. 31101 ABB York 1993–1994. –/86 1T. 28.0 t.

**Notes:** 465 014 and 465 041 are currently misformed with 64849 ex-465 041 in 465 014 and 64822 ex-465 014 in 465 041.

465 007 and 465 179 are currently misformed with 65828 ex-465 179 in 465 007 and 64815 ex-465 007 in 465 179.

**Class 465/0.** Built by BREL/ABB.

| | | | | | | | | |
|---|---|---|---|---|---|---|---|---|
| 465 001 | **CN** | H | *SE* | SG | 64759 | 72028 | 72029 | 64809 |
| 465 002 | **CN** | H | *SE* | SG | 64760 | 72030 | 72031 | 64810 |
| 465 003 | **CN** | H | *SE* | SG | 64761 | 72032 | 72033 | 64811 |
| 465 004 | **CN** | H | *SE* | SG | 64762 | 72034 | 72035 | 64812 |
| 465 005 | **CN** | H | *SE* | SG | 64763 | 72036 | 72037 | 64813 |
| 465 006 | **CN** | H | *SE* | SG | 64764 | 72038 | 72039 | 64814 |
| 465 007 | **CN** | H | *SE* | SG | 64765 | 72040 | 72041 | 65828 |
| 465 008 | **CN** | H | *SE* | SG | 64766 | 72042 | 72043 | 64816 |
| 465 009 | **CN** | H | *SE* | SG | 64767 | 72044 | 72045 | 64817 |
| 465 010 | **CN** | H | *SE* | SG | 64768 | 72046 | 72047 | 64818 |
| 465 011 | **CN** | H | *SE* | SG | 64769 | 72048 | 72049 | 64819 |
| 465 012 | **CN** | H | *SE* | SG | 64770 | 72050 | 72051 | 64820 |
| 465 013 | **CN** | H | *SE* | SG | 64771 | 72052 | 72053 | 64821 |
| 465 014 | **CN** | H | *SE* | SG | 64772 | 72054 | 72055 | 64849 |
| 465 015 | **CN** | H | *SE* | SG | 64773 | 72056 | 72057 | 64823 |
| 465 016 | **CN** | H | *SE* | SG | 64774 | 72058 | 72059 | 64824 |
| 465 017 | **CN** | H | *SE* | SG | 64775 | 72060 | 72061 | 64825 |
| 465 018 | **CN** | H | *SE* | SG | 64776 | 72062 | 72063 | 64826 |
| 465 019 | **CN** | H | *SE* | SG | 64777 | 72064 | 72065 | 64827 |
| 465 020 | **CN** | H | *SE* | SG | 64778 | 72066 | 72067 | 64828 |
| 465 021 | **CN** | H | *SE* | SG | 64779 | 72068 | 72069 | 64829 |
| 465 022 | **CN** | H | *SE* | SG | 64780 | 72070 | 72071 | 64830 |
| 465 023 | **CN** | H | *SE* | SG | 64781 | 72072 | 72073 | 64831 |
| 465 024 | **CN** | H | *SE* | SG | 64782 | 72074 | 72075 | 64832 |
| 465 025 | **CN** | H | *SE* | SG | 64783 | 72076 | 72077 | 64833 |
| 465 026 | **CN** | H | *SE* | SG | 64784 | 72078 | 72079 | 64834 |
| 465 027 | **CN** | H | *SE* | SG | 64785 | 72080 | 72081 | 64835 |
| 465 028 | **CN** | H | *SE* | SG | 64786 | 72082 | 72083 | 64836 |
| 465 029 | **CN** | H | *SE* | SG | 64787 | 72084 | 72085 | 64837 |
| 465 030 | **CN** | H | *SE* | SG | 64788 | 72086 | 72087 | 64838 |
| 465 031 | **CN** | H | *SE* | SG | 64789 | 72088 | 72089 | 64839 |
| 465 032 | **CN** | H | *SE* | SG | 64790 | 72090 | 72091 | 64840 |
| 465 033 | **CN** | H | *SE* | SG | 64791 | 72092 | 72093 | 64841 |
| 465 034 | **CN** | H | *SE* | SG | 64792 | 72094 | 72095 | 64842 |
| 465 035 | **CN** | H | *SE* | SG | 64793 | 72096 | 72097 | 64843 |
| 465 036 | **CN** | H | *SE* | SG | 64794 | 72098 | 72099 | 64844 |
| 465 037 | **CN** | H | *SE* | SG | 64795 | 72100 | 72101 | 64845 |
| 465 038 | **CN** | H | *SE* | SG | 64796 | 72102 | 72103 | 64846 |
| 465 039 | **CN** | H | *SE* | SG | 64797 | 72104 | 72105 | 64847 |
| 465 040 | **CN** | H | *SE* | SG | 64798 | 72106 | 72107 | 64848 |
| 465 041 | **CN** | H | *SE* | SG | 64799 | 72108 | 72109 | 64822 |
| 465 042 | **CN** | H | *SE* | SG | 64800 | 72110 | 72111 | 64850 |
| 465 043 | **CN** | H | *SE* | SG | 64801 | 72112 | 72113 | 64851 |
| 465 044 | **CN** | H | *SE* | SG | 64802 | 72114 | 72115 | 64852 |
| 465 045 | **CN** | H | *SE* | SG | 64803 | 72116 | 72117 | 64853 |
| 465 046 | **CN** | H | *SE* | SG | 64804 | 72118 | 72119 | 64854 |
| 465 047 | **CN** | H | *SE* | SG | 64805 | 72120 | 72121 | 64855 |
| 465 048 | **CN** | H | *SE* | SG | 64806 | 72122 | 72123 | 64856 |
| 465 049 | **CN** | H | *SE* | SG | 64807 | 72124 | 72125 | 64857 |
| 465 050 | **CN** | H | *SE* | SG | 64808 | 72126 | 72127 | 64858 |

**Class 465/1.** Built by BREL/ABB. Similar to Class 465/0 but with detail differences.

| | | | | | | | | |
|---|---|---|---|---|---|---|---|---|
| 465 151 | CN | H | *SE* | SG | 65800 | 72900 | 72901 | 65847 |
| 465 152 | CN | H | *SE* | SG | 65801 | 72902 | 72903 | 65848 |
| 465 153 | CN | H | *SE* | SG | 65802 | 72904 | 72905 | 65849 |
| 465 154 | CN | H | *SE* | SG | 65803 | 72906 | 72907 | 65850 |
| 465 155 | CN | H | *SE* | SG | 65804 | 72908 | 72909 | 65851 |
| 465 156 | CN | H | *SE* | SG | 65805 | 72910 | 72911 | 65852 |
| 465 157 | CN | H | *SE* | SG | 65806 | 72912 | 72913 | 65853 |
| 465 158 | CN | H | *SE* | SG | 65807 | 72914 | 72915 | 65854 |
| 465 159 | CN | H | *SE* | SG | 65808 | 72916 | 72917 | 65855 |
| 465 160 | CN | H | *SE* | SG | 65809 | 72918 | 72919 | 65856 |
| 465 161 | CN | H | *SE* | SG | 65810 | 72920 | 72921 | 65857 |
| 465 162 | CN | H | *SE* | SG | 65811 | 72922 | 72923 | 65858 |
| 465 163 | CN | H | *SE* | SG | 65812 | 72924 | 72925 | 65859 |
| 465 164 | CN | H | *SE* | SG | 65813 | 72926 | 72927 | 65860 |
| 465 165 | CN | H | *SE* | SG | 65814 | 72928 | 72929 | 65861 |
| 465 166 | CN | H | *SE* | SG | 65815 | 72930 | 72931 | 65862 |
| 465 167 | CN | H | *SE* | SG | 65816 | 72932 | 72933 | 65863 |
| 465 168 | CN | H | *SE* | SG | 65817 | 72934 | 72935 | 65864 |
| 465 169 | CN | H | *SE* | SG | 65818 | 72936 | 72937 | 65865 |
| 465 170 | CN | H | *SE* | SG | 65819 | 72938 | 72939 | 65866 |
| 465 171 | CN | H | *SE* | SG | 65820 | 72940 | 72941 | 65867 |
| 465 172 | CN | H | *SE* | SG | 65821 | 72942 | 72943 | 65868 |
| 465 173 | CN | H | *SE* | SG | 65822 | 72944 | 72945 | 65869 |
| 465 174 | CN | H | *SE* | SG | 65823 | 72946 | 72947 | 65870 |
| 465 175 | CN | H | *SE* | SG | 65824 | 72948 | 72949 | 65871 |
| 465 176 | CN | H | *SE* | SG | 65825 | 72950 | 72951 | 65872 |
| 465 177 | CN | H | *SE* | SG | 65826 | 72952 | 72953 | 65873 |
| 465 178 | CN | H | *SE* | SG | 65827 | 72954 | 72955 | 65874 |
| 465 179 | CN | H | *SE* | SG | 65875 | 72956 | 72957 | 64815 |
| 465 180 | CN | H | *SE* | SG | 65829 | 72958 | 72959 | 65876 |
| 465 181 | CN | H | *SE* | SG | 65830 | 72960 | 72961 | 65877 |
| 465 182 | CN | H | *SE* | SG | 65831 | 72962 | 72963 | 65878 |
| 465 183 | CN | H | *SE* | SG | 65832 | 72964 | 72965 | 65879 |
| 465 184 | CN | H | *SE* | SG | 65833 | 72966 | 72967 | 65880 |
| 465 185 | CN | H | *SE* | SG | 65834 | 72968 | 72969 | 65881 |
| 465 186 | CN | H | *SE* | SG | 65835 | 72970 | 72971 | 65882 |
| 465 187 | CN | H | *SE* | SG | 65836 | 72972 | 72973 | 65883 |
| 465 188 | CN | H | *SE* | SG | 65837 | 72974 | 72975 | 65884 |
| 465 189 | CN | H | *SE* | SG | 65838 | 72976 | 72977 | 65885 |
| 465 190 | CN | H | *SE* | SG | 65839 | 72978 | 72979 | 65886 |
| 465 191 | CN | H | *SE* | SG | 65840 | 72980 | 72981 | 65887 |
| 465 192 | CN | H | *SE* | SG | 65841 | 72982 | 72983 | 65888 |
| 465 193 | CN | H | *SE* | SG | 65842 | 72984 | 72985 | 65889 |
| 465 194 | CN | H | *SE* | SG | 65843 | 72986 | 72987 | 65890 |
| 465 195 | CN | H | *SE* | SG | 65844 | 72988 | 72989 | 65891 |
| 465 196 | CN | H | *SE* | SG | 65845 | 72990 | 72991 | 65892 |
| 465 197 | CN | H | *SE* | SG | 65846 | 72992 | 72993 | 65893 |

**Class 465/2.** Built by Metro-Cammell.
**Dimensions:** 20.80/20.15 x 2.81 m.

| | | | | | | | | |
|---|---|---|---|---|---|---|---|---|
| 465 235 | CN | A | *SE* | SG | 65734 | 72787 | 72788 | 65784 |
| 465 236 | CN | A | *SE* | SG | 65735 | 72789 | 72790 | 65785 |
| 465 237 | CN | A | *SE* | SG | 65736 | 72791 | 72792 | 65786 |
| 465 238 | CN | A | *SE* | SG | 65737 | 72793 | 72794 | 65787 |
| 465 239 | CN | A | *SE* | SG | 65738 | 72795 | 72796 | 65788 |
| 465 240 | CN | A | *SE* | SG | 65739 | 72797 | 72798 | 65789 |
| 465 241 | CN | A | *SE* | SG | 65740 | 72799 | 72800 | 65790 |
| 465 242 | CN | A | *SE* | SG | 65741 | 72801 | 72802 | 65791 |
| 465 243 | CN | A | *SE* | SG | 65742 | 72803 | 72804 | 65792 |
| 465 244 | CN | A | *SE* | SG | 65743 | 72805 | 72806 | 65793 |
| 465 245 | CN | A | *SE* | SG | 65744 | 72807 | 72808 | 65794 |
| 465 246 | CN | A | *SE* | SG | 65745 | 72809 | 72810 | 65795 |
| 465 247 | CN | A | *SE* | SG | 65746 | 72811 | 72812 | 65796 |
| 465 248 | CN | A | *SE* | SG | 65747 | 72813 | 72814 | 65797 |
| 465 249 | CN | A | *SE* | SG | 65748 | 72815 | 72816 | 65798 |
| 465 250 | CN | A | *SE* | SG | 65749 | 72817 | 72818 | 65799 |

**Class 465/9.** Built by Metro-Cammell. Refurbished at Wabtec, Doncaster in 2005 for longer distance services, with the addition of First Class seating areas and wheelchair spaces. Details as Class 465/0 unless stated.

**Formation:** DMCO–TSO(A)–TSO(B)–DMCO.
**Seating Layout:** 1: 2+2 facing/unidirectional, 2: 3+2 facing/unidirectional.

**65700–65733. DMCO(A).** Lot No. 31103 Metro-Cammell 1991–1993. 12/68. 39.2 t.
**72719–72785 (odd nos.) TSO(A).** Lot No. 31104 Metro-Cammell 1991–1992. –/76 1T 2W. 30.3 t.
**72720–72786 (even nos.) TSO(B).** Lot No. 31105 Metro-Cammell 1991–1992. –/90. 29.5 t.
**65750–65783. DMCO(B).** Lot No. 31103 Metro-Cammell 1991–1993. 12/68. 39.2 t.

| | | | | | | | | | |
|---|---|---|---|---|---|---|---|---|---|
| 465 901 | (465 201) | CN | A | *SE* | SG | 65700 | 72719 | 72720 | 65750 |
| 465 902 | (465 202) | CN | A | *SE* | SG | 65701 | 72721 | 72722 | 65751 |
| 465 903 | (465 203) | CN | A | *SE* | SG | 65702 | 72723 | 72724 | 65752 |
| 465 904 | (465 204) | CN | A | *SE* | SG | 65703 | 72725 | 72726 | 65753 |
| 465 905 | (465 205) | CN | A | *SE* | SG | 65704 | 72727 | 72728 | 65754 |
| 465 906 | (465 206) | CN | A | *SE* | SG | 65705 | 72729 | 72730 | 65755 |
| 465 907 | (465 207) | CN | A | *SE* | SG | 65706 | 72731 | 72732 | 65756 |
| 465 908 | (465 208) | CN | A | *SE* | SG | 65707 | 72733 | 72734 | 65757 |
| 465 909 | (465 209) | CN | A | *SE* | SG | 65708 | 72735 | 72736 | 65758 |
| 465 910 | (465 210) | CN | A | *SE* | SG | 65709 | 72737 | 72738 | 65759 |
| 465 911 | (465 211) | CN | A | *SE* | SG | 65710 | 72739 | 72740 | 65760 |
| 465 912 | (465 212) | CN | A | *SE* | SG | 65711 | 72741 | 72742 | 65761 |
| 465 913 | (465 213) | CN | A | *SE* | SG | 65712 | 72743 | 72744 | 65762 |
| 465 914 | (465 214) | CN | A | *SE* | SG | 65713 | 72745 | 72746 | 65763 |
| 465 915 | (465 215) | CN | A | *SE* | SG | 65714 | 72747 | 72748 | 65764 |
| 465 916 | (465 216) | CN | A | *SE* | SG | 65715 | 72749 | 72750 | 65765 |
| 465 917 | (465 217) | CN | A | *SE* | SG | 65716 | 72751 | 72752 | 65766 |
| 465 918 | (465 218) | CN | A | *SE* | SG | 65717 | 72753 | 72754 | 65767 |
| 465 919 | (465 219) | CN | A | *SE* | SG | 65718 | 72755 | 72756 | 65768 |

| 465 920 | (465 220) | CN | A | *SE* | SG | 65719 | 72757 | 72758 | 65769 |
| 465 921 | (465 221) | CN | A | *SE* | SG | 65720 | 72759 | 72760 | 65770 |
| 465 922 | (465 222) | CN | A | *SE* | SG | 65721 | 72761 | 72762 | 65771 |
| 465 923 | (465 223) | CN | A | *SE* | SG | 65722 | 72763 | 72764 | 65772 |
| 465 924 | (465 224) | CN | A | *SE* | SG | 65723 | 72765 | 72766 | 65773 |
| 465 925 | (465 225) | CN | A | *SE* | SG | 65724 | 72767 | 72768 | 65774 |
| 465 926 | (465 226) | CN | A | *SE* | SG | 65725 | 72769 | 72770 | 65775 |
| 465 927 | (465 227) | CN | A | *SE* | SG | 65726 | 72771 | 72772 | 65776 |
| 465 928 | (465 228) | CN | A | *SE* | SG | 65727 | 72773 | 72774 | 65777 |
| 465 929 | (465 229) | CN | A | *SE* | SG | 65728 | 72775 | 72776 | 65778 |
| 465 930 | (465 230) | CN | A | *SE* | SG | 65729 | 72777 | 72778 | 65779 |
| 465 931 | (465 231) | CN | A | *SE* | SG | 65730 | 72779 | 72780 | 65780 |
| 465 932 | (465 232) | CN | A | *SE* | SG | 65731 | 72781 | 72782 | 65781 |
| 465 933 | (465 233) | CN | A | *SE* | SG | 65732 | 72783 | 72784 | 65782 |
| 465 934 | (465 234) | CN | A | *SE* | SG | 65733 | 72785 | 72786 | 65783 |

**Name:** 465 903   Remembrance

## CLASS 466          NETWORKER          GEC-ALSTHOM

Inner/outer suburban units.

**Formation:** DMSO–DTSO.
**Construction:** Welded aluminium alloy.
**Traction Motors:** Four GEC-Alsthom G352AY asynchronous of 280 kW.
**Wheel Arrangement:** Bo-Bo + 2-2.
**Braking:** Disc, rheostatic & regenerative.
**Dimensions:** 20.80 x 2.80 m.
**Bogies:** BREL P3/T3.                   **Couplers:** Tightlock.
**Gangways:** Within unit.                 **Control System:** 1992-type GTO Inverter.
**Doors:** Sliding plug.                    **Maximum Speed:** 75 m.p.h.
**Seating Layout:** 3+2 facing/unidirectional.
**Multiple Working:** Within class and with Class 465.

**DMSO.** Lot No. 31128 Birmingham 1993–1994. –/86. 40.6 t.
**DTSO.** Lot No. 31129 Birmingham 1993–1994. –/82 1T. 31.4 t.

| 466 001 | CN | A | *SE* | SG | 64860 | 78312 |
| 466 002 | CN | A | *SE* | SG | 64861 | 78313 |
| 466 003 | CN | A | *SE* | SG | 64862 | 78314 |
| 466 004 | CN | A | *SE* | SG | 64863 | 78315 |
| 466 005 | CN | A | *SE* | SG | 64864 | 78316 |
| 466 006 | CN | A | *SE* | SG | 64865 | 78317 |
| 466 007 | CN | A | *SE* | SG | 64866 | 78318 |
| 466 008 | CN | A | *SE* | SG | 64867 | 78319 |
| 466 009 | CN | A | *SE* | SG | 64868 | 78320 |
| 466 010 | CN | A | *SE* | SG | 64869 | 78321 |
| 466 011 | CN | A | *SE* | SG | 64870 | 78322 |
| 466 012 | CN | A | *SE* | SG | 64871 | 78323 |
| 466 013 | CN | A | *SE* | SG | 64872 | 78324 |
| 466 014 | CN | A | *SE* | SG | 64873 | 78325 |
| 466 015 | CN | A | *SE* | SG | 64874 | 78326 |
| 466 016 | CN | A | *SE* | SG | 64875 | 78327 |

| 466 017 | CN | A | *SE* | SG | 64876 | 78328 |
| 466 018 | CN | A | *SE* | SG | 64877 | 78329 |
| 466 019 | CN | A | *SE* | SG | 64878 | 78330 |
| 466 020 | CN | A | *SE* | SG | 64879 | 78331 |
| 466 021 | CN | A | *SE* | SG | 64880 | 78332 |
| 466 022 | CN | A | *SE* | SG | 64881 | 78333 |
| 466 023 | CN | A | *SE* | SG | 64882 | 78334 |
| 466 024 | CN | A | *SE* | SG | 64883 | 78335 |
| 466 025 | CN | A | *SE* | SG | 64884 | 78336 |
| 466 026 | CN | A | *SE* | SG | 64885 | 78337 |
| 466 027 | CN | A | *SE* | SG | 64886 | 78338 |
| 466 028 | CN | A | *SE* | SG | 64887 | 78339 |
| 466 029 | CN | A | *SE* | SG | 64888 | 78340 |
| 466 030 | CN | A | *SE* | SG | 64889 | 78341 |
| 466 031 | CN | A | *SE* | SG | 64890 | 78342 |
| 466 032 | CN | A | *SE* | SG | 64891 | 78343 |
| 466 033 | CN | A | *SE* | SG | 64892 | 78344 |
| 466 034 | CN | A | *SE* | SG | 64893 | 78345 |
| 466 035 | CN | A | *SE* | SG | 64894 | 78346 |
| 466 036 | CN | A | *SE* | SG | 64895 | 78347 |
| 466 037 | CN | A | *SE* | SG | 64896 | 78348 |
| 466 038 | CN | A | *SE* | SG | 64897 | 78349 |
| 466 039 | CN | A | *SE* | SG | 64898 | 78350 |
| 466 040 | CN | A | *SE* | SG | 64899 | 78351 |
| 466 041 | CN | A | *SE* | SG | 64900 | 78352 |
| 466 042 | CN | A | *SE* | SG | 64901 | 78353 |
| 466 043 | CN | A | *SE* | SG | 64902 | 78354 |

## CLASS 483                                     METRO-CAMMELL

Built 1938 onwards for LTE. Converted 1989–1990 for the Isle of Wight Line.

**Formation:** DMSO–DMSO.
**System:** 660 V DC third rail.
**Construction:** Steel.
**Traction Motors:** Two Crompton Parkinson/GEC/BTH LT100 of 125 kW.
**Braking:** Tread.                          **Dimensions:** 16.15 x 2.69 m.
**Bogies:** LT design.                       **Couplers:** Wedglock.
**Gangways:** None. End doors.
**Control System:** Pneumatic Camshaft Motor (PCM).
**Doors:** Sliding.                          **Maximum Speed:** 45 m.p.h.
**Seating Layout:** Longitudinal or 2+2 facing/unidirectional.
**Multiple Working:** Within class.

**Notes:** The last three numbers of the unit number only are carried.

Former London Underground numbers are shown in parentheses.

**DMSO (A).** Lot No. 31071. –/40. 27.4 t.
**DMSO (B).** Lot No. 31072. –/42. 27.4 t.

| 483 002 | LT | SW | *SW* | RY | 122 | (10221) | 225 | (11142) |
| 483 004 | LT | SW | *SW* | RY | 124 | (10205) | 224 | (11205) |

| 483 006 | IL | SW | *SW* | RY | 126 | (10297) | 226 | (11297) |
|---------|----|----|------|----|-----|---------|-----|---------|
| 483 007 | LT | SW | *SW* | RY | 127 | (10291) | 227 | (11291) |
| 483 008 | LT | SW | *SW* | RY | 128 | (10255) | 228 | (11255) |
| 483 009 | LT | SW | *SW* | RY | 129 | (10289) | 229 | (11229) |

# CLASS 507            BREL YORK

Suburban units.

**Formation:** BDMSO–TSO–DMSO.
**Construction:** Steel underframe, aluminium alloy body and roof.
**Traction Motors:** Four GEC G310AZ of 82.125 kW.
**Wheel Arrangement:** Bo-Bo + 2-2 + Bo-Bo.
**Braking:** Disc & rheostatic.      **Dimensions:** 20.33/20.18 x 2.82 m.
**Bogies:** BX1.      **Couplers:** Tightlock.
**Gangways:** Within unit + end doors.      **Control System:** Camshaft.
**Doors:** Sliding.      **Maximum Speed:** 75 m.p.h.
**Seating Layout:** All refurbished with 2+2 high-back facing seating.
**Multiple Working:** Within class and with Class 508.

**BDMSO.** Lot No. 30906 1978–1980. –/56(3) 1W. 37.0 t.
**TSO.** Lot No. 30907 1978–1980. –/74. 25.5 t.
**DMSO.** Lot No. 30908 1978–1980. –/56(3) 1W. 35.5 t.

**Advertising liveries:**
507 008 Liverpool European Capital of Culture (Maritime theme – blue).
507 019 Liverpool European Capital of Culture (Sport theme – red).
507 033 Liverpool European Capital of Culture (Heritage theme – green).

| 507 001 | ME | A | *ME* | BD | 64367 | 71342 | 64405 | |
|---------|----|----|------|----|-------|-------|-------|---|
| 507 002 | ME | A | *ME* | BD | 64368 | 71343 | 64406 | |
| 507 003 | ME | A | *ME* | BD | 64369 | 71344 | 64407 | |
| 507 004 | ME | A | *ME* | BD | 64388 | 71345 | 64408 | Bob Paisley |
| 507 005 | ME | A | *ME* | BD | 64371 | 71346 | 64409 | |
| 507 006 | ME | A | *ME* | BD | 64372 | 71347 | 64410 | |
| 507 007 | ME | A | *ME* | BD | 64373 | 71348 | 64411 | |
| 507 008 | AL | A | *ME* | BD | 64374 | 71349 | 64412 | |
| 507 009 | ME | A | *ME* | BD | 64375 | 71350 | 64413 | Dixie Dean |
| 507 010 | ME | A | *ME* | BD | 64376 | 71351 | 64414 | |
| 507 011 | ME | A | *ME* | BD | 64377 | 71352 | 64415 | |
| 507 012 | ME | A | *ME* | BD | 64378 | 71353 | 64416 | |
| 507 013 | ME | A | *ME* | BD | 64379 | 71354 | 64417 | |
| 507 014 | ME | A | *ME* | BD | 64380 | 71355 | 64418 | |
| 507 015 | ME | A | *ME* | BD | 64381 | 71356 | 64419 | |
| 507 016 | ME | A | *ME* | BD | 64382 | 71357 | 64420 | |
| 507 017 | ME | A | *ME* | BD | 64383 | 71358 | 64421 | |
| 507 018 | ME | A | *ME* | BD | 64384 | 71359 | 64422 | |
| 507 019 | AL | A | *ME* | BD | 64385 | 71360 | 64423 | |
| 507 020 | ME | A | *ME* | BD | 64386 | 71361 | 64424 | John Peel |
| 507 021 | ME | A | *ME* | BD | 64387 | 71362 | 64425 | Red Rum |
| 507 023 | ME | A | *ME* | BD | 64389 | 71364 | 64427 | |
| 507 024 | ME | A | *ME* | BD | 64390 | 71365 | 64428 | |

| 507 025 | **ME** | A | *ME* | BD | 64391 | 71366 | 64429 |
| 507 026 | **ME** | A | *ME* | BD | 64392 | 71367 | 64430 |
| 507 027 | **ME** | A | *ME* | BD | 64393 | 71368 | 64431 |
| 507 028 | **ME** | A | *ME* | BD | 64394 | 71369 | 64432 |
| 507 029 | **ME** | A | *ME* | BD | 64395 | 71370 | 64433 |
| 507 030 | **ME** | A | *ME* | BD | 64396 | 71371 | 64434 |
| 507 031 | **ME** | A | *ME* | BD | 64397 | 71372 | 64435 |
| 507 032 | **ME** | A | *ME* | BD | 64398 | 71373 | 64436 |
| 507 033 | **AL** | A | *ME* | BD | 64399 | 71374 | 64437 |

# CLASS 508                                          BREL YORK

Suburban units.

**Formation:** DMSO–TSO–BDMSO.
**Construction:** Steel underframe, aluminium alloy body and roof.
**Traction Motors:** Four GEC G310AZ of 82.125 kW.
**Wheel Arrangement:** Bo-Bo + 2-2 + Bo-Bo.
**Braking:** Disc & rheostatic.          **Dimensions:** 20.33/20.18 x 2.82 m.
**Bogies:** BX1.                          **Couplers:** Tightlock.
**Gangways:** Within unit + end doors.   **Control System:** Camshaft.
**Doors:** Sliding.                       **Maximum Speed:** 75 m.p.h.
**Seating Layout:** All Merseyrail units have been refurbished with 2+2 high-back facing seating. SE and London Overground units have 3+2 low-back facing seating.
**Multiple Working:** Within class and with Class 507.

**DMSO.** Lot No. 30979 1979–1980. –/56(3) 1W. 36.0 t.
**TSO.** Lot No. 30980 1979–1980. –/74. 26.5 t.
**BDMSO.** Lot No. 30981 1979–1980. –/56(3) 1W. 36.5 t.

**Note:** 508 139 and 508 143 are currently misformed with 64734 in 508 139 instead of 64730 which is in 508 143. 508 139 is undergoing repairs at Eastleigh following accident damage.

**Advertising livery:**
508 134 Liverpool European Capital of Culture (Creativity theme – purple).

**Class 508/1.** Merseyrail units.

| 508 103 | **ME** | A | *ME* | BD | 64651 | 71485 | 64694 |
| 508 104 | **ME** | A | *ME* | BD | 64652 | 71486 | 64695 |
| 508 108 | **ME** | A | *ME* | BD | 64656 | 71490 | 64699 |
| 508 110 | **ME** | A | *ME* | BD | 64658 | 71492 | 64701 |
| 508 111 | **ME** | A | *ME* | BD | 64659 | 71493 | 64702 |
| 508 112 | **ME** | A | *ME* | BD | 64660 | 71494 | 64703 |
| 508 114 | **ME** | A | *ME* | BD | 64662 | 71496 | 64705 |
| 508 115 | **ME** | A | *ME* | BD | 64663 | 71497 | 64706 |
| 508 117 | **ME** | A | *ME* | BD | 64665 | 71499 | 64708 |
| 508 120 | **ME** | A | *ME* | BD | 64668 | 71502 | 64711 |
| 508 122 | **ME** | A | *ME* | BD | 64670 | 71504 | 64713 |
| 508 123 | **ME** | A | *ME* | BD | 64671 | 71505 | 64714 |
| 508 124 | **ME** | A | *ME* | BD | 64672 | 71506 | 64715 |

| 508 125 | **ME** | A | *ME* | BD | 64673 | 71507 | 64716 | |
| 508 126 | **ME** | A | *ME* | BD | 64674 | 71508 | 64717 | |
| 508 127 | **ME** | A | *ME* | BD | 64675 | 71509 | 64718 | |
| 508 128 | **ME** | A | *ME* | BD | 64676 | 71510 | 64719 | |
| 508 130 | **ME** | A | *ME* | BD | 64678 | 71512 | 64721 | |
| 508 131 | **ME** | A | *ME* | BD | 64679 | 71513 | 64722 | |
| 508 134 | **AL** | A | *ME* | BD | 64682 | 71516 | 64725 | |
| 508 136 | **ME** | A | *ME* | BD | 64684 | 71518 | 64727 | Capital of Culture |
| 508 137 | **ME** | A | *ME* | BD | 64685 | 71519 | 64728 | |
| 508 138 | **ME** | A | *ME* | BD | 64686 | 71520 | 64729 | |
| 508 139 | **ME** | A | | ZG | 64687 | 71521 | 64734 | |
| 508 140 | **ME** | A | *ME* | BD | 64688 | 71522 | 64731 | |
| 508 141 | **ME** | A | *ME* | BD | 64689 | 71523 | 64732 | |
| 508 143 | **ME** | A | *ME* | BD | 64691 | 71525 | 64730 | |

**Class 508/2.** Units facelifted for the South Eastern lines by Wessex Traincare/
Alstom, Eastleigh 1998–1999.

**DMSO.** Lot No. 30979 1979–1980. –/66. 36.0 t.
**TSO.** Lot No. 30980 1979–1980. –/79 1W. 26.5 t.
**BDMSO.** Lot No. 30981 1979–1980. –/74. 36.5 t.

| 508 201 | (508 101) | **CX** | A | | AF | 64649 | 71483 | 64692 |
| 508 202 | (508 105) | **CX** | A | | AF | 64653 | 71487 | 64696 |
| 508 203 | (508 106) | **CN** | A | | RM | 64654 | 71488 | 64697 |
| 508 204 | (508 107) | **CX** | A | | AF | 64655 | 71489 | 64698 |
| 508 205 | (508 109) | **CN** | A | | RM | 64657 | 71491 | 64700 |
| 508 206 | (508 113) | **CX** | A | | AF | 64661 | 71495 | 64704 |
| 508 207 | (508 116) | **CN** | A | | RM | 64664 | 71498 | 64707 |
| 508 208 | (508 119) | **CN** | A | | GI | 64667 | 71501 | 64710 |
| 508 209 | (508 121) | **CX** | A | | AF | 64669 | 71503 | 64712 |
| 508 210 | (508 129) | **CN** | A | | GI | 64677 | 71515 | 64720 |
| 508 211 | (508 132) | **CN** | A | | GI | 64680 | 71514 | 64723 |
| 508 212 | (508 133) | **CX** | A | | GI | 64681 | 71525 | 64724 |

**Class 508/3.** Units facelifted units for use on Euston–Watford Junction services
by Alstom, Eastleigh 2002–2003.

**DMSO.** Lot No. 30979 1979–1980. –/68 1W. 36.0 t.
**TSO.** Lot No. 30980 1979–1980. –/86. 26.5 t.
**BDMSO.** Lot No. 30981 1979–1980. –/68 1W. 36.5 t.

| 508 301 | (508 102) | **SL** | A | | ZG | 64650 | 71484 | 64693 |
| 508 302 | (508 135) | **SL** | A | *LO* | WN | 64683 | 71517 | 64726 |
| 508 303 | (508 142) | **SL** | A | *LO* | WN | 64690 | 71524 | 64733 |

# 4.3. EUROSTAR UNITS (CLASS 373)

Eurostar units were built for and are normally used on services between Britain and Continental Europe via the Channel Tunnel. Apart from such workings units may be used as follows:

SNCF-owned units 3203/04, 3225/26 and 3227/28 have been removed from the Eurostar pool and only operate SNCF-internal services between Paris and Lille. In addition six of the former Regional Eurostar sets are now on hire to SNCF for use on Pairis–Lille services and also a Paris–Douai/Valanciennes turn.

Each train consists of two 10-car units coupled, with a motor car at each driving end (the sets built for Regional Eurostar services are 8-car). All units are articulated with an extra motor bogie on the coach adjacent to the motor car.

Sets marked "r" have been refurbished. This now includes all sets used by Eurostar, but not 3101/02 (in store) or the sets used by SNCF.

**Formation:** DM–MSO–4TSO–RB–2TFO–TBFO or DM–MSO–3TSO–RB–TFO–TBFO. Gangwayed within pair of units. Air conditioned.
**Construction:** Steel.
**Supply Systems:** 25 kV AC 50 Hz overhead or 3000 V DC overhead (* also equipped for 1500 V DC overhead operation).
**Control System:** GTO–GTO Inverter on UK 750 V DC and 25 kV AC, GTO Chopper on SNCB 3000 V DC.
**Wheel Arrangement:** Bo–Bo + Bo–2–2–2–2–2–2–2–2–2.
**Length:** 22.15 m (DM), 21.85 m (MS & TBF), 18.70 m (other cars).
**Couplers:** Schaku 10S at outer ends, Schaku 10L at inner end of each DM and outer ends of each sub set.
**Maximum Speed:** 186 m.p.h. (300 km/h.)
**Built:** 1992–1993 by GEC-Alsthom/Brush/ANF/De Dietrich/BN Construction/ACEC.
**Note:** DM vehicles carry the set numbers indicated below.

**Class 373/0. 10-Car sets.** Built for services starting from/terminating in London Waterloo. Individual vehicles in each set are allocated numbers 373xxx0 + 373xxx1 + 373xxx2 + 373xxx3 + 373xxx4 + 373xxx5 + 373xxx6 + 373xxx7 + 373xxx8 + 373xxx9, where 3xxx denotes the set number.

**Non-standard livery (0):** Grey with silver ends, TGV symbol & green/blue doors.

**373xxx0 series. DM.** Lot No. 31118 1992–1995. 68.5 t.
**373xxx1 series. MSO.** Lot No. 31119 1992–1995. –/48 2T. 44.6 t.
**373xxx2 series. TSO.** Lot No. 31120 1992–1995. –/58 1T (r –/56 1T). 28.1 t.
**373xxx3 series. TSO.** Lot No. 31121 1992–1995. –/58 2T (r –/56 2T). 29.7 t.
**373xxx4 series. TSO.** Lot No. 31122 1992–1995. –/58 1T (r –/56 1T). 28.3 t.
**373xxx5 series. TSO.** Lot No. 31123 1992–1995. –/58 2T (r –/56 2T). 29.2 t.
**373xxx6 series. RB.** Lot No.31124 1992–1995. 31.1 t.
**373xxx7 series. TFO.** Lot No. 31125 1992–1995. 39/– 1T. 29.6 t.
**373xxx8 series. TFO.** Lot No. 31126 1992–1995. 39/– 1T. 32.2 t.
**373xxx9 series. TBFO.** Lot No. 31127 1992–1995. 25/– 1TD. 39.4 t.

| | | | | | | | | | |
|---|---|---|---|---|---|---|---|---|---|
| 3001 r | **EU** | EU | *EU* | TI Tread Lightly | | 3004 r | **EU** | EU | *EU* | TI |
| 3002 r | **EU** | EU | *EU* | TI Voyage Vert | | 3005 r | **EU** | EU | *EU* | TI |
| 3003 r | **EU** | EU | *EU* | TI | | 3006 r | **EU** | EU | *EU* | TI |

| Set | | | | | Name |
|---|---|---|---|---|---|
| 3007 r | **EU** | EU | *EU* | TI | Waterloo Sunset |
| 3008 r | **EU** | EU | *EU* | TI | Waterloo Sunset |
| 3009 r | **EU** | EU | *EU* | TI | |
| 3010 r | **EU** | EU | *EU* | TI | |
| 3011 r | **EU** | EU | *EU* | TI | |
| 3012 r | **EU** | EU | *EU* | TI | |
| 3013 r | **EU** | EU | *EU* | TI | LONDON 2012 |
| 3014 r | **EU** | EU | *EU* | TI | LONDON 2012 |
| 3015 r | **EU** | EU | *EU* | TI | |
| 3016 r | **EU** | EU | *EU* | TI | |
| 3017 r | **EU** | EU | *EU* | TI | |
| 3018 r | **EU** | EU | *EU* | TI | |
| 3019 r | **EU** | EU | *EU* | TI | |
| 3020 r | **EU** | EU | *EU* | TI | |
| 3021 r | **EU** | EU | *EU* | TI | |
| 3022 r | **EU** | EU | *EU* | TI | |
| 3101 | **EU** | SB | | TI | |
| 3102 | **EU** | SB | | TI | |
| 3103 r | **EU** | SB | *EU* | FF | |
| 3104 r | **EU** | SB | *EU* | FF | |
| 3105 r | **EU** | SB | *EU* | FF | |
| 3106 r | **EU** | SB | *EU* | FF | |
| 3107 r | **EU** | SB | *EU* | FF | |
| 3108 r | **EU** | SB | *EU* | FF | |
| 3201 r* | **EU** | SF | *EU* | LY | |
| 3202 r* | **EU** | SF | *EU* | LY | |
| 3203 | **0** | SF | *SF* | LY | |
| 3204 | **0** | SF | *SF* | LY | |
| 3205 r | **EU** | SF | *EU* | LY | |
| 3206 r | **EU** | SF | *EU* | LY | |
| 3207 r* | **EU** | SF | *EU* | LY | MICHEL HOLLARD |
| 3208 r* | **EU** | SF | *EU* | LY | MICHEL HOLLARD |
| 3209 r* | **EU** | SF | *EU* | LY | THE DA VINCI CODE |
| 3210 r* | **EU** | SF | *EU* | LY | THE DA VINCI CODE |
| 3211 r | **EU** | SF | *EU* | LY | |
| 3212 r | **EU** | SF | *EU* | LY | |
| 3213 r* | **EU** | SF | *EU* | LY | |
| 3214 r* | **EU** | SF | *EU* | LY | |
| 3215 r* | **EU** | SF | *EU* | LY | |
| 3216 r* | **EU** | SF | *EU* | LY | |
| 3217 r* | **EU** | SF | *EU* | LY | |
| 3218 r* | **EU** | SF | *EU* | LY | |
| 3219 r | **EU** | SF | *EU* | LY | |
| 3220 r | **EU** | SF | *EU* | LY | |
| 3221 r* | **EU** | SF | *EU* | LY | |
| 3222 r* | **EU** | SF | *EU* | LY | |
| 3223 r* | **EU** | SF | *EU* | LY | |
| 3224 r* | **EU** | SF | *EU* | LY | |
| 3225 | **0** | SF | *SF* | LY | |
| 3226 | **0** | SF | *SF* | LY | |
| 3227 | **0** | SF | *SF* | LY | |
| 3228 | **0** | SF | *SF* | LY | |
| 3229 r* | **EU** | SF | *EU* | LY | |
| 3230 r* | **EU** | SF | *EU* | LY | |
| 3231 r | **EU** | SF | *EU* | LY | |
| 3232 r | **EU** | SF | *EU* | LY | |

**Class 373/2. 8-Car sets. Built for Regional Eurostar services, now on long-term hire to SNCF.** Individual vehicles in each set are allocated numbers 373xxx0 + 373xxx1 + 373xxx2 + 373xxx3 + 373xxx5 + 373xxx6 + 373xxx7 + 373xxx9, where 3xxx denotes the set number.

**3733xx0 series. DM.** 68.5 t.
**3733xx1 series. MSO.** –/48 1T. 44.6 t.
**3733xx2 series. TSO.** –/58 2T. 28.1 t.
**3733xx3 series. TSO.** –/58 1T. 29.7 t.
**3733xx5 series. TSO.** –/58 1T. 29.2 t.
**3733xx6 series. RB.** 31.1 t.
**3733xx7 series. TFO.** 39/– 1T. 29.6 t.
**3733xx9 series. TBFO.** 18/– 1TD. 39.4 t.

| Set | | | | | | Set | | | | |
|---|---|---|---|---|---|---|---|---|---|---|
| 3301 | **EU** | EU | *SF* | LY | | 3308 | **EU** | EU | | TI |
| 3302 | **EU** | EU | *SF* | LY | | 3309 | **EU** | EU | *SF* | LY |
| 3303 | **EU** | EU | *SF* | LY | | 3310 | **EU** | EU | *SF* | LY |
| 3304 | **EU** | EU | *SF* | LY | | 3311 | **EU** | EU | *SF* | LY |
| 3305 | **EU** | EU | *SF* | LY | | 3312 | **EU** | EU | *SF* | LY |
| 3306 | **EU** | EU | *SF* | LY | | 3313 | **EU** | EU | *SF* | LY |
| 3307 | **EU** | EU | | LY | | 3314 | **EU** | EU | *SF* | LY |

**Spare DM:**
| 3999 | **EU** | EU | *EU* | TI |
|---|---|---|---|---|

# 4.4. INTERNAL USE EMUS

**Class 423 "Vep" Service Units**

The following units are used by Bombardier Transportation as tractor units at Chart Leacon. They have been fitted with special couplers for moving intermediate EMU vehicles.

| 3905 | **CX** | BT | AF | 76398 | 62266 | 70904 | 76397 |
|------|--------|----|----|-------|-------|-------|-------|
| 3918 | **CX** | BT | AF | 76528 | 62321 | 70950 | 76527 |

**Class 930 Service Units**

The following unit (converted from Class 405) is in use by East Midlands Trains at Derby as a Staff Coach (975600) and as a Training Room (975601).

| 930 010 | **RK** | EM | DY | 975600 (10988) 975601 (10843) |
|---------|--------|----|----|-------------------------------|

The following units (converted from Class 416s) are used by Southern for de-icing within the confines of Selhurst depot.

| 930 204 | **RK** | SN | SU | 977874 (65302) 977875 (65304) |
|---------|--------|----|----|-------------------------------|
| 930 206 | **RK** | SN | SU | 977924 (65382) 977925 (65379) |

# 4.5. EMUS AWAITING DISPOSAL

The list below comprises vehicles awaiting disposal which are stored on the National Railway network.

**IMPORTANT NOTE:** EMUs still intact but already at scrapyards, unless specifically there for storage purposes, are not included in this list.

# 25 kV AC 50 Hz OVERHEAD UNITS:

**Non-standard livery:** 960 101 and 960 102 – Light blue & white.

**Note:** 390 033 has been written off following the Lambrigg accident of February 2007. It is expected that some vehicles will be used for training purposes.

| 390 033 | **VT** | VI | LM | 69133 | 69433 | 69533 | 69633 | 68833 |
|---------|--------|----|----|-------|-------|-------|-------|-------|
|         |        |    |    | 69733 | 69833 | 69933 | 69233 |       |

| 960 101 | **O** | A | SN | 977962 (75642) 977963 (61937) 977964 (75981) |
|---------|-------|---|----|-----------------------------------------------|
| 960 102 | **O** | A | SN | 977965 (75965) 977966 (61928) 977967 (75972) |

**Spare cars:**

| Cl. 309 | **RR** | WC | CS | 71758 |       |       |       |
|---------|--------|----|----|-------|-------|-------|-------|
| Cl. 310 | **N**  | H  | SN | 62075 | 62076 | 70736 | 76135 |

## 750 V DC THIRD RAIL UNITS:

**Note:** Vehicles shown as owned by KN have been purchased by Knights Rail Services with a view to returning two units (one of which will be 1881) to main line condition.

**Non-standard liveries:**
1304, 1881, 1884 & 3536 – Old Stagecoach (as **N** but with an orange stripe).
930 101 – Used for paint trials.

| | | | | | | | | |
|---|---|---|---|---|---|---|---|---|
| 1304 | 0 | KN | ZG | 76583 | 62289 | 70969 | 76613 | |
| 1881 | 0 | KN | ZG | 76762 | 62400 | 71080 | 76833 | |
| 1884 | 0 | KN | ZG | 76767 | | | 76838 | |
| 3417 | B | SW | ZG | 76262 | 62236 | 70797 | 76263 | Gordon Pettitt |
| 3536 | 0 | KN | ZG | | 62207 | 70897 | | |
| 930 101 | 0 | NR | AF | 977207 | (61658) | 977609 | (65414) | |

**Spare cars:**

**Non-standard liveries:**
70293 – Used for paint trials.
76112 – Silver (prototype Class 424 "Networker Classic" conversion).
64709 – Old Merseytravel (yellow & white with grey & black stripes).

| | | | | | |
|---|---|---|---|---|---|
| Cl. 411 | 0 | H | ZI | 70293 | |
| Cl. 424 | 0 | BT | ZD | 76112 | |
| Cl. 508 | 0 | A | Reid Freight, Stoke-on-Trent | 64709 | |
| Cl. 930 | RO | NR | AF | 975598 (10989) | 975605 (10940) |
| | RO | NR | SE | 977364 (10400) | |

# 5. UK LIGHT RAIL & METRO SYSTEMS

This section lists the rolling stock of the various light rail and metro systems in the UK. Passenger carrying vehicles only are covered (not works vehicles). This listing does not cover the London Underground network.

## 5.1. BLACKPOOL & FLEETWOOD TRAMWAY

Until the opening of Manchester Metrolink, the Blackpool Tramway was the only urban/inter-urban tramway system left in Britain. The infrastructure is owned by the local authorities and the tramway is operated by Blackpool Transport Services Ltd., using a mixture of trams dating back to the 1930s, as well as some newer vehicles dating from the 1980s. The line runs for 11½ miles from Fleetwood in the north to Starr Gate in the south. There is an extensive summer service between North Pier and Pleasure Beach.
**System:** 550 V DC overhead.
**Depot & Workshops:** Rigby Road, Blackpool.
**Standard livery:** Cream & green except where stated otherwise.

All cars are single-deck unless stated otherwise. For advertising liveries predominate colours are given.

(S) – Stored out of service. At the end of the 2004 season several trams were stood down (or "mothballed") at Rigby Road depot as surplus to requirements.

The status of individual trams is flexible and is varied to meet traffic requirements and each season.

## OPEN BOAT CARS                                          A1-1A

Used during the summer season!
**Built:** 1934 by English Electric. 12 built.
**Traction Motors:** Two EE327 of 30 kW.
**Seats:** 56 (* 52).

| | | |
|---|---|---|
| 600 | 604 *(S) | 607 (S)  Yellow & Green |
| 602  *  Yellow & Black | 605 *    Green & Cream | |

**Named:** 600 "THE DUCHESS OF CORNWALL".

## BRUSH RAILCOACHES                                       A1-1A

Most of the Brush Railcoaches are now mothballed and only five remained in use at the time of writing.
**Built:** 1937 by Brush, Loughborough. 20 built.
**Traction Motors:** Two EE305 of 40 kW.
**Seats:** 48 (* 46).
**Note:** 636 has been withdrawn for testing of new traction equipment.
**Advertising liveries:**

621 – Hot Ice Show, Pleasure Beach (blue)
622 – Pontins (blue & yellow)

626 – Blackpool Zoo & Dinosaur Safari (white, black & green)
627 – Buccaneer Family Bar (black)
630 – Karting 2000 (yellow & purple)
631 – Walls ice cream (red)
632 – Blackpool Sealife Centre (blue)
634 – Cala Gran Holiday Park (blue)
637 – Blackpool Zoo (green & white)

| 621 (S) | **AL** | 626 * | **AL** | 632 (S) | **AL** |
|---|---|---|---|---|---|
| 622 | **AL** | 627 (S) | **AL** | 634 (S) | **AL** |
| 623 | **Green & Cream** | 630 | **AL** | 636 (S) | **Yellow/green** |
| 625 (S) | | 631 | **AL** | 637 (S) | **AL** |

## CENTENARY CLASS                                      A1-1A

The newest trams in use, these are used all year round.
**Built:** 1984–1987. Body by East Lancs. Coachbuilders, Blackburn. Driver-only operated.
**Traction Motors:** Two EE305 of 40 kW.
**Seats:** 53.                          † Rebuilt from GEC car 651.
**Advertising liveries:**

641 – Orion Bingo, Cleveleys (blue)
643 – "G" Casino (black)
644 – Farmer Parrs Animal World/Fleetwood Market (yellow)
645 – Palm Beach Hotel (blue)
646 – Paul Gaunt Furniture (blue)
648 – Vue Cinema, Cleveleys (blue)

| 641 | **AL** | 643 | **AL** | 645 | **AL** | 647 | **Yellow** |
|---|---|---|---|---|---|---|---|
| 642 | **Yellow** | 644 | **AL** | 646 | **AL** | 648 † | **AL** |

## PROGRESS TWIN CARS                          A1-1A + 2-2

These cars mainly see use during the "illuminations" season.
**Built:** Motor cars (671–676) rebuilt 1958–1960 from English Electric Railcoaches by Blackpool Corporation Transport. Driving trailers (681–687) built 1960 by Metro-Cammell.
**Traction Motors:** Two EE305 of 40 kW.          **Seats:** 53 + 61.

**Note:** Following the scrapping of 677 in 2007, trailer 687 is now used as a store room at Rigby Road depot.

| 671+681 | **Green/yellow** | 673+683 | **Turquoise/yellow** | 675+685 | **Red/yellow** |
|---|---|---|---|---|---|
| 672+682 | **Orange/yellow** | 674+684 | **Blue/yellow** | 676+686 | **(S)** |

## ENGLISH ELECTRIC RAILCOACHES                    A1-1A

**Built:** Rebuilt 1958–1960 from EE Railcoaches. Originally ran with trailers.
**Traction Motors:** Two EE305 of 40 kW.          **Seats:** 48.
**Advertising livery:**

678 – Radiowave (black & blue)

| 678 (S) | **AL** | 680 | **Blue** |
|---|---|---|---|

# "BALLOON" DOUBLE DECKERS A1-1A

The "Balloon" cars are still the mainstay of the fleet during the summer months and are also used in lesser numbers during the winter.
**Built:** 1934–1935 by English Electric. 700–712 were originally built with open tops and 706 has now reverted to that condition.
**Traction Motors:** Two EE305 of 40 kW.      **Seats:** 94 (*† 92, ‡ 90, ¶ 88).

**Notes:** 717 is named "PHILLIP R THORPE"
720 is undergoing a major overhaul.
* Rebuilt with a new flat front end design and air-conditioned cabs. Known as "Millennium Class".
o Rebuilt as an open-topped double-decker seating 92. Named "PRINCESS ALICE". Also carries original number 243.

**Advertising liveries:**

701 – Palm Beach Hotel (gold & purple)
704 – Eclipse at the Globe, Pleasure Beach (black & orange)
707 – Coral Island – The Jewel on the Mile (black)
709 – Blackpool Sealife Centre (blue)
719 – Blackpool Pleasure Beach (Fusion ride) (two tone blue)
721 – "Hot Ice" Blackpool Pleasure Beach (white)
722 – Transport & General Workers Union (white)
726 – HM Coastguard (blue & yellow)

| 700 | Green & Cream | 709 | * AL | 718 | * | Yellow/blue |
|---|---|---|---|---|---|---|
| 701 | ‡ AL | 710 (S) | Yellow/purple | 719 | | AL |
| 702 | ¶ | 711 † | Yellow/green | 720 (S) | | |
| 703 | | 712 | | 721 | | AL |
| 704 (S) | AL | 713 | Yellow/purple | 722 (S)‡ | | AL |
| 706 | o | 715 | Yellow/blue | 723 | † | |
| 707 | * AL | 716 (S) | | 724 | * | Yellow/red |
| 708 (S) | ‡ | 717 | | 726 | | AL |

# JUBILEE CLASS DOUBLE DECKERS

**Built:** Rebuilt 1979/1982 from Balloon cars 725 and 714 respectively. Standard bus ends, thyristor control and stairs at each end. 761 has one door per side whereas 762 has two. Suitable for driver-only operation.
**Traction Motors:** Two EE305 of 40 kW.      **Seats:** 104 (*86).
**Note:** 762 is named "STUART L PILLAR"
**Advertising liveries:**

761 – Wynsors World of Shoes (orange)
762 – Unison (yellow)

| 761 | AL | 762 * | AL |
|---|---|---|---|

## ILLUMINATED CARS

| | | | |
|---|---|---|---|
| 732 (S) | The Rocket | Built: 1961 | Seats: 47 |
| 733 | Western Train loco & tender | Built: 1962 | Seats: 35 |
| 734 | Western Train coach | Built: 1962 | Seats: 60 |
| 736 | "Warship" HMS Blackpool | Built: 1965 | Seats: 71 |
| 737 | Illuminated Trawler – "Fisherman's Friend" | Built: 1937 | Seats: 48 |

## VINTAGE CARS

These trams are used for special services as well as for occasional normal services, particularly during the "illuminations" season.

**Note:** 147 is named "MICHAEL AIREY"

| | | |
|---|---|---|
| Stockport 5 | Open-top double-decker | Built: 1901 |
| Blackpool & Fleetwood 40 | Single deck "box car" | Built: 1914 |
| Bolton 66 | Bogie double-decker | Built: 1901 |
| Blackpool 147 | Standard double-decker | Built: 1924 |
| Blackpool 304 | Coronation Class single decker | Built: 1952 |
| Sheffield "Roberts Car" 513 | Double-decker | Built: 1950 |
| Blackpool 619 | Single deck Replica Vanguard | Built: 1987 |
| Blackpool 660 | Coronation Class single decker | Built: 1953 |

# 5.2. SHEFFIELD SUPERTRAM

This system opened in 1994 and has three lines radiating from Sheffield City Centre. These run to Halfway in the south east, with a spur from Gleadless Townend to Herdings Park, to Middlewood in the north with a spur from Hillsborough to Malin Bridge and to Meadowhall Interchange in the north east, adjacent to the large shopping complex. The total route mileage is 18 miles. The system is a mixture of on-street and segregated running.

The cars are owned by South Yorkshire Light Rail Ltd., a subsidiary of South Yorkshire PTE. The operating company, South Yorkshire Supertram Ltd. is leased to Stagecoach who operate the system as Stagecoach Supertram.

Because of severe gradients in Sheffield (up to 1 in 10) all axles are powered on the vehicles.

**System:** 750 DC overhead.
**Depot & Workshops:** Nunnery.
**Standard livery:** All over blue with red & orange ends.

**Advertising livery:**

104 – MySheffieldjobs.co.uk (orange & white).

# EIGHT-AXLE ARTICLUATED UNITS B–B–B–B

**Built:** 1993–1994 by Duewag, Dusseldorf, Germany.
**Traction Motors:** Four monomotors of 250 kW.
**Seats:** 80 + 6 tip-up.
**Weight:** 52 t.
**Dimensions:** 34.75 x 2.65 m.
**Couplers:** Not equipped.
**Doors:** Sliding plug.
**Braking:** Rheostatic, regenerative, disc and emergency track.
**Max. Speed:** 50 m.p.h.

| | | | | | |
|---|---|---|---|---|---|
| 101 | 106 | 110 | 114 | 118 | 122 |
| 102 | 107 | 111 | 115 | 119 | 123 |
| 103 | 108 | 112 | 116 | 120 | 124 |
| 104 **AL** | 109 | 113 | 117 | 121 | 125 |
| 105 | | | | | |

# 5.3. DOCKLANDS LIGHT RAILWAY

This system now runs for a total of 19 route miles, with more extensions in the pipeline. Lines run from termini at Bank and Tower Gateway, central London to Lewisham, Stratford, Beckton and King George V (on the new London City Airport line). The next extensions will be from King George V under the Thames to Woolwich Arsenal (opened in January 2009) and from Stratford to Canning Town (due to open mid 2010). The first line was opened in 1987 from Tower Gateway to Island Gardens.

Originally owned by London Transport, it is now owned by DLR Ltd. and operated by Serco Docklands. Cars are normally "driven" automatically using the Alcatel "Seltrack" moving block signalling system.

**Notes:** Original P86 and P89 Class vehicles 01–21 were withdrawn from service in 1991 (01–11) and 1995 (12–21) and sold for use in Essen, Germany.

The first of 55 new cars from Bombardier in Germany are now entering service. These new cars will enable 3-car trains to start operation on Bank–Lewisham services as well as providing the additional vehicles required for extensions to the network. Longer term they will meet higher projected passenger demand during the 2012 Olympics and beyond.

**System:** 750 V DC third rail (bottom contact).
**Depots:** Beckton (main depot) and Poplar.
**Livery:** Red with a curving blue stripe to represent the River Thames.

## CLASS B90                                      B–2–B

**Built:** 1991–1992 by BN Construction, Brugge, Belgium. Chopper control.
**Traction Motors:** Two Brush of 140 kW.
**Seats:** 52 + 4 tip-up.                 **Weight:** 37 t.
**Dimensions:** 28.80 x 2.65 m.          **Braking:** Rheostatic.
**Couplers:** Scharfenberg.               **Max. Speed:** 50 m.p.h.
**Doors:** Sliding. End doors for staff use.

| | | | | | |
|----|----|----|----|----|----|
| 22 | 26 | 30 | 34 | 38 | 42 |
| 23 | 27 | 31 | 35 | 39 | 43 |
| 24 | 28 | 32 | 36 | 40 | 44 |
| 25 | 29 | 33 | 37 | 41 | |

## CLASS B92                                      B–2–B

**Built:** 1992–1995 by BN Construction, Brugge, Belgium. Chopper control.
**Traction Motors:** Two Brush of 140 kW.
**Seats:** 52 + 4 tip-up.                 **Weight:** 37 t.
**Dimensions:** 28.80 x 2.65 m.          **Braking:** Rheostatic.
**Couplers:** Scharfenberg.               **Max. Speed:** 50 m.p.h.
**Doors:** Sliding. End doors for staff use.

| | | | | | |
|----|----|----|----|----|----|
| 45 | 53 | 61 | 69 | 77 | 85 |
| 46 | 54 | 62 | 70 | 78 | 86 |
| 47 | 55 | 63 | 71 | 79 | 87 |
| 48 | 56 | 64 | 72 | 80 | 88 |
| 49 | 57 | 65 | 73 | 81 | 89 |
| 50 | 58 | 66 | 74 | 82 | 90 |
| 51 | 59 | 67 | 75 | 83 | 91 |
| 52 | 60 | 68 | 76 | 84 | |

## CLASS B2K                                      B–2–B

**Built:** 2002–2003 by Bombardier Transportation, Brugge, Belgium.
**Traction Motors:** Two Brush of 140 kW.
**Seats:** 52 + 4 tip-up.                 **Weight:** 37 t.
**Dimensions:** 28.80 x 2.65 m.          **Braking:** Rheostatic.
**Couplers:** Scharfenberg.               **Max. Speed:** 50 m.p.h.
**Doors:** Sliding. End doors for staff use.

| | | | | | |
|----|----|----|----|----|----|
| 92 | 96 | 01 | 05 | 09 | 13 |
| 93 | 97 | 02 | 06 | 10 | 14 |
| 94 | 98 | 03 | 07 | 11 | 15 |
| 95 | 99 | 04 | 08 | 12 | 16 |

## CLASS B07                                      B–2–B

55 new vehicles now being delivered. 24 cars were ordered in 2005, these
will be numbered 101–124. 31 extra cars were ordered in 2006 in prospect of
the "London 2012" Olympic Games. These will be numbered 125–155.

**Built:** 2007–2009 by Bombardier Transportation, Bautzen, Germany.
**Traction Motors:**
**Seats:** 52 + 4 tip-up.                    **Weight:** 37 t.
**Dimensions:**                              **Braking:** Rheostatic.
**Couplers:** Scharfenberg.                  **Max. Speed:** 50 m.p.h.
**Doors:** Sliding. End doors for staff use.

| | | | | | |
|---|---|---|---|---|---|
| 101 | 105 | 109 | 113 | 117 | 121 |
| 102 | 106 | 110 | 114 | 118 | 122 |
| 103 | 107 | 111 | 115 | 119 | 123 |
| 104 | 108 | 112 | 116 | 120 | 124 |

| | | | | | |
|---|---|---|---|---|---|
| 125 | 131 | 136 | 141 | 146 | 151 |
| 126 | 132 | 137 | 142 | 147 | 152 |
| 127 | 133 | 138 | 143 | 148 | 153 |
| 128 | 134 | 139 | 144 | 149 | 154 |
| 129 | 135 | 140 | 145 | 150 | 155 |
| 130 | | | | | |

# 5.4. LONDON TRAMLINK

This system runs through central Croydon via a one-way loop, with lines radiating out to Wimbledon, New Addington and Beckenham Junction/Elmers End with the total route mileage being 18½ miles. It opened in 2000 and is now operated by Transport for London. Formerly called "Croydon Tramlink".

**System:** 750 V DC overhead.
**Depot & Workshops:** Therapia Lane, Croydon.

# SIX AXLE ARTICULATED CARS                 Bo–2–Bo

**Built:** 1998–1999 by Bombardier-Wien Schienenfahrzeuge, Austria.
**Traction Motors:** Four of 120 kW each.
**Seats:** 70.                               **Dimensions:** 30.1 x 2.65 m.
**Couplers:** Scharfenberg.                  **Doors:** Sliding plug.
**Weight:** 36.3 t.                          **Max. Speed:** 50 m.p.h.
**Braking:** Disc, regenerative and magnetic track.

**Standard livery:** Red & white unless stated.
**TL** – New London Tramlink livery (light grey & lime green with a blue solebar).

**Note:** 2534 is out of traffic following collision damage at the time of writing.

| | | | | | |
|---|---|---|---|---|---|
| 2530 | 2534 (S) | 2538 | 2542 | 2546 **TL** | 2550 |
| 2531 **TL** | 2535 | 2539 **TL** | 2543 | 2547 | 2551 |
| 2532 **TL** | 2536 | 2540 **TL** | 2544 **TL** | 2548 **TL** | 2552 **TL** |
| 2533 **TL** | 2537 | 2541 **TL** | 2545 | 2549 **TL** | 2553 **TL** |

**Name:** 2535 STEPHEN PARASCANDOLO 1980–2007

# 5.5. GREATER MANCHESTER METROLINK

Metrolink was the first modern tramway system in the UK, combining on-street running with longer distance running over former BR lines. The system opened in 1992 from Bury to Altrincham through the streets of Manchester, with a spur to Piccadilly station. A second line opened in 2000 from Cornbrook to Eccles extending the total route mileage to 23 miles.

Further extensions ("Phase 3a") have now been authorised to Rochdale station via Oldham to the north of Manchester (involving converting a National Rail line to light rail use), Droylsden to the east (on a line which will eventually reach Ashton-under-Lyne) and St. Werburgh's Road, Chorlton to the south (on a line which will eventually reach Manchester Airport). A short spur off the Eccles line to mediacity:uk has also been authorised. "Phase 3b" will consist of Oldham and Rochdale town centre sections, and the extension of above lines to Ashton-under-Lyne and Manchester Airport and East Didsbury.

The system is operated by Stagecoach Metrolink.

**System:** 750 V DC overhead.
**Depot & Workshops:** Queens Road, Manchester.

# SIX-AXLE ARTICULATED CARS     Bo–2–Bo

**Built:** 1991–1992 by Firema, Italy. Chopper control.
**Traction Motors:** Four GEC of 130 kW.
**Seats:** 82 + 4 tip-up.
**Dimensions:** 29.00 x 2.65 m.     **Couplers:** Scharfenberg.
**Doors:** Sliding.     **Weight:** 45 t.
**Braking:** Rheostatic, regenerative, disc and emergency track.
**Max. Speed:** 50 m.p.h.

**Livery:** White, dark grey & blue with light blue doors.

* Fitted with front-end valances, retractable couplers and controllable magnetic track brakes for running to Eccles.

| | | | | |
|---|---|---|---|---|
| 1001 | | SYSTEM ONE | 1014 | | THE GREAT MANCHESTER RUNNER |
| 1002 | | | 1015 | * | BURMA STAR |
| 1003 | | | 1016 | | |
| 1004 | | THE ROBERT OWEN | 1017 | | BURY HOSPICE |
| 1005 | * | THE RAILWAY MISSION | 1018 | | |
| 1006 | | | 1019 | | |
| 1007 | * | | 1020 | | LANCASHIRE FUSILIER |
| 1008 | | | 1021 | | |
| 1009 | | VIRGIN MEGASTORES | 1022 | | POPPY APPEAL |
| 1010 | * | | 1023 | | |
| 1011 | | SYSTEM ONE | 1024 | | |
| 1012 | | | 1025 | | |
| 1013 | | | 1026 | | |

## SIX-AXLE ARTICULATED CARS                    Bo–2–Bo

**Built:** 1999 by Ansaldo, Italy. Chopper control. Fitted with front-end valances, retractable couplers and controllable magnetic track brakes for running to Eccles. Can also be used on the Bury–Altrincham route.
**Traction Motors:** Four GEC of 130 kW.
**Seats:** 82 + 4 tip-up.
**Dimensions:** 29.00 x 2.65 m.                **Couplers:** Scharfenberg.
**Doors:** Sliding.                             **Weight:** 45 t.
**Braking:** Rheostatic, regenerative, disc and magnetic track.
**Max. Speed:** 50 m.p.h.

**Livery:** White, dark grey & blue with light blue doors.

| | | | |
|---|---|---|---|
| 2001 | | 2004 | |
| 2002 | | 2005 | WHSMITH WEST ONE |
| 2003 | TRAVELLER 2000 | 2006 | |

## SIX-AXLE ARTICULATED CARS

40 trams under construction for Manchester Metrolink from the Bombardier B5000 "Flexity Swift" family. The first eight cars will be delivered from May 2009 for use on existing routes. The remaining 32 cars are for the extensions mentioned above. Full details awaited.
**Built:** 2008–2011 by Bombardier, Bautzen, Germany & Vienna, Austria.
**Traction Motors:** Four Bombardier 3-phase.
**Seats:**
**Dimensions:** 28.4 x 2.65 m.                 **Couplers:** Scharfenberg.
**Doors:** Sliding.                             **Weight:**
**Braking:**
**Max. Speed:** 50 m.p.h.

**Livery:** New Manchester Metrolink silver & yellow.

| | | | | |
|---|---|---|---|---|
| 3001 | 3003 | 3005 | 3007 | 3008 |
| 3002 | 3004 | 3006 | | |

| | | | | |
|---|---|---|---|---|
| 3009 | 3016 | 3023 | 3029 | 3035 |
| 3010 | 3017 | 3024 | 3030 | 3036 |
| 3011 | 3018 | 3025 | 3031 | 3037 |
| 3012 | 3019 | 3026 | 3032 | 3038 |
| 3013 | 3020 | 3027 | 3033 | 3039 |
| 3014 | 3021 | 3028 | 3034 | 3040 |
| 3015 | 3022 | | | |

# 5.6. NOTTINGHAM EXPRESS TRANSIT

This is the newest light rail system in the UK, opened in 2004. Line 1 runs for 8¾ miles from Station Street, Nottingham (alongside Nottingham station) to Hucknall, including a short spur to Phoenix Park. There is around three miles of on-street running through Nottingham. Extensions are planned to Clifton (Line 2) to the south of Nottingham and Chilwell via Beeston to the west (Line 3).

The system is operated by the Arrow Light Rail Ltd. consortium (Transdev, Nottingham City Transport, Carillion, Bombardier, Innsfree and Galaxy).

**System:** 750 V DC overhead.
**Depot & Workshops:** Wilkinson Street.

# SIX AXLE ARTICULATED CARS

**Built:** 2002–2003 by Bombardier, Derby Litchurch Lane Works. Branded "Bombardier Incentros".
**Traction Motors:** 8 Asynchronous.
**Seats:** 54 + 4 tip-up.            **Dimensions:** 33.0 x 2.4 m
**Couplers:** Not equipped.          **Doors:** Sliding plug.
**Weight:** 36.7 t.                  **Max. Speed:** 50 m.p.h.
**Braking:** Disc, regenerative and magnetic track for emergency use.

**Standard livery:** Black, silver & green unless stated.
**Advertising livery:**

201 – MyNottinghamjobs.co.uk (orange & white).

| | | | | |
|---|---|---|---|---|
| 201 | **AL** | Torvill and Dean | 209 | Sid Standard |
| 202 | | DH Lawrence | 210 | Sir Jesse Boot |
| 203 | | Bendigo Thompson | 211 | Robin Hood |
| 204 | | Erica Beardsmore | 212 | William Booth |
| 205 | | Lord Byron | 213 | Mary Potter |
| 206 | | Angela Alcock | 214 | Dennis McCarthy |
| 207 | | Mavis Worthington | 215 | Brian Clough |
| 208 | | Dinah Minton | | |

# 5.7. MIDLAND METRO

This system opened in 1999 and has one 12½ mile line from Birmingham Snow Hill to Wolverhampton along the former GWR line to Wolverhampton Low Level. On the approach to Wolverhampton it deviates from the former railway alignment to run on-street to the St. George's terminus. It is operated by Travel West Midlands Ltd. Extensions are proposed from Snow Hill through Birmingham to Five Ways and from Wednesbury to Brierley Hill and Dudley.

**System:** 750 V DC overhead.     **Depot & Workshops:** Wednesbury.

## SIX AXLE ARTICULATED CARS                    Bo–2–Bo

**Built:** 1998–1999 by Ansaldo Transporti, Italy.

| | |
|---|---|
| **Traction Motors:** Four. | **Seats:** 52 + 4 tip-up. |
| **Dimensions:** 24.00 x 2.65 m. | **Couplers:** Not equipped. |
| **Doors:** Sliding plug. | **Weight:** 35.6 t. |

**Braking:** Rheostatic, regenerative, disc and magnetic track.
**Max. Speed:** 43 m.p.h.

**Standard livery:** Dark blue & light grey with green stripe, yellow doors & red front end.

**MW:** New Network West Midlands tram livery (silver & pink).
**Note:** 01 is currently stored out of use and used for spares.

| | | | | | |
|---|---|---|---|---|---|
| 01 | (S) | SIR FRANK WHITTLE | 09 | MW | JEFF ASTLE |
| 02 | | | 10 | MW | JOHN STANLEY WEBB |
| 03 | | RAY LEWIS | 11 | | THERESA STEWART |
| 04 | | | 12 | | |
| 05 | MW | SISTER DORA | 13 | | ANTHONY NOLAN |
| 06 | | ALAN GARNER | 14 | | JIM EAMES |
| 07 | MW | BILLY WRIGHT | 15 | | AGENORIA |
| 08 | | JOSEPH CHAMBERLAIN | 16 | | GERWYN JOHN |

# 5.8. TYNE & WEAR METRO

The Tyne & Wear Metro system covers 48 route miles and can be described as the UK's first modern light rail system. However it is not a true light rail system, but more of a hybrid system, with elements of light rail, underground metro and outer suburban heavy rail operations.

The initial network opened between 1980 and 1984 consisting of a line from South Shields via Gateshead and Newcastle Central station to Bank Foot (later extended to Newcastle Airport in 1991) and the North Tyneside loop (over former BR lines) serving North Shields, Tynemouth and Whitley Bay with a terminus at St. James in Newcastle city centre. A more recent extension came from Pelaw to Sunderland and South Hylton in 2002, making use of existing heavy rail infrastructure between Heworth and Sunderland.

The system is owned and operated by Nexus – the Tyne & Wear PTE.

**System:** 1500 V DC overhead.     **Depot & Workshops:** South Gosforth.

## SIX-AXLE ARTICULATED UNITS B–2–B

**Built:** 1978–1981 by Metropolitan Cammell, Birmingham (Prototype cars 4001 and 4002 were built by Metropolitan Cammell in 1976 and rebuilt 1984–1987 by Hunslet TPL, Leeds).
**Traction Motors:** Two Siemens of 187 kW each.

| | |
|---|---|
| **Seats:** 68. | **Dimensions:** 27.80 x 2.65 m. |
| **Couplers:** BSI. | **Doors:** Sliding plug. |
| **Weight:** 39.0 t. | **Maximum Speed:** 50 m.p.h. |

**Standard livery:** Red & yellow unless otherwise indicated.
**B** Blue & yellow
**G** Green & yellow.
**O (4001)** Original 1975 Tyne & Wear Metro livery of yellow & cream.
**O (4027)** Original North Eastern Railway style (red & white).
**Advertising liveries:**

4002 – Tyne & Wear Metro (orange & black).
4020 – Modern Apprenticeships (white, red & blue).
4038 – Talktofrank.com (white).
4040 – Cut your $CO_2$ day (blue & white).
4042 – Metro Radio (blue & pink).
4045 – Newcastle Racecourse (green).
4049 – Kidd & Spoor Harper Solicitors (blue).
4055 – European Regional Development Fund (blue & yellow).
4075 – Tyne & Wear Public Services (purple & white).
4080 – South Shields market (white).

| | | | | | | | | | | |
|---|---|---|---|---|---|---|---|---|---|---|
| 4001 | **O** | 4019 | | 4037 | | 4055 | **AL** | 4073 | |
| 4002 | **AL** | 4020 | **AL** | 4038 | **AL** | 4056 | | 4074 | |
| 4003 | | 4021 | | 4039 | **B** | 4057 | | 4075 | **AL** |
| 4004 | **G** | 4022 | | 4040 | **AL** | 4058 | **B** | 4076 | **B** |
| 4005 | | 4023 | **G** | 4041 | | 4059 | | 4077 | |
| 4006 | | 4024 | **B** | 4042 | **AL** | 4060 | | 4078 | |
| 4007 | | 4025 | **G** | 4043 | | 4061 | | 4079 | |
| 4008 | | 4026 | | 4044 | | 4062 | **G** | 4080 | **AL** |
| 4009 | | 4027 | **O** | 4045 | **AL** | 4063 | | 4081 | **B** |
| 4010 | | 4028 | | 4046 | | 4064 | | 4082 | |
| 4011 | | 4029 | **B** | 4047 | **B** | 4065 | | 4083 | **B** |
| 4012 | | 4030 | | 4048 | | 4066 | **B** | 4084 | |
| 4013 | | 4031 | **B** | 4049 | **AL** | 4067 | | 4085 | |
| 4014 | | 4032 | | 4050 | | 4068 | | 4086 | |
| 4015 | | 4033 | | 4051 | **G** | 4069 | | 4087 | |
| 4016 | **B** | 4034 | | 4052 | | 4070 | | 4088 | |
| 4017 | | 4035 | **B** | 4053 | **B** | 4071 | | 4089 | |
| 4018 | **G** | 4036 | **G** | 4054 | **B** | 4072 | **B** | 4090 | |

**Names:**

| | | | |
|---|---|---|---|
| 4026 | George Stephenson | 4065 | DAME Catherine Cookson |
| 4041 | HARRY COWANS | 4073 | Danny Marshall |
| 4060 | Thomas Bewick | 4077 | Robert Stephenson |
| 4064 | Michael Campbell | 4078 | Ellen Wilkinson |

# 5.9. GLASGOW SUBWAY

This circular 4 foot gauge underground line is the smallest metro system in the UK, running for just over six miles. It is generally referred to as the "Subway" or the "Clockwork Orange". Operated by Strathclyde PTE the system has 15 stations. The entire passenger railway is underground, contained in twin tunnels, allowing for clockwise operation on the "outer" circle and anticlockwise operation on the "inner" circle.

Trains are formed of 3-cars – either three power cars or two power cars sandwiching one of the newer trailer cars.

**System:** 600 V DC third rail.
**Depot & Workshops:** Broomloan.
**Livery:** Strathclyde PTE carmine & cream unless stated.

## SINGLE POWER CARS                                    Bo–Bo

**Built:** 1977–1979 by Metro-Cammell, Birmingham. Refurbished 1993–1995 by ABB Derby.
**Traction Motors:** Four GEC G312AZ of 35.6 kW each.
**Seats:** 36.                          **Dimensions:** 12.81 m x 2.34 m.
**Couplers:** Wedglock.                **Doors:** Sliding.
**Weight:** 19.6 t.                    **Maximum Speed:** 33.5 m.p.h.

| | | | | |
|---|---|---|---|---|
| 101 | 108 | 115 | 122 | 128 |
| 102 | 109 | 116 | 123 | 129 |
| 103 | 110 | 117 | 124 | 130 |
| 104 | 111 | 118 | 125 | 131 |
| 105 | 112 | 119 | 126 | 132 |
| 106 | 113 | 120 | 127 | 133 |
| 107 | 114 | 121 | | |

## INTERMEDIATE TRAILERS                                    2–2

**Built:** 1992 by Hunslet Barclay, Kilmarnock.
**Seats:** 40.                          **Dimensions:** 12.70 m x 2.34 m.
**Couplers:** Wedglock.                **Doors:** Sliding.
**Weight:** 17.2 t.                    **Maximum Speed:** 33.5 m.p.h.

**Advertising liveries:**

203 – Radio Clyde (red).
204 – SPT zonecard ticket (blue).
205 & 208 – Glasgow 2014 – "back the bid" (blue with various images).

| | | | | | | | |
|---|---|---|---|---|---|---|---|
| 201 | 203 | **AL** | 205 | **AL** | 207 | 208 | **AL** |
| 202 | 204 | **AL** | 206 | | | | |

# Keep right up to date with....

# Today's
**UK**
# Railways

## The UK railway magazine from Platform 5 Publishing.

Read all the very latest news from Britain and Ireland and unrivalled coverage of UK rolling stock news, every month.

**On sale 2nd Monday of EVERY MONTH**

Subscribe to Today's Railways UK TODAY!

---

### Never miss an issue!
- Your copy delivered to your door at no extra cost.
- Recieve every issue hot off the press.
- No price increase for the duration of your subscription.
- Exclusive reduced prices on selected books and videos from the Platform 5 Mail Order Department

---

Today's Railways UK subscriptions:

☎: (+44) 0114 255 8000     Fax: (+44) 0114 255 2471

# Subscription order form

To subscribe, please complete the form below (or a copy) and return it with your remittance to:

**Today's Railways UK (Dept. LCS), 3 Wyvern House, Sark Road, SHEFFIELD, S2 4HG, ENGLAND.**

**BLOCK CAPITALS PLEASE**

(All prices include postage and packing.)

---

**Today's Railways UK: Subscription (12 issues)**

☐ UK £45.00 (post free);     ☐ Overseas Airmail £54.60.

JAN   FEB   MAR   APR   MAY   JUN   JUL   AUG   SEP   OCT   NOV   DEC

Please circle start issue required

---

**Name:** ................................................................................................

**Address:** ............................................................................................

...........................................................................................................

................................................ **Postcode:** ....................................

**Daytime Tel. No:** ...............................................................................

**E-mail:** ..............................................................................................

---

I enclose my cheque/UK postal order for £ ..............................................

made payable to **'PLATFORM 5 PUBLISHING LTD.'**

**Please debit my Visa/Mastercard/Maestro**

**Card No:** ..................................................... **Expiry Date:** ................

**Card Issue No./Date (Maestro only):** ................ **Security No.:** .............

**for £** .................................................................. **Date:** ..................

**Signature:** ..........................................................................................

---

or if ordering by debit/credit card, telephone our subscription department on the numbers opposite.

**Special note:** Subscriptions may begin with the current issue or the next to be published. Subscriptions cannot be backdated.

# 6. CODES

## 6.1. LIVERY CODES

Livery codes are used to denote the various liveries carried. It is impossible to list every livery variation which currently exists. In particular items ignored for this publication include:

- Minor colour variations.
- Omission of logos.
- All numbering, lettering and brandings.

Descriptions quoted are thus a general guide only. Logos as appropriate for each livery are normally deemed to be carried.

The colour of the lower half of the bodyside is stated first. Minor variations to these liveries are ignored.

Coaches are in **IC** livery as standard (i.e. a blank livery code space means that vehicle is in **IC** livery).

*Code Description*

| | |
|---|---|
| **1** | "One" (metallic grey with a broad black bodyside stripe. White National Express interim stripe as branding). |
| **AB** | Arriva Trains "executive" dark & light blue. |
| **ACT** | ACTS {Netherlands} (deep blue with a broad yellow stripe). |
| **AI** | Aggregate Industries (green, light grey & blue). |
| **AL** | Advertising/promotional livery (see class heading for details). |
| **AN** | Anglia Railways Class 170s (white & turquoise with blue vignette). |
| **AR** | Anglia Railways (turquoise blue with a white stripe). |
| **AV** | Arriva Trains (turquoise blue with white doors & a cream "swish"). |
| **AW** | Revised Arriva Trains {Class 175} (turquoise blue with white vignette & two yellow stripes). |
| **AZ** | Advenza Freight (deep blue with green Advenza brandings). |
| **B** | BR blue. |
| **BG** | BR blue & grey lined out in white. |
| **BI** | "Visit Bristol" promotional livery (deep blue with various images). |
| **BL** | BR Revised blue with yellow cabs, grey roof, large numbers & logo. |
| **BP** | Blue Pullman ("Nanking" blue & white). |
| **BS** | Serco Railtest blue (deep blue with white Serco brandings). |
| **C2** | c2c Rail (blue with metallic grey doors & pink c2c branding). |
| **CC** | BR Carmine & Cream. |
| **CD** | Cotswold Rail (silver with blue & red logo). |
| **CE** | BR Civil Engineers (yellow & grey with black cab doors & window surrounds). |
| **CH** | BR Western Region/GWR (chocolate & cream lined out in gold). |
| **CI** | New Centro {Class 150} (light green with a broad blue lower bodyside band & blue cab end sections). |
| **CM** | Revised old Midland Mainline (Midland Mainline teal green with white Central logos). |
| **CN** | Southeastern (white with black window surrounds & grey lower band). |
| **CON** | Continental Rail (blue with a yellow stripe). |

**CR**    Chiltern Railways (blue & white with a thin red stripe).

**CS**    Colas Rail (yellow, orange & black).

**CT**    Central Trains (two-tone green with yellow doors. Blue flash & red stripe at vehicle ends).

**CU**    Corus (silver with red logos).

**CX**    Connex (white with yellow lower body & blue solebar).

**DB**    DB Schenker (Deutsch Bahn red with grey roof & solebar).

**DC**    Scenic lines of Devon & Cornwall promotional livery (black with gold cantrail stripe).

**DG**    BR Departmental (dark grey with black cab doors & window surrounds).

**DR**    Direct Rail Services (dark blue with light blue or dark grey roof).

**DS**    Revised Direct Rail Services (dark blue, light blue & green. "Compass" logo).

**E**    English Welsh & Scottish Railway (maroon bodyside & roof with a broad gold bodyside band).

**EB**    Eurotunnel (two-tone grey with a broad blue stripe).

**ECR**    Euro Cargo Rail {France} (light grey).

**EG**    "EWS grey" (As **F** but with large yellow & red EWS logo).

**EP**    European Passenger Services (two-tone grey with dark blue roof).

**EM**    East Midlands Trains {Connect} (blue with red & orange swish at unit ends).

**EU**    Eurostar (white with dark blue & yellow stripes).

**F**    BR Trainload Freight (two-tone grey with black cab doors & window surrounds. Various logos).

**FA**    Fastline Freight (grey & black with white & orange stripes).

**FB**    First Group dark blue.

**FD**    First Great Western "Dynamic Lines" (dark blue with thin multi-coloured lines on the lower bodyside).

**FE**    Railfreight Distribution International (two tone-grey with black cab doors & dark blue roof).

**FER**    Fertis (light grey with a dark grey roof & solebar).

**FF**    Freightliner grey (two-tone grey with black cab doors & window surrounds. Freightliner logo).

**FG**    First Group Inter-City (indigo blue with a white roof & gold, pink & white stripes).

**FI**    First Great Western "Local Lines" DMU (varying blue with local visitor attractions applied to the lower bodyside).

**FL**    Freightliner (dark green with yellow cabs).

**FP**    Old First Great Western (green & ivory with thin green & broad gold stripes).

**FR**    Fragonset Railways (black with silver roof & a red bodyside band lined out in white).

**FS**    First Group (indigo blue with pink & white stripes).

**FT**    First Trans-Pennine Express "Dynamic Lines" (varying blue with thin multi-coloured lines on the lower bodyside).

**FU**    First Group "Urban Lights" (varying blue with pink, white and blue markings on the lower bodyside).

**FY**    Foster Yeoman (blue & silver. Cast numberplates).

**G¹**    BR Green (plain green, with white stripe on main line locomotives).

**G²**    BR Southern Region/SR or BR DMU green.

**GB**    GB Railfreight (blue with orange cantrail & solebar stripes, orange cabs).

**GC**  Grand Central (all over black).
**GE**  First Great Eastern (grey, green, blue & white).
**GG**  BR green (two-tone green).
**GIF**  GIF {Spain} light blue with dark blue band.
**GL**  First Great Western locos (green with a gold stripe).
**GN**  Great North Eastern Railway {modified} (dark blue with a white (was red) stripe).
**GS**  Royal Scotsman/Great Scottish & Western Railway (maroon).
**GV**  Gatwick Express EMU (red, white & indigo blue with mauve & blue doors).
**GW**  Great Western Railway (green, lined out in black & orange. Cast numberplates).
**GX**  Gatwick Express InterCity (dark grey/white/burgundy/white).
**GY**  Eurotunnel (grey & yellow).
**HA**  Hanson Quarry Products (dark blue/silver with oxide red roof).
**HB**  HSBC Rail (Oxford blue & white).
**HC**  Heathrow Connect (grey with a broad deep blue bodyside band & orange doors).
**HE**  Heathrow Express (grey & indigo blue with black window surrounds).
**HN**  Harry Needle Railroad Company (orange & grey, lined out in black).
**HT**  Hull Trains (dark green & silver with two gold stripes).
**IC**  BR InterCity (dark grey/white/red/white).
**IL**  Island Line (light blue, with illustrations featuring dinosaurs etc).
**IM**  BR InterCity Mainline (dark grey/white/red/light grey & yellow lower cabsides except shunters).
**K**  Black.
**LH**  BR Loadhaul (black with orange cabsides).
**LM**  London Midland (white/grey & green with broad black stripe around the windows).
**LN**  LNER Tourist (green & cream).
**LO**  London Overground (all over white with a blue solebar & black window surrounds).
**LT**  London Transport maroon & cream.
**M**  BR maroon (maroon lined out in straw & black).
**MA**  Maintrain (blue).
**ME**  Merseyrail Electrics (metallic silver with yellow doors).
**ML**  BR Mainline Freight (aircraft blue with a silver stripe).
**MM**  Old Midland Mainline (teal green with grey lower body sides & three tangerine stripes).
**MN**  Midland Mainline (thin tangerine stripe on the lower bodyside, ocean blue, grey & white).
**MT**  First GBRf Metronet (blue with orange cabsides).
**N**  BR Network South East (white & blue with red lower bodyside stripe, grey solebar & cab ends).
**NO**  Northern (deep blue, lilac & white). Some units have area-specific promotional vinyls (see class headings for details).
**NR**  Network Rail (blue with a red stripe).
**NS**  Northern Spirit (turquoise blue with a lime green "N").
**NW**  North Western Trains (blue with gold cantrail stripe & star).
**NX**  National Express (white with grey ends).
**O**  Non standard livery (see class heading for details).
**P**  Porterbrook Leasing Company (white or grey & purple).

**PC** Pullman Car Company (umber & cream with gold lettering lined out in gold).
**RG** BR Parcels (dark grey & red).
**RK** Railtrack (green & blue).
**RM** Royal Mail (red with yellow stripes above solebar).
**RO** Old Railtrack (orange with white & grey stripes).
**RP** Royal Train (claret, lined out in red & black).
**RR** Regional Railways (dark blue & grey with light blue & white stripes, three narrow dark blue stripes at vehicle ends).
**RT** RT Rail (black, lined out in red).
**RV** Riviera Trains (Oxford blue & cream lined out in gold {blue only for locos}).
**RX** Rail Express Systems (dark grey & red with or without blue markings).
**RZ** Royal Train revised (plain claret, no lining).
**S** Old Strathclyde PTE (orange & black lined out in white).
**SB** Southeastern all over blue.
**SC** Strathclyde PTE (carmine & cream lined out in black & gold).
**SD** South West Trains outer suburban {Class 450 style} (deep blue with red doors & orange & red cab sides).
**SCO** Seco-Rail (orange with a broad yellow bodyside band).
**SL** Silverlink (indigo blue with white stripe, green lower body & yellow doors).
**SP** Strathclyde PTE {Class 334 style} (carmine & cream, with a turquoise stripe).
**SN** Southern (white & dark green with light green semi-circles at one end of each vehicle. Light grey band at solebar level).
**SO** Serco Railtest (red & grey).
**SR** ScotRail – Scotland's Railways (dark blue with Scottish Saltire flag & white/light blue flashes).
**SS** South West Trains inner suburban {Class 455 style} (red with blue & orange flashes at unit ends).
**ST** Stagecoach {long-distance stock} (white & dark blue with dark blue window surrounds and red & orange swishes at unit ends).
**SU** Revised Stansted Express (light blue with a dark blue lower bodyside stripe & light grey doors).
**SX** Stansted Express (two-tone metallic blue with grey doors).
**TC** Revised Trans-Pennine Express (all over plum).
**TL** New Thameslink (silver with blue window surrounds & ends).
**TSO** TSO (all over yellow with a blue solebar).
**TW** Modified Thameslink (dark blue with broad white lower bodyside stripe).
**U** Plain white or grey undercoat.
**V** Virgin Trains (red with black doors extending into bodysides, three white lower bodysides stripes).
**VP** Virgin Trains shunters (black with a large black & white chequered flag on the bodyside).
**VN** Venice Simplon Orient Express "Northern Belle" (crimson lake & cream).
**VT** Virgin Trains silver (silver, with black window surrounds, white cantrail stripe & red roof. Red swept down at unit ends. Black & white striped doors on units).
**WA** Wabtec Rail (black).
**WB** Wales & Borders Alphaline (metallic silver with blue doors).
**WC** West Coast Railway Co. maroon (57601 carries a black bodyside stripe).
**WM** Network West Midlands (light blue with green lower bodyside stripe and white stripe at cantrail level).

**WN** Old West Anglia Great Northern (white with blue, grey & orange stripes).
**WP** West Anglia Great Northern (deep purple with white or light purple doors).
**WS** Wrexham & Shropshire (two-tone grey & silver).
**WX** Heart of Wessex Line promotional livery (cerise pink).
**WZ** Wessex Trains claret promotional livery with various images.
**XC** Cross-Country (two-tone silver with deep crimson ends and pink doors).
**Y** Network Rail yellow.
**YN** Old West Yorkshire PTE EMUs (red with light grey "N").
**YR** West Yorkshire PTE/Northern EMUs (red, lilac & grey).
**YP** West Yorkshire PTE DMUs (red with grey semi-circles).

# 6.2. OWNER CODES

The following codes are used to define the ownership details of the locomotives or rolling stock listed in this book. Codes shown indicate either the legal owner or "responsible custodian" of each vehicle.

*Code  Owner*

20    Class 20189 Ltd.
24    6024 Preservation Society
40    The Class 40 Preservation Society
47    The Stratford 47 Group
50    Class 50 Alliance
62    The Princess Royal Locomotive Trust
67    Tangmere Locomotive Company
70    7029 Clun Castle Ltd.
92    City of Wells Supporters Association
A     Angel Trains
A4    The A4 Locomotive Society
AC    The AC Locomotive Group
AI    Aggregate Industries
AM    Alstom
AW    Arriva Trains Wales
B1    Thompson B1 Locomotive Society
BC    Bridgend County Borough Council/Rhondda Cynon Taff District Council
BE    Bert Hitchins
BK    The Scottish Railway Preservation Society
BM    BTMU Capital Corporation
BS    Bressingham Steam Museum
BT    Bombardier Transportation
BU    The Bulgarian Railway Company
CC    Cardiff City Council
CD    Cotswold Rail
CG    Cargo-D

| | |
|---|---|
| CR | Chiltern Railways |
| CS | Colas Rail |
| DB | DB Schenker (was EWS) / DB Regio |
| DG | Duke of Gloucester Steam Locomotive Trust |
| DM | Dartmoor Railway |
| DR | Direct Rail Services |
| DT | The Diesel Traction Group |
| EM | East Midlands Trains |
| EP | Europhoenix |
| ET | Eurotunnel |
| EU | Eurostar (UK) |
| FA | Fastline |
| FG | First Group |
| FL | Freightliner |
| GB | First GBRf |
| GD | Garsdale Railtours |
| GS | The Great Scottish & Western Railway Company |
| GW | The Great Western Society |
| H | HSBC Rail (UK) |
| HA | Hanson Group |
| HD | Hastings Diesels |
| HE | British Airports Authority |
| HJ | Howard Johnston Engineering |
| HN | Harry Needle Railroad Company |
| HS | Hanson Traction |
| HX | Halifax Bank of Scotland |
| IR | Ian Riley Engineering |
| JC | John Cameron |
| JH | Jeremy Hosking |
| KN | Knights Rail Services |
| LM | London Midland |
| LR | Les Ross |
| LW | London & North Western Railway Company (owned by Arriva) |
| LY | Lloyds TSB |
| MN | Merchant Navy Locomotive Preservation Society |
| MW | Martin Walker (Beaver Sports) |
| NE | North Eastern Locomotive Preservation Group |
| NM | National Railway Museum |
| NR | Network Rail |
| NY | North Yorkshire Moors Railway |
| NX | National Express |
| P | Porterbrook Leasing Company |
| PO | Other private owner |
| PU | Pullman Rail |
| QW | QW Rail Leasing |
| RA | Railfilms |
| RE | Railway Vehicle Engineering |
| RI | Rail Assets Investments |
| RL | RMS Locotec |
| RM | Royal Mail |
| RP | Rampart Carriage & Wagon Services |

| | |
|---|---|
| RV | Riviera Trains |
| SB | SNCB/NMBS (Société Nationale des Chemins de fer Belges/ Nationale Maatschappij der Belgische Spoorwegen) |
| SF | SNCF (Société Nationale des Chemins de fer Français) |
| SM | Siemens Transportation |
| SN | Southern |
| SO | Serco Railtest |
| SR | Swift Rail |
| ST | Sovereign Trains |
| SV | Severn Valley Railway |
| SW | South West Trains |
| TT | Type Three Traction Group |
| VI | Virgin Trains |
| VS | Venice-Simplon Orient Express |
| VT | Vintage Trains |
| WA | Wabtec Rail |
| WC | West Coast Railway Company |
| WT | Wessex Trains |
| X | Sold for scrap/further use and awaiting collection or owner unknown |

# 6.3. LOCOMOTIVE POOL CODES

Locomotives are split into operational groups ("pools") for diagramming and maintenance purposes. The official codes used to denote these pools are shown in this publication.

*Code*    *Pool*

| | |
|---|---|
| ACAC | AC Locomotive Group operational locomotives. |
| ADFL | Advenza Freight locomotives. |
| ATLO | Alstom Class 08. |
| ATTB | Alstom Class 57. |
| ATZZ | Alstom locos for disposal. |
| CDJD | Serco Railtest Class 08. |
| CFOL | Class 50 Operations locomotives. |
| COLO | Colas Rail operational locomotives. |
| CREL | Cotswold Rail operational locomotives – contract hire. |
| CRRH | Cotswold Rail operational locomotives – spot-hire contracts. |
| DFFT | Freightliner Class 66 (route learning). |
| DFGC | Freightliner Intermodal Class 86/5. |
| DFGM | Freightliner Intermodal Class 66. |
| DFHG | Freightliner Heavy Haul modified Class 66 (general). |
| DFHH | Freightliner Heavy Haul Class 66. |
| DFIM | Freightliner Intermodal modified Class 66. |
| DFIN | Freightliner Intermodal Class 66 (low emission). |
| DFLC | Freightliner Intermodal Class 90. |
| DFLH | Freightliner Heavy Haul Class 47 ("super shunters"). |

| | |
|---|---|
| DFLS | Freightliner Class 08. |
| DFNC | Freightliner Intermodal Class 86/6. |
| DFNR | Freightliner Heavy Haul modified Class 66. Infrastructure services. |
| DFRT | Freightliner Heavy Haul Class 66. Infrastructure services. |
| DHLT | Freightliner locomotives awaiting maintenance/repair/disposal. |
| EFOO | First Great Western Class 57. |
| EFPC | First Great Western Class 43. |
| EFSH | First Great Western Class 08. |
| EHPC | Cross-Country Class 43. |
| EJLO | London Midland Class 08. |
| ELRD | East Lancashire Railway-based main line registered locos. |
| EMPC | East Midlands Trains Class 43. |
| EMSL | East Midlands Trains Class 08. |
| EPXX | Europhoenix Class 86. |
| GBCM | First GBRf Class 66. General. |
| GBED | First GBRf Class 73. |
| GBRT | First GBRf Class 66. Network Rail contracts. |
| GBZZ | First GBRf. Stored locomotives. |
| GCHP | Grand Central Class 43. |
| GPSN | Eurostar (UK) Class 73. |
| GPSS | Eurostar (UK) Class 08. |
| HBSH | Wabtec hire shunting locomotives. |
| HNRL | Harry Needle Railroad Company hire locomotives. |
| HNRS | Harry Needle Railroad Company stored locomotives. |
| HTLX | Hanson Traction locomotives. |
| HWSU | Southern Class 09. |
| HYWD | South West Trains Class 73 standby locomotives. |
| IANA | National Express East Anglia Class 90. |
| IECA | National Express East Coast Class 91. |
| IECP | National Express East Coast Class 43. |
| IVGA | Gatwick Express Class 73 (standby use). |
| MBDL | Non TOC-owned diesel locomotives. |
| MBED | Non TOC-owned electro-diesel locomotives. |
| MBEL | Non TOC-owned electric locomotives. |
| MRSO | RMS Locotec Class 08. |
| PTXX | Europorte2 locomotives. |
| QACL | Network Rail Class 86. |
| QADD | Network Rail diesel locomotives. |
| QAED | Network Rail Class 73. |
| QCAR | Network Rail New Measurement Train Class 43. |
| QETS | Network Rail Class 37. |
| QSTR | Network Rail stored locomotives. |
| RCJA | Fastline Class 56. |
| RCJB | Fastline Class 66. |
| RFSH | Wabtec Rail locomotives. |
| RTLO | Riviera Trains operational fleet. |
| RTLS | Riviera Trains stored locomotives. |
| RVLO | Rail Vehicle Engineering operational locomotives. |
| SAXL | HSBC Rail (UK) off-lease locomotives. |
| SBXL | Porterbrook Leasing Company off-lease locomotives. |
| SRLO | Swift Rail locomotive (stored). |

| | |
|---|---|
| TTTC | Type Three Traction Group Class 37. |
| WAAN | DB Schenker Network Class 67. |
| WABN | DB Schenker Network Class 67. RETB fitted. |
| WAFN | DB Schenker Network Class 67 for hire to First Great Western. |
| WAWN | DB Schenker Network Class 67 for Wrexham & Shropshire services. |
| WBAI | DB Schenker Industrial Class 66. |
| WBAK | DB Schenker Construction Class 66. |
| WBAM | DB Schenker Energy Class 66. |
| WBAN | DB Schenker Network Class 66. |
| WBBK | DB Schenker Construction Class 66. RETB fitted. |
| WBBN | DB Schenker Network Class 66. RETB fitted. |
| WBEN | DB Schenker Class 66 for Euro Cargo Rail, France. |
| WBLI | DB Schenker Industrial Class 66. Dedicated locos for Lickey Incline banking duties. |
| WCAI | DB Schenker Industrial Class 60. |
| WCAK | DB Schenker Construction Class 60. |
| WCAM | DB Schenker Energy Class 60. |
| WCAN | DB Schenker Network Class 60. |
| WCBI | DB Schenker Industrial Class 60. Extended-range fuel tanks. |
| WCBK | DB Schenker Construction Class 60. Extended-range fuel tanks. |
| WCBM | DB Schenker Energy Class 60. Extended-range fuel tanks. |
| WCBN | DB Schenker Network Class 60. Extended-range fuel tanks. |
| WDAK | DB Schenker Construction Class 59. |
| WEFE | DB Schenker Network Class 90. |
| WFMU | DB Schenker Fleet Management Unit locomotives. |
| WKBN | DB Schenker Network Class 37. |
| WNSO | DB Schenker locomotives – sold awaiting collection. |
| WNTR | DB Schenker locomotives – tactical reserve. |
| WNTS | DB Schenker locomotives – tactical stored unserviceable. |
| WNXX | DB Schenker locomotives – stored unserviceable. |
| WNYX | DB Schenker locomotives – authorised for component recovery. |
| WSEN | DB Schenker/Euro Cargo Rail shunting locomotives. |
| WSSA | DB Schenker/Axiom Rail operational Shunters. |
| WSSI | DB Schenker Industrial operational Shunters. |
| WSSK | DB Schenker Construction operational Shunters. |
| WSSM | DB Schenker Energy operational Shunters. |
| WSSN | DB Schenker Network operational Shunters. |
| WSXX | DB Schenker shunting locomotives – internal/depot use. |
| WTAE | DB Schenker Network Class 92. |
| WZFF | DB Schenker Class 58 – former hire locomotives France (stored). |
| WZFH | DB Schenker Class 58 – hire locomotives The Netherlands. |
| WZFS | DB Schenker Class 58 – hire locomotives Spain. |
| WZGF | DB Schenker Class 56 – former hire locomotives France (stored). |
| WZKS | DB Schenker Class 37 – hire locomotives Spain. |
| WZTS | DB Schenker locomotives – tactical stored. |
| XHHP | Direct Rail Services locomotives – holding pool. |
| XHIM | Direct Rail Services locomotives – Intermodal traffic. |
| XHNC | Direct Rail Services locomotives – nuclear traffic/general. |
| XHSS | Direct Rail Services stored locomotives. |
| XYPA | Mendip Rail Class 59/1. |
| XYPO | Mendip Rail Class 59/0. |

# 6.4. OPERATOR CODES

Operator codes are used to denote the organisation that facilitates the use of that vehicle, and may not be the actual Train Operating Company which runs the train. Where no operator code is shown, vehicles are currently not in use.

| Code | Operator |
|------|----------|
| 62 | The Princess Royal Locomotive Trust |
| AW | Arriva Trains Wales |
| BK | The Scottish Railway Preservation Society |
| C2 | c2c Rail |
| CD | Cotswold Rail |
| CG | Cargo-D |
| CR | Chiltern Railways |
| CS | Colas Rail |
| DB | DB Schenker |
| DR | Direct Rail Services |
| EA | National Express East Anglia |
| EC | National Express East Coast |
| EM | East Midlands Trains |
| EU | Eurostar (UK) |
| FC | First Capital Connect |
| FL | Freightliner |
| GB | First GBRf |
| GC | Grand Central |
| GS | The Great Scottish & Western Railway Company |
| GW | First Great Western |
| HC | Heathrow Connect |
| HD | Hastings Diesels |
| HE | Heathrow Express |
| HT | First Hull Trains |
| LO | London Overground |
| LM | London Midland |
| ME | Merseyrail |
| NO | Northern |
| NY | North Yorkshire Moors Railway |
| RP | Royal Train |
| RV | Riviera Trains |
| SE | Southeastern |
| SF | SNCF (French Railways) |
| SN | Southern |
| SO | Serco Railtest |
| SR | First ScotRail |
| SW | South West Trains |
| TP | First Trans-Pennine Express |
| VS | Venice-Simplon Orient Express |
| VT | Vintage Trains |
| VW | Virgin Trains |
| WC | West Coast Railway Company |
| WS | Wrexham, Shropshire & Marylebone Railway |

*WT*     Wessex Trains
*XC*     Cross-Country

# 6.5. ALLOCATION & LOCATION CODES

Allocation codes are used in this publication to denote the normal maintenance base ("depots") of each operational locomotive, multiple unit or coach. However, maintenance may be carried out at other locations and may also be carried out by mobile maintenance teams.

Location codes are used to denote common storage locations whilst the full place name is used for other locations. The designation (S) denotes stored. However, when a locomotive pool code denotes that a loco is stored anyway then the (S) is not shown.

| Code | Depot | Operator |
|------|-------|----------|
| AD | Ashford (Hitachi) | Hitachi/Southeastern |
| AF | Ashford Chart Leacon Works (Kent) | Bombardier Transportation |
| AK | Ardwick (Manchester) | Siemens |
| AL | Aylesbury | Chiltern Railways |
| AN | Allerton (Liverpool) | DB Schenker |
| AP* | Ashford Rail Plant (Kent) | Balfour Beatty Rail Services |
| AY | Ayr | DB Schenker |
| BA | Basford Hall Yard (Crewe) | *Storage location only* |
| BD | Birkenhead North | Merseyrail |
| BH | Barrow Hill (Chesterfield) | Barrow Hill Engine Shed Society |
| BF | Bedford Cauldwell Walk | First Capital Connect |
| BI | Brighton Lovers Walk | Southern |
| BK | Bristol Barton Hill | DB Schenker |
| BM | Bournemouth | South West Trains |
| BN | Bounds Green (London) | National Express East Coast |
| BR* | MoD DSDC Bicester | Ministry of Defence |
| BQ | Bury (Greater Manchester) | East Lancashire Railway |
| BS | Bescot (Walsall) | DB Schenker |
| BT | Bo'ness (West Lothian) | Bo'ness & Kinneil Railway |
| BY | Bletchley | London Midland |
| BZ | St. Blazey (Par) | DB Schenker |
| CD | Crewe Diesel | DB Schenker |
| CE | Crewe International | DB Schenker |
| CF | Cardiff Canton | Arriva Trains Wales/Pullman Rail |
| CH | Chester | Alstom |
| CJ | Clapham Yard (London) | South West Trains |
| CK | Corkerhill (Glasgow) | First ScotRail |
| CO | Coquelles (France) | Eurotunnel |
| CP | Crewe Carriage | LNWR (Arriva) |
| CQ | Crewe (The Railway Age) | LNWR |
| CR | Crewe Gresty Lane | Direct Rail Services |
| CS | Carnforth | West Coast Railway Company |

| CZ | Central Rivers (Burton) | Bombardier Transportation |
| DC* | Didcot Yard | DB Schenker |
| DF | Derby | Railway Vehicle Engineering |
| DI | Didcot Railway Centre | Great Western Society |
| DR | Doncaster | DB Schenker |
| DY | Derby Etches Park | East Midlands Trains |
| DW* | Doncaster West Yard | *Storage location only* |
| EC | Edinburgh Craigentinny | National Express East Coast |
| EH | Eastleigh | DB Schenker |
| EM | East Ham (London) | c2c |
| ES* | On hire to GIF, Spain | GIF |
| EX | Exeter | First Great Western |
| FB | Ferrybridge | DB Schenker |
| FD | Freightliner diesels nationwide | Freightliner |
| FE | Freightliner electrics nationwide | Freightliner |
| FF* | Forest (Brussels) | SNCB/NMBS |
| FN* | Locos in use in France | Euro Cargo Rail/SNCF |
| GI | Gillingham (Kent) | Southeastern |
| GL | Gloucester Horton Road | Cotswold Rail |
| GW | Glasgow Shields Road | First ScotRail |
| HA | Haymarket (Edinburgh) | First ScotRail |
| HE | Hornsey (London) | First Capital Connect |
| HG | Hither Green (London) | DB Schenker |
| HM | Healey Mills (Wakefield) | DB Schenker |
| HP* | Hope Cement Works | Lafarge |
| HT | Heaton (Newcastle) | Northern |
| IM | Immingham | DB Schenker |
| IL | Ilford (London) | National Express East Anglia |
| IP | Ipswich stabling point | Freightliner |
| IS | Inverness | First ScotRail |
| KM | Carlisle Kingmoor | Direct Rail Services |
| KR | Kidderminster | Severn Valley Railway |
| KT | MoD Kineton (Warwickshire) | Ministry of Defence |
| KY | Knottingley | DB Schenker |
| LA | Laira (Plymouth) | First Great Western |
| LB | Loughborough Works | Brush Traction |
| LD | Leeds Midland Road | Freightliner |
| LE | Landore (Swansea) | First Great Western |
| LG | Longsight (Manchester) | Northern |
| LH* | LH Group, Barton-under-Needwood | LH Group Services |
| LL | Edge Hill (Liverpool) | Alstom |
| LM | Long Marston (Warwickshire) | Motorail Logistics |
| LU* | MoD Ludgersall | Ministry of Defence |
| LW* | Leeming Bar | Wensleydale Railway |
| LY* | Le Landy (Paris) | SNCF |
| MA | Manchester Longsight | Alstom |
| MD | Merehead | Mendip Rail |
| ME | Mossend Yard | DB Schenker |
| MG | Margam (Port Talbot) | DB Schenker |
| MH | Millerhill (Edinburgh) | DB Schenker |
| ML | Motherwell (Glasgow) | DB Schenker |

| | | |
|---|---|---|
| MN | Machynlleth | Arriva Trains Wales |
| MQ* | Meldon Quarry (Okehampton) | *Storage locaation only* |
| NC | Norwich Crown Point | National Express East Anglia |
| NH | Newton Heath (Manchester) | Northern |
| NL | Neville Hill (Leeds) | East Midlands Trains/Northern |
| NM | Nottingham Eastcroft | East Midlands Trains |
| NN | Northampton King's Heath | Siemens |
| NT | Northam (Southampton) | Siemens |
| NY | Grosmont (North Yorkshire) | North Yorkshire Moors Railway |
| OC | Old Oak Common locomotive (London) | DB Schenker |
| OH | Old Oak Common Heathrow | Heathrow Express |
| OO | Old Oak Common HST | First Great Western |
| OM | Old Oak Common carriage | Riviera Trains/DB Schenker |
| OY | Oxley (Wolverhampton) | Alstom |
| PB | Peterborough Yards | DB Schenker/First GBRf |
| PM | St. Philip's Marsh (Bristol) | First Great Western |
| PZ | Penzance | First Great Western |
| RG | Reading | First Great Western |
| RM | Ramsgate | Southeastern |
| RR | Doncaster Robert's Road | Fastline |
| RU | Rugby Rail Plant | Colas Rail |
| RY | Ryde (Isle of Wight) | South West Trains |
| SA | Salisbury | South West Trains |
| SE | St. Leonards (Hastings) | St. Leonards Railway Engineering |
| SG | Slade Green (London) | Southeastern |
| SI | Soho (Birmingham) | London Midland |
| SK | Swanwick Junction (Derbyshire) | Midland Railway-Butterley |
| SL | Stewarts Lane (London) | Southern/VSOE |
| SM* | Swansea Maliphant Sidings | *Storage location only* |
| SN* | MoD Shoeburyness | Ministry of Defence |
| SO | Southall (Greater London) | Jeremy Hosking |
| SP | Springs Branch (Wigan) | DB Schenker |
| SU | Selhurst (Croydon) | Southern |
| SZ | Southampton Maritime | Freightliner |
| TB* | Tilburg (Netherlands) | NedTrain |
| TE | Thornaby (Middlesbrough) | DB Schenker |
| TI | Temple Mills (London) | Eurostar |
| TJ | Tavistock Junction (Plymouth) | Colas Rail |
| TM | Tyseley Locomotive Works | Birmingham Railway Museum |
| TN | Thornton (Fife) | John Cameron |
| TO | Toton (Nottinghamshire) | DB Schenker |
| TS | Tyseley (Birmingham) | London Midland |
| TW* | Tonbridge West Yard | First GBRf |
| TY | Tyne Yard (Newcastle) | DB Schenker |
| WA | Warrington | DB Schenker |
| WB | Wembley (London) | Alstom |
| WD | Wimbledon (London) | South West Trains |
| WE | Willesden Brent sidings | *Storage location only* |
| WF | Wansford (Cambridgeshire) | Nene Valley Railway |
| WN | Willesden (London) | London Overground |
| WY* | Wembley Yard | DB Schenker |

| | | |
|---|---|---|
| XW | Crofton (Wakefield) | Bombardier Transportation |
| YK | National Railway Museum (York) | Science Museum |
| YJ | Yeovil Junction Railway Centre | The Yeovil Country Railway |
| ZA | RTC Business Park (Derby) | Serco Railtest/Delta Rail |
| ZB | Doncaster Works | Wabtec Rail |
| ZC | Crewe Works | Bombardier Transportation |
| ZD | Derby Works | Bombardier Transportation |
| ZG | Eastleigh Works | Knights Rail Services/Wabtec |
| ZH | Springburn Works (Glasgow) | Railcare |
| ZI | Ilford Works | Bombardier Transportation |
| ZJ | Marcroft, Stoke | Turners/DB Axiom Rail |
| ZK | Kilmarnock Works | Brush-Barclay |
| ZN | Wolverton Works | Railcare |
| ZR | York (Holgate Works) | Network Rail |

* unofficial code.

# Keep right up to date with....

# Today's Railways

**EUROPE**

## The only UK railway magazine exclusively devoted to events on Mainland Europe's railways.

Every issue is packed with the latest news, informative articles and comprehensive features, plus useful travel information, heritage news, light rail news, diary of events, readers letters and much much more!

**On sale 4th Monday of EVERY MONTH**

## Subscribe to Today's Railways Europe TODAY!

### Never miss an issue!
- Your copy delivered to your door at no extra cost.
- Recieve every issue hot off the press.
- No price increase for the duration of your subscription.
- Exclusive reduced prices on selected books and videos from the Platform 5 Mail Order Department

Today's Railways Europe subscriptions:

☎: (+44) 0114 255 8000    Fax: (+44) 0114 255 2471

# Subscription order form

To subscribe, please complete the form below (or a copy) and return it with your remittance to:

**Today's Railways Europe (Dept. LCS), 3 Wyvern House, Sark Road, SHEFFIELD, S2 4HG, ENGLAND.**

**BLOCK CAPITALS PLEASE**

(All prices include postage and packing.)

---

**Today's Railways Europe: Subscription (12 issues)**

☐ **UK £45.00 (post free);**  ☐ **Overseas Airmail £54.60.**

**JAN  FEB  MAR  APR  MAY  JUN  JUL  AUG  SEP  OCT  NOV  DEC**

Please circle start issue required

---

**Name:** ....................................................................

**Address:** ................................................................

..............................................................................

.......................................... **Postcode:** ..................

**Daytime Tel. No:** ....................................................

**E-mail:** ..................................................................

---

I enclose my cheque/UK postal order for £ ...........................

made payable to **'PLATFORM 5 PUBLISHING LTD.'**

**Please debit my Visa/Mastercard/Maestro**

**Card No:** ................................... **Expiry Date:** ...........

**Card Issue No./Date (Maestro only):** ............ **Security No.:** ........

**for £** ............................. **Date:** .........................

**Signature:** ..............................................................

---

or if ordering by debit/credit card, telephone our subscription department on the numbers opposite.

**Special note:** Subscriptions may begin with the current issue or the next to be published. Subscriptions cannot be backdated.

# 6.6. ABBREVIATIONS

**The following general abbreviations are used in this book:**

| | |
|---|---|
| AC | Alternating Current (i.e. Overhead supply) |
| AFD | Air Force Department |
| BAA | British Airports Authority |
| BR | British Railways |
| BSI | Bergische Stahl Industrie |
| CRDC | Component Recovery & Disposal Centre |
| C&W | Carriage & Wagon |
| DC | Direct Current (i.e. Third Rail) |
| DEMU | Diesel Electric Multiple Unit |
| DERA | Defence Evaluation & Research Agency |
| DfT | Department for Transport |
| Dia. | Diagram number |
| DMU | Diesel Multiple Unit (general term) |
| DSDC | Defence Storage & Distribution Centre |
| DRS | Direct Rail Services |
| EMU | Electric Multiple Unit (general term) |
| GWR | Great Western Railway |
| H-B | Hunslet-Barclay |
| h.p. | Horse power |
| HNRC | Harry Needle Railroad Company |
| Hz | Hertz |
| kN | Kilonewtons |
| km/h | Kilometres per hour |
| kW | Kilowatts |
| lbf | Pounds force |
| LT | London Transport |
| LUL | London Underground Limited |
| m. | Metres |
| mm. | Millimetres |
| m.p.h. | Miles per hour |
| NPCCS | Non Passenger Carrying Coaching Stock |
| PTE | Passenger Transport Executive |
| RCH | Railway Clearing House |
| r.p.m. | Revolutions per minute |
| RR | Rolls Royce |
| RSL | Rolling Stock Library |
| SR | BR Southern Region |
| t. | Tonnes |
| T | Toilet |
| TD | Toilet suitable for disabled passengers |
| TDM | Time Division Multiplex |
| TOPS | Total Operations Processing System |
| V | Volts |
| W | Wheelchair space |